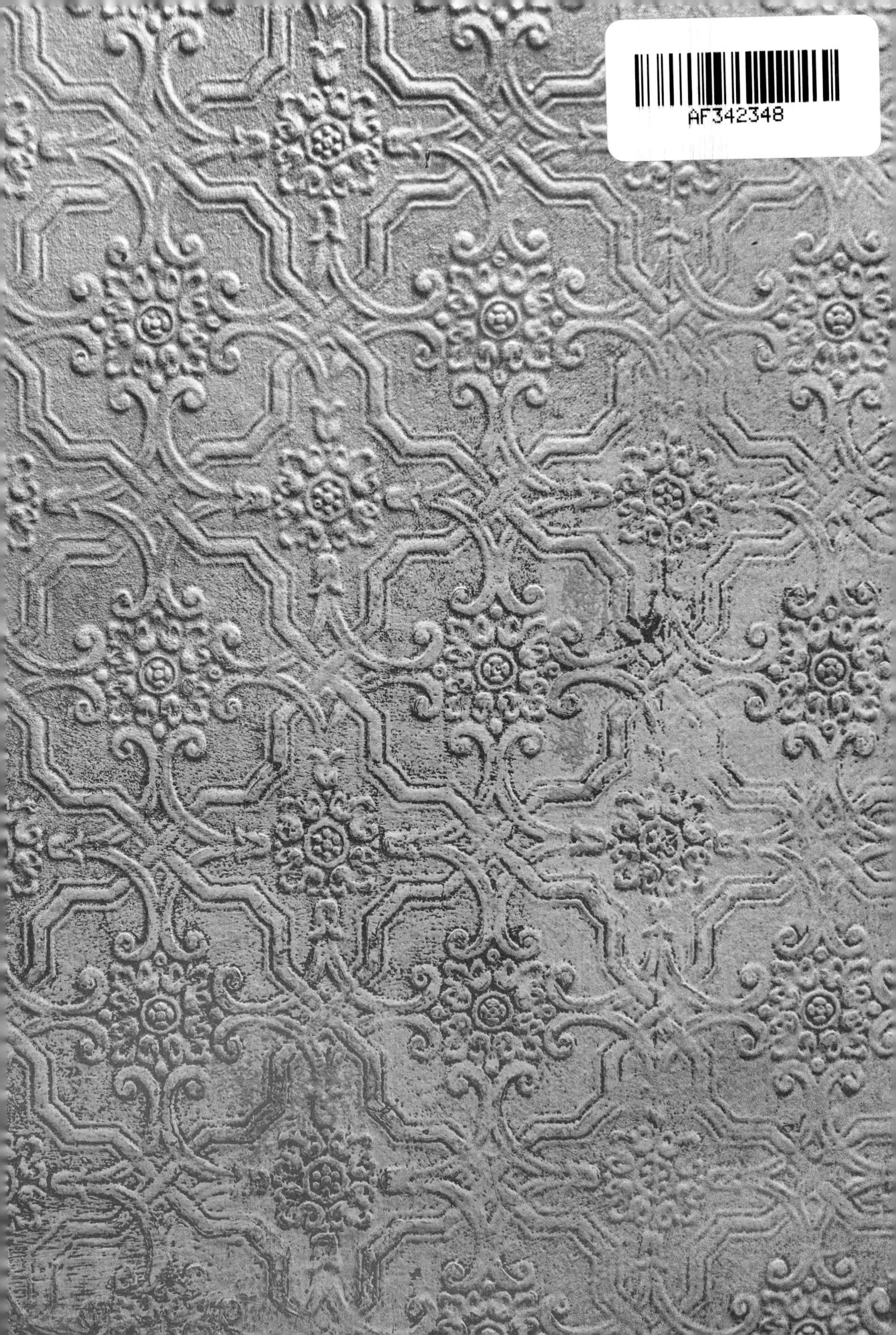
AF342348

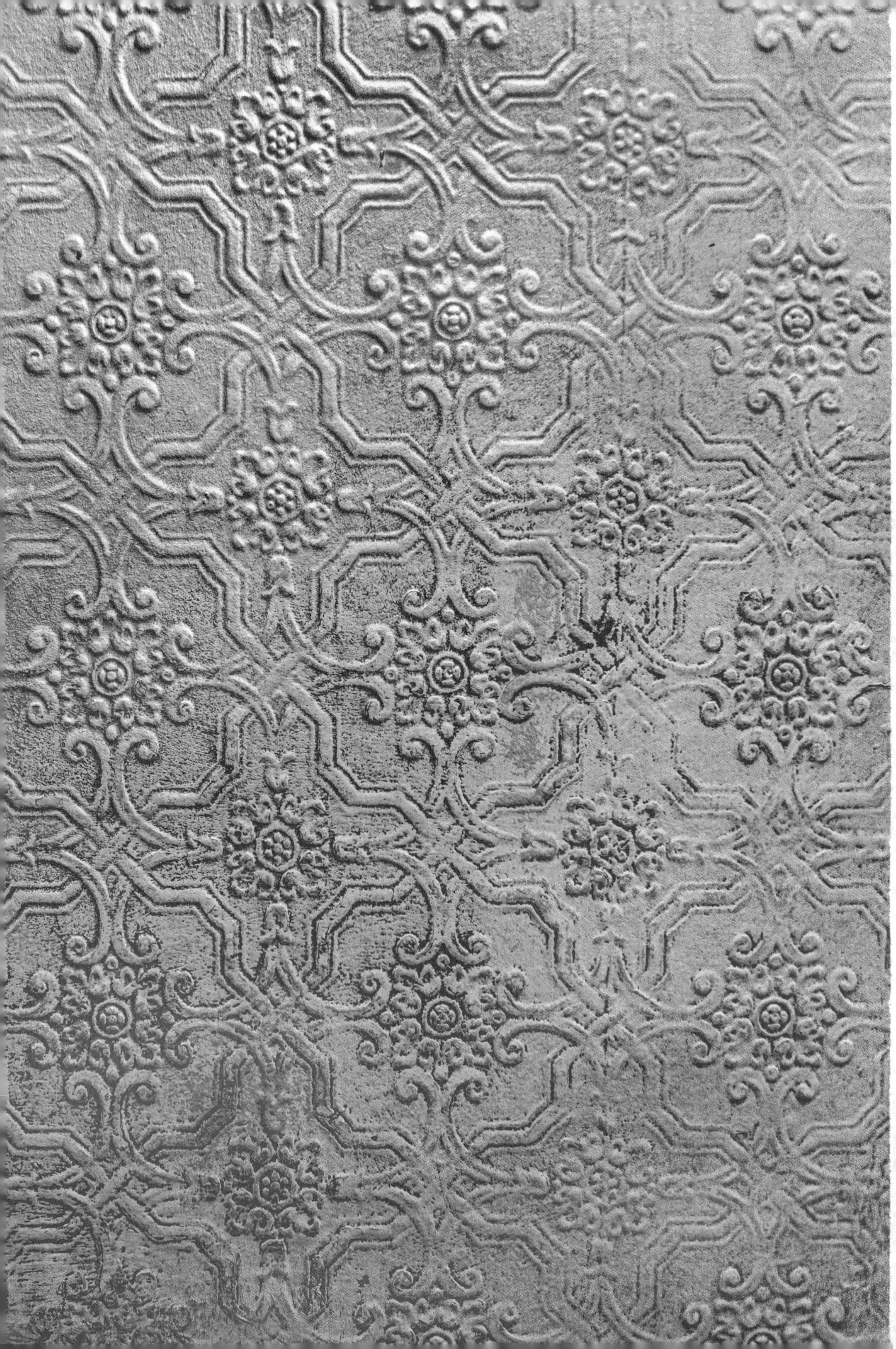

LOCAL LEGENDS

THE HIDDEN PUBS OF LONDON

HORST A. FRIEDRICHS

JOHN WARLAND

PRESTEL

MUNICH   LONDON   NEW YORK

CONTENTS

LOCAL LEGENDS: HIDDEN PUBS OF LONDON

Foreword by Suggs — 5
A Love Story — 7

CITY SLICKERS & SURROUNDS
Ye Olde Mitre — 10
The Cockpit — 18
The Seven Stars — 28
The Hand & Shears — 38
The Duke — 48
The Holy Tavern — 54
The Jamaica Wine House — 60

UP WEST
The Nags Head — 68
Cask & Glass — 76
The Barley Mow — 82
The Champion — 92
Bradley's Spanish Bar — 100
The Toucan — 108
The Golden Eagle — 114
The Cross Keys — 118
The Nell Gwynne Tavern — 128
The Heron — 136

EASTENDERS
The Pride of Spitalfields — 146
Princess of Prussia — 156
Turner's Old Star — 164

The Auld Shillelagh — 174
The Palm Tree — 184
The Eleanor Arms — 196

NORTHERN STARS
The Wenlock Arms — 204
King Charles I — 212
The Shakespeare's Head — 222
The Hemingford Arms — 234
The Queen's Head — 246

SOUTH OF THE RIVER
The Lord Clyde — 252
The Kings Arms — 264
The Plume of Feathers — 270
The Prince of Wales — 276
The Dog & Bell — 282

**DON'T FORGET
YOUR TRAVELCARD**
The Masons Arms — 290
Blythe Hill Tavern — 300
The Bricklayer's Arms — 310
The Park Tavern — 314
The Dacre Arms — 324

Authors — 334
Acknowledgements — 335

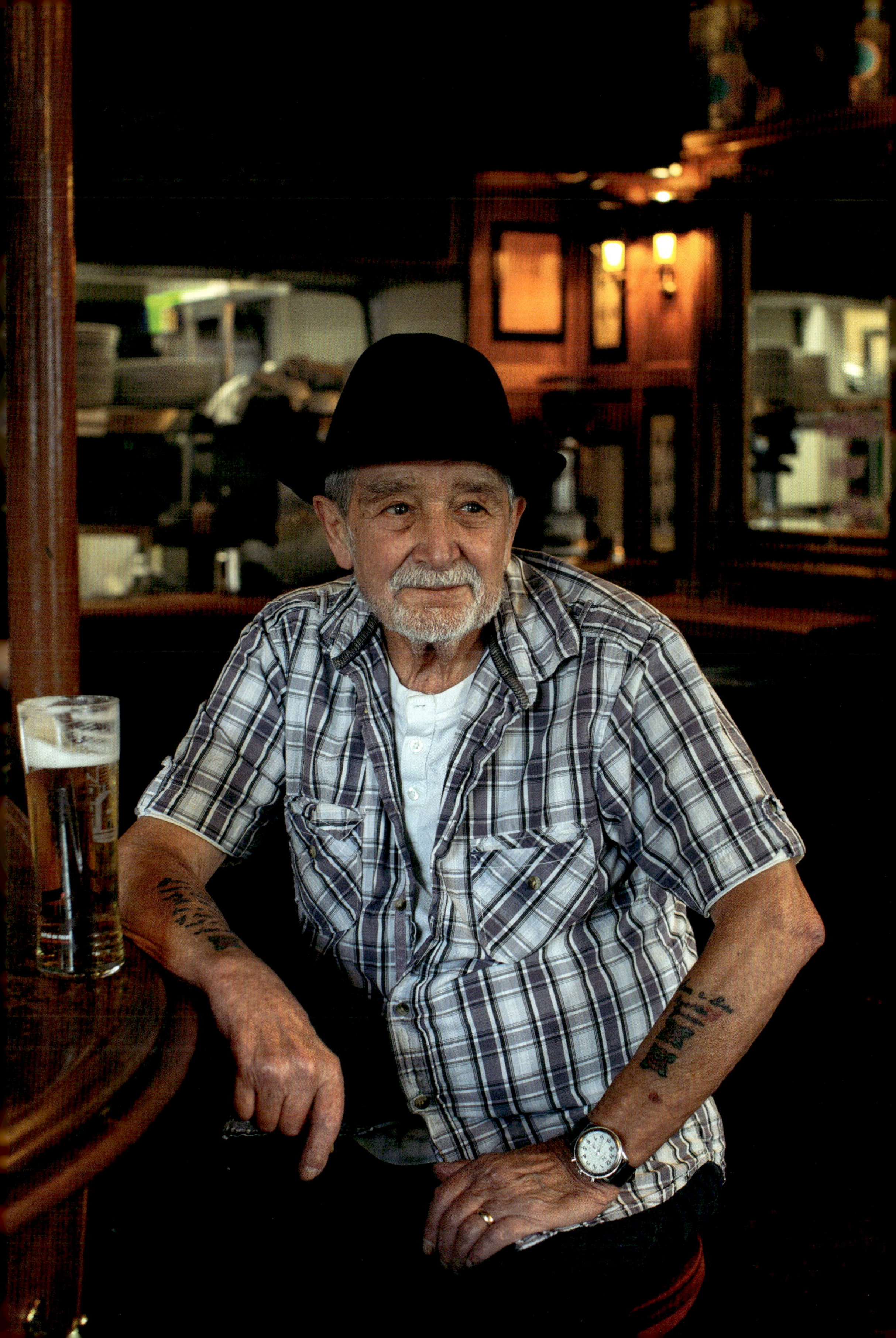

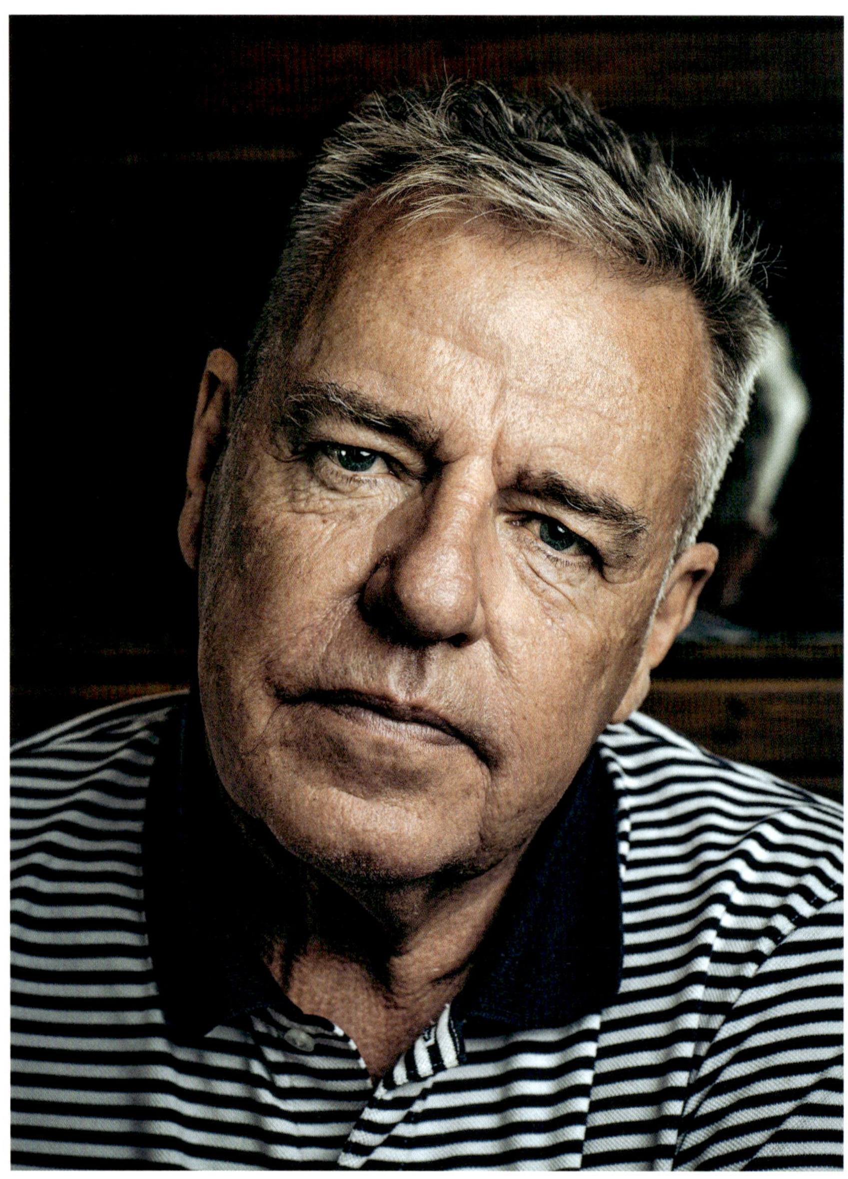

Suggs — The French House, 2023

FOREWORD BY SUGGS

I love April Fool's Day. You'll find me pouring the first 568 millilitres of the day behind the bar of The French House. Every other day of the year, it's half pints only in this bohemian boozer frequented by the likes of Francis Bacon and Lucian Freud. But for one day only, we get to pull the pints. Auctioning them off for good causes, we then run for the hills, as the pints can be not just beer, but wine and even gin.

My Mum was a singer in the pubs and clubs, including The French, so Soho became our home. After being greeted by the benevolent witch Muriel Belcher at the door of The Colony Club as "Little Cunty", I would pluck my way across the sticky carpet, passing rows of fishnet-clad knees – and that was just the fellas. Soho and its pubs and clubs were a magnet for all sorts of misfits: jazz musicians, painters, writers, poets, strippers, prostitutes, coppers and toffs, plain old deviants and transvestites. From "good time" George Melly to Jeffrey Bernard being unwell, you could be anything – the only house rule was that you just couldn't be boring.

I wouldn't have had a career without pubs. I would have been a busker or butcher's boy to eternity. Pubs were the firmament of our culture. The pubs gave us a platform. They gave us a place to hone our performance, and they gave us a fanbase. Without our ancestral home at The Dublin Castle in Camden, it's quite possible that the nascent Nutty Boys would never have left NW1.

London has been my life, my love, and my muse. It evolves continually, and the pubs shapeshift to mirror the moving sands of society around them. They offer the perfect houses of fun to chew the cud, debate the dream back four line-up at my beloved Chelsea FC, or simply get pissed with your mates. Now whose round is it?

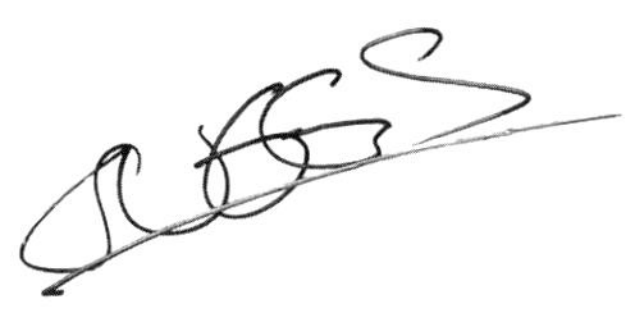

"There's a pub in London that I really adore, but I won't say what it is. It's divided into a lounge and a public bar and it's small and obscure. Hardly anyone goes there. I'm bracing myself against the thought that someone will soon take it over and rip it up. Although in a way I can understand people doing that, if it means they end up making more money. I suppose if I was a publican wanting to make a living, then I would probably do the same. That's just the way the world is going, I suppose. It's a case of: what can anyone do about it?"

Bill Bryson, *The Times*

A LOVE STORY

London is full of iconic alehouses. These timeless taverns are the perfect portal to the past. The cultural conduits through which to conjure history. Visitors can pop for a pint in the pubs where Shakespeare once performed in the courtyard or Dickens penned *A Tale of Two Cities*. These are the legendary pubs where you really should enjoy at least one pint in your life.

But are these the ones that linger longest in the memory? Great as they are, there is a different breed of pub with its own reverential following. It is special breed of pub that informed our alcoholic odyssey across The Big Smoke and inspired us to capture their idiosyncratic qualities and share their richly woven histories through the evocative images captured here.

It's always worth noting the name of the gaffer above the door as you enter. They are usually quite the character, with a reputation that precedes them by a country mile.

Discreetly located far from maddening tourist crowds and noisy out-of-towners, these hubris-free charmers are worth seeking out; side-street specials where eccentric landlords attract an equally characterful clientele. The welcome is warmer, the beer better kept, and a carefully curated ambience keeps the "rowdies" at arm's length.

These hidden gems are happy to live in the shadow of the easily found, modern-misery chain pubs hoovering up the occasional drinker. Visiting these more elusive pubs takes you out of your natural way, through less familiar parts of town, but suddenly you'll duck through an archway or turn a corner, and then! Alcoholic Xanadu! The hand-painted sign, the proudly polished brass and the light burble of chit-chat give you a feeling of warm contentment before you've even set foot inside.

It's always worth noting the name of the gaffer above the door as you enter. They are usually quite the character, with a reputation that precedes them by a mile. The walls and ceiling are regularly adorned with vintage ephemera and there's often a house pet somewhere too. As forces of nature, battling the bland by the hour, these landlords can of course be polarising, with 1★ reviews as likely as 5★. But it's their eccentric way or the homogenised highway, and I've seen a few people told to "bugger off down to Wetherspoons" if they can't respect the house rules. These landlords often see themselves merely as the caretaker of these fine pubs, ready to hand the keys on to the next generation when the time is right.

Eating can be viewed as cheating in these wet-led boozers, and why waste valuable stomach space when there's more wonderful cask ale to fill your belly with? Patrons are connoisseurs of the carb. From crisps to scratchings, pork pies, toasties or cling-filmed rolls, it's all up for grabs. When you see the bar staff nonchalantly dropping a pickled egg into a bag of ready salted crisps, then you know that you've found yourself a proper fucking boozer.

Long before the advent of GPS, these were pubs of legend and lore. Locations shared by word of mouth or ringed on a well-thumbed copy of the *London A–Z*. Even to this day, they rarely feature in lists of the most famous or must-visit pubs of London, and they certainly don't seek such accolades. Most don't even have a website and, with almost zero social media presence, you'll soon realise that the pubs themselves are the social network.

Shakespeare, Dickens, Freud or Bacon are unlikely to have drunk in any of these pubs. In fact, it's you, the drinker, that makes the story as soon as you enter stage right. Patronise these establishments regularly and you're likely to find your own tankard or brass plaque above the bar. These pubs invite the locals to curate the jukebox playlist, suggest a new ale or trial a case of wine they've stumbled on during their recent travels. Each pub has an area or run of bar stools where the hardcore locals find their place. These are the pubs that both serve and support the local community, for business or leisure. You'll find charity tins, quirky quiz nights and perhaps an order of service for a local wedding or funeral behind the bar. Local cricket or special interest groups host their monthly meets here, and that's when the ominous hanging yard-of-ale glass might see some serious action.

The more time you spend in these pubs, the more addicted you become. No longer content with catching up in your tried-and-tested classic corner pubs, you'll seek these out. Perhaps the best thing about these discoveries is imagining what other beauties might be hiding across the capital. With 3,500 pubs still pulling pints, the thought that there might be 30 or 40 drinking diamonds in the rough, ready to be unearthed, is a thrilling prospect. The Hope in Carshalton, The Eagle Ale House in Battersea, The Warwick Castle in Maida Vale, The Ship in Fitzrovia, The Victoria in Bermondsey, The Anchor & Hope in Clapton: all mouth-watering prospects for the avid pint-chaser and easily enough to fill another book... if only our livers could keep up.

But this rare breed of pub is possibly the one most at risk of extinction. Will the new work-from-home ways allow these rare face-to-face forums a viable future? With past performance being no guarantee of future survival, please consider this book a call to arms to spread the love around and spend your pounds in the fabulous freehouses listed and photographed so richly within these pages.

The baton now passes to you, the reader. It's time to push open the brass-handled pub door, pull up a bar stool, order a pint 'n pickled egg and join us on our trundle through the glorious world of London's finest backstreet boozers. Just remember not to sit on the cat.

Cheers!
John & Horst

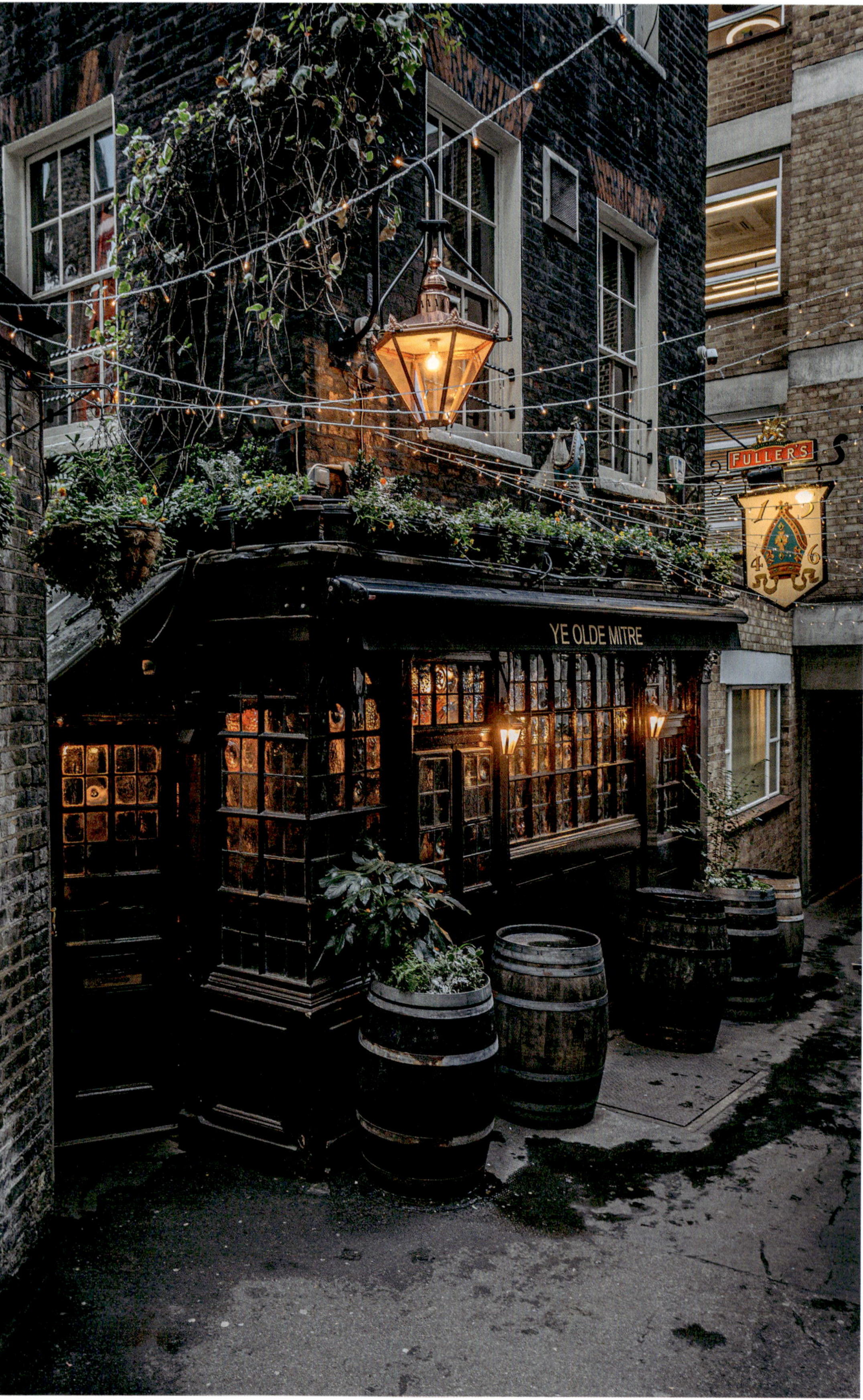
FULLER'S
YE OLDE MITRE

YE OLDE MITRE

Being touted as the hardest-to-find pub in London certainly keeps the hoi polloi at arm's length, and not opening on the weekend often catches out the uninitiated. Simply finding the pub for the first time can evoke a small euphoric glow. It's possible for the first-timer to wander past Hatton Garden's diamond dealers several times before noticing the uniquely handsome bishop's mitre pub sign and squeezing through the shady archway to a very fine pub indeed.

You certainly can visit for the history, dating back to 1546, and many do indeed come to seek out the fossilised ancient cherry tree that Elizabeth I allegedly once danced around on May Day. You will also no doubt listen to the legend of the pub being legally assigned as part of Cambridge under the Bishop of Ely. And whilst all this legend and lore certainly has merit, at the heart lies a truly cracking pub. A place where connoisseurs of the cask congregate, with the Society for the Preservation of Beers from the Wood designating The Mitre as its hallowed headquarters. Campaigning since 1963 against the rise of the fizzy filth dispensed from "sealed dustbins", members have their own tankards shelved behind the bar, and revel in The Mitre's very own wooden beer casks filled regularly with gravity-fed devil juice.

This is the kind of magical spot that, once discovered, makes it hard to return to the real world

Ship brokers holding court over lunchtime pints give way to an after-work throng filling this urban crevice with full-throttle beery burble. Suitable sustenance is found in the finest pork pies from Mr Barrick's in Yorkshire, which are, in addition to the toasties, the Platonic ideal of bar snacks. Heaven can indeed wait. Living above the shop after ten years is the ever-welcoming landlady, Judith Norman. This is the kind of magical spot that, once discovered, makes it hard to return to the real world.

The newest recruit to the team asked for a job on his very first visit to the pub. When asked "Why the enthusiasm?", he simply replied: "Because I love great beer!" Quite.

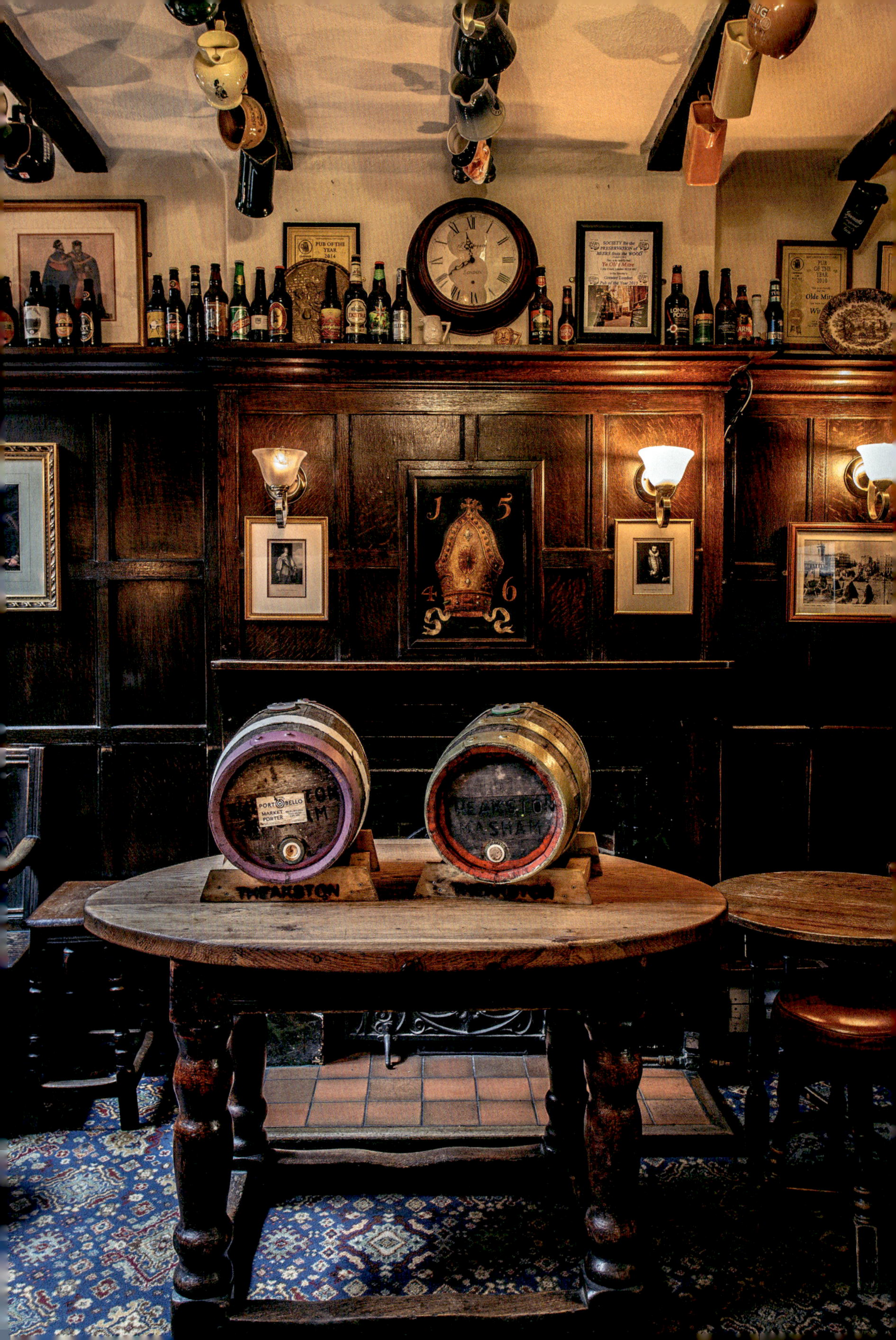

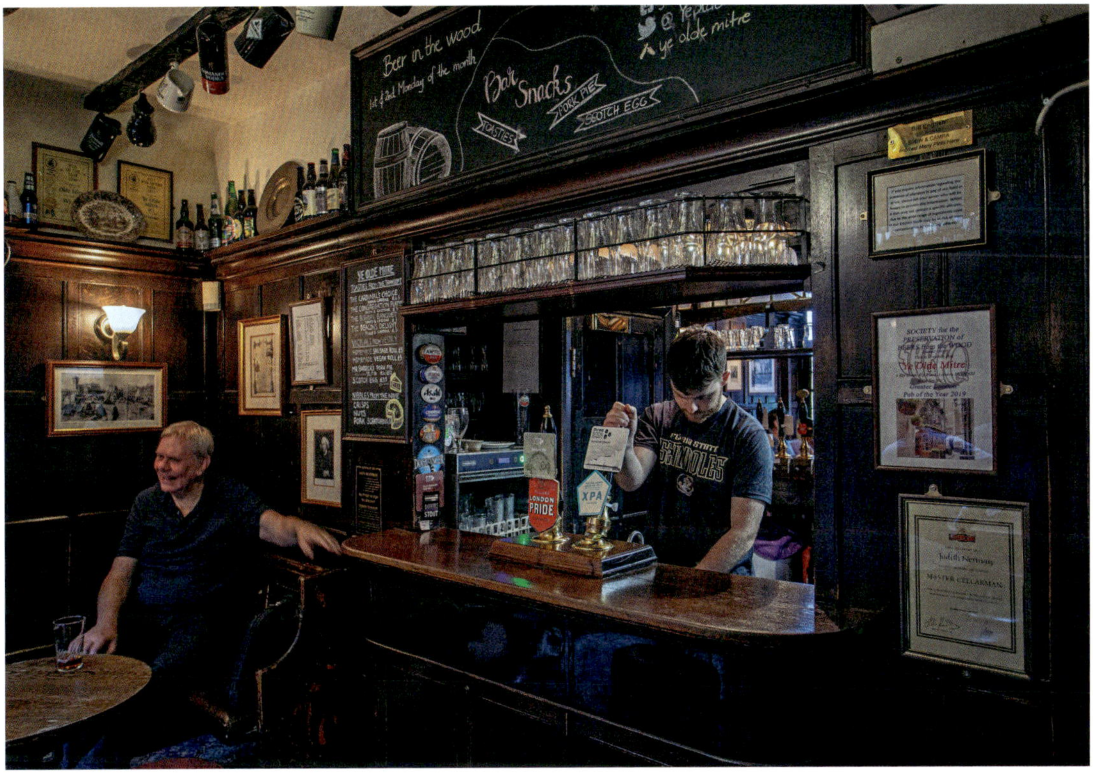

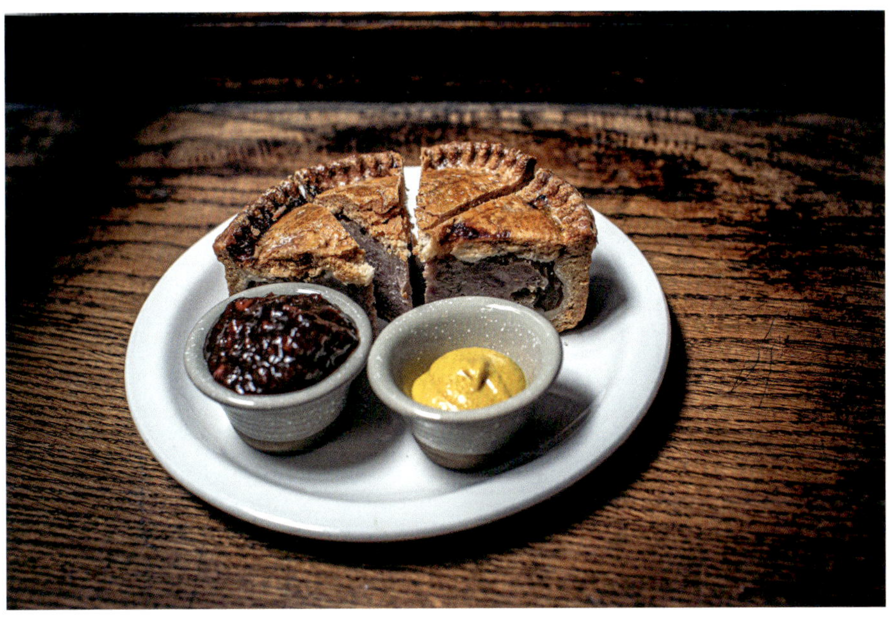

Traditional pork pies and hand-pulled pints make for perfect bedfellows

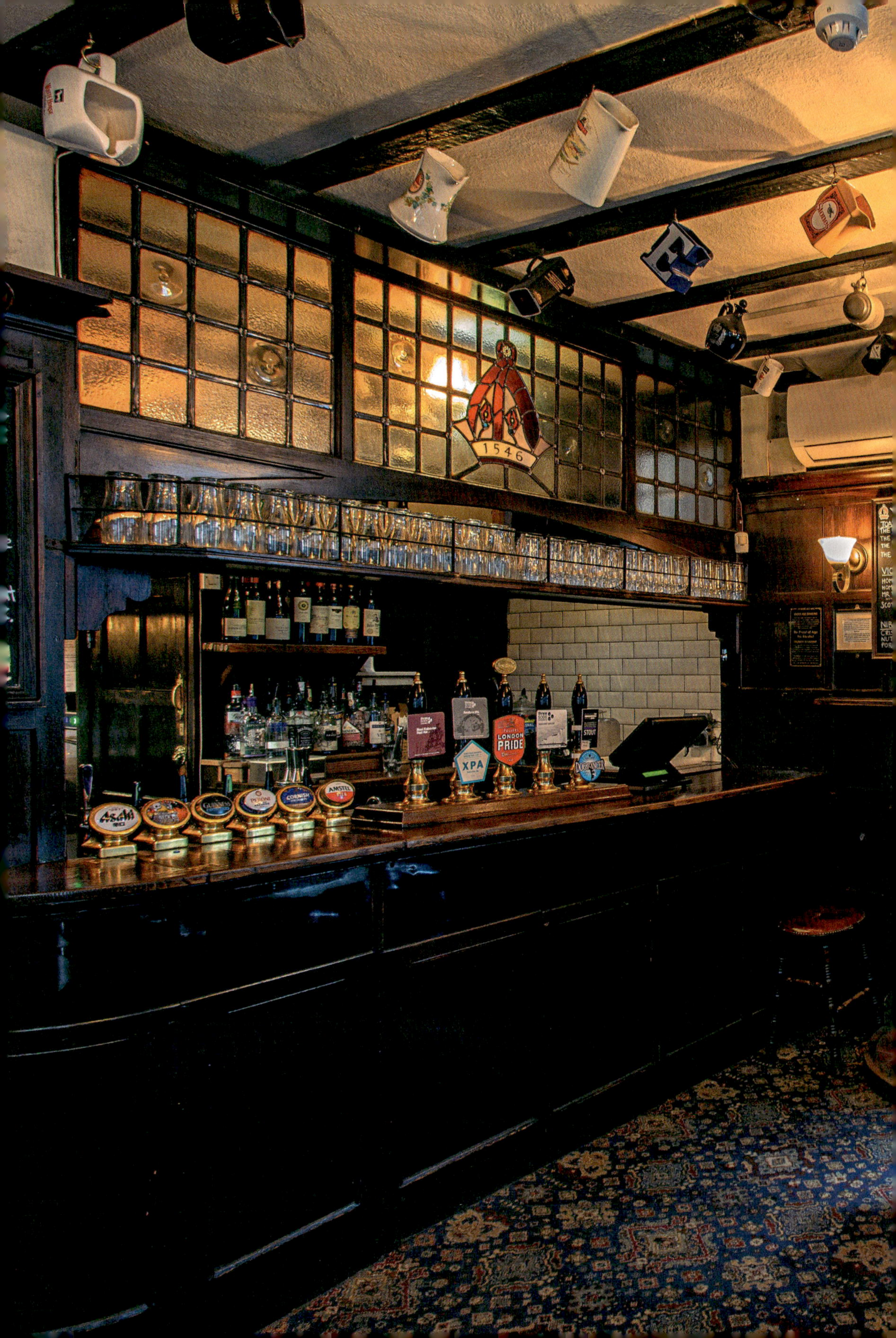

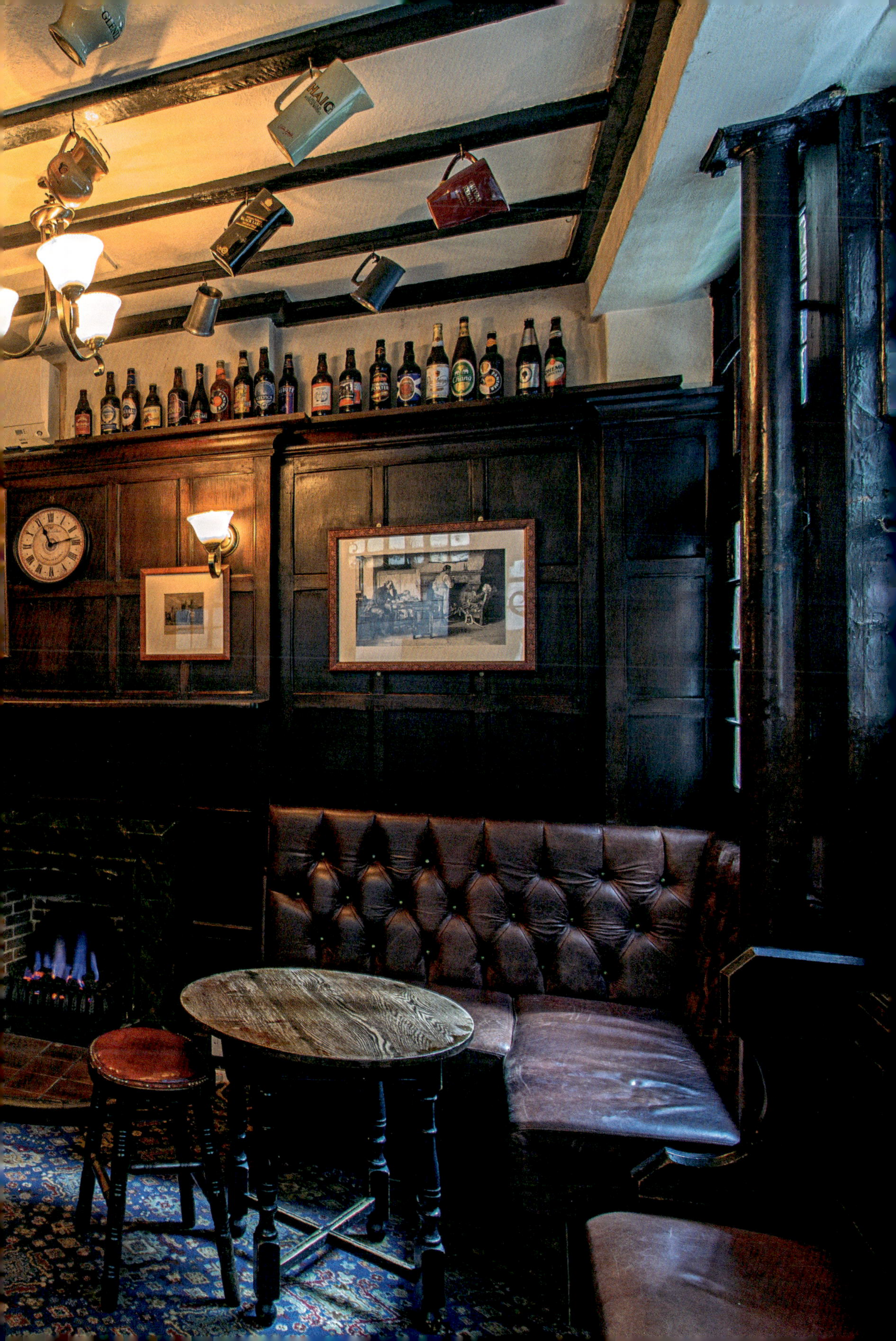

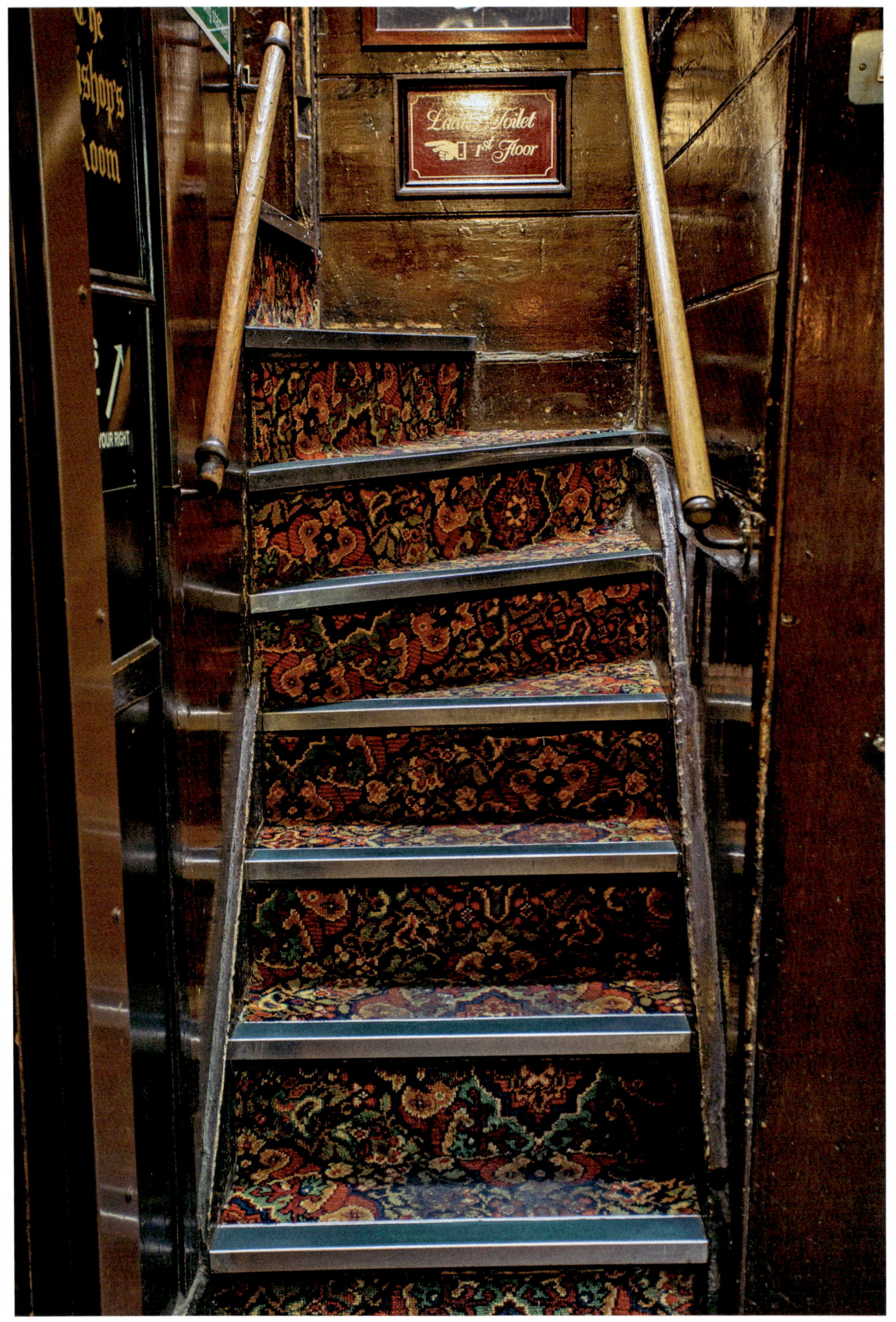

Head upstairs to escape the post-work-pint hubbub

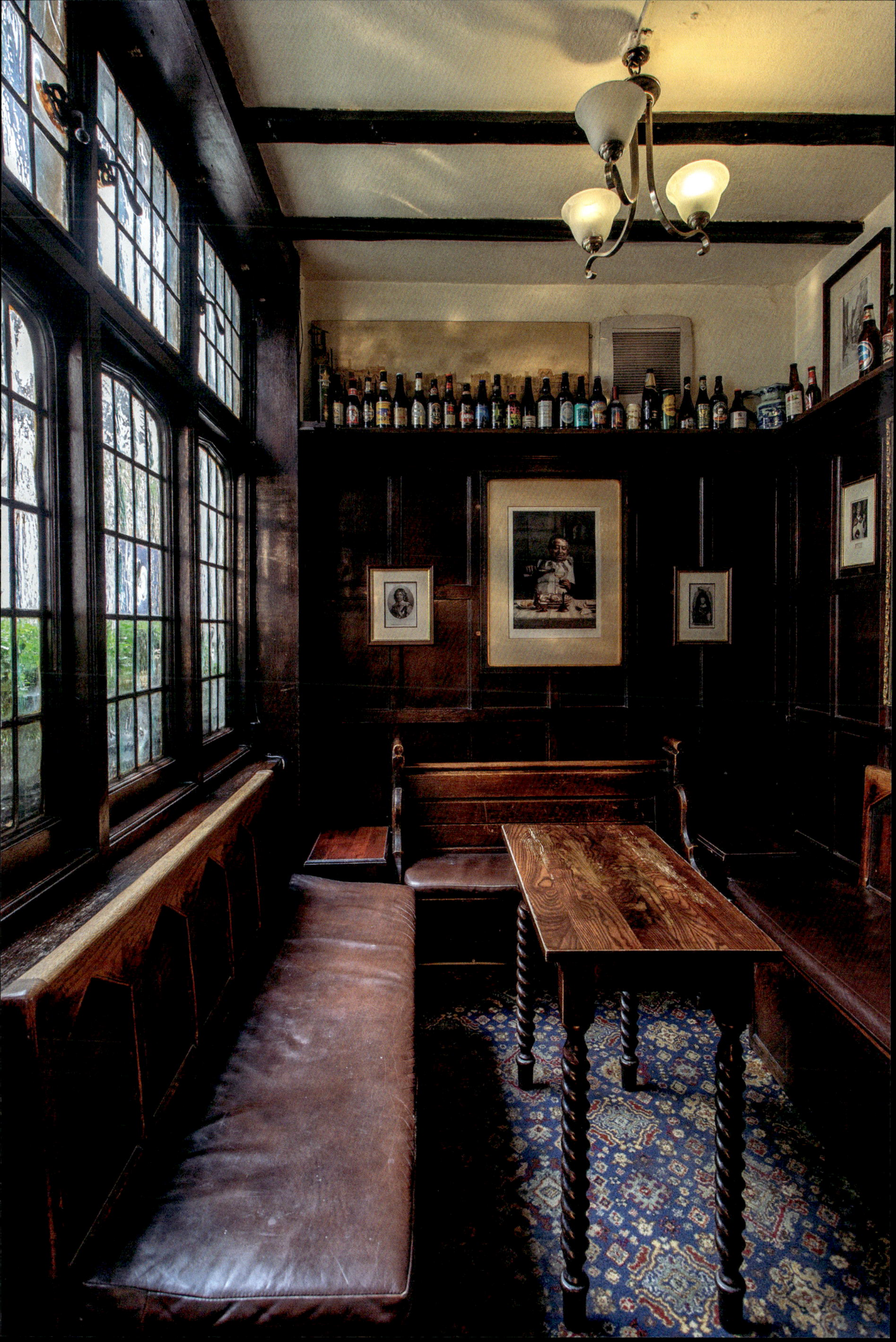

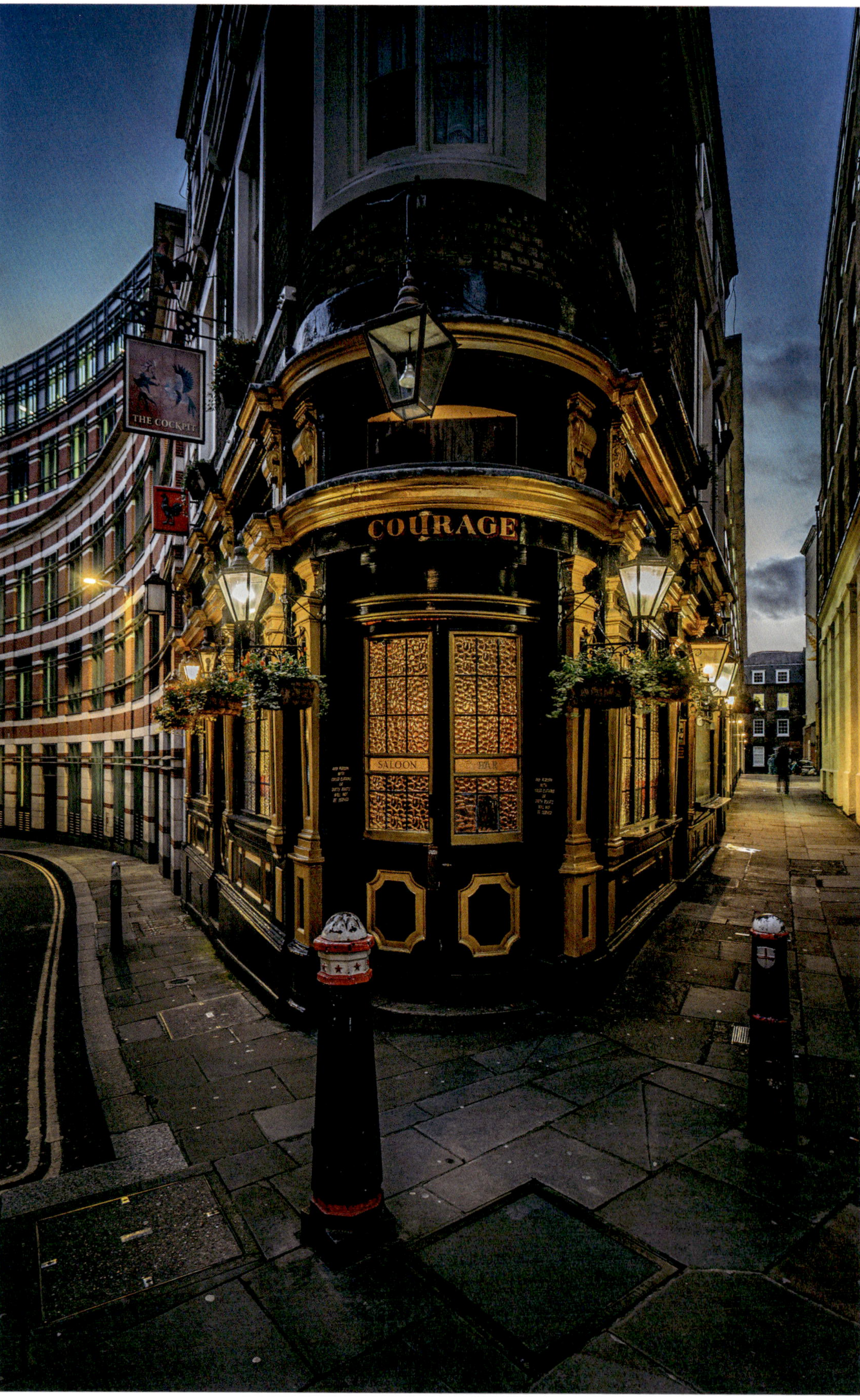
THE COCKPIT
COURAGE
SALOON BAR

THE COCKPIT

Sheltering in the shadow of St Paul's Cathedral, this is a pub with traditional East End hospitality running through its veins at the beating heart of the moral-munching Square Mile.

The signage recalls the pub's bloody cock-fighting history, when cocks would scrap to the death whilst the booze and bets flowed freely all around. The keeper of the losing bird would find themselves hoisted up by bucket into the gallery and pelted with glass bottles, often full of bodily fluids supplied by the baying crowds.

The current clientele are rather more genteel, with the Cathedral bell-ringers often seen indulging in post-peal refreshments. There's usually a gaggle of regular bar-huggers in situ, but with almost no one living in the Square Mile they must travel a long way to call this their "local".

Mr Cook – Dave, or Cookie to his friends – has run this pub with his wife for over thirty years, and it feels that little has been touched for a decade or two. The place is a rich whirl of colourful carpets, natty upholstery, burnished wood and rudimentary bogs. A vintage Shove Ha'penny board acts as a reminder of simpler times. The perfect template for a backstreet boozer? Quite possibly.

The doors open here nearly every day of the year, making it a treasured anomaly in the deserted weekend City streets. It is a fine antidote to modern capitalism; when you sit sheltered inside its opaque windows, you forget that you're in one of the pre-eminent financial centres of the world.

Enveloped by historic mercantile exchanges, investment banks and insurance multinationals, the real estate here is amongst the most expensive on the planet. Buildings rarely last long in the City, with Great Fires, Great Wars and even greater financial pressures ripping through it. The corporate world has little time for architectural nostalgia, but this pub is a place of constant and quiet refuge.

But when the captain of this Cockpit rings his own last orders and throws in the (beer) towel, what comes next? Who knows what will become of such old-world boozers cast adrift in the new age of digital finance, when the days of long liquid lunches are fast disappearing?

Perhaps the hand-painted word "Courage" over the exquisite curving front doors is a call to arms rather than a reference to the once-famous brewery. The Cockpit has seen plenty of bloodshed over the centuries, but, with Cookie at the helm, this good ship shall sail on.

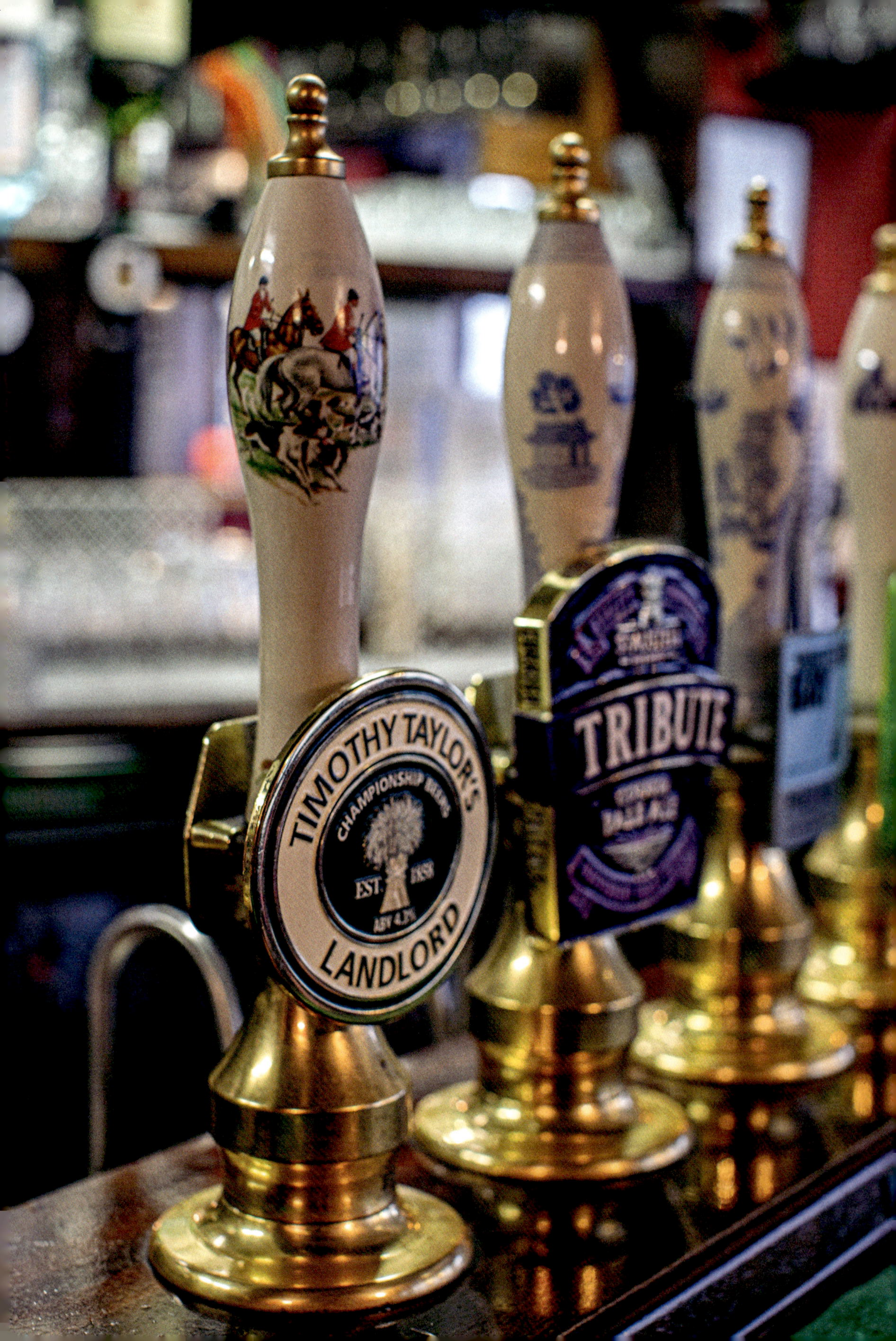

TIMOTHY TAYLOR'S
CHAMPIONSHIP BEERS
EST. 1858
ABV 4.3%
LANDLORD
TRIBUTE

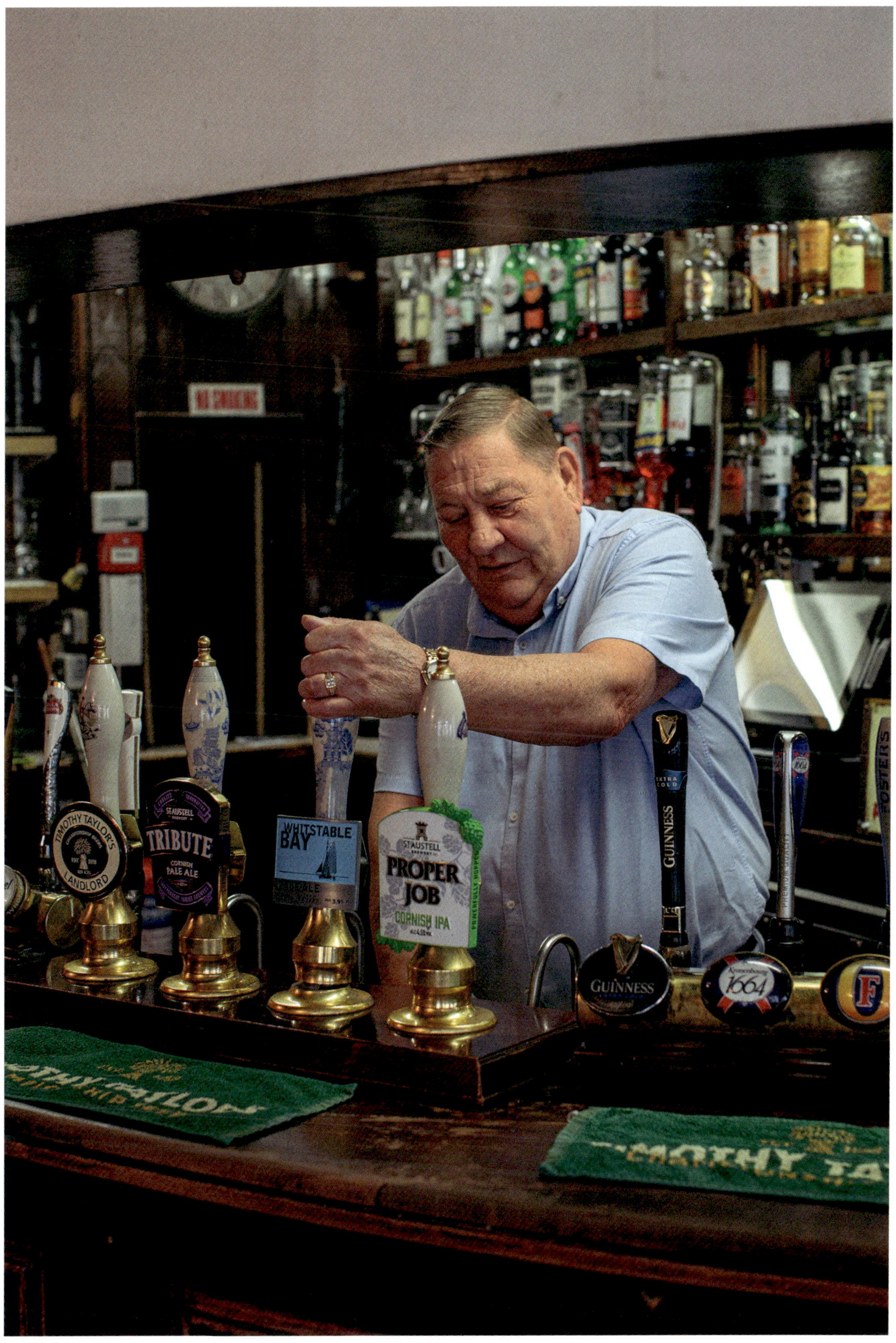

Cookie ruling his roost

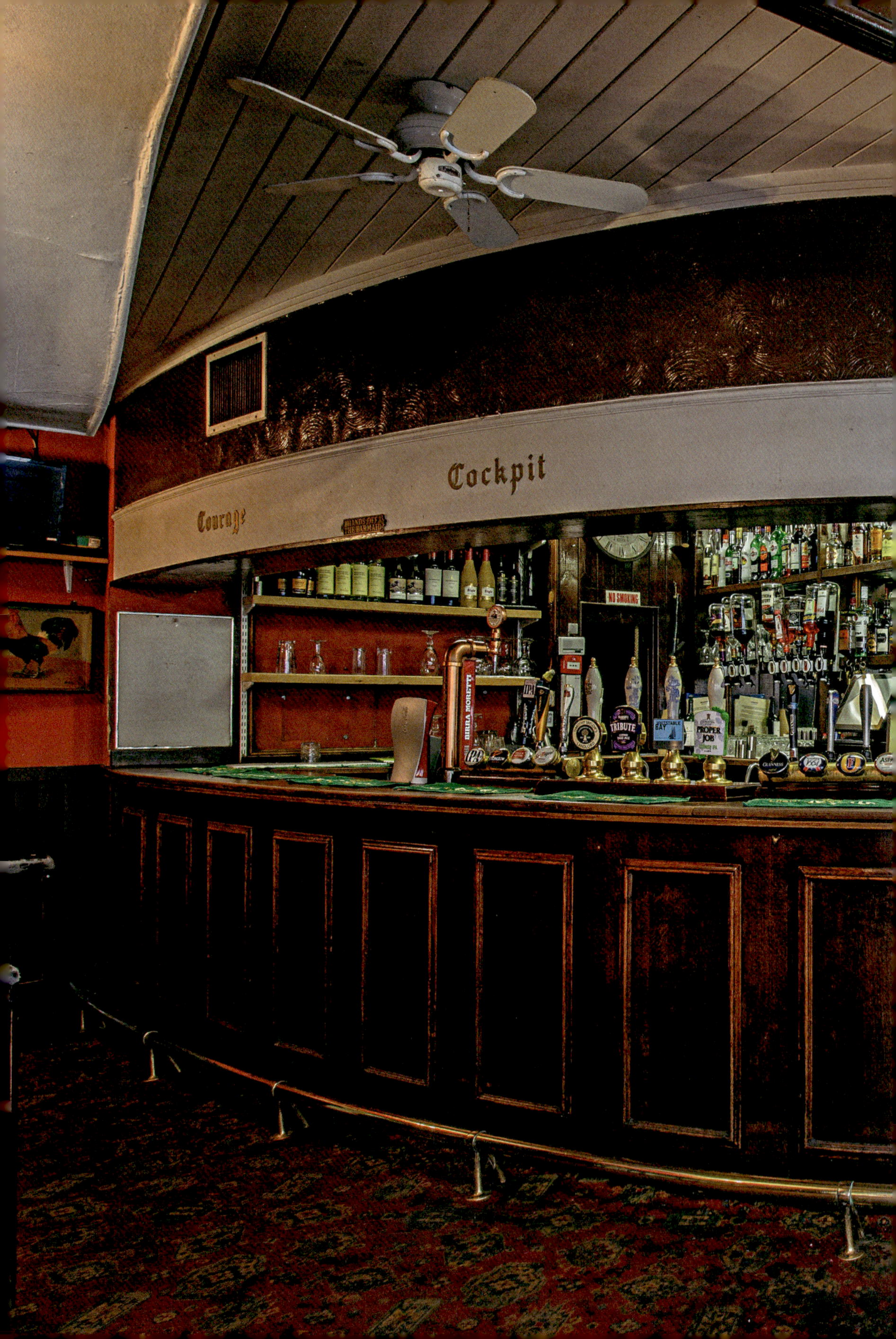
Cockpit
Courage
HANDS OFF THE BARMAID
NO SMOKING

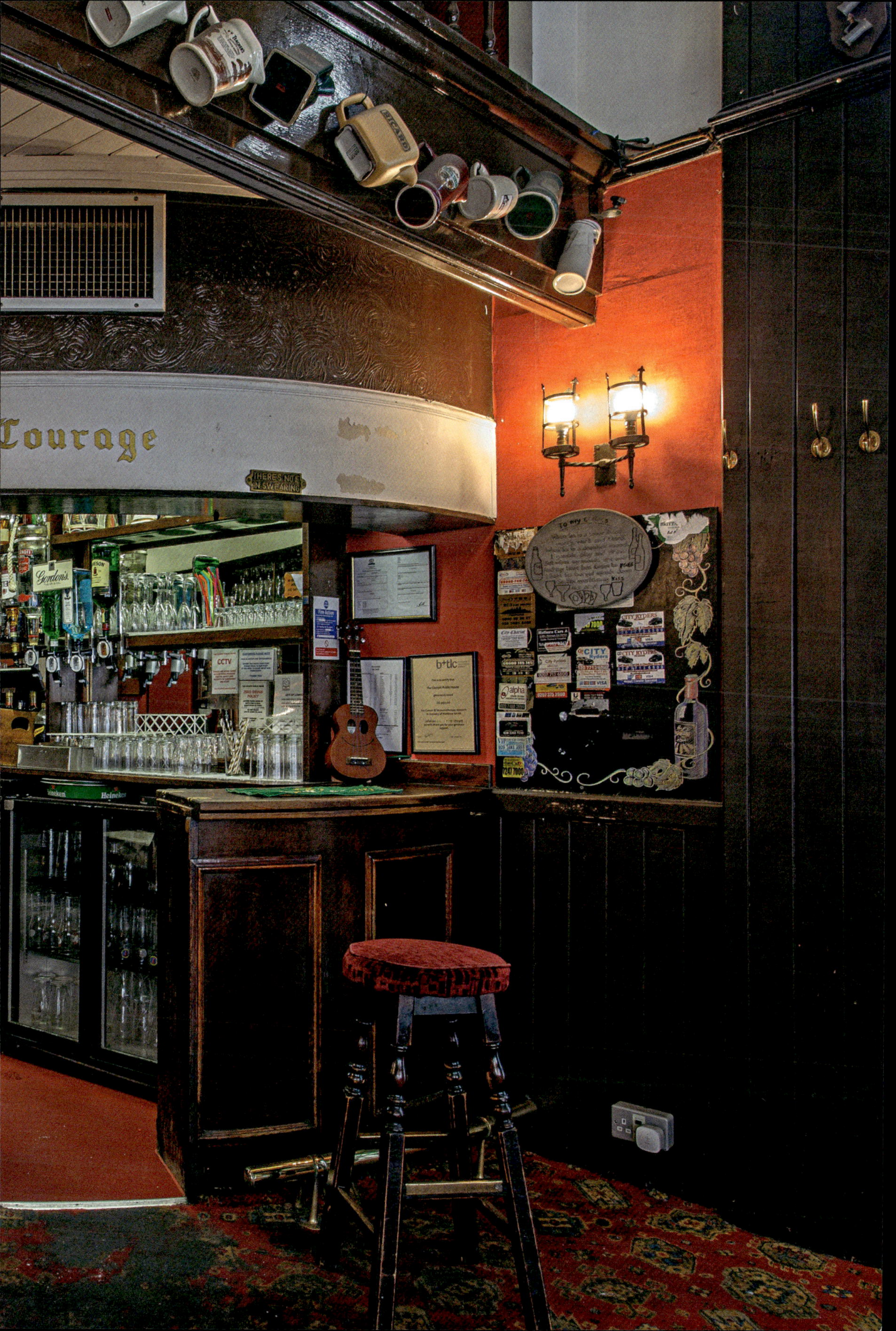

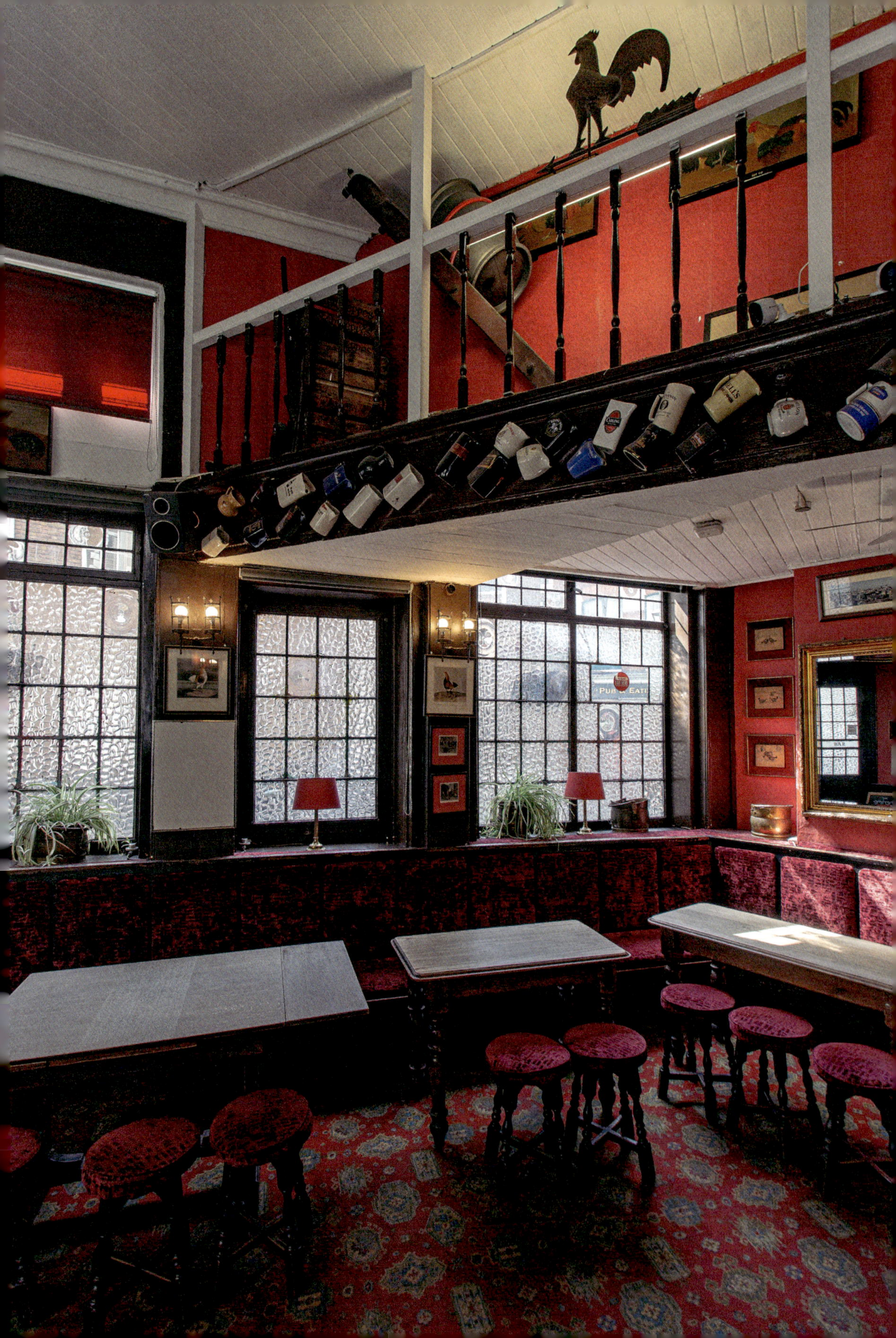

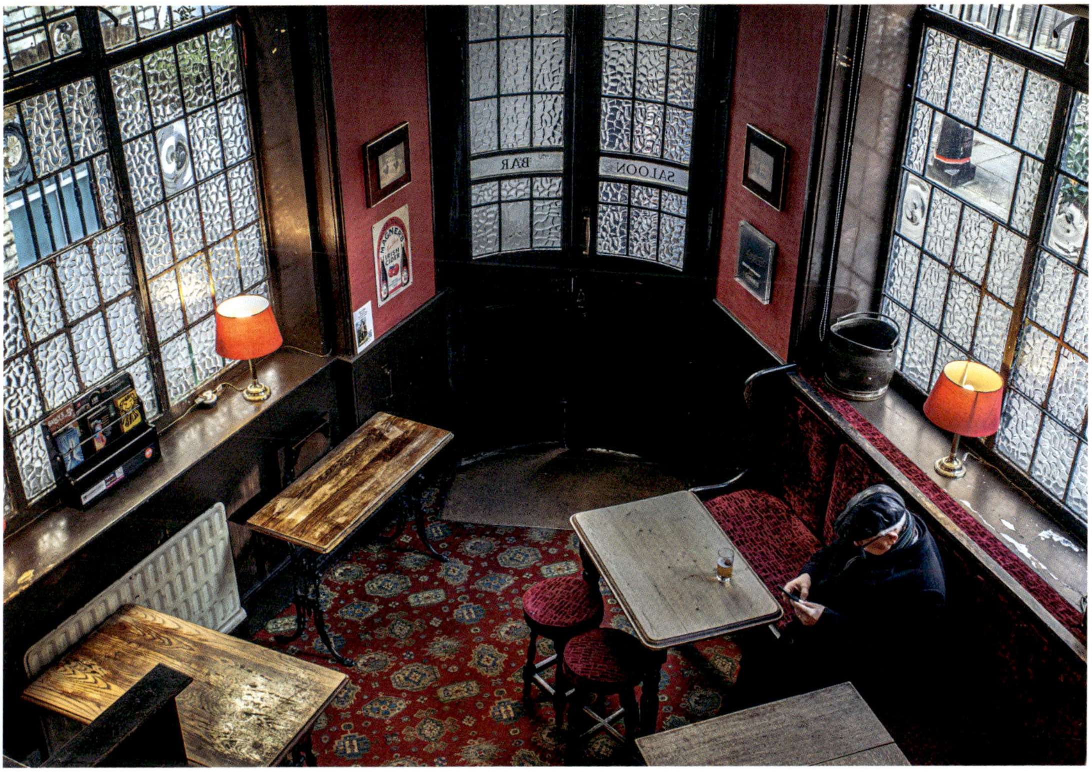

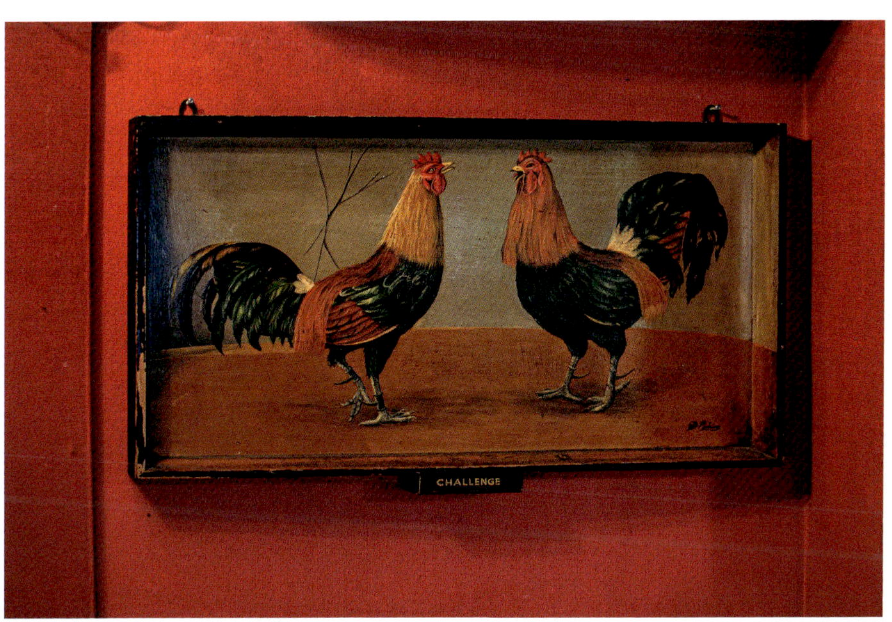

Old-school charm in the heart of the City

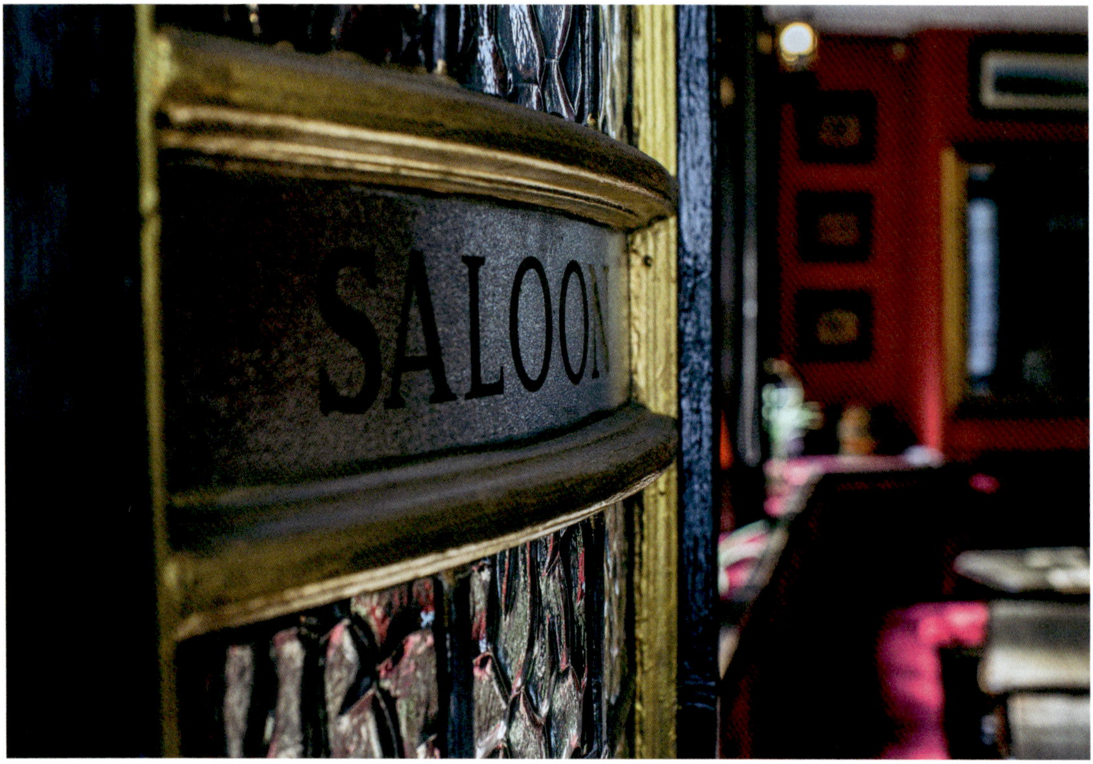

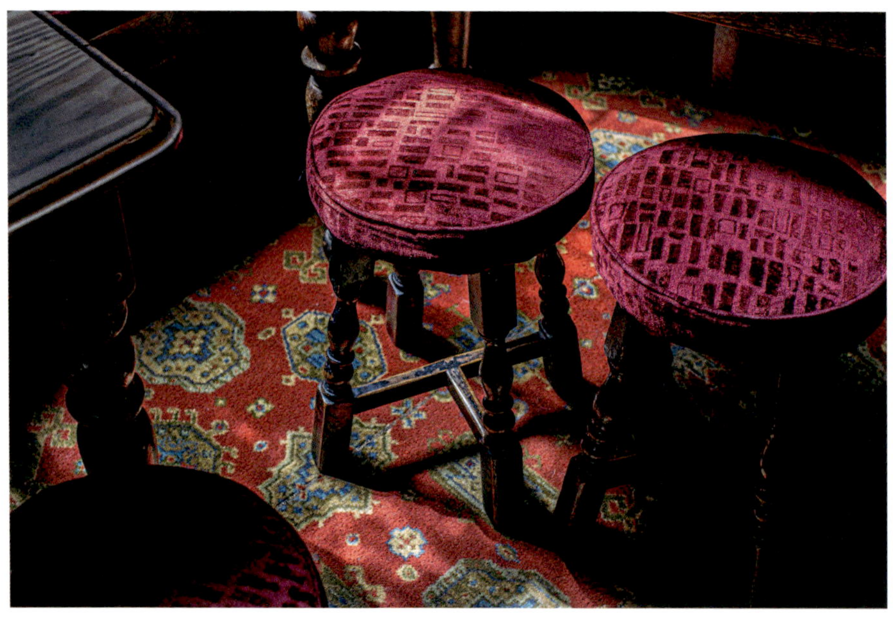

A carpeted cocoon apart from the modern world

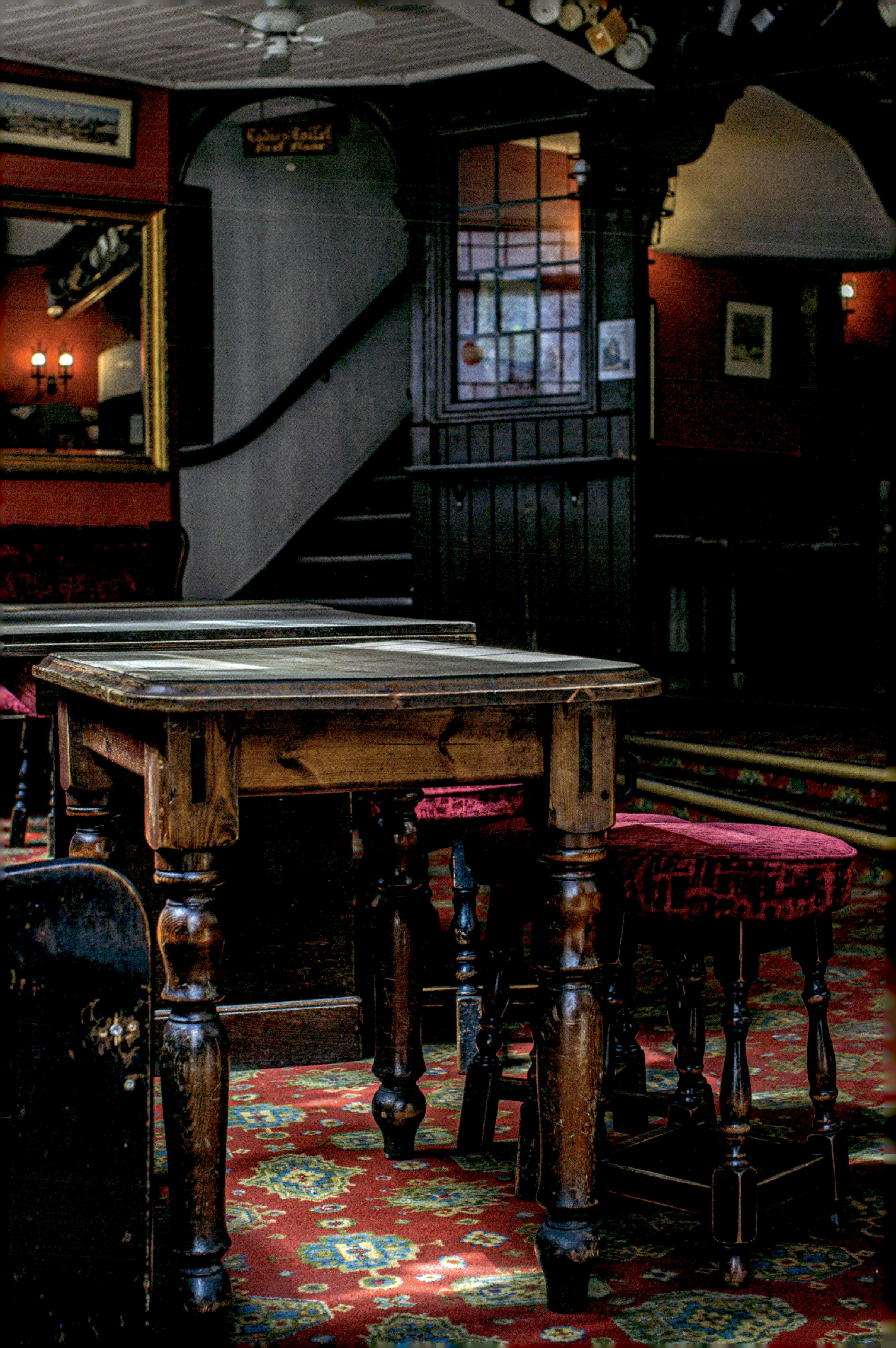

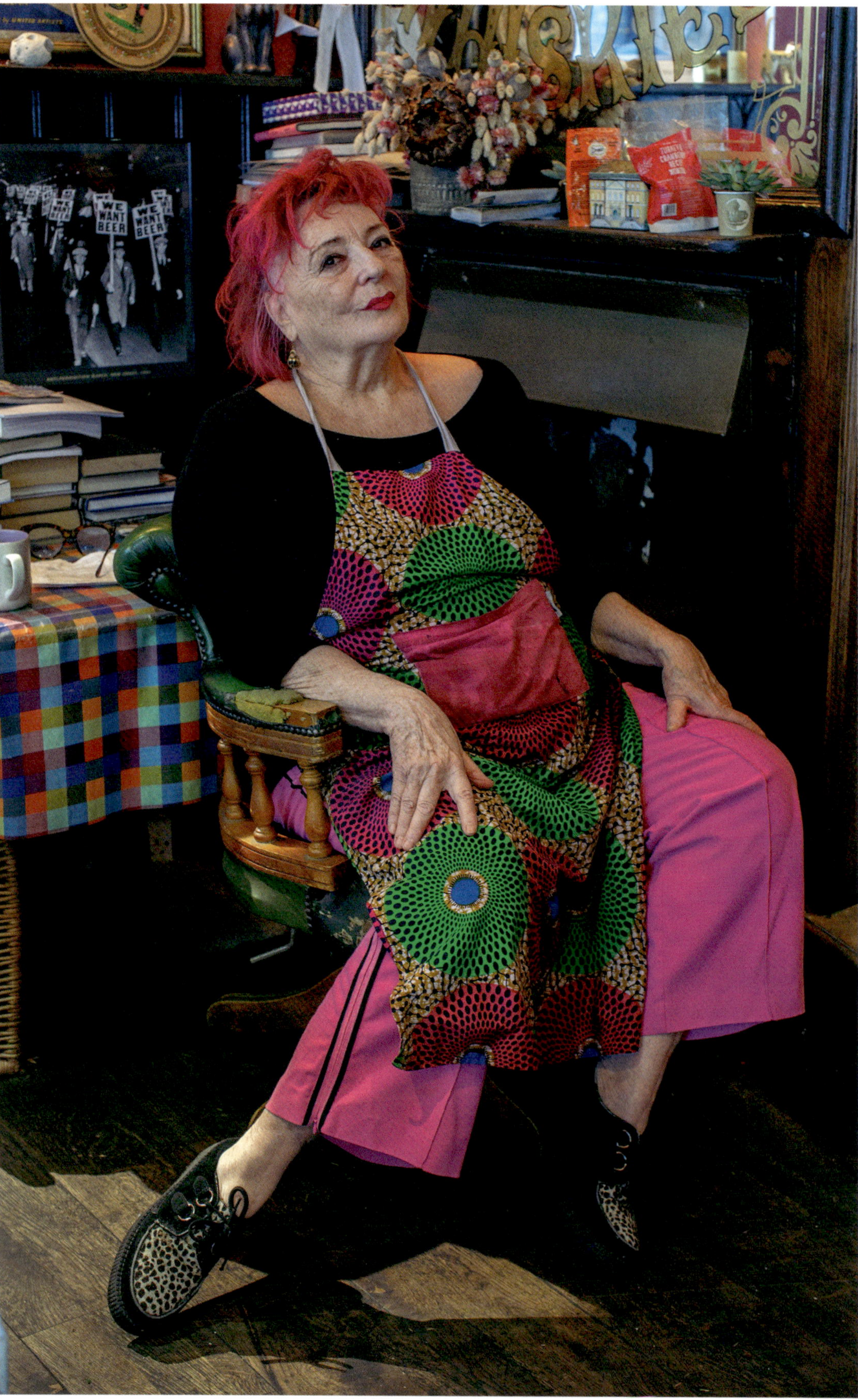
WE WANT BEER
WE WANT BEER

THE SEVEN STARS

LEGAL LONDON'S BOHEMIAN BOLTHOLE

53 CAREY ST, LINCOLN'S INN WC2A 3QS

Being barred from a pub is rarely one of life's highlights. But I certainly wasn't the first, and definitely won't be the last, to be shown the door by the legendary "ale wife for the ages" that is Roxy Beaujolais.

It really is her way or the highway, so a reasonable amount of riff-raff are given their marching orders. But stay just the right side of this full-bodied and fruity Beaujolais, and you're in for a real treat.

The Stars is a cosy, three-roomed railway carriage of a pub. Dating to 1602, legend suggests that it can stake a claim to be the oldest pub in London. Shakespeare himself might have popped in after premiering *Twelfth Night* across the way at Middle Temple Hall in the very same year. Had Roxy been working the pumps, I like to think she would have shouted "You're bard, too!"

A pub is egalitarian: anyone can come in. Until I say they can't.

Roxy Beaujolais

But for all its quirky architecture (and death-trap Elizabethan staircase) it's a wonderful legal backwater to sink a few jars in. It enjoys a unique Parisian bistro-meets-jazz-club ambience, dotted with checked tablecloths and windows lined with linen curtains. Roxy's showbiz razzmatazz permeates every corner of the pub, from the vintage legal movie posters to the Elizabethan ruff-wearing cat *du jour*. (Never ever eat the bar snacks at The Stars. Why? Because they're cat food.)

Whilst Roxy once held sway at Ronnie Scott's, her clientele at The Stars generally decant straight out the back door of the Royal Courts or Lincoln's Inn. Highbrow legal chit-chat might not be quite your thing, but this crowd ensures that a good bottle of red is never far away, and a strong dry martini is ready to pour straight from the chiller.

If all this quaffing amongst the legal eagles and bigwigs is making you peckish, then Roxy still dishes up some top gastro nosh. Think proper home cooking with a twist, akin to a posh aristocrat's dinner party.

So take a canter down Carey Street to revel in one of London's last legendary landladies holding court in her own bon vivant way. I might even see you at the bar. If Roxy ever lets me back in again.

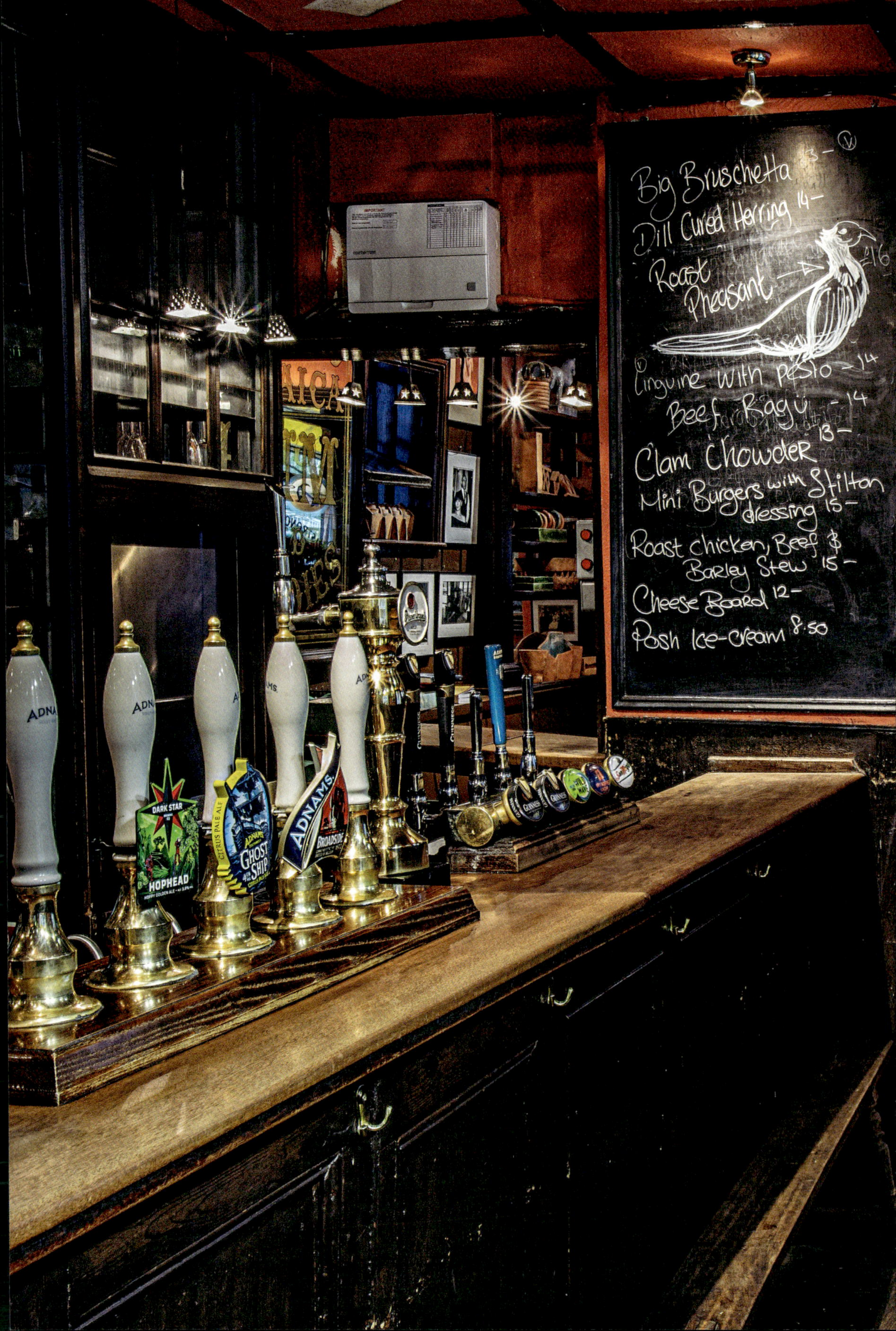
Big Bruschetta 13 - Ⓥ
Dill Cured Herring 14 -
Roast Pheasant → 16
Linguine with pesto - 14
Beef Ragù - 14
Clam Chowder 13 -
Mini Burgers with Stilton dressing 15 -
Roast chicken, Beef & Barley Stew 15 -
Cheese Board 12 -
Posh Ice-cream 8.50
DARK STAR
HOPHEAD
HOPPY GOLDEN ALE
CITRUS PALE ALE
ADNAMS
GHOST SHIP
4.5% PALE ALE
CITRUS PALE ALE
ADNAMS
BROADSIDE
ADNAMS

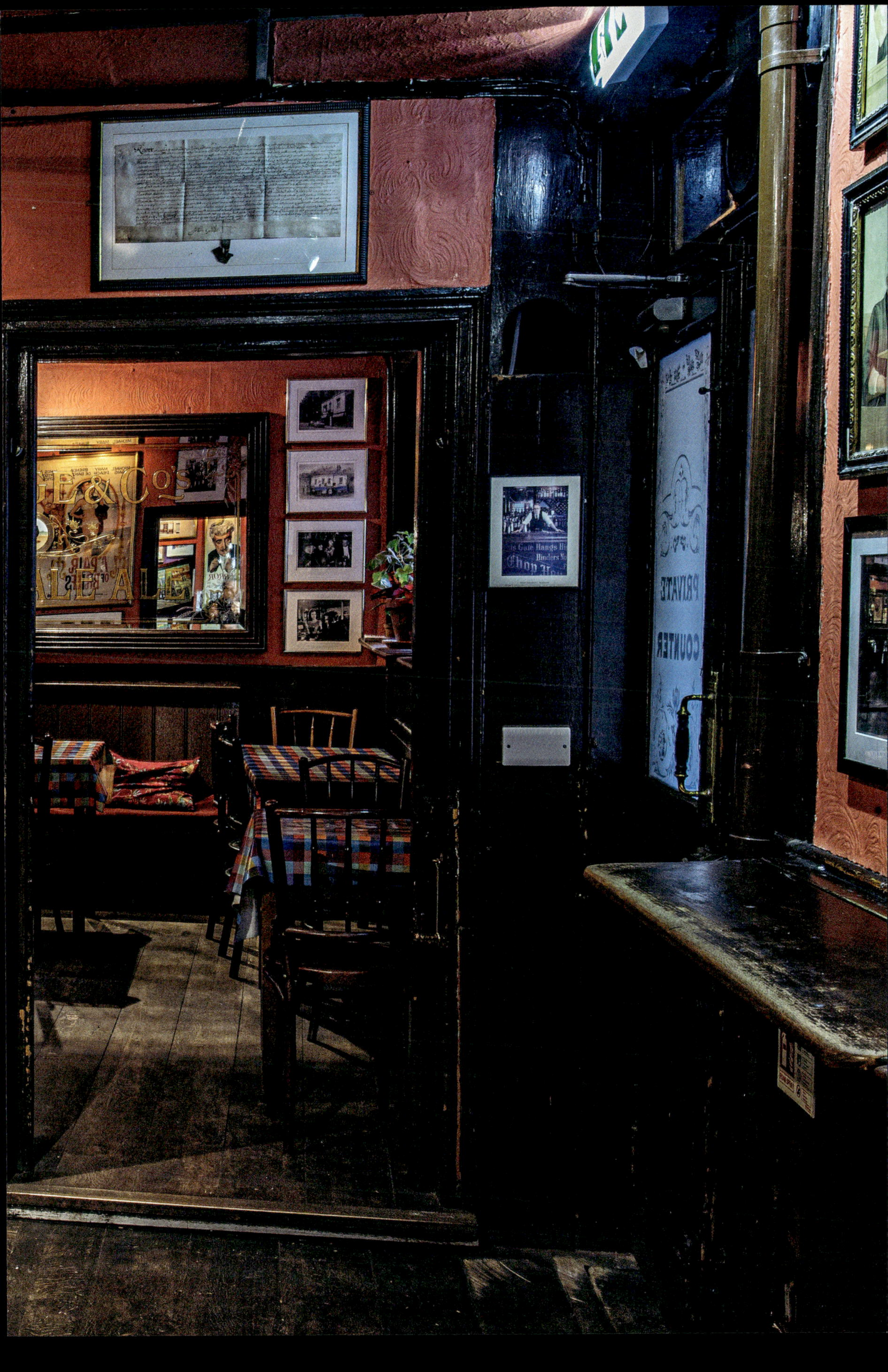

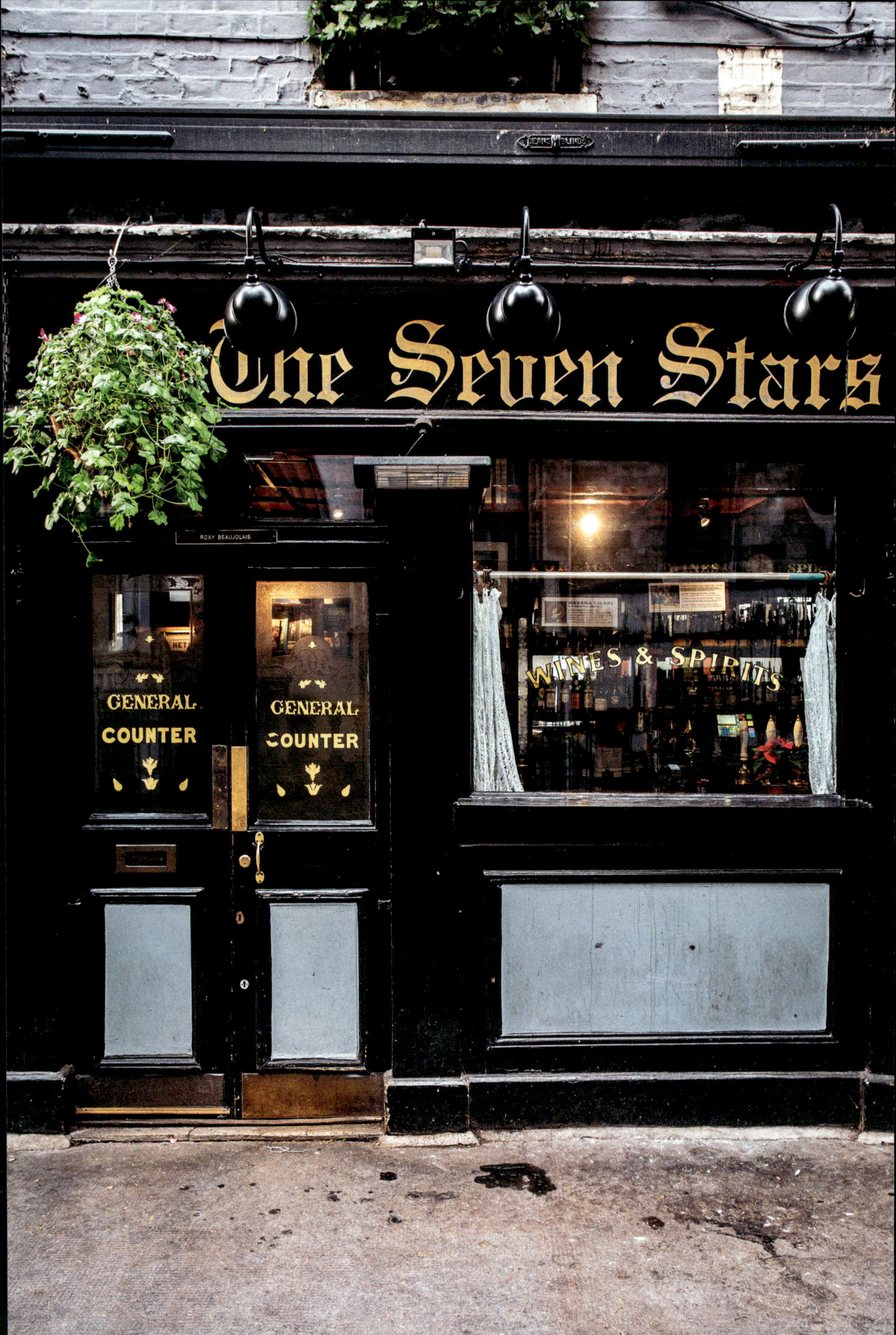
The Seven Stars
ROXY BEAUJOLAIS
GENERAL COUNTER
GENERAL COUNTER
WINES & SPIRITS
HAVANA CIGARS

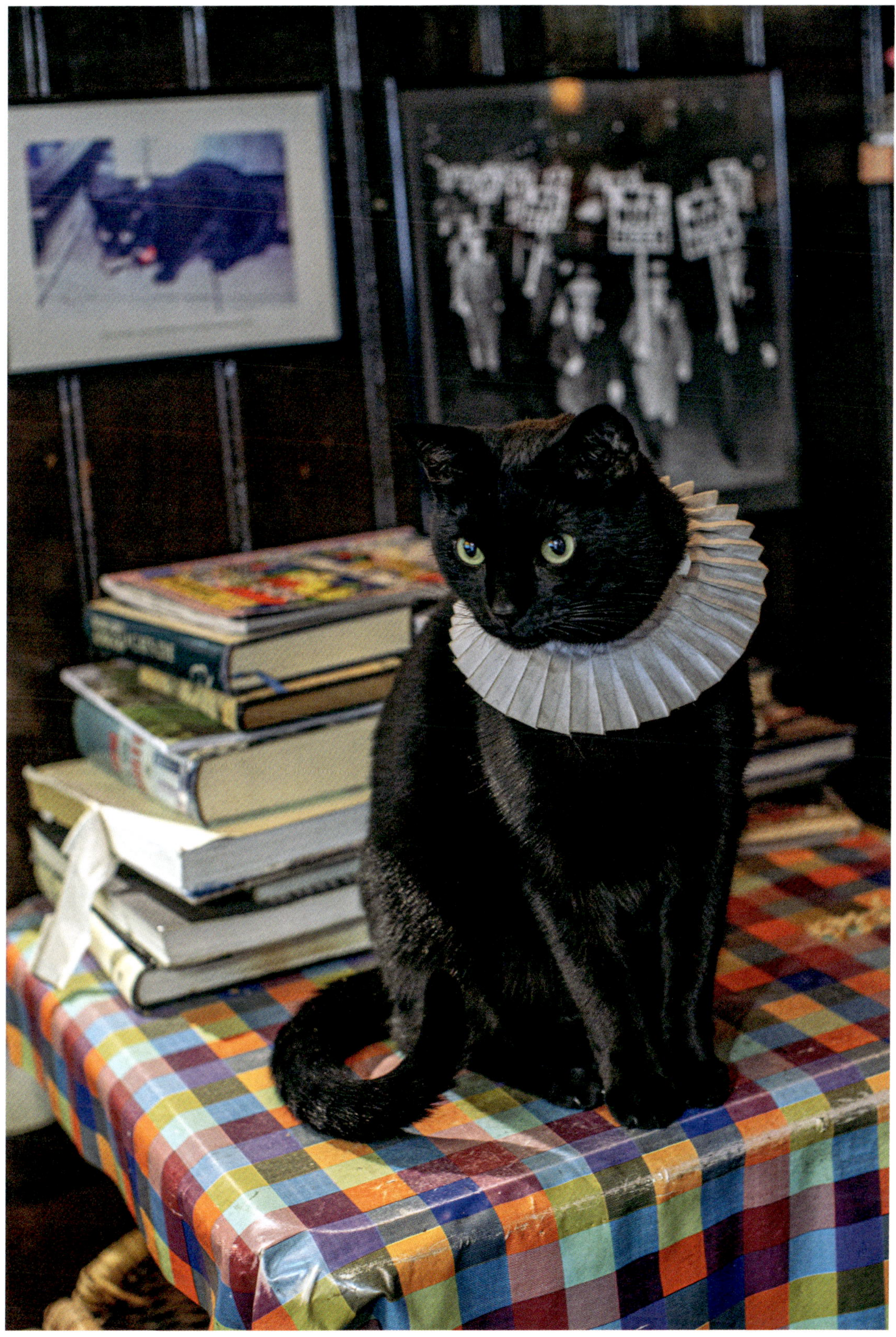

Because we're in show business darling!

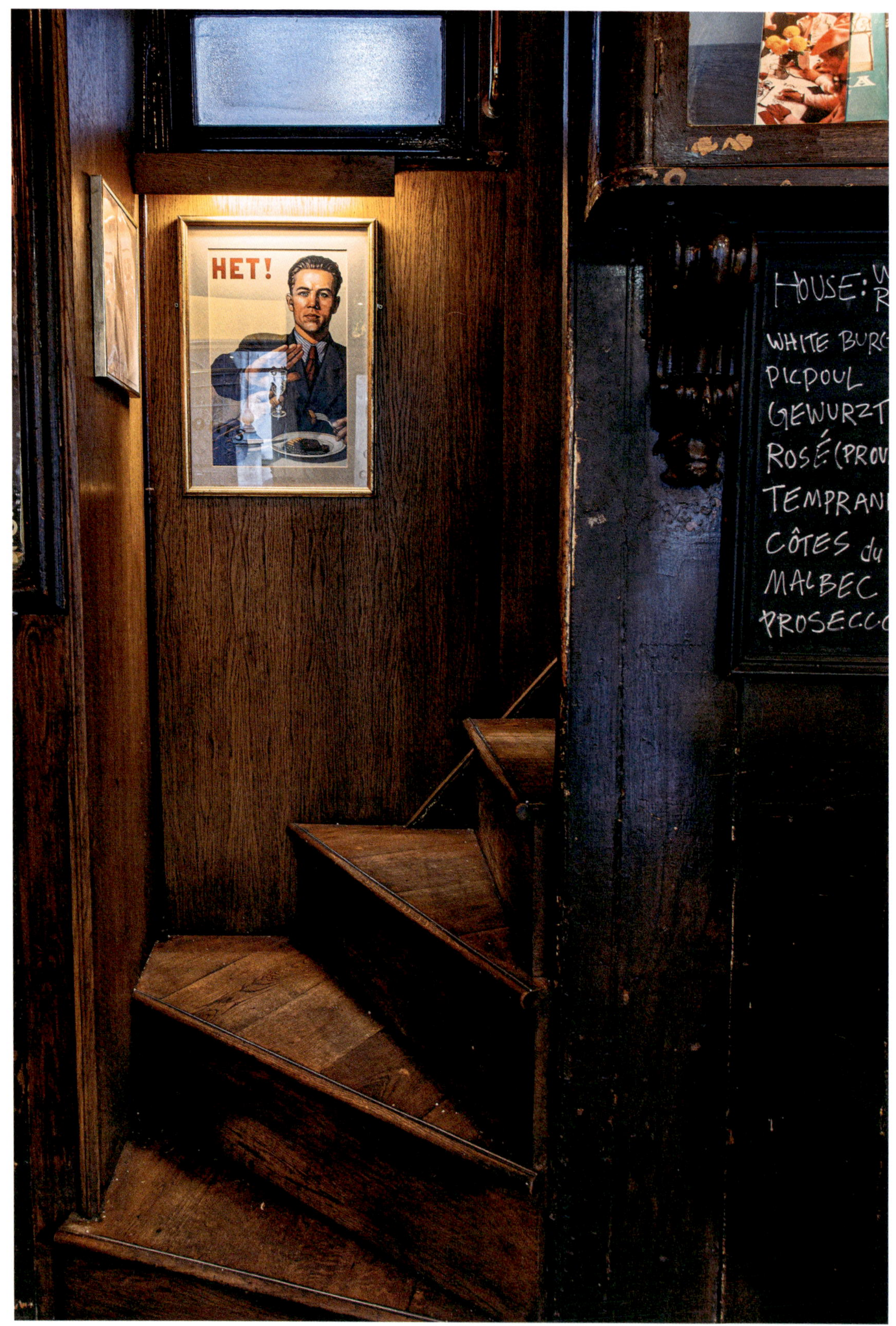

Ancient Elizabethan architecture underlies the bohemian bistro vibes

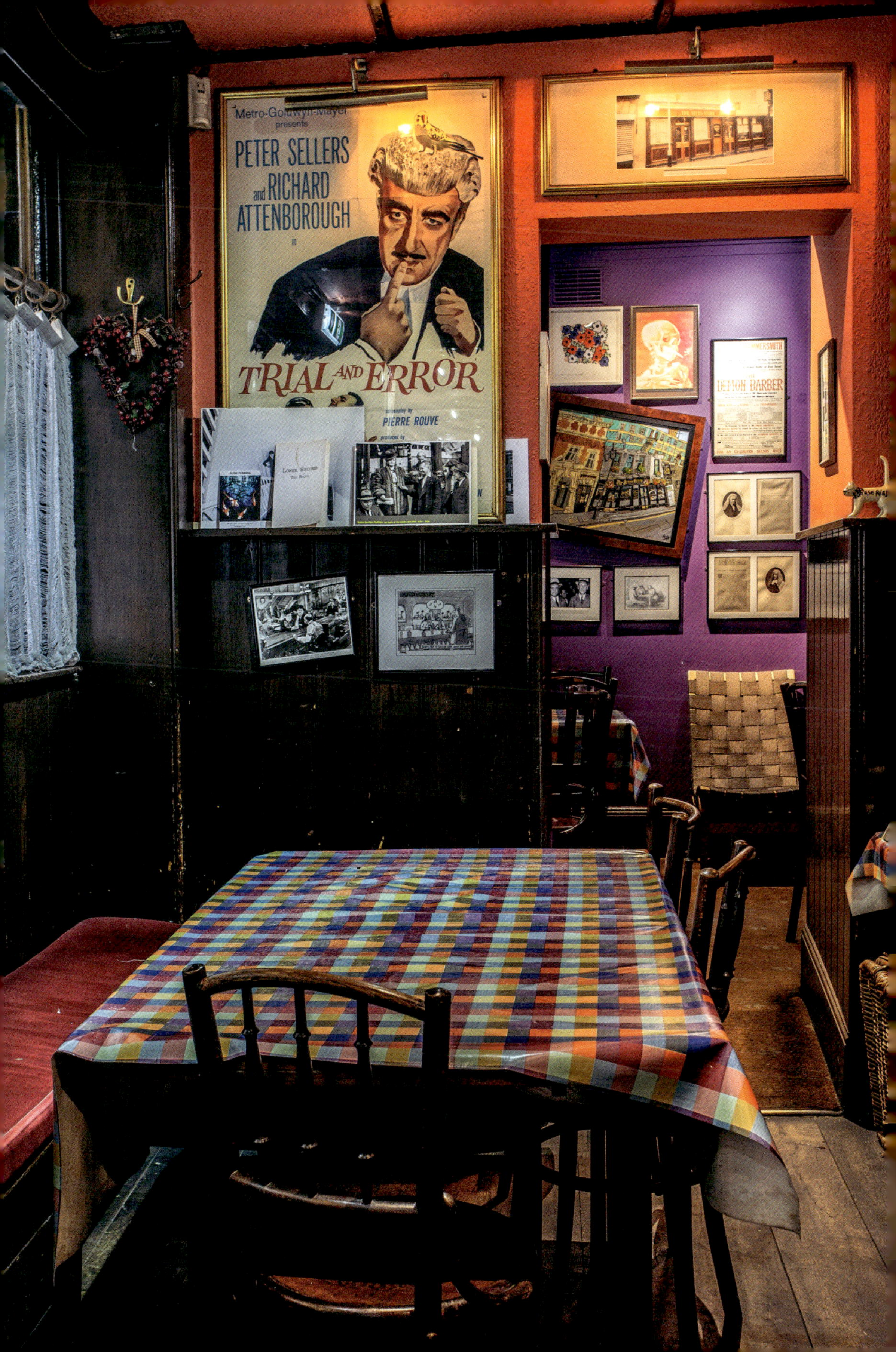
Metro-Goldwyn-Mayer
presents
PETER SELLERS
and RICHARD
ATTENBOROUGH
in
TRIAL AND ERROR
screenplay by
PIERRE ROUVE
produced by

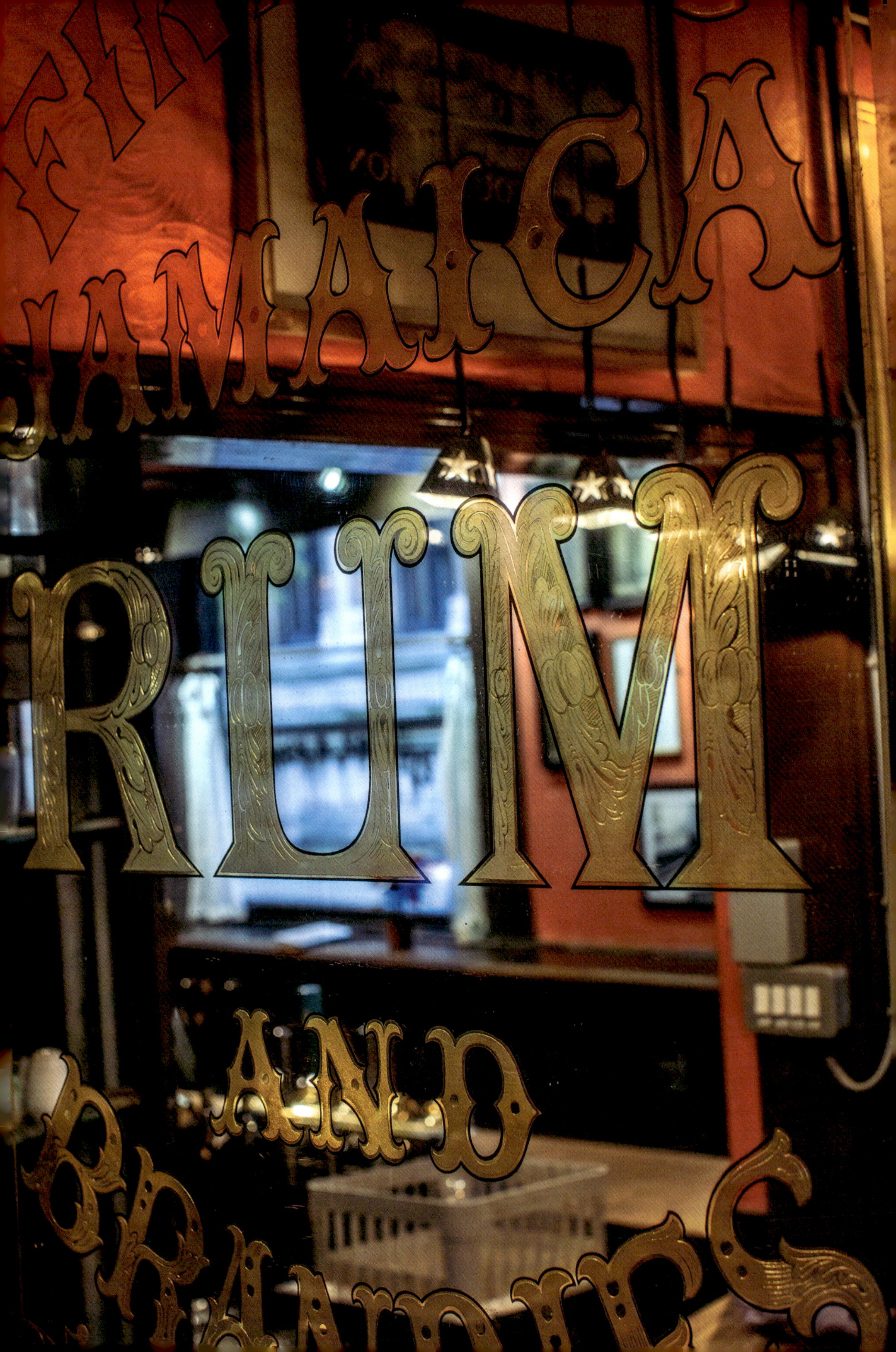
JAMAICA
RUM
AND

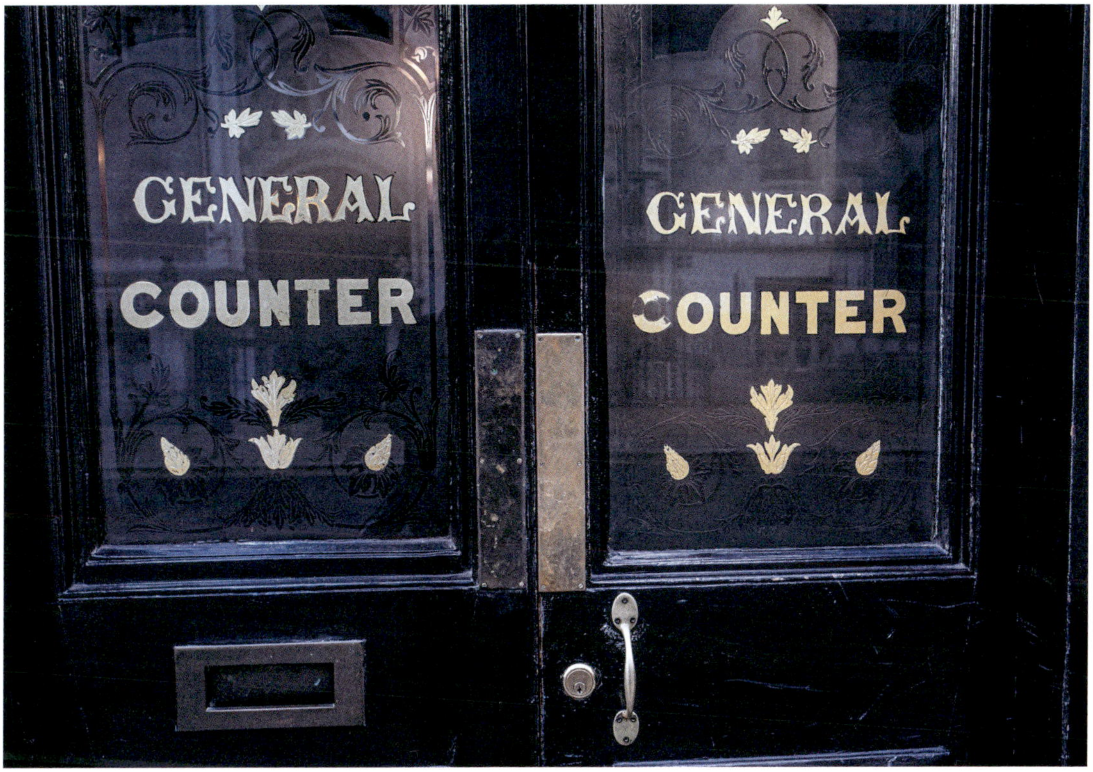

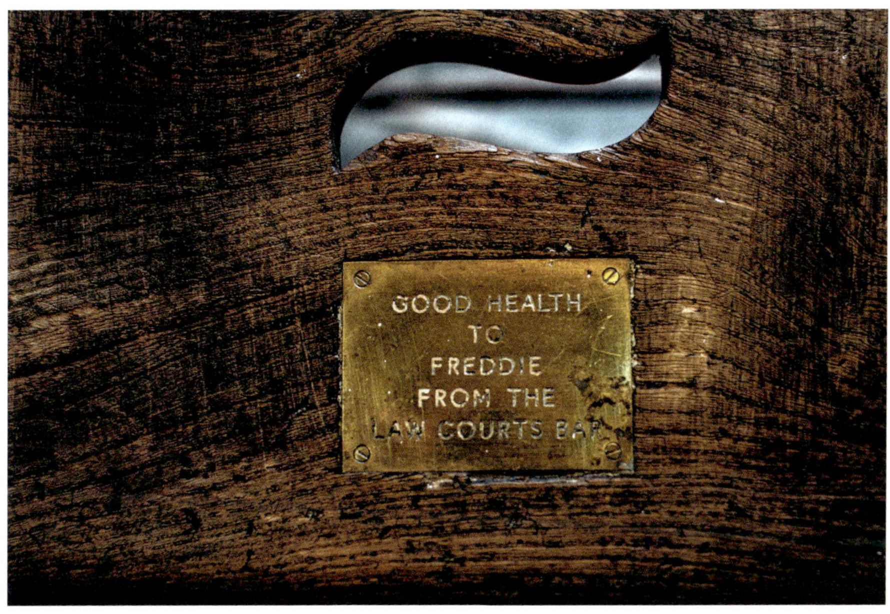

London's legal eagles flock to this watering hole

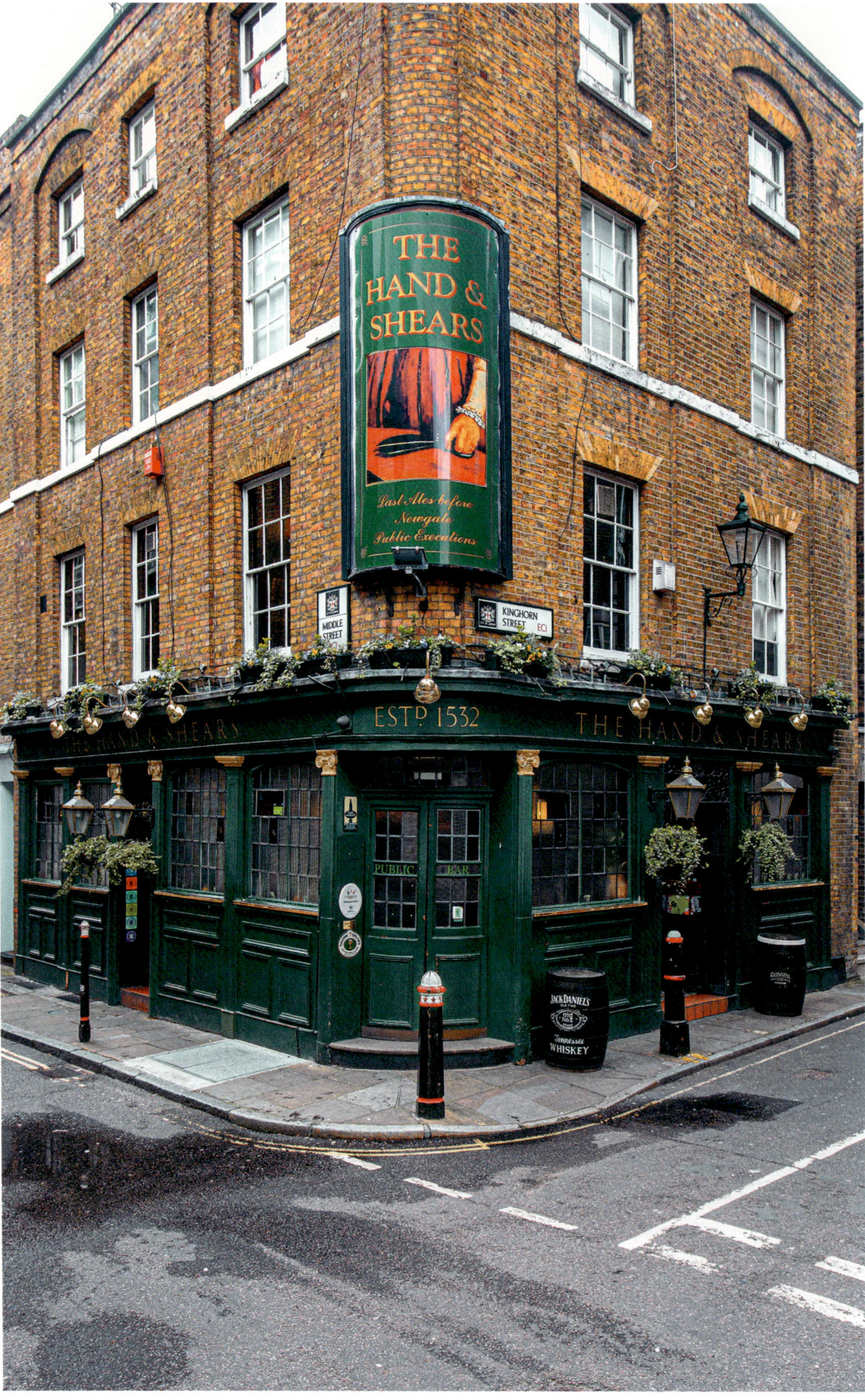

THE HAND & SHEARS
Last Ales before
Newgate
Public Executions
MIDDLE STREET
KINGHORN STREET EC1
ESTD. 1532
THE HAND & SHEARS
THE HAND & SHEARS
PUBLIC BAR
JACK DANIELS
OLD NO. 7
Tennessee
WHISKEY

THE HAND & SHEARS

The poet laureate Sir John Betjeman was a true connoisseur and discerning man about town. This is the chap who helped save the splendid Arts and Crafts Black Friar pub. He also thought a few "friendly bombs" should rain down on Slough, so it's probably lucky that he was a poet rather than part-time RAF pilot. Sir John loved and knew London better than most, so where he chose to live is worth noting. He took lost-in-time lodgings just off the medieval Cloth Fair. The ancient parish church frames Cloth Fair along one side, whilst across the way you'll find the oldest residential houses in the City of London. And in the snicket next door, you'll find Sir John Betjeman's house where he once came for lunch in 1954 and stayed for twenty blissful years.

... the solidity of bare and burnished dark wood holds firm here.

As a poet, he was interested in places and faces more than highfalutin, abstracted states of mind. Here he could be immersed in the "physical chaff and clutter" of the meat market and follow the associated fallout to the bar at the "fist 'n' clippers". Once his mackintosh and trilby hat were safely hung, this would be his realm: the place where prisoners would take a "last drop" before execution at nearby Newgate Gaol and where the Lord Mayor of London would open the bawdy Bartholomew Fair by cutting ribbon on these tavern steps.

The pub remains remarkably unchanged to this day. A central bar dispenses to every panelled nook and cranny of its four rooms, and sepia tones drown every space. The real ales are taken seriously, with the usual suspects of Theakston's and Landlord often up top, whilst peckish pub-goers might find a sausage roll or meat pie locally sourced from the market a few yards away. Where other pubs of the era would be all etched glass and razzle dazzle, the solidity of bare and burnished dark wood holds firm here.

With Smithfield Market on the brink of closure, it's all change for this quiet corner of the City, and the modern world appears to be attacking from all sides. But wait! It's the twenty-first century and both Cloth Fair and The Hand and Shears are still there. Go now. Go quickly. For one day they shall both be gone.

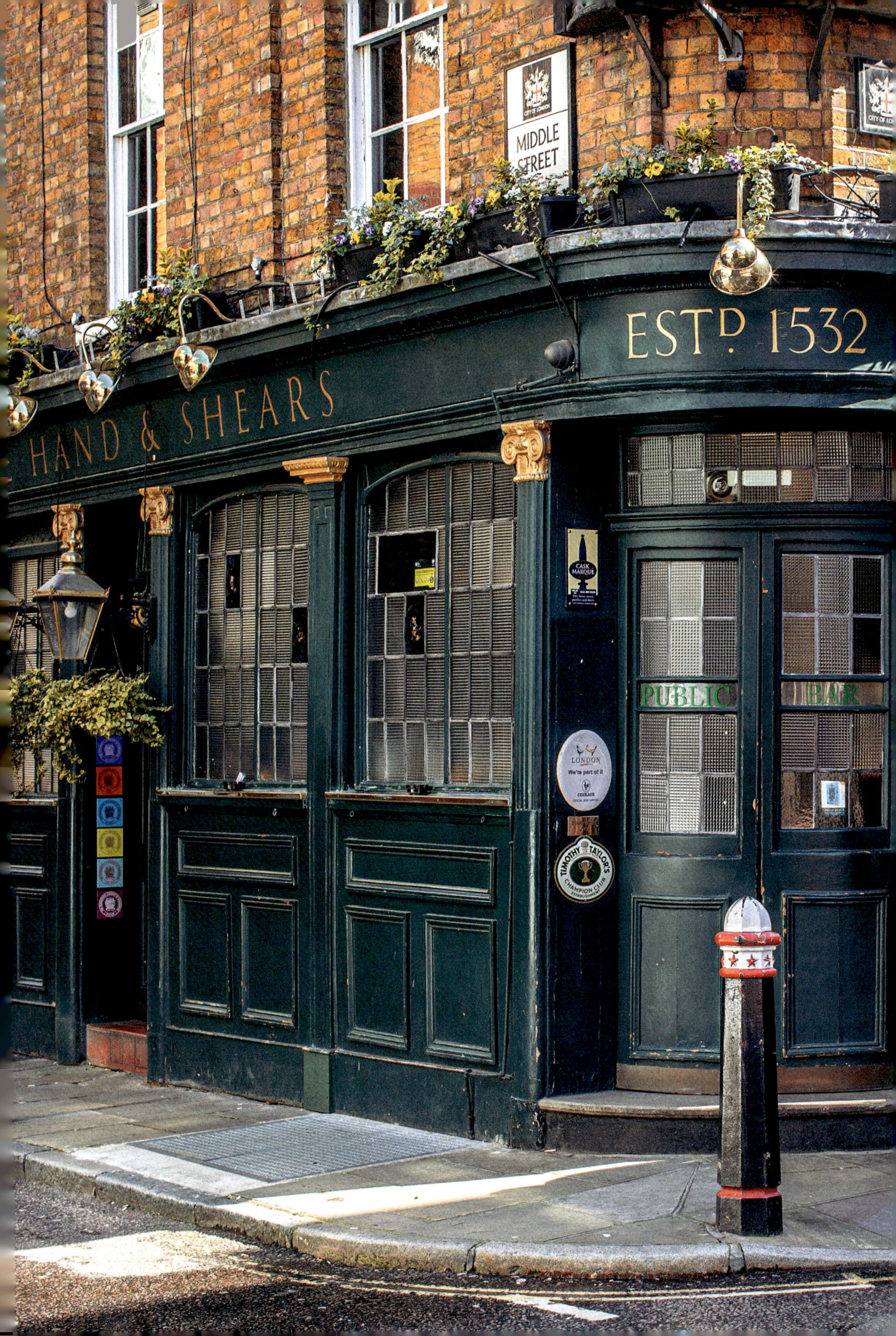

CITY OF LONDON
MIDDLE STREET
ESTᴰ 1532
HAND & SHEARS
PUBLIC BAR
CASK MARQUE
LONDON
We're part of it
COURAGE
TIMOTHY TAYLOR'S
CHAMPION CLUB

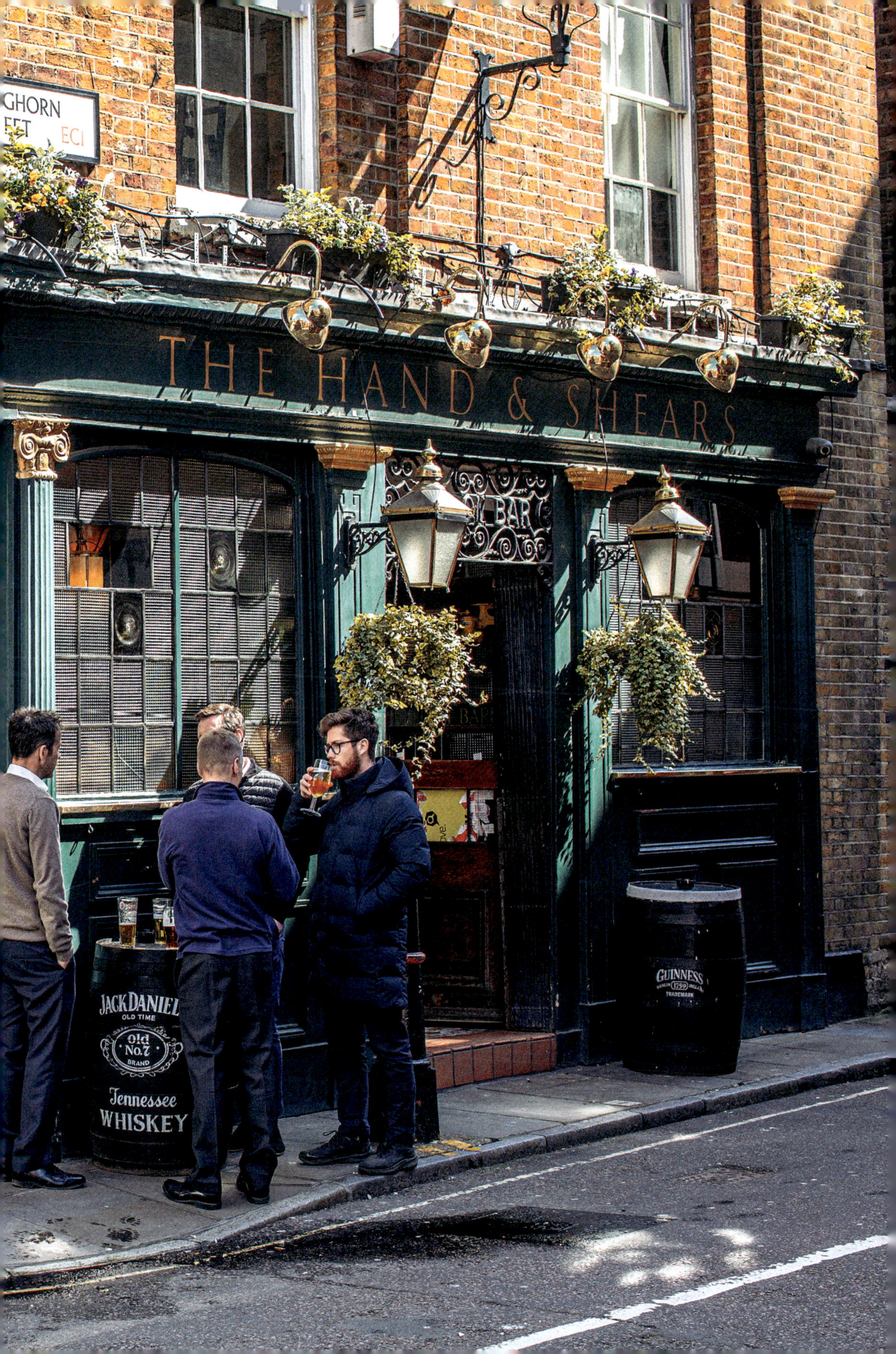
GHORN
EET EC1
THE HAND & SHEARS
BAR
BAR
JACK DANIEL'S
OLD TIME
Old
NO.7
BRAND
Tennessee
WHISKEY
GUINNESS
1759 DUBLIN
TRADEMARK

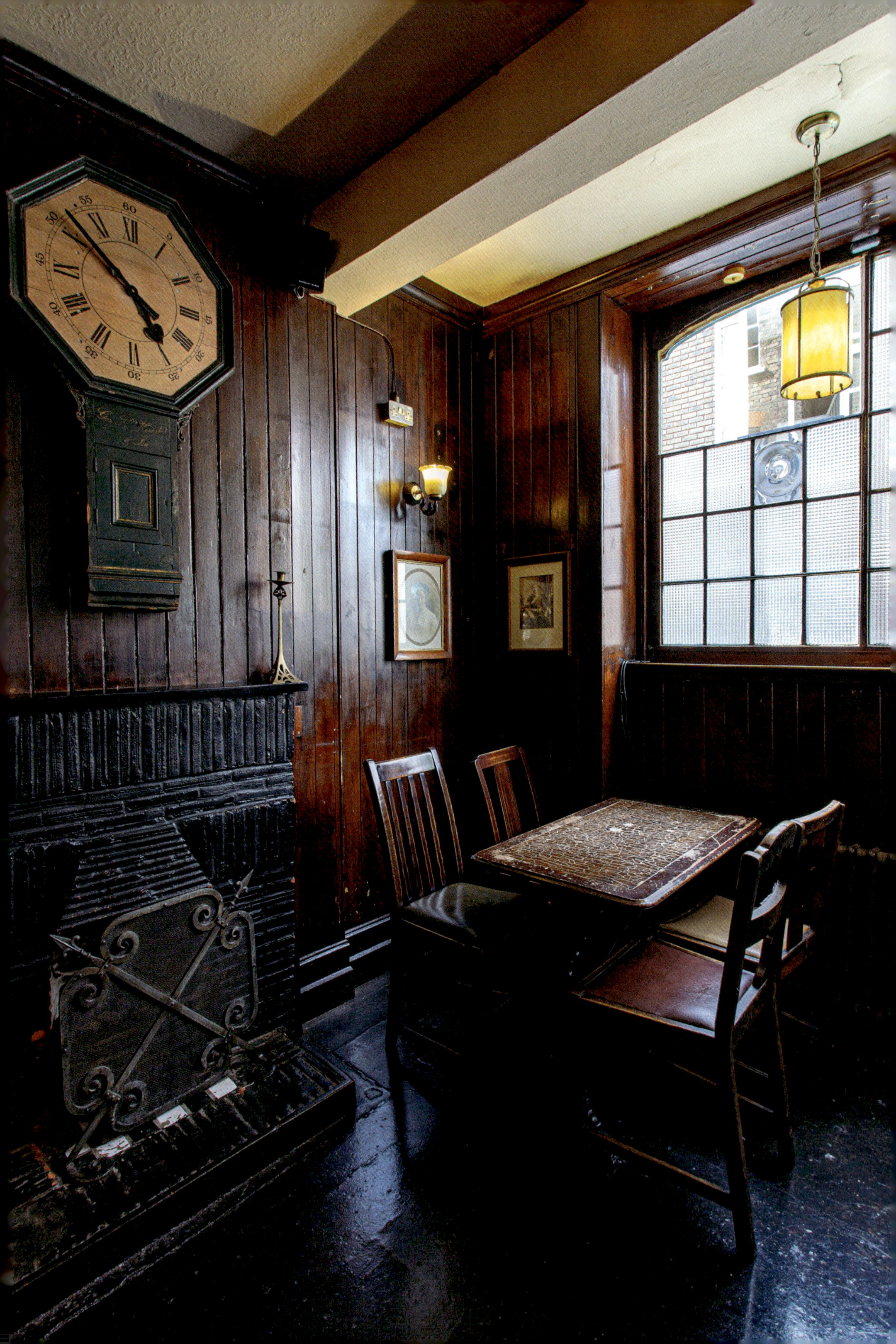

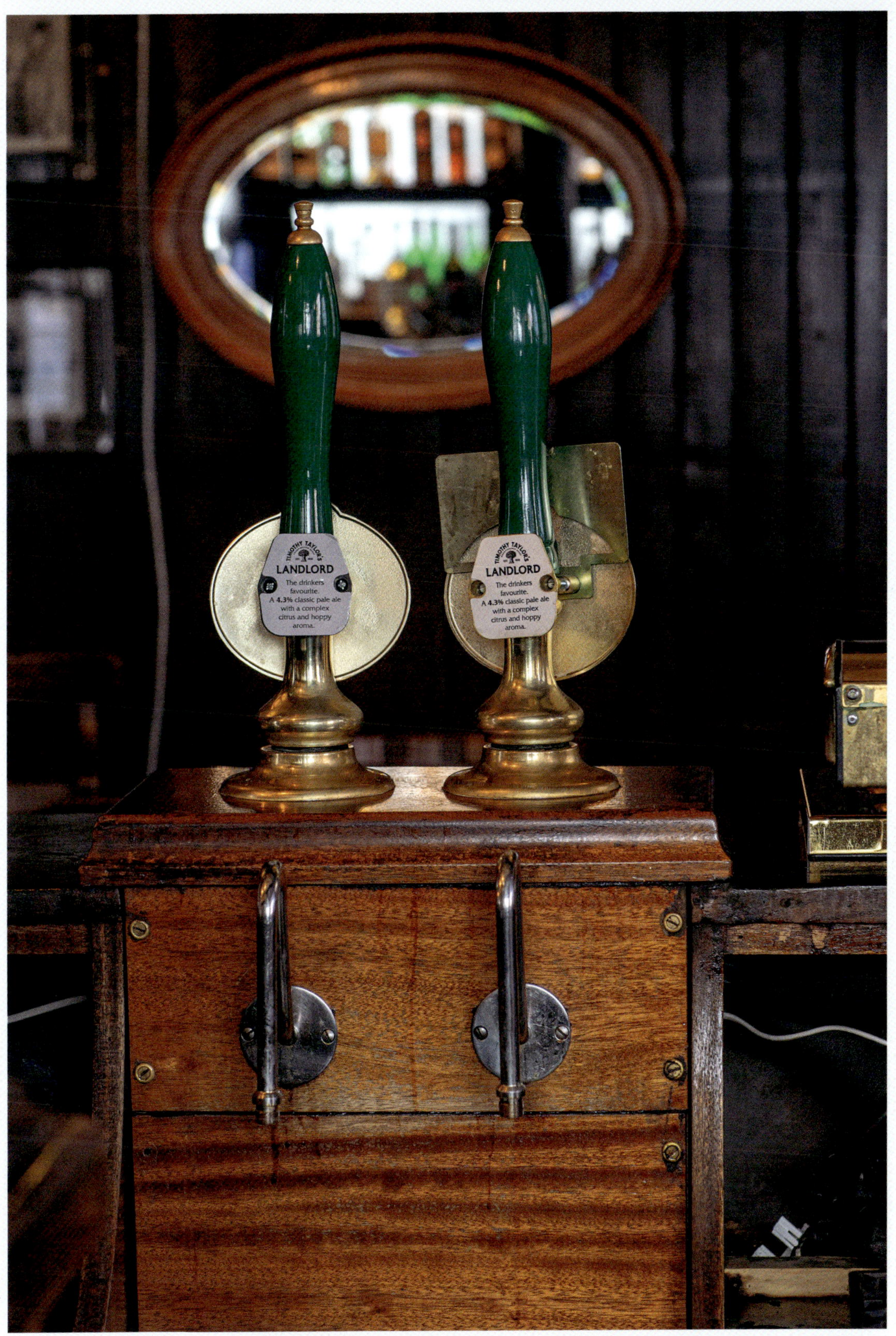

Little-changed since Betjeman's days

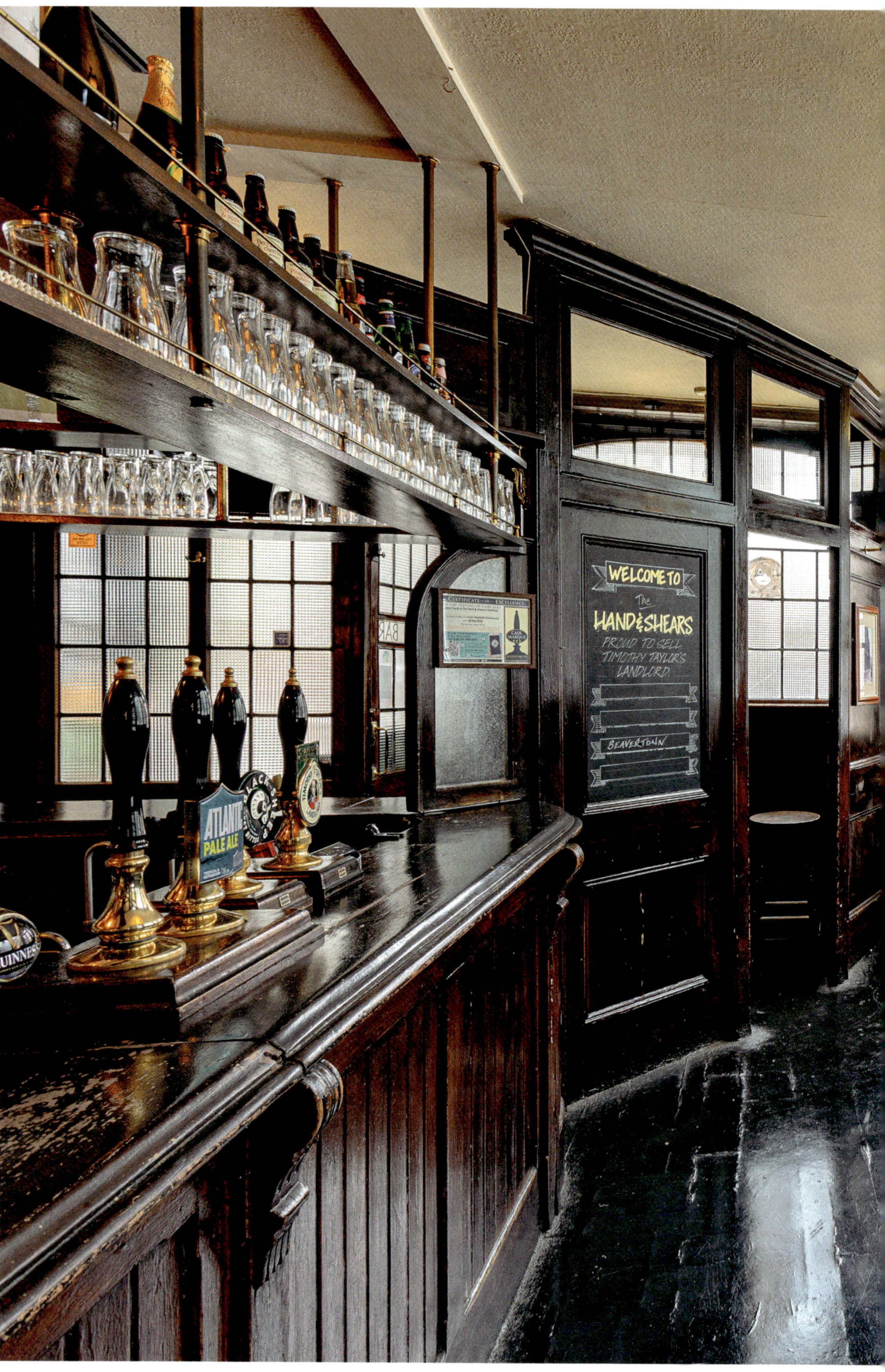

WELCOME TO
The
HAND & SHEARS
PROUD TO SELL
TIMOTHY TAYLOR'S
LANDLORD
BEAVERTOWN
ATLANTIC
PALE ALE
GUINNESS

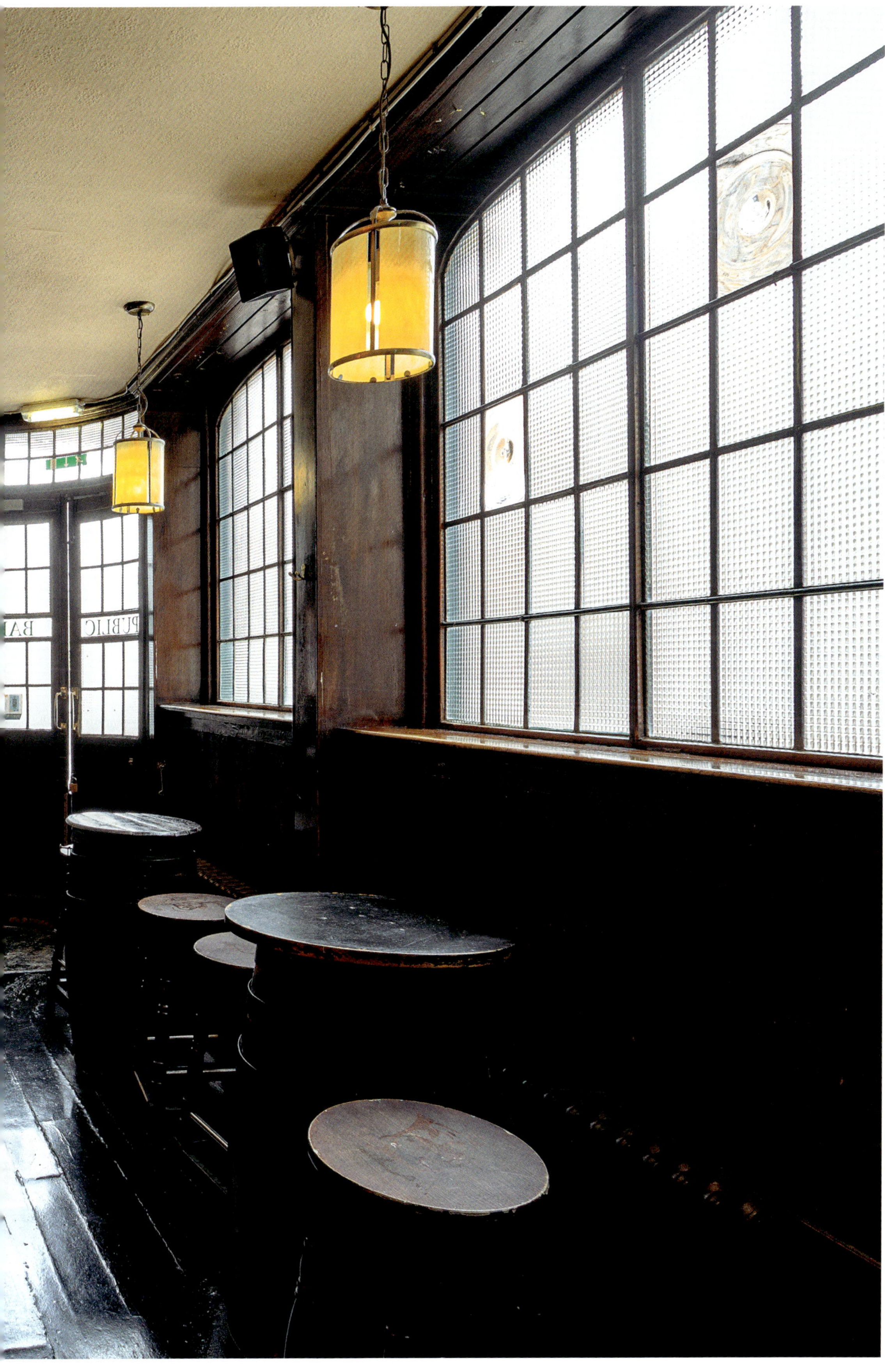

PUBLIC
BA

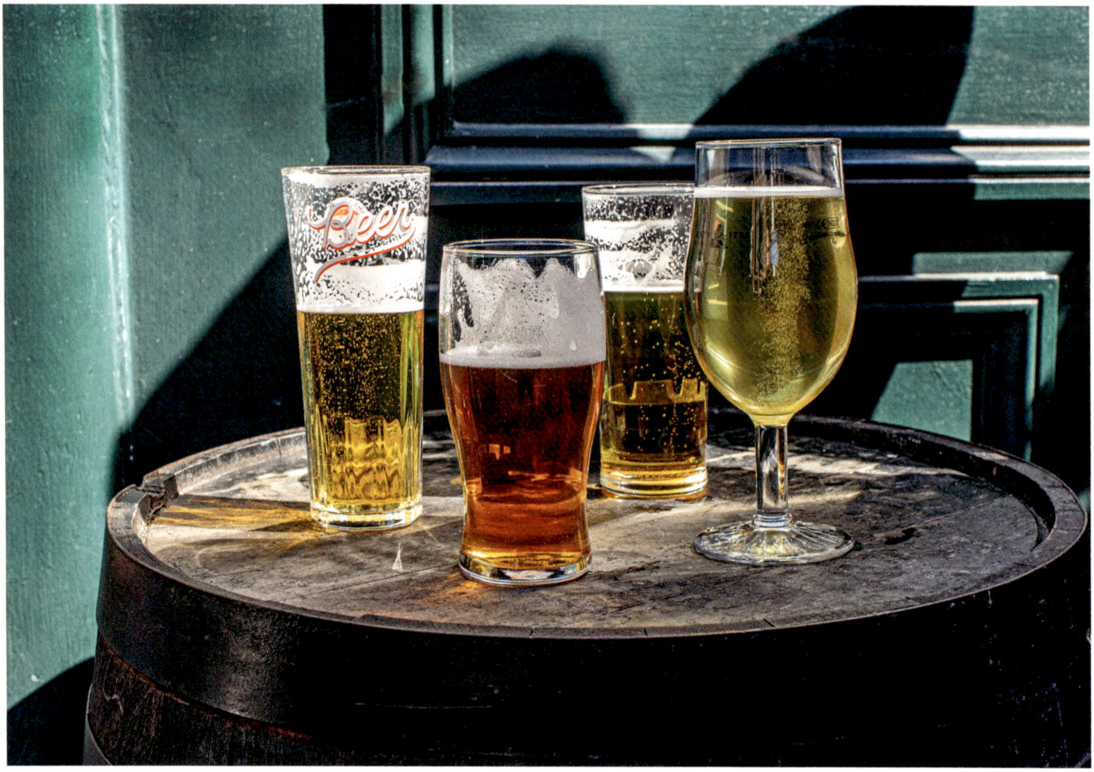

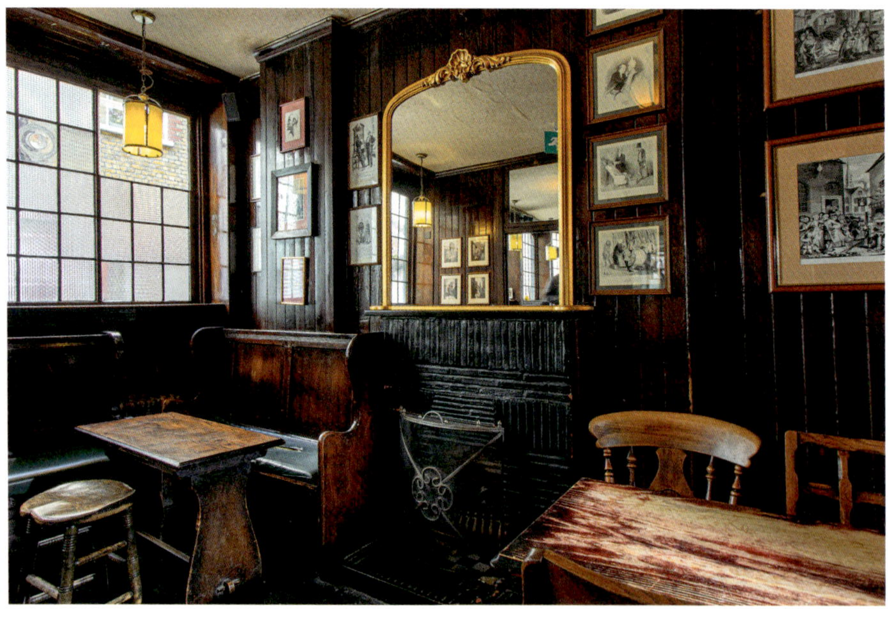

A most agreeable lost-in-time interior

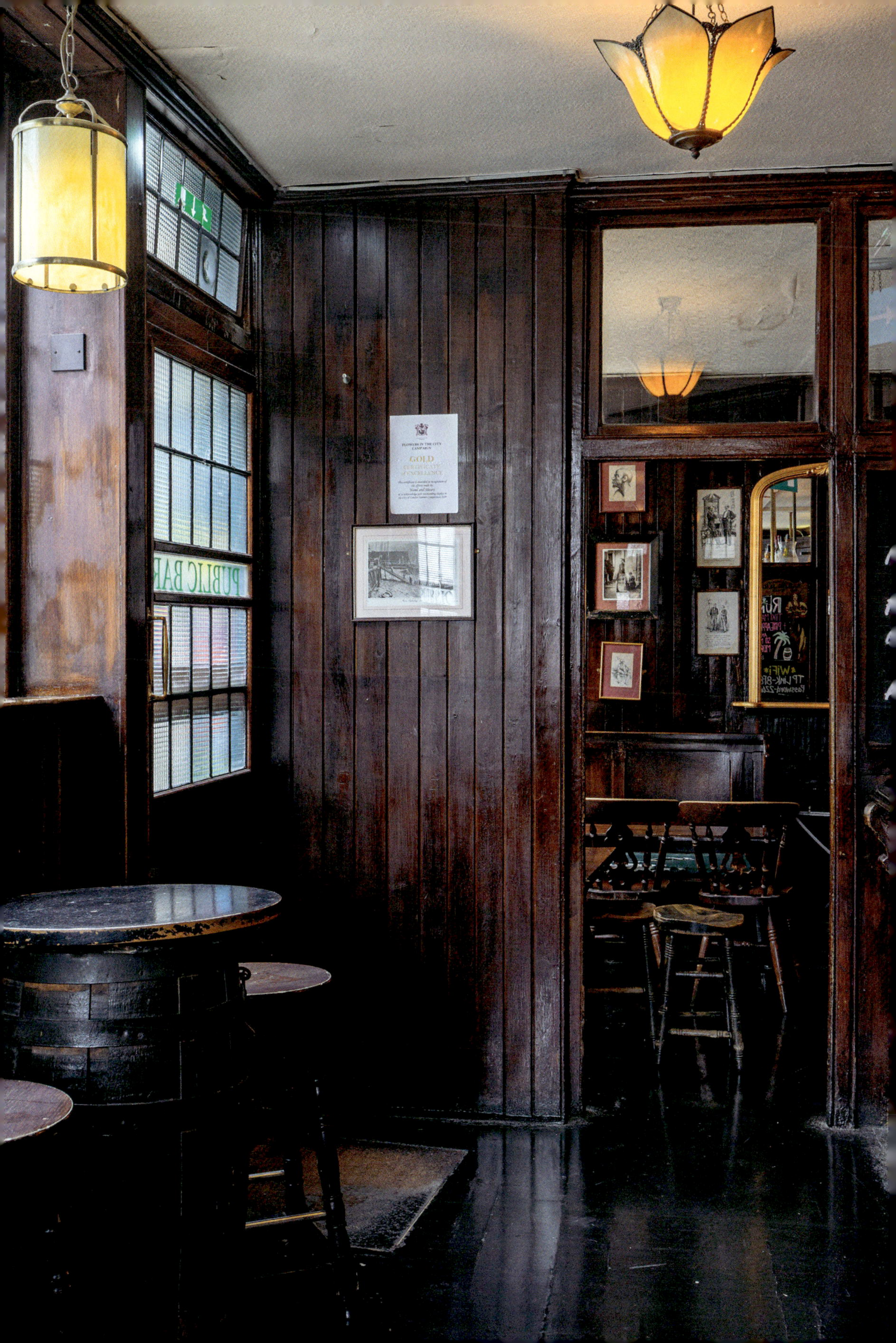

THE DUKE

LONDON'S LAST REMAINING ART DECO PUB

7 ROGER ST, BLOOMSBURY WC1N 2PB

Art Deco pubs are few and far between in London. This indulgent architectural style is best enjoyed over a Gin Rickey with a Great Gatsby side serve at The Savoy, Claridge's or the Rivoli Bar of The Ritz.

The short inter-war period allowed little time to pamper the more proletariat pubs with Deco's smooth walls and sharp-edged symmetry. It's a style built on confidence (and deep pockets), and by the mid-1930s there were some serious storm clouds gathering. The year of this pub's completion, 1938, was not a classic. *Time* magazine made Adolf Hitler their "Man of the Year" as he rolled into Austria and the Sudetenland. And whilst Neville Chamberlain declared a "Peace for our time", the RAF were secretly building early-warning radar stations along our coastline.

Jitterbug tunes fill the airwaves, and the stuttering hum of doodlebugs haunts the imagination

The Duke is a pub that hides its face well in this quiet corner of Bloomsbury. You're primarily visiting for the architecture, so a stroll around the block is the order of the day. Revel in the Eric Gill-esque reliefs, imagine Hercules Poirot and Hastings pontificating in the penthouse, and lust after the curved brick balconies next door. It's a remarkably forward-thinking mixed-use development: the pub imagined as a hub for office workers, posh apartment owners or perhaps the frazzled primary school teachers across the way.

Inside, it's a classic. Not a pub classic per se. But The Duke is a unique and spacious two-roomer in which to sink a couple of jars and decant to the rear room for a pie and mash. Savour the soaring ceilings, crisp steel window lines, and Double Diamond frosted glass. The veneered wood bar and streamlined booths keep the modernist dream alive for local workers and hospital staff. Garnished lightly with a sprinkling of period mirrors and lamps, the lack of ornamental overkill lets the architecture do the talking, and you feel like you've stepped into a Second World War movie set. Jitterbug tunes fill the airwaves, and the stuttering hum of doodlebugs haunts the imagination. Thankfully, the forces of fascism were kept at arm's length by "The Few", but the war determined that the Art Deco style would also be extinguished. We would never build like this ever again. The Duke may not look like a pub. It may not even feel like a pub. But it is a portal to the near past and a fine example of a brave new pub world that never quite came into being.

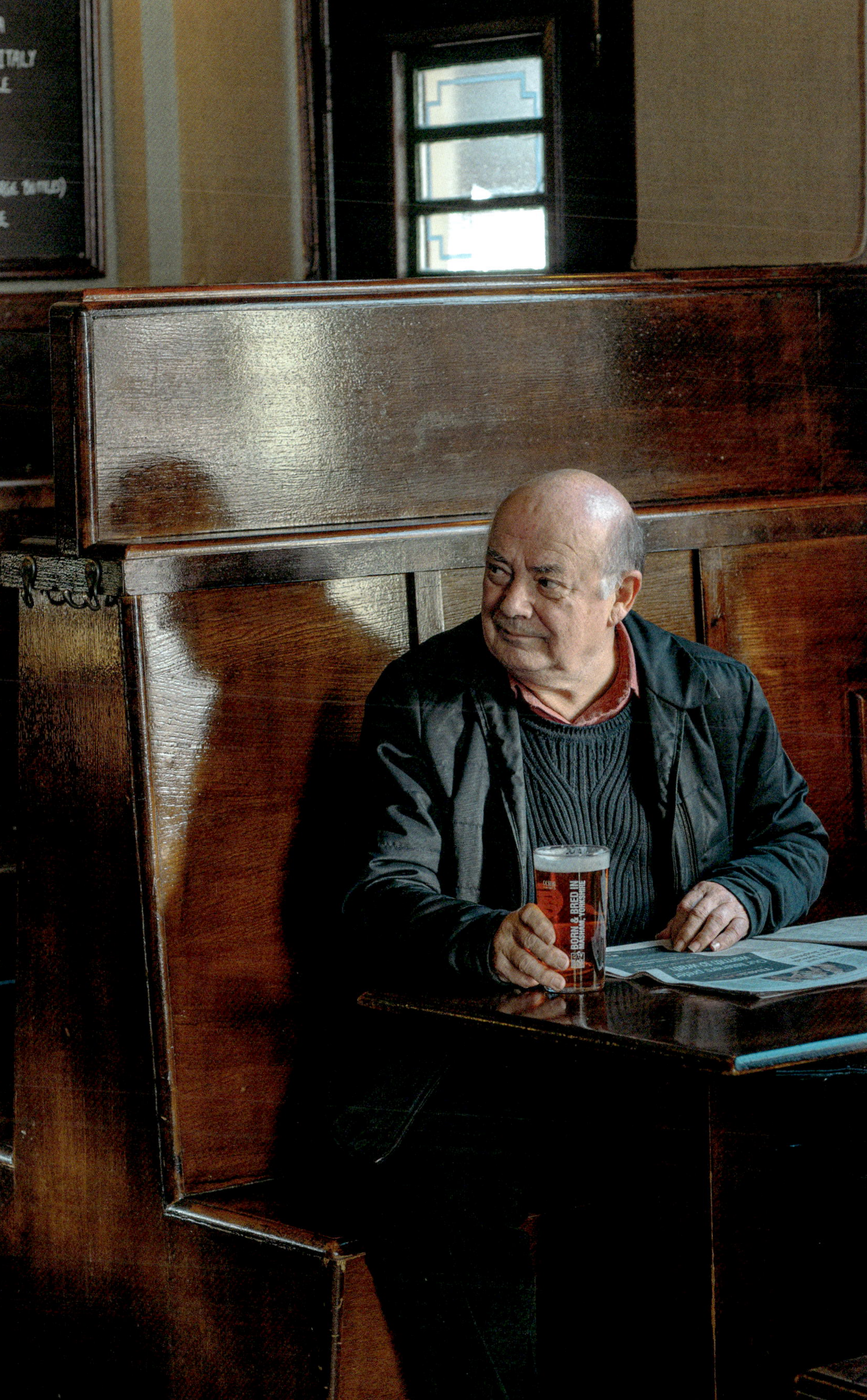

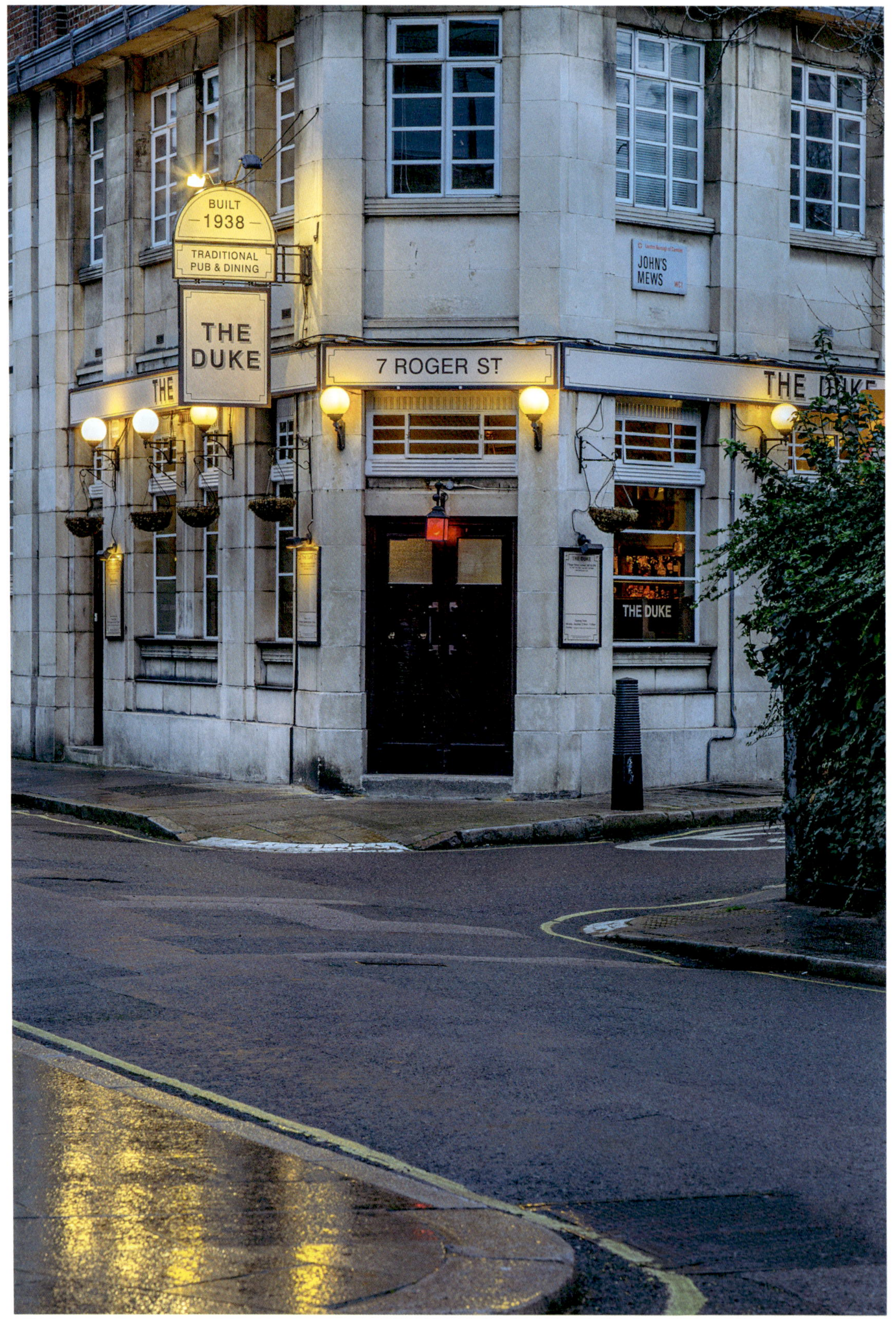

An architectural treasure

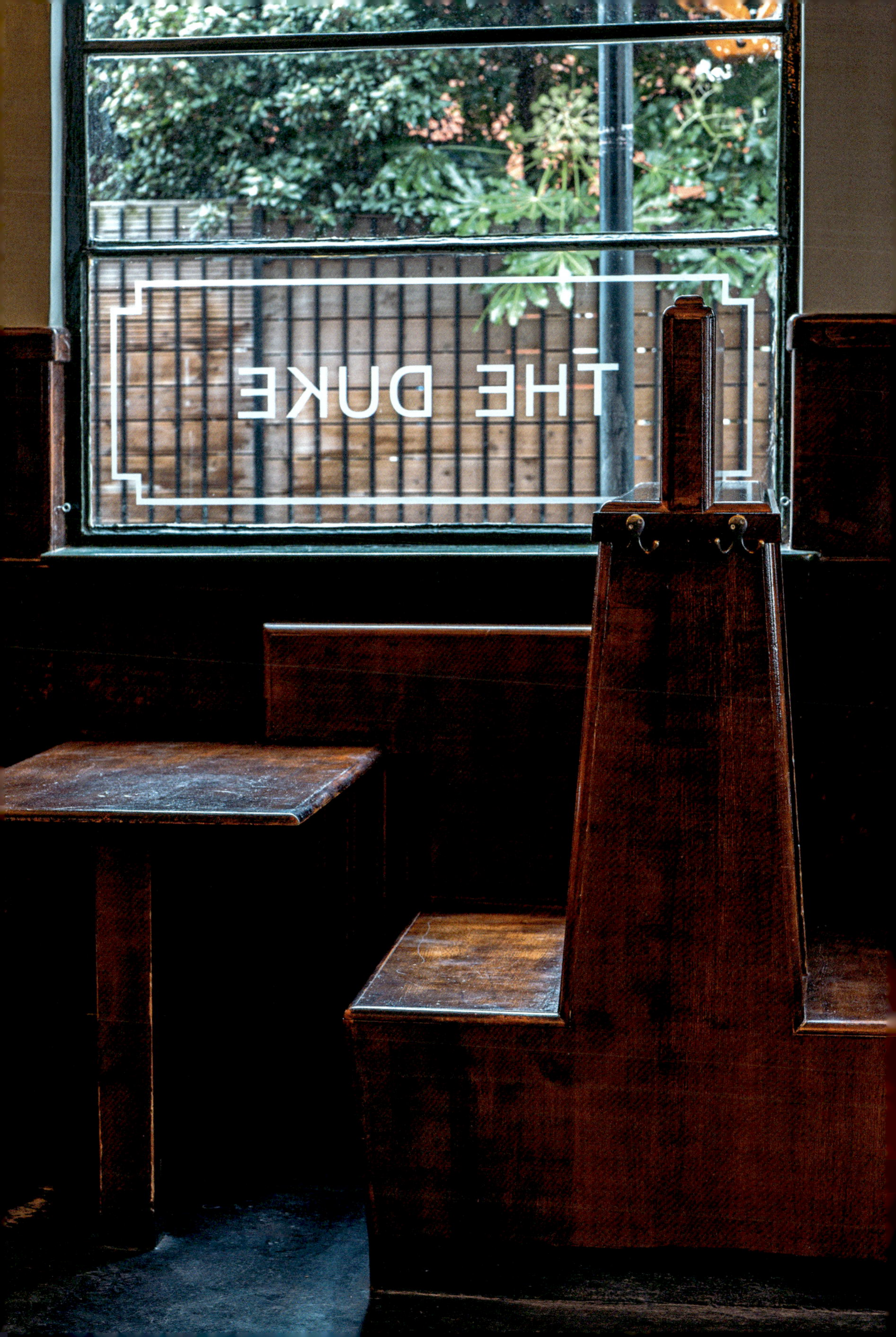
THE DUKE

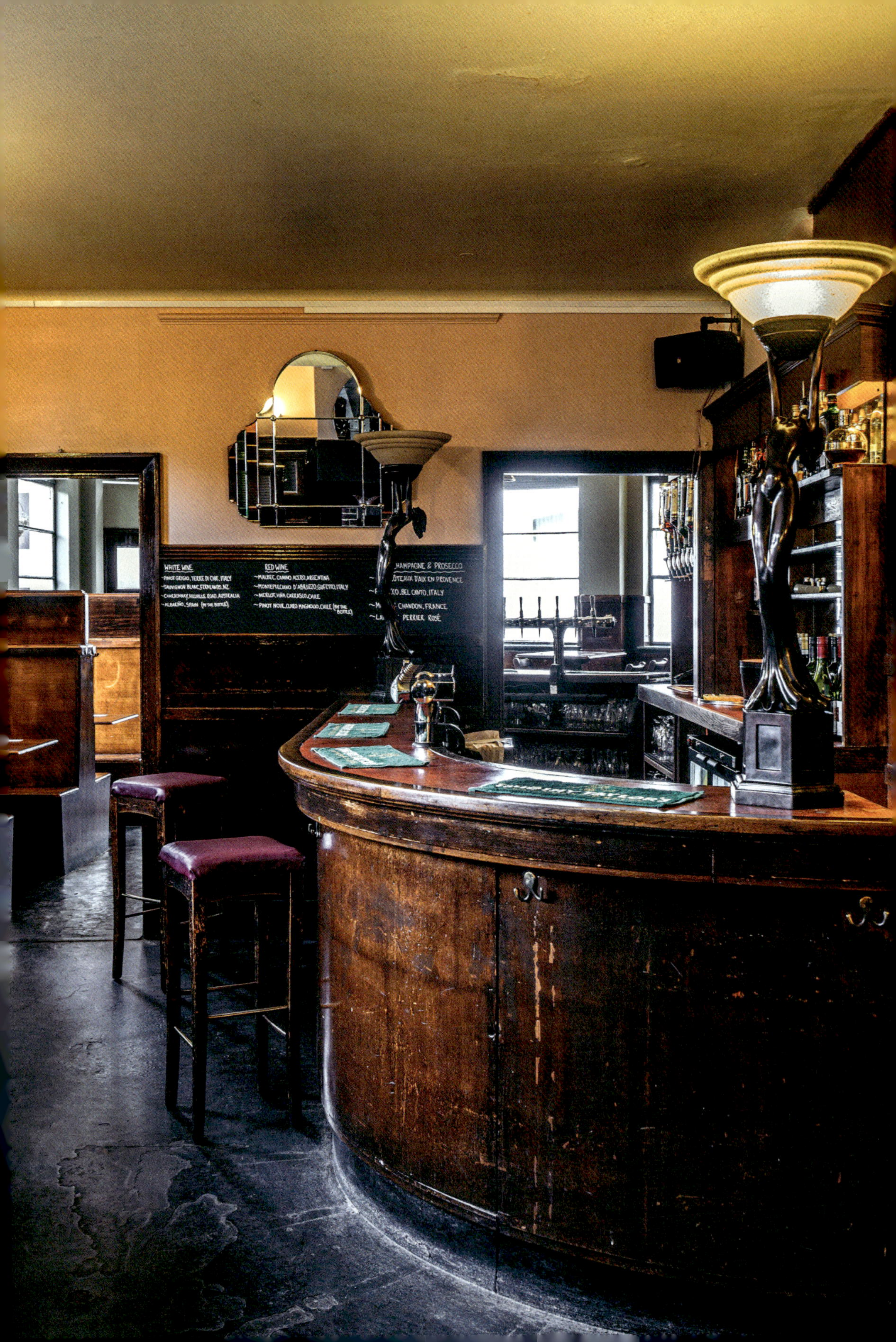

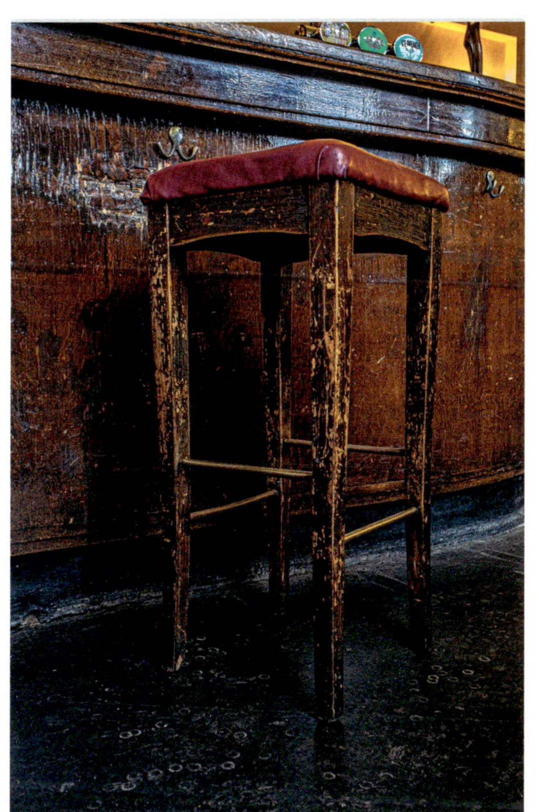

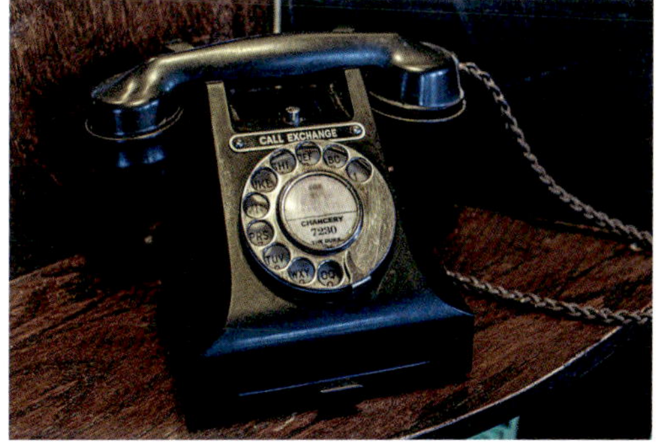

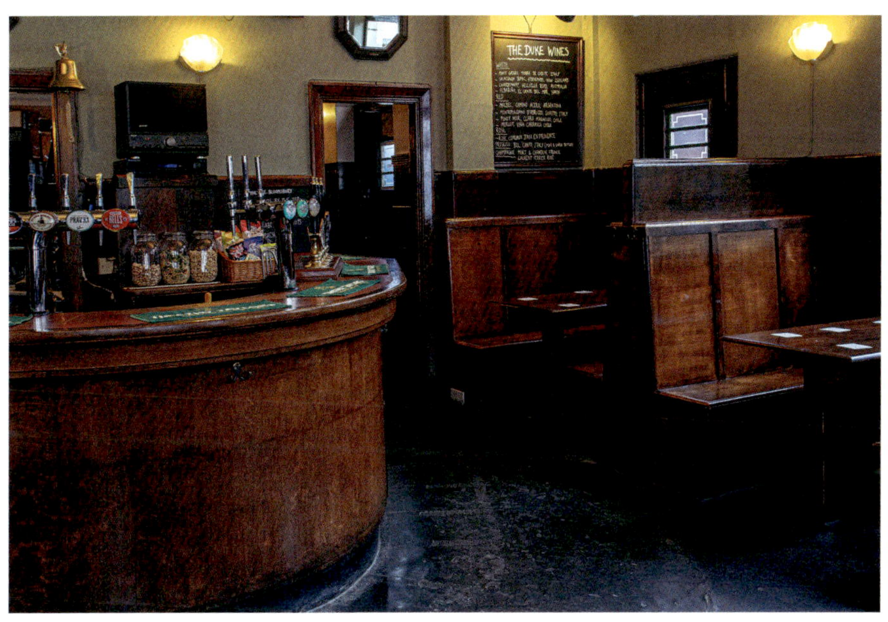

Inter-war aesthetics conjure a movie-set ambience

THE HOLY TAVERN

CLERKENWELL'S CHARLATAN COFFEE-HOUSE

Nobody likes being hoodwinked. Being taken down an alley with the best of intentions, only to have your pants pulled down and be spanked with a rotten kipper whilst the culprits make their getaway. Or do they?

The majority of visitors to The Holy Tavern (née Jerusalem Tavern) seem delighted to indulge in one of the best acts of chicanery this side of the Square Mile. It all begins with the date above the door reading "Anno 1720", often shortly followed by "Blimey, well that IS an old pub."

Alas! It's all a hoax. A gentle josh. A bit of creative accounting. For this ancient tavern dates back to around "Anno 1996". To add some perspective, Tim Martin was opening his 150th Wetherspoon in the very same year: his oldest 'Spoons dates back to the relatively historic 1979.

But any comparison ends there, for this is a quirky cracker. It has been hewn from a genuinely old building and given a design makeover so understated that it can tease and play with the most discerning of architectural eyes. The closest comparison I can think of would be a brown café in Old Amsterdam. When you know that one of the owners, Hendrick, was a Dutch policeman, the penny begins to drop and the Delft tiling begins to make a little more sense. It also starts to feel like a historic coffee-house, as this was how it was originally conceived in the early nineties.

This charlatan is best visited during daylight hours when shards of sunlight penetrate the dark wood interior. Grab a well-worn wooden seat beside the fireplace, the communal single-tabled snug to the rear or the comedically jaunty crow's-nest table for the ultimate tête-à-tête. Smart-suited City gents, ale lovers and the Clerkenwell creatives drift to this neither-here-nor-there location. Quiet conversation is the order of the day, and the occasional candlelit soirée completes this timeless deception. Reminiscent of the remarkable Dennis Severs' House, patrons can watch the ghosts of Dr Johnson and others frequent the tavern to take coffee or something a little stronger to keep the chill at bay.

For over twenty-five years, cask hunters converged at The Jerusalem Tavern for the estimable St Peter's Brewery booze pouring from the pumps. But alas, apparently all great things must come to an end, so a new name and a refreshed line-up awaits you at the bar. But the confidence trick remains intact, and the charm persists.

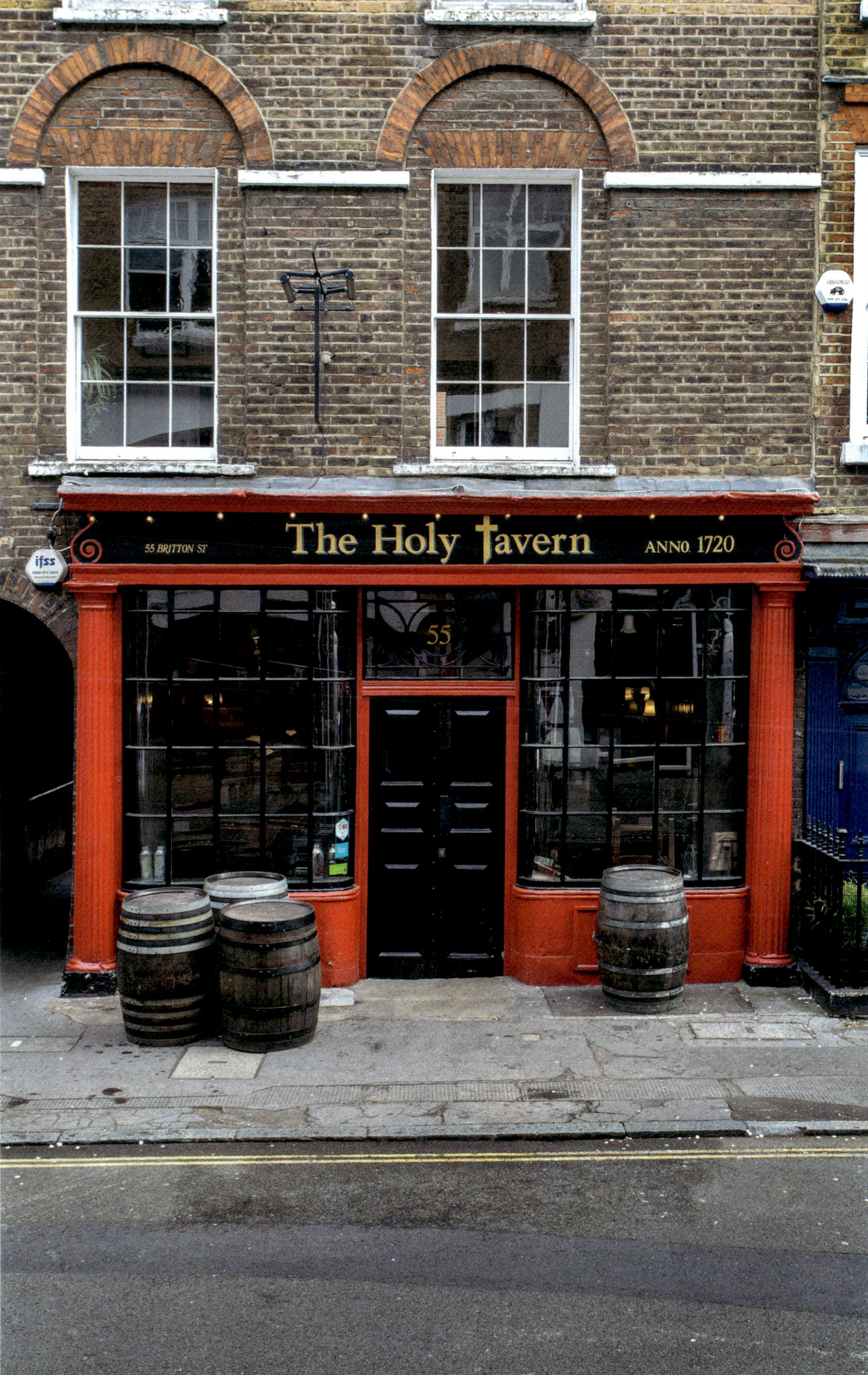

The Holy Tavern
55 BRITTON ST
ANNO. 1720
55
ifss

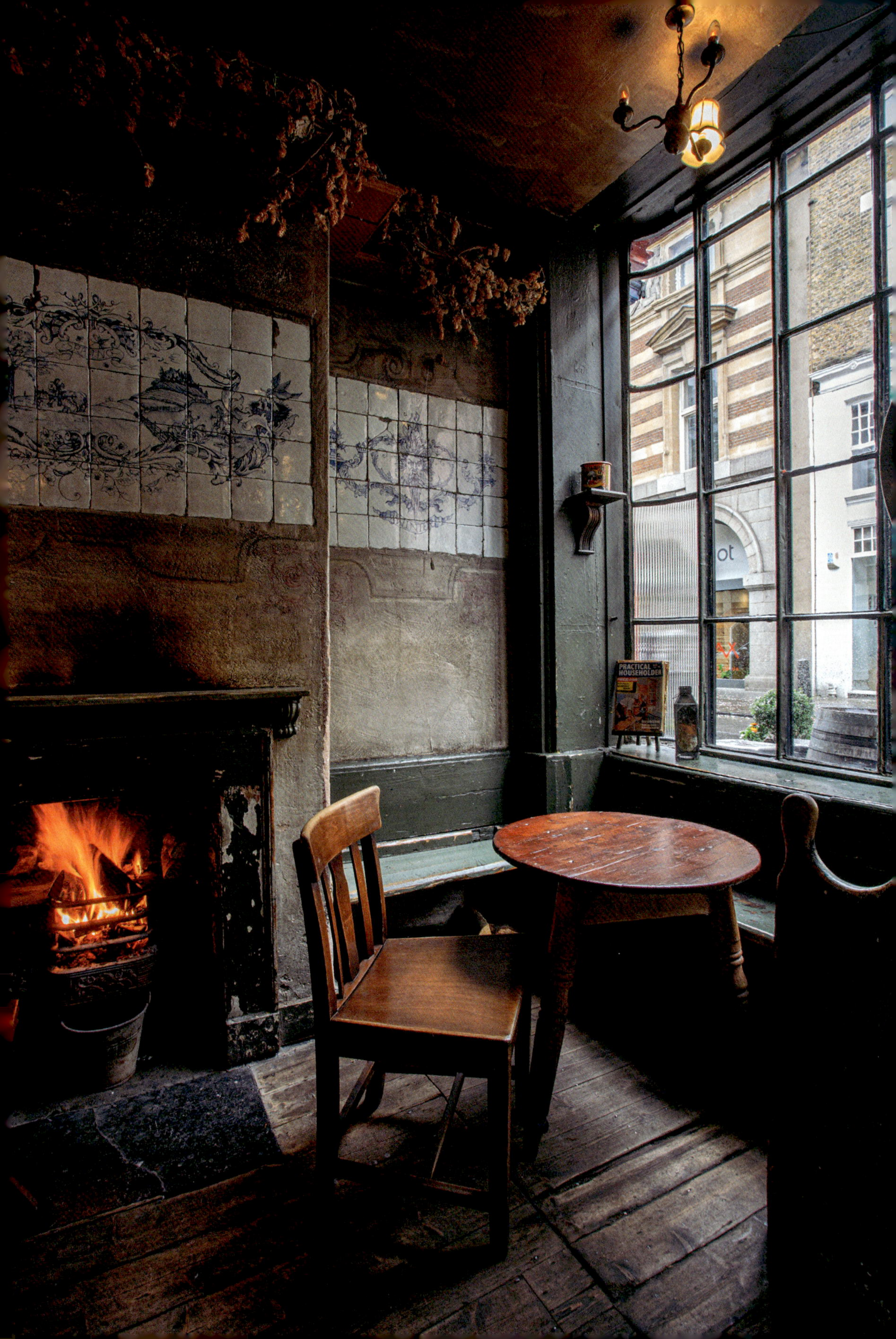

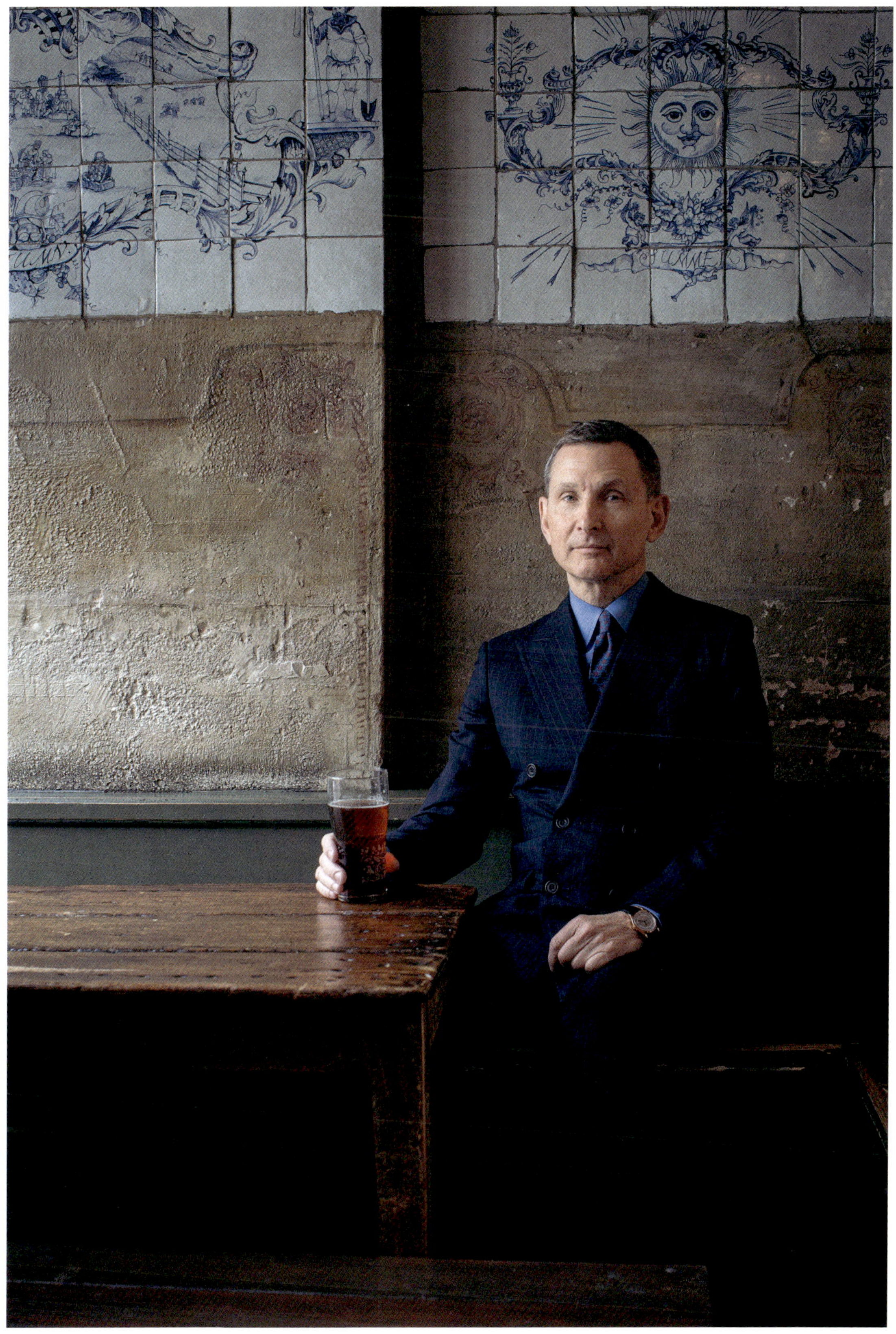

Melting pot for City gents and Clerkenwell creatives

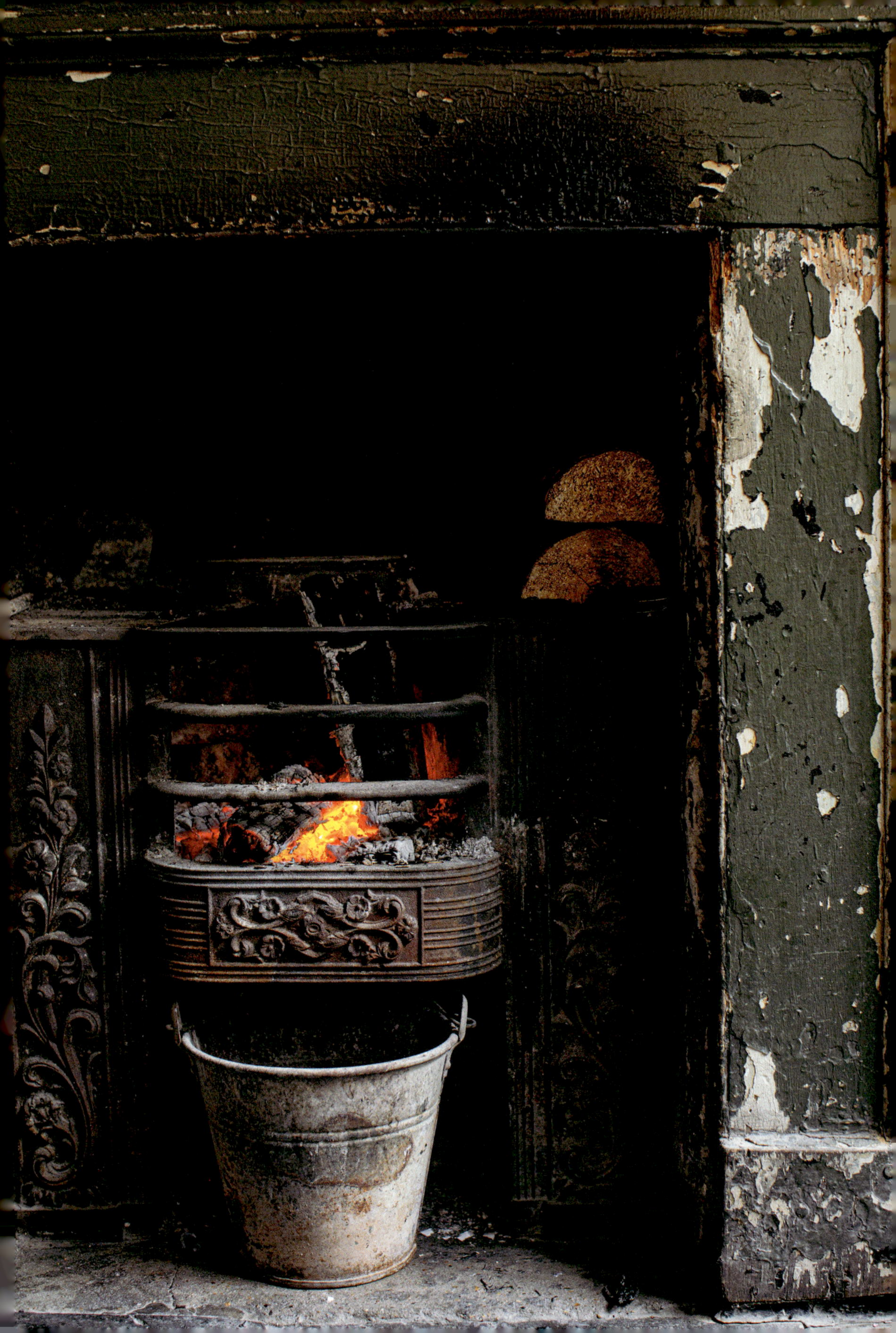

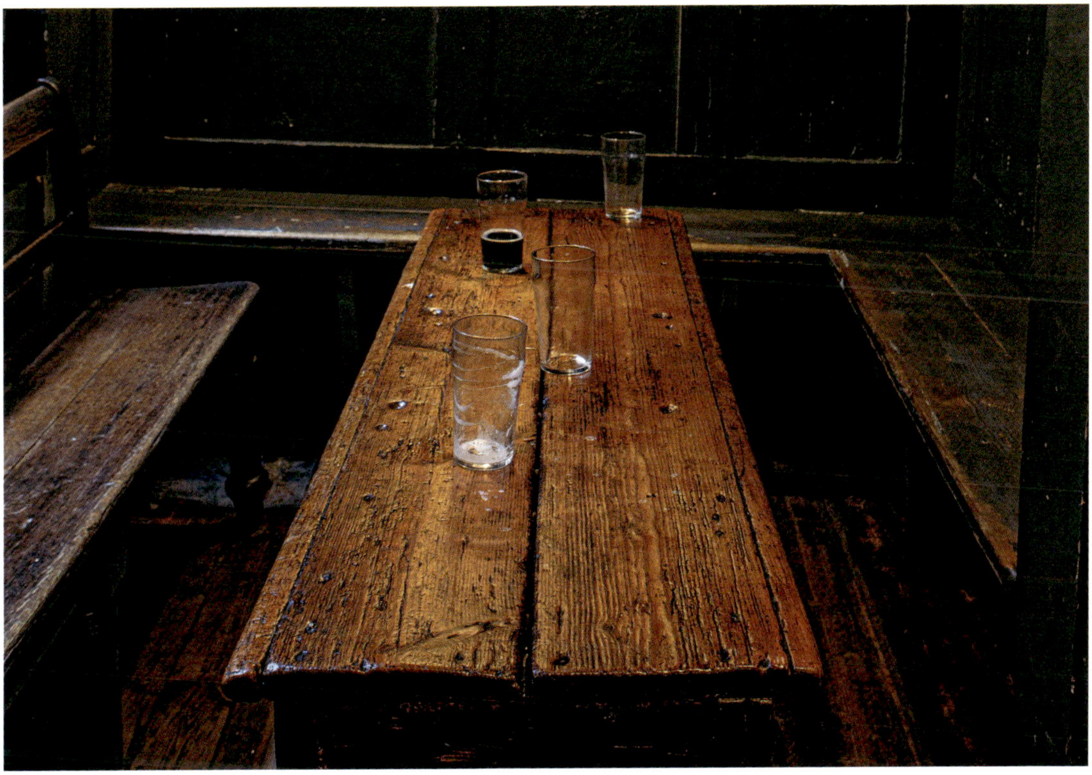

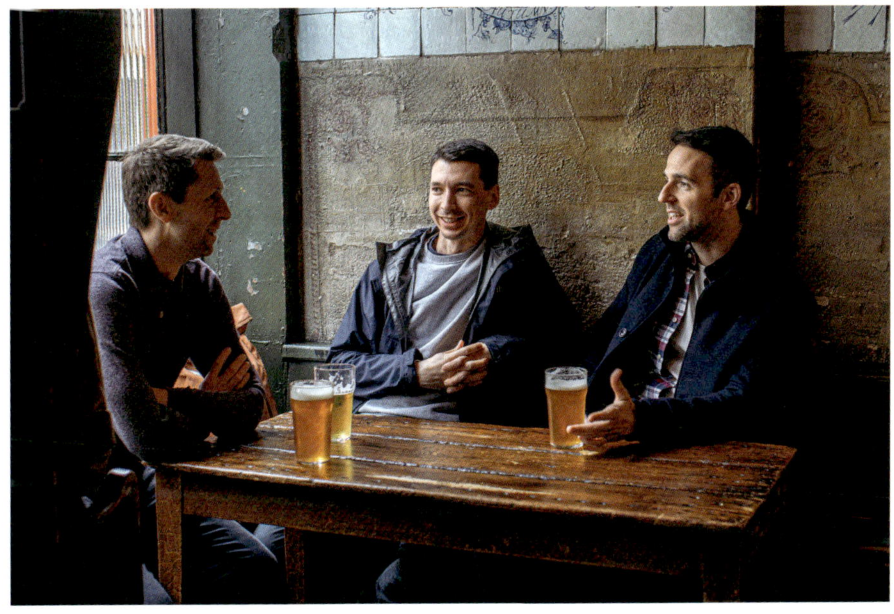

The much-coveted fireside cubby holes go early

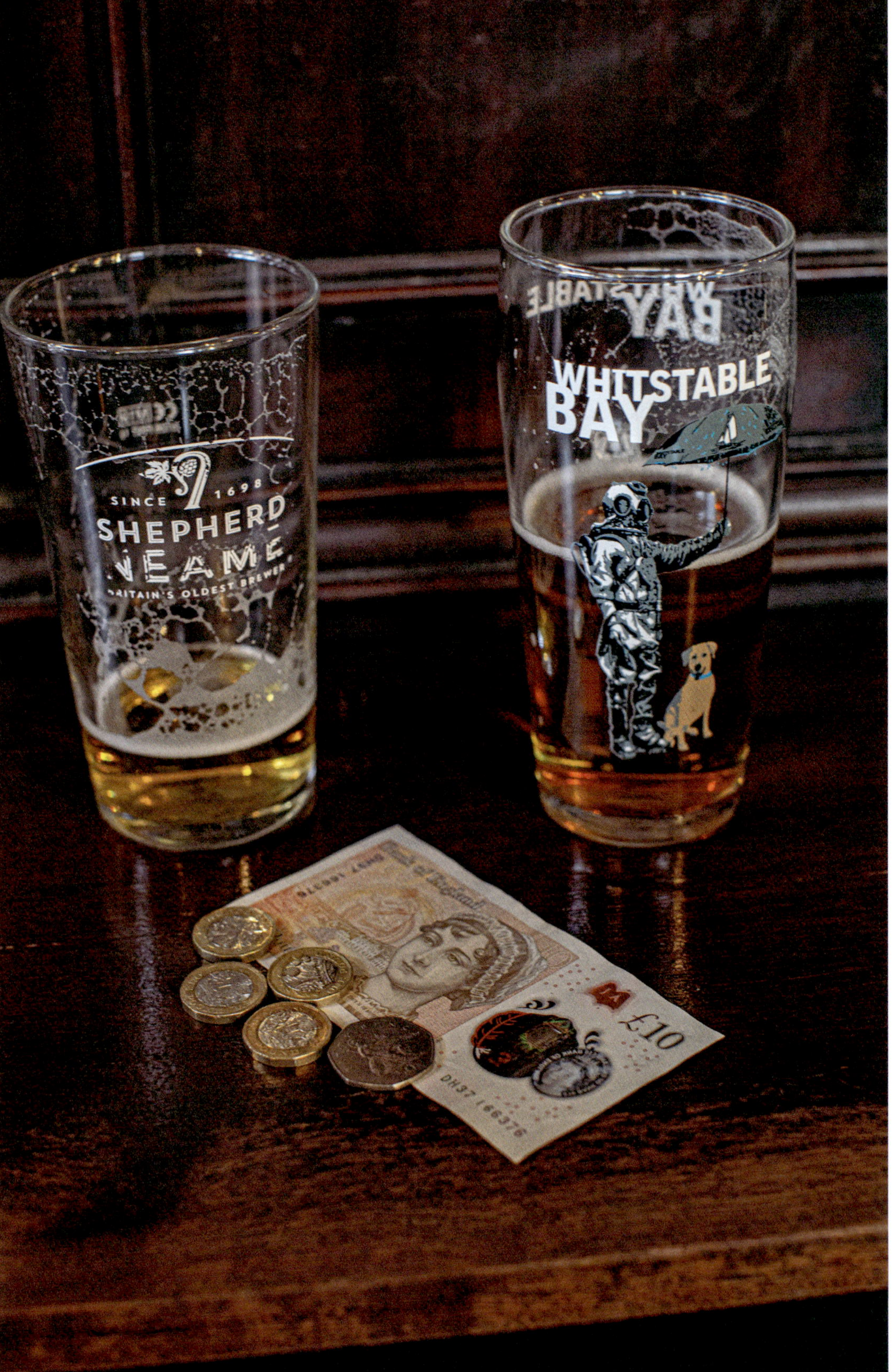
SHEPHERD
NEAME
SINCE 1698
BRITAIN'S OLDEST BREWER
WHITSTABLE
BAY
£10

THE JAMAICA WINE HOUSE

SQUARE MILE COFFEE-HOUSE, WINE-HOUSE AND TAVERN

ST MICHAEL'S ALLEY, CITY OF LONDON EC3V 9DS

No great pub story ever started with a coffee. Except this one. Travel back to 1652 and The Jampot offered a discreet backstreet location for merchants to commune, conspire and make caffeine-fuelled clandestine deals. Coffee, sugar, tobacco, indigo and cotton were the conversational commodities whilst hand-bills plastering the walls noted every type of vessel in the pool of London, its seaworthiness and expected date of departure. A boy would stand in the corner of the pub to announce new port arrivals or share word-of-mouth intel on the movements of a particular ship's captain. And even when the formal Royal Exchange and Lloyd's of London opened, with all their fancy floors and rules and regulations, the merchants would still slip away to the pub to share surreptitious side-chat and seal the deal.

With nothing written down or recorded in The Jampot, your word is still your bond

Fast forward to the present day and, under the ever-taller skyscrapers, The Jampot's *genius loci* holds firm. Coffee is no longer the tipple of choice, with most patrons choosing a pint of Spitfire as their liquid asset. Three-hour, two-bottle liquid lunches in the City might be a thing of the past, but wander these secret streets Monday to Friday if you want to pick up the latest gossip from the trading floors. Suited and booted City slickers still fill these passageways, escaping the open-plan eavesdroppers and digital email trail to look their colleague or client in the eye and indulge in word-of-mouth confabulation. It's these informal "water-cooler" moments that still join the dots of business. With nothing written down or recorded in The Jampot, your word is still your bond.

The pub itself is a handsome 1869 pink sandstone rebuild, apparently retaining an original stone step worn by the ravages of time and tipsy traders. The inside is all dark and brooding, with a spectacular ceiling and wood-partitioned rooms in which to rest your pint. People still make a beeline for the basement, but really this pub is all about the al fresco imbibing.

We can only concur with London's great drinking diarist Samuel Pepys, who visited in 1660 and "found much pleasure in it through the diversity of company – and discourse."

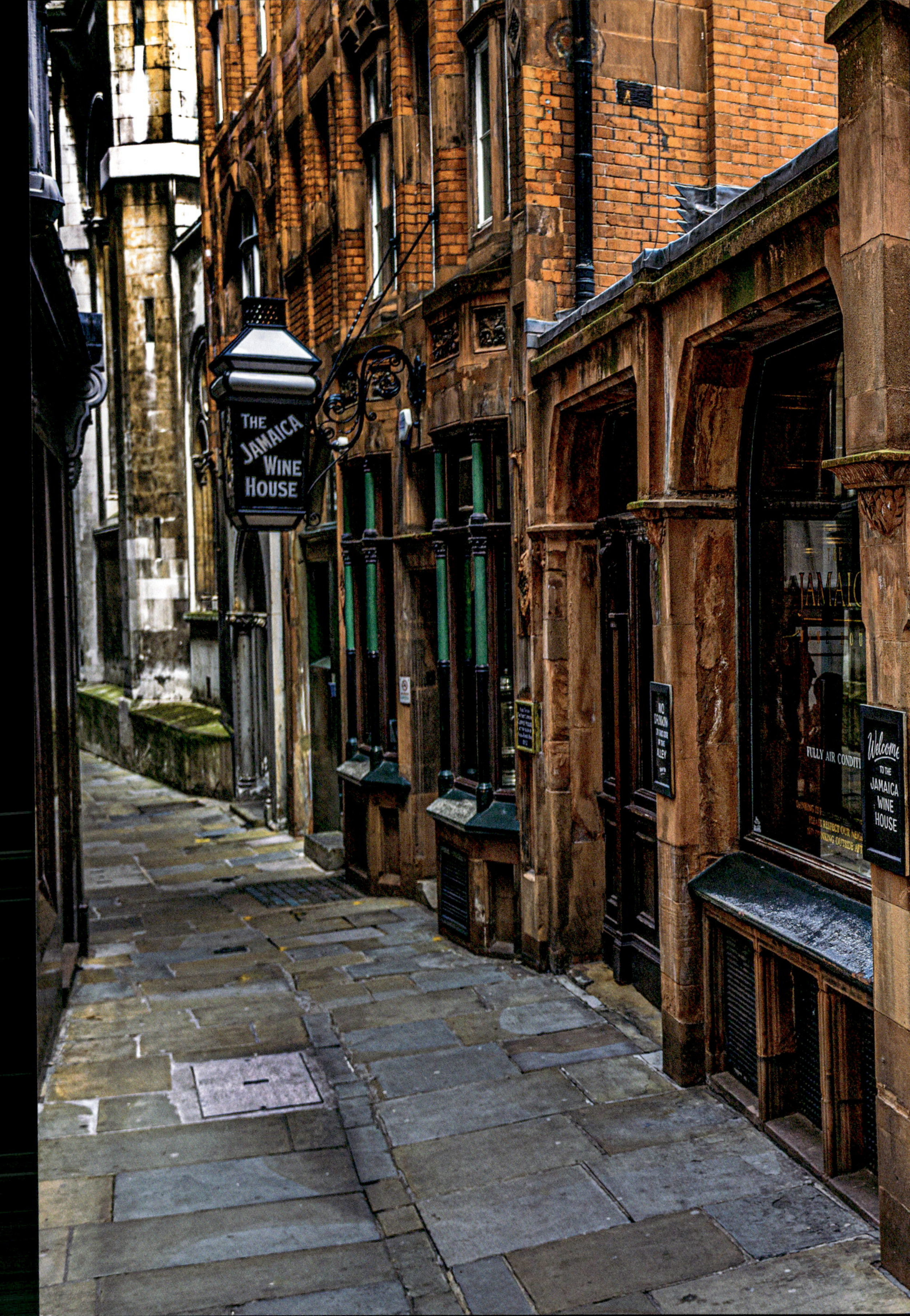

THE
JAMAICA
WINE
HOUSE

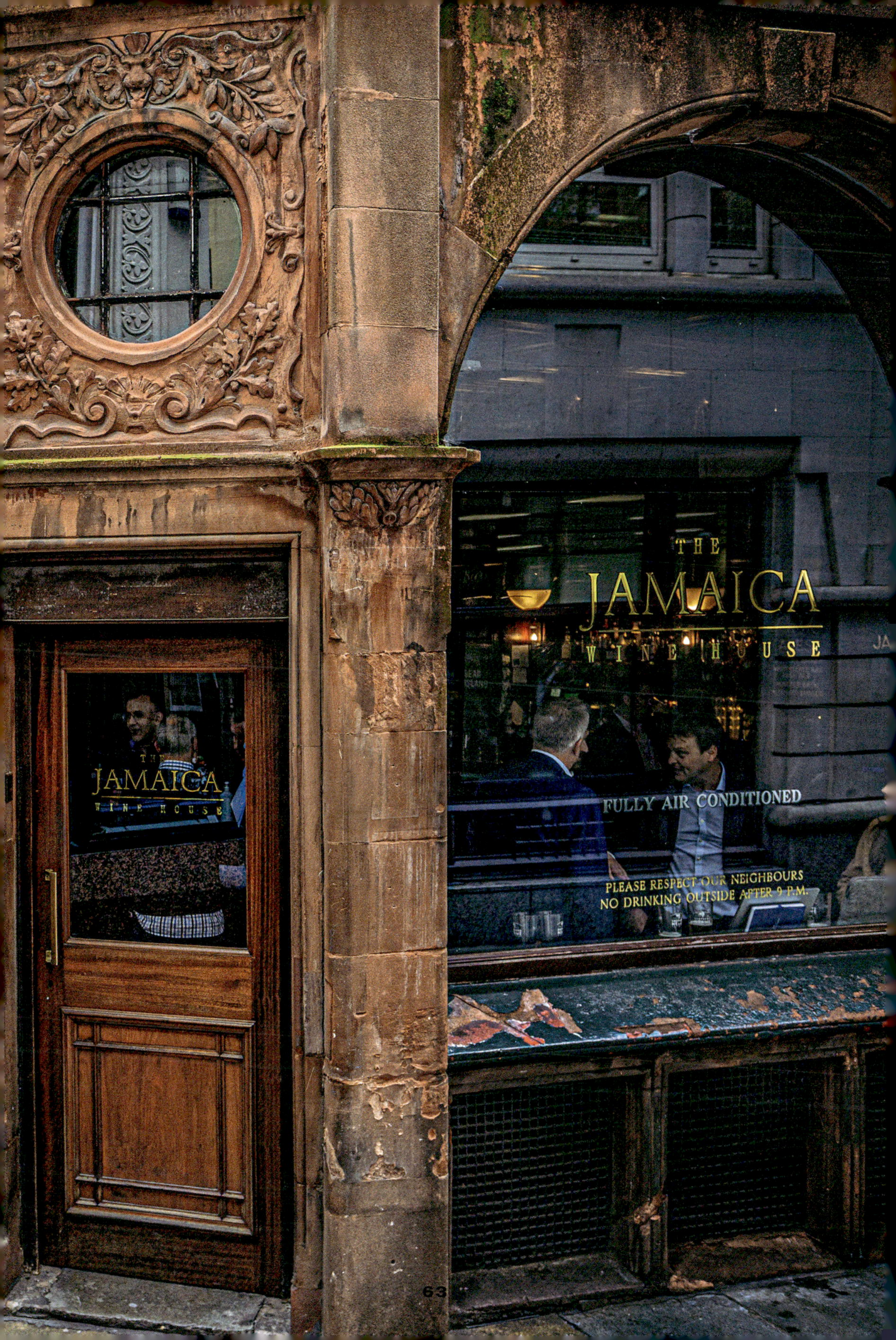

THE
JAMAICA
WINE HOUSE
JAMAICA
WINE HOUSE
FULLY AIR CONDITIONED
PLEASE RESPECT OUR NEIGHBOURS
NO DRINKING OUTSIDE AFTER 9 P.M.
63

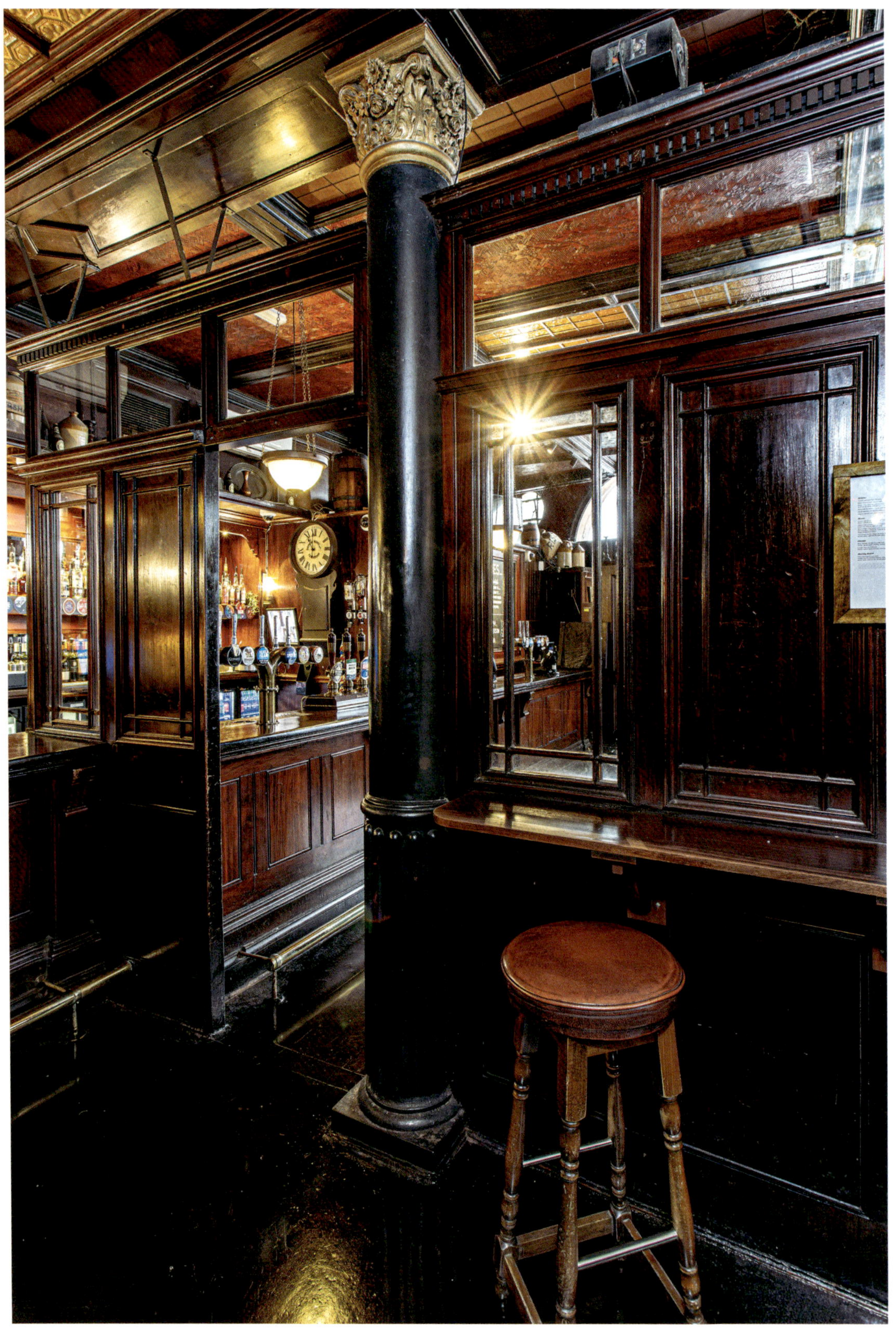

Look up to savour the sumptuous ceilings

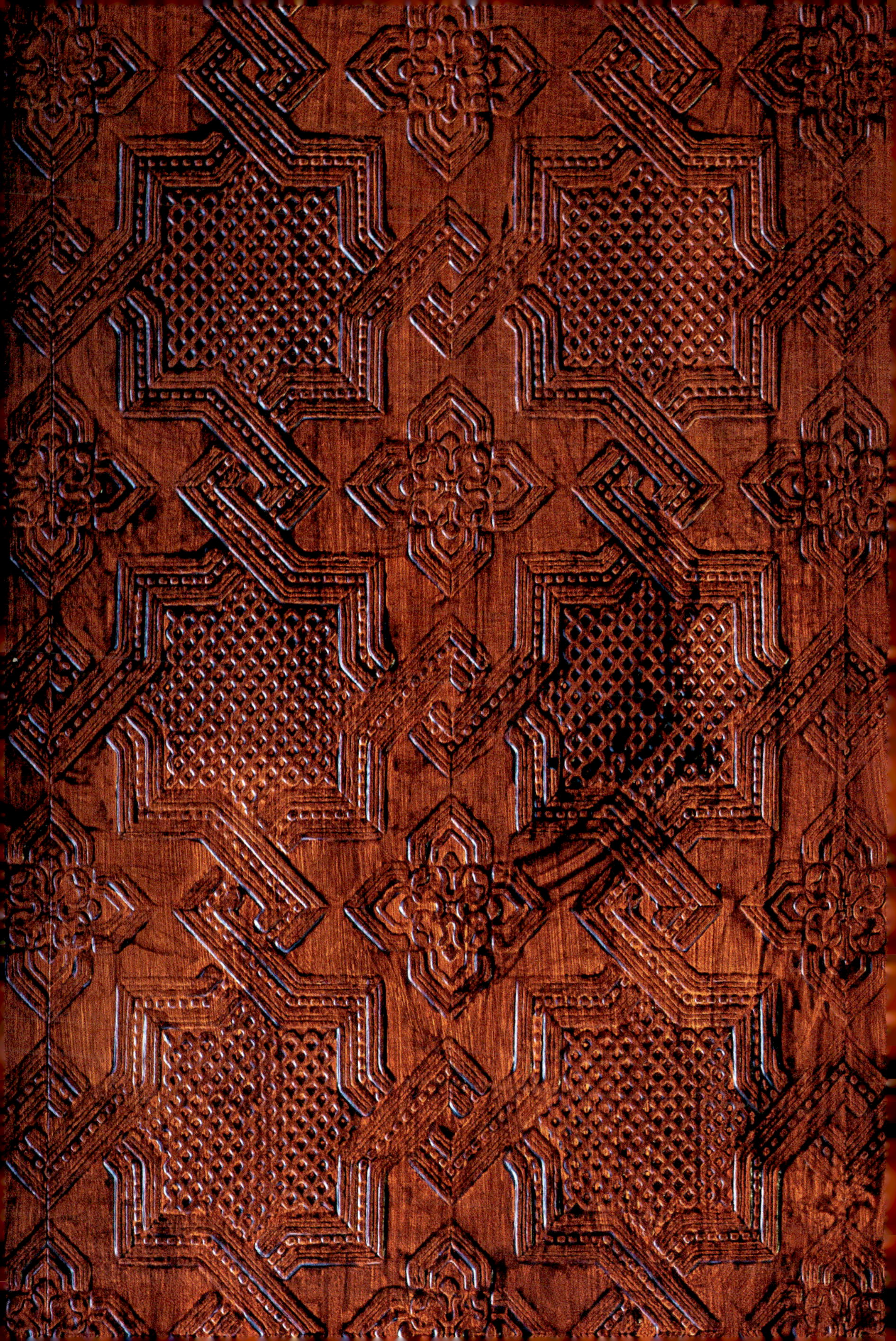

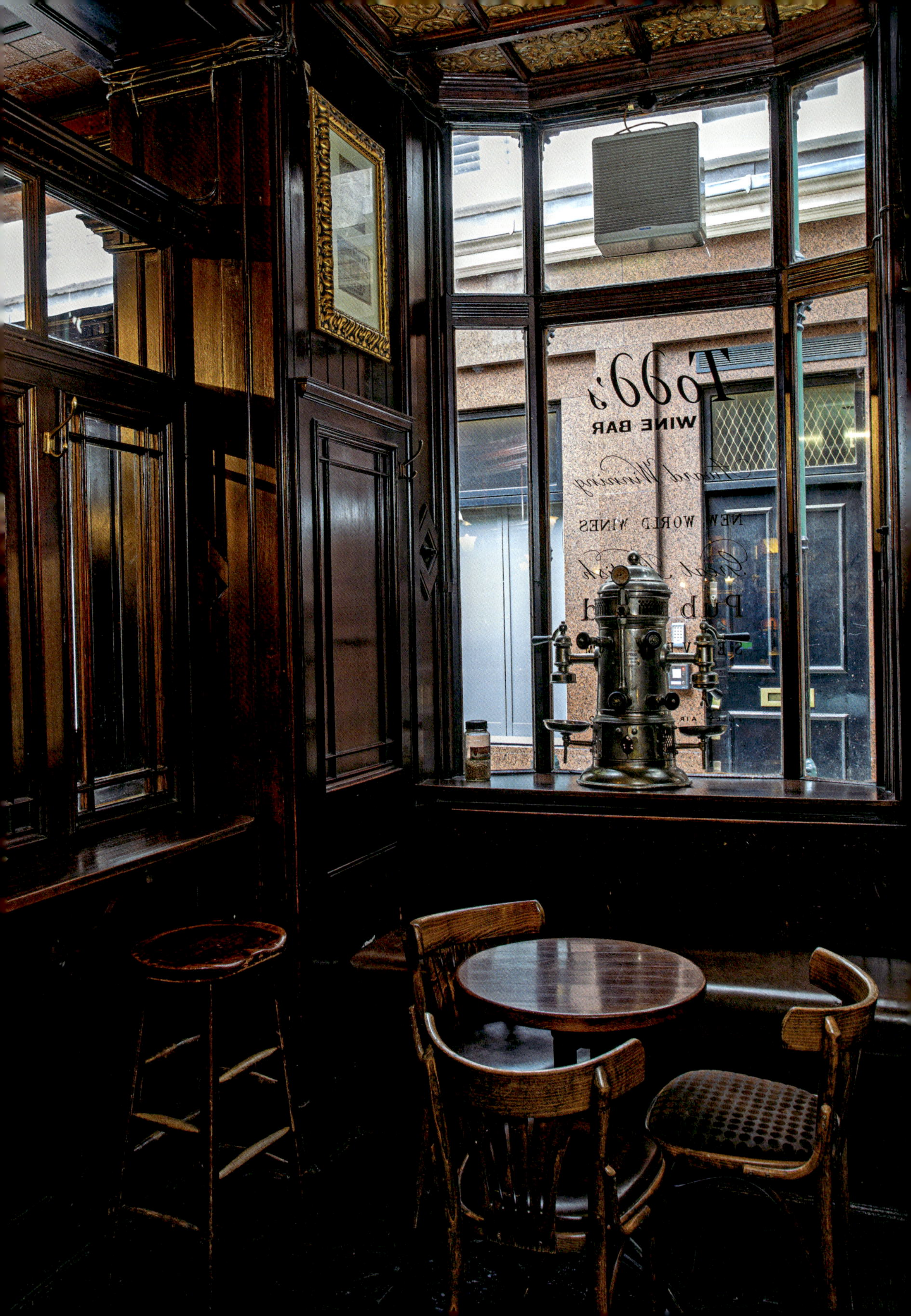
Fogg's
WINE BAR
NEW WORLD WINES

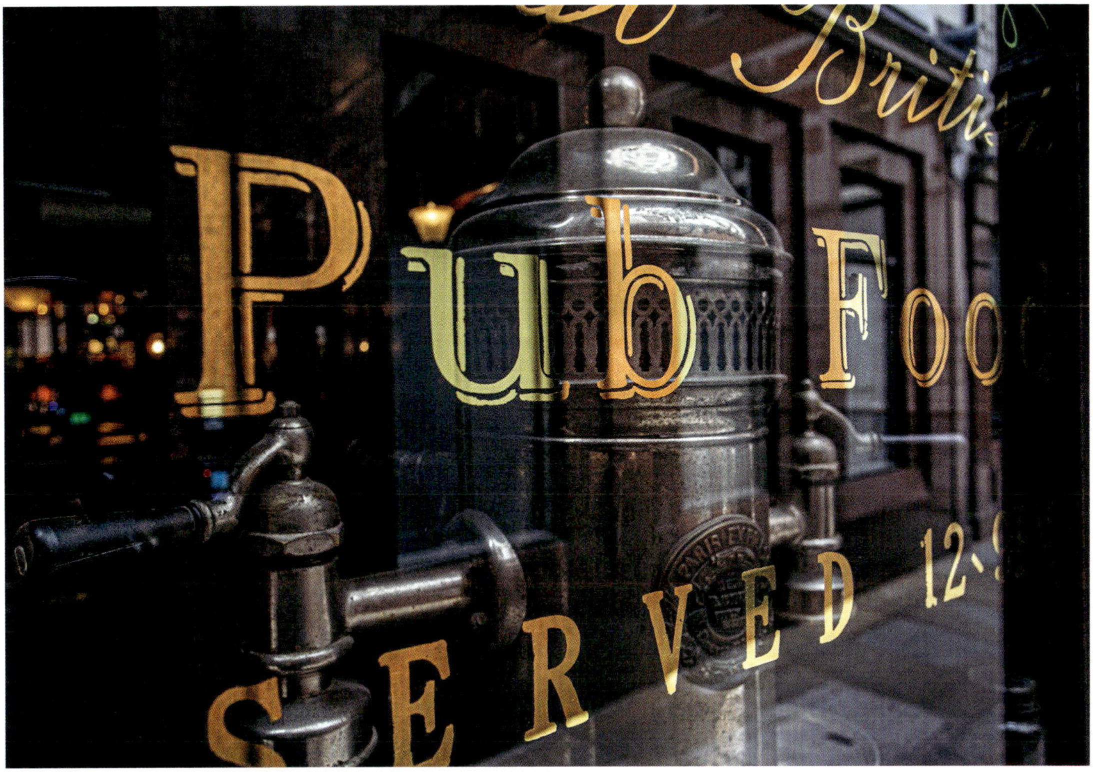

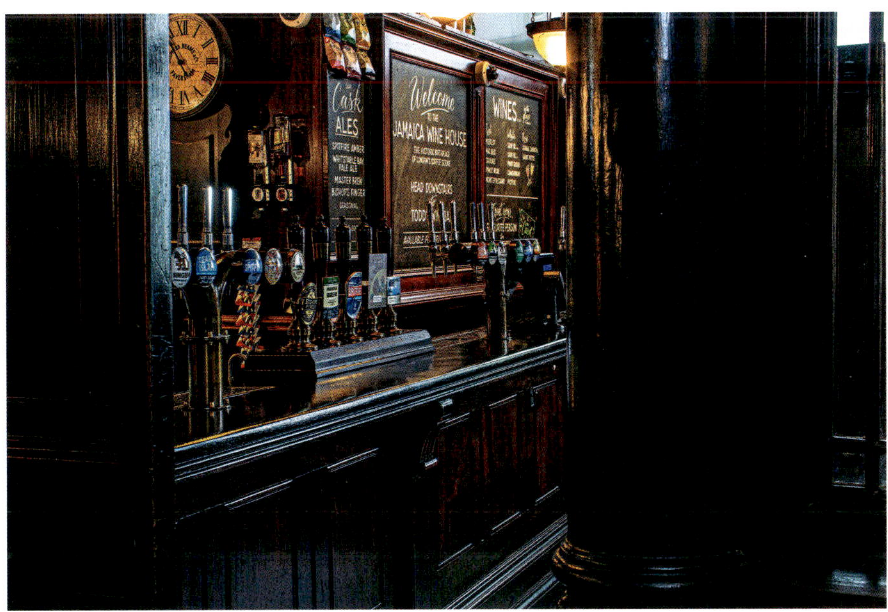

A boozy bolthole for City brokers

THE NAGS HEAD

53 KINNERTON ST, BELGRAVIA SW1X 8ED

Kevin Moran was mining in County Durham aged just fourteen before being dispatched to London by his father. Scooped up by a recruiting sergeant, he went on to serve in the Scots Guards, protecting the monarchy as a self-proclaimed "Fenian bastard". Guzzling with Peter O'Toole and Richard Harris in bohemian Soho earned Kevin his Equity card and a few roles in *Doctor Who* to subsidise his military stipend.

This book celebrates the "characters" of London's pubs. Its measuring stick is far from a Tripadvisor rating. But just have a look at the reviews of this place. "Well worth a visit to get insulted." "Avoid like the plague." "Very rude landlord." I could make a wager that, right now, someone is furiously typing a 1★ review based on how they were treated by Kevin Moran.

"If you don't like it, don't come here."

Kevin Moran

Wander in with clattering suitcases and kids in tow and you might not even make it across the threshold. Kevin's verbal volleys start early. Twiddle on your phone or query the pricing strategy and a second salvo will soon head your way. Those who manage to survive the opening barrage and are happy to cover the minimum card spend, whilst keeping their phone firmly planted in their pocket, rarely want to go anywhere else. Kevin attracts more than his fair share of drama in one of the poshest postcodes on the planet. Prince William hoicked younger brother Harry out by the ear during his misspent youth, the house opposite is owned by the Maxwell family (yes, the same house where "that photo" of Prince Andrew was taken) and a young Robbie Williams hid out here as the press scavenged for a scoop on the Take That fallout.

Kevin runs a tight ship and, with his military background and over forty years at the helm, perhaps rightly so. The pub is full of disarmingly low bars, salacious slide shows and famous photography. The wall of the dead remembers his fallen comrades, 1930s jazz makes the musical wallpaper and the ancient cash till rings out until last orders are called. With his name proudly displayed across the pub awning, the octogenarian is still pulling pints of cask from the 150-year-old Chelsea china handpumps when not acting as pub gatekeeper. So if the rudest landlord in London does decide to kick you out, then don't worry: you're in fine company. Oliver Reed was shown the door at least twice.

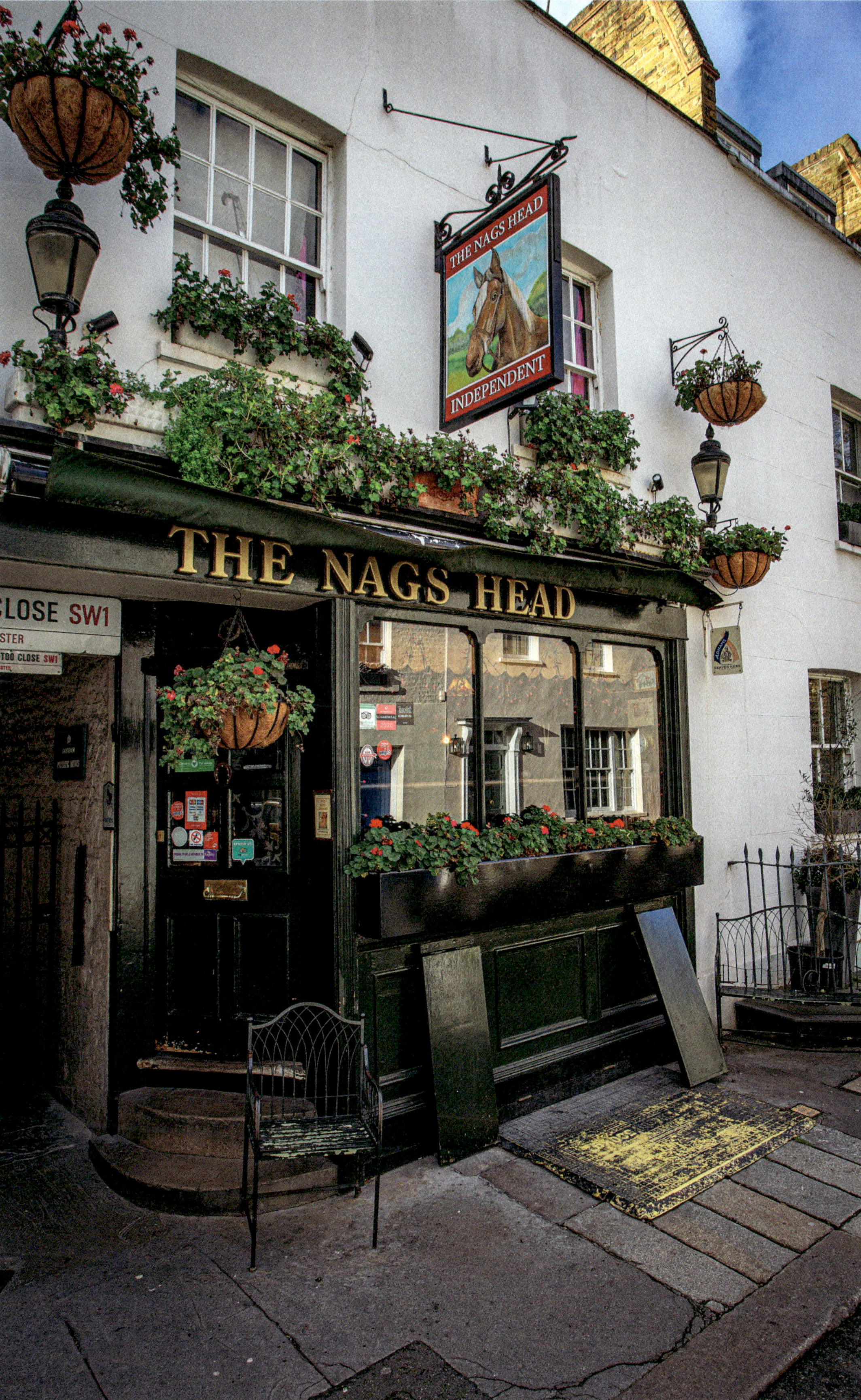
THE NAGS HEAD
INDEPENDENT
THE NAGS HEAD
CLOSE SW1
TOO CLOSE SW1

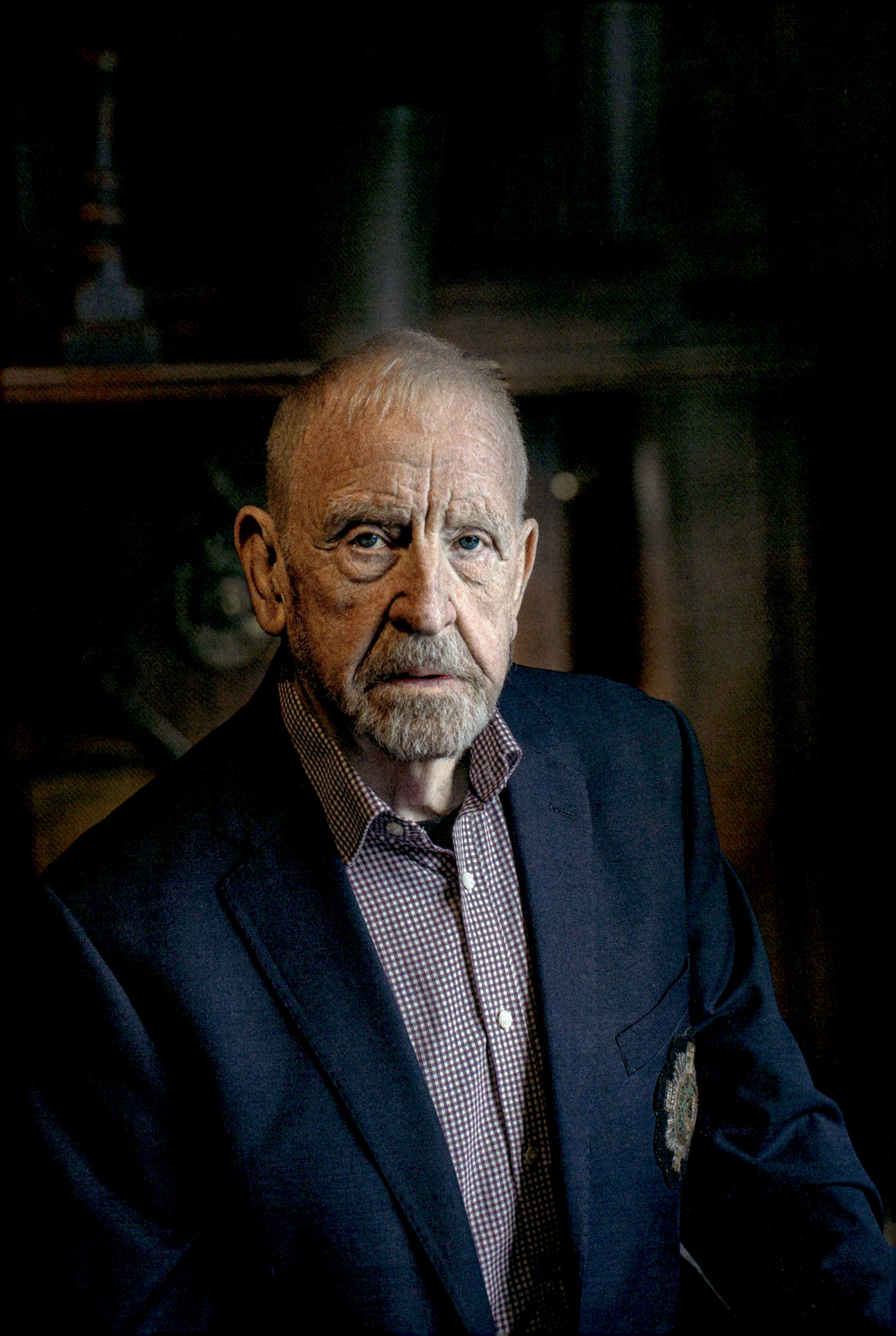

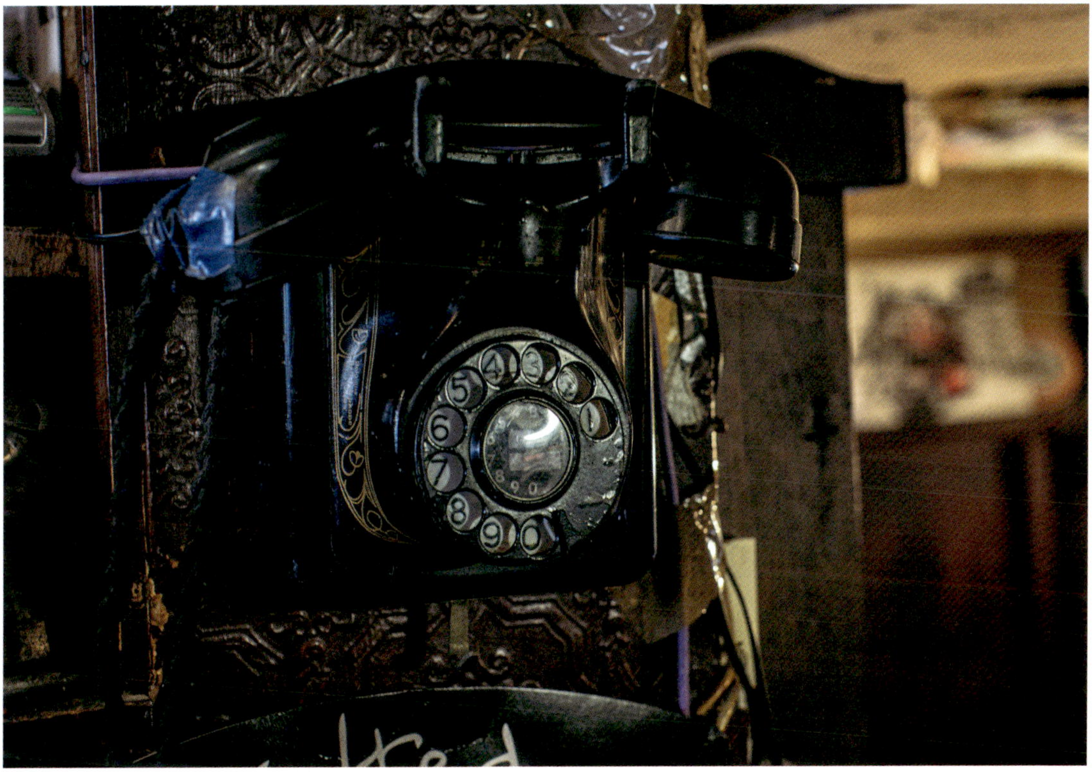

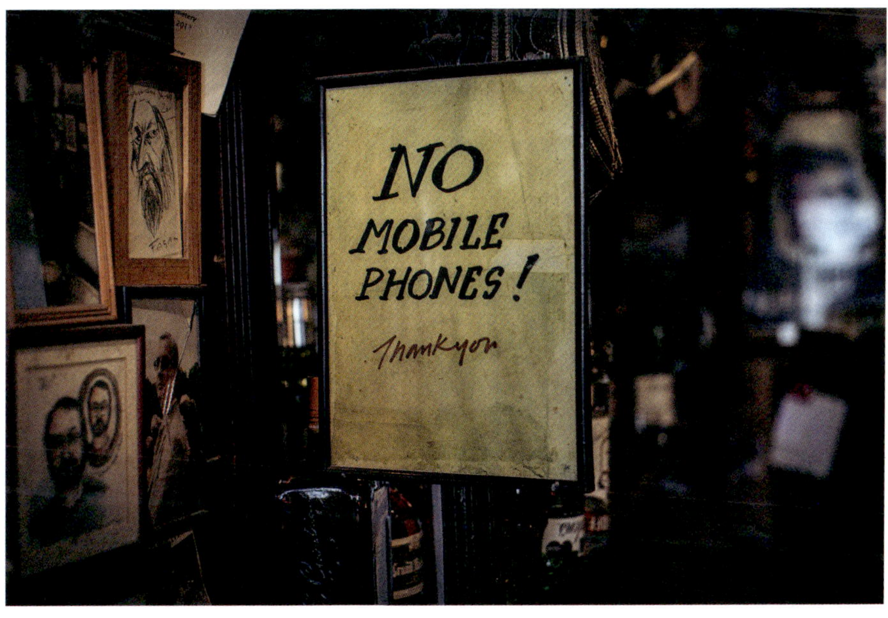

You have been warned!

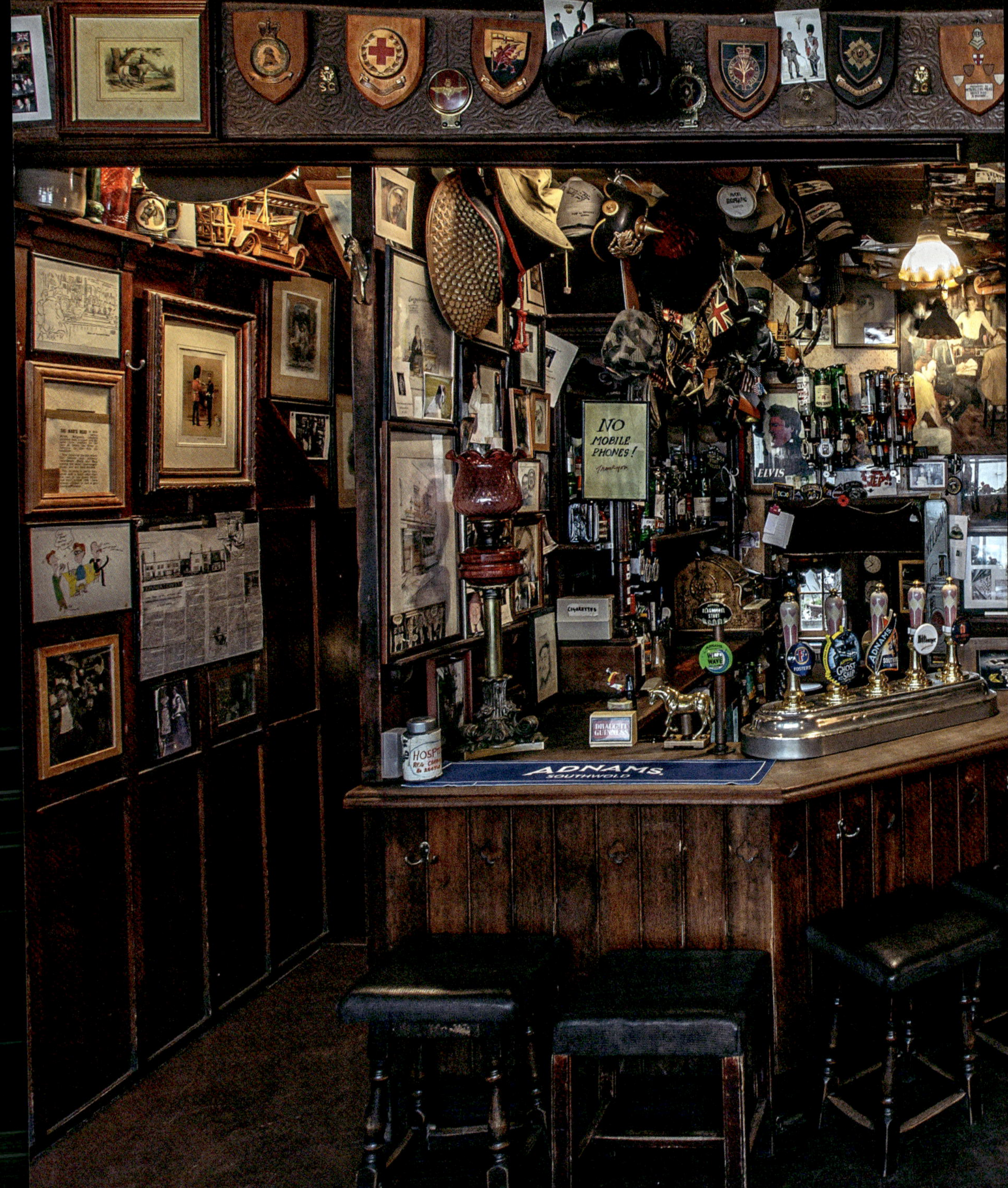
NO
MOBILE
PHONES !
Thank you
ELVIS
CIGARETTES
ADNAMS
SOUTHWOLD
DRAUGHT
GUINNESS
GHOST
SHIP
ADNAMS
FOSTERS

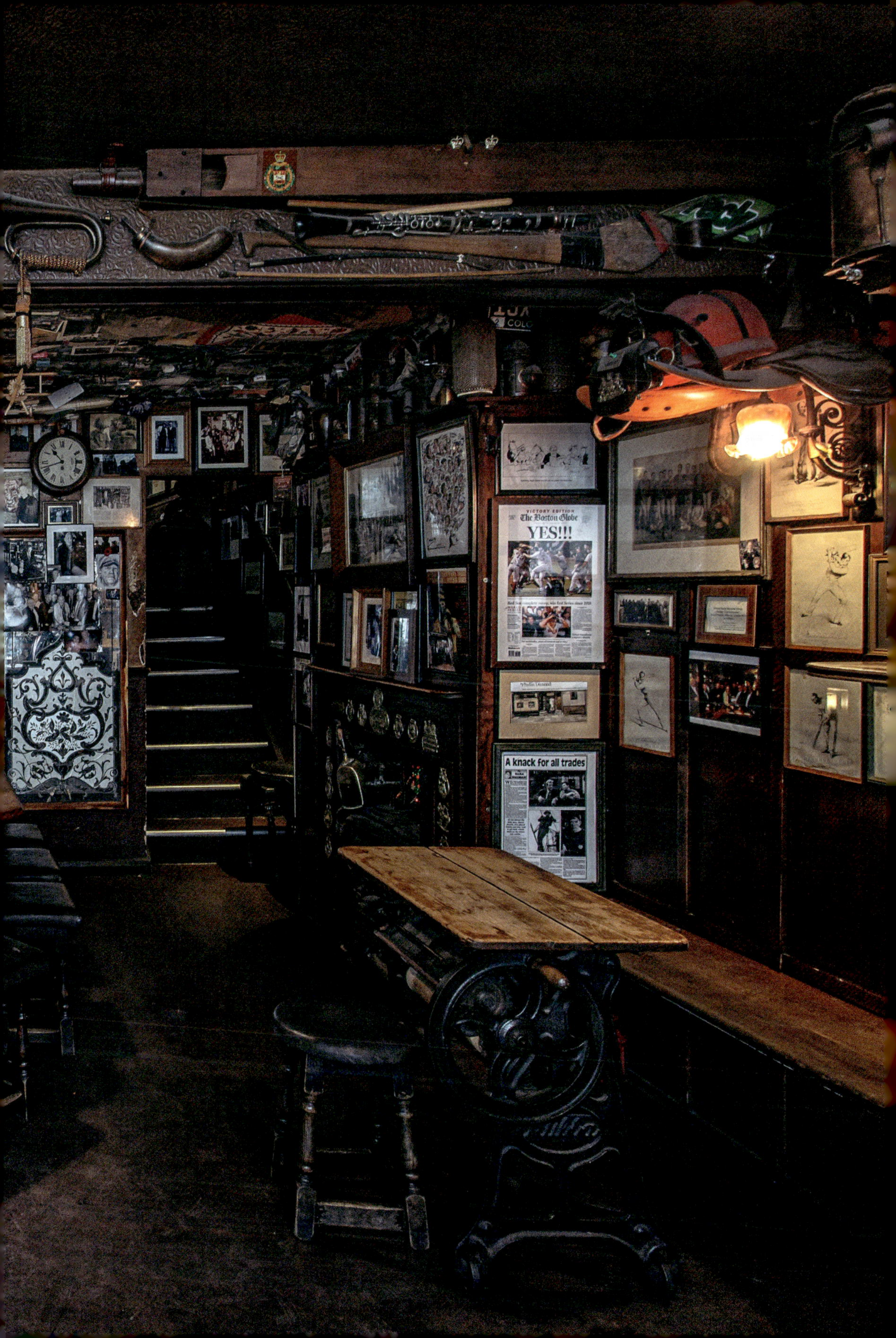

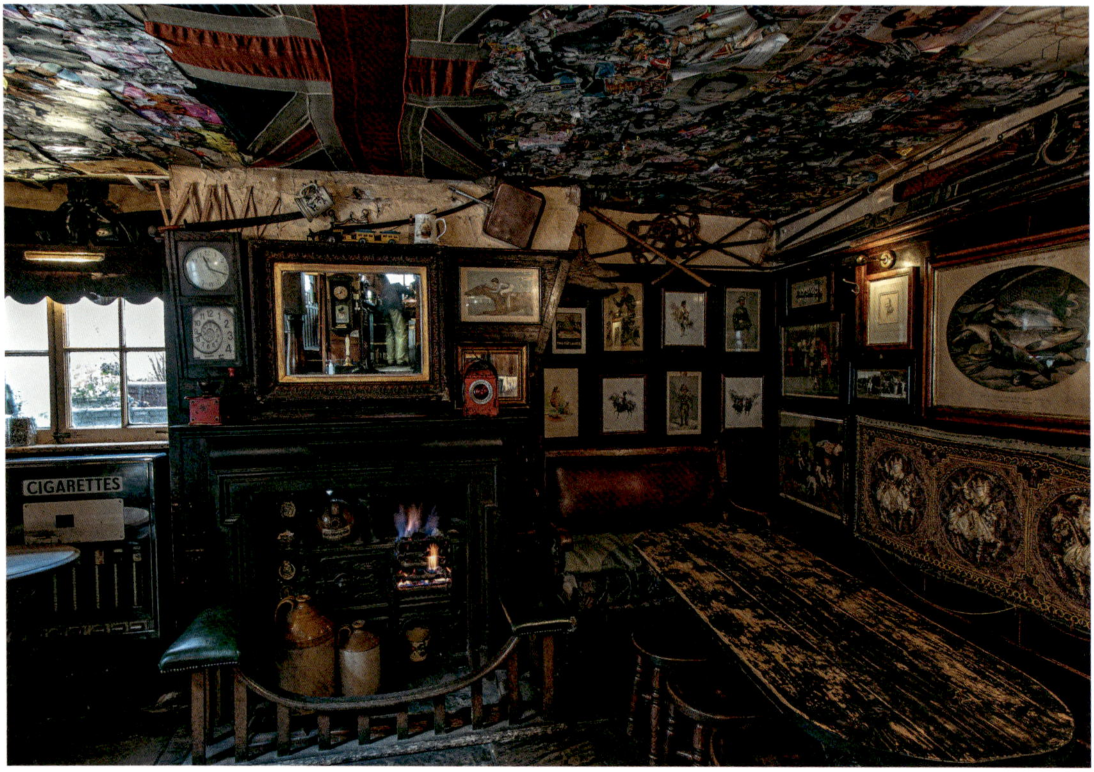

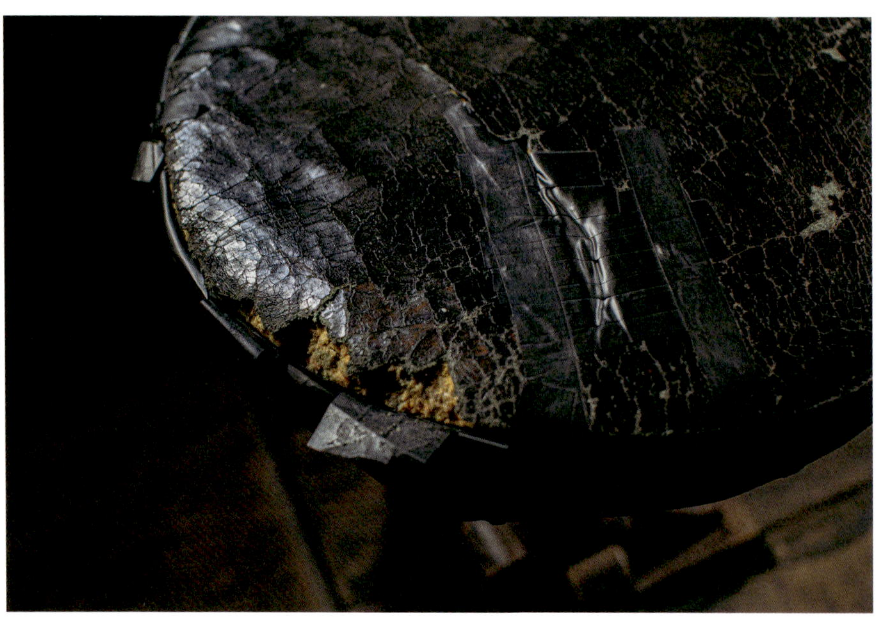

... as mad as a box of frogs

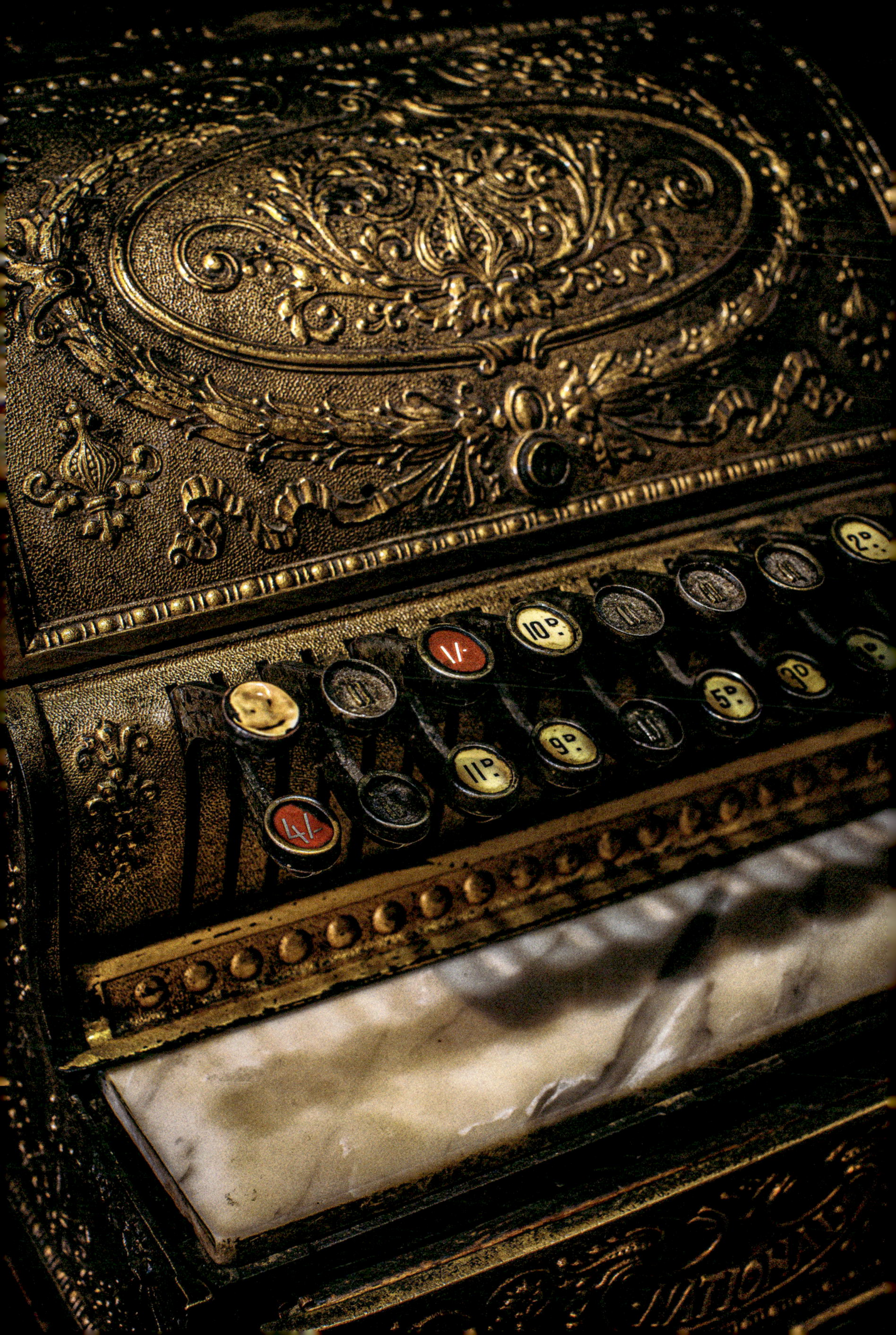

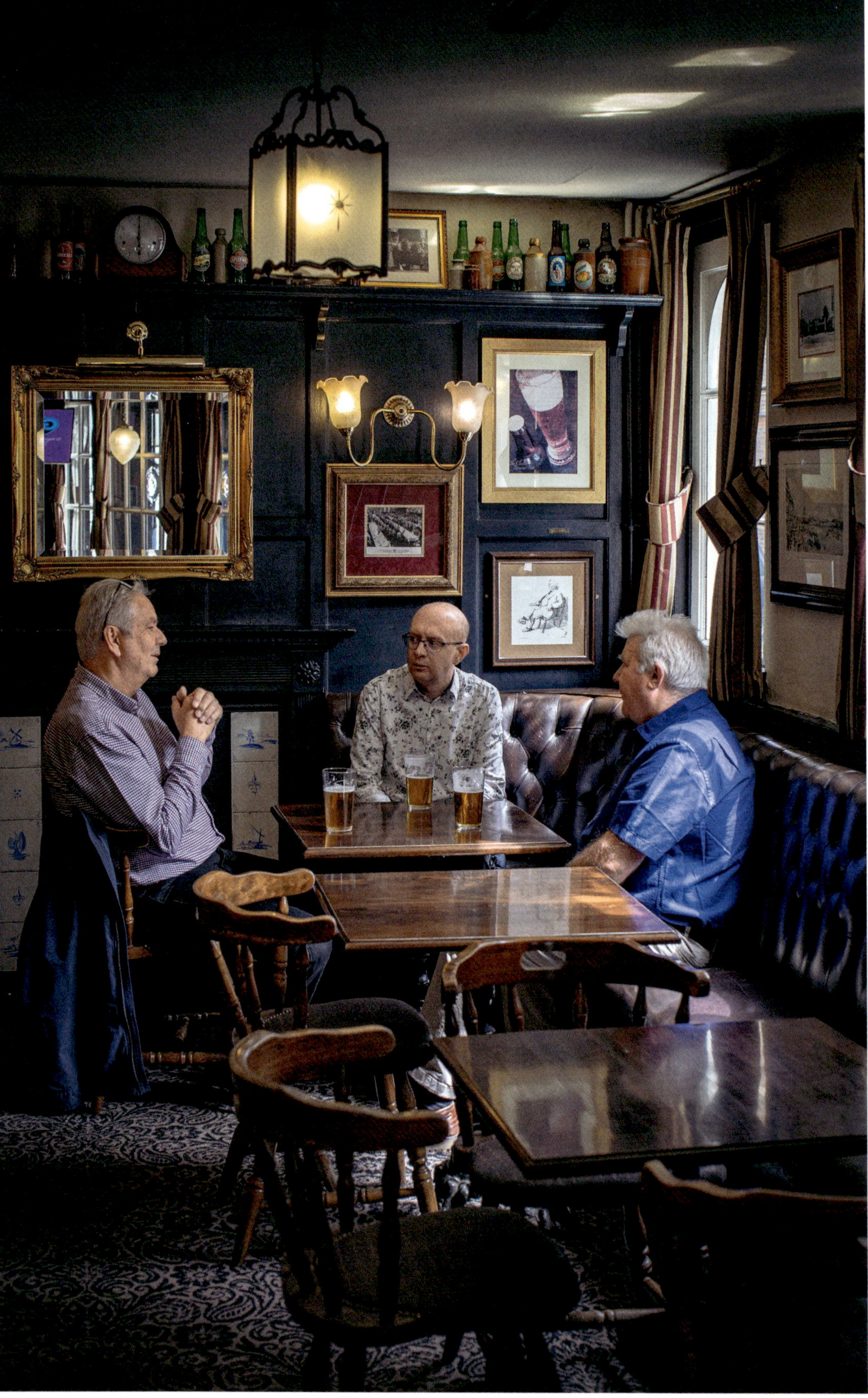

CASK & GLASS

Real ale fans love to exclaim that "Cask is king!", and this pub is often described as the King's local. Being only a three-minute trot from the golden gates of Buckingham Palace, if the monarch did fancy getting merry with his minions, this would be a fine choice indeed. He would be swapping out his 775-roomed palace for a wedgy one-room wonder hidden in the heart of Victoria.

The title for London's smallest boozer is always widely contested, but this postage stamp of a pub could only be politely described as bijou. With no straight lines, no garden and no tea or coffee, you just have to be thankful if they manage to squeeze out a toastie for you. It has a wonderfully domestic air to it all, and the ale wife *du jour*, Sally, still lives upstairs.

Quiet daytime drinking inside surrounded by political cartoons, Royal Household workers and a few military types from the barracks nearby is a simple pleasure. Britain's oldest brewer proffers traditional fare from the boomerang bar, and life ticks over very nicely.

With the Royal Warrant Holders Association located right next door, they pop in and conduct regular and thorough quality control sessions. You're in safe hands when it's all poured by royal appointment.

Cometh the end of the working day, and this cosy village pub transforms into a serving hatch for the massed pavement lizards. This is when the pub can clean its feet financially and pour forth from the pumps to keep the lights on. The capacity of the place doubles or even trebles as pint-holding punters cling to the corner of Palace Street in search of their daily dose of vitamin D, all washed down with a pint or three of Master Brew.

But the pavement crush might prove too much for the licensing authorities. The pub's single lifeline for financial security might be severed or cut off entirely one day, and then this people's palace would fall by the wayside and no doubt be converted back into the lovely small corner house it was crafted from a century or two ago.

So when the day comes that they try to limit the street-side drinking and close this little beauty forever, then don't forget to write to your local MP. Or perhaps just harangue them over a pint of Spitfire at the bar, as they're quite likely to be propping it up when not round the corner at The Speaker.

The Cask & Glass is king. Long live the King!

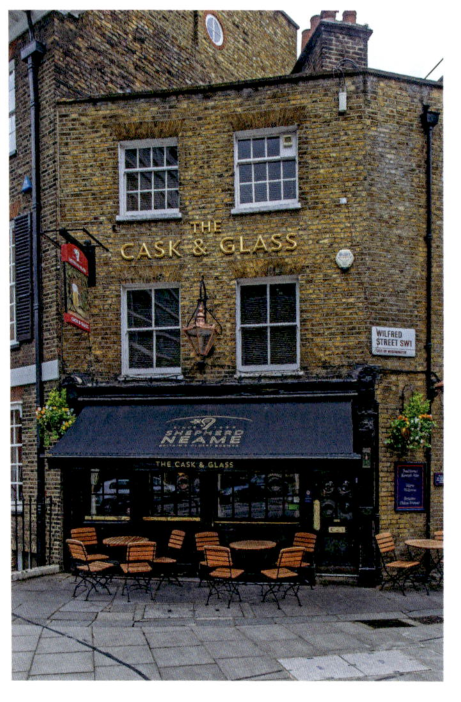

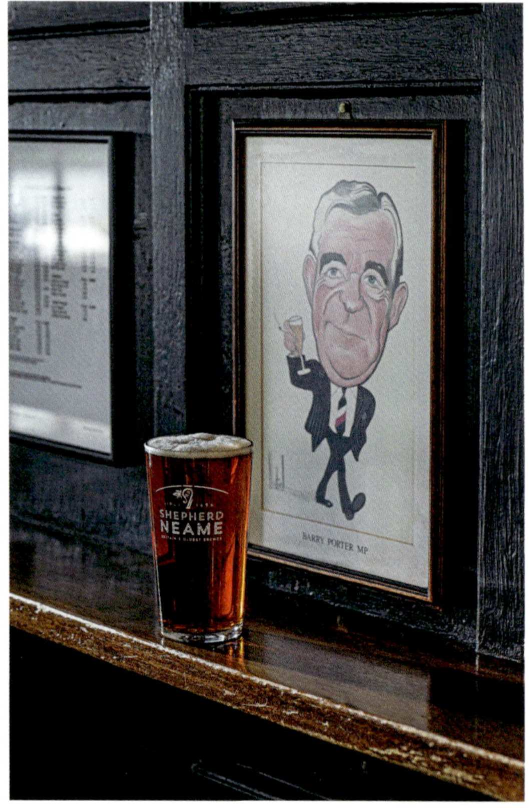

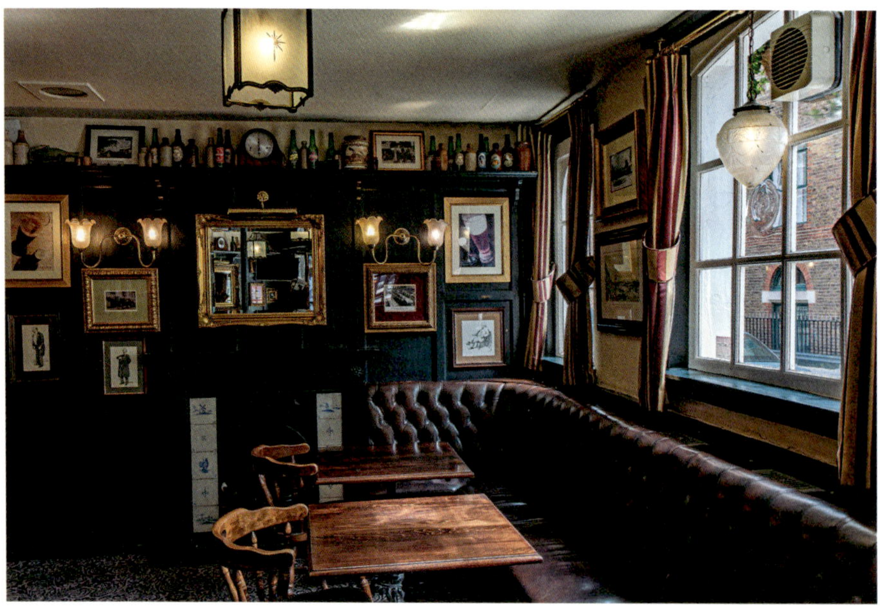

Bijou boozing in the shadow of Buckingham Palace

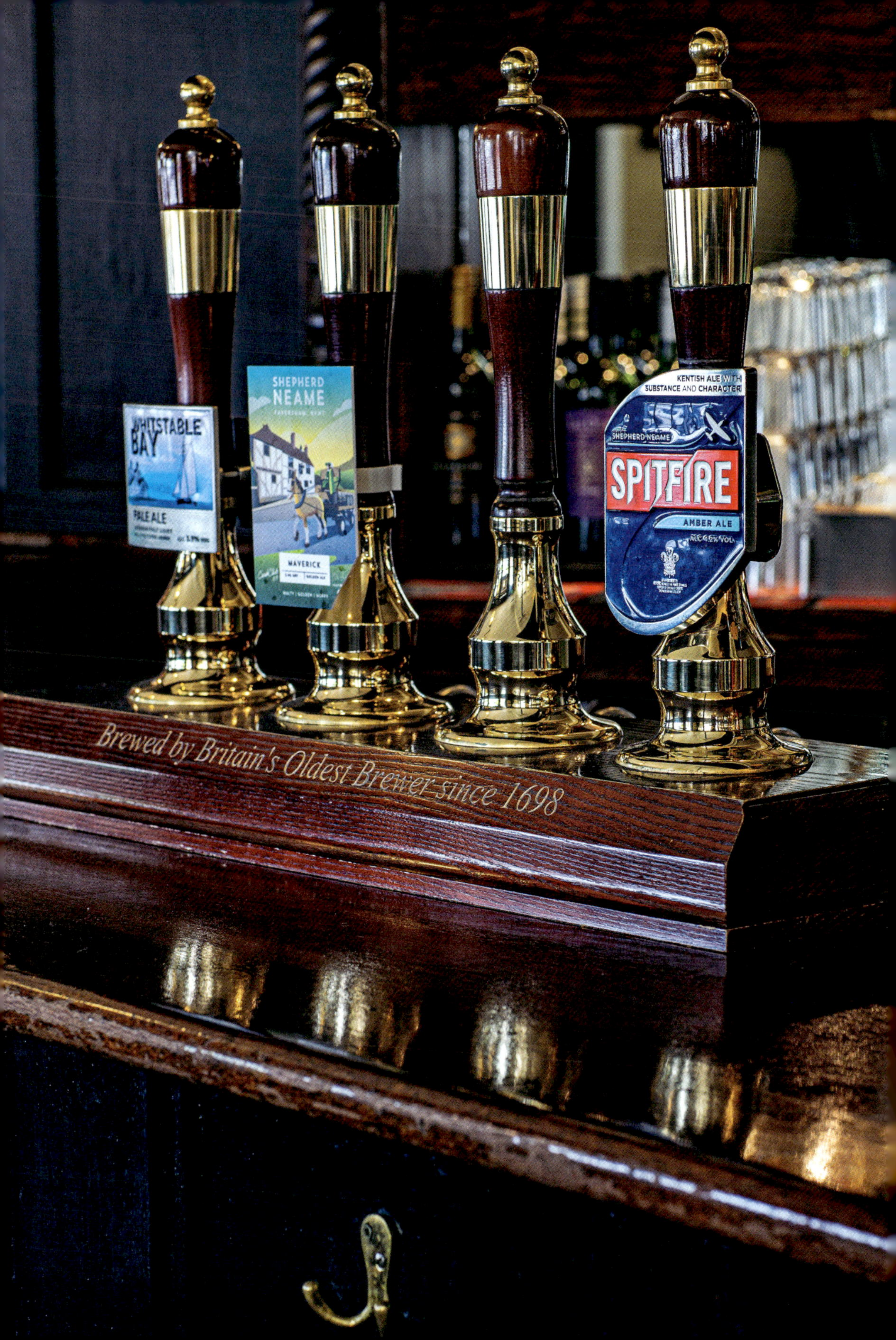
WHITSTABLE BAY
PALE ALE
SHEPHERD NEAME
MAVERICK
KENTISH ALE WITH SUBSTANCE AND CHARACTER
SHEPHERD NEAME
SPITFIRE
AMBER ALE
Brewed by Britain's Oldest Brewer since 1698

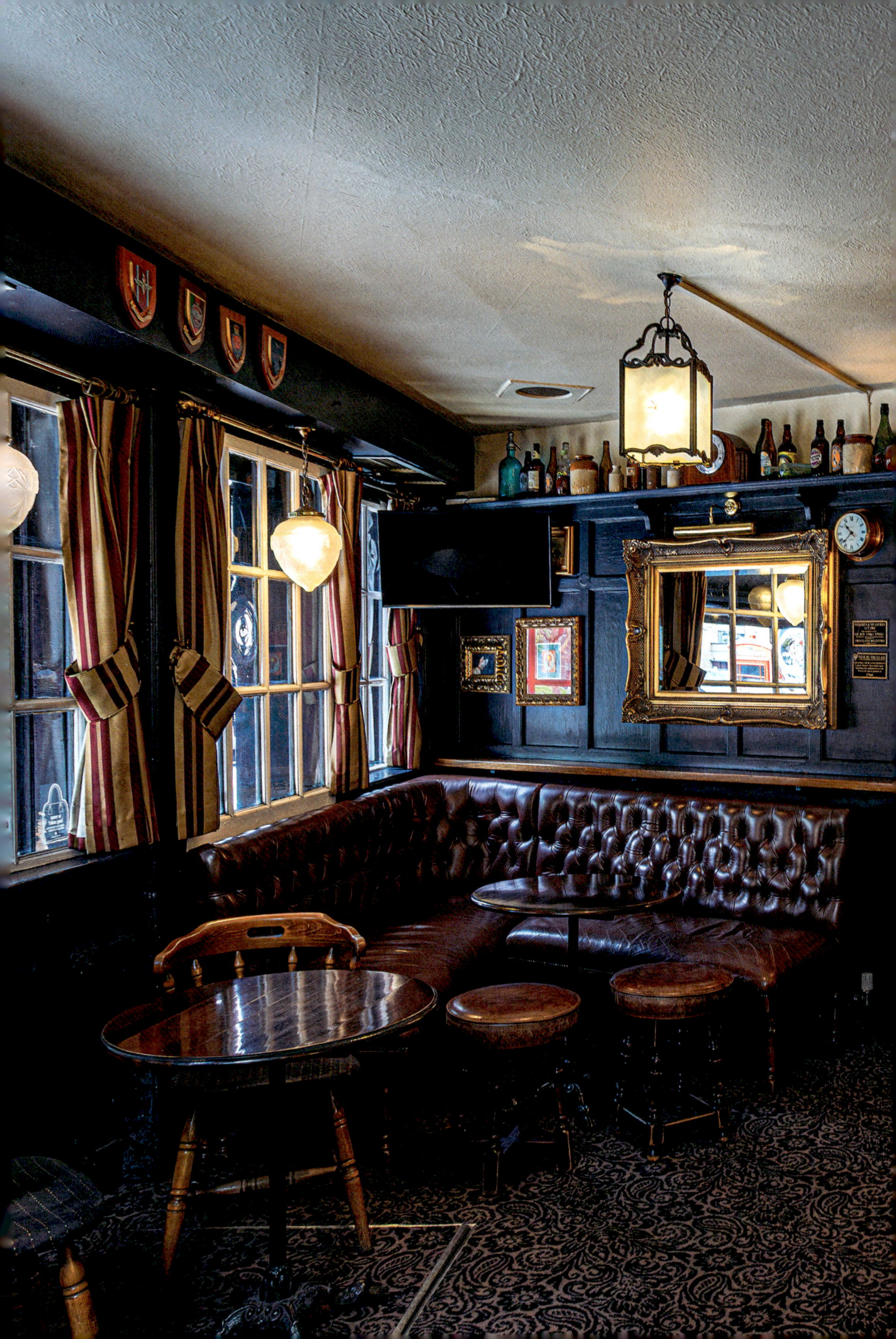

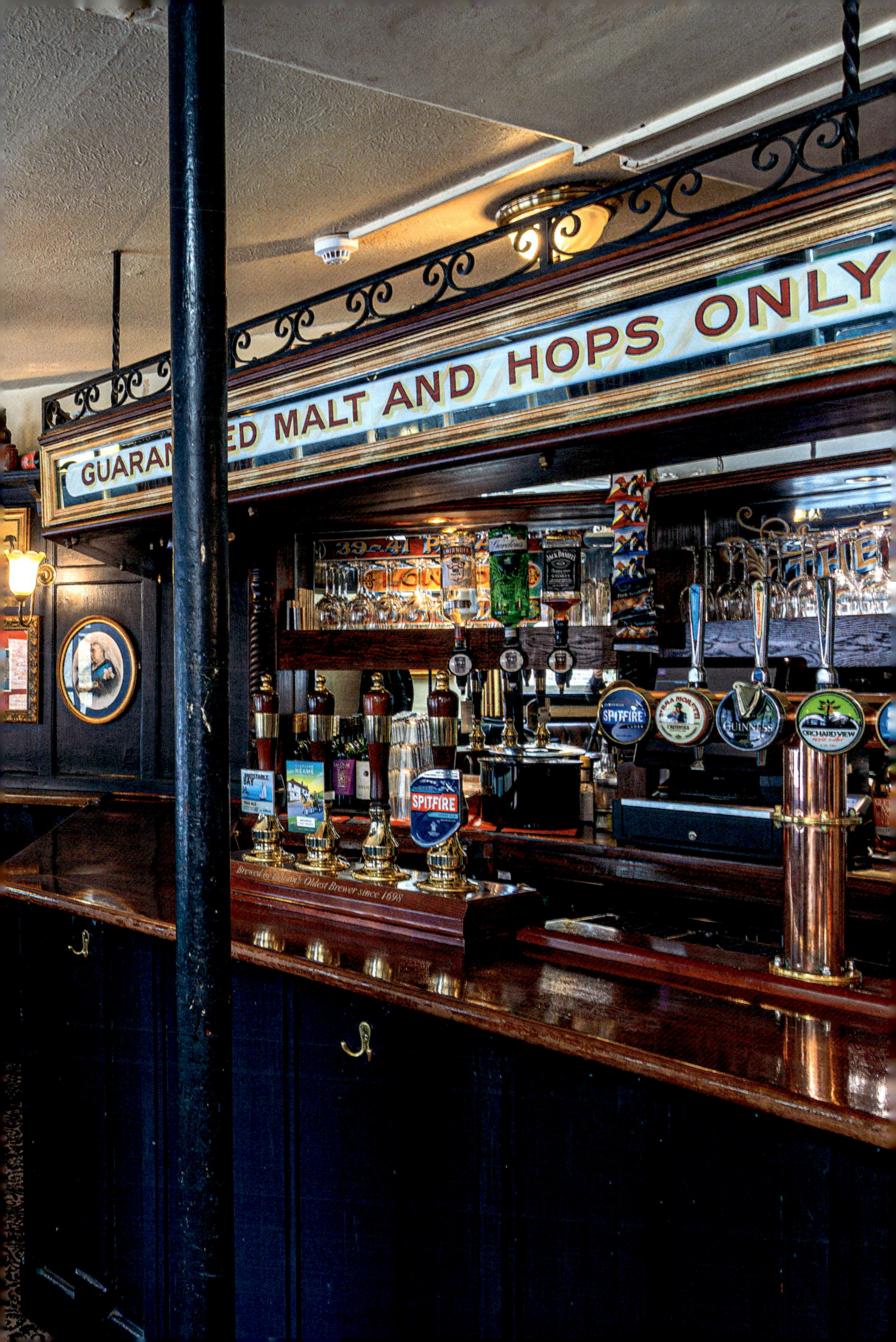

GUARAN[TE]ED MALT AND HOPS ONLY
SPITFIRE
GUINNESS
ORCHARD VIEW
Brewed by Britain's Oldest Brewer since 1698

THE BARLEY MOW

The whole world may be a stage, but most of an actor's life is spent hanging around waiting for the director's call that never comes. So, in between the training at RADA and sleeping on floors at the Edinburgh Festival, they often need a bit of cash to keep the dream alive. The itinerant and anti-social hours of bar work fit almost perfectly. Cast all day and cask all night, as it were.

The thespian crowd is as wide and diverse as the people who can be found pulling the pints at "The Mow". They've never had to advertise for a job, and people simply trickle through the door on word-of-mouth referrals. It makes for a jolly set-up and the team here, led by Will and Clare, are conjuring a beautiful community pub in the heart of central London.

It's a classic-looking layout: all loud and proud from the outside, with its famous boxy pawnbroking booths adorning the innards. Every black cabbie reckons the Beatles used to drink in here, but as Marylebone became fashionable and land values upwardly mobile, the freeholders tried to close The Mow down and convert it into residential use. The pub closed for three years until finally the righteous won and the pub reopened. Hurrah, for the god of good beer!

With fourteen investors chipping in, the future, certainly for the short-term, has been secured. Even Will's young daughter got a share in the pub, so it really is a family affair, run with a genuine passion for quality, creativity and, most importantly, fun.

If you fancy going to a "world-famous" pub quiz introduced by Dame Judi Dench or have the next Doctor Who pull your pint, then this might be the place for you. Even 007 and his quartermaster have popped in when not on Her Majesty's Service. Open mic nights are a broad church, and the legendary darts league is named in honour of former Mow manager and lauded actor Alex Beckett. The award-winning short film *The Lock-In* was filmed right here, with the shillelagh behind the bar playing a lead role in dispatching over-bearing and odious pub customers to their deaths in the cellar below. You have been warned.

It's a beautiful pub, doing beautiful things. By the time you visit, they might even have expanded into the room upstairs and be offering the best family-style Sunday roasts in town. Bravo and encore!

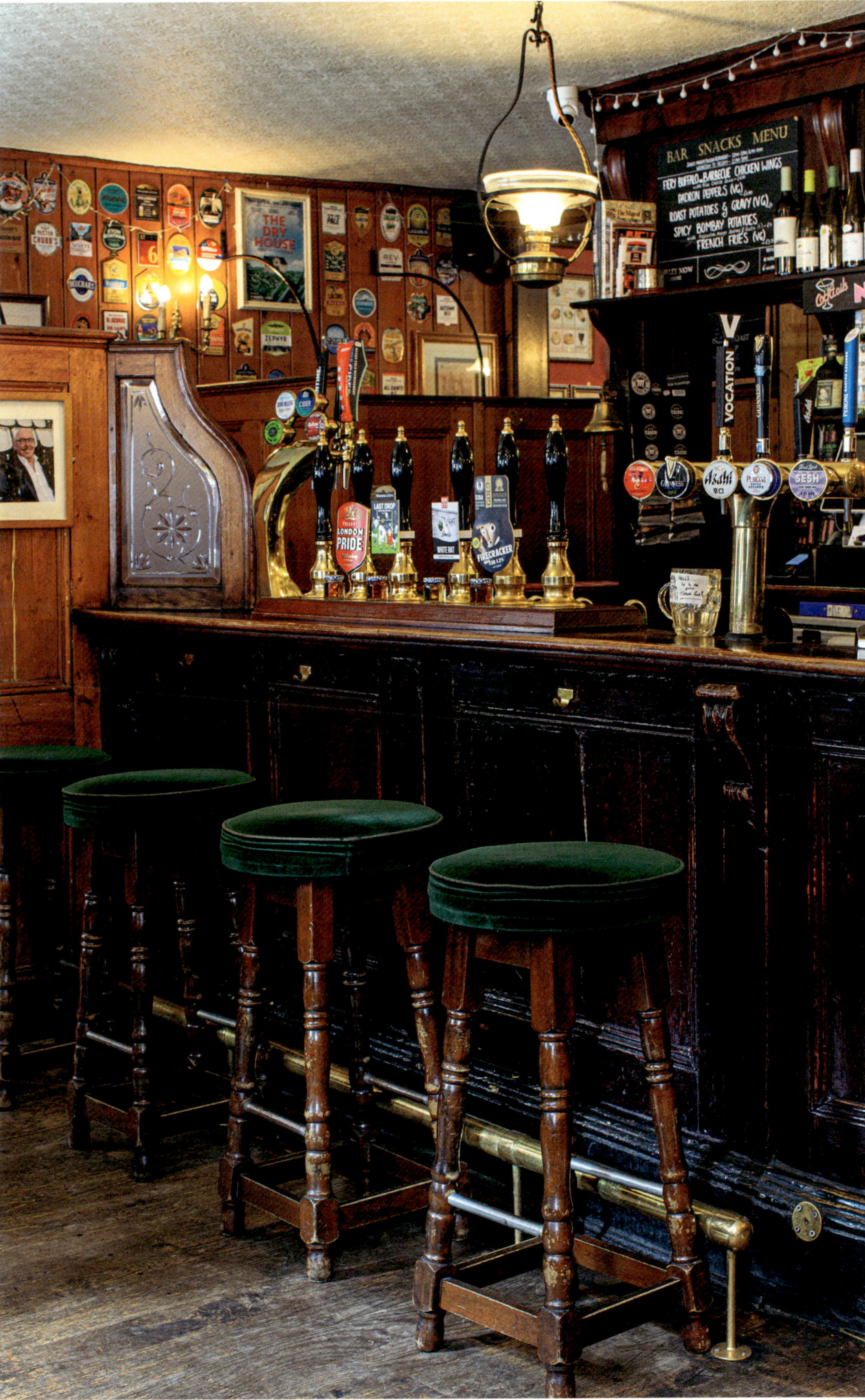

BAR SNACKS MENU
FIERY BUFFALO or BARBECUE CHICKEN WINGS
PADRON PEPPERS (VG)
ROAST POTATOES & GRAVY (VG)
SPICY BOMBAY POTATOES
FRENCH FRIES (VG)
THE DRY HOUSE
LONDON PRIDE
LAST DROP
WHITE RAT
FIRECRACKER
VOCATION
GUINNESS
Asahi
PERONI
SESH

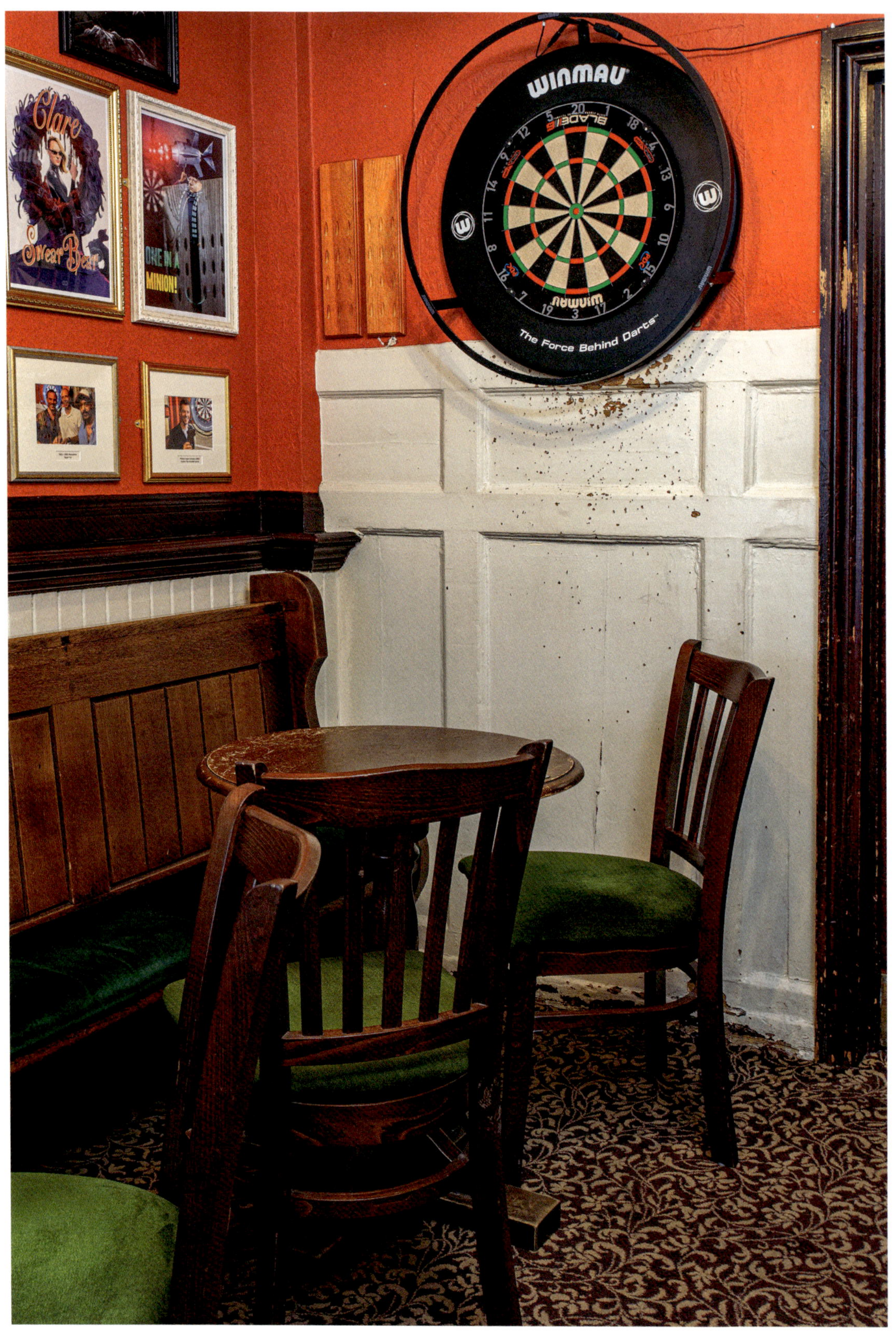

The art of arrow-chucking is a serious pastime here

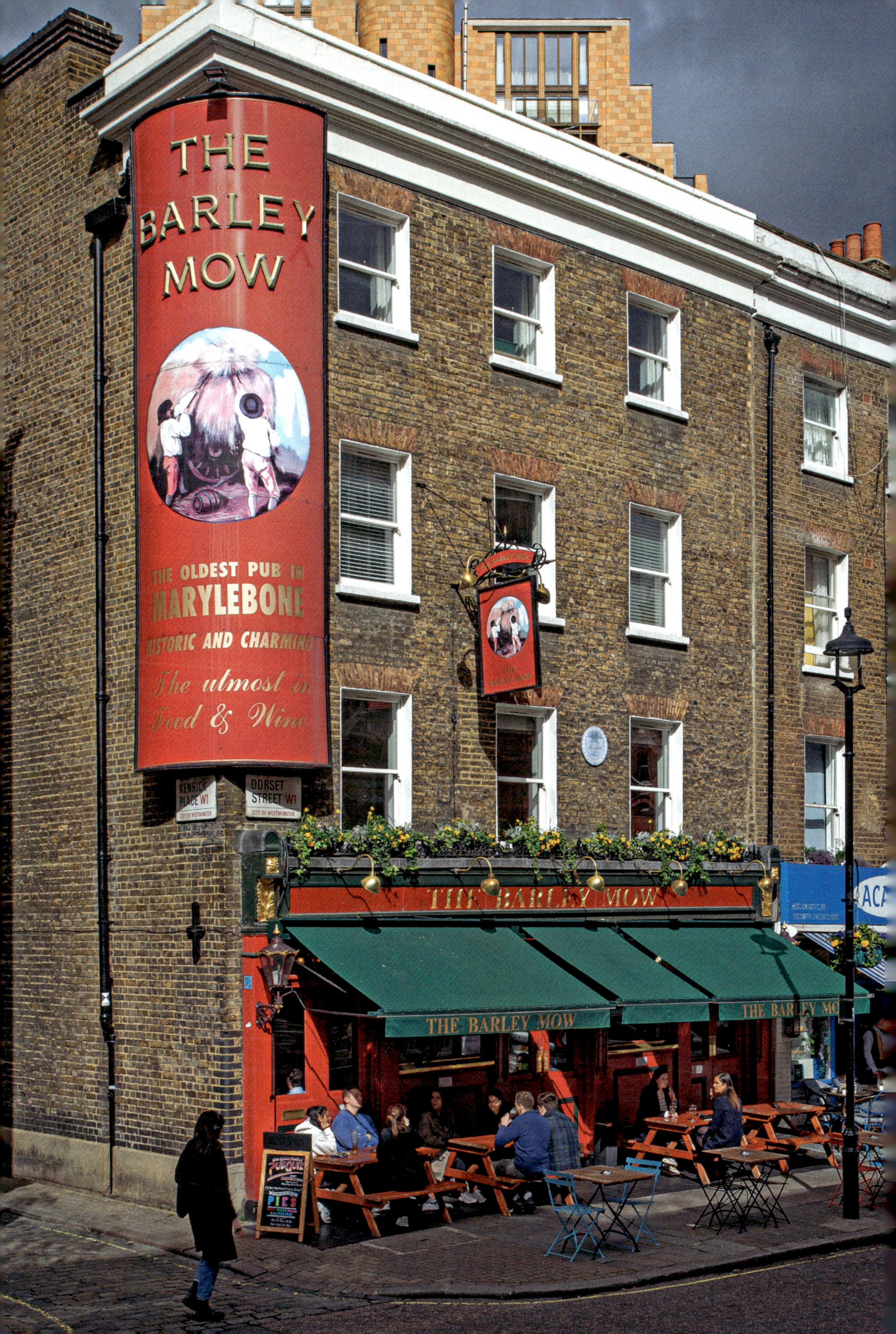
THE
BARLEY
MOW
THE OLDEST PUB IN
MARYLEBONE
HISTORIC AND CHARMING
The utmost in
Food & Wine
KENRICK
PLACE W1
CITY OF WESTMINSTER
DORSET
STREET W1
CITY OF WESTMINSTER
THE BARLEY MOW
THE BARLEY MOW
THE BARLEY MOW
PIES

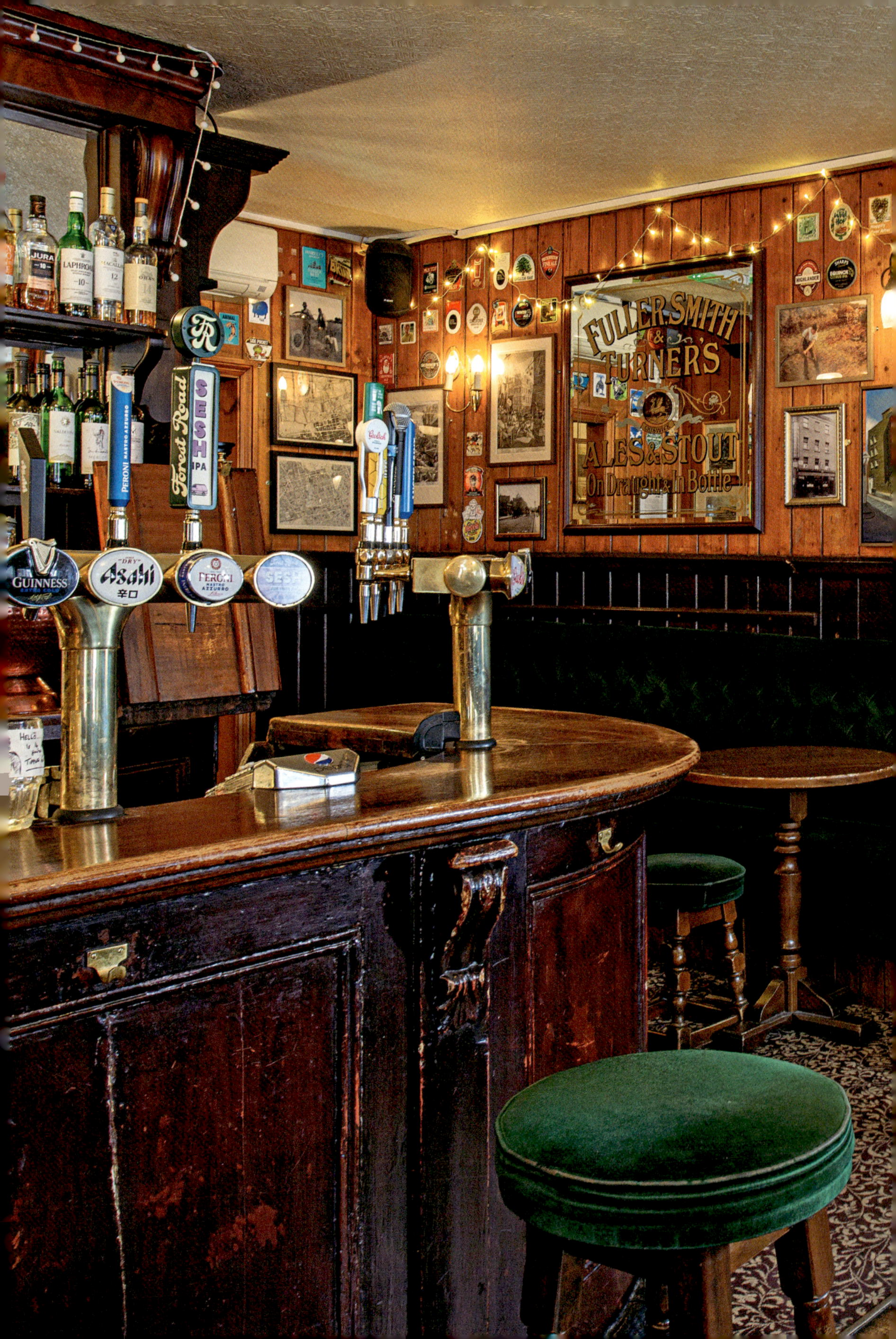

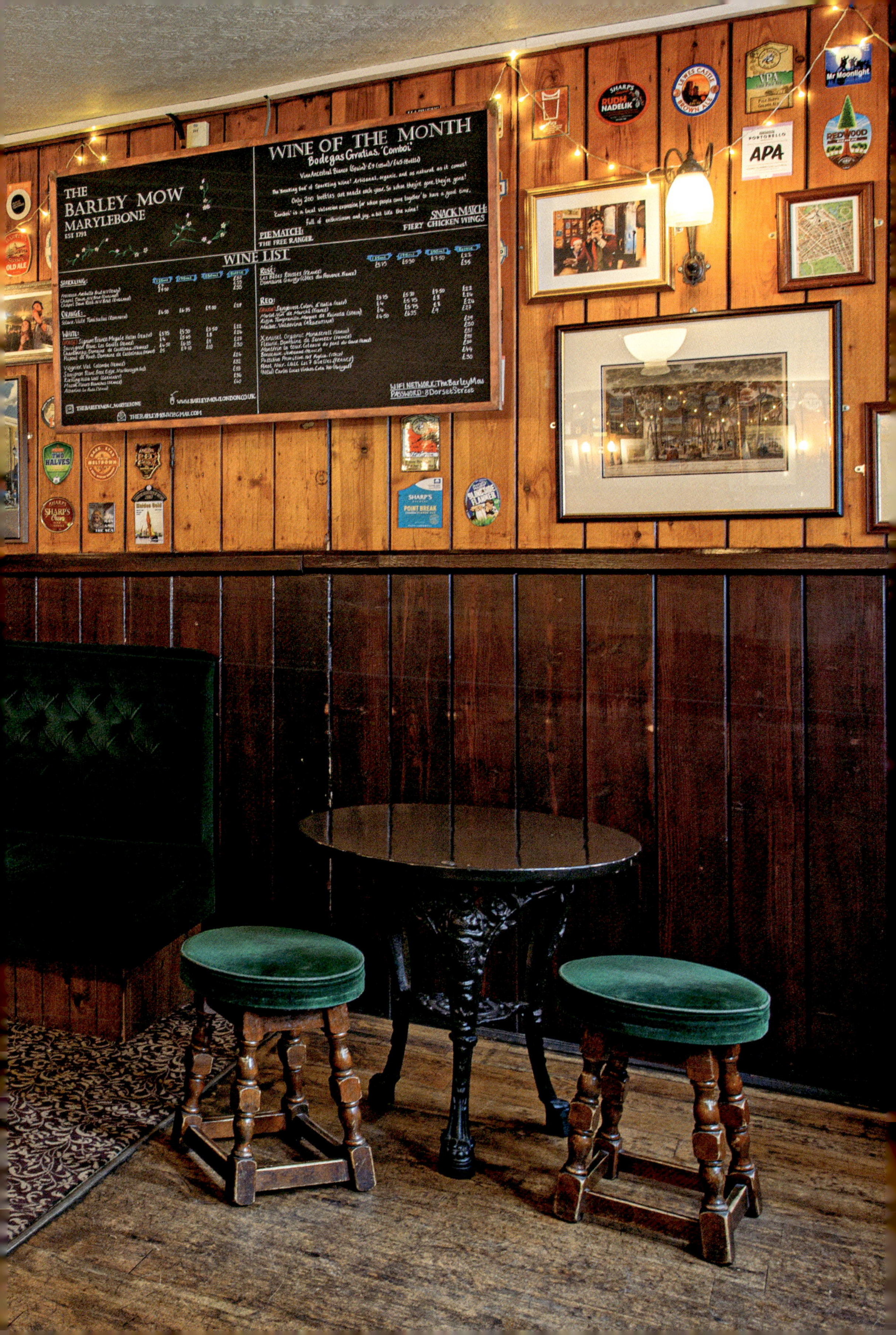

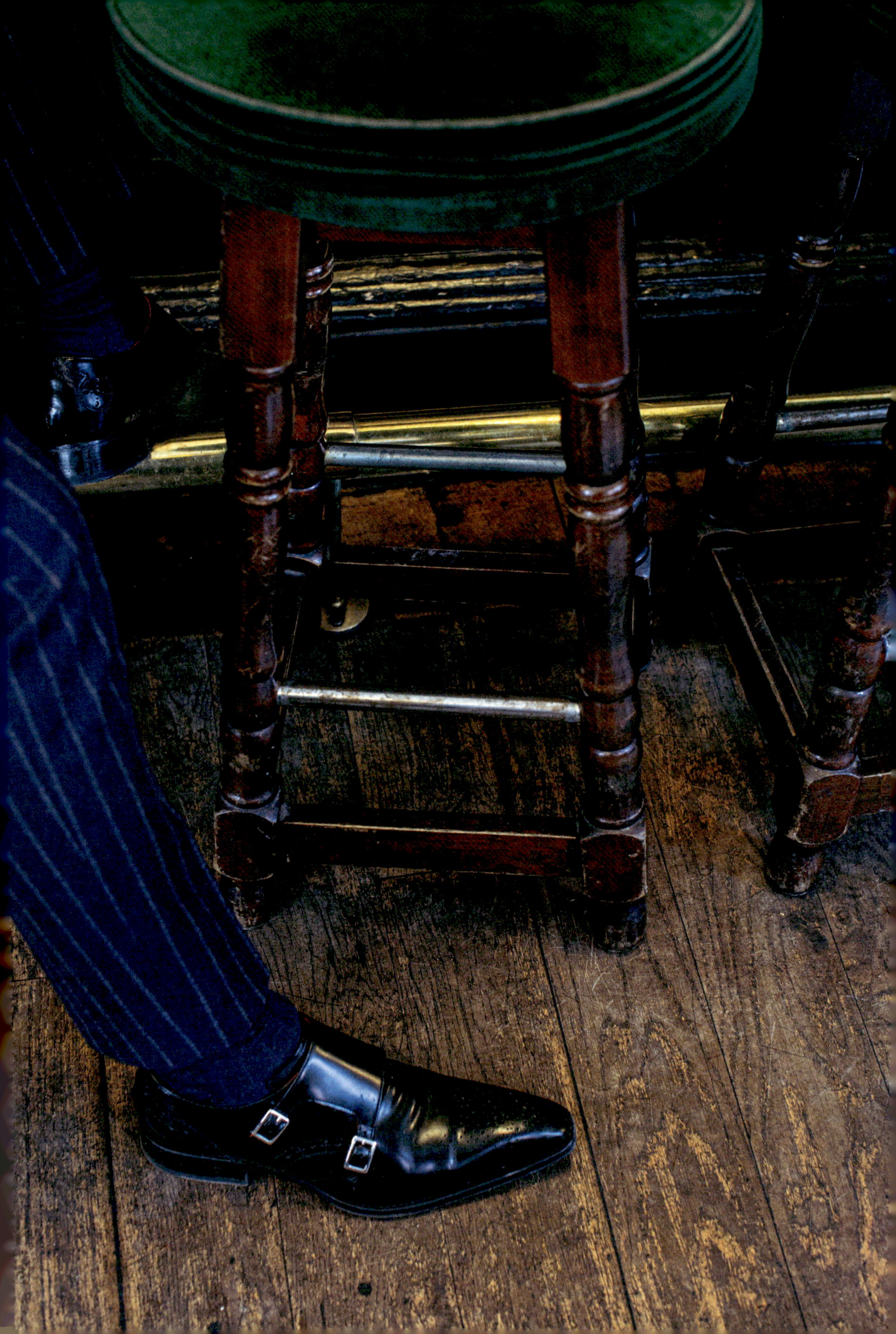

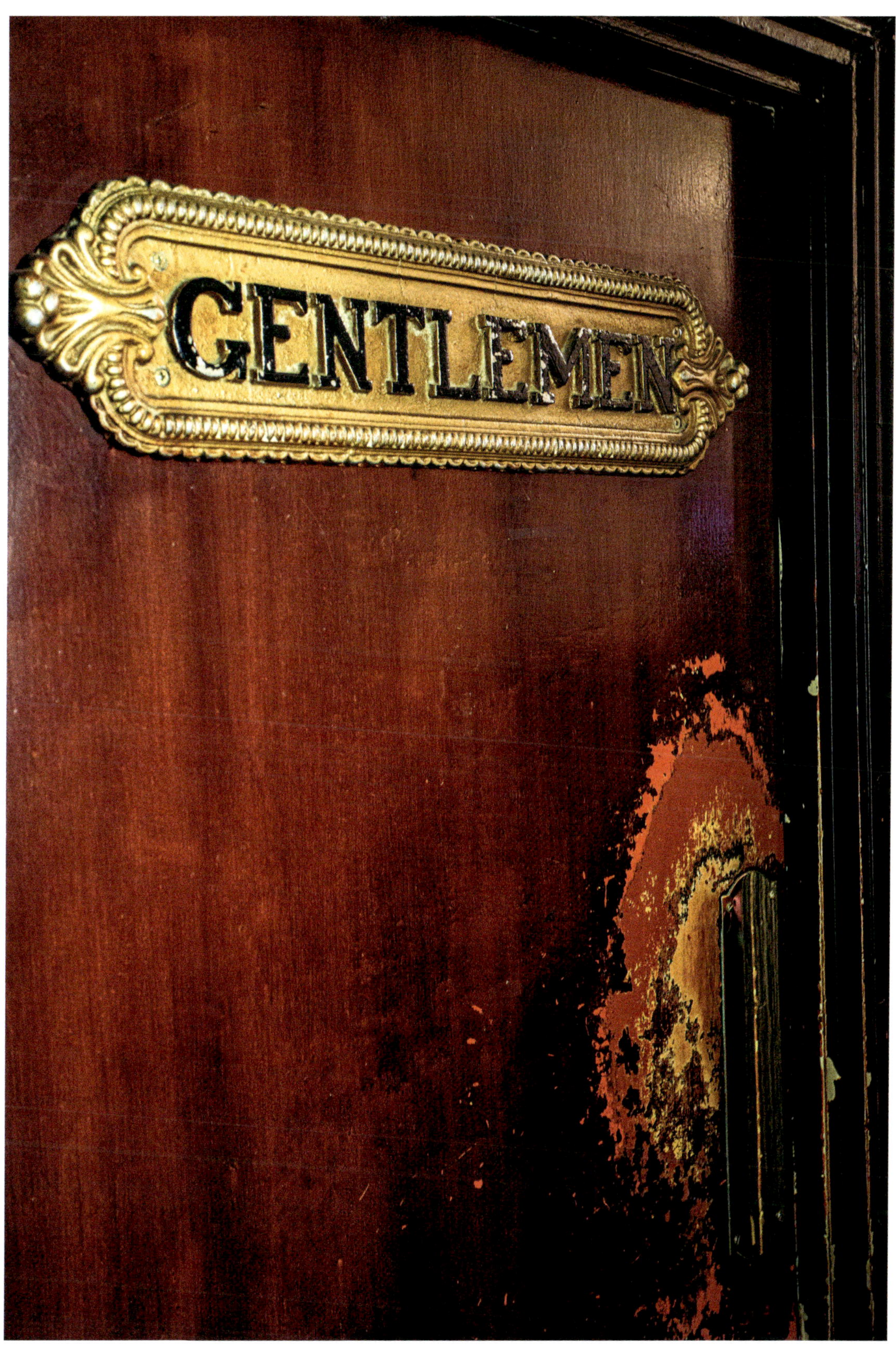

An eclectic crowd of elbow-benders throng to this Baker Street backwater

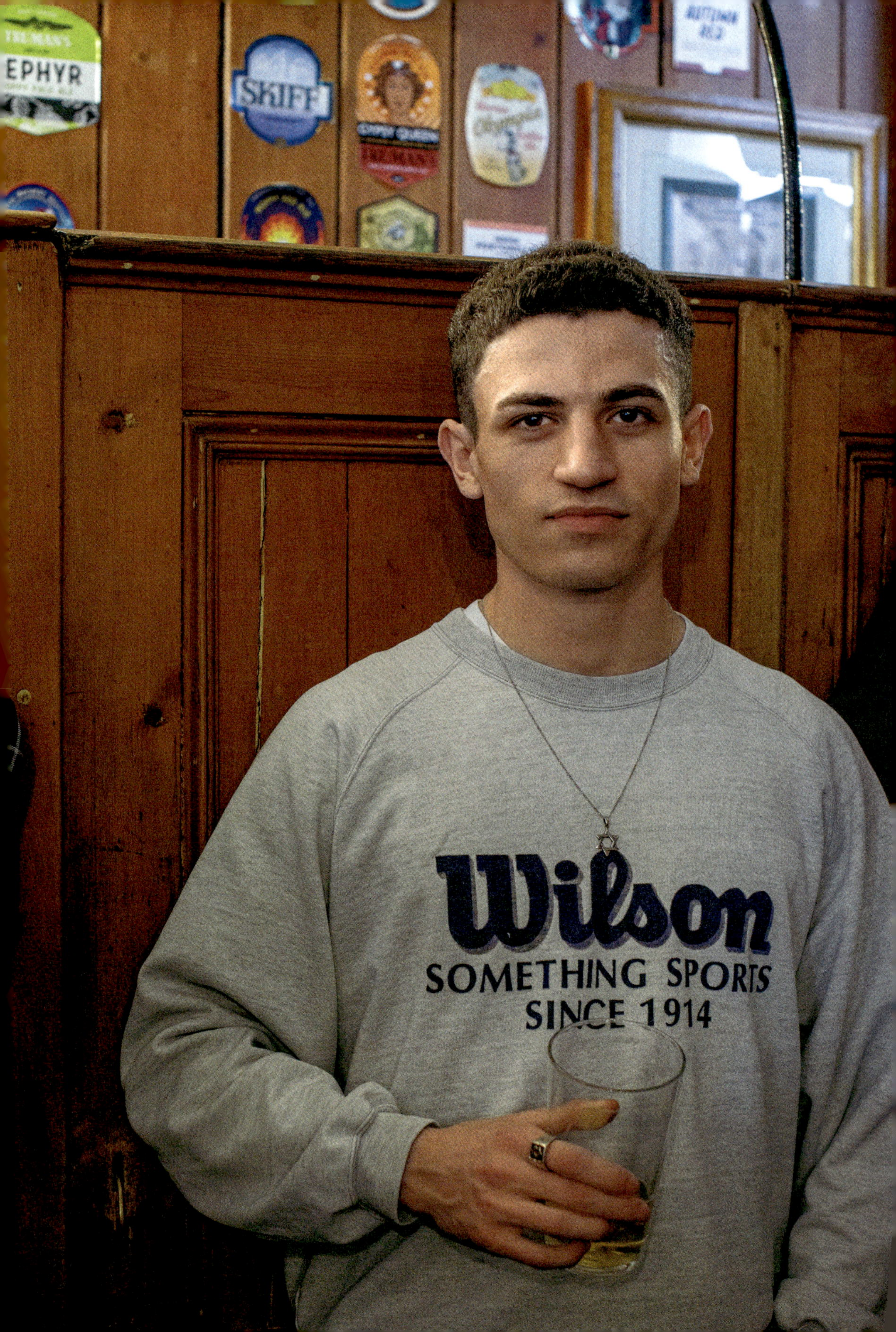
EPHYR
SKIFF
TRUMAN'S
AUTUMN
RED
Wilson
SOMETHING SPORTS
SINCE 1914

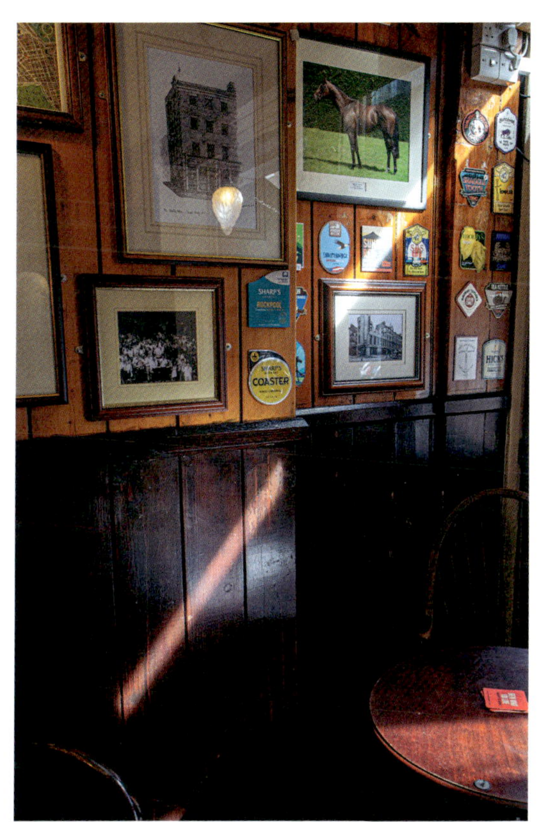

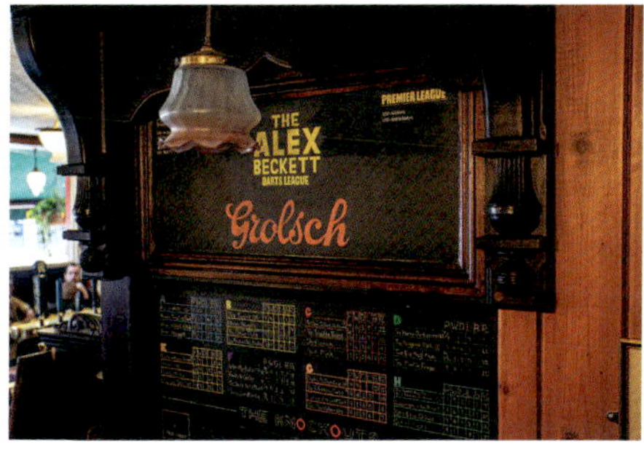

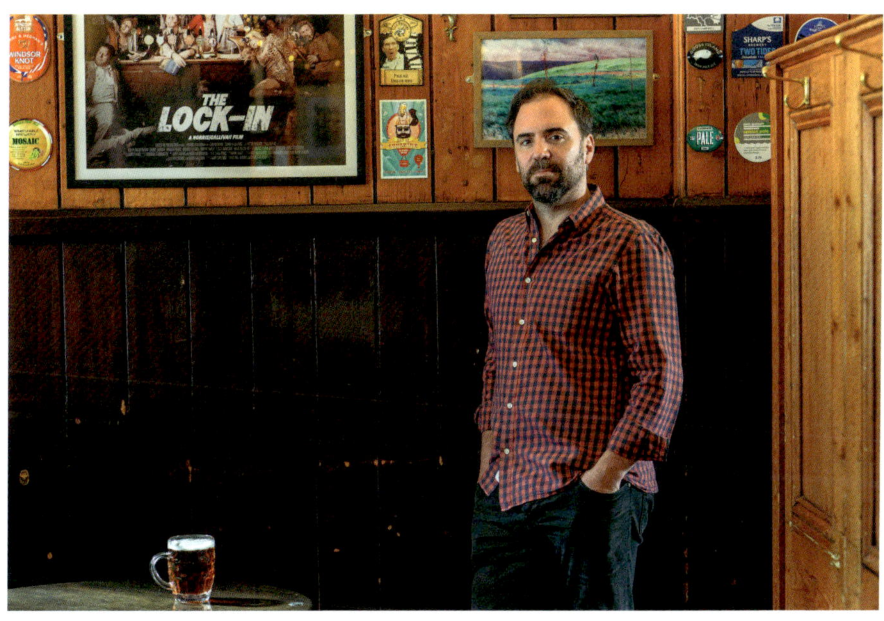

Darts leagues and world-famous quizzes bring the buzz

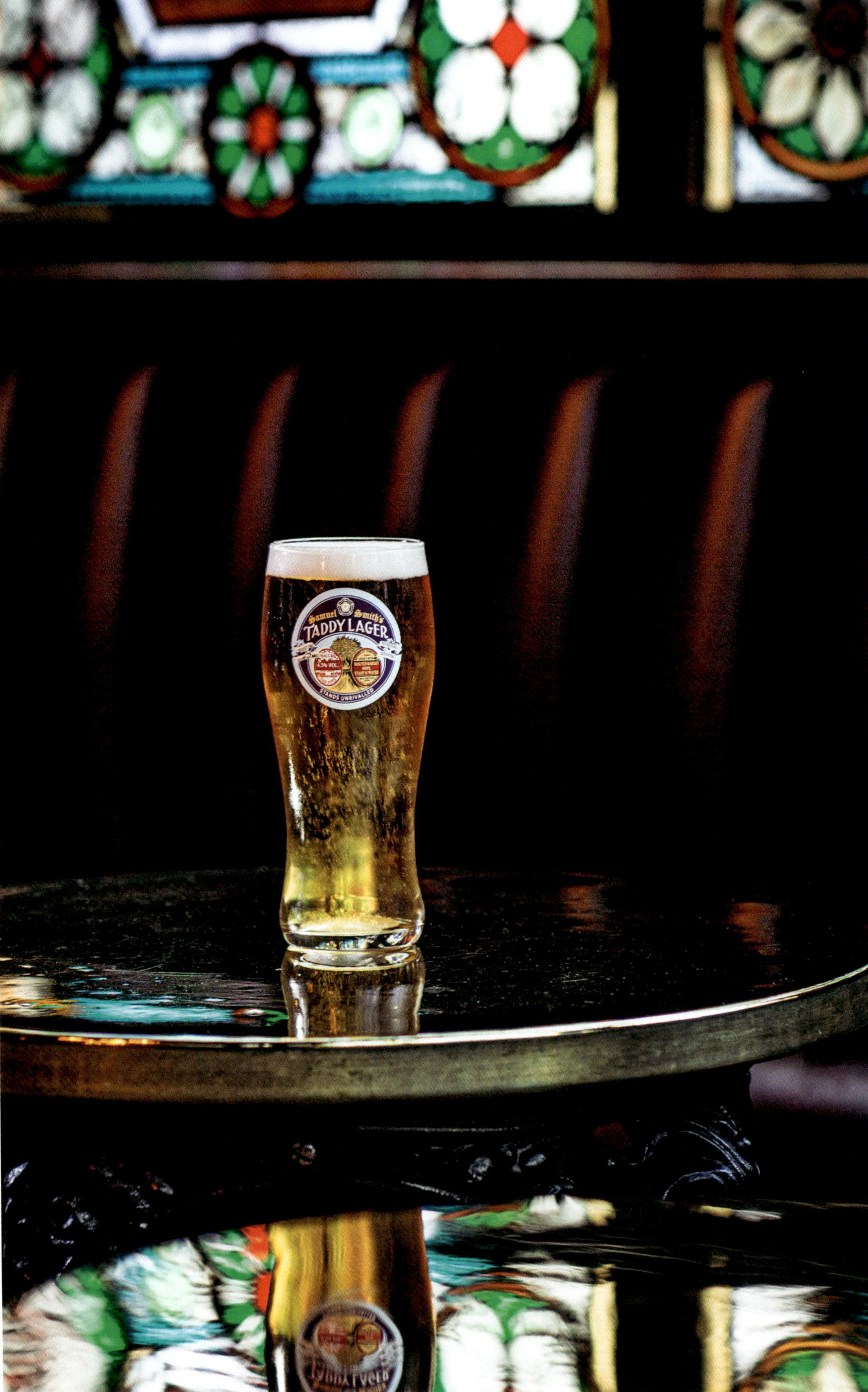

Samuel Smith's
TADDY LAGER
4.5% VOL.
STANDS UNRIVALLED

THE CHAMPION

A FITZROVIAN CATHEDRAL OF GLASS

12–13 WELLS ST, FITZROVIA W1T 3PA

Samuel Smith's hostelries can be polarising places, with many real ale drinkers loving to hate this fifth-generation Yorkshire brewer. Providing a comforting solidity and tradition to everything they do, they make no excuses for their historic inertia, slowly sailing through a rapidly changing world. Drawing water from historic wells, fermenting in traditional slate Yorkshire squares, decanting into oak casks and then delivering locally by horse-drawn drays to the town of Tadcaster are all part of the stoic DNA at work here.

It would be easy to walk past The Champion every day and never be tempted in by the quiet exterior. Its opaque glass and wood façade give no intimation of the grandeur within. But my Lord, what majesty! It oozes cathedral-like light, and you won't be surprised to hear that the very same stained-glass artist works on the world-famous windows at York Minster.

Samuel Smith understands that they don't own any of their pubs but are mere custodians for the next generation.

The windows commemorate a who's who of the British Empire during the 1800s, when the pub first opened. Featuring the great and good, they depict famous explorers, world-champion pugilists, cross-Channel swimmers, Cresta Run daredevils and Matterhorn summiteers. Florence Nightingale is honoured for her Crimean nursing exploits, whilst W. G. Grace is noted for his prowess at the cricketing crease. It's an eclectic selection, and your mind drifts easily to the question of which icons might merit inclusion in these windows if they were recommissioned for the twentieth or twenty-first century.

Samuel Smith understands that they don't own any of their pubs but are mere custodians for the next generation. They spared no inconsiderable expense when commissioning this stained-glass magnificence in the late 1980s, and it's not easy to think of any other landlord who would lavish their real estate with such decorative indulgence.

But with no shareholders to service and no dividends to pay, they can invest for the long term. A classical understanding that pleasant environs, simple beer and good conversation will hold appeal until time immemorial.

As they might say up north,
"Totally champion!"

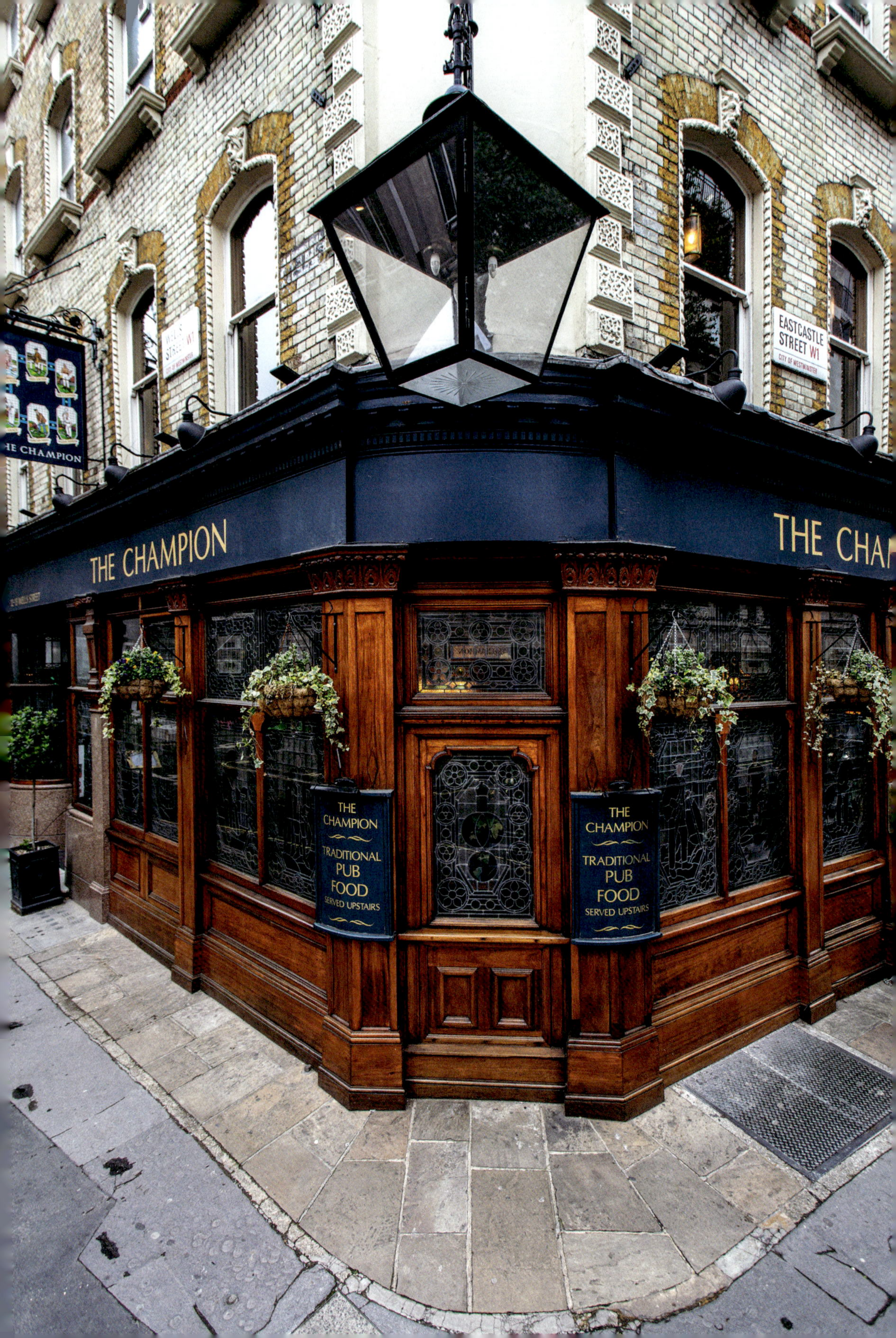
EASTCASTLE
STREET W1
CITY OF WESTMINSTER
THE CHAMPION
THE CHAMPION
THE CHA
THE CHAMPION
TRADITIONAL
PUB
FOOD
SERVED UPSTAIRS
THE
CHAMPION
TRADITIONAL
PUB
FOOD
SERVED UPSTAIRS

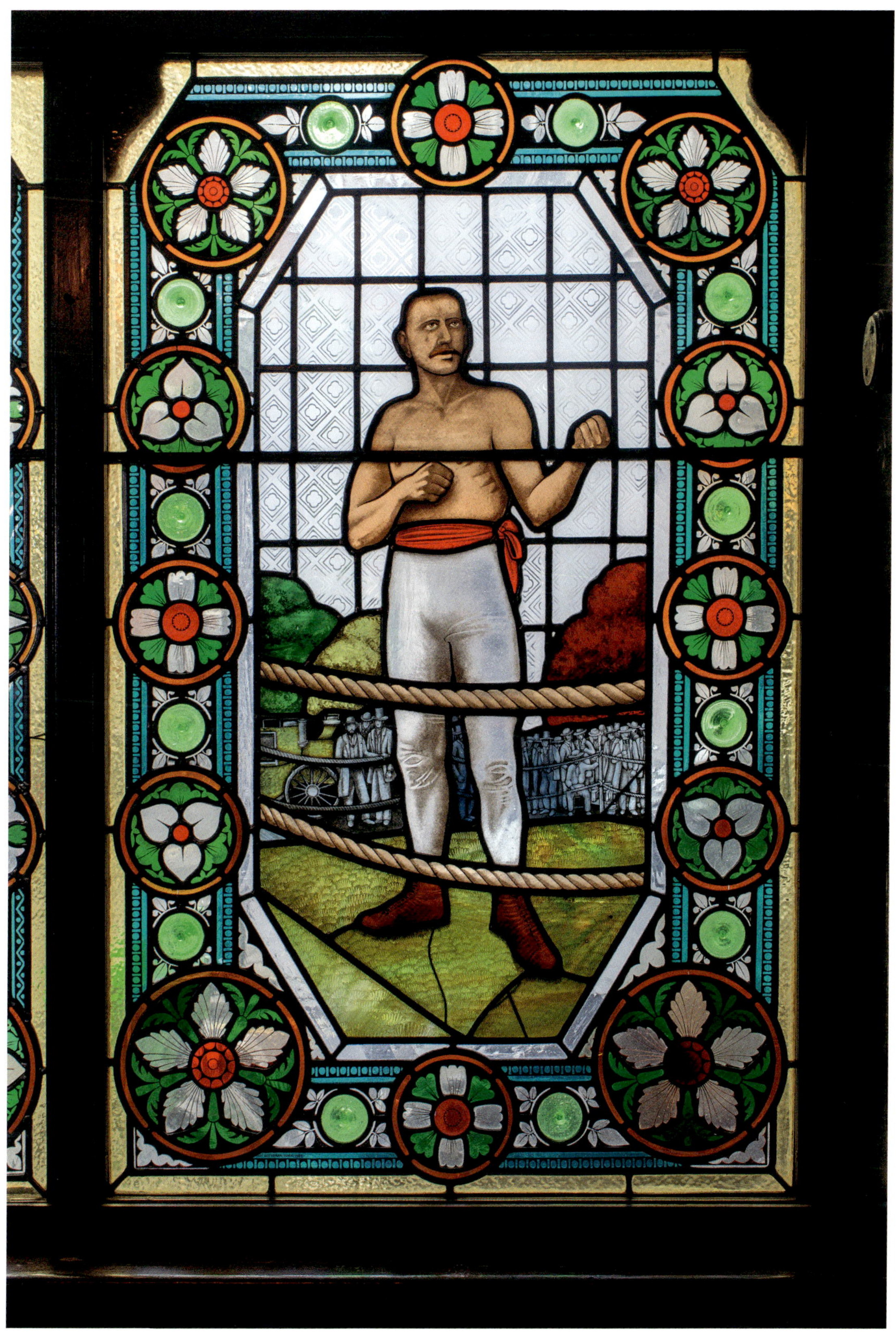

Prize-fighting pugilists watch over your pint

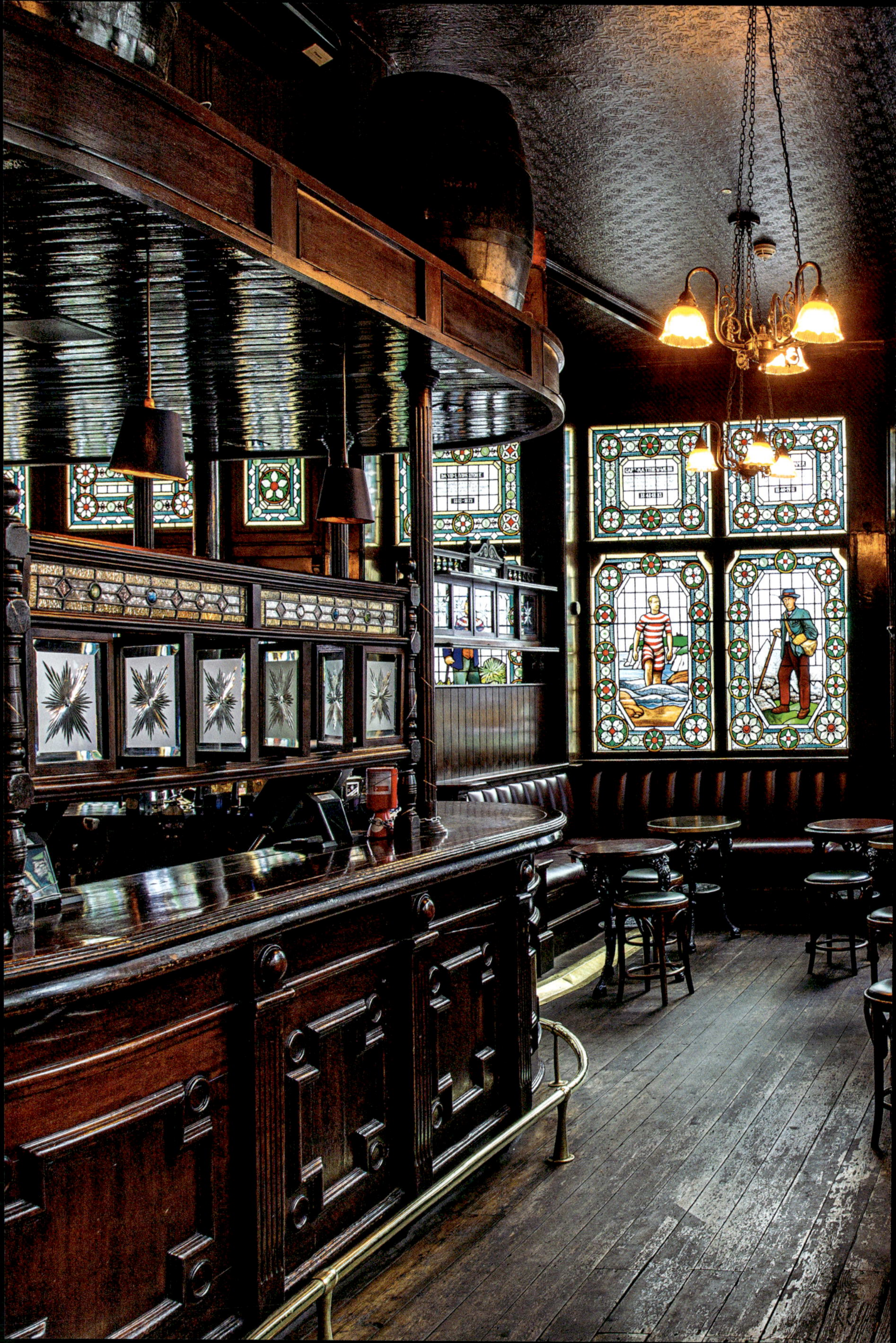

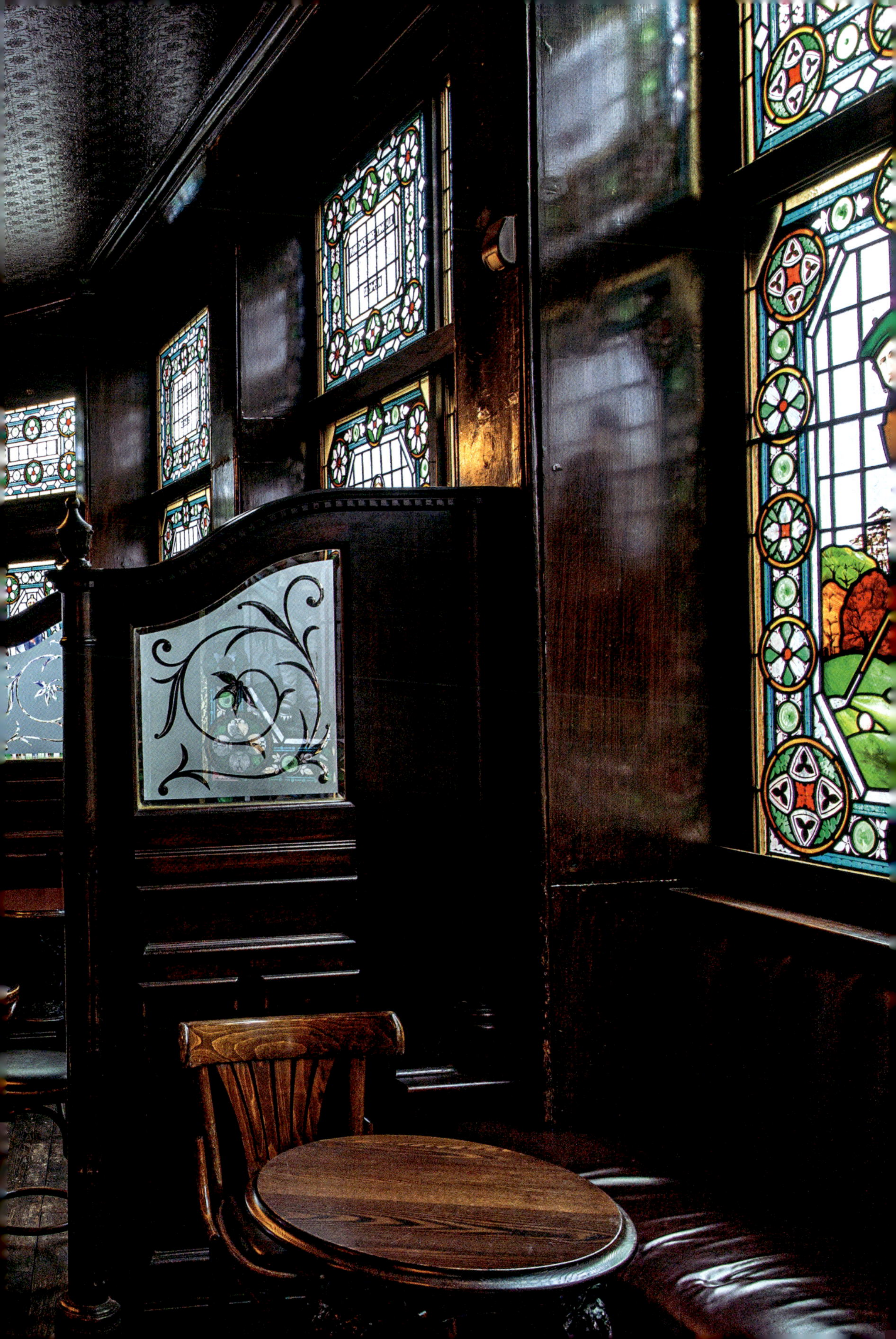

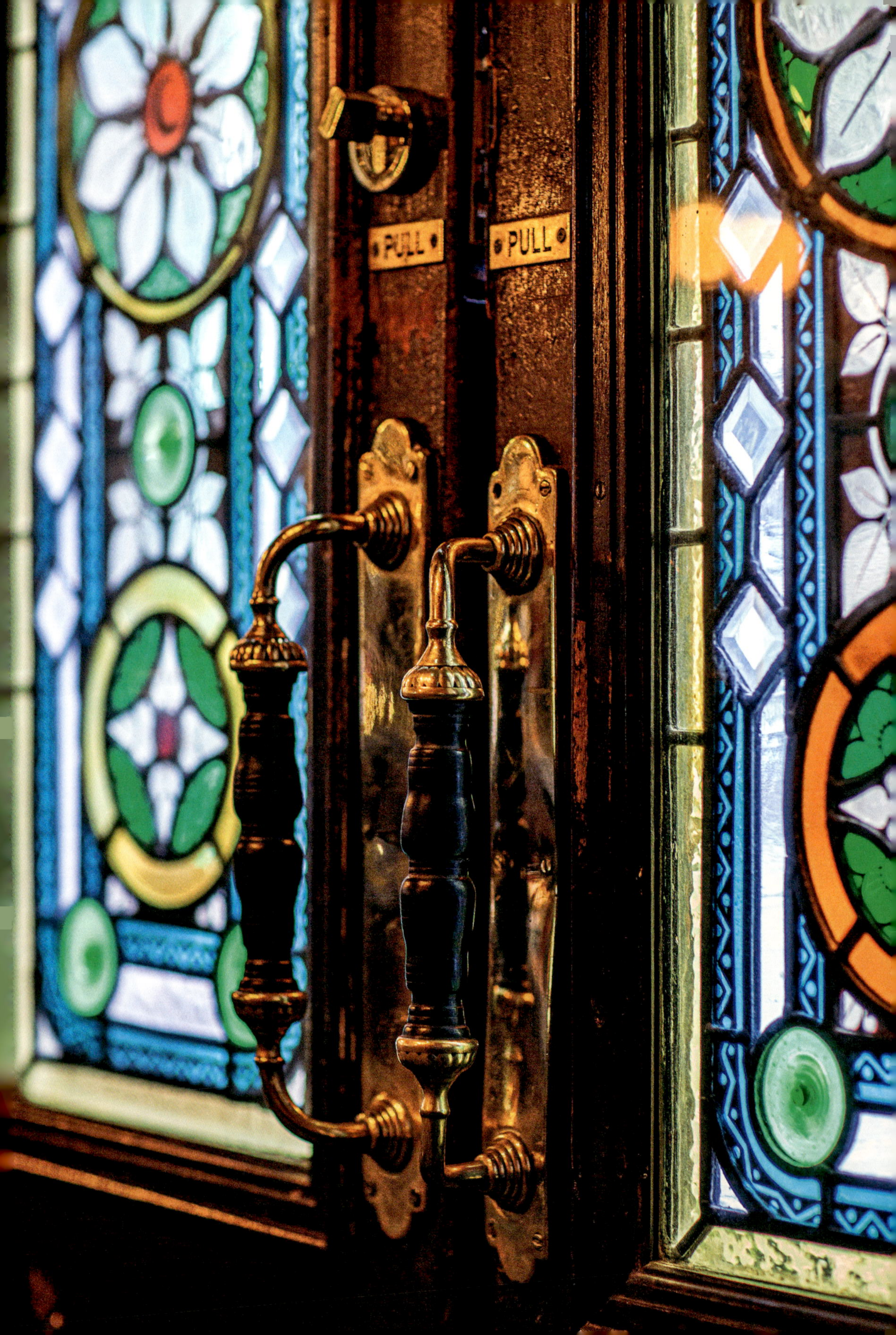
PULL
PULL

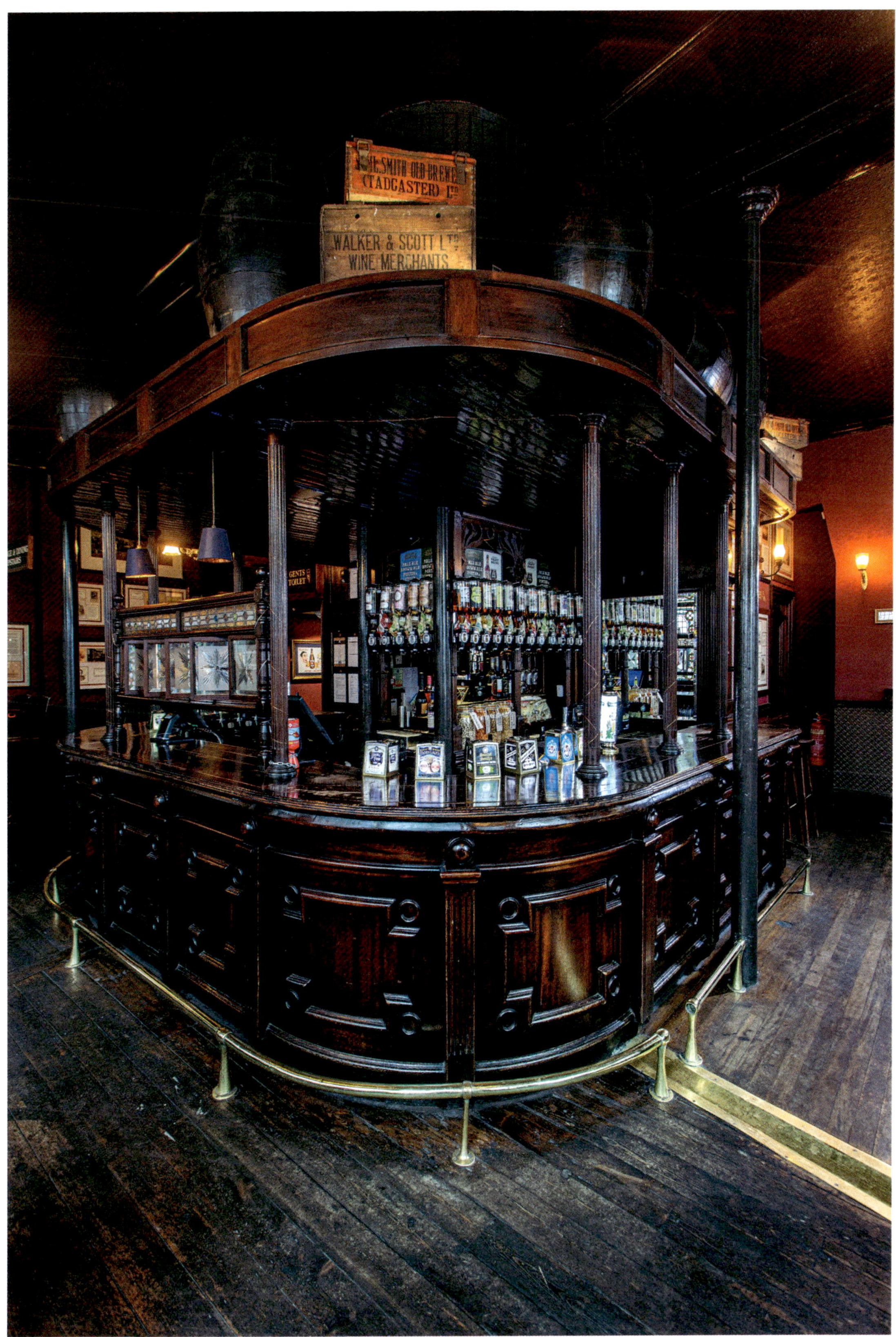

Brass rails and burnished wood complete the scene

BRADLEY'S SPANISH BAR

When is a pub not a pub? When it's Bradley's Spanish Bar, of course. The sign says "bar" but your heart says "pub". Sure, it serves a few cervezas, but who doesn't proffer a San Miguel or Mahou on the ramp these days? There's also no food, so it can't be a tapas bar. To be honest, you rarely find a Spaniard in here, and a few La Liga football scarves and pictures of matadors are fooling nobody. What once was a fine wine and sherry bar is now officially a pub, a cavern of compact chaos. Bradley's is the least secret secret escape for those tired of the two kilometres of commerce on Oxford Street.

It seems that every epic night always begins, or more than likely ends, on Hanway Place.

If you are a fan of the Irish madness at The Toucan not far away, then you'll love its exotic Spanish cousin. The one who went on a foreign language exchange, had a wild fling and never returned. Good times flow either in the cramped bars inside or out on the street, dicing with death from rat-running cabbies. It seems that every epic night always begins, or more than likely ends, on Hanway Place. The cosy compression means that, no matter where you drink, conversation flows in every direction. It's not really a place to be alone, and it's perennially staffed by people who popped in for a pint and simply forgot to leave.

The true fulcrum of fun is of course the jukebox. It continues to spin the vinyl 45s from a back catalogue of over 20,000 singles. That's enough groove to play continually for over a month, and it's wall-to-wall nostalgic bangers. The iPod generation look on in wonder at those clunky buttons, flashing lights and whirring discs.

Thank goodness that the regulars (past and present) crowdfunded Bradley's' survival through the pandemic, and with the commercial threat of Crossrail mere yards away, you must join this party whilst the jukebox still plays.

As the bar – sorry, pub – itself proclaims:

"At the end of the day, night or afternoon, you'll have stayed longer than expected, drank more than you wanted and will generally have had a good time. That's a promise."

Olé!

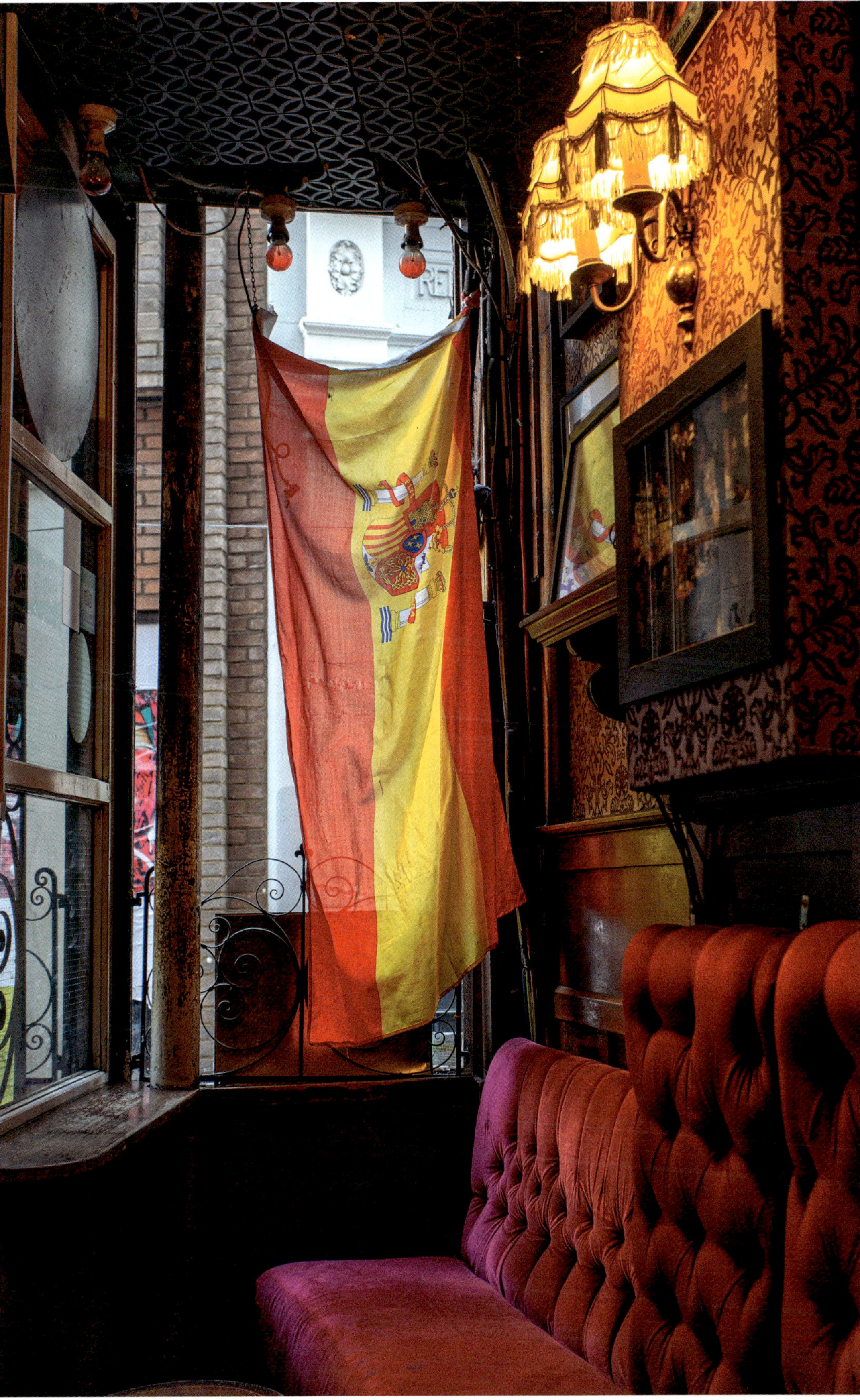

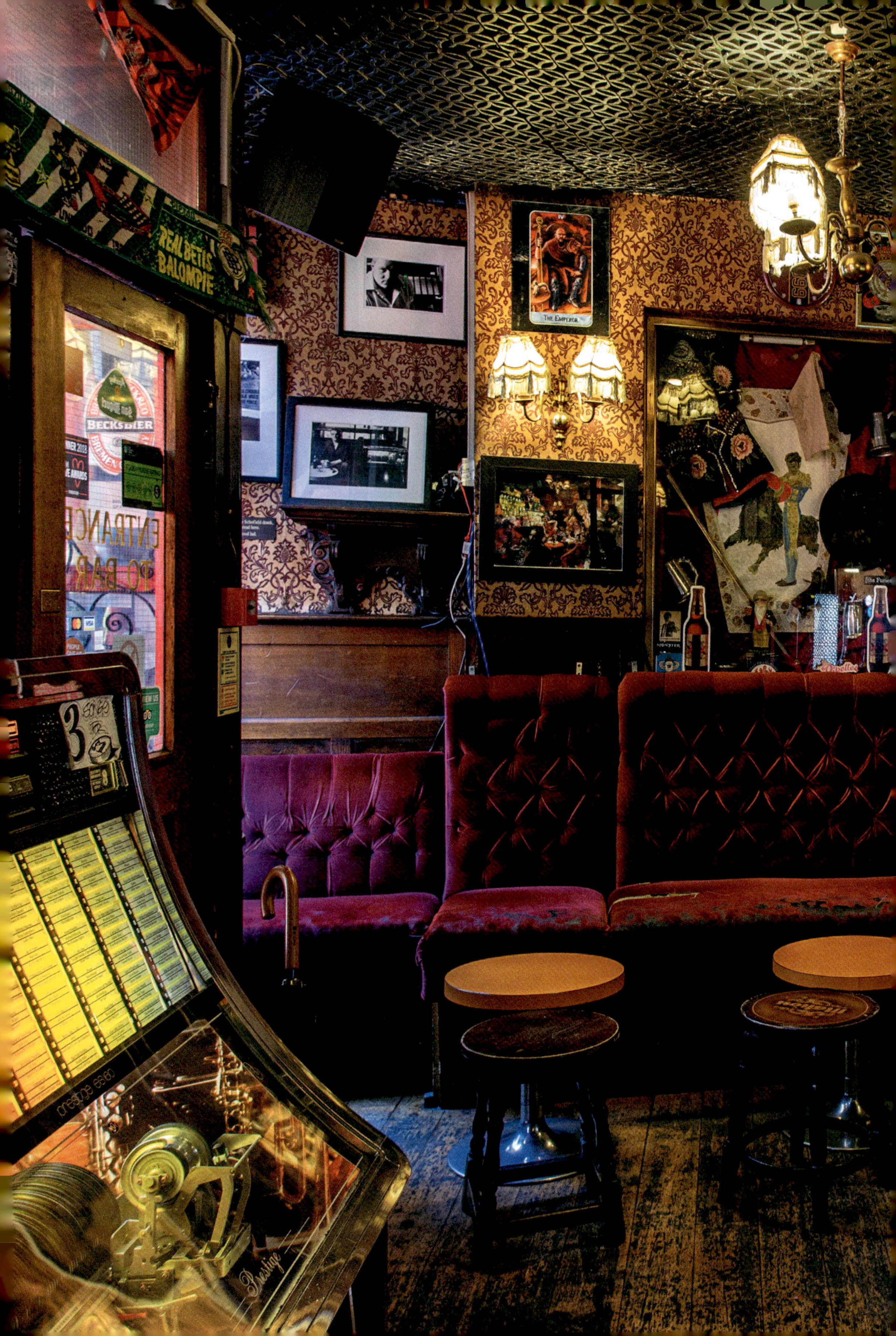

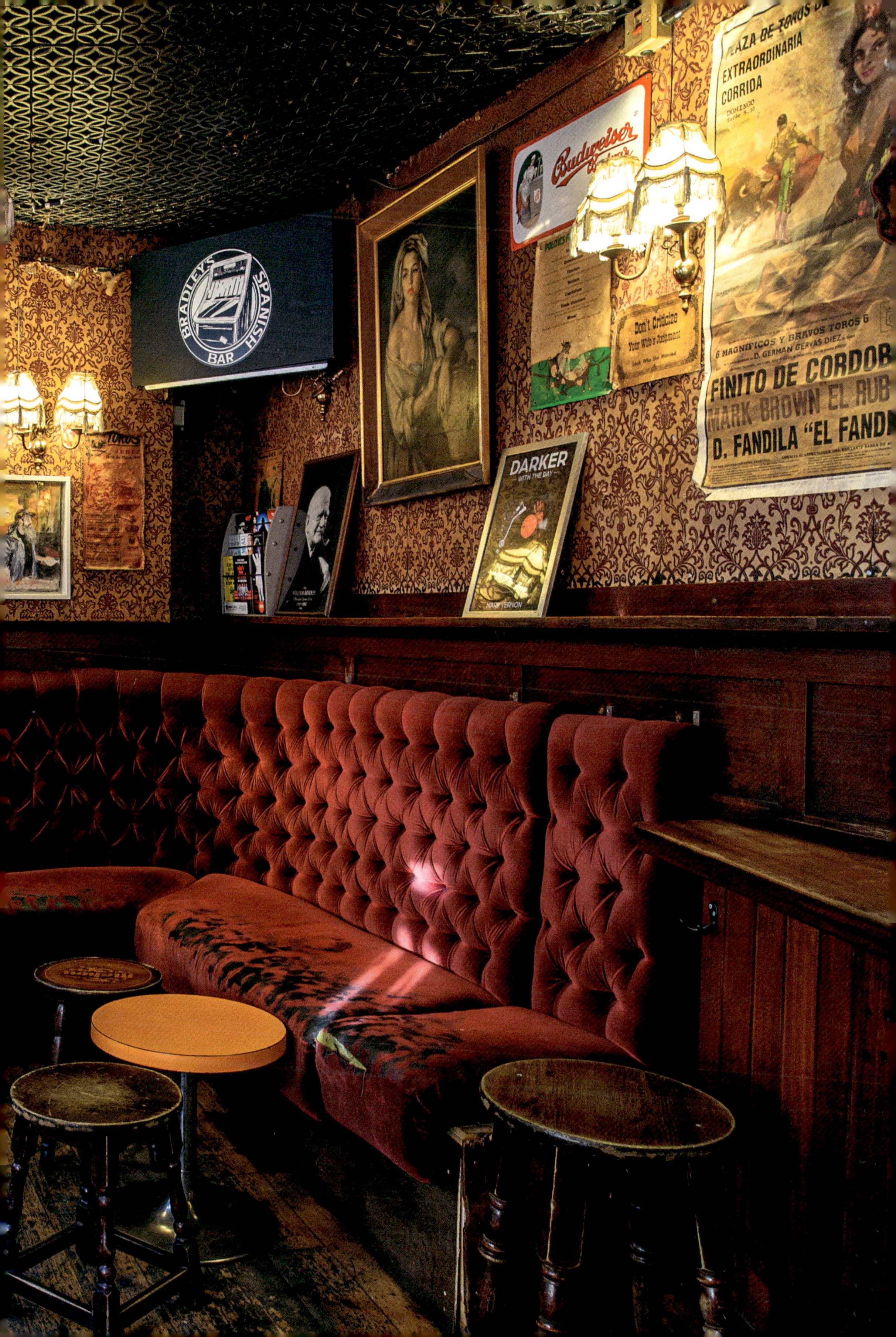
BRADLEY'S SPANISH BAR
Budweiser
DARKER
WITH THE DAY
PLAZA DE TOROS
EXTRAORDINARIA
CORRIDA
6 MAGNIFICOS Y BRAVOS TOROS 6
D. GERMAN GERVAS DIEZ
FINITO DE CORDOB
MARK BROWN EL RUB
D. FANDILA "EL FANDI
Don't Criticize
Your Wife's Judgment

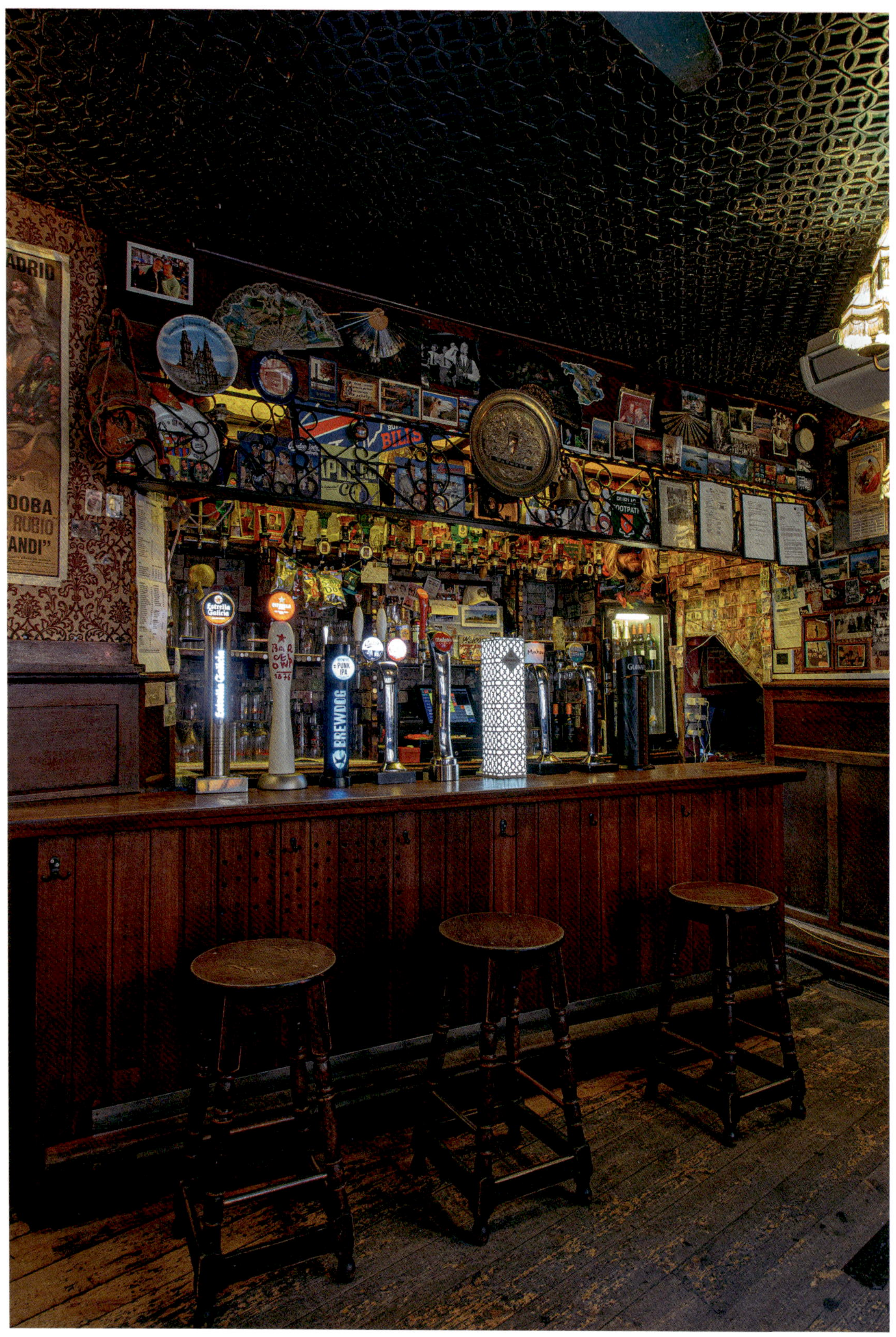

A nostalgic push-button playlist gets the party started

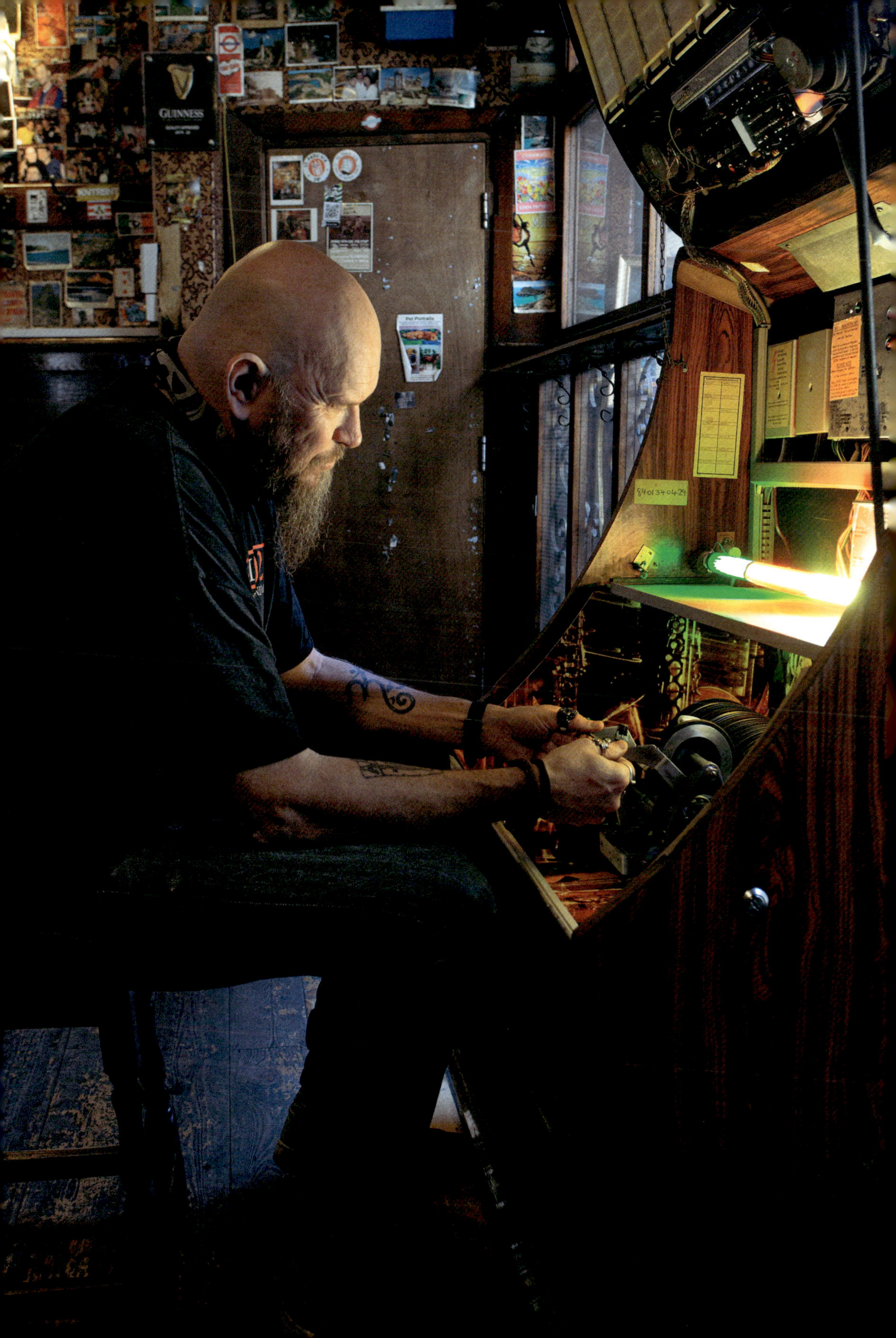

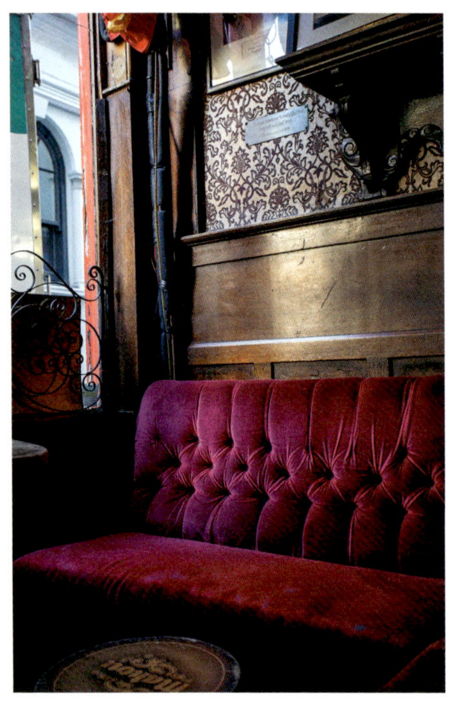

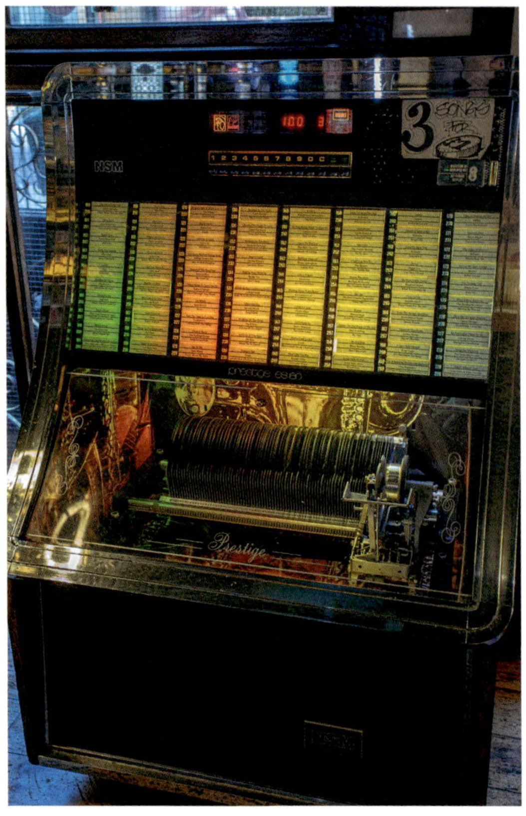

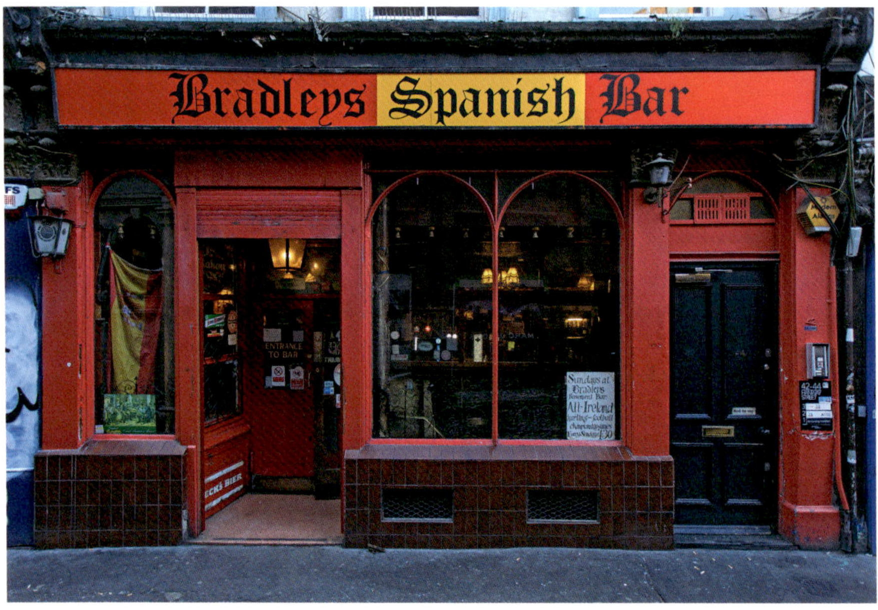

The sign says "bar" but your heart says "pub"

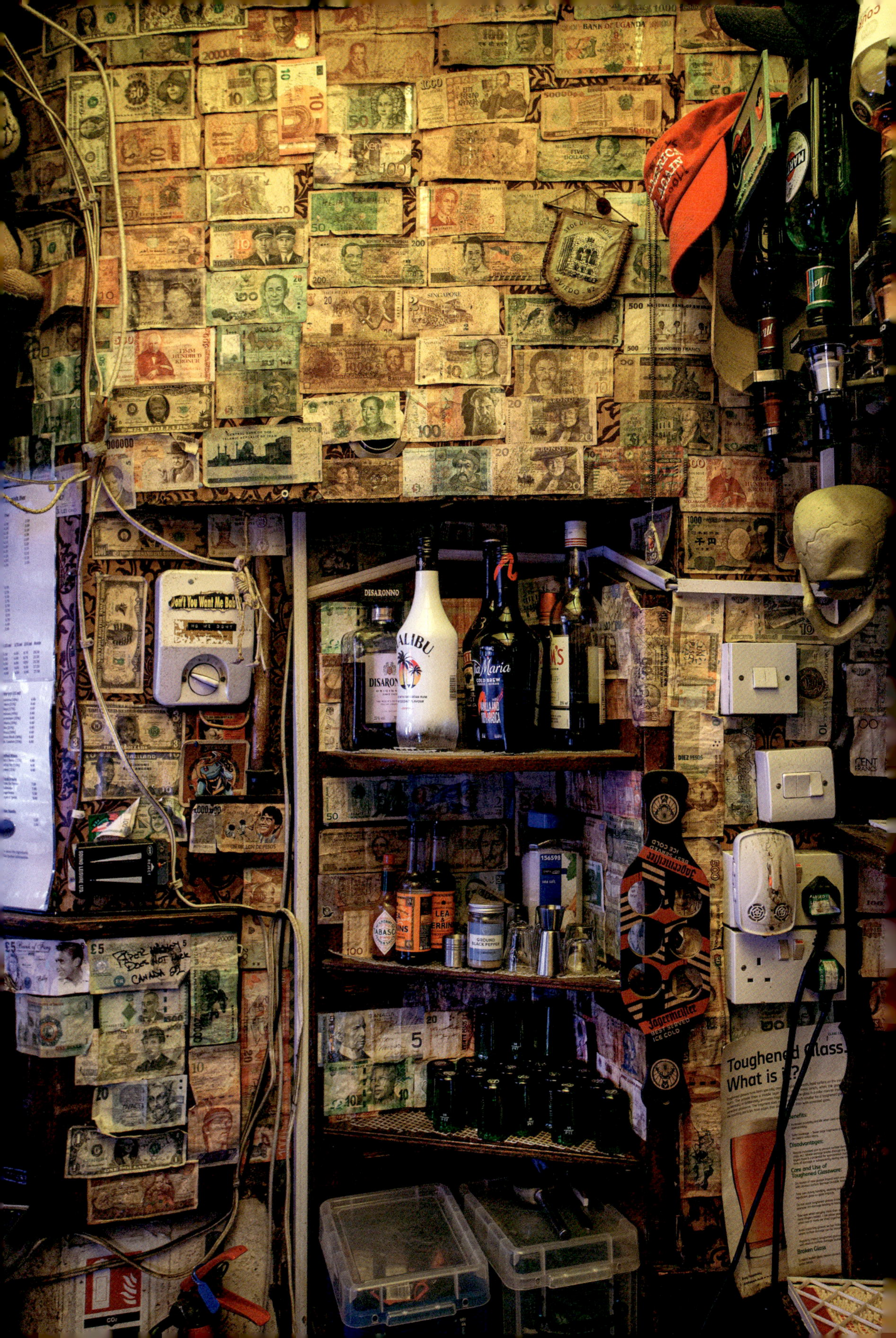

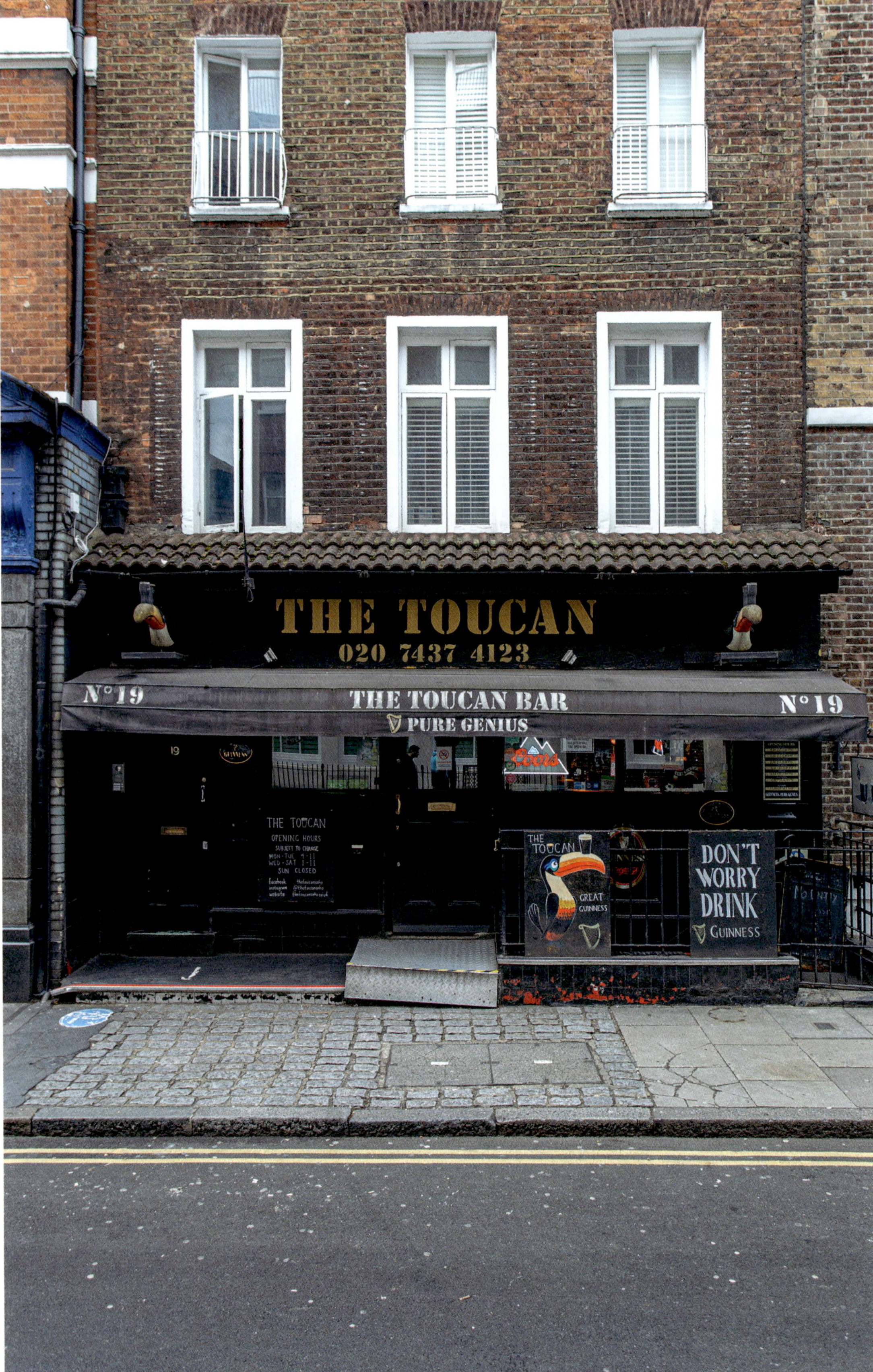
THE TOUCAN
020 7437 4123
N°19
THE TOUCAN BAR
PURE GENIUS
N°19
THE TOUCAN
OPENING HOURS
SUBJECT TO CHANGE
MON-TUE 9-11
WED-SAT 1-11
SUN CLOSED
THE TOUCAN
GREAT
GUINNESS
DON'T
WORRY
DRINK
GUINNESS

THE TOUCAN

A SHRINE TO STOUT

19 CARLISLE ST, SOHO W1D 3BY

The history of Guinness is not quite as black and white as one might assume. It's likely there would be no Guinness at all without London porter. With the brown malts blending perfectly with the chalky London water, these dark arts were first enjoyed by the several thousand London market porters glugging this poor man's pint. The London porter beer legend grew, and by the early 1700s casks of the stuff were finding their way over to, you guessed it, Dublin. It was given a stronger ABV, a shortened moniker, acquired a legendary 9,000-year brewery lease, created one hell of a global advertising campaign and boom! Three hundred years later we find ourselves in an uncompromising Soho shed paying homage to this porter-inspired pint of black magic.

Tulip pint glasses, 45-degree pours and a 18-20mm creamy dome will always make an Irishman feel at home

But there are no beating drums, white horses or men on surfboards to be seen here in Soho. Just a ramshackle shebeen in which to savour the iconic 119.5-second, two-part pour and 30 million bubbles tumbling into each glass. Tulip pint glasses, 45-degree pours and an 18–20mm creamy dome will always make an Irishman feel at home.

The Toucan is bedecked in all things Guinness, making it a micro-museum for pilgrims of this mythical pint. Like its namesake bird, The Toucan is noisy and social, with flocks congregating on Carlisle Street. Fight your way through the stout-fuelled game of sardines, slurp an oyster, line the stomach with stew and take an Irish whiskey as a digestif. The Toucan has morphed from Greek restaurant to sandwich bar and caff, but the basement has always hosted bohemian giggers, including the great Jimi Hendrix, with traditional music sessions continuing to this day. Simply slink onto a bar stool and roll into the best Guinness dive bar this side of the Irish Sea.

Does The Toucan pour the best pint of Guinness in London? Far from it: it's simply too busy. But it's a fine place to take down 568ml of Liffey water on a sunny Soho evening, enjoying the hustle, bustle and banter. It's rammed. It's rough. But it sure is fun. Down at heel, rough around the edges: much-missed Soho, we raise our pint of Guinness and salute you. Sláinte!

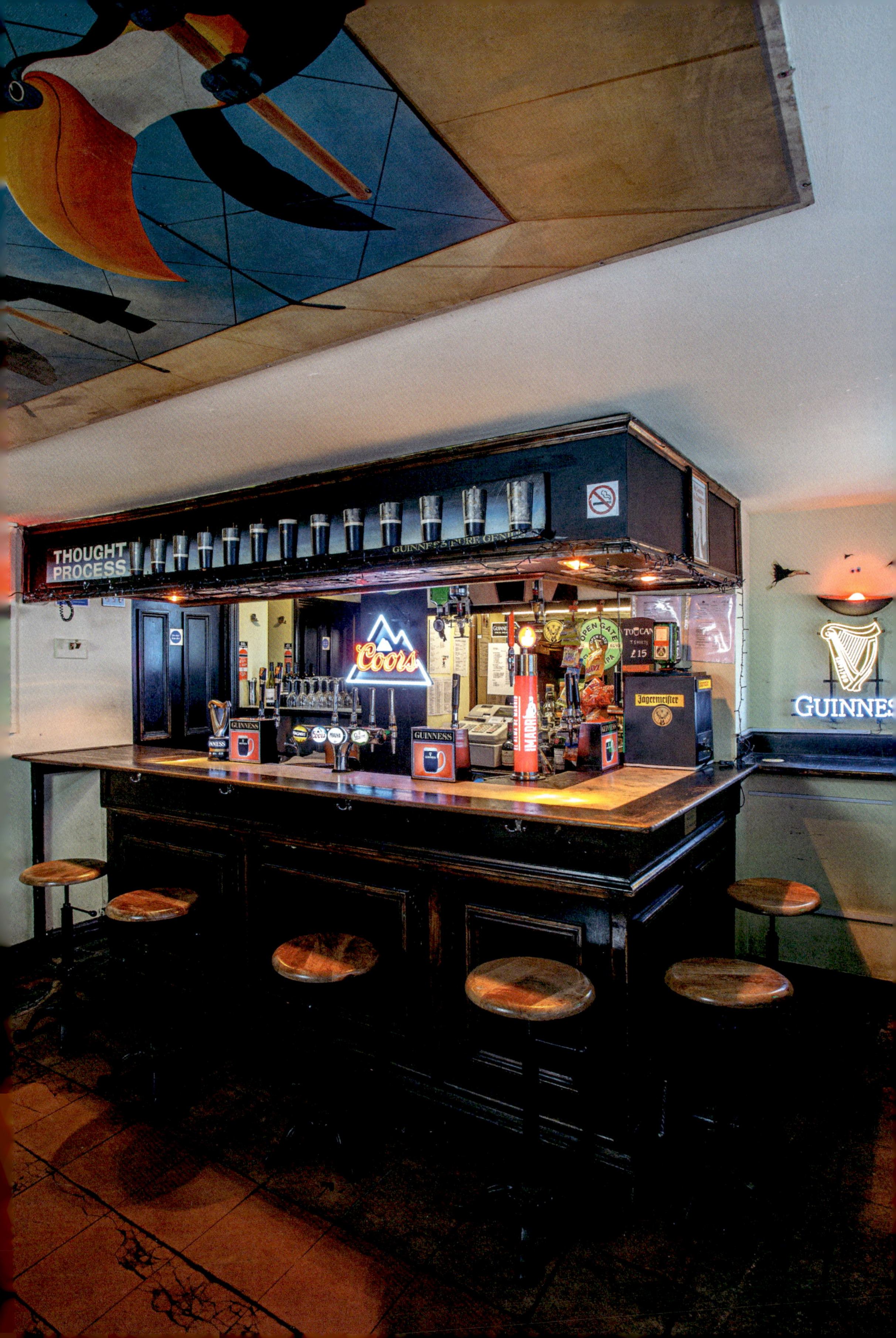

THOUGHT
PROCESS
Coors
GUINNESS
Jägermeister
OPEN GATE
TOUCAN
T SHIRTS
£15

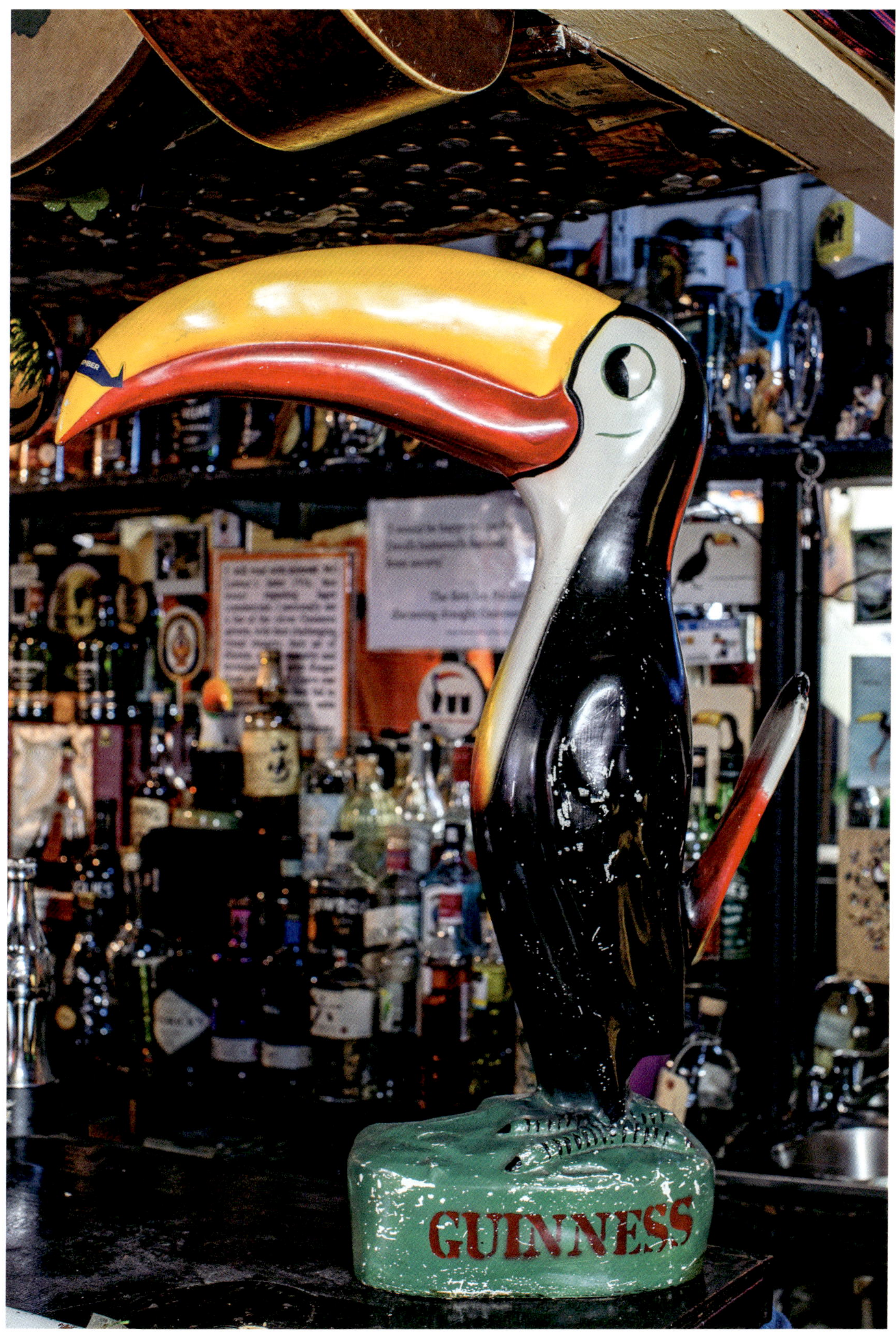

The finest Guinness-themed dive bar this side of the Irish Sea

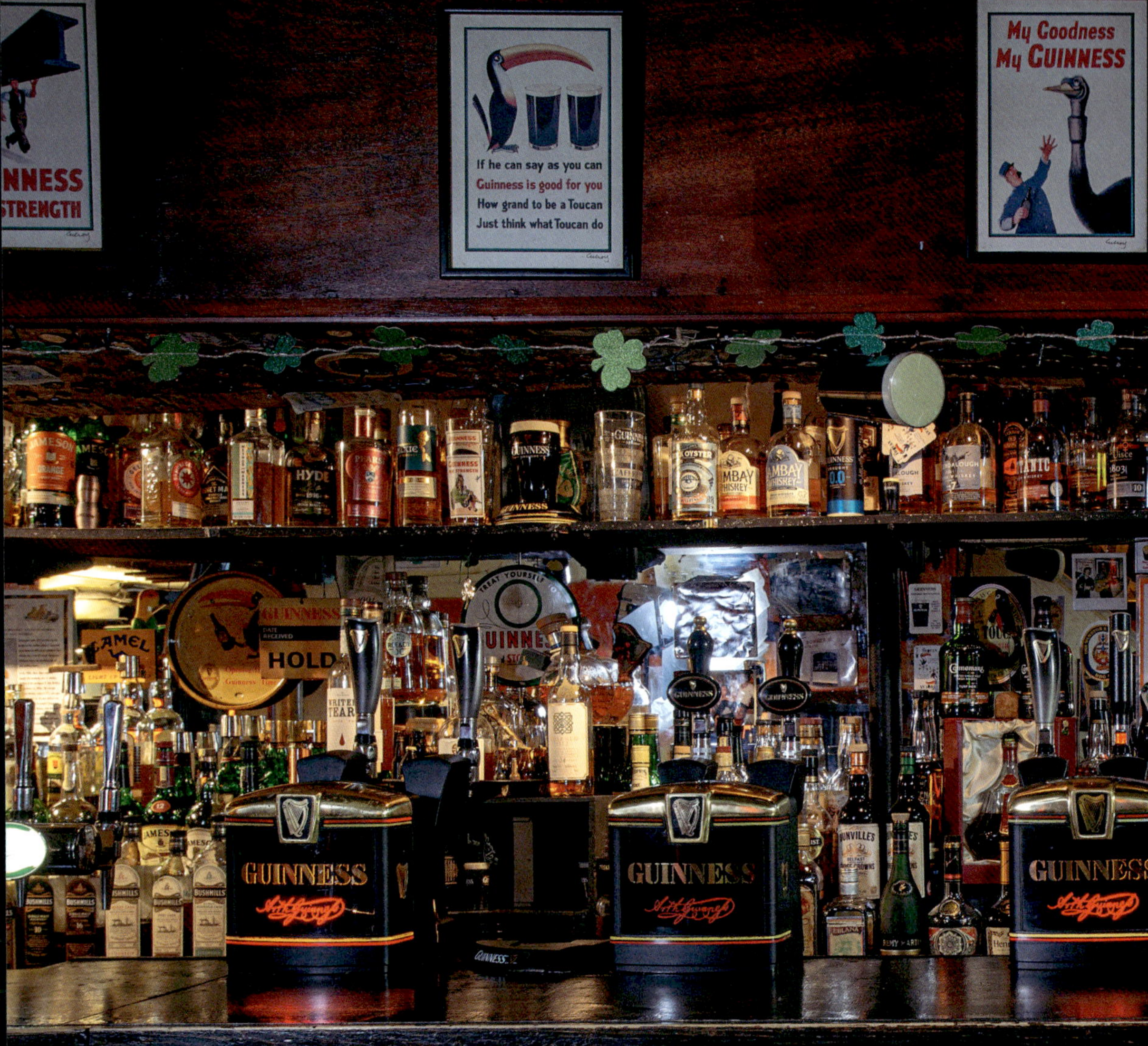
GUINNESS
STRENGTH
If he can say as you can
Guinness is good for you
How grand to be a Toucan
Just think what Toucan do
My Goodness
My GUINNESS
GUINNESS
HOLD
GUINNESS
GUINNESS
GUINNESS

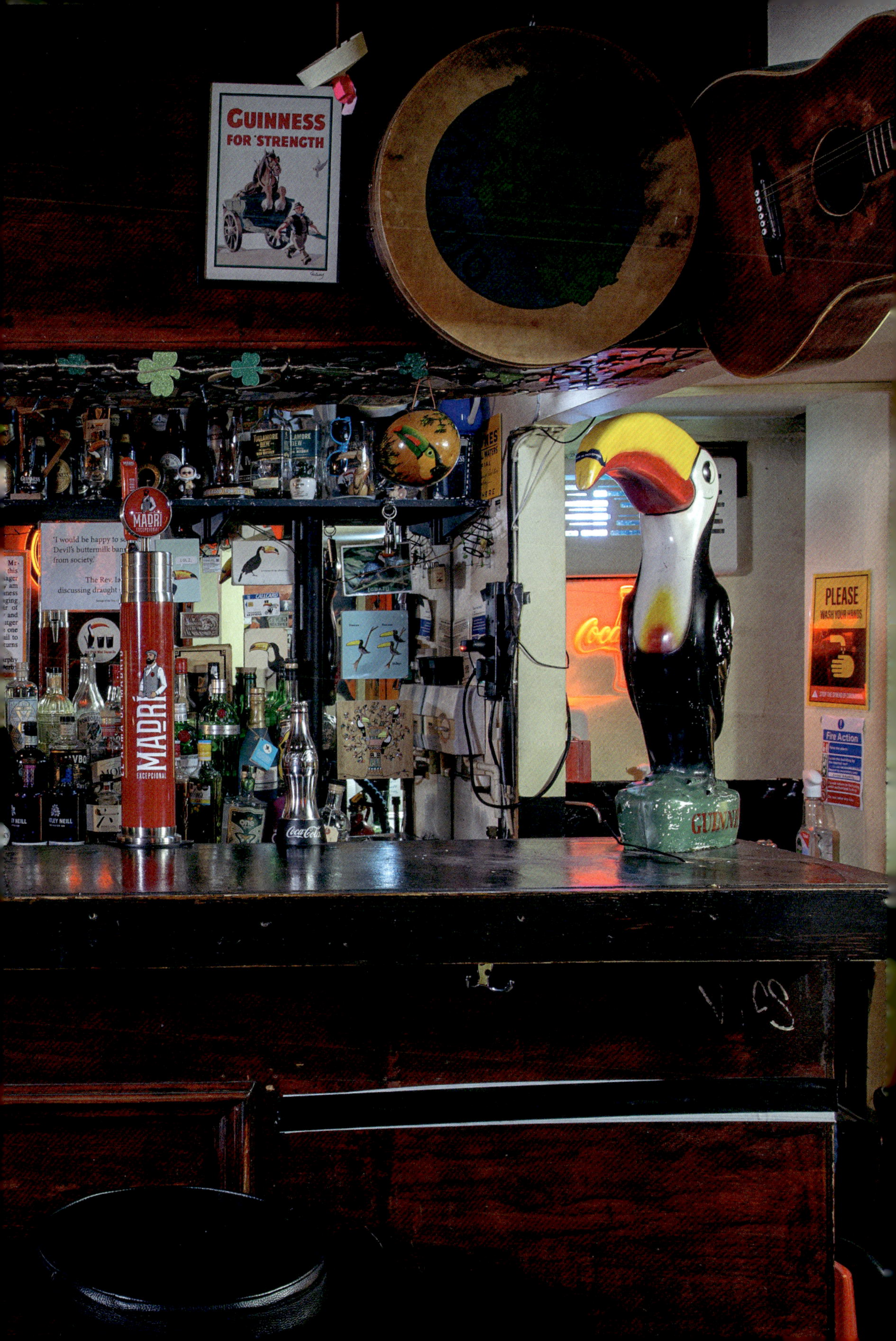

GUINNESS
FOR STRENGTH
MADRÍ
EXCEPCIONAL
Coca-Cola
PLEASE
WASH YOUR HANDS
Fire Action
GUINNA

THE GOLDEN EAGLE

MARYLEBONE'S VILLAGE PUB

59 MARYLEBONE LANE, MARYLEBONE W1U 2NY

People always bang on about London being a collection of interjoined villages. And they're right. Pop up in Blackheath, Dulwich or Hampstead and it really can feel like a green idyll full of church spires and pretty people whizzing around like Mary Poppins. At the heart of every self-respecting village is of course the pub (sorry, vicar!).

The Golden Eagle pub is well-known as "the heart of Marylebone Village". You'd have to go back to the early eighteenth century to find fields and a sprinkling of agricultural buildings in these parts, with the River Tyburn trickling downhill to the Thames. But then you'd have to wait until 1842 for this village pub to be built and the bucolic country scenes supplanted by fine Georgian houses and fancy physicians over in Harley Street. The River Tyburn has long been tunnelled over but it continues to flow quietly beneath these streets, whilst Marylebone has transformed into a boutique-shopping mecca, awash with design hotels and Michelin-starred munch-houses.

A straight-up interior and no fancy nonsense need apply. Please just leave your ego at the door and indulge.

The more the world spirals around it, the more people yearn for the fail-safe comfort of falling through The Eagle's opaque doors. The silliness of the Insta-Tok snapperati can be left at the door and good village folk can escape for a damn good pint. Gina Vernon and her family have been nesting here for over thirty-two years, with at least one of the offspring born in the room upstairs. Golden eagles enjoy the quiet life, stay loyal to their patch and improve their eyrie year on year.

You couldn't wish for a more handsome pub. It spreads its wings across the street corner, all perfectly painted exterior and traditional leaded windows. A straight-up interior and no fancy nonsense need apply. Please just leave your ego at the door and indulge.

The stalwart piano offers regular singalong sessions, and the pub comes alive when Tony "Fingers" Vernon taps away at the ivories like there's no tomorrow. And there will be a tomorrow. And it will be bountiful. For the secret of a village's survival lies not in the buildings but the beauty of the souls it holds: a close-knit community sewn together by tradition, customs and a simpler way of life. This eagle shall be soaring for some time to come.

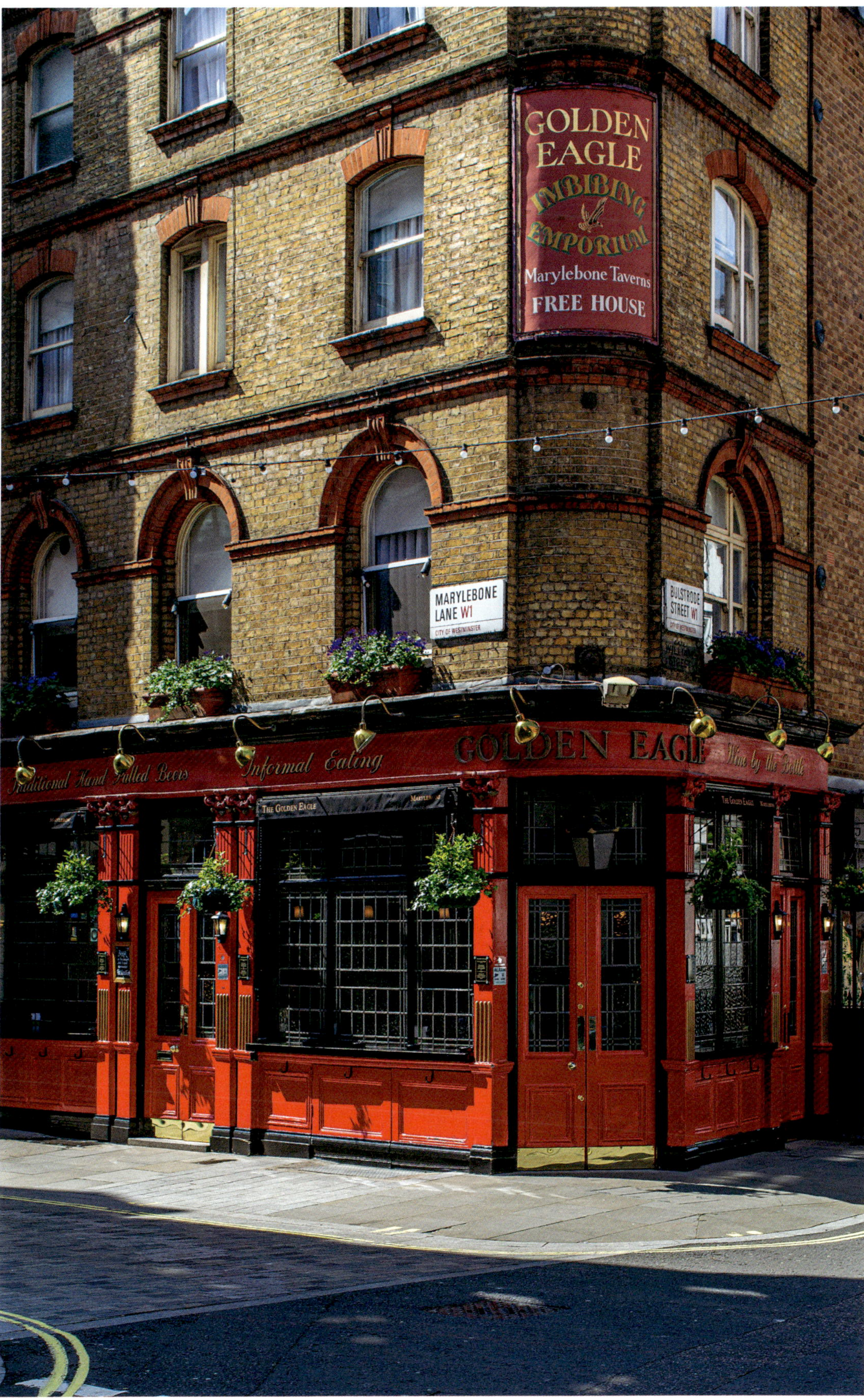

GOLDEN EAGLE
IMBIBING EMPORIUM
Marylebone Taverns
FREE HOUSE
MARYLEBONE LANE W1
CITY OF WESTMINSTER
BULSTRODE STREET W1
CITY OF WESTMINSTER
Traditional Hand Pulled Beers
Informal Eating
GOLDEN EAGLE
Wine by the Bottle
THE GOLDEN EAGLE

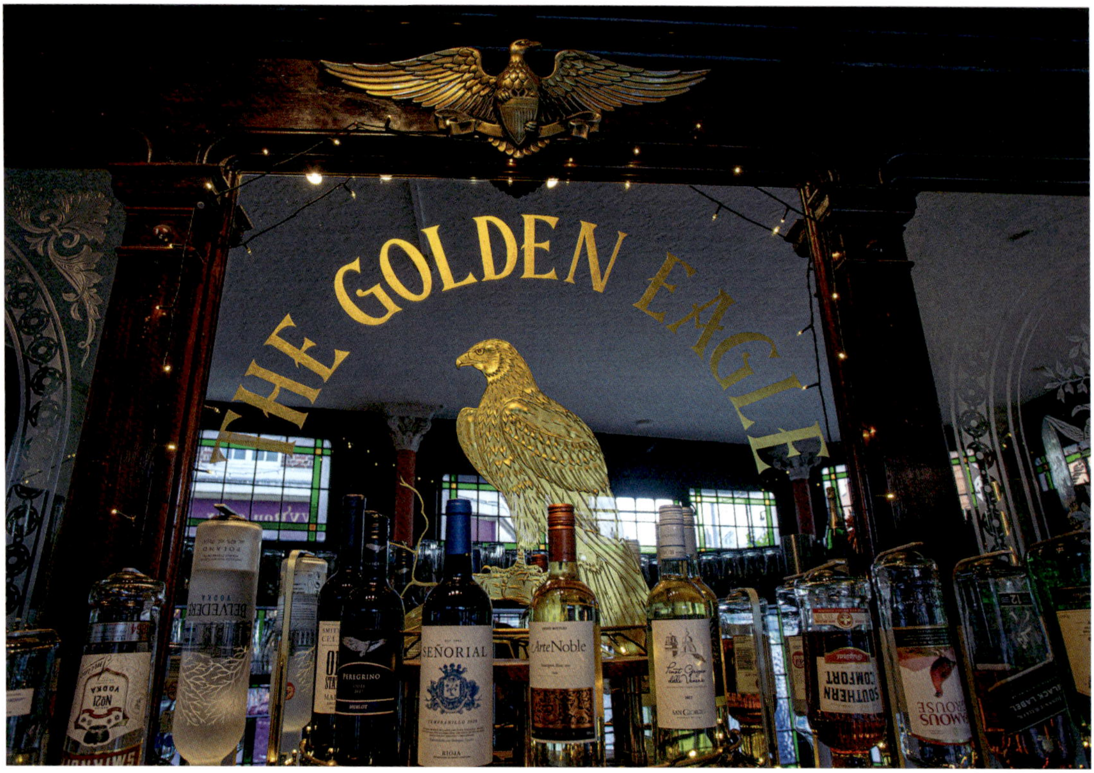

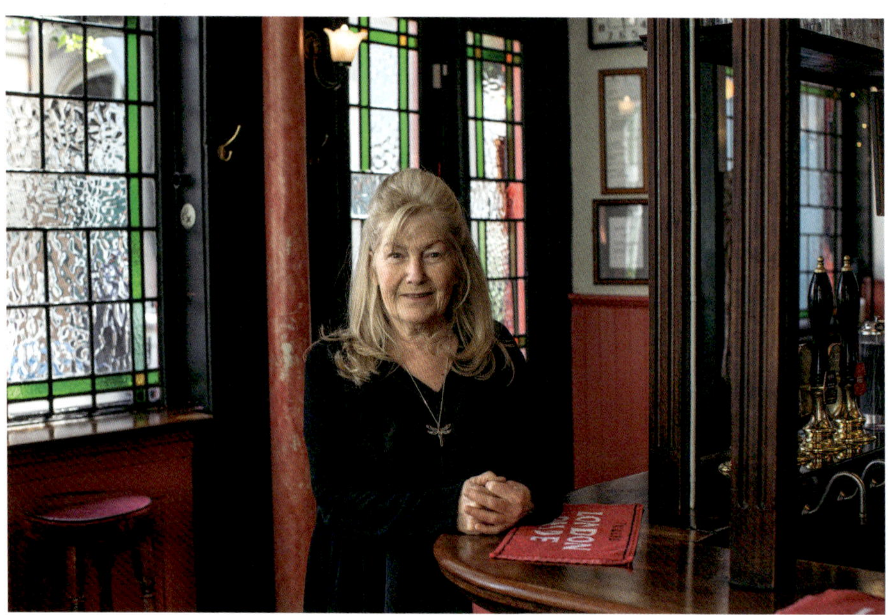

Enter to enjoy over thirty years of traditional innkeeping experience

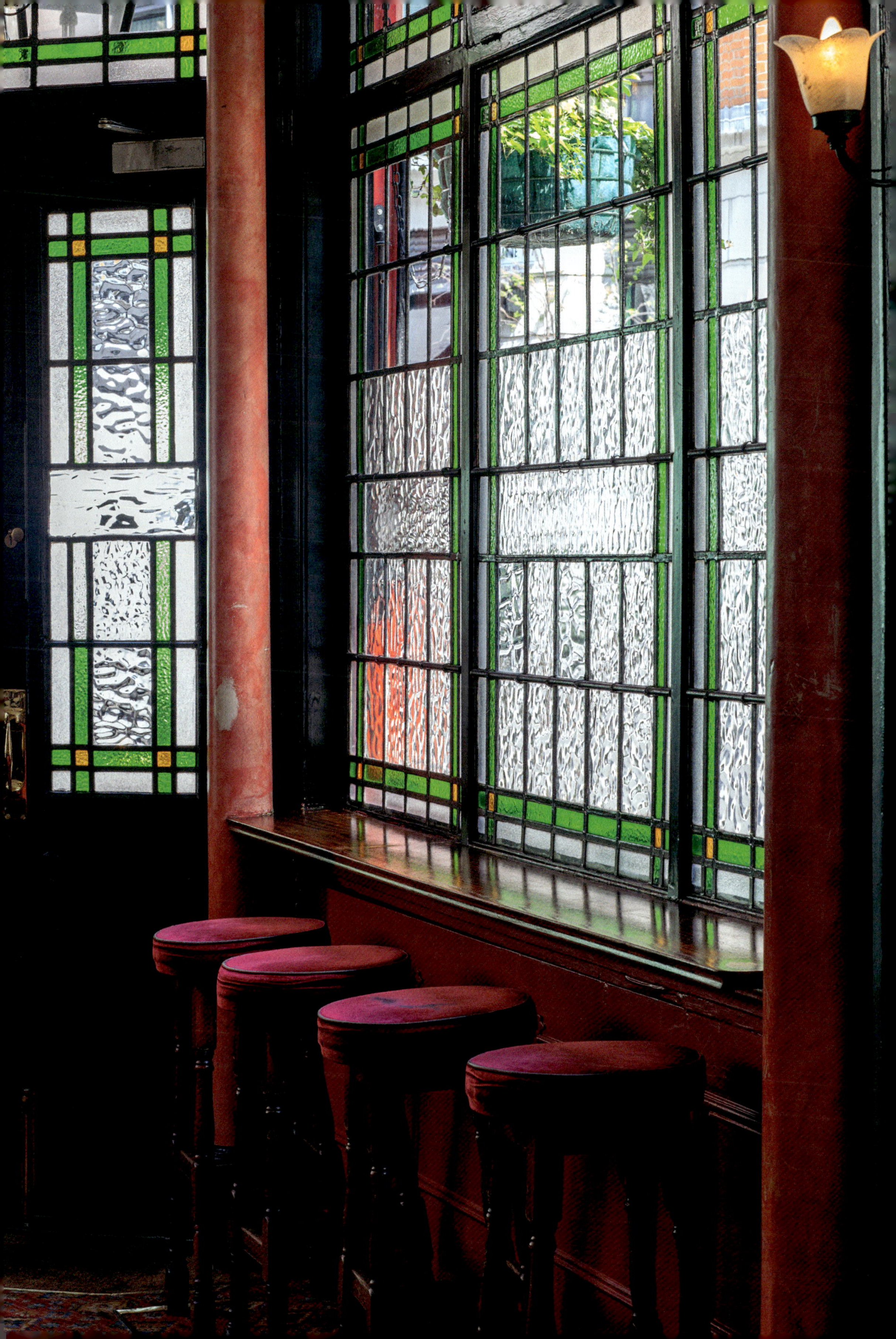

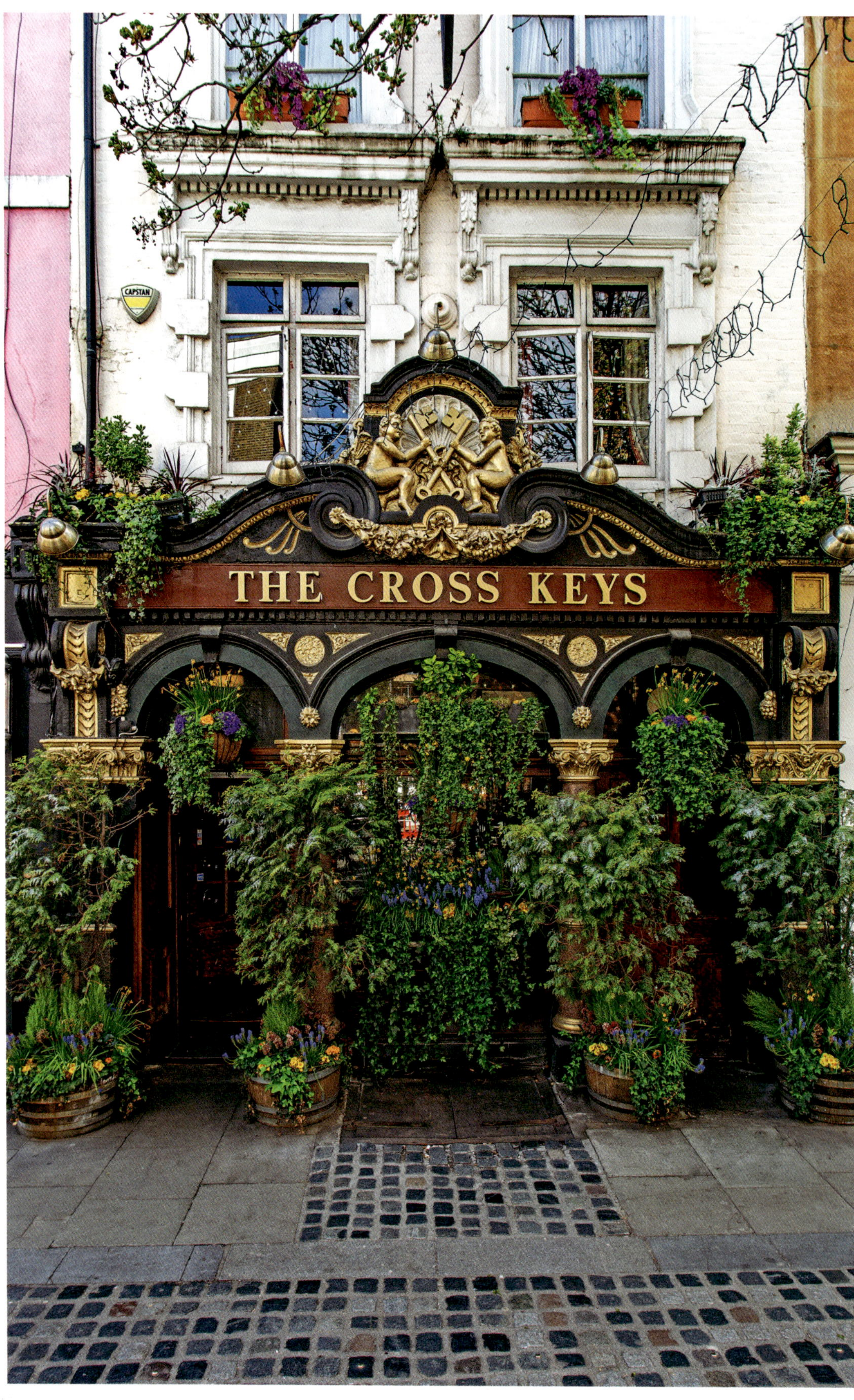

CAPSTAN
THE CROSS KEYS

THE CROSS KEYS

The Cross Keys has politely turned its back on Covent Garden. Whilst shoppers and snappers plough the Piazza, this pub ticks to its own time. It's a locals' pub in a locale few call home; so close to the centre of terminal tourism yet feeling so far away. It's an amazing trick, and a lovely Aladdin's cave in which to retreat. Squeeze through the hanging gardens of Babylon and emerge into a dark yet cacophonic collection of the weird and the truly wonderful. Pub landlords seem to inherit a particular strain of OCD that compels them to collect the curious, filling every available space with what the casual observer might call tat, bric-a-brac or simply "stuff". But to the owner, this is their magnum opus. A life's work. Carefully curated, shelved and even occasionally dusted on special occasions.

Pub landlords seem to inherit a particular strain of OCD that compels them to collect the curious, filling every available space with what the casual observer might call tat, bric-a-brac or simply "stuff".

Legend suggests that when the landlord of The Keys made a few bob, instead of putting it into the hands of the taxman or local bank manager, he would pop round to the local auction house. John Lennon's glasses? Just imagine! A signed napkin by Elvis? Uh-huh. One of legendary willow-wafter Donald Bradman's bats? Howzat! A few Beatles bits and bobs. Well, you can't buy me love, so I'll take it. Deep-sea diver's helmet, copper kettles, brass band instruments: no doubt it all seemed like a good idea at the time. It makes for a unique rhapsody of quirkiness and gives you a few things to squint at and wonder "What on earth were they drinking?" whilst you muse your next drink selection.

This pub wears its wealth well, as a rare and dimly lit oasis of authenticity patronised by all and sundry. Thick carpets and brass rails everywhere. Lovely. Perfect for a snifter before watching Papageno over at the Royal Opera House or holding fort outside enjoying a pavement pint in the most wonderful city on earth.

Look up and you'll see a set of keys the klepto-landlord didn't acquire at auction, held aloft by a couple of cheeky cherubs and belonging to the mighty St Peter. Luckily for us, he left us the keys to the promised land, and if you end up pausing for a pint here you would be entitled to think that you've found your own little slice of heaven on earth. Blessed indeed!

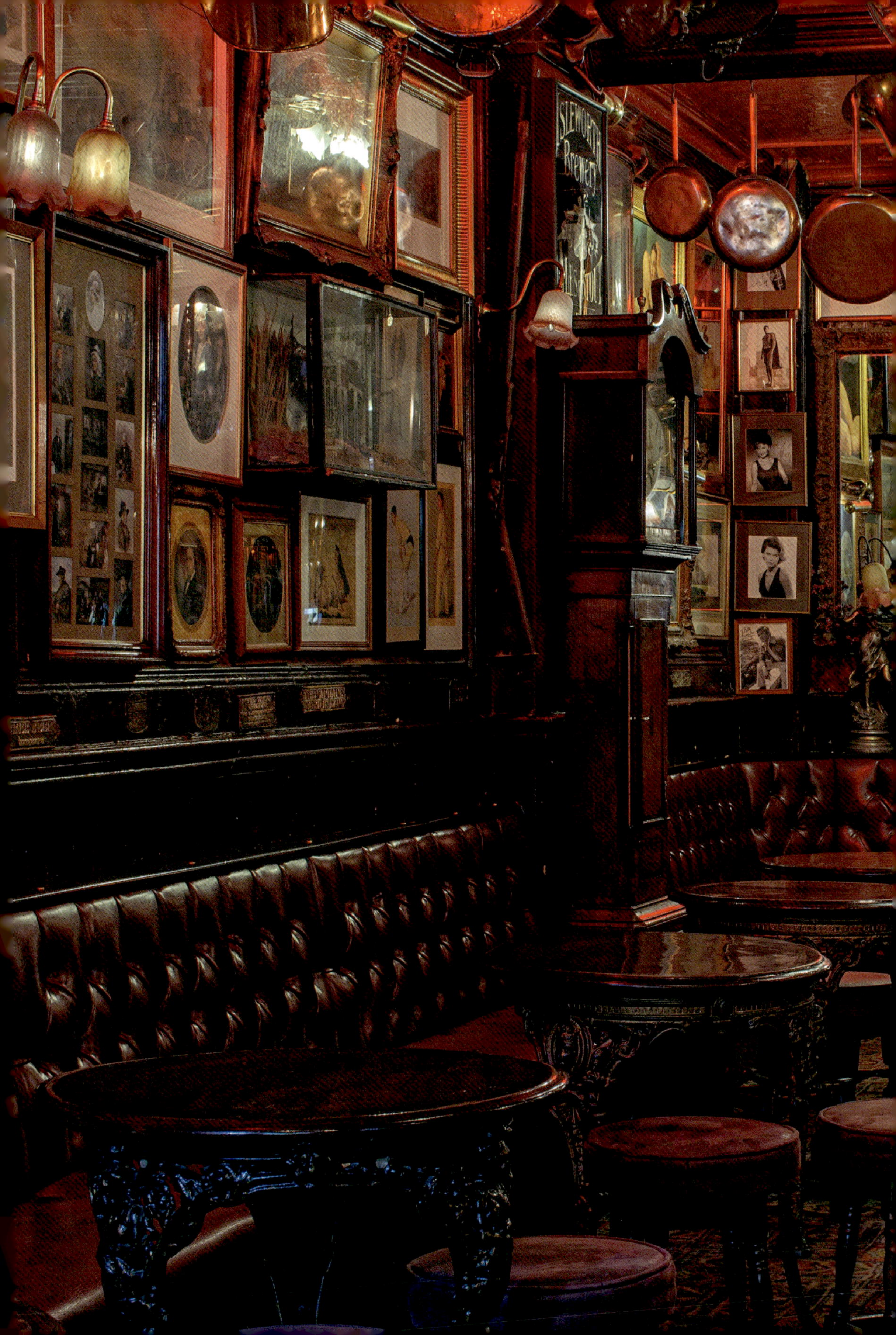

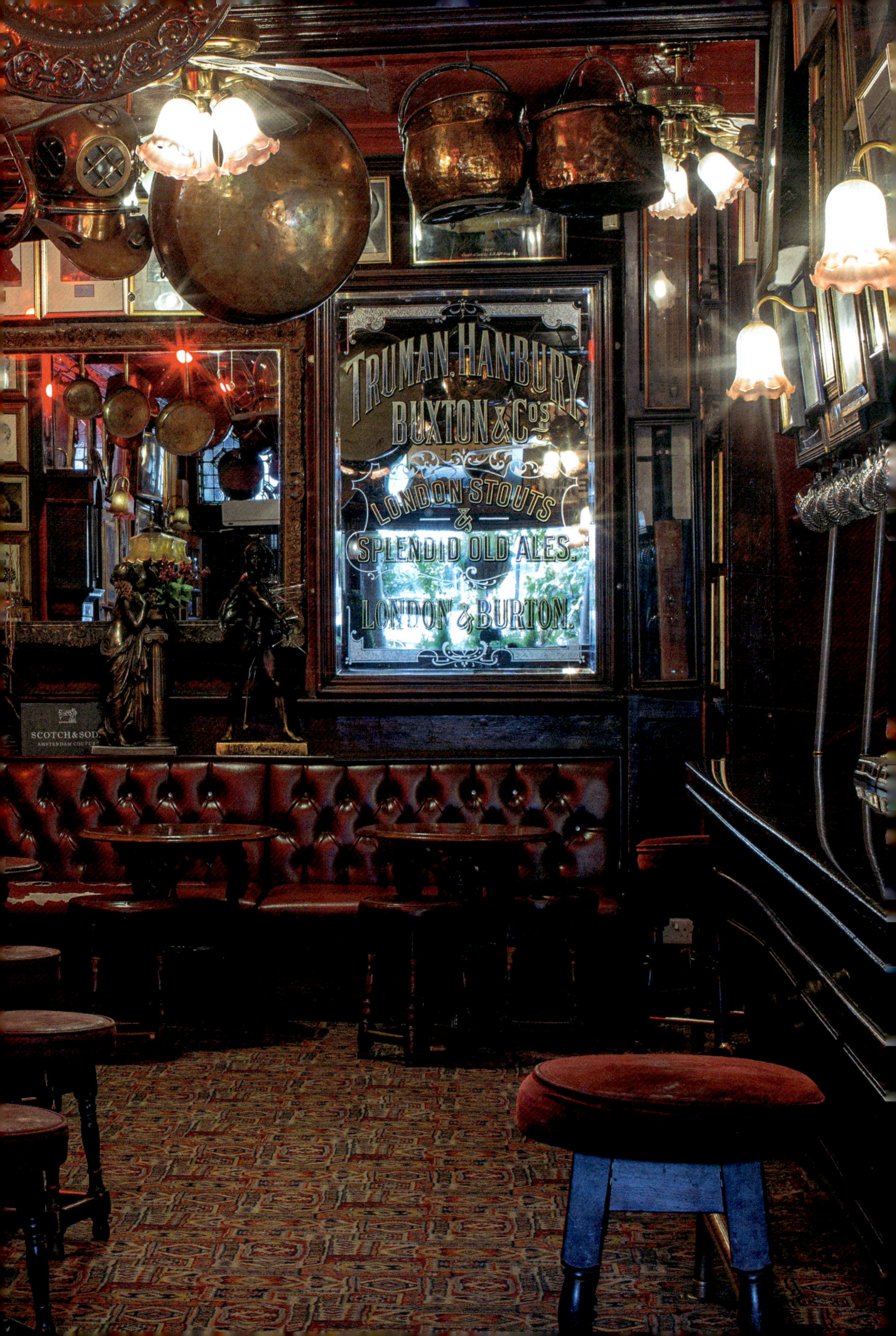
TRUMAN, HANBURY,
BUXTON & Cos.
LONDON STOUTS
&
SPLENDID OLD ALES.
LONDON & BURTON.
SCOTCH & SODA
AMSTERDAM COUTURE

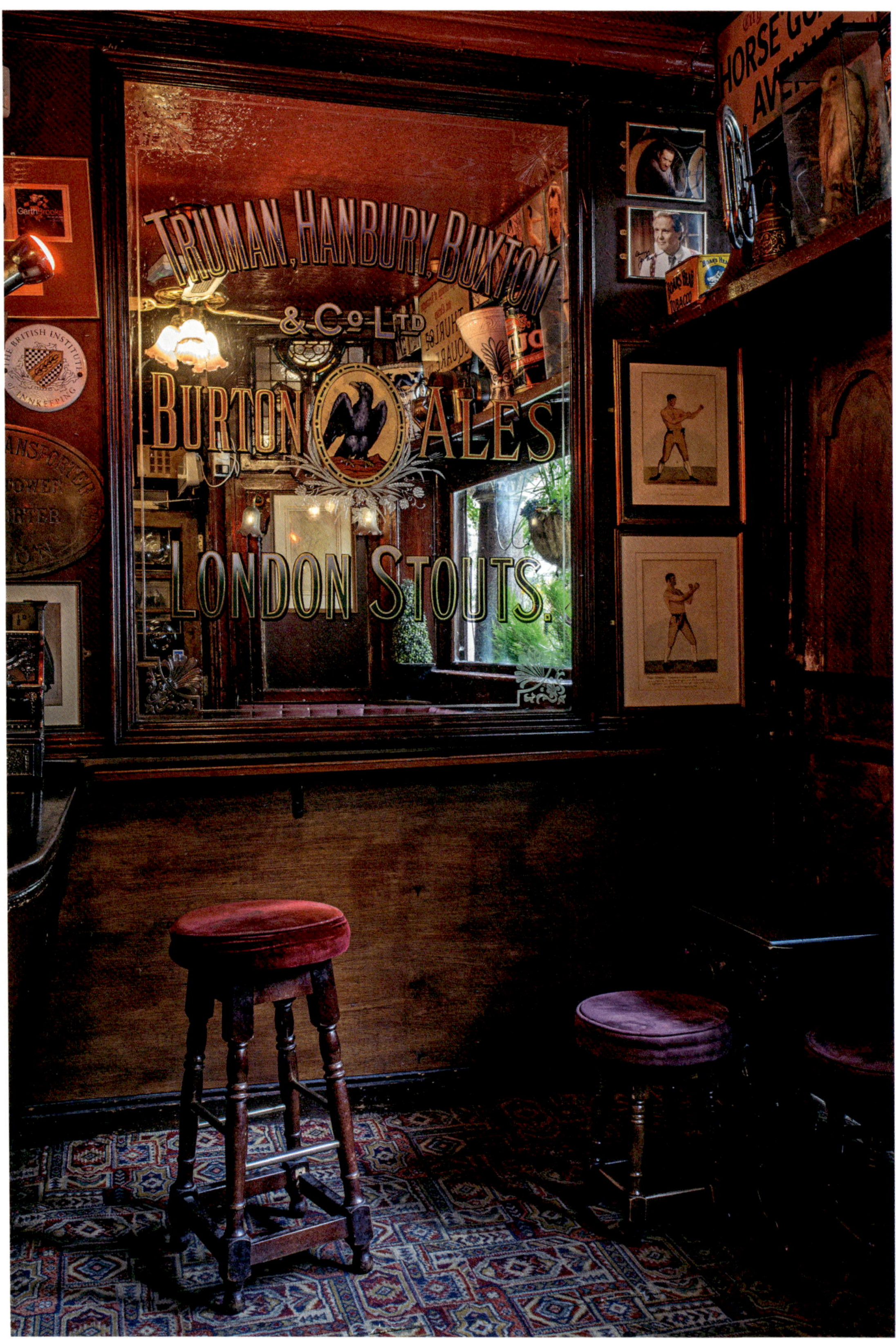

An Aladdin's cave of ephemera

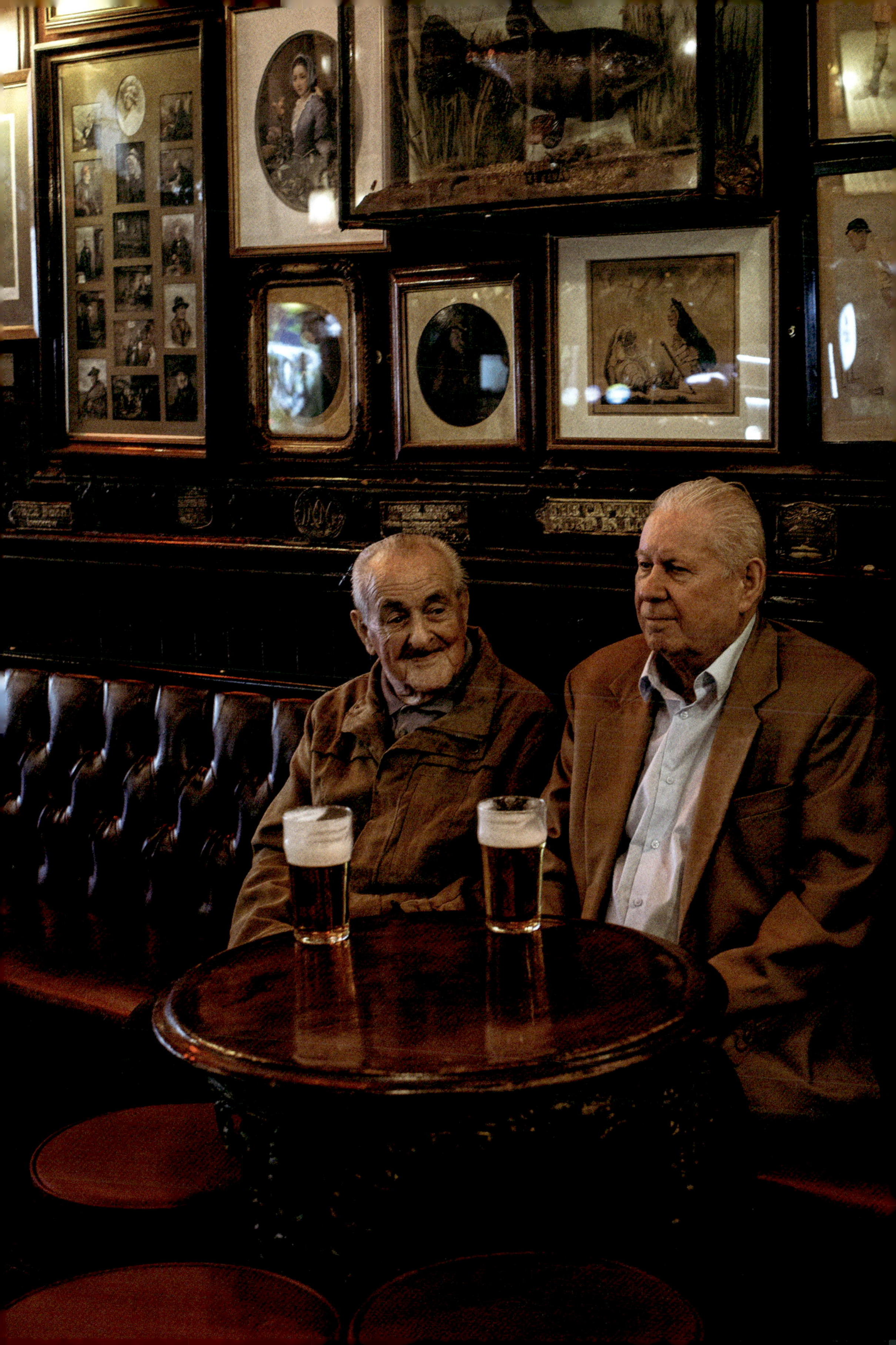

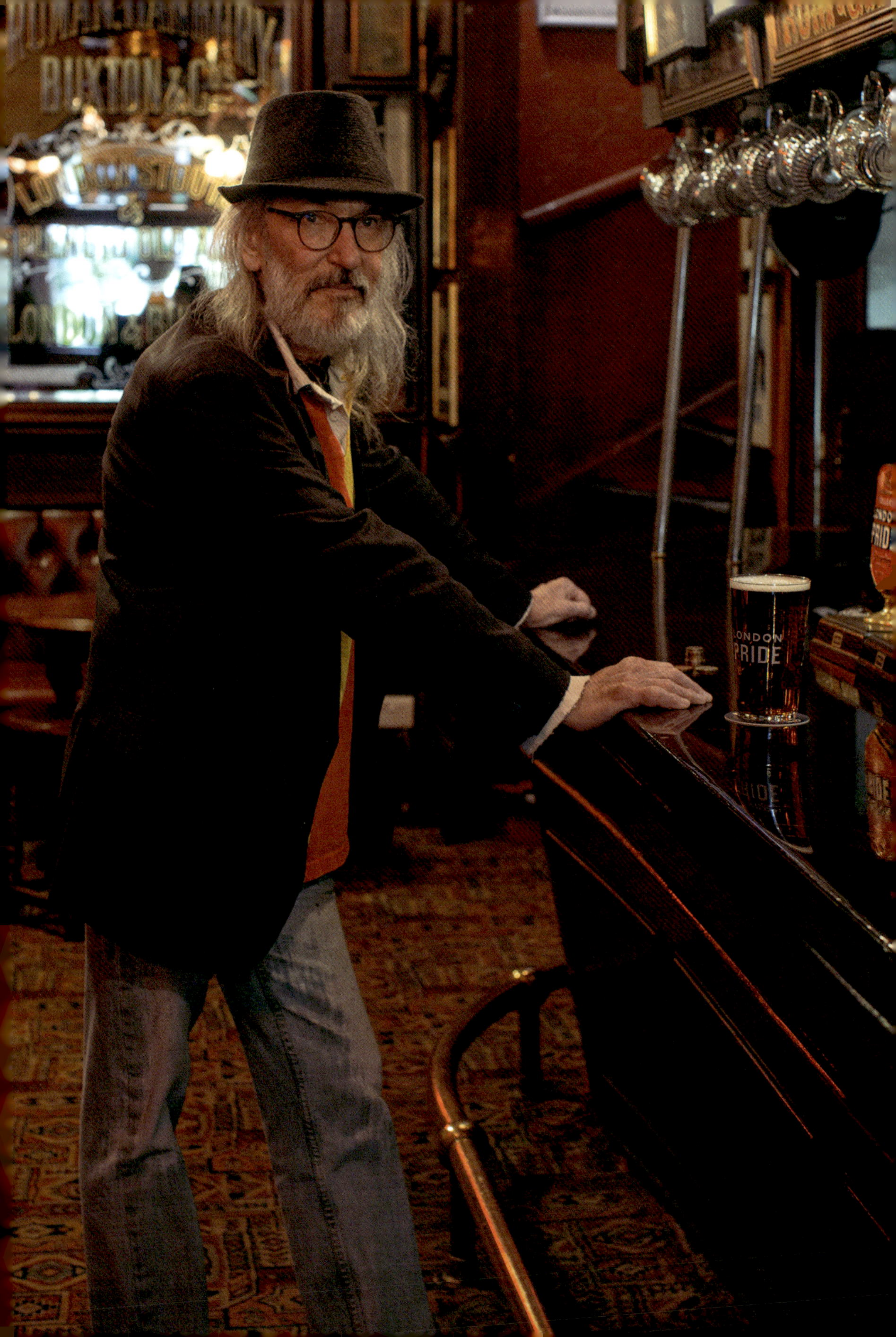

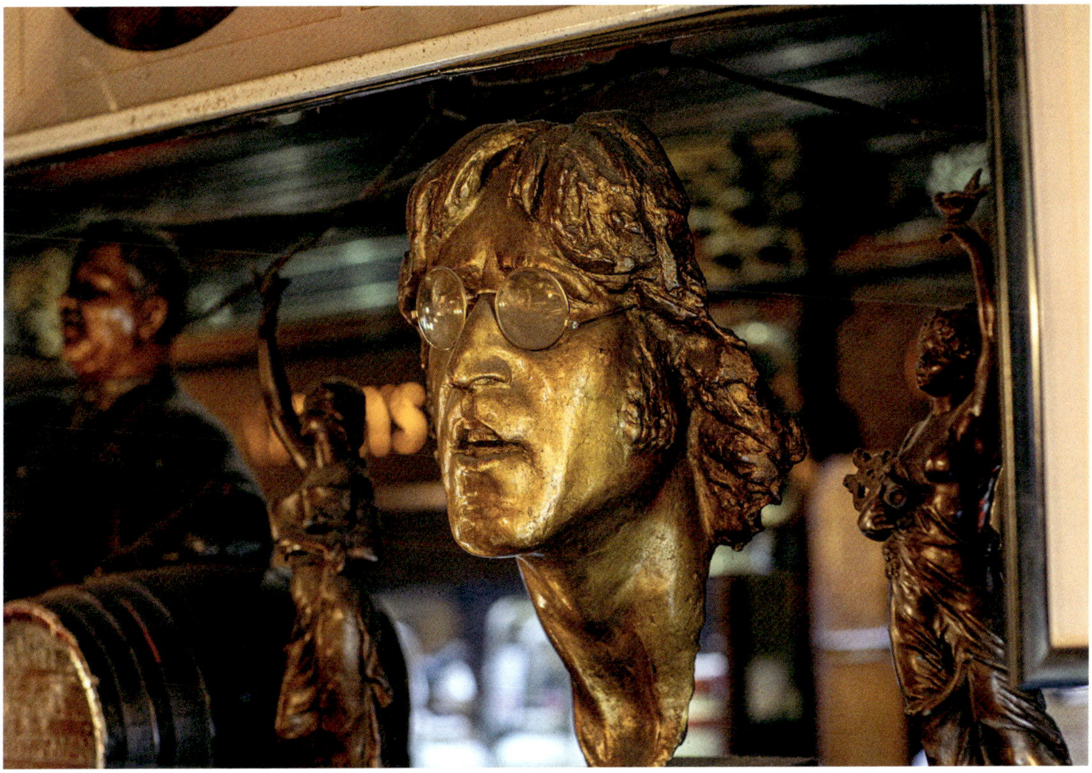

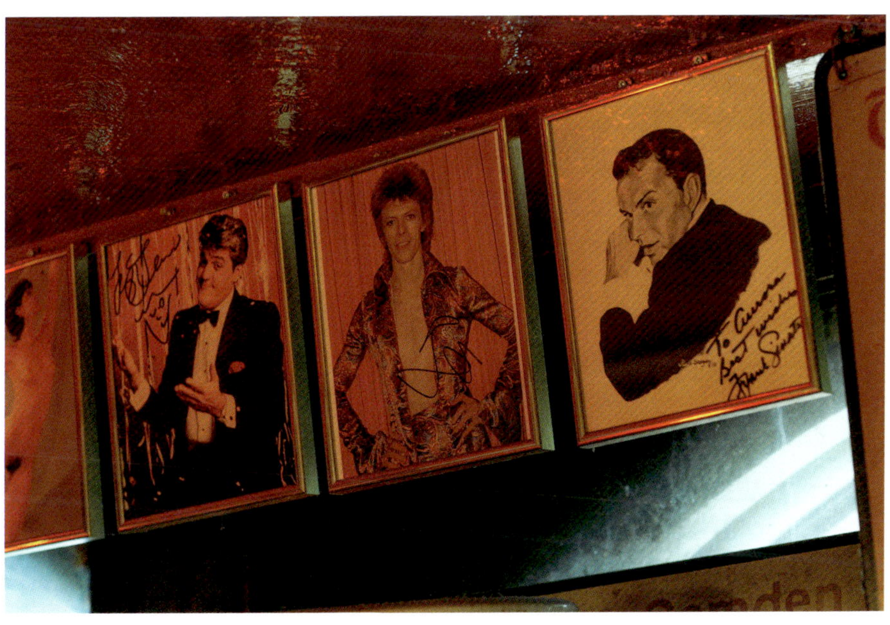

Elvis, Lennon, Sinatra... you shall find them here

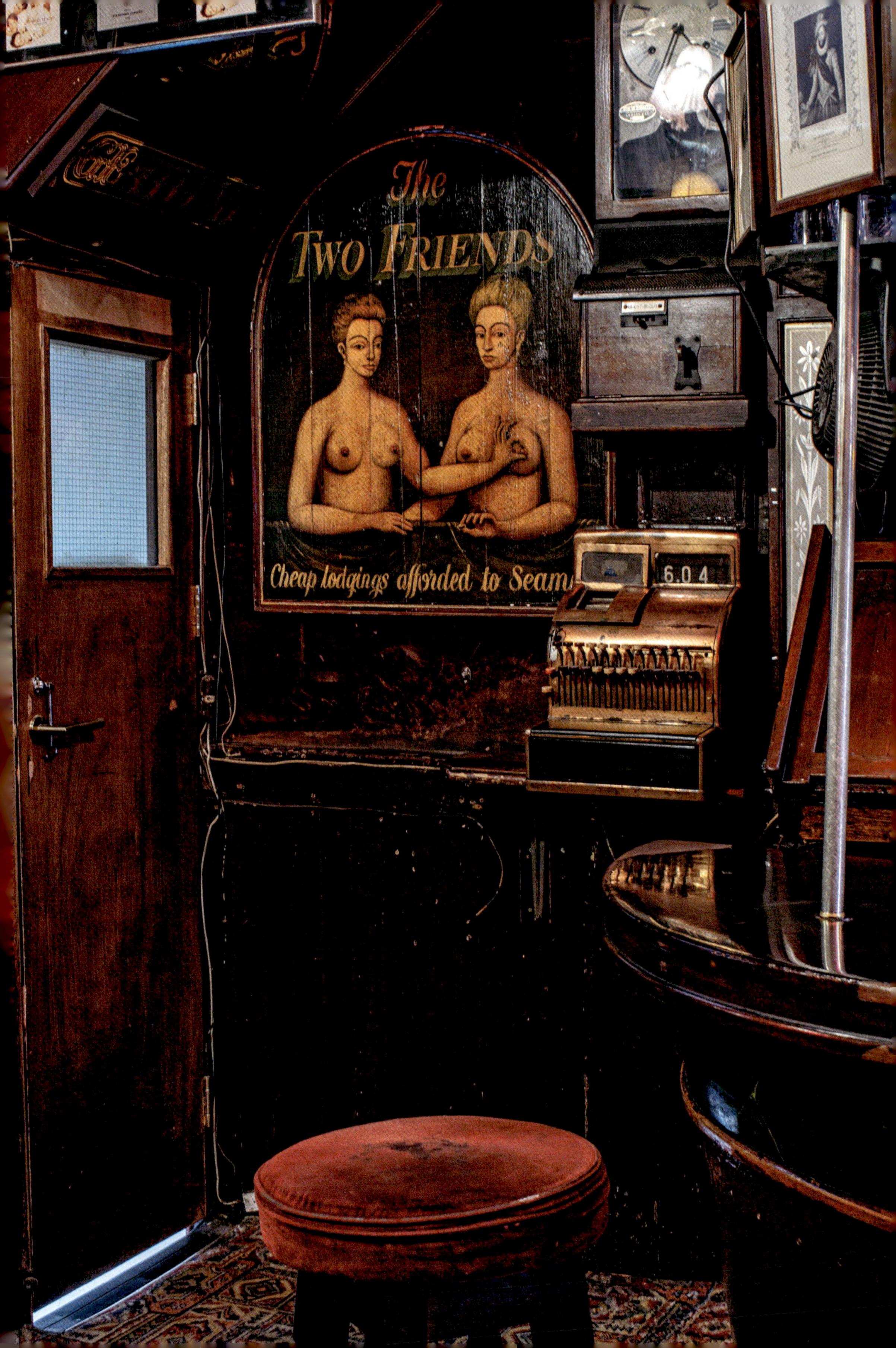
The
TWO FRIENDS
Cheap lodgings afforded to Seam

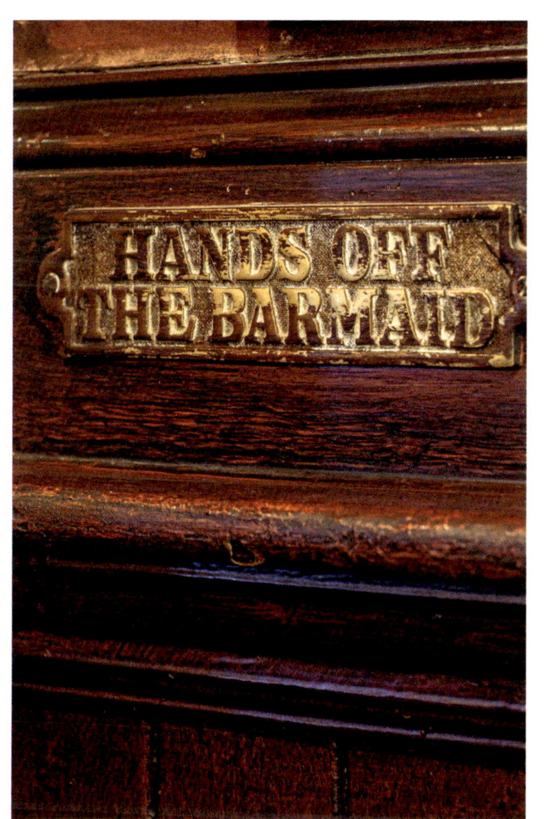

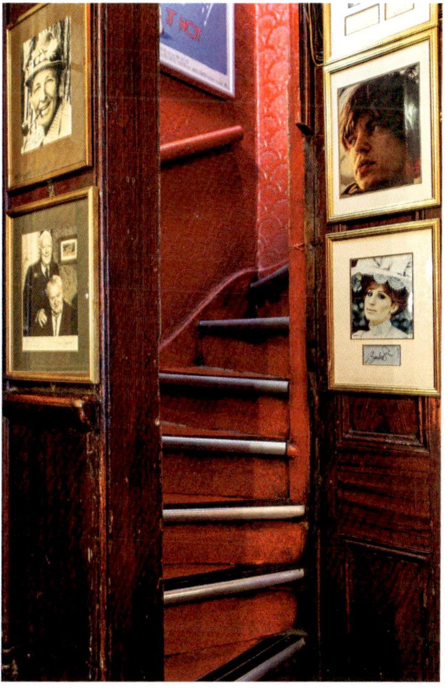

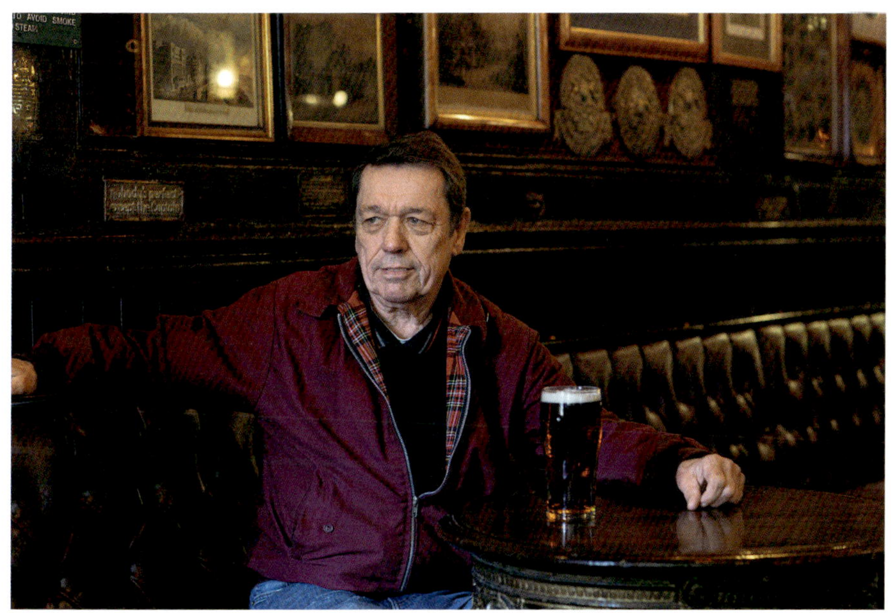

One of Covent Garden's last great boozers

THE NELL GWYNNE TAVERN

THEATRELAND'S ENGINE ROOM

2 BULL INN CT, THE STRAND WC2R 0NP

The bright lights of London's West End theatreland don't call for a high head count of cracking pubs. The glut of tourists and the weekend "bridge and tunnel" crowd zig-zag from one mediocre pleasure palace to another, soaking up the homogenised opiate for the masses.

But there are a select few authentic boltholes in which to escape the undiscerning throngs. The Nell is secreted between the Adelphi and Vaudeville theatres. A place where stage-hands can convene just before curtain up, sous chefs sup once they've cooked their last order or star-crossed celebrity lovers can conduct their extra-marital infidelities. A portrait of Edward VII's mistress Lillie Langtry can be found on the walls, acting as a reminder of the dangerous liaisons possibly taken here.

The pub's snickleway location means the rowdies rarely stumble across it, and once you've found the pub it does seem to have more than a whiff of a whore's boudoir about it all. It's of course entirely befitting for a pub named after the infamous Protestant mistress of Charles II. Nell Gwynne was indeed one of the era's most upwardly mobile ladies in between earning her keep in the horizontal position.

Almost everything at The Nell is painted red, giving it a vague cabaret-cum-house-of-ill-repute vibe. You can plonk a few well-curated vinyls on the free jukebox. People head here to spin their favourite record, and don't forget to grab a pickled egg (eat three in a row and a free pint is on the house!). It's no wonder that legendary rabble-rouser Richard Harris nursed some of his final pints of Guinness here. It was the perfect antidote to the excess of his residential trappings at the Savoy Hotel just across the road.

The pint-in-hand human spillage across the outside snook and along Bull Inn Court is frequent and extensive. Drinking *en plein air* is certainly a safer bet than attempting a run at the basement bogs. As they are seemingly conjured by M. C. Escher into a vertiginous vortex of architectural twists and pump clip wallpaper, just allow mild inebriation and gravity to spiral you into the ablutionary black hole at the bottom of the stairs.

So, whether you're an illiterate purveyor of oranges to the King, or just fancy a quick pre-theatre tipple, take one step off the main drag and allow this beautiful little battle cruiser to provide the perfect fillip for either prince or pauper.

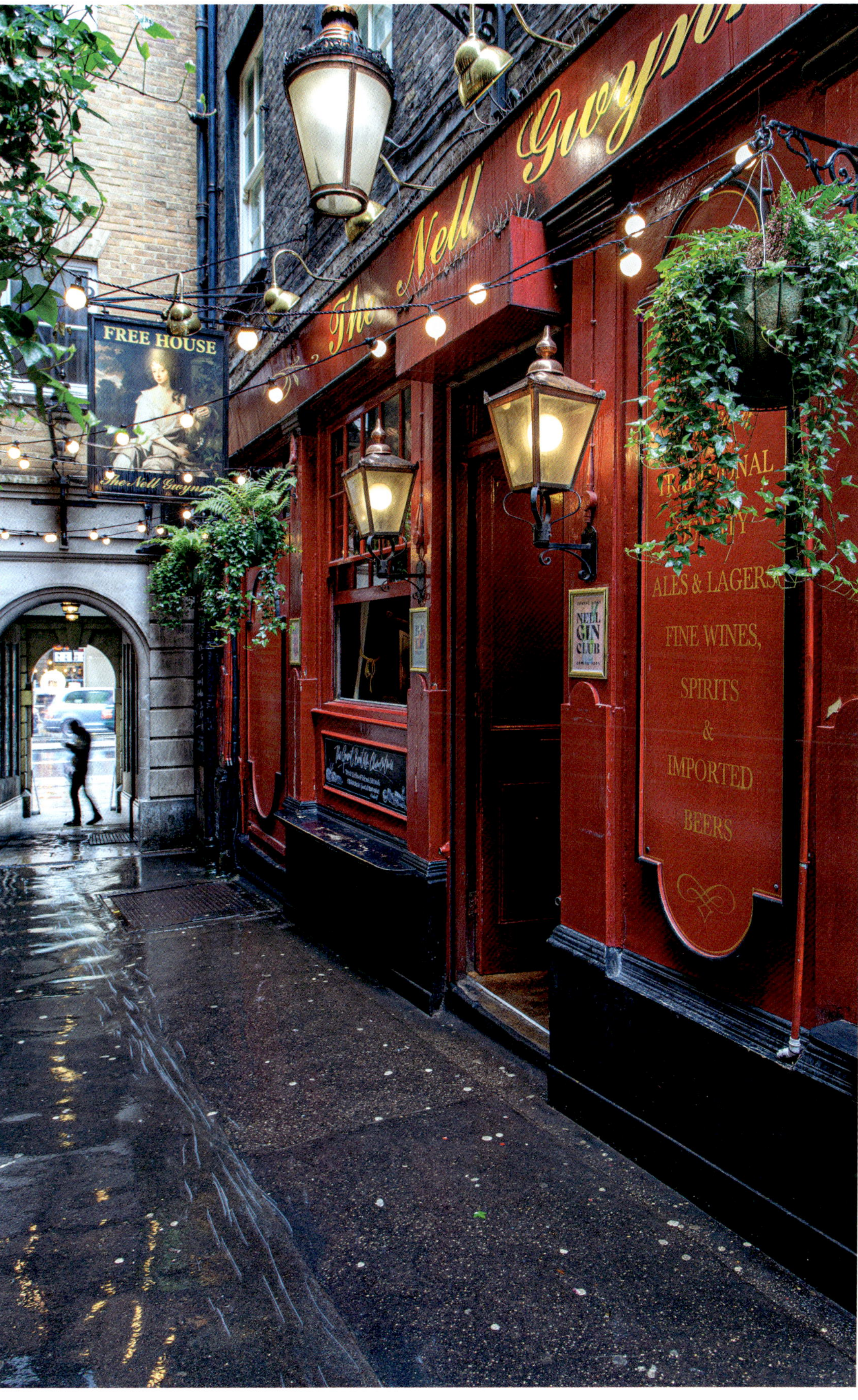
Gwynn
The Nell
FREE HOUSE
The Nell Gwynne
NELL
GIN
CLUB
TRADITIONAL
ALES & LAGERS
FINE WINES,
SPIRITS
&
IMPORTED
BEERS

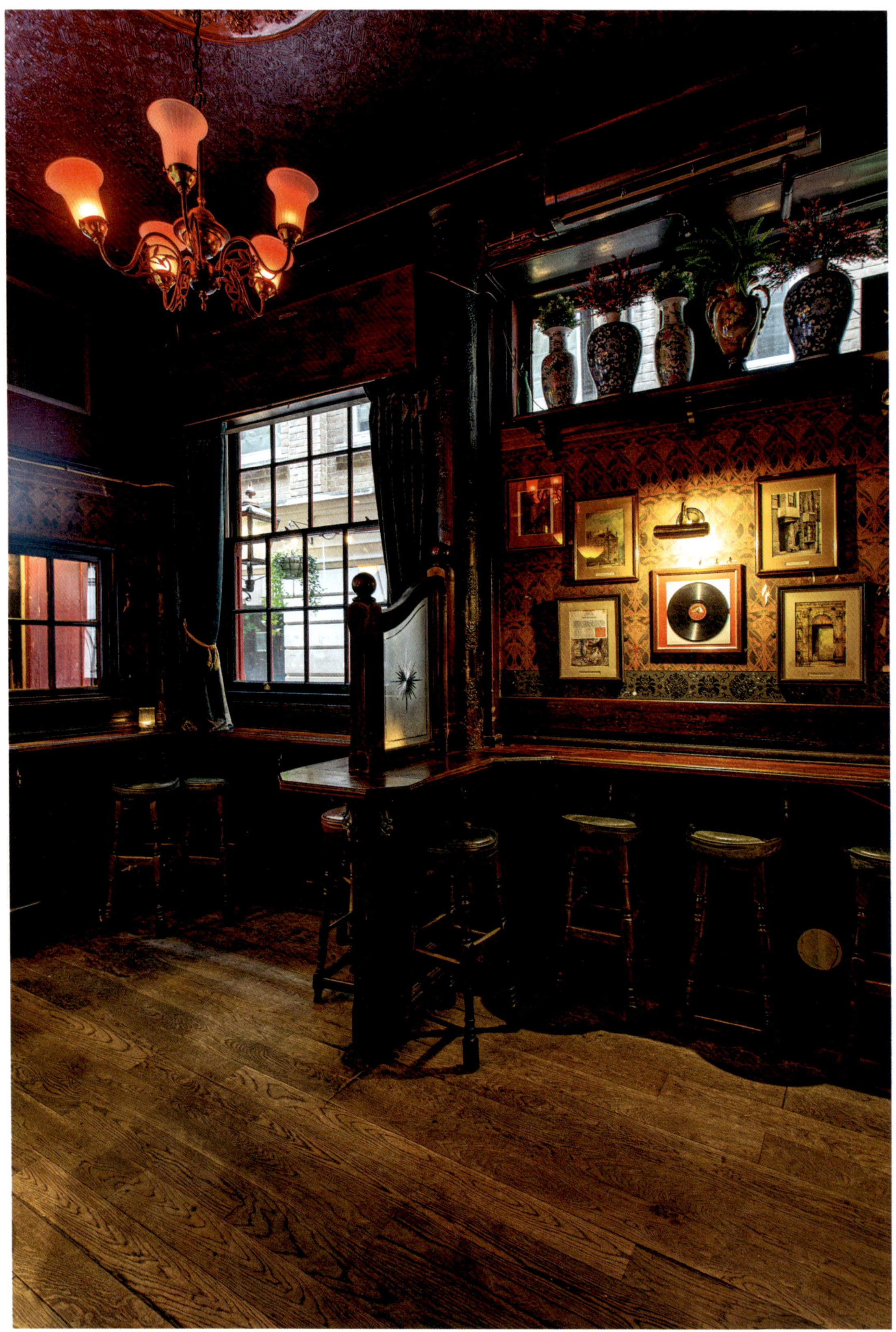

Theatreland's side-street refuge

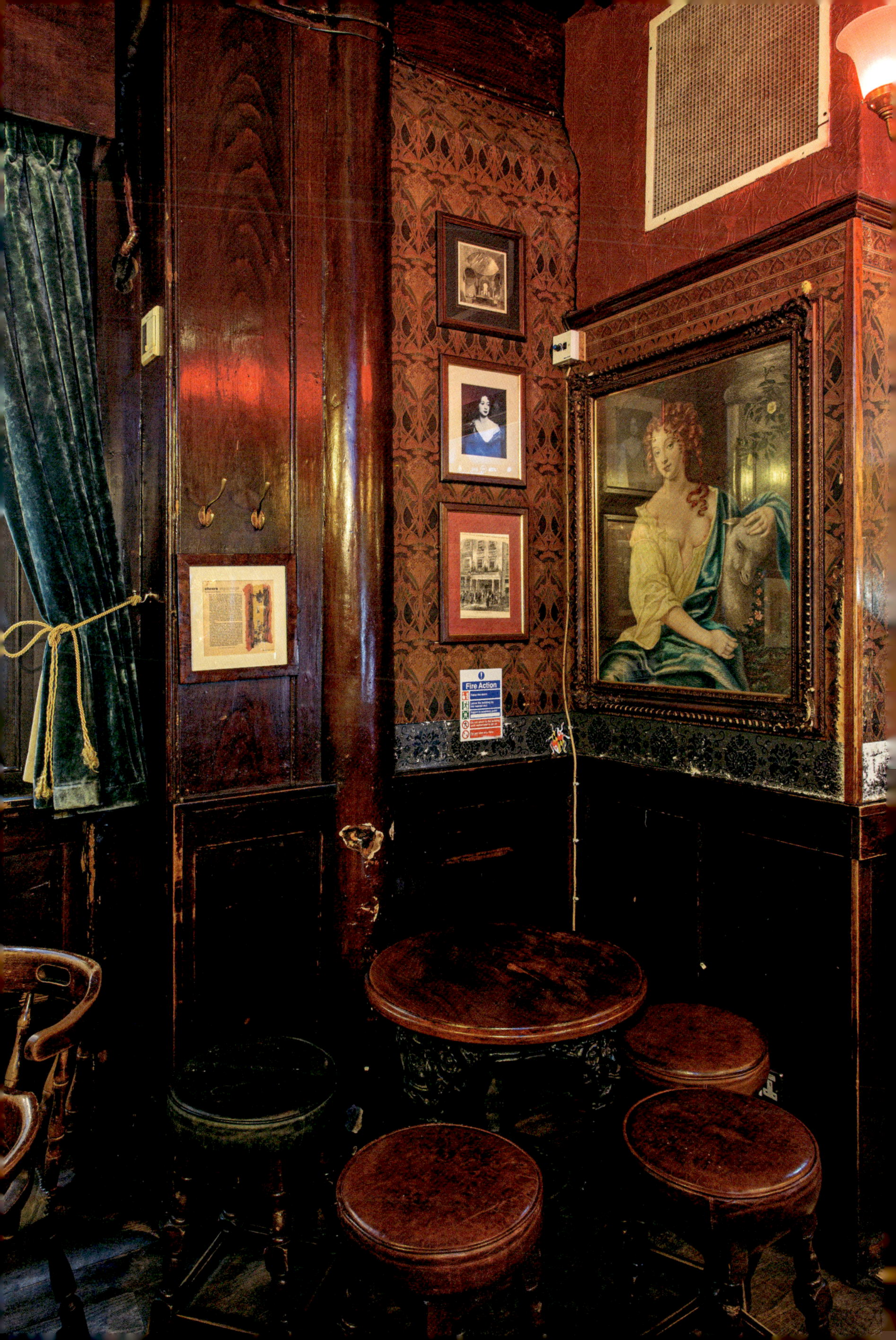

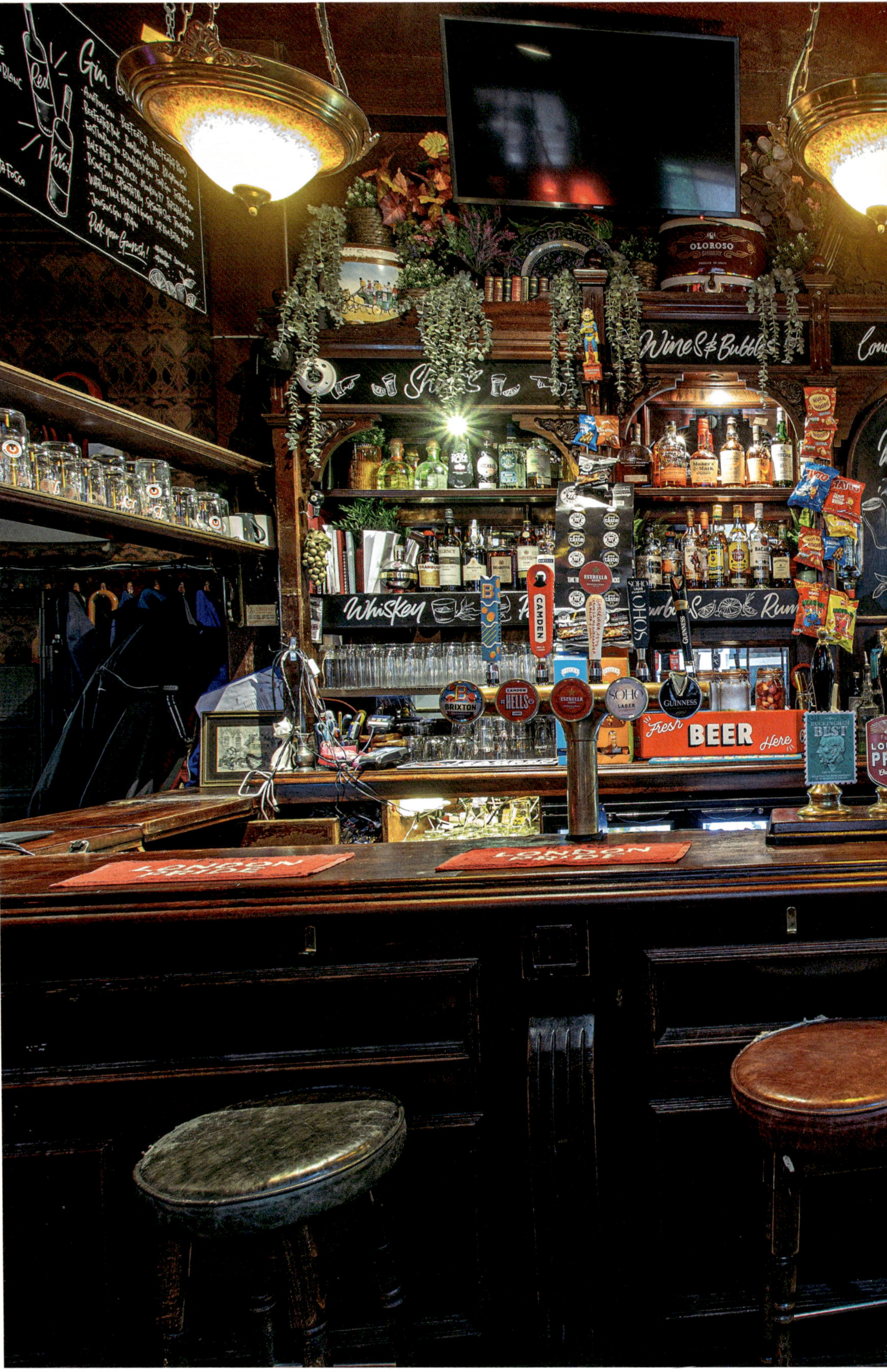

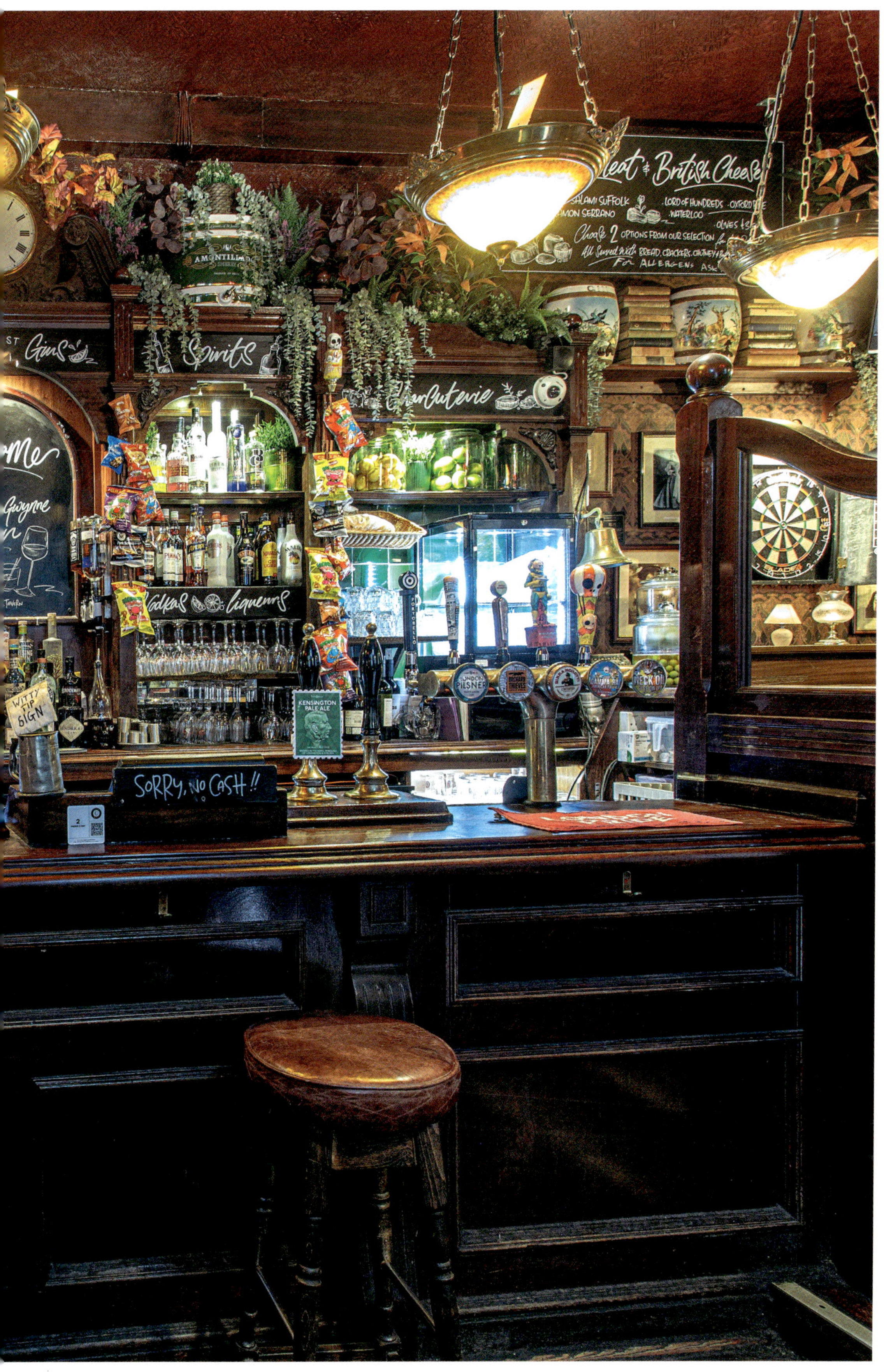
Gins
Spirits
Charcuterie
eat & British Cheese
Vodkas Liqueurs
KENSINGTON PALE ALE
SORRY, NO CASH !!
WITTY TIP SIGN

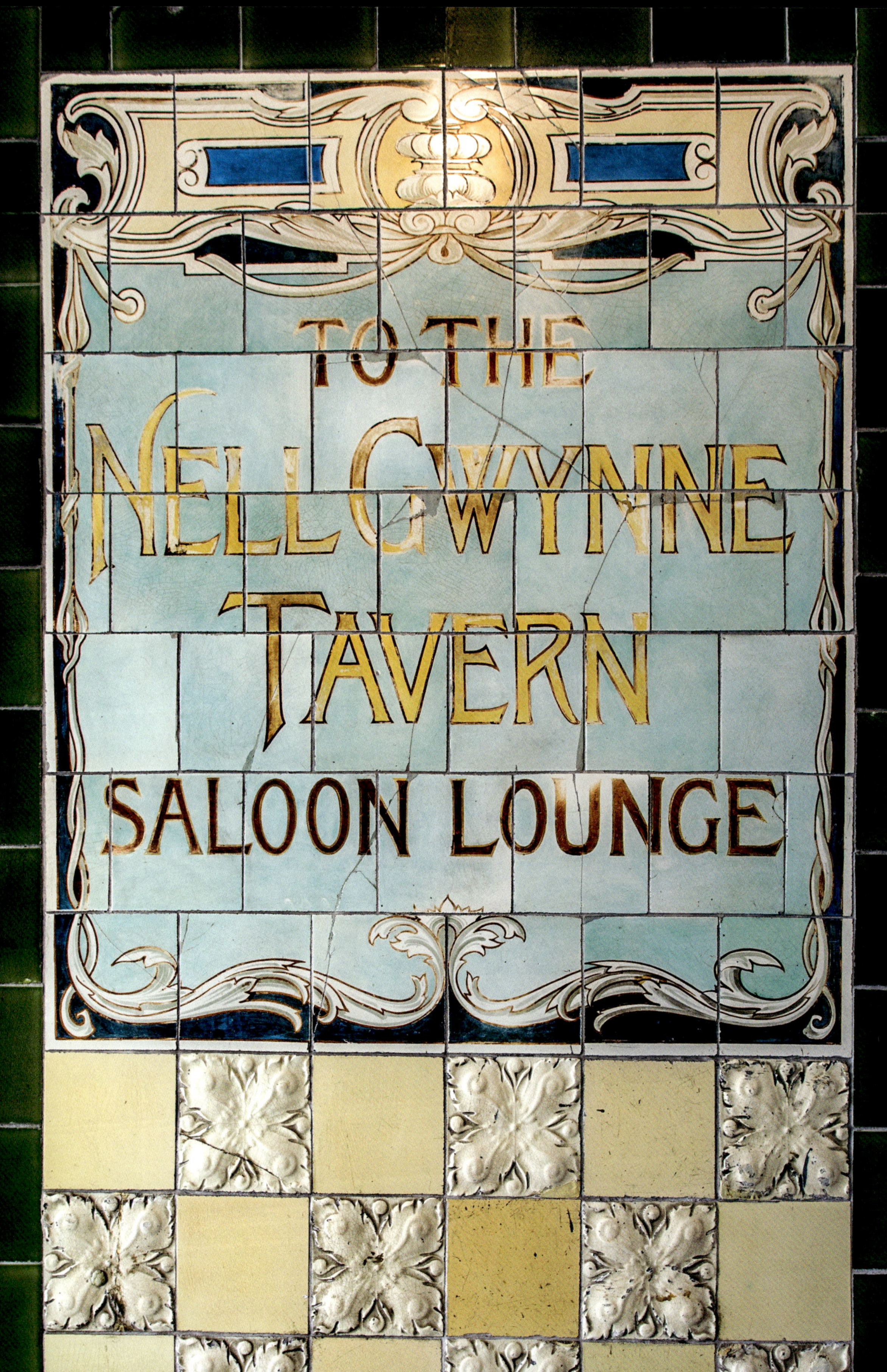

TO THE
NELL GWYNNE
TAVERN
SALOON LOUNGE

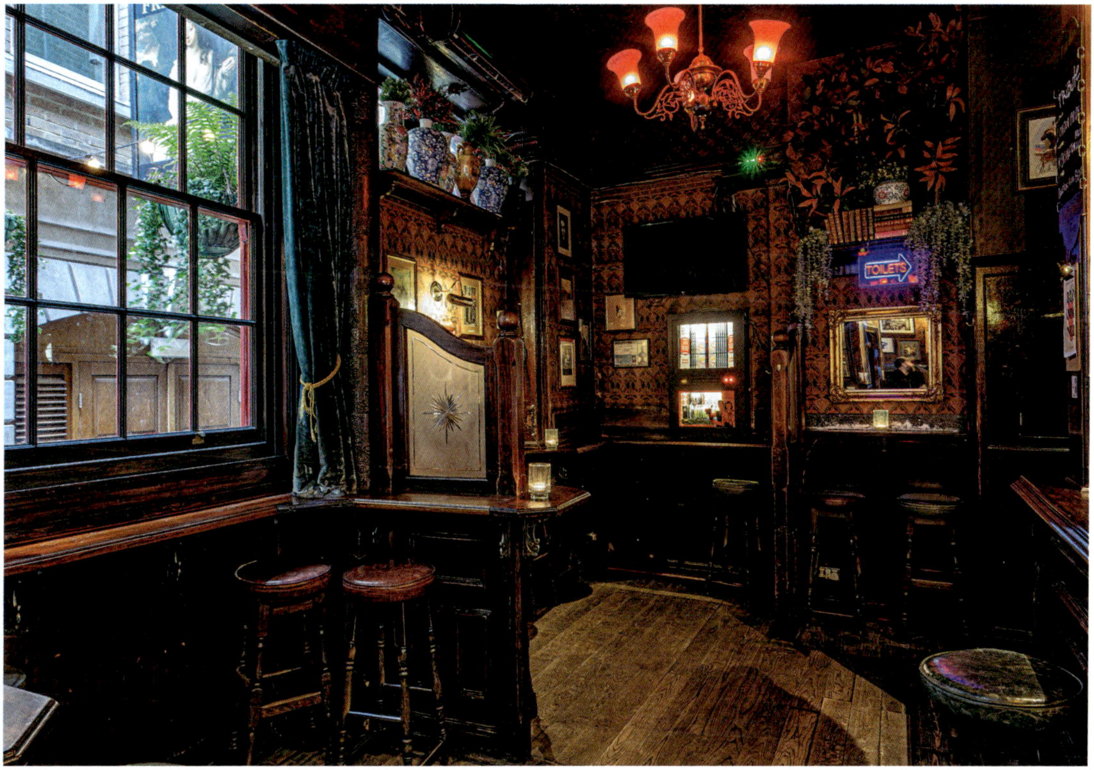

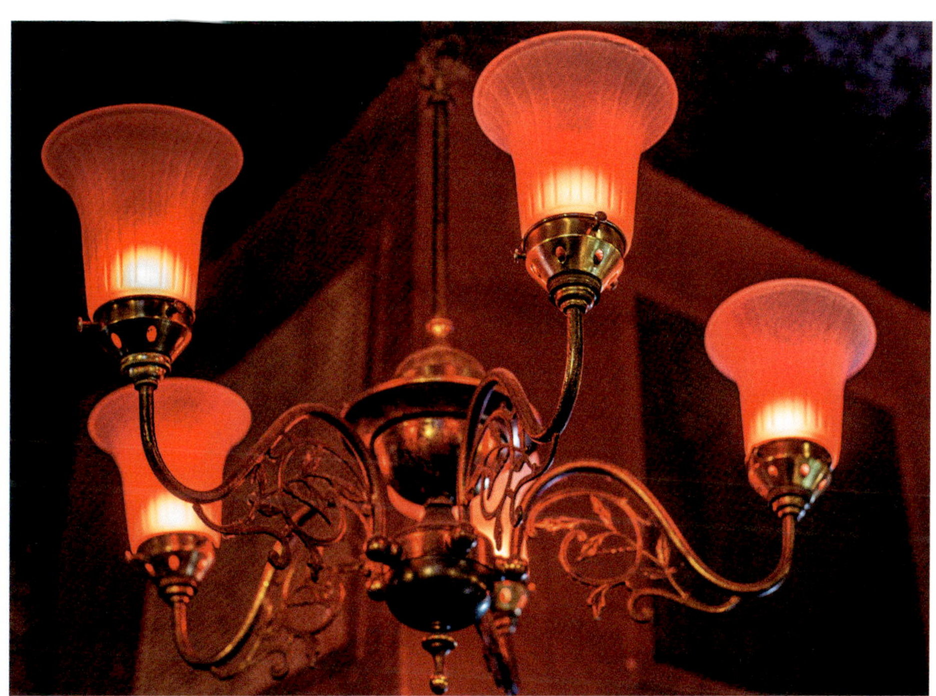

The casual whiff of a whore's boudoir

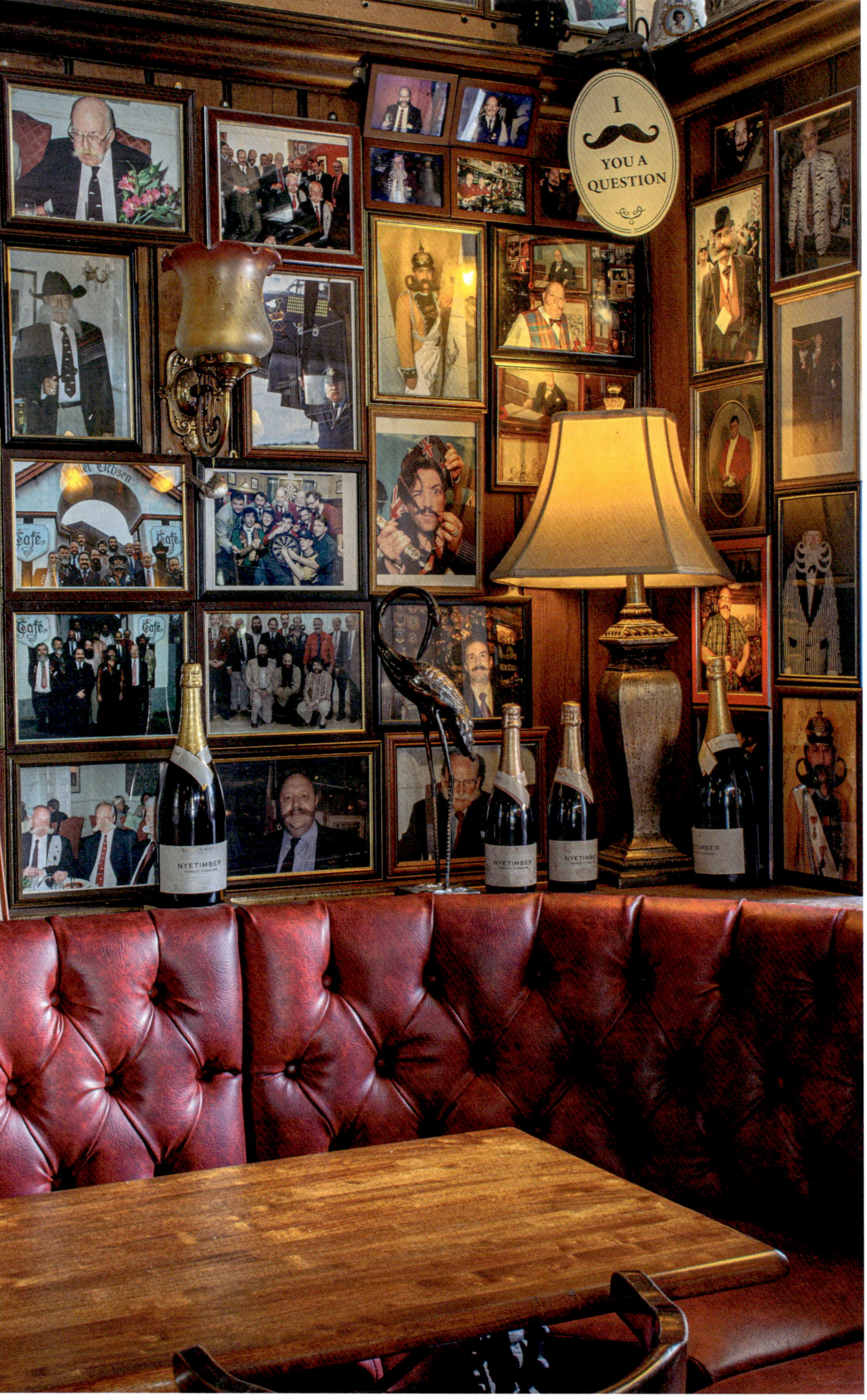

I
YOU A
QUESTION

THE HERON

Can a pub be born again? Can you simply lock the doors one last time, box up the assorted ephemera, move a quarter of the mile down the road and yet keep the essence of the pub the same? Of course you can! But the longevity of a pub and loyalty of its patrons can never be guaranteed.

So, when the much-loved Windsor Castle on Crawford Place shut up shop in the summer of 2016 due to an expiring lease and rapacious property developer, who knew what might happen? Thankfully, the cornucopia of quirky delights and royal bric-a-brac were scooped up and poured into this humble saviour just down the road.

The architecture is certainly perfunctory, but it's living proof that you can indeed polish a flat-roofed turd once in a while. The Royal Guardsman continues to keep watch at the front door, and the interior is flooded with the same royal tat. The new home allows this unique collection to breathe a little, but the pleasantly eccentric vibe holds true and the whiff of spicy tom yum soup just adds to the eclectic mix.

And if you just happen to sport "a hirsute appendage of the upper lip and with graspable extremities", then you've just stumbled into the spiritual home of the Handlebar Moustache Club. Founded in the heart of post-war Soho with the aim of keeping armed-forces camaraderie alive, the club still meet here on the first Friday of every month, with members sporting their burgundy club tie. Brought together through a shared passion for sport and a quest for general conviviality, their support for charities whilst whisker-twiddling is unsurpassed. It takes a certain type of man to cultivate, hone and maintain such facial finery. Just navigating your face furniture through some of the frothier pints on offer up top requires a certain discipline. But such an eccentric club, convening in such characterful surroundings just off the Edgware Road, seems a suitably ad hoc home for such indulgences. The clear aversion to beards of any kind is also worth applauding (hipsters, please take note).

The Heron is emblematic of what makes a great pub. For it isn't just the polished brass and beer that keep people coming back; it's the publicans and, more importantly, the characterful punters that give a pub its magnetic qualities. Pubs are for people, so treat your patrons well and, when you are forced to move 600 paces down the road, they might just follow you. Handlebar moustache in tow.

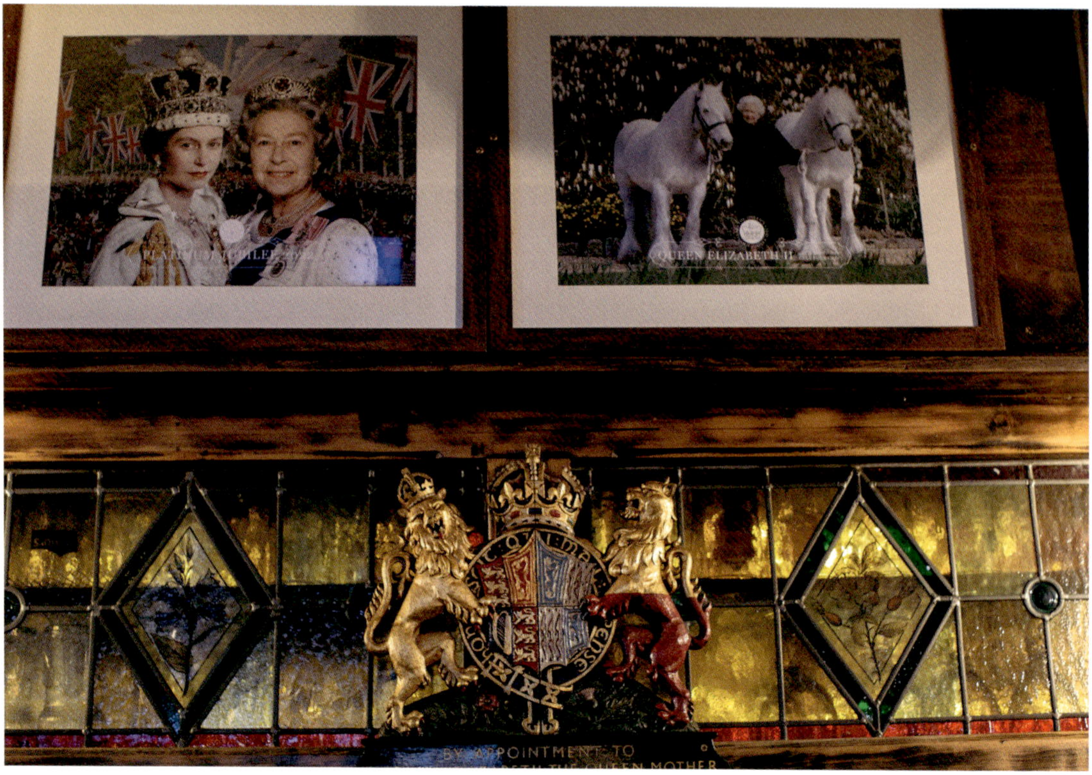

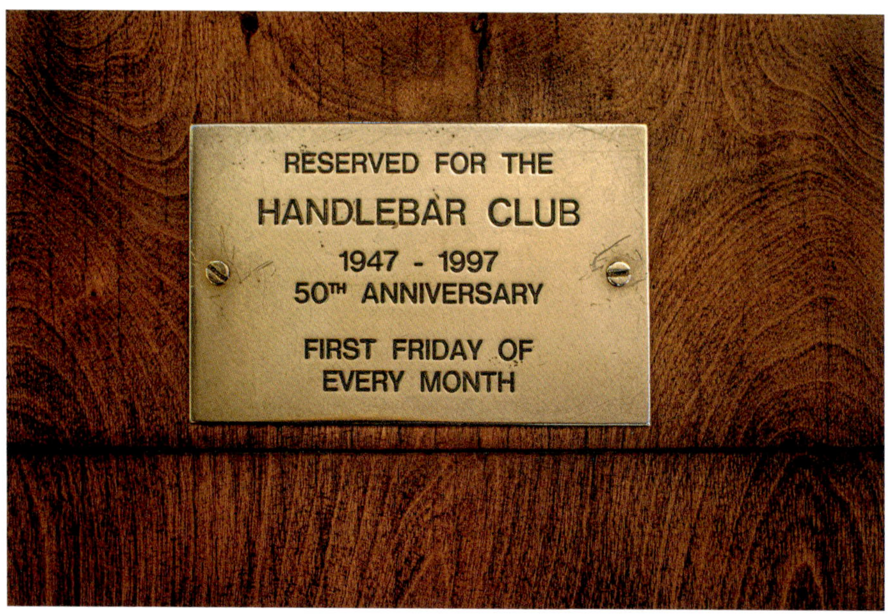

Home to hirsute appendages of the upper lip, with graspable extremities

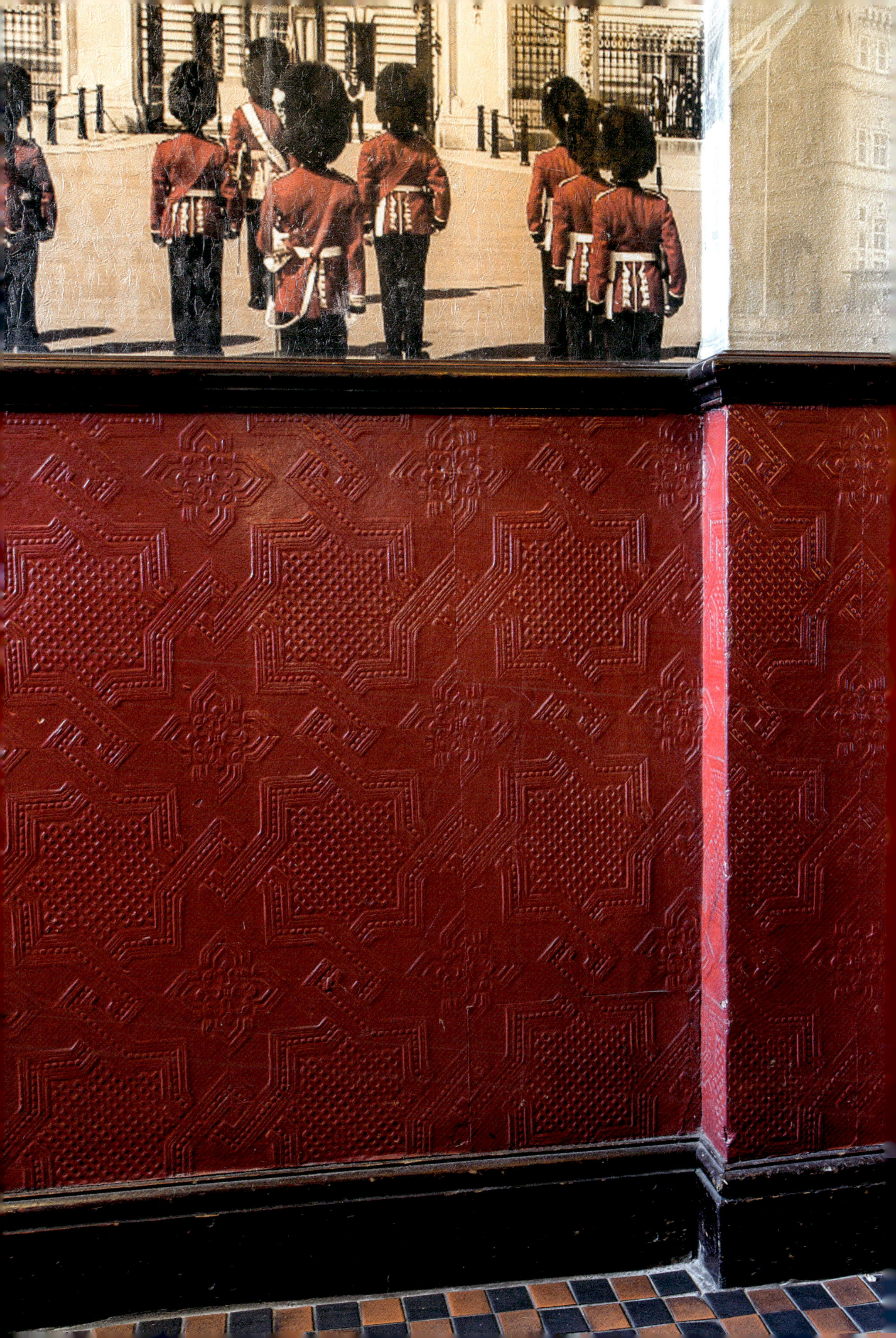

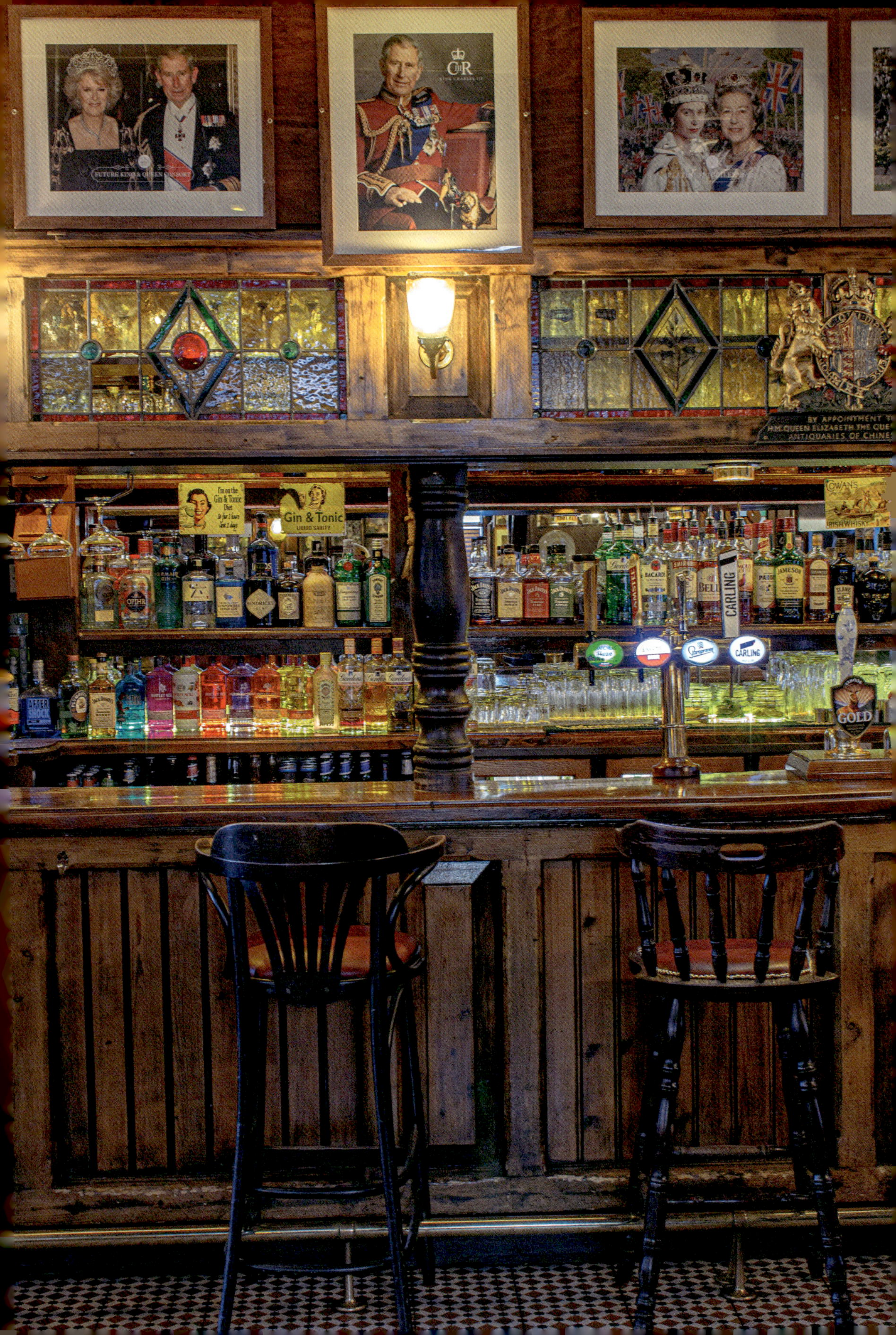

CIIIR
KING CHARLES III
Gin & Tonic
I'm on the Gin & Tonic Diet
CARLING
GOLD
IRISH WHISKY
BY APPOINTMENT
H.M. QUEEN ELIZABETH THE QUEEN
ANTIQUARIES OF CHINE

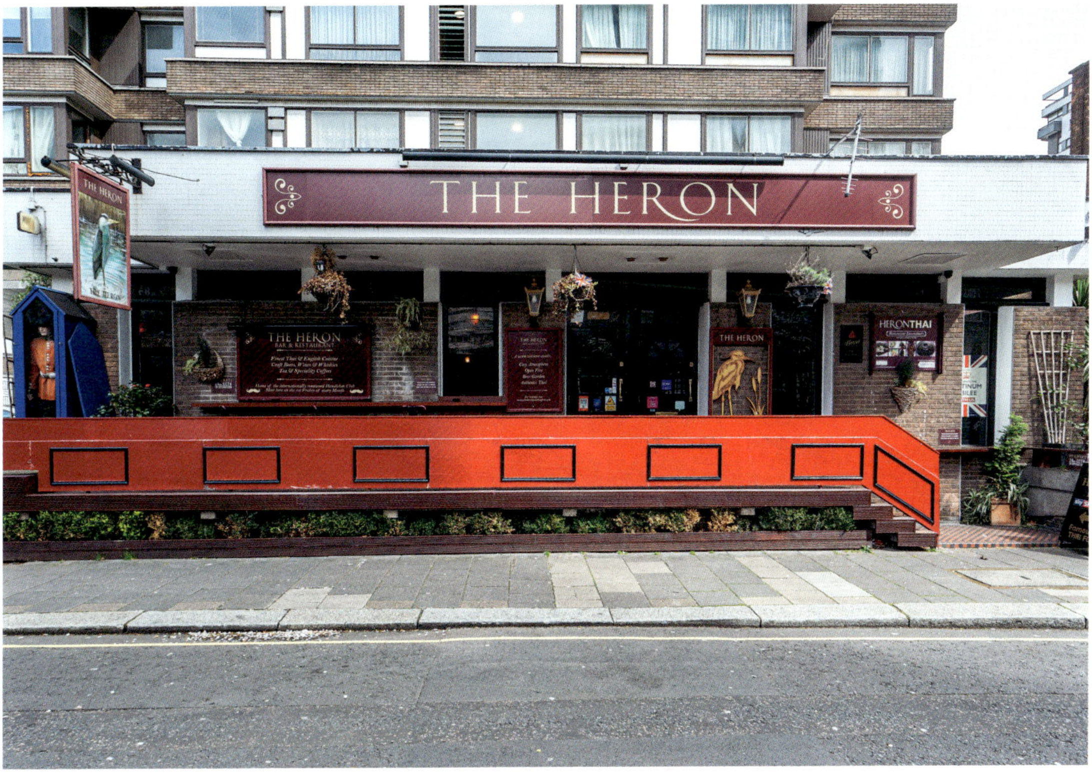

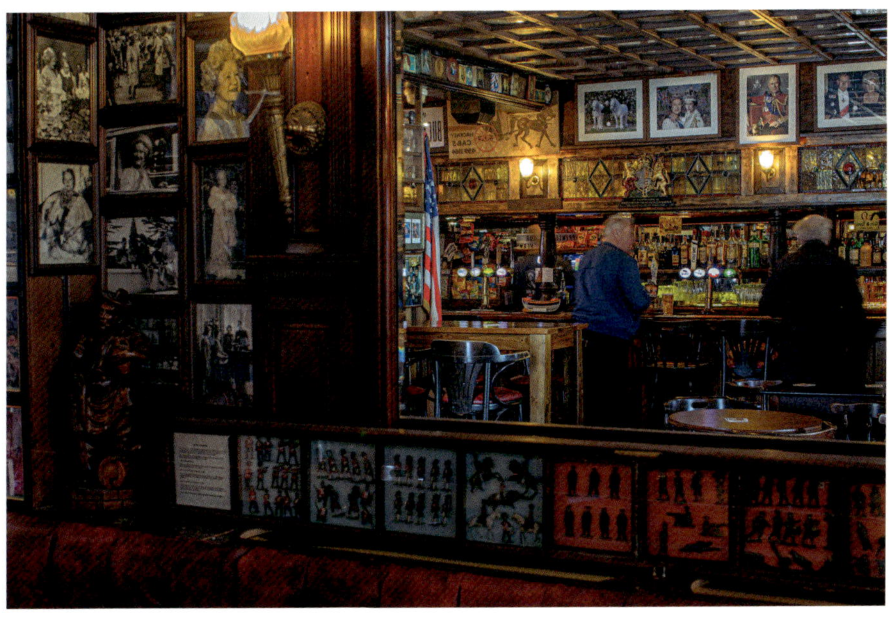

A foreboding flat roof gives little intimation of the right royal knees-up inside

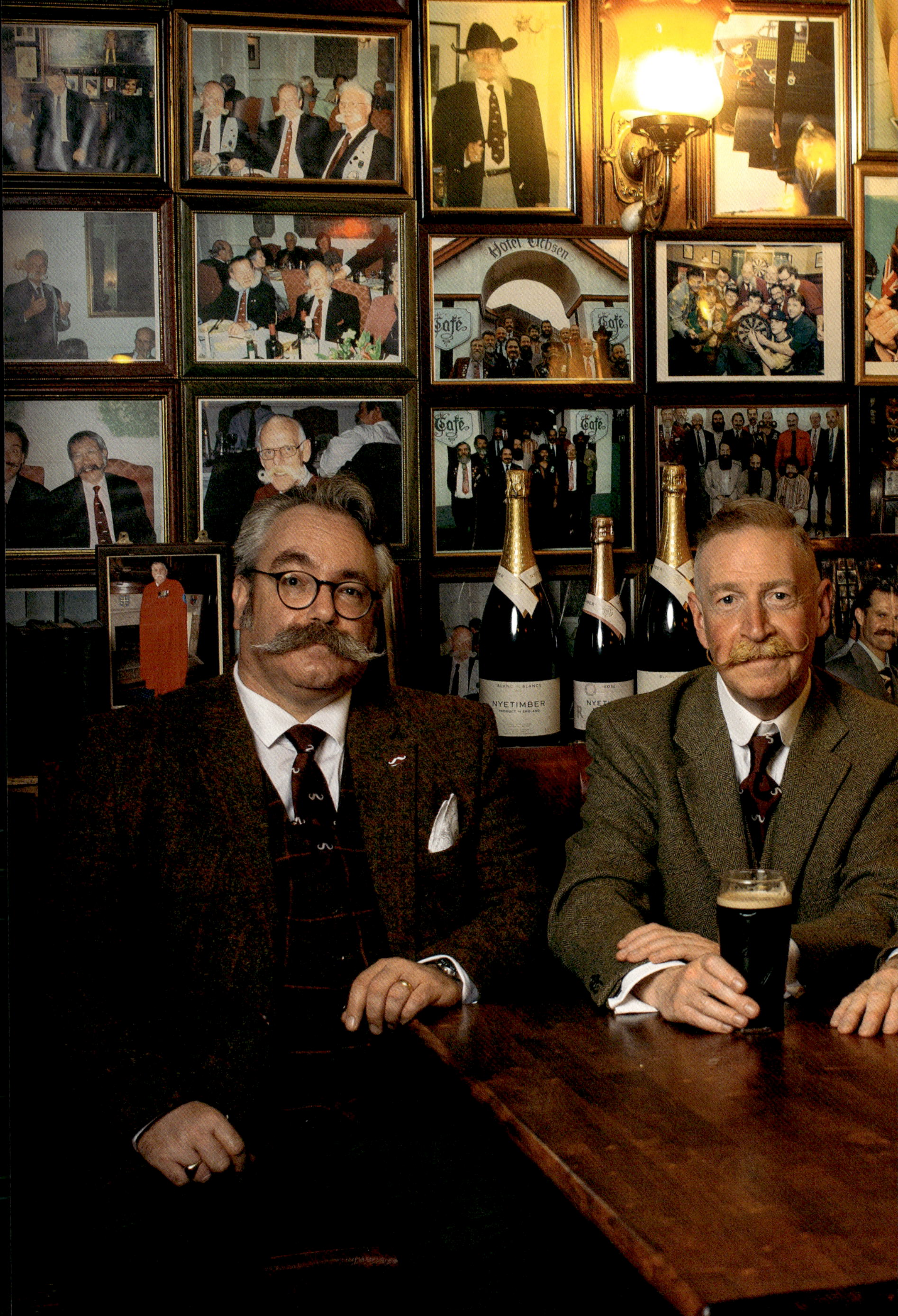

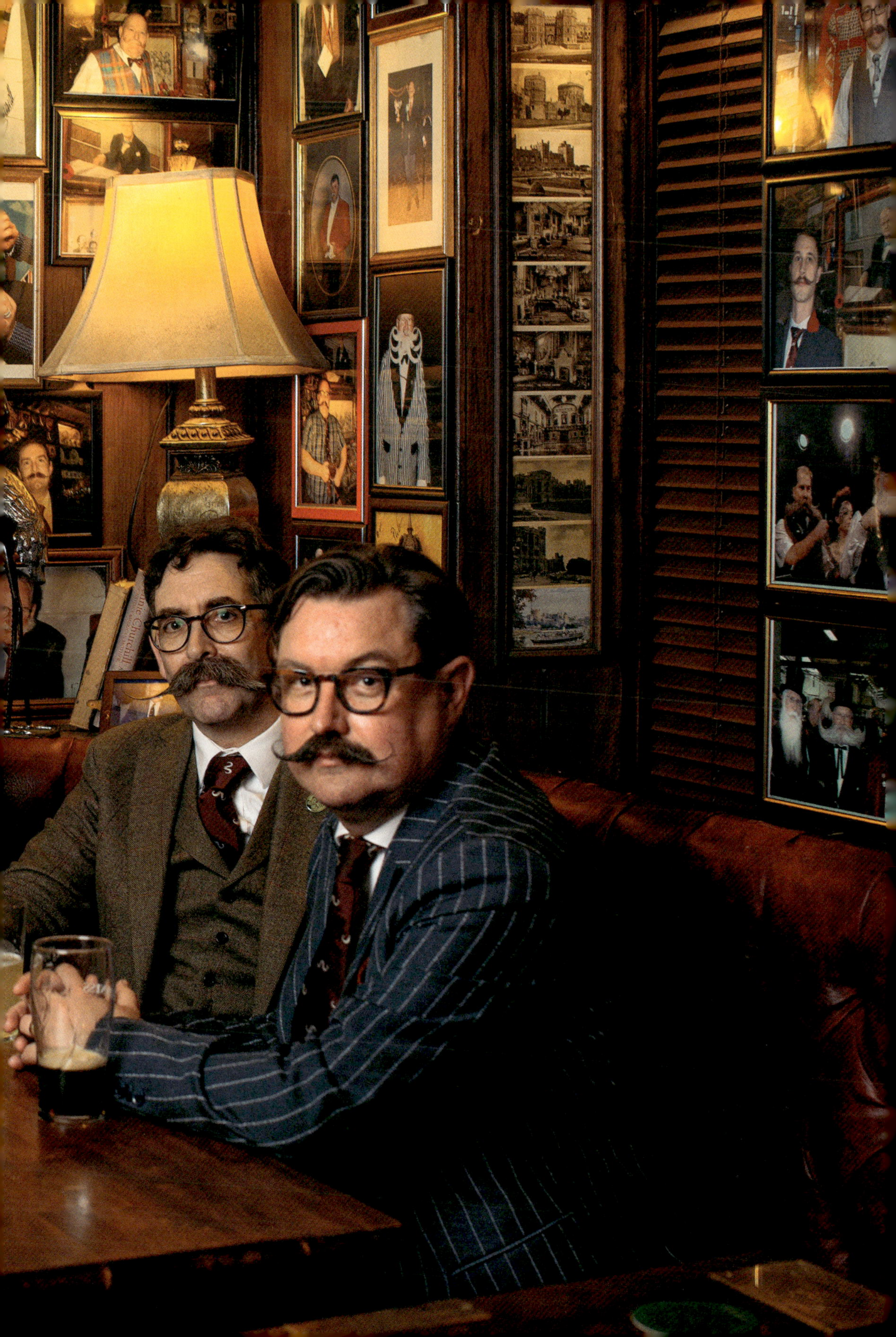

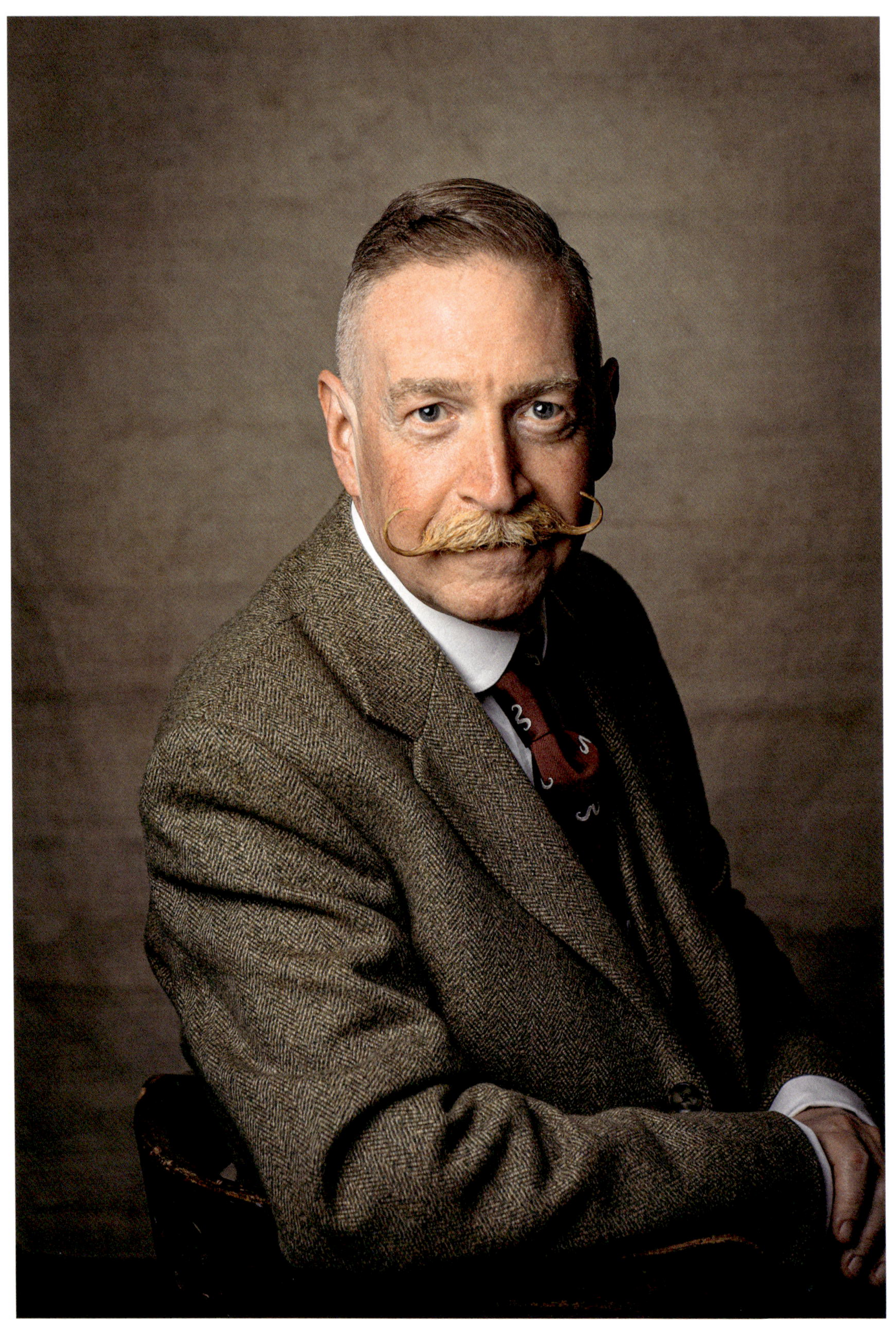

The home of exceptional face furniture

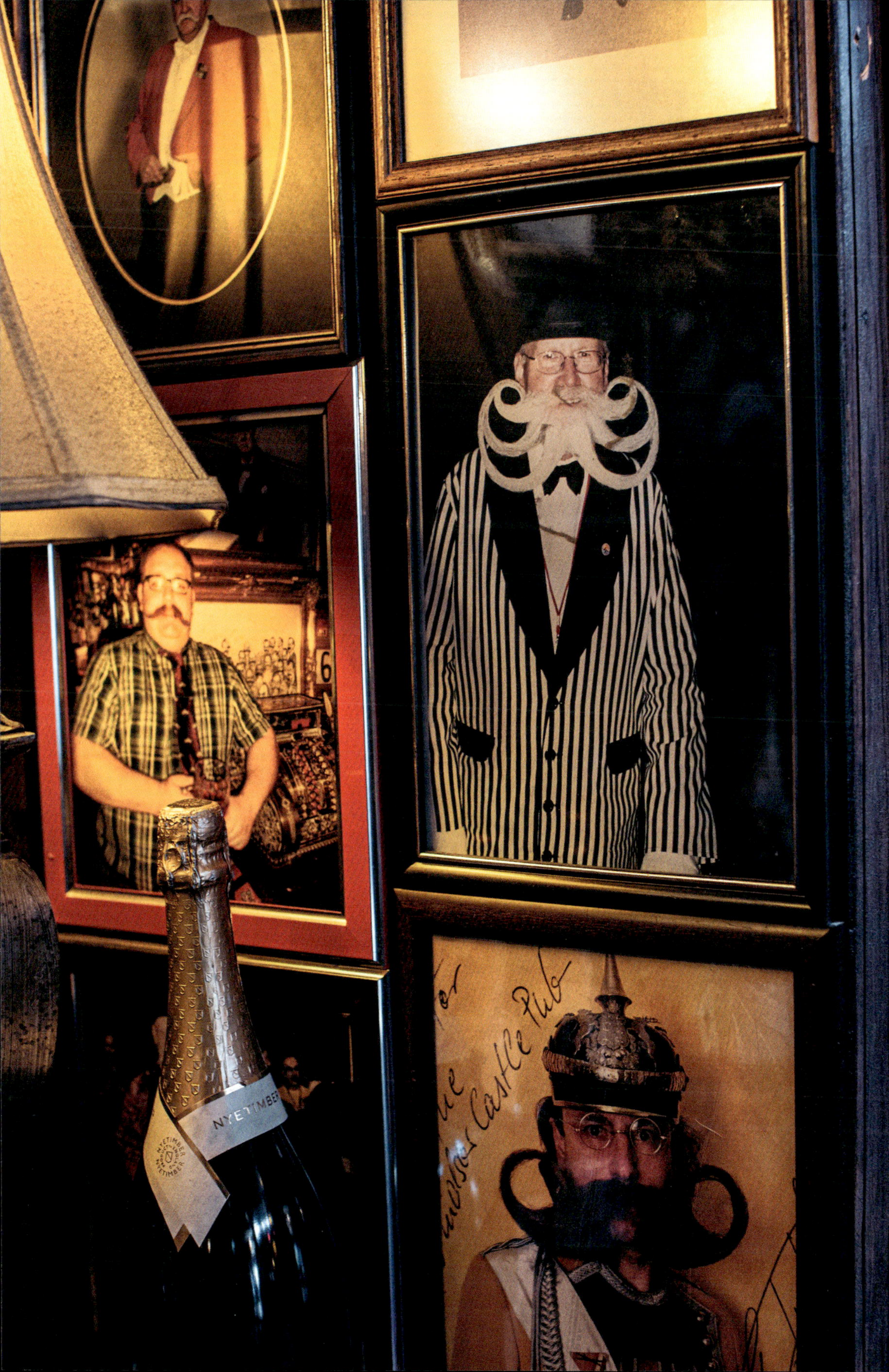
NYETIMBER

THE PRIDE OF SPITALFIELDS

The legend of the beer London Pride was forged in the firestorms of the Blitz. As the city burnt and bomb-sites lay undeveloped for years, one plant learnt to grow amongst the ashes. This plant, known simply as "London Pride", became a symbol of hope. London's most iconic ale was named in its honour and was first brewed beside the River Thames in 1958.

Although London Pride's birthplace is the Griffin Brewery in Chiswick, when Kerry and Ann Butler took over The Romford Arms just off Brick Lane in the mid-1980s they immediately renamed the pub in honour of this West London beer. Nearly forty years later it still has literal pride of place on the bar.

It's this consistency of custodianship under Ann that gives this pub its understated charm. Marooned in a sea of cool kids and fashionistas, this old man's oasis has chiselled a soft spot in almost every London drinker's heart. As the City seeps ever further eastwards, it's a final bastion against gentrification.

The East End, like this pub, accepts all comers. From artistic provocateurs Gilbert and George resident next door to a building only yards away that has functioned as an eighteenth-century Protestant chapel for Huguenot weavers, a nineteenth-century synagogue and, by the late twentieth century, a mosque. So, from Mr Gupta helping with the pub's annual accounts to Mark keeping the cellar ship-shape, it's a real community effort. One staff member would take an annual loan out to pay the year's tax bill and have it repaid over the next eleven months before starting again come January. And when drug dealers burnt the pub to the ground, it was Ann's mum who sent her life savings down from Liverpool to cover the shortfall in the insurance payout.

Daytime sees the bar tick over with a steady stream of old-time pint-shufflers. But come Monday's vinyl night (or any evening, to be honest) and the diminutively proportioned pub takes on a different dimension. With room for only three behind the bar, it's a tightly crewed operation. Jobs are never advertised, and recommendations often come directly from patrons. It runs on no fuss and no pretension, just like the garish tongue-in-cheek Christmas decorations that make it look ready for a good knees-up round the piano. The biggest change greeting regular patrons of The Pride is the loss of the legendary pub cat. Lenny from Liverpool rarely left the comforts of the carpet in the front room and offered an informal meet-and-greet to every new arrival. With fans from all over the world, you'll see his ashes resting above the fireplace where he spent many happy an hour. This is a pub that serves Pride and runs on pride. It's not just the Pride of Spitalfields. This is the blimmin' Pride of London.

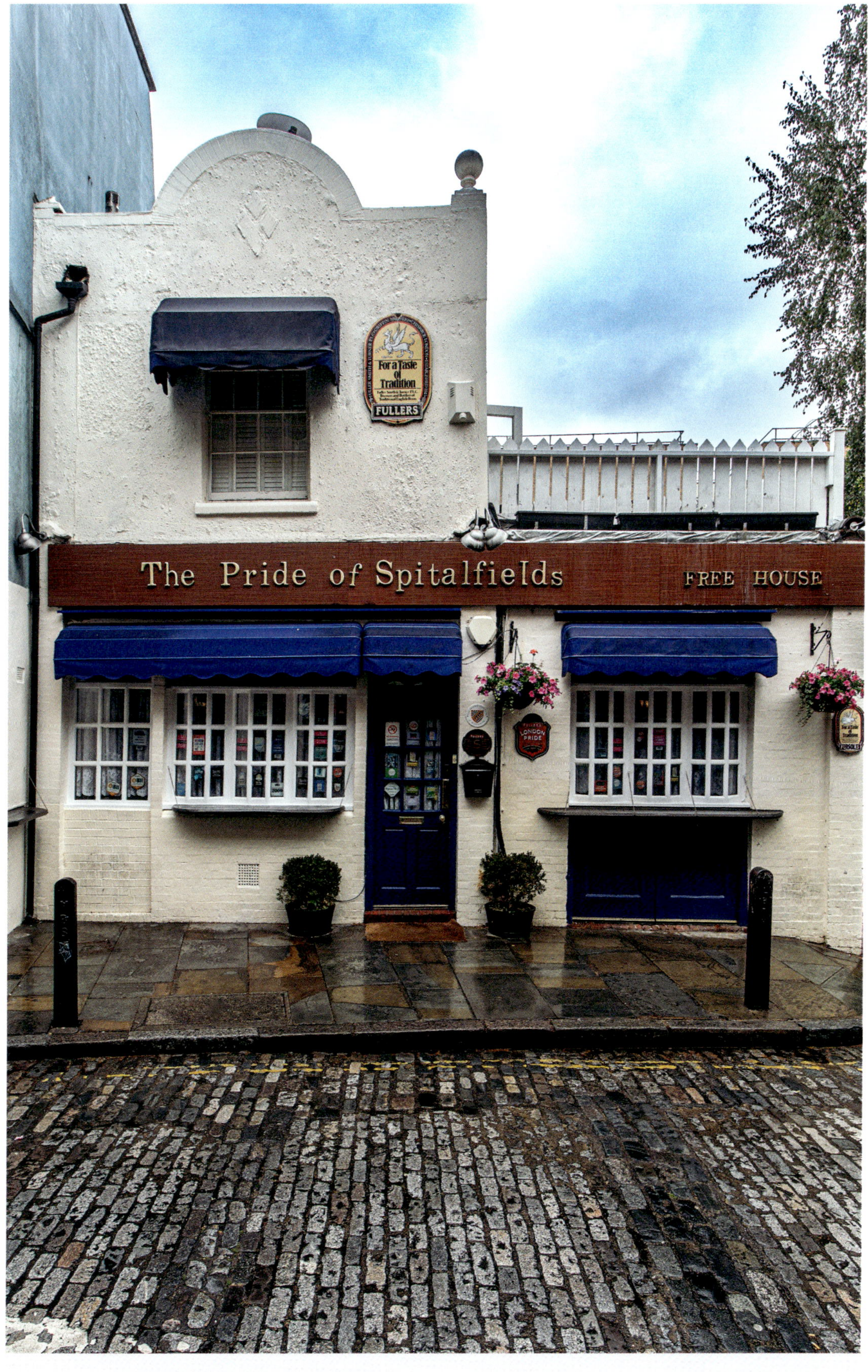
For a Taste of Tradition
FULLERS
The Pride of Spitalfields
FREE HOUSE
LONDON PRIDE

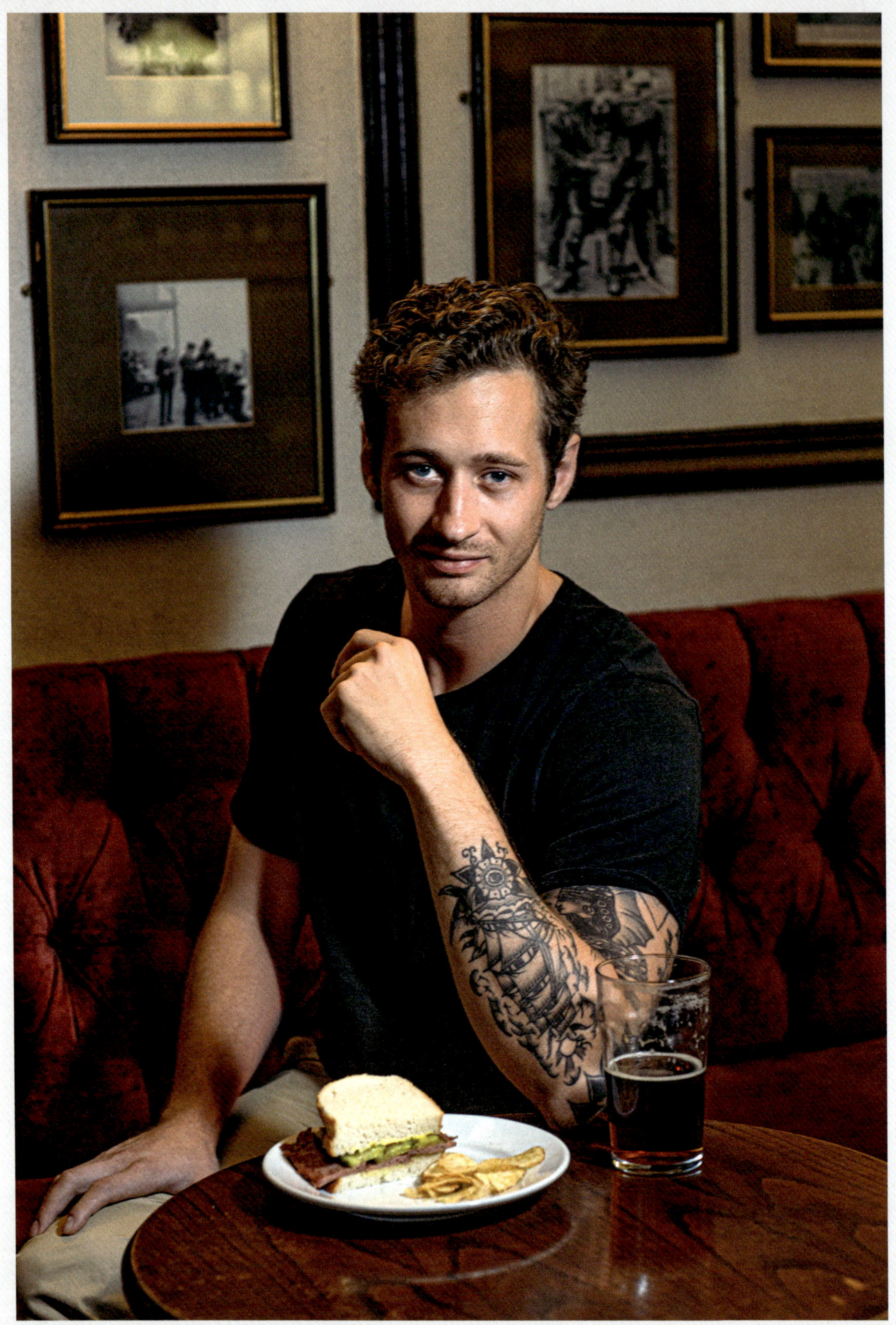

Marooned in a sea of cool kids and fashionistas

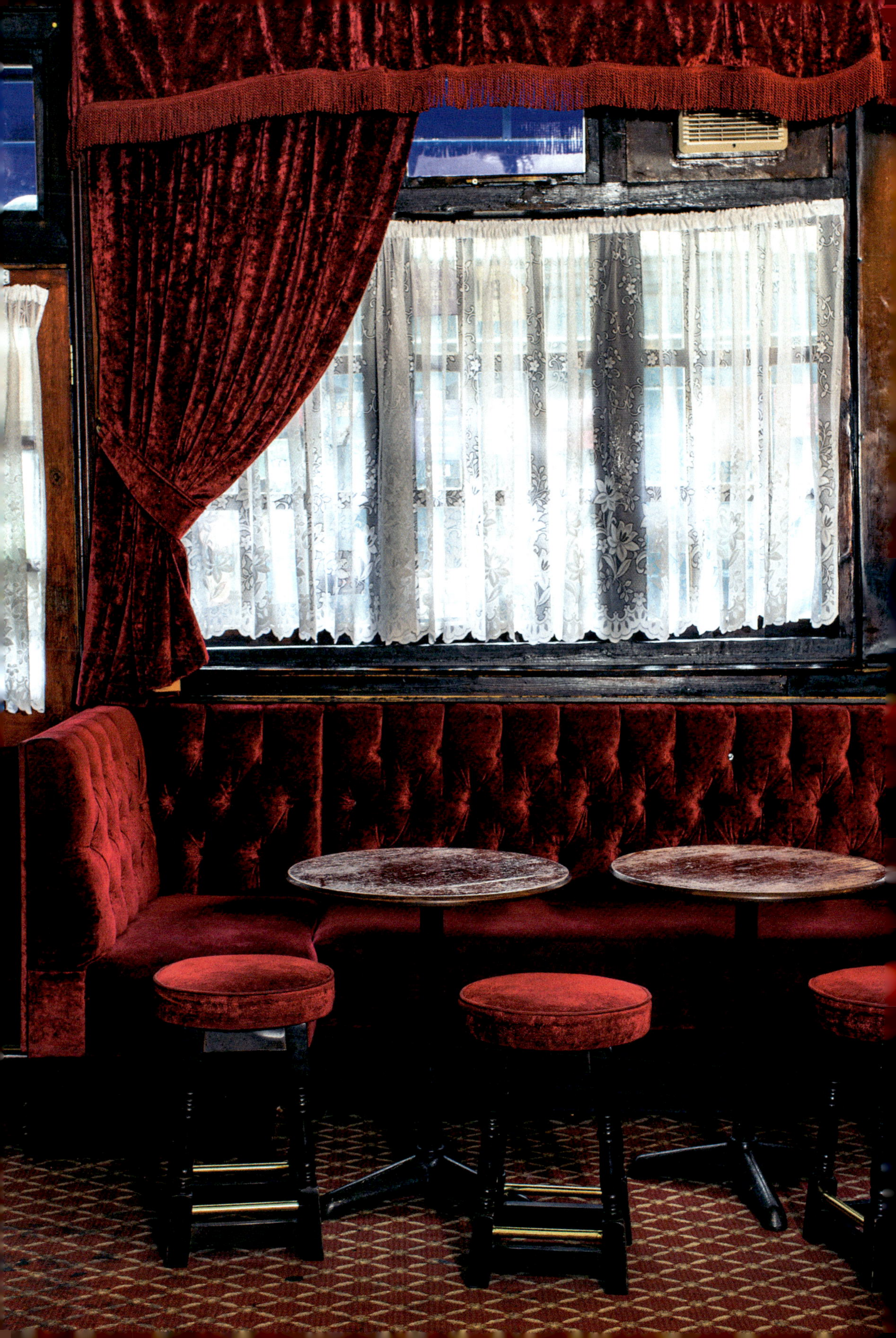

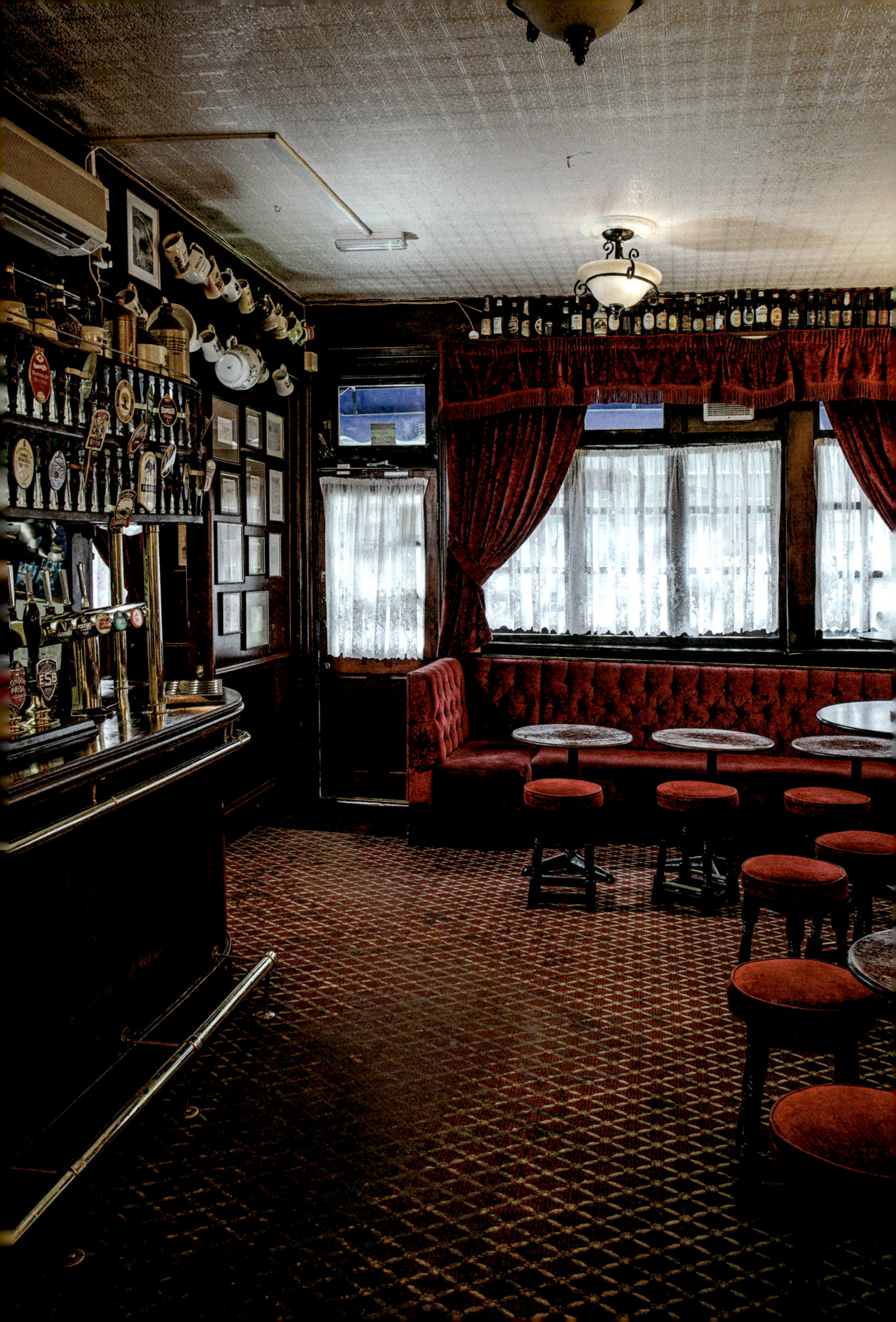

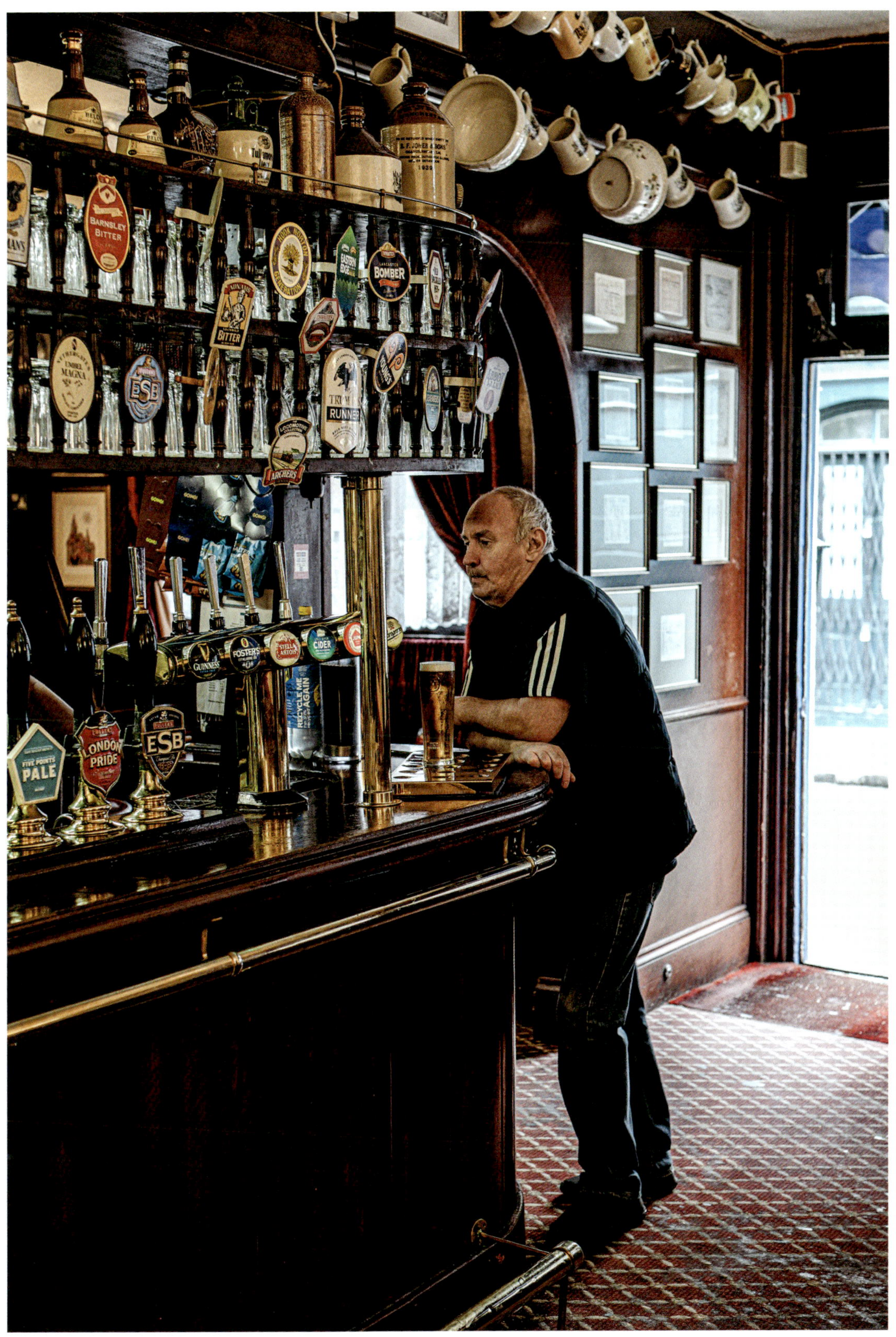

A classic British boozer in the heart of Banglatown

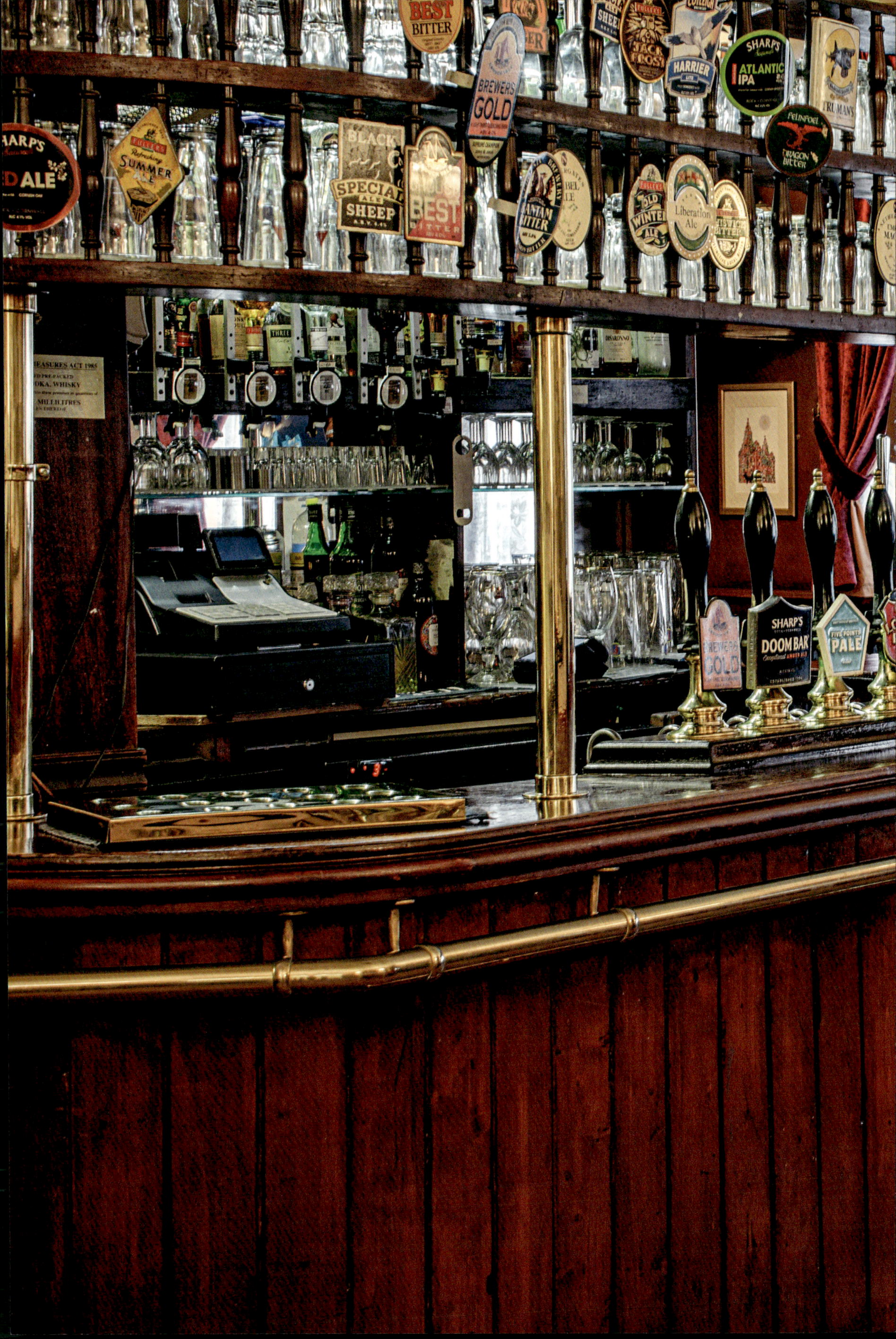

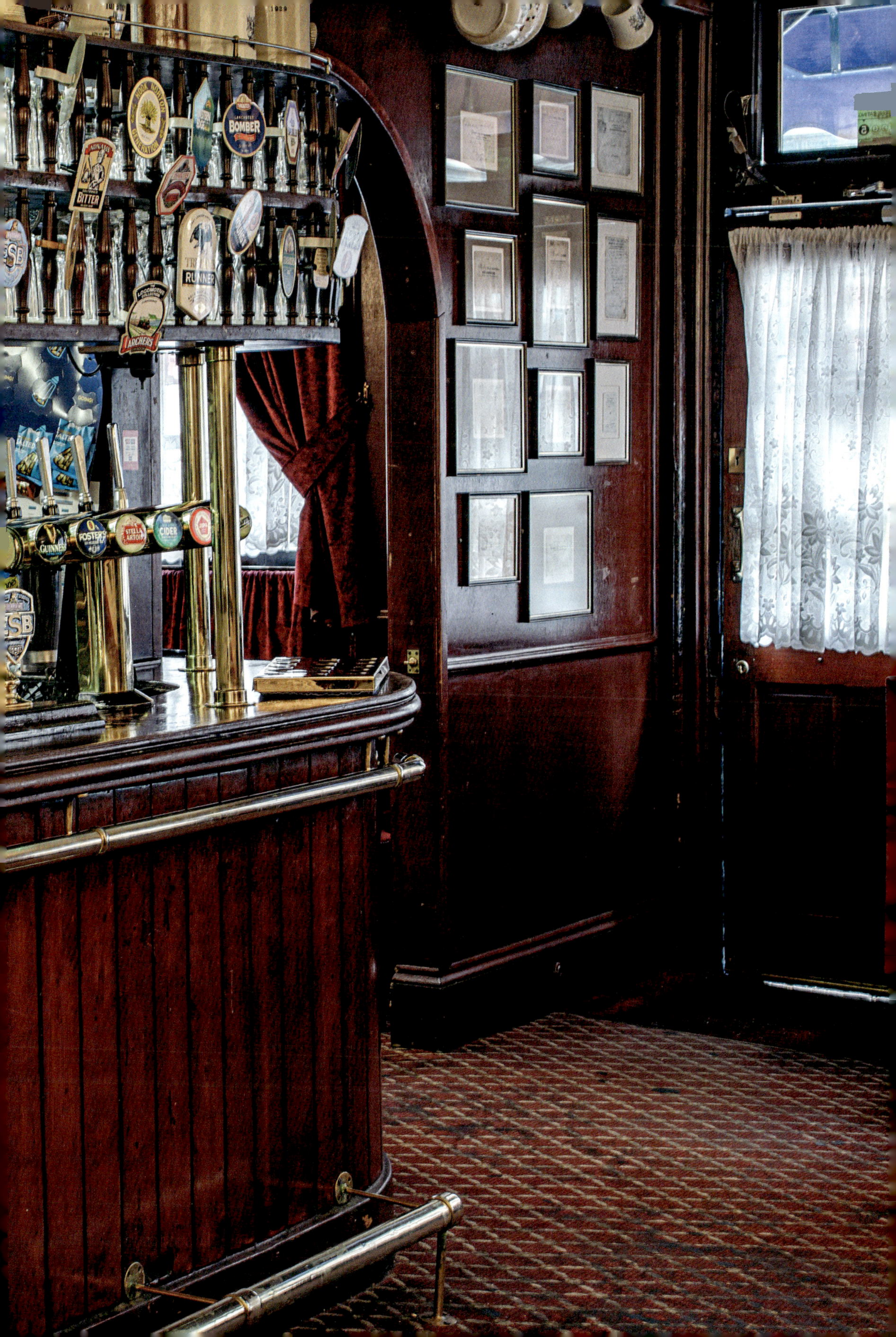

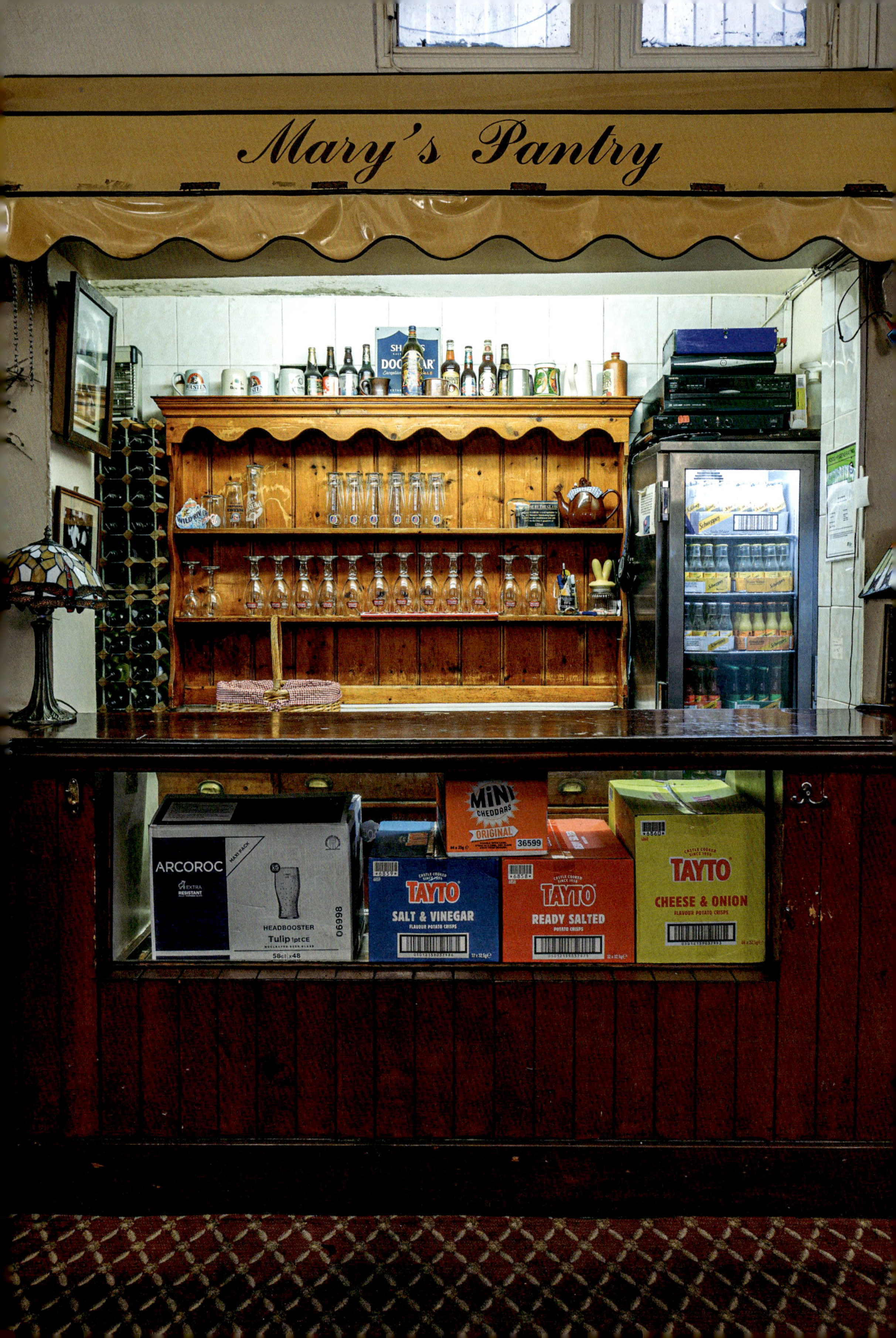

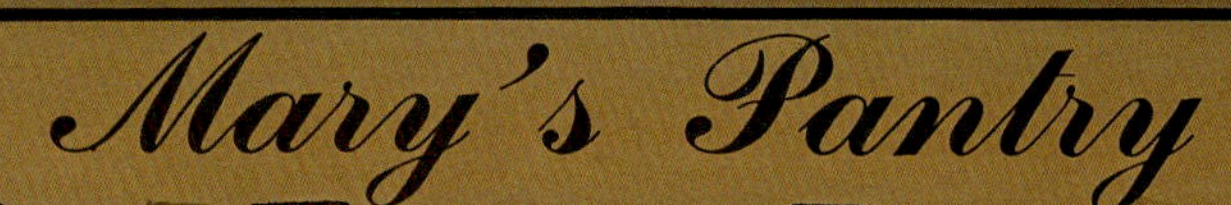

Mary's Pantry

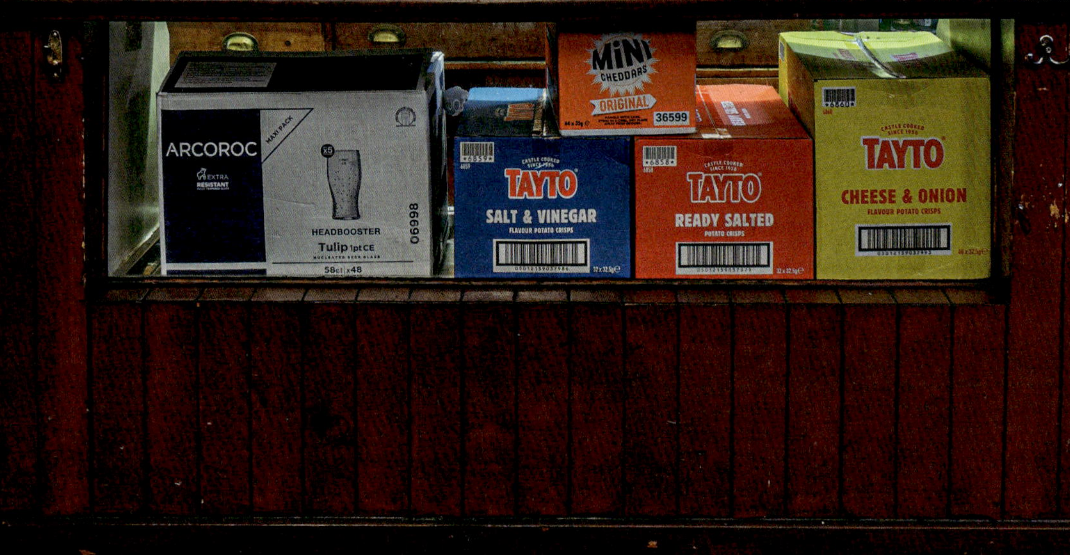

ARCOROC
HEADBOOSTER
Tulip 1pce
TAYTO
SALT & VINEGAR
FLAVOUR POTATO CRISPS
MINI
CHEDDARS
ORIGINAL
36599
TAYTO
READY SALTED
POTATO CRISPS
TAYTO
CHEESE & ONION
FLAVOUR POTATO CRISPS

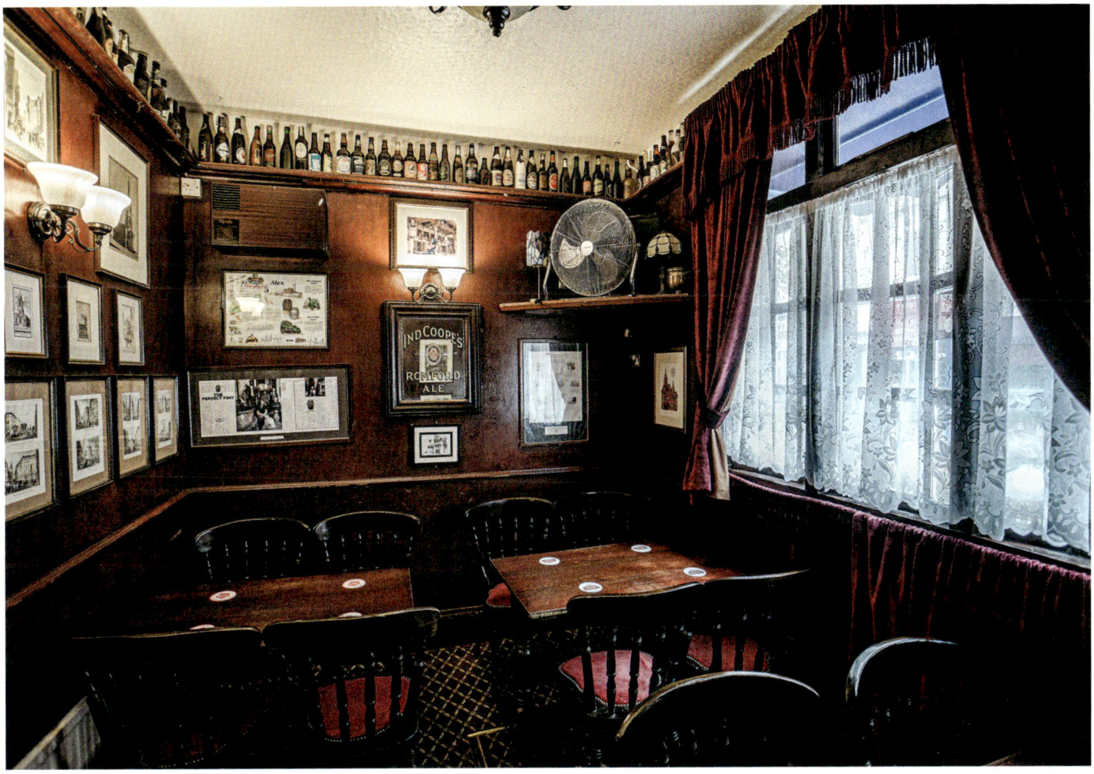

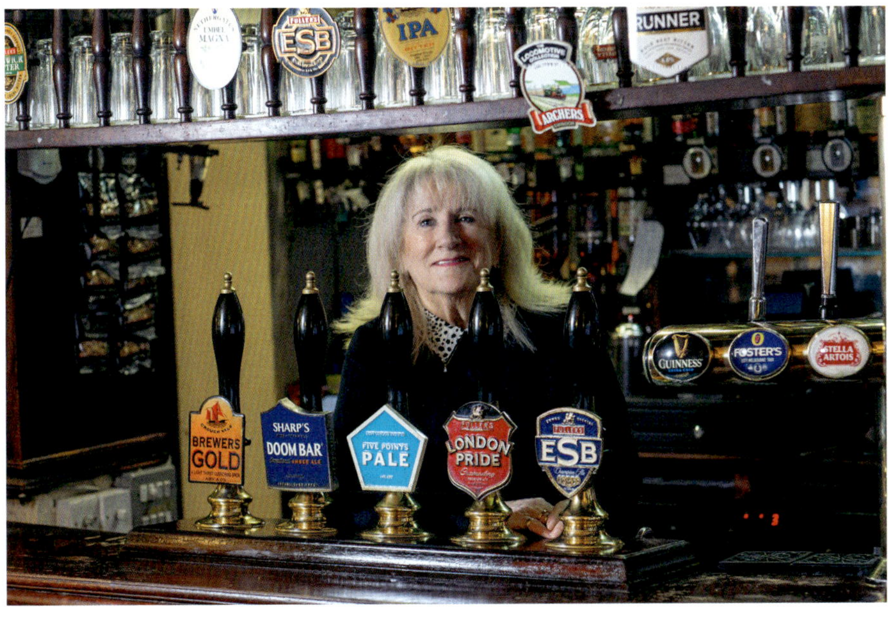

Run on pride...

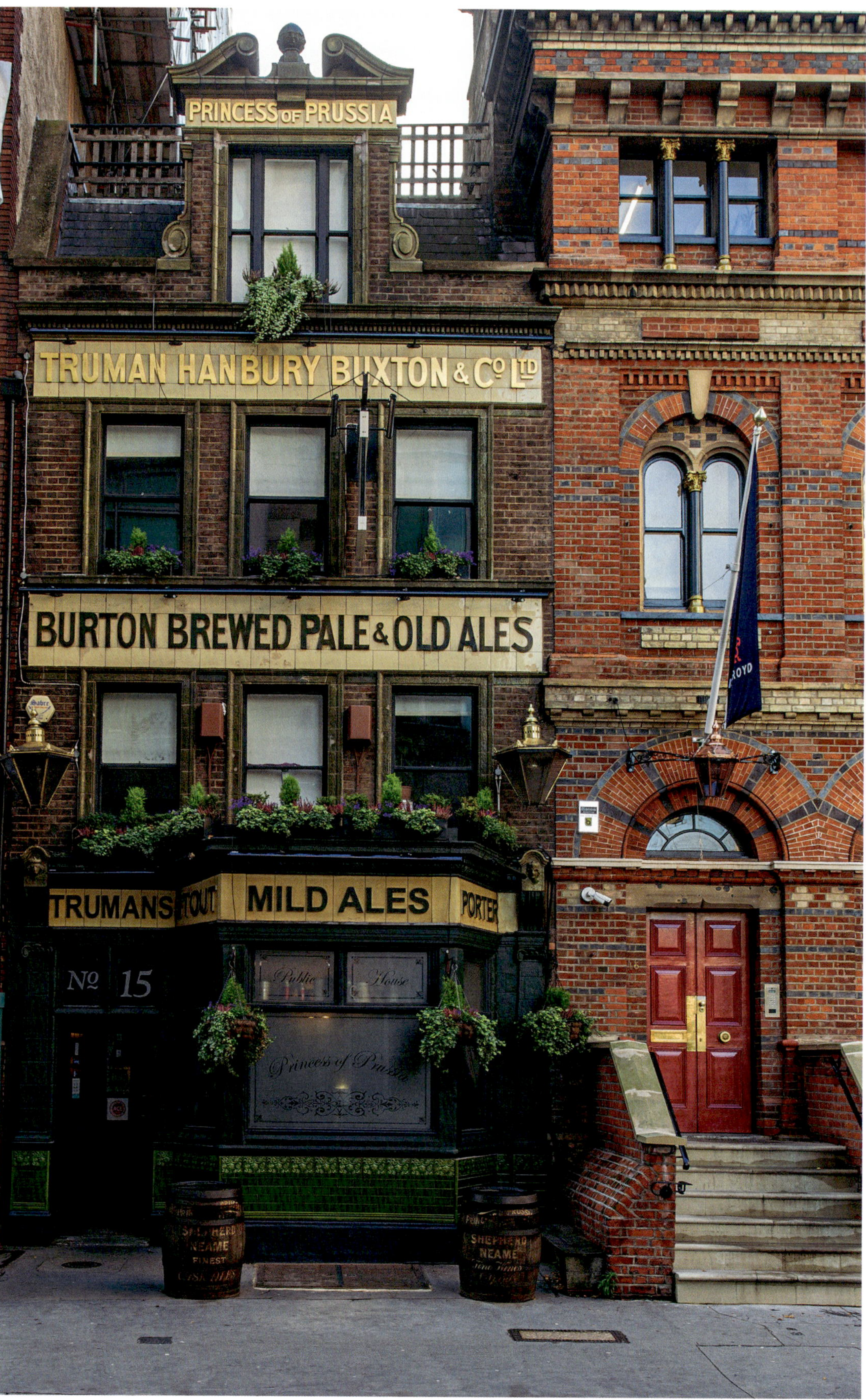

PRINCESS OF PRUSSIA
TRUMAN HANBURY BUXTON & Cº Lᵀᴰ
BURTON BREWED PALE & OLD ALES
TRUMANS STOUT
MILD ALES
PORTER
Nº 15
Public House
Princess of Prussia
SHEPHERD NEAME
SHEPHERD NEAME

PRINCESS OF PRUSSIA

THE PERFECT NIGHT ON THE TILES

Should you judge a book by its cover? A pub from its façade? Looking at all this magnificence, we'd certainly be willing to give it a go. This architectural jewel is reminiscent of a New York townhouse shoehorned in between light industrial warehousing, all loud and proud, with the top-to-bottom Truman's exterior tiling being amongst the finest of its kind. The large sans serif ceramic font allows the pub to deliver exactly what it says on the tin, with the gentle promise of enticing Burton pale ales or pints of mild within.

Tiling was a legacy from the Victorian heyday that continued into the early twenty-first century. Although an expensive finish, these were competitive times for attracting punters through your doors, and such a durable material was a good investment for the big breweries of the day. Tiles also imposed one of the first forms of corporate house style across the urban landscape, and happening upon a tiled Truman pub still brings a moment of joy.

> **As one visitor noted, it's mercifully bereft of "poseurs and gobshites", and for this we can only be truly grateful.**

Once the jaw-dropping curb value has stopped you in your tracks, you'll find a largely unspoilt, two-room Victorian pub, understated ephemera and the added bonus of a secluded beer garden to the rear. The George Orwell "Moon Under Water" bingo card is close to a full house here.

The Princess of Prussia herself had quite the inglorious entry to this world. Queen Victoria, on being informed that her firstborn was a female, simply retorted "Never mind, next time it will be a prince!" But perhaps then we would never have received this most splendid pub…

Rarely passed by accident and not close enough to the high footfall at the Tower of London and St Katharine Docks only a few minutes away, it was probably as rough as old boots when the river porters used to throng here for their libations. But nowadays, people seek it out for a quiet and unfussy pint in traditional surrounds. Generally omitted from guidebooks and missed by the social media vultures, as one visitor noted, it's mercifully bereft of "poseurs and gobshites", and for this we can only be truly grateful. Shepherd Neame pours forth quality brews from the pumps, and traditional good times abound. A leisurely afternoon or night on the tiles has never been more perfect.

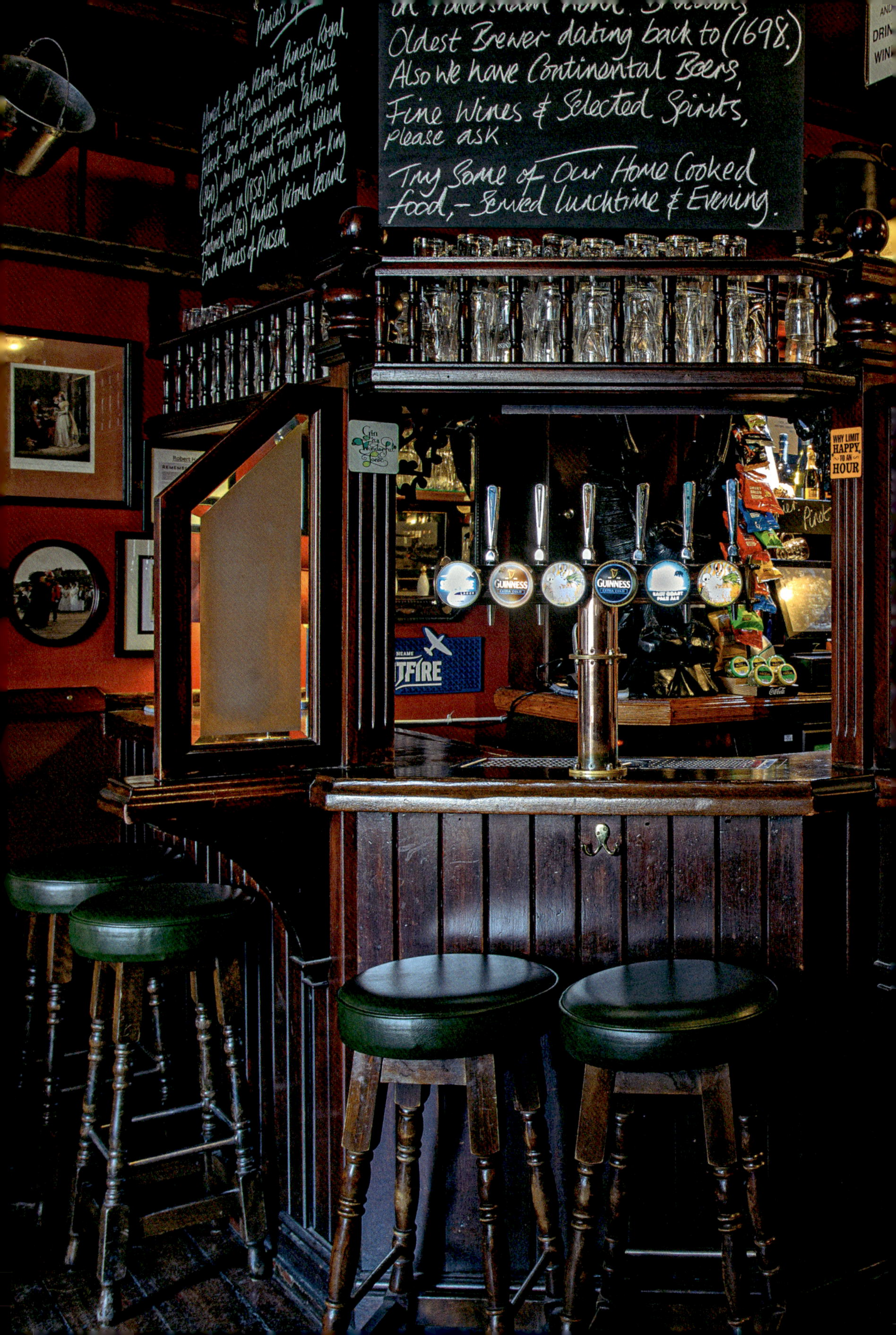

Princess of...
Named So after Victoria Princess Royal, Eldest Child of Queen Victoria & Prince Albert. Born at Buckingham Palace in (1840) who later married Frederick William of Prussia in (1858.) On the death of King Frederick in (1861) Princess Victoria became Crown Princess of Prussia.
...in Faversham Kent, Britains Oldest Brewer dating back to (1698.) Also we have Continental Beers, Fine Wines & Selected Spirits, please ask.
Try Some of Our Home Cooked food, - Served Lunchtime & Evening.
Gin is a Wonderful Tonic
WHY LIMIT HAPPY TO AN HOUR
GUINNESS EXTRA COLD
SPITFIRE

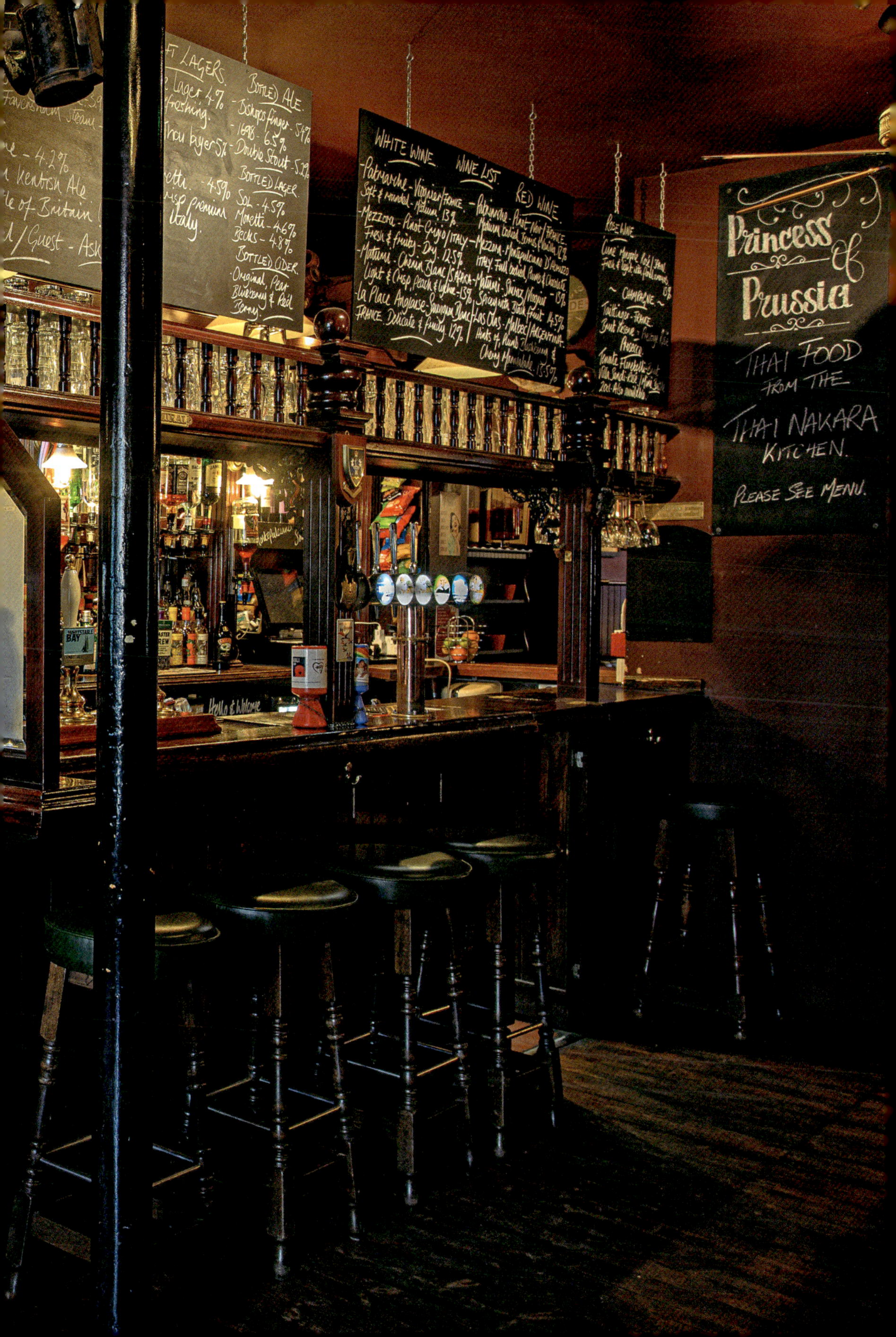

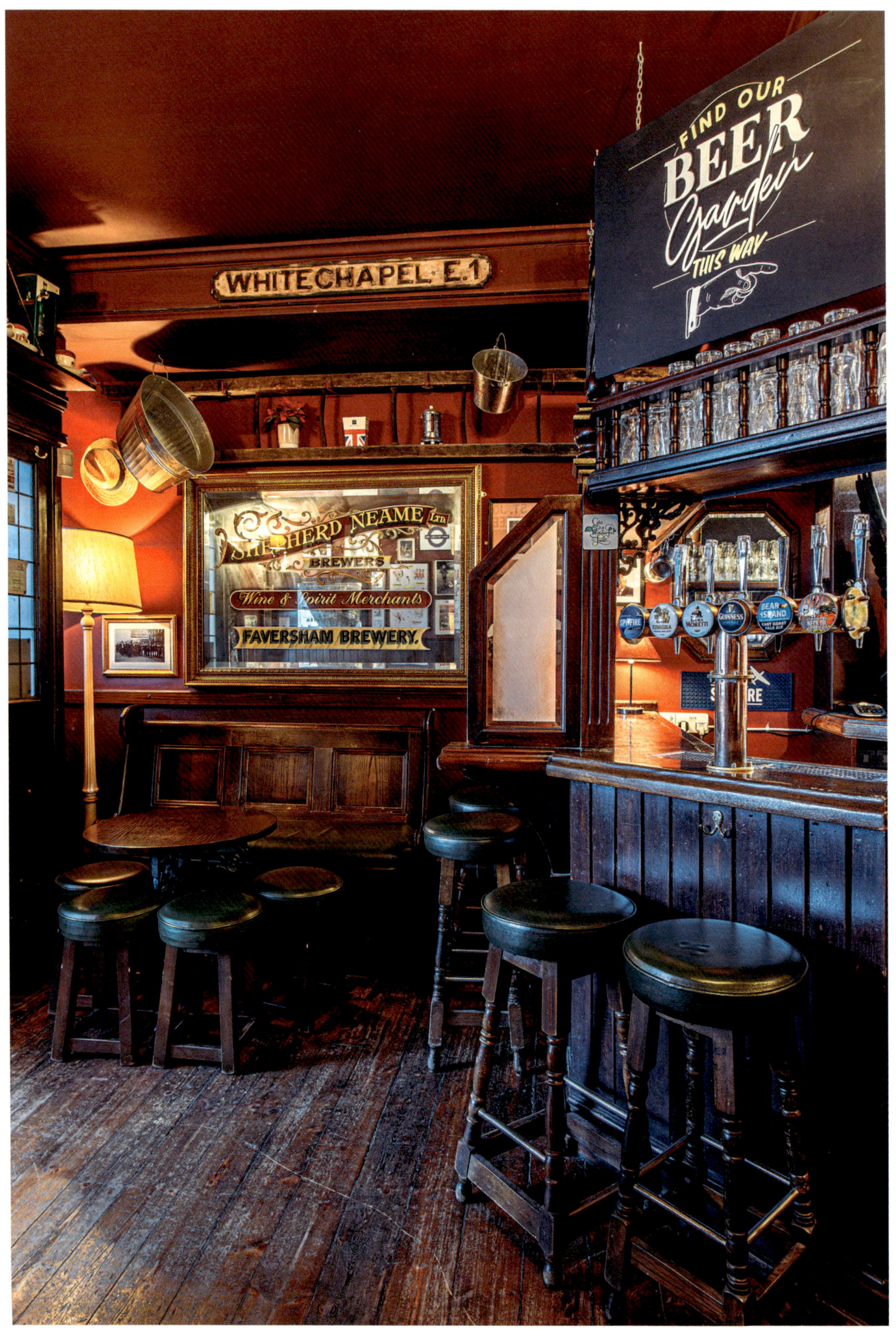

Simple pub pleasures far from the maddening crowds

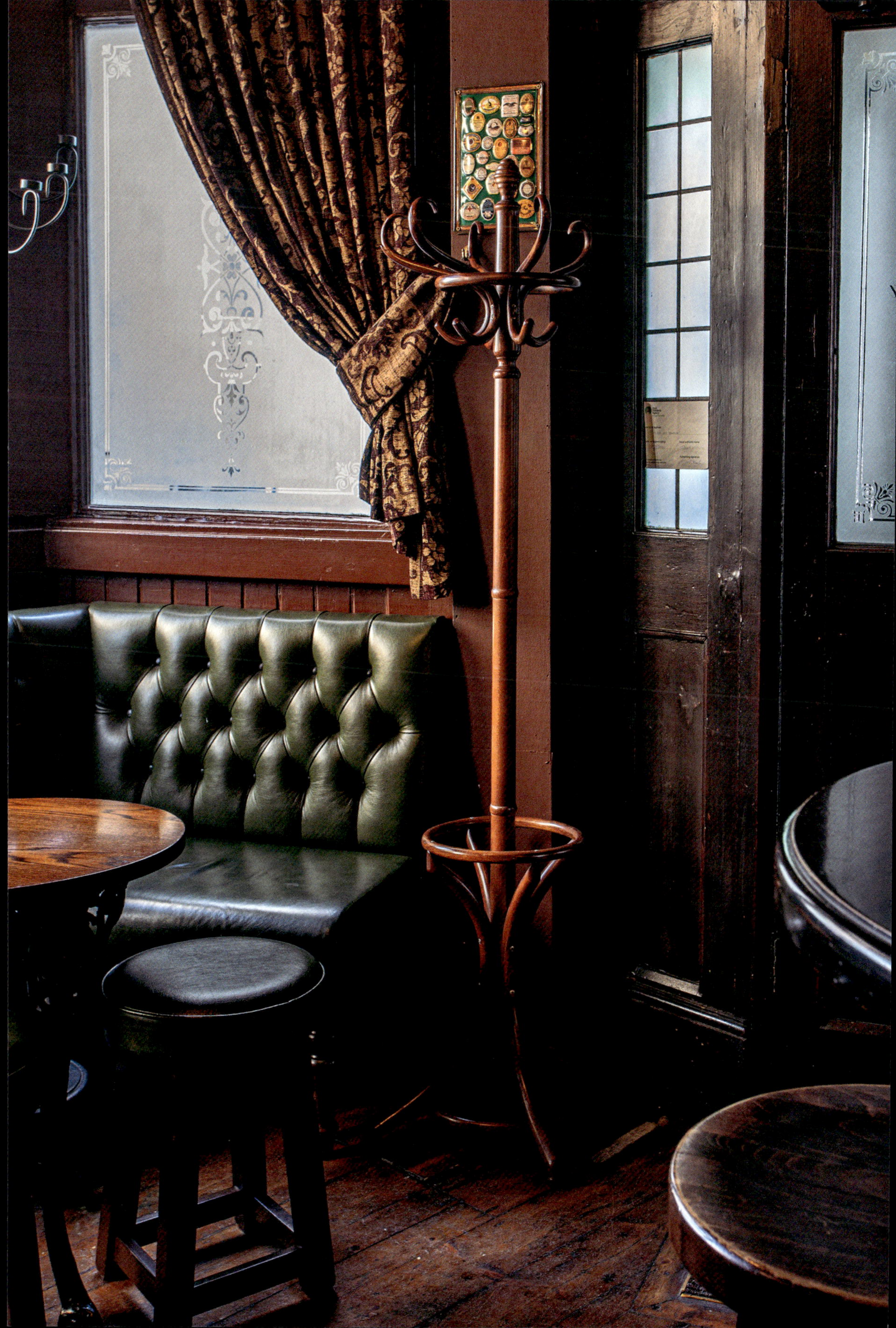

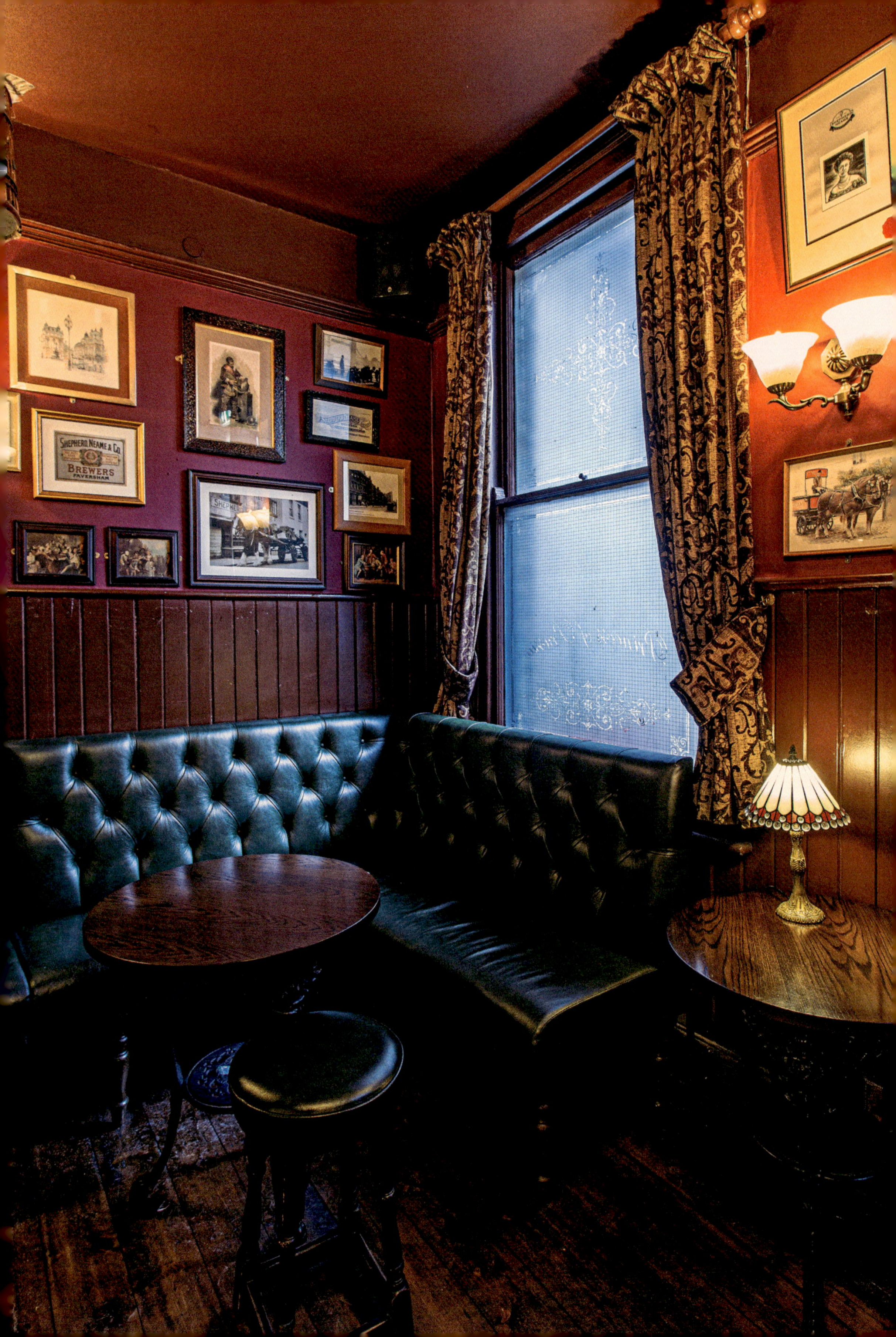

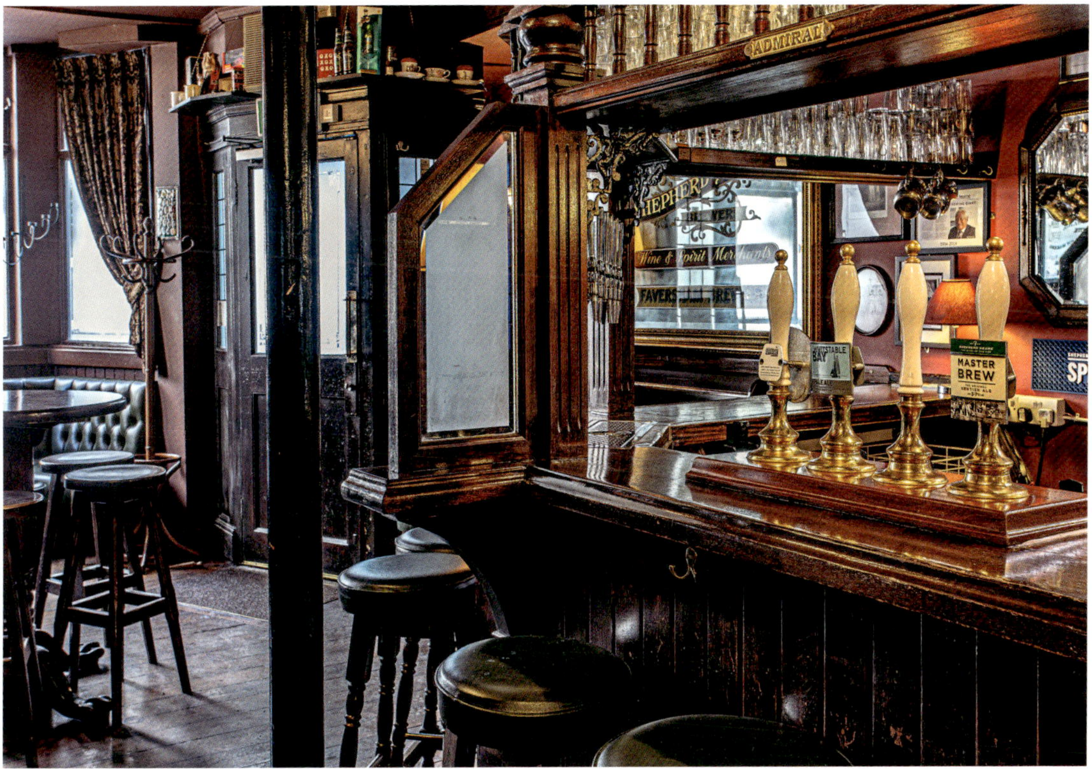

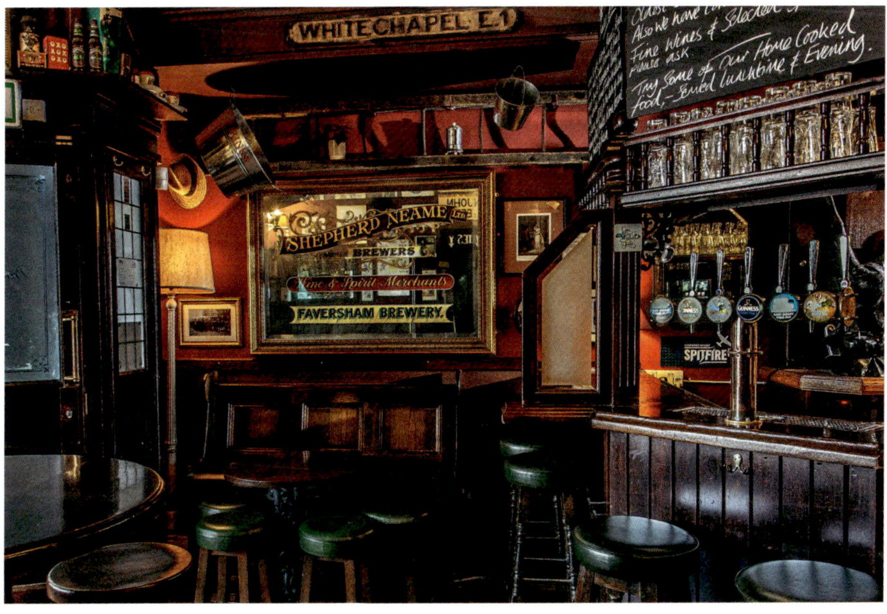

... a secluded beer garden awaits you to the rear

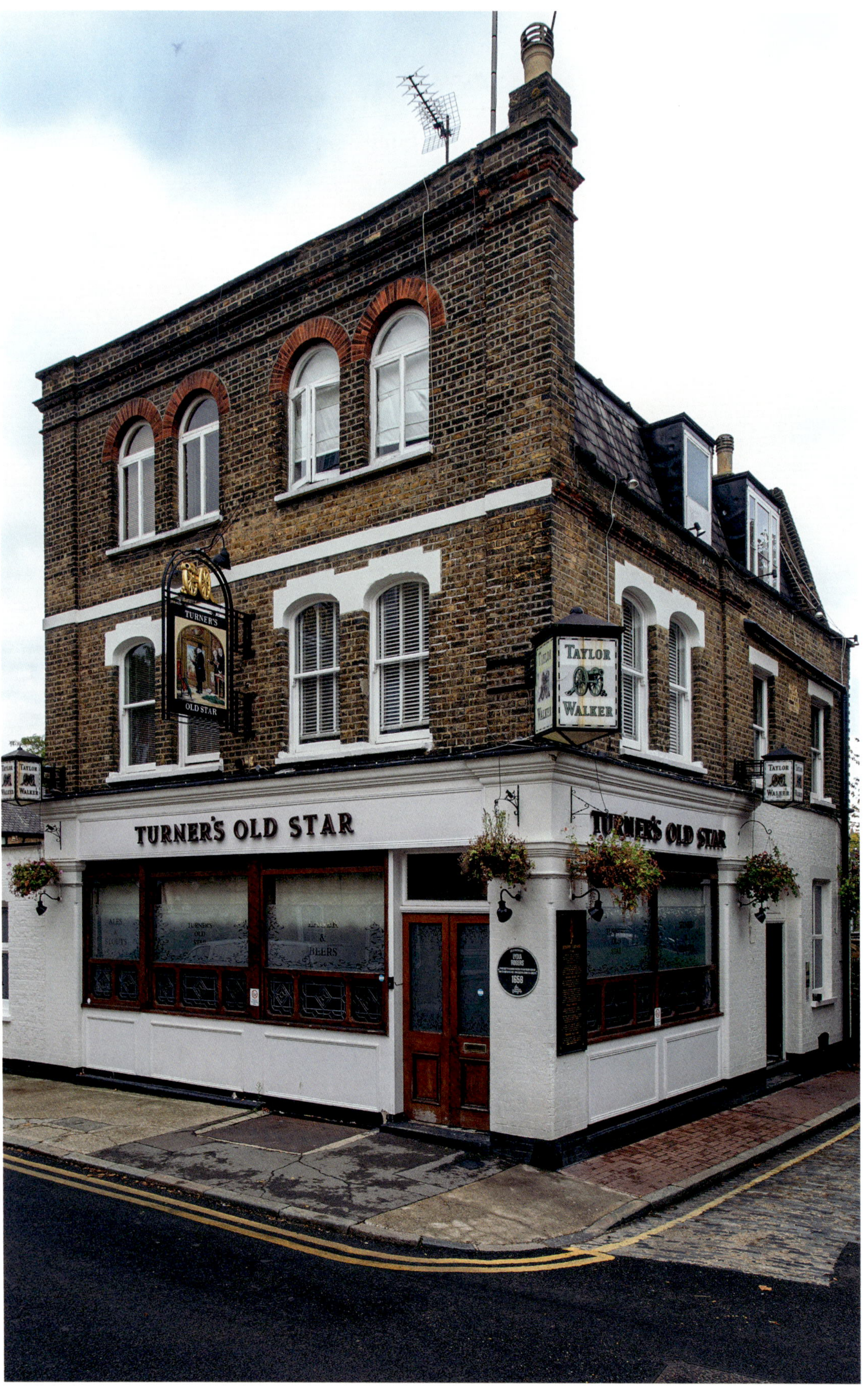
TURNER'S
OLD STAR
TAYLOR
WALKER
TAYLOR
WALKER
TAYLOR
WALKER
TURNER'S OLD STAR
TURNER'S OLD STAR

TURNER'S OLD STAR

Wapping is not short of world-famous pubs. This timeless curve in the Thames has hosted a wild band of pirates, pilgrims and press-gangs over the centuries. Modern-day travellers flock here to drink in the history at these waterside taverns. The light certainly dances in mystical ways here, but the artist J. M. W. Turner was drawn here for its darker side. He bought this pub for one of his mistresses and would visit at the weekend to escape his West London high life for a bit of low-life East London lovin'.

Take one step back from the water and it's a whole different world. No longer commanding riverside views or nosebleed price tags, this is the real Wapping and a fast-disappearing vignette of East London. Pass the chippie and cross Wapping Green to find a real pub run for a real community.

It's a handsome beast with Taylor Walker lanterns dangling like Angie Watts's earrings from every corner. Step inside and you might expect a few death stares from territorial locals or a re-enactment of the seminal Krays dust-up filmed here for the *Legend* biopic, but you'll receive the exact opposite. Greeted by one of the widest smiles in showbiz from Paul or his missus Bernice, all are welcomed warmly to their manor. These are genuine, sparkly-eyed, salt-of-the-earth types. Spend a few minutes in their upbeat company and you'll start hoping they might consider adopting you.

There are no trendy beers to tempt the itinerant drinker. They stick to what they know best and what their punters love. Crowd-pleasing cask, keg and Guinness keep the decision simple at below-average prices. You can order pie and chips if you missed their belt-busting breakfast. Then just take a pew and let the easy-going banter begin. TV sports, karaoke nights, quizzes and pool leagues complete the rhythm for the week. Escape to the secret beer garden if you must.

It's all no-frills, family-orientated fun, filled rolls and fancy dress. Hearts are worn proudly on the sleeve, so when England are playing or the monarch is having a moment, they'll fly the flag for a right old-fashioned knees-up. For those wishing to see J. M. W. Turner's true masterpiece, head not for the National Gallery but his salacious stomping ground down Wapping way for a nailed-on stellar time at his one-time true "darling".

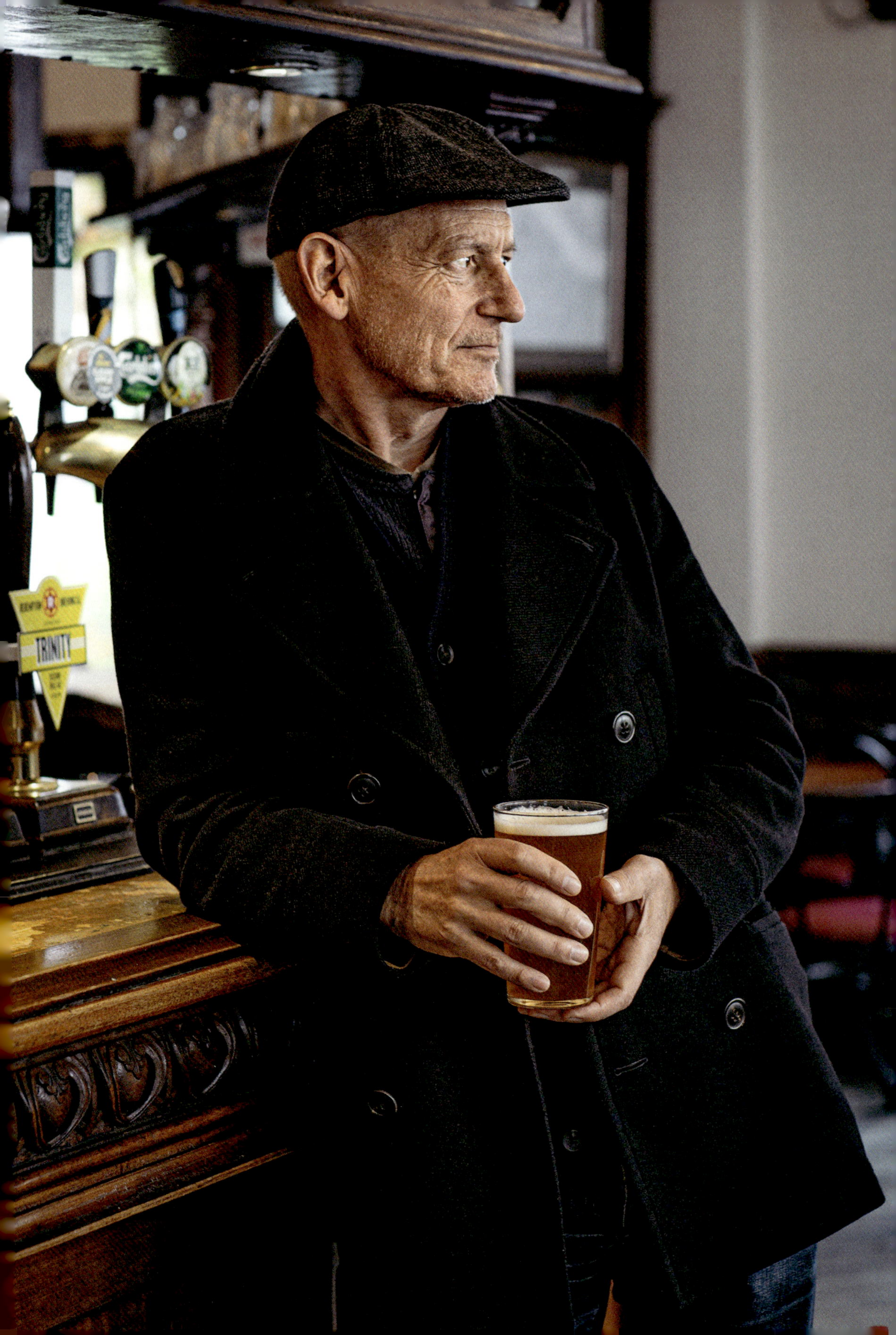

TRINITY

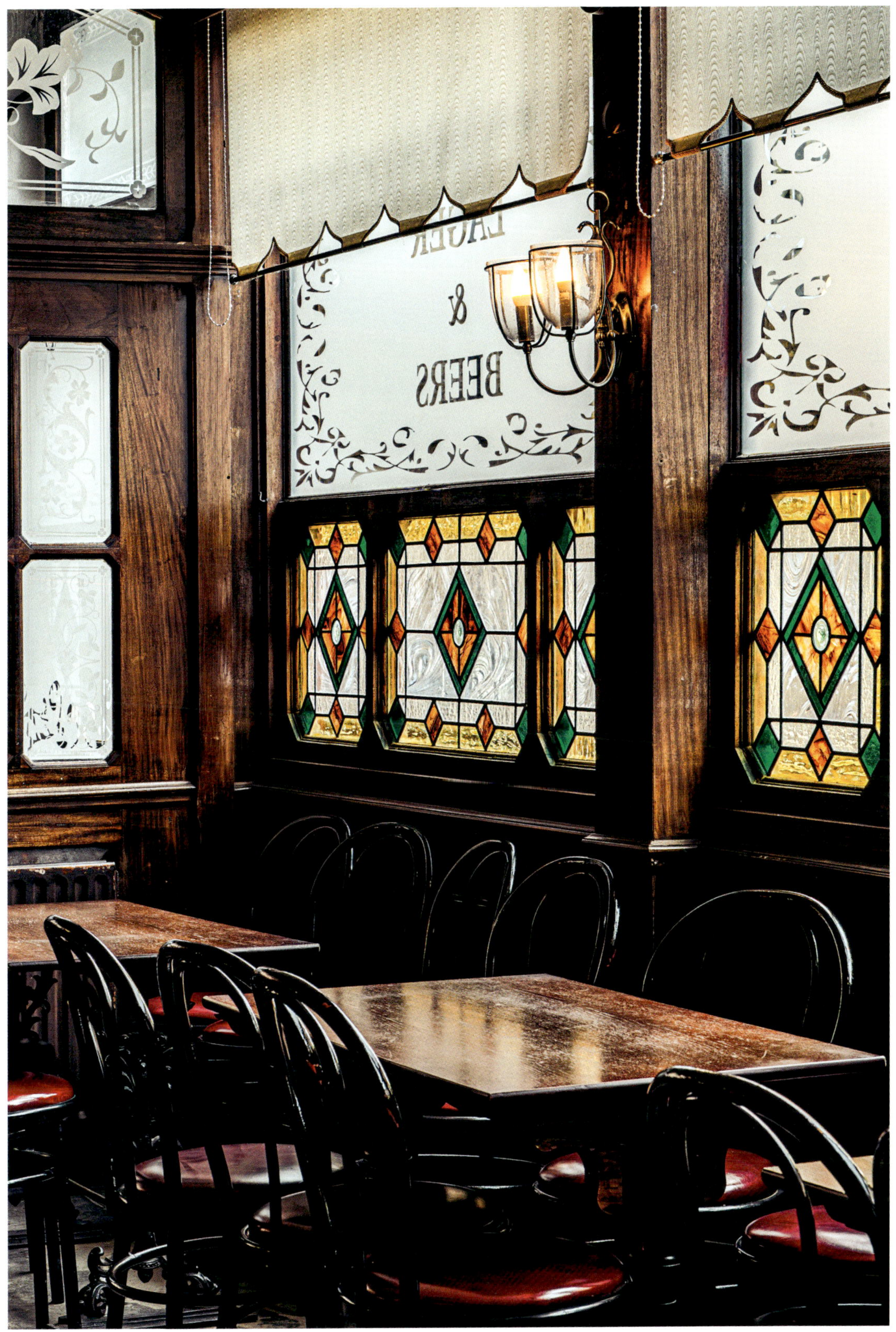

Welcome to Wapping's finest

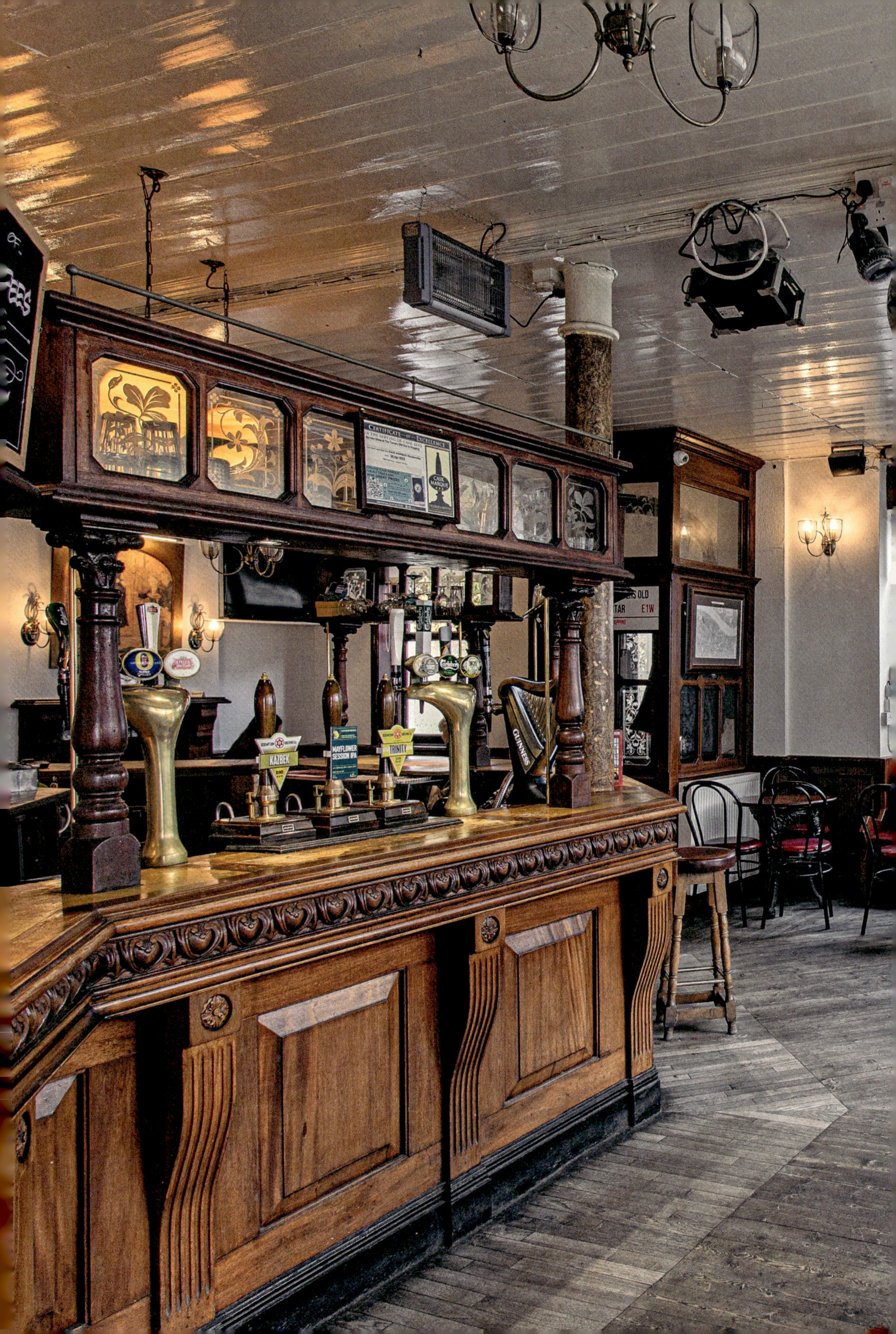

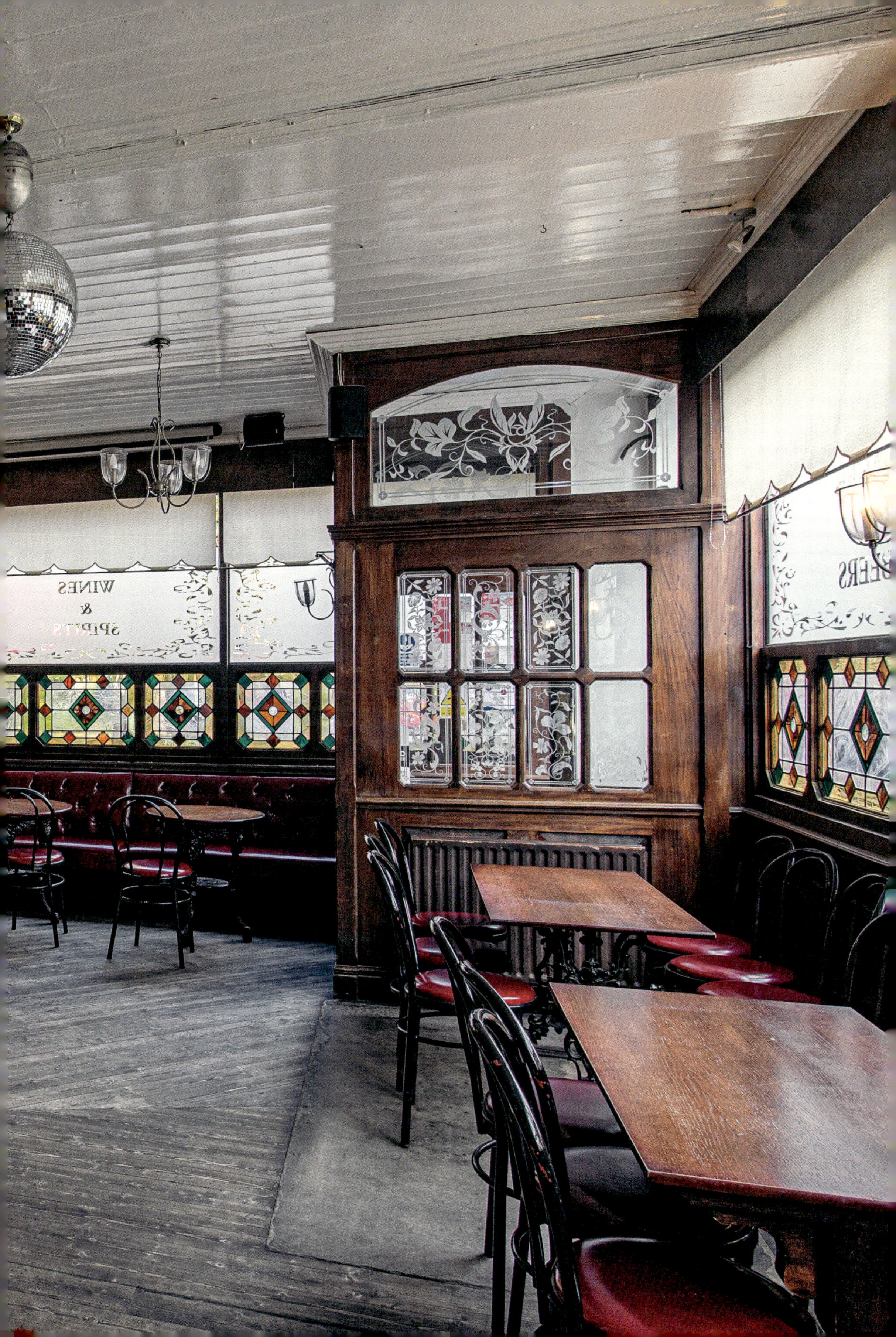

WINES
&
SPIRITS
BEERS

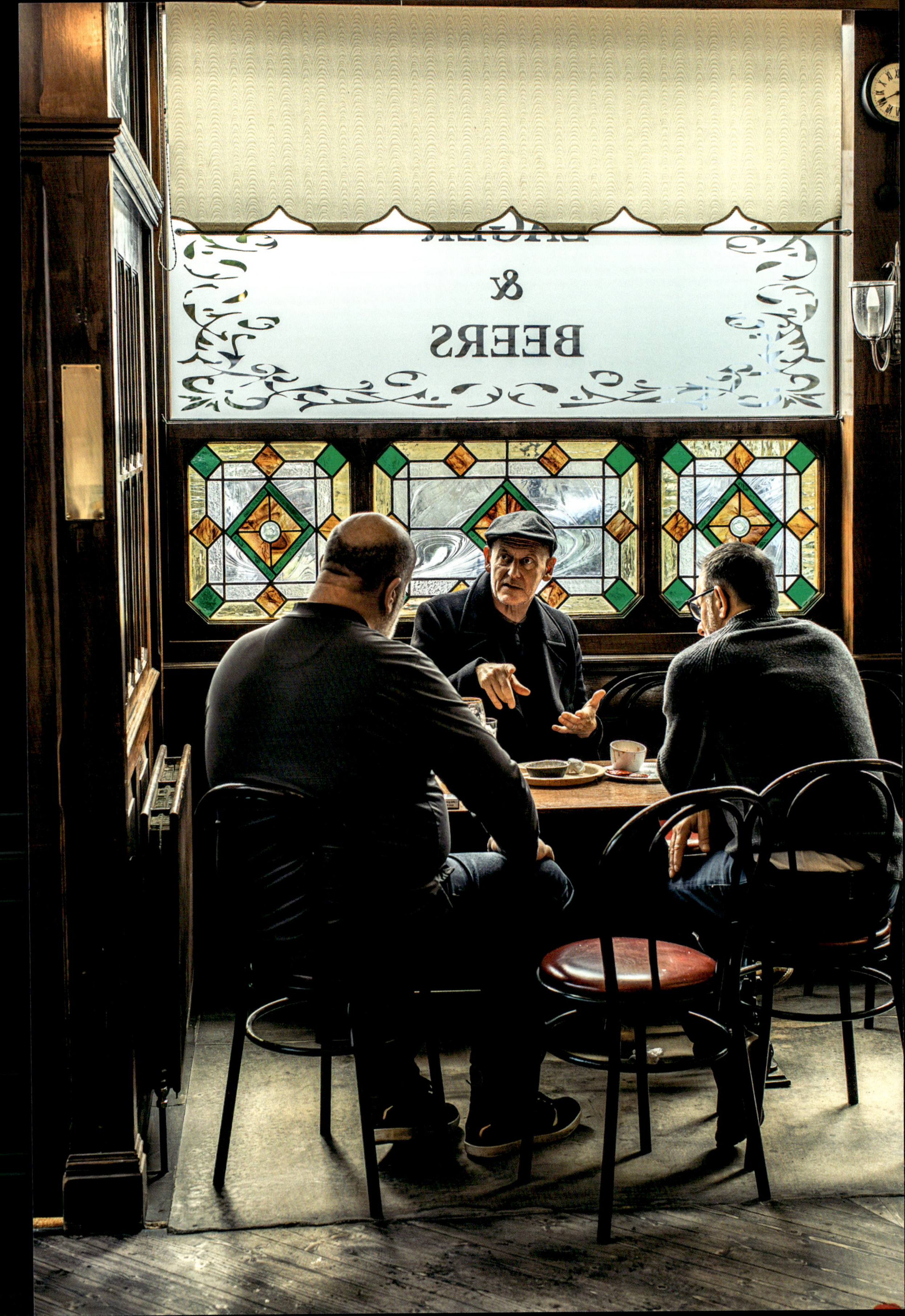
LAGER
&
BEERS

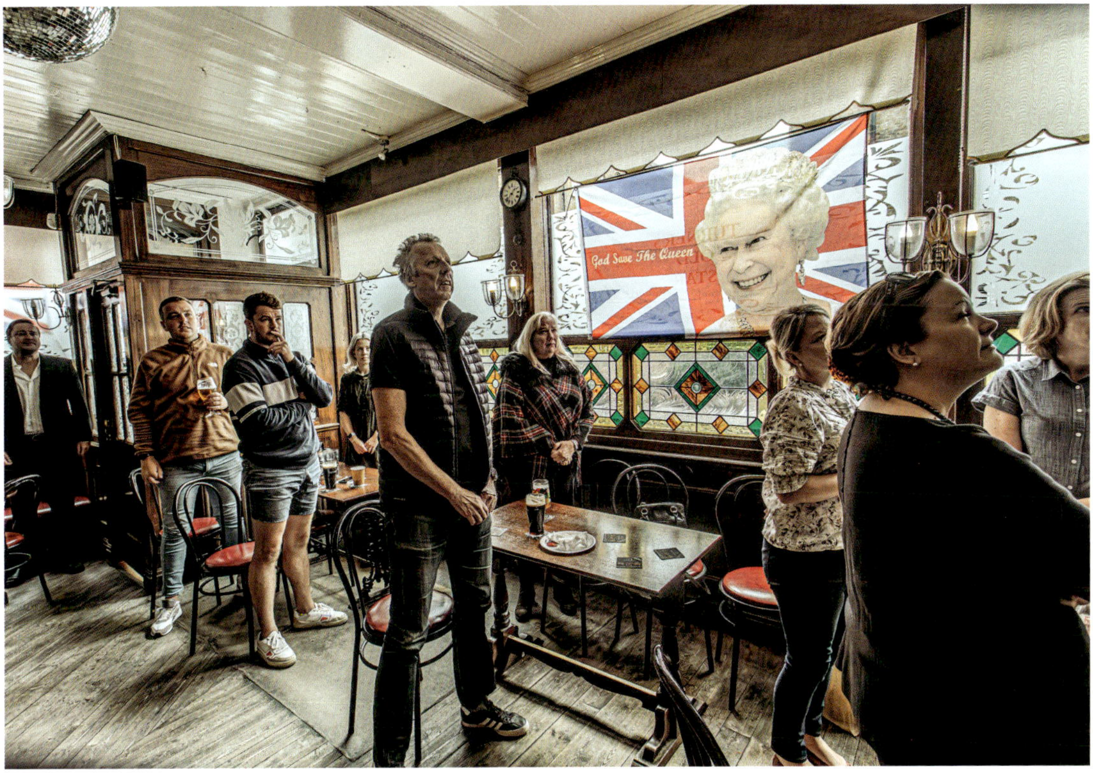

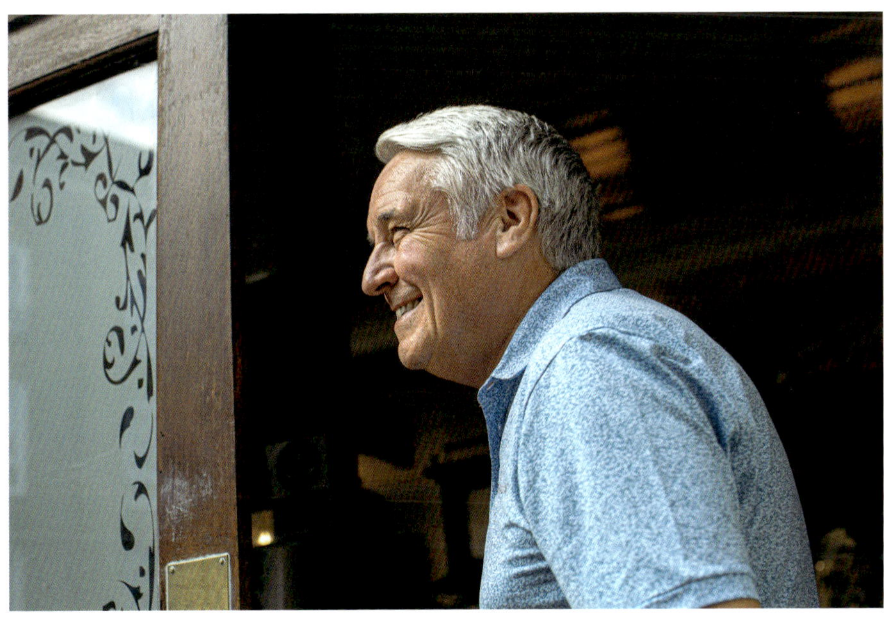

An ever-sparkly-eyed welcome from the guvnor

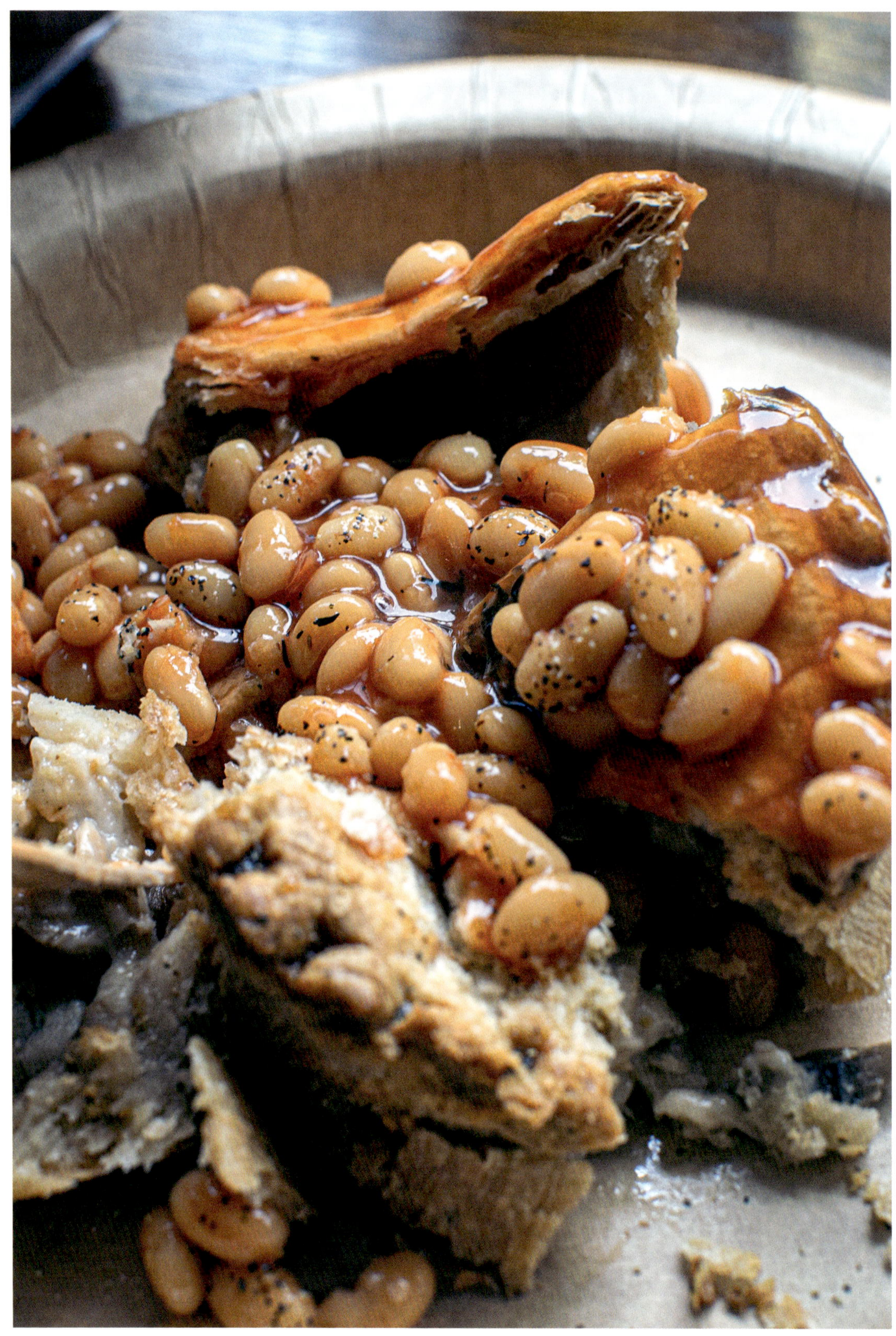

Oozing with East End charm

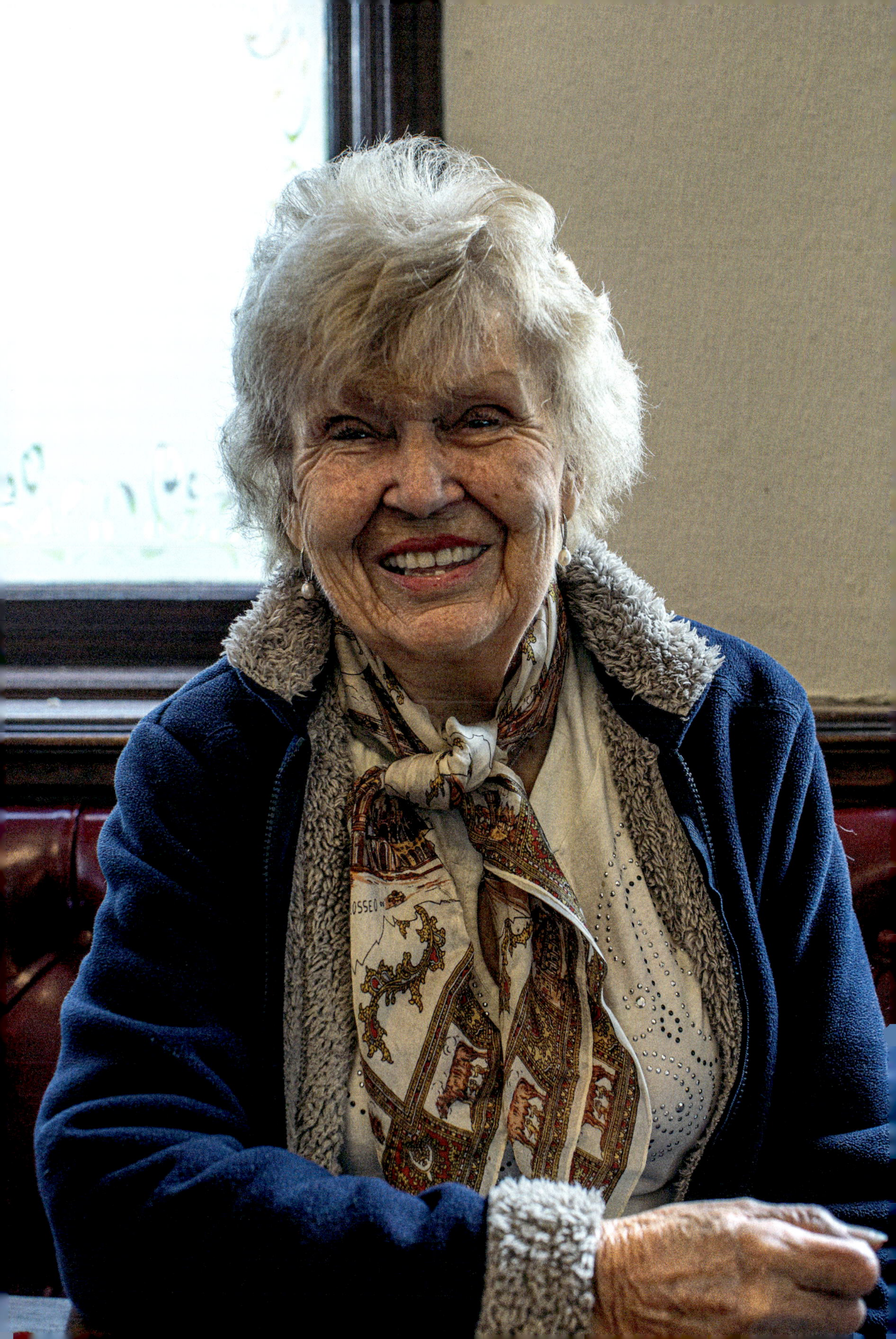

THE AULD SHILLELAGH

Crisps. They're a tricky subject down the pub. Die-hard crunchers suggest that you should look no further than a lightly salted varietal. The salt is an acceptable gateway drug to the full potatoey hit, and to mask this simple starch in a new-fangled flavour is a simple no-no. The role of the humble crisp is to provide simple refuge from the early pangs of hunger but to not interfere with the main liquid attractions. Beer can be a delicate thing, so there's often little desire to muddy the subtle hop-fuggled pleasures.

So, if you're the landlord of what the *Irish Times* calls the "Most authentic Irish pub in the world outside Ireland", then you'd better get the crisp selection right. For that, there can only be one choice: the mighty Tayto. The true taste of home. The ultimate tabletop tear and share. A brand so strong for the roaming Irish diaspora that the word "Taytos" is synonymous with crisps in Ireland. The fictional figurehead and mainstay mascot Mr Tayto has run as a candidate in the general election, released a best-selling autobiography and even had a theme park named in his honour. It's a cultural phenomenon of a crisp.

To get the true taste of Ireland, urban legend states that the landlording Leydon brothers have been known to import the real-deal Taytos directly from the Republic. Drinkers even bring their own white-sliced loaf and Kerrygold Irish Butter to the bar to create the seminal snack that is the classic cheese and onion Tayto crisp sandwich.

Just imagine how good the Guinness is going to be if they take their crisp game this seriously. From the vintage black stuff bar fonts to a classically two-stage poured pint of plain with obligatory domed head, it's a resolutely Irish pub. The service is swift, and the pumps pour like fury when the hurling or Gaelic football finals are on.

Tomás Leydon was a mere seventeen years old when he joined his brother Aonghus at The Auld Shillelagh, and Stoke Newington was a very different place in the early nineties. For over thirty years now the brothers from Roscommon have provided fine hospitality both to homesick Irish and the rest of the world looking to enjoy a warm welcome, a cracking pint and, of course, plenty of craic. And the order of the day? Two pints of Guinness and a packet of Taytos...

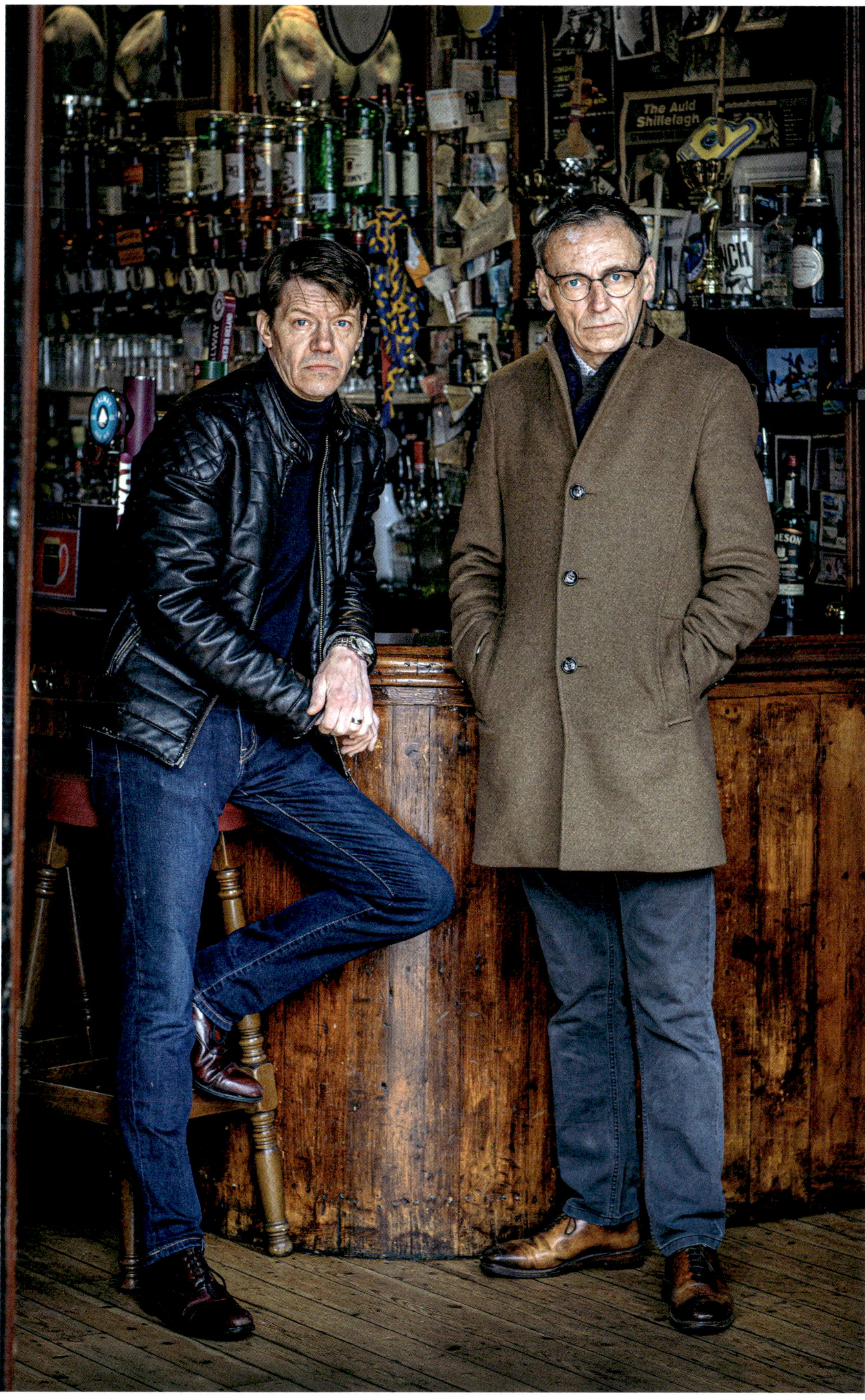

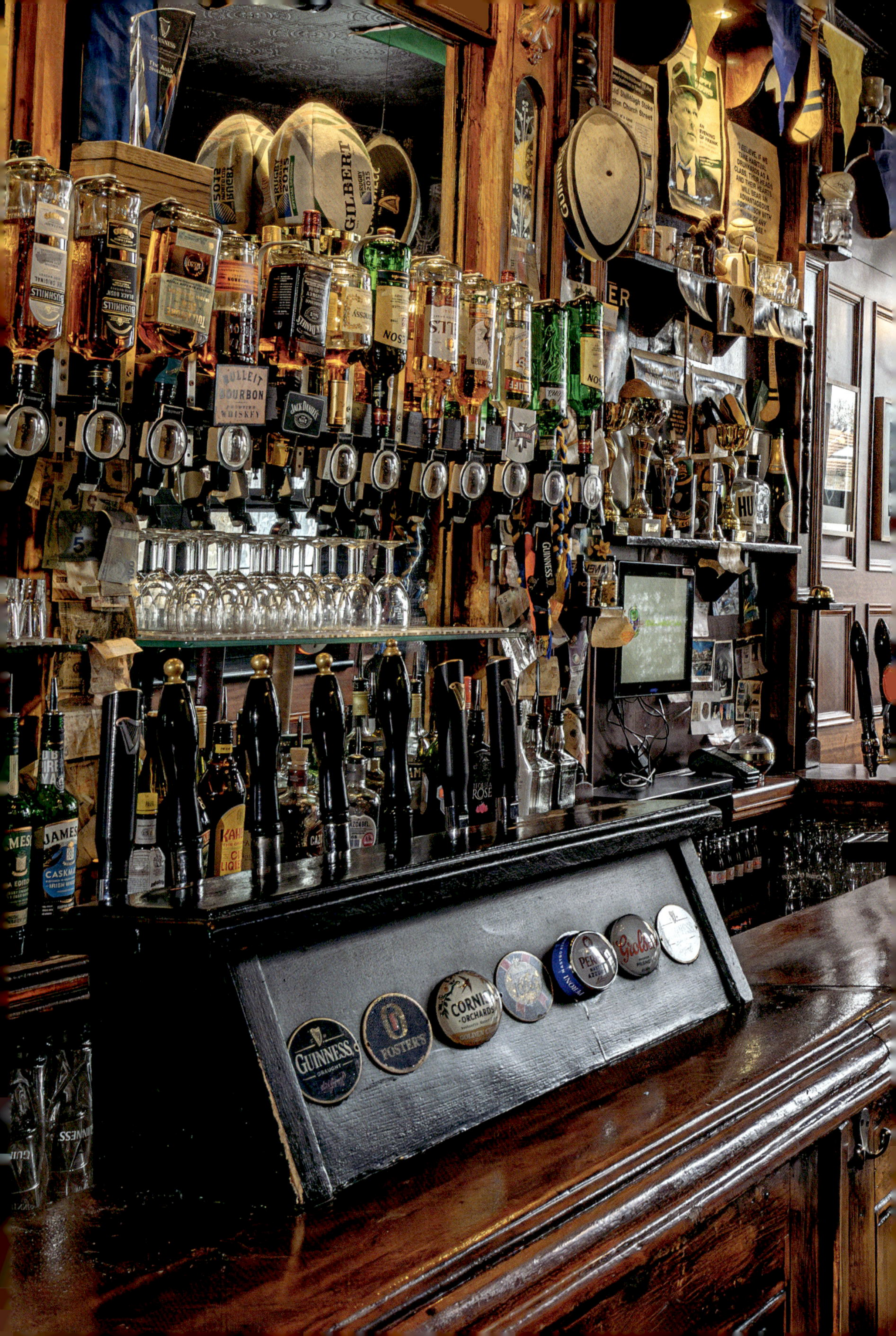

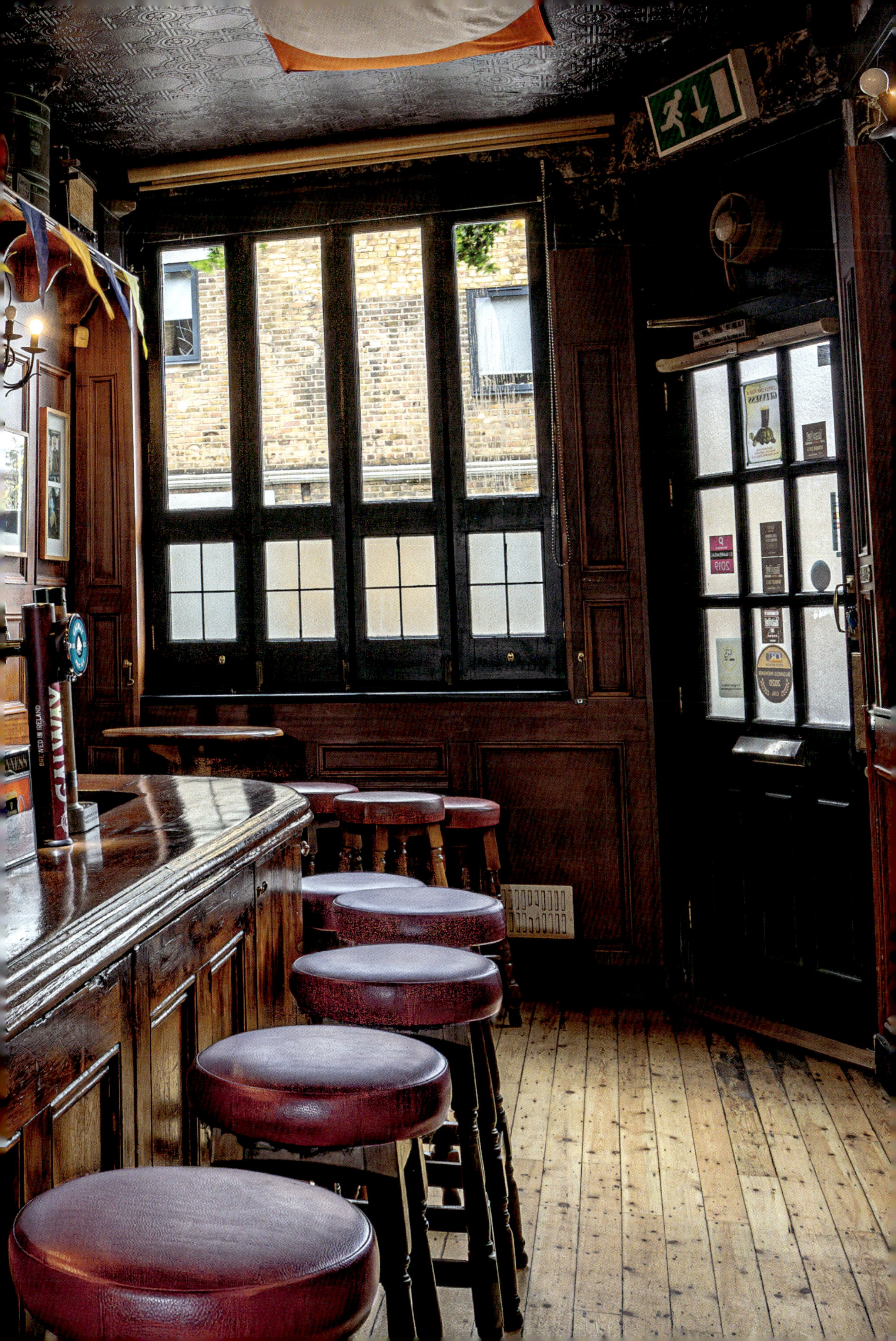

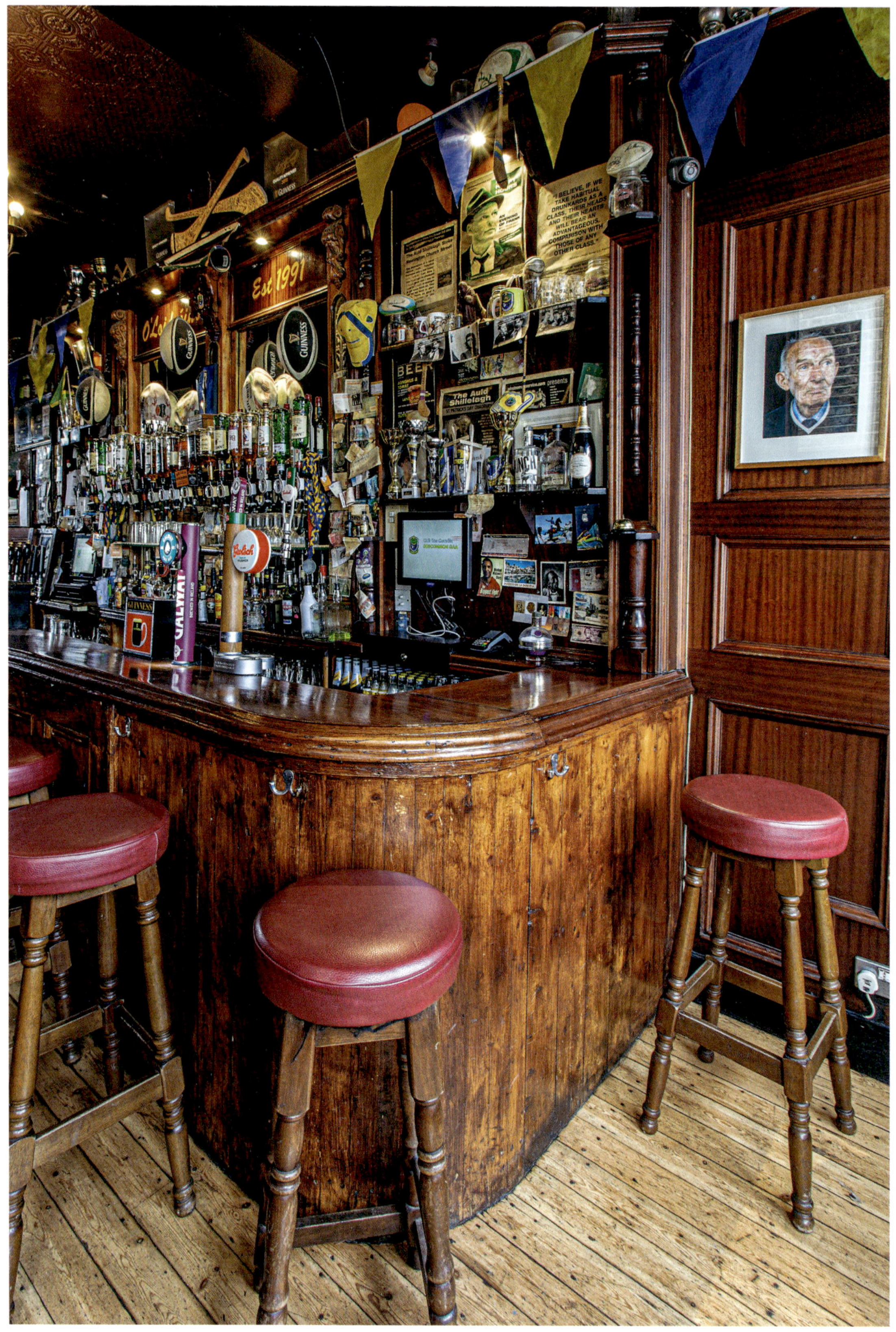

Get ready for the craic

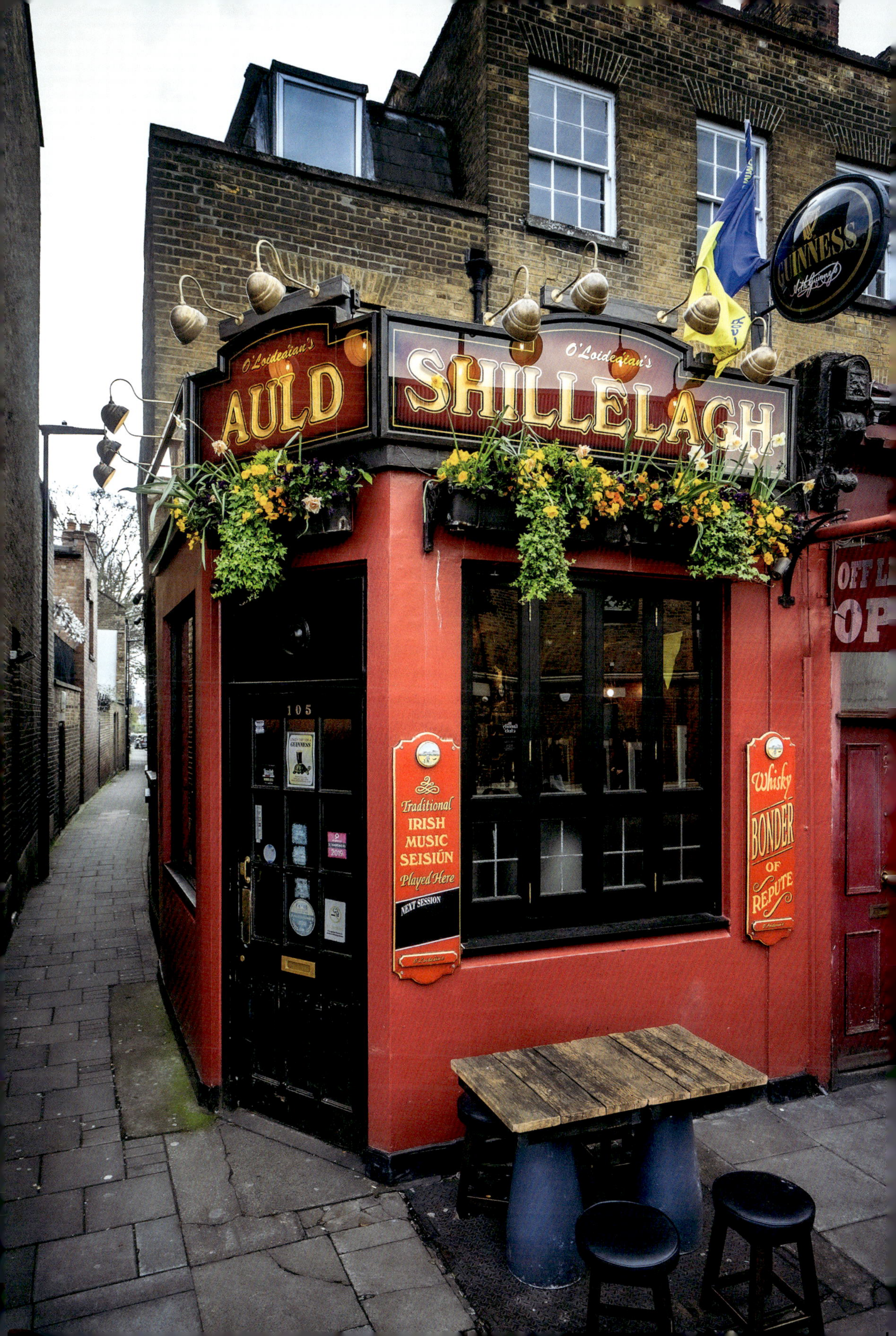
O'Loideáin's
AULD
O'Loideáin's
SHILLELAGH
GUINNESS
105
Traditional
IRISH
MUSIC
SEISIÚN
Played Here
NEXT SESSION
Whisky
BONDER
OF
REPUTE
OFF L
OP

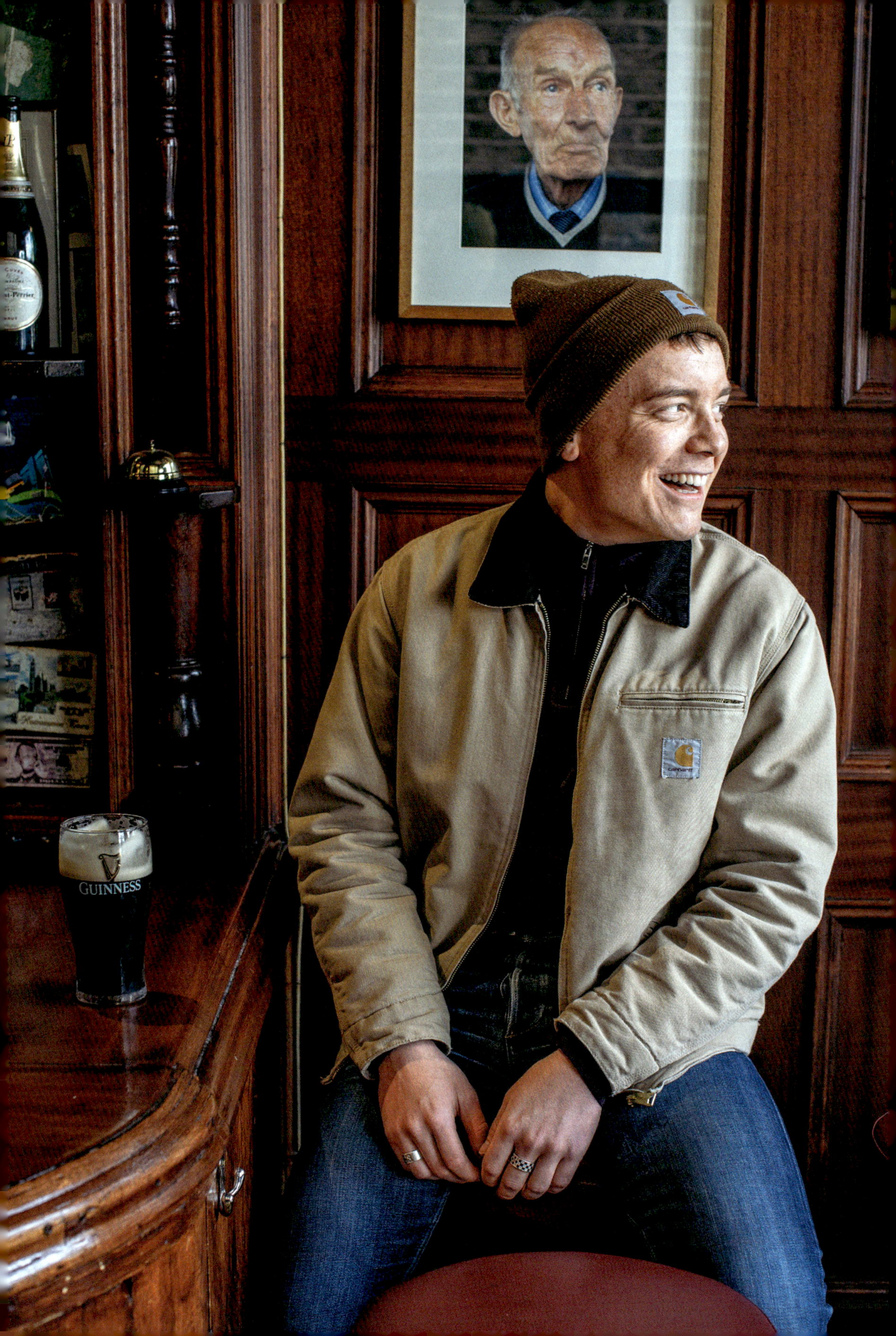

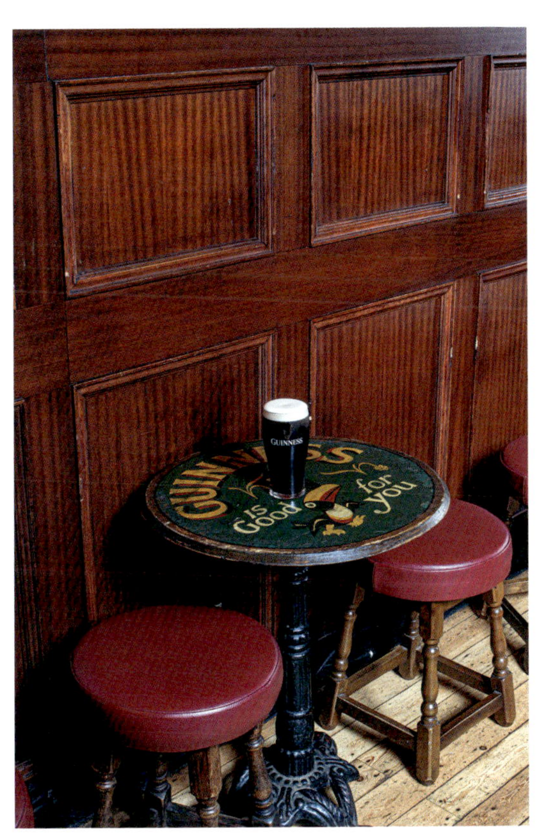

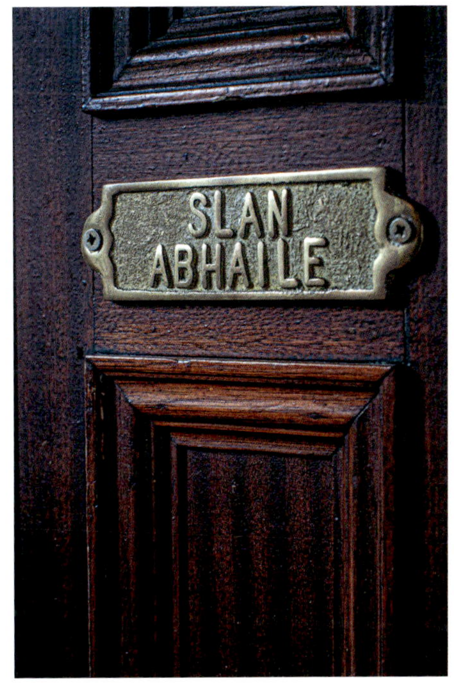

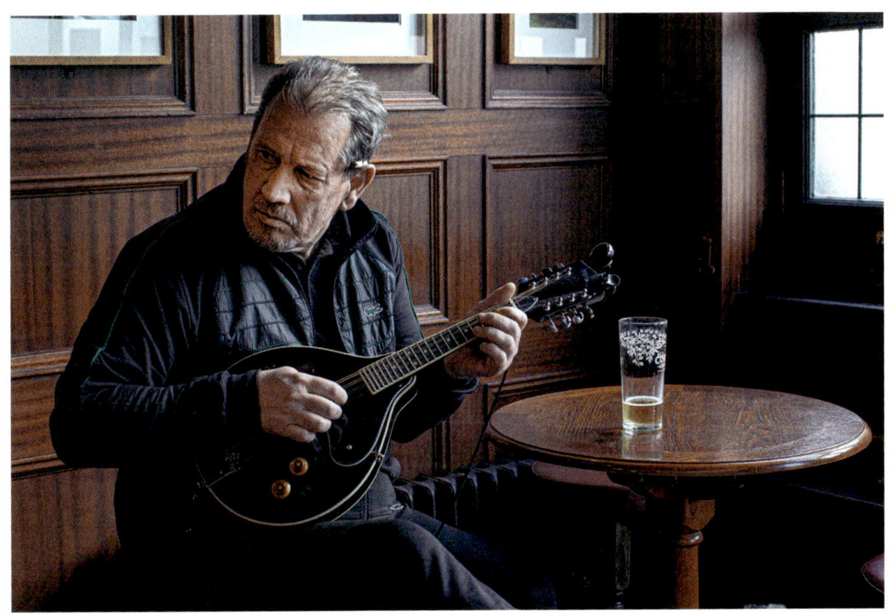

Home is where the harp is

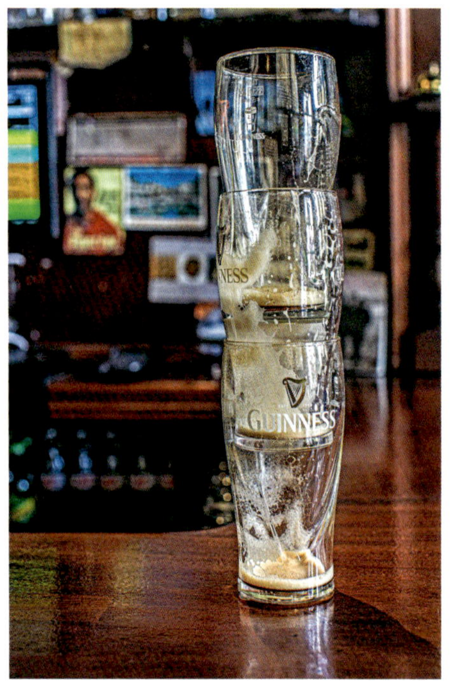

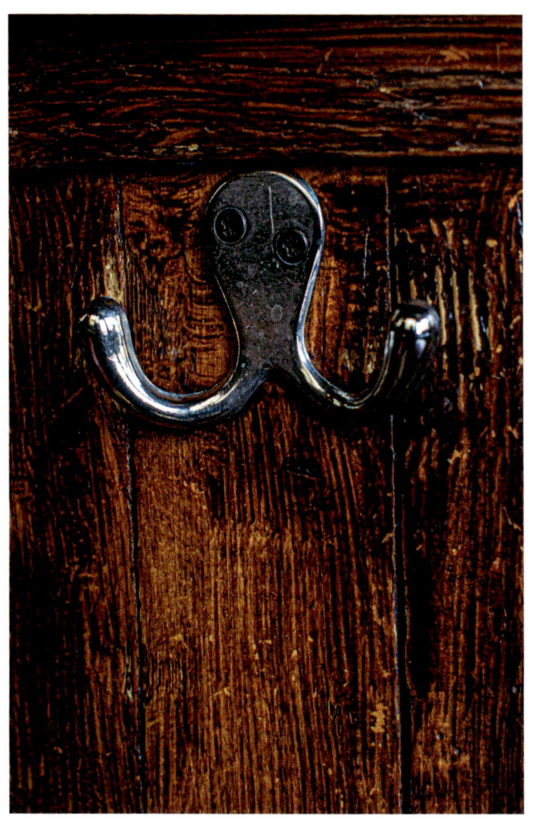

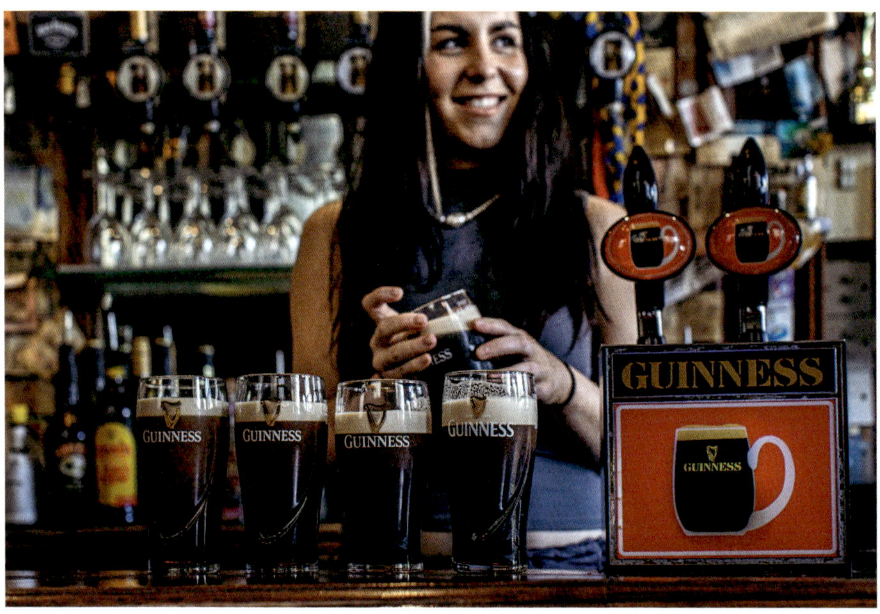

Omnipresent pints of plain line the ramp

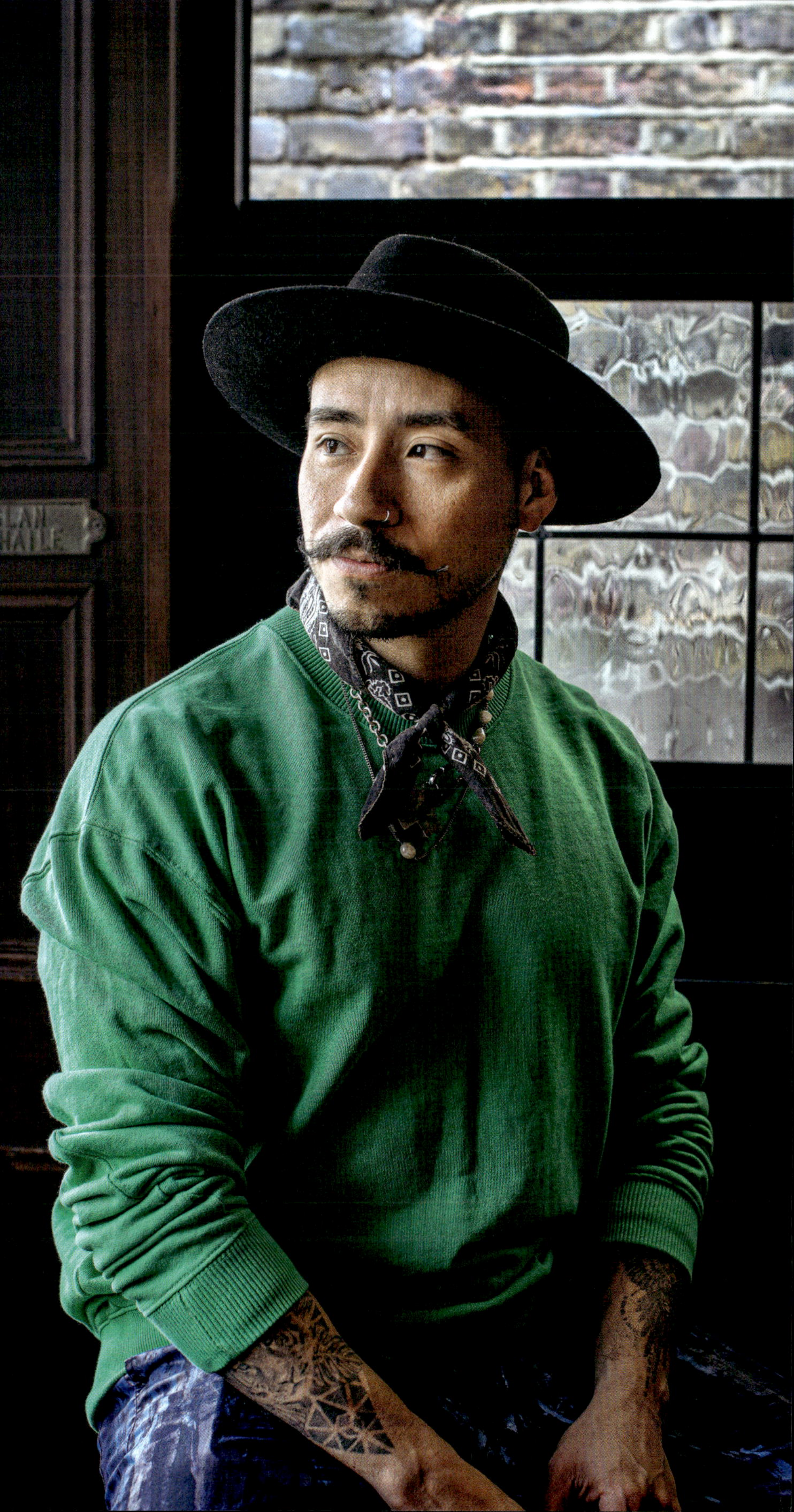

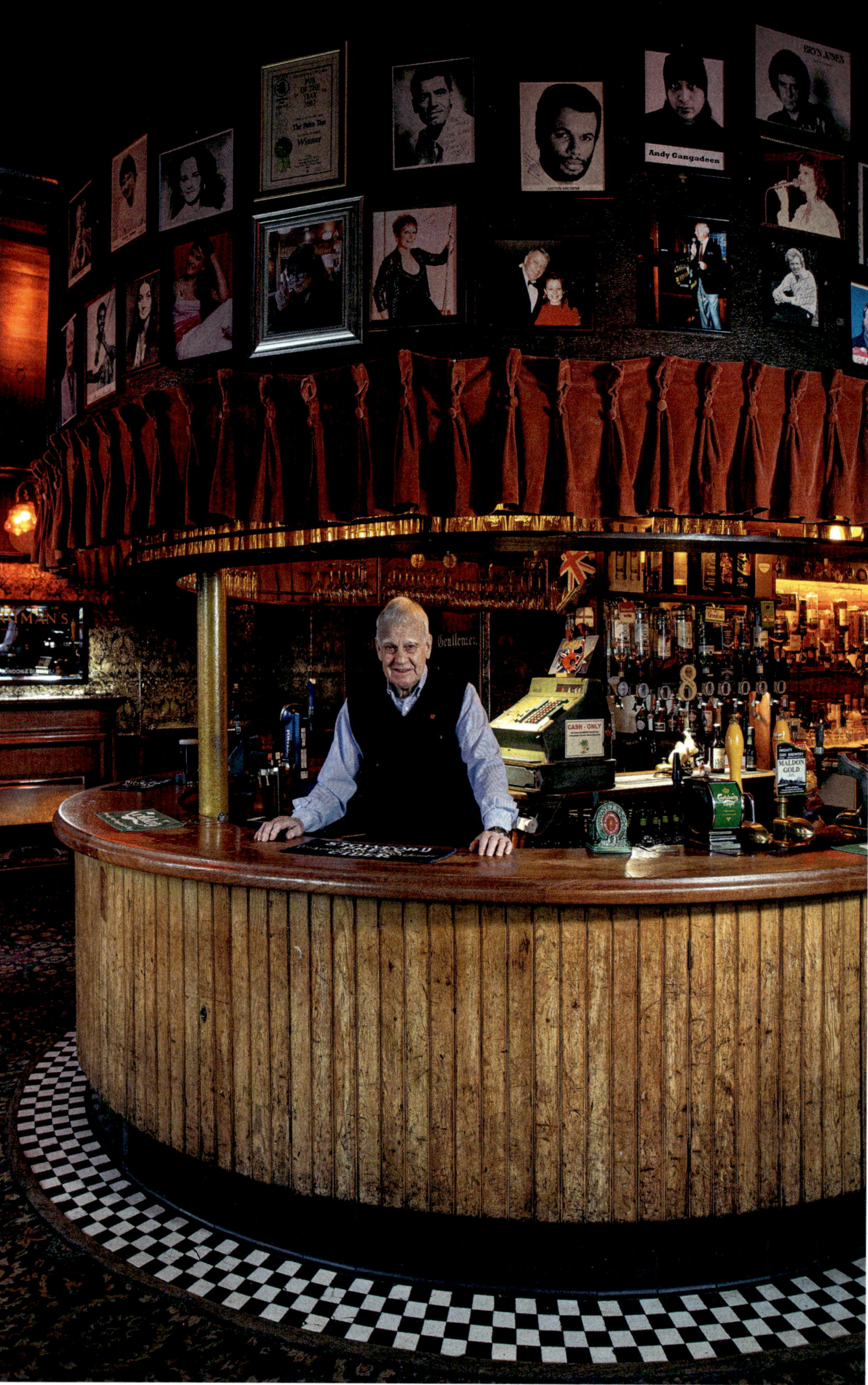

THE PALM TREE

127 GROVE RD, BOW E3 5BH

The Palm Tree is famously cash-only, and this is a beautiful thing. At worst, consider it an inconvenient conversation starter. Contactless checkout certainly has its place in the modern world, but you've entered a 1970s twilight zone here. So, make sure you come loaded with a healthy roll of Lady Godivas or Ayrton Sennas. It's a lonely trudge of shame to the nearest ATM. And you'll be thirsty by the time you make it back to the pub, but don't ask for a glass of water. "It's pumped straight from the canal" will come the retort, and then you'll be charged for the pleasure. Don't phone Trading Standards. Just send over the spondoolies for a simple drink priced on the higher side of random. Libations shall be poured and the ancient till register shall finally ring out, often swiftly followed by the incorrect change. Don't worry, you won't even blink, as just coming here means that you're quids-in already.

Welcome to 1977! This is the year that Val (RIP) and Alf moved in and they have successfully held the barbarian progressive world at bay ever since. One wonders if Alf even knows that James Callaghan is no longer in office and that we entered the European Union, let alone left it? It matters not, for this is Alf's anachronistic kingdom. Master and commander of all this red-hued majesty. Quiet daytime pints taken canal-side are replaced by more up-tempo evening sessions. Whilst the back bar accumulates the locals and arrow throwers, the front bar has hosted some of the best jazz singers and performers over the last forty years. No tickets or entrance fee required, just throw some brass behind the oval bar and get those toes a-tapping. These are genuinely old-timers sharing their craft, perfected right here over the past decade or two. Flirtatious octogenarians know how to get the party started, and with no NIMBY neighbours nearby, the band plays on into the night.

It's hard to imagine Mile End without The Palm Tree, and even harder to imagine The Palm Tree without Alf. You somehow miss him before he's even cashed out. The day that The Palm Tree accepts card payments and the till at The Palm Tree no longer rings, will be a loss to London. A pub that survived bombing raids, demolition and encircling gentrification. The ravens might as well flee the Tower, for Alf's old-world kingdom shall have fallen.

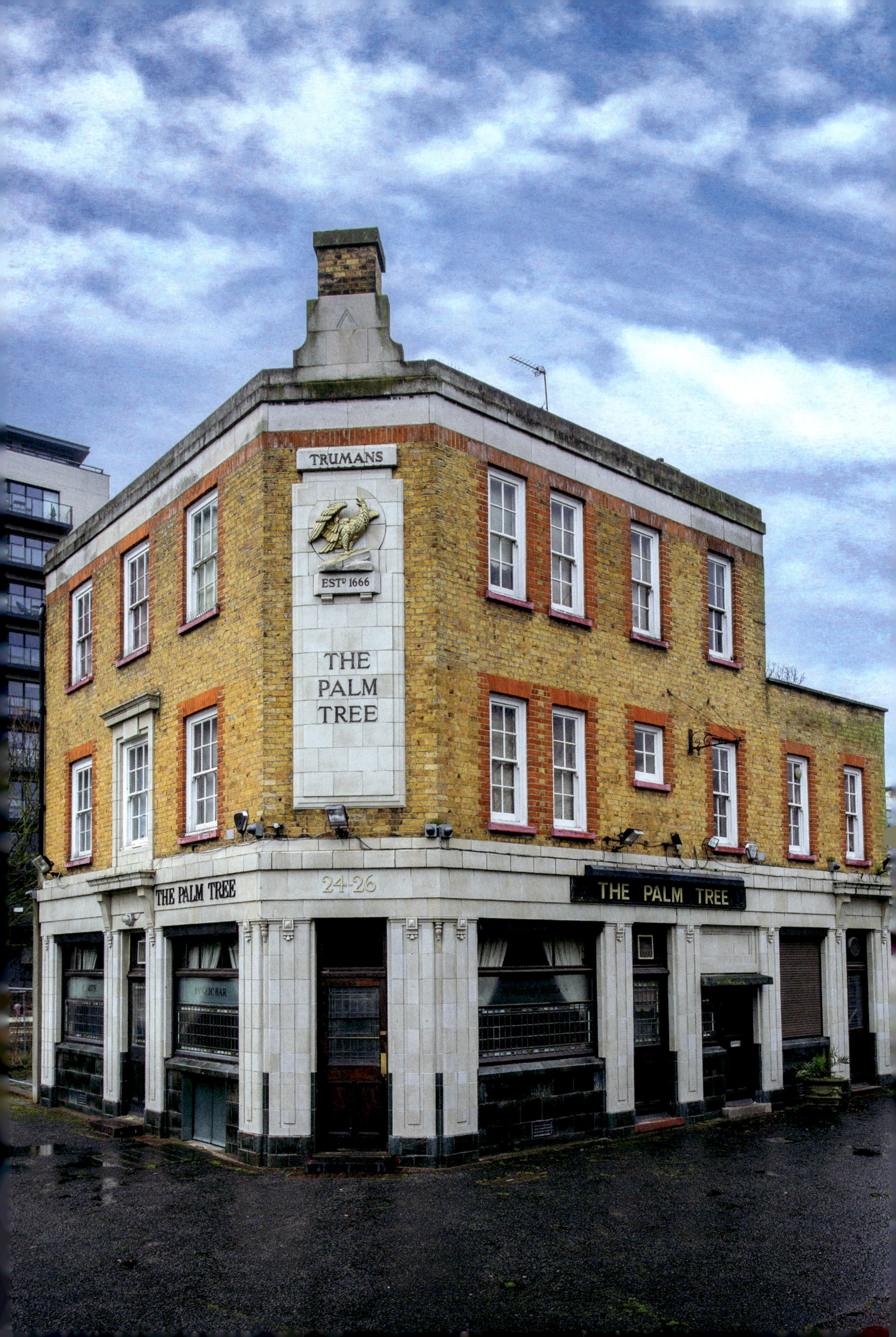
TRUMANS
ESTD 1666
THE
PALM
TREE
THE PALM TREE
24-26
THE PALM TREE
PUBLIC BAR

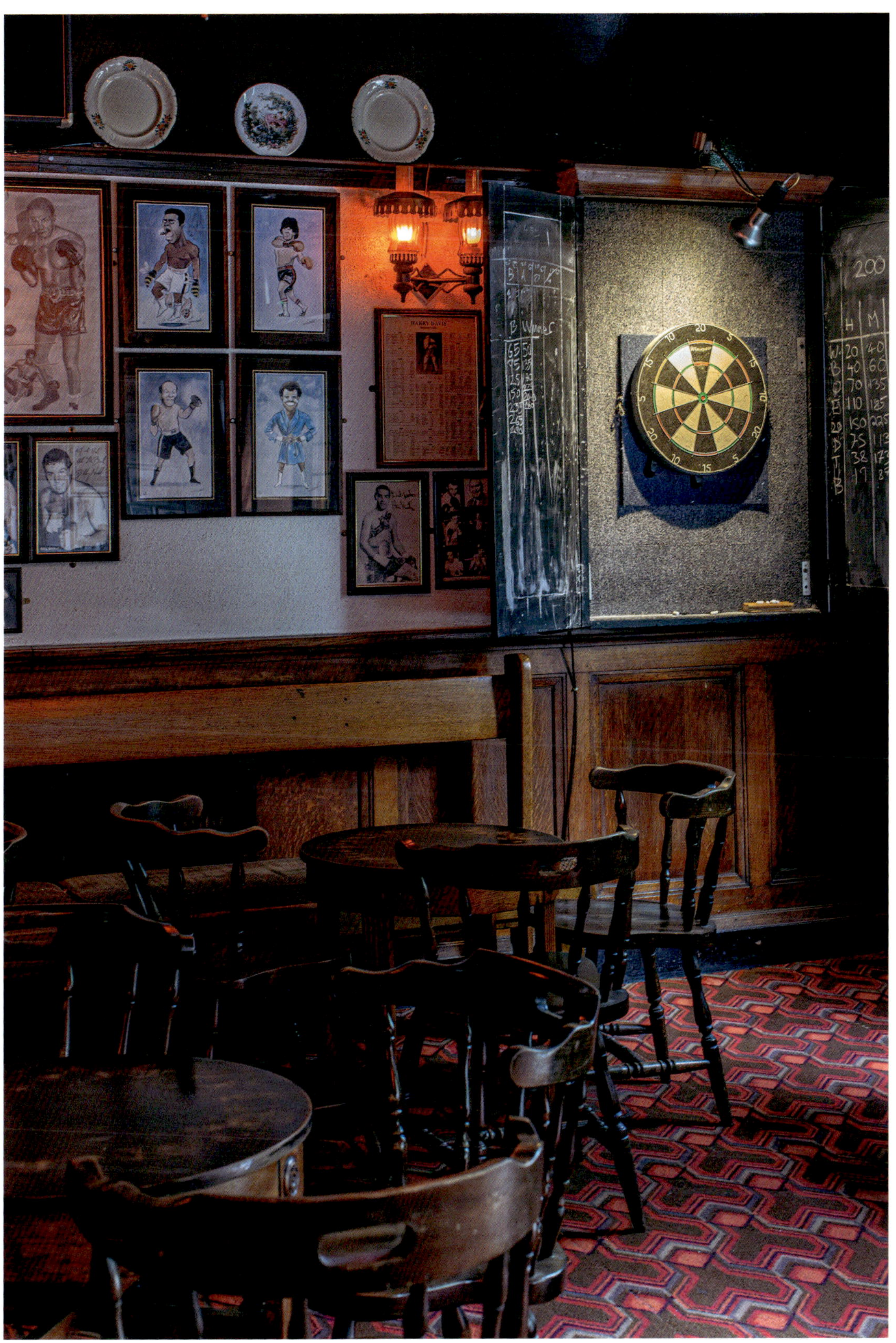

An understated oasis a world away from twenty-first-century foibles

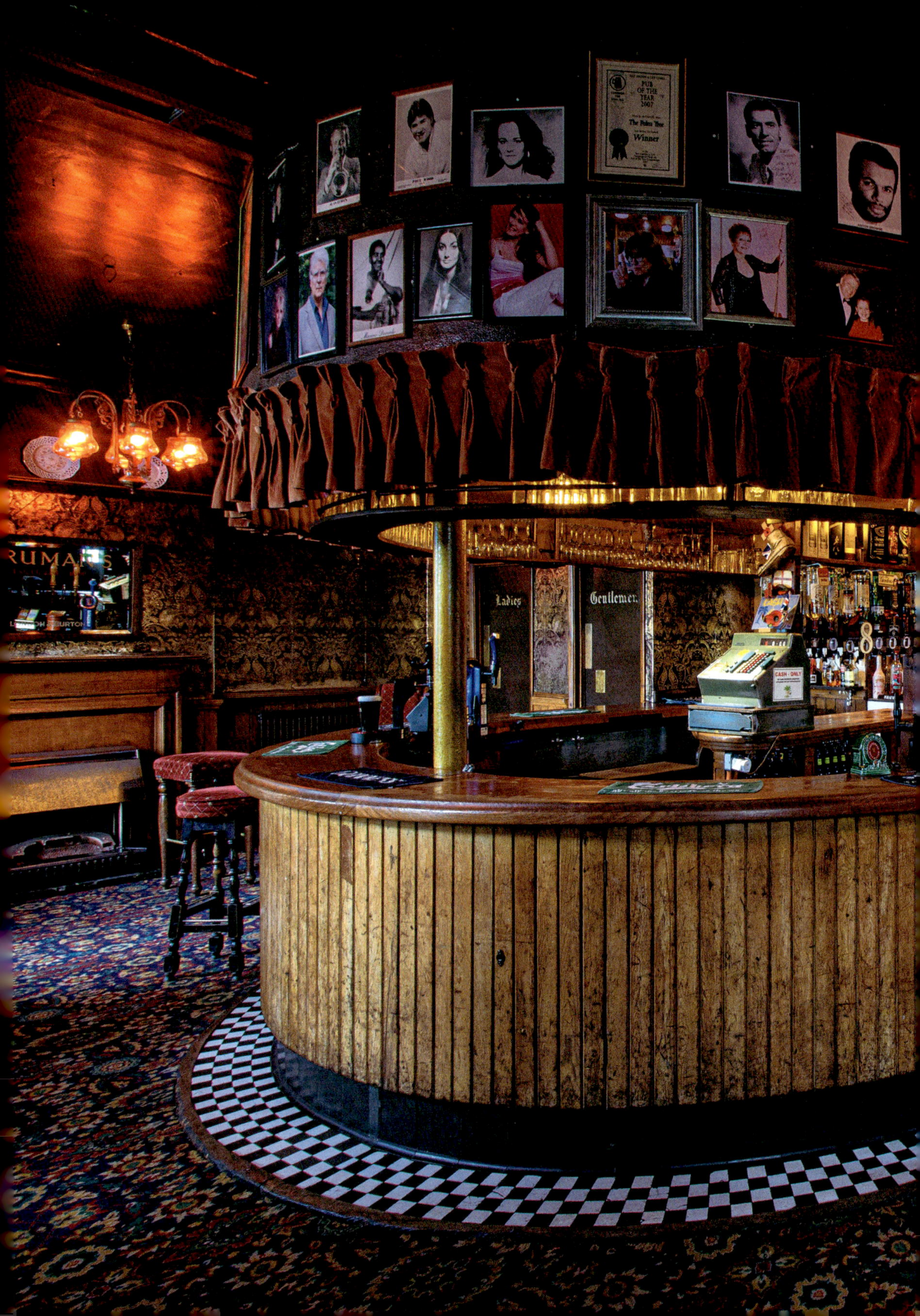

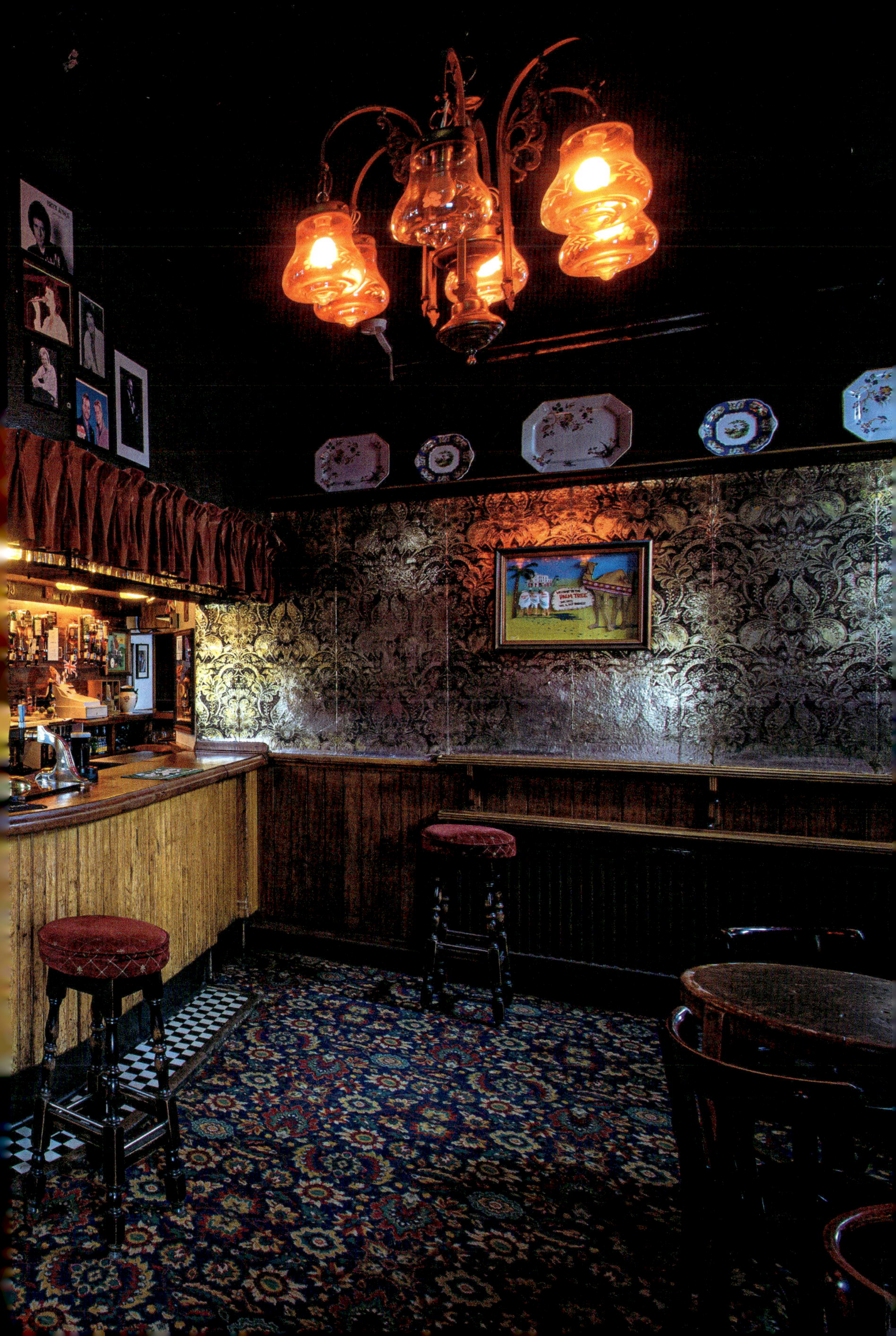

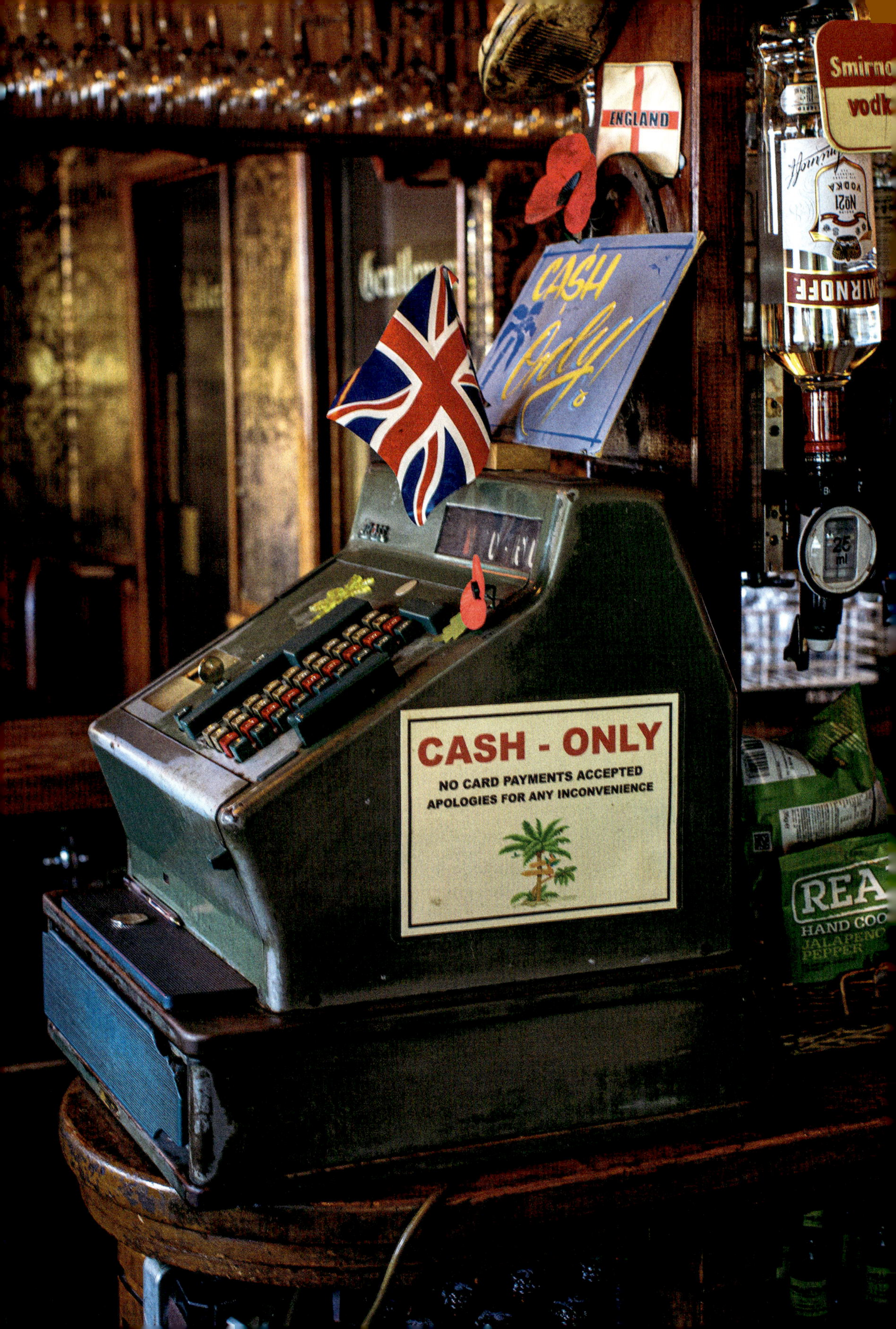

ENGLAND
Smirno
vodk
No21
VODKA
SMIRNOFF
25 ml
CASH
CASH - ONLY
NO CARD PAYMENTS ACCEPTED
APOLOGIES FOR ANY INCONVENIENCE
REA
HAND COO
JALAPENO
PEPPER

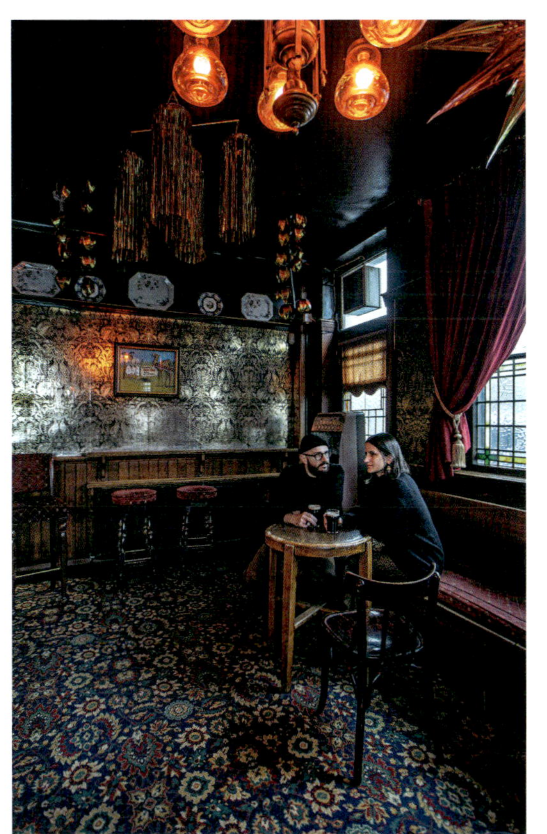

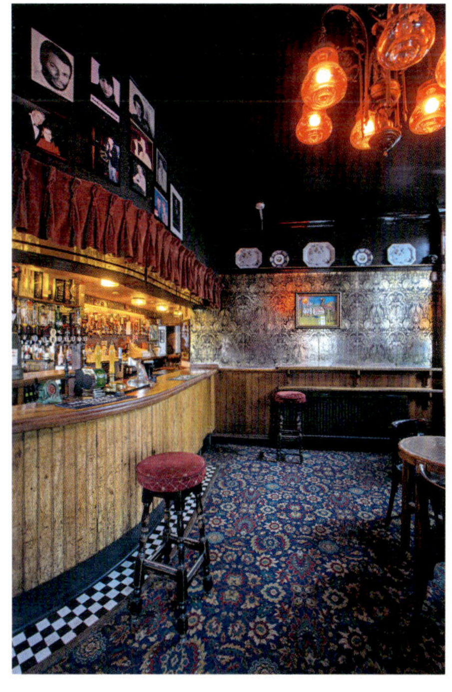

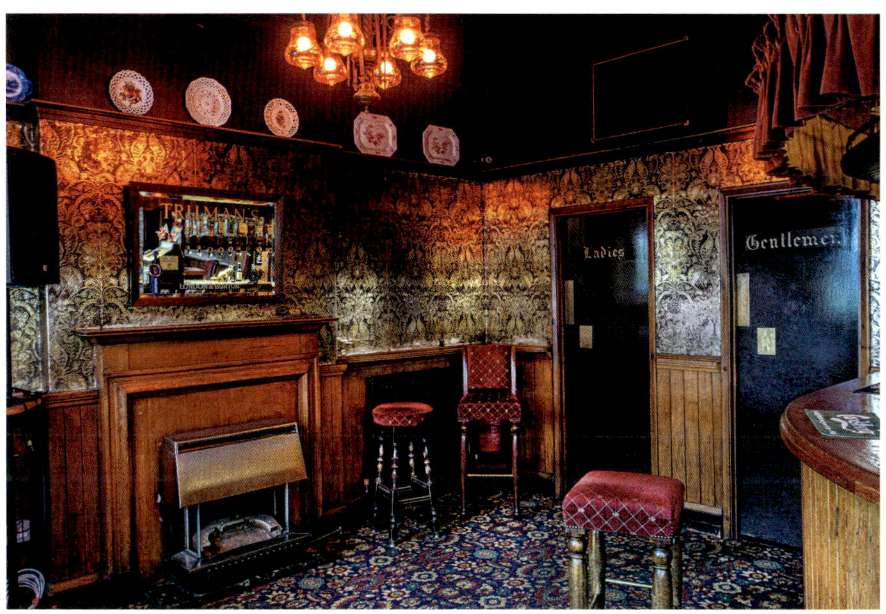

Cash is always king at The Palm Tree

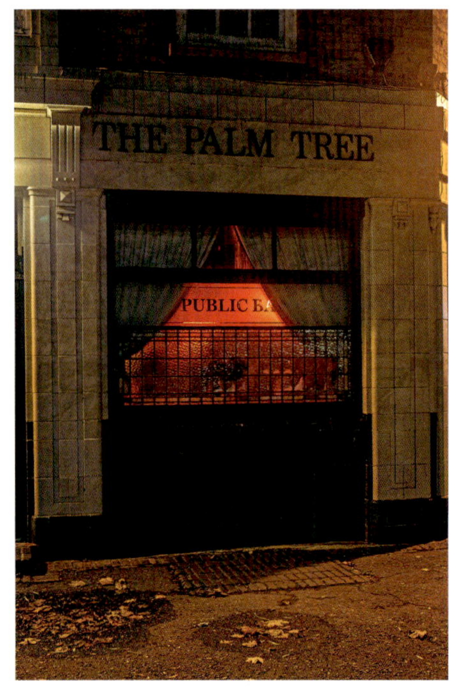

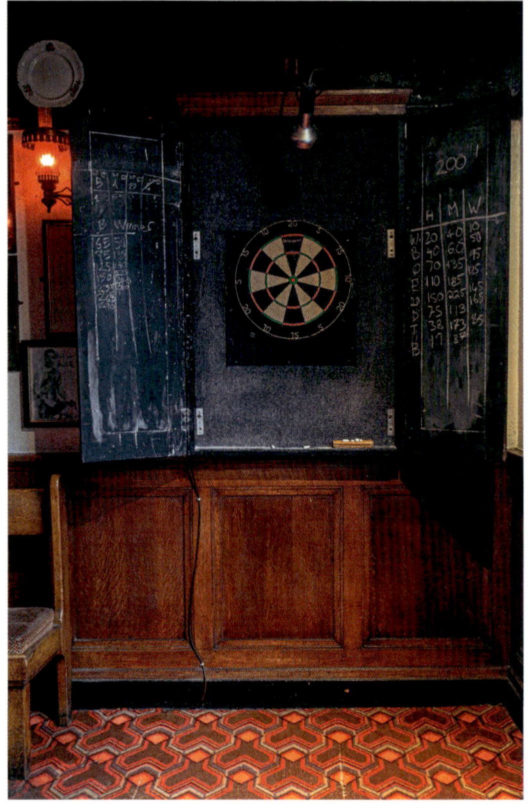

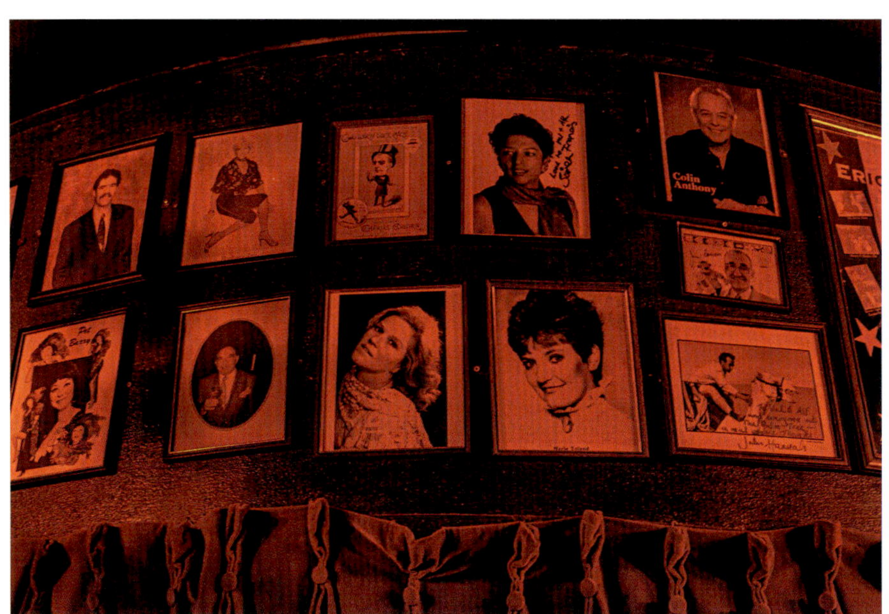

A red-alert ambience pervades the space

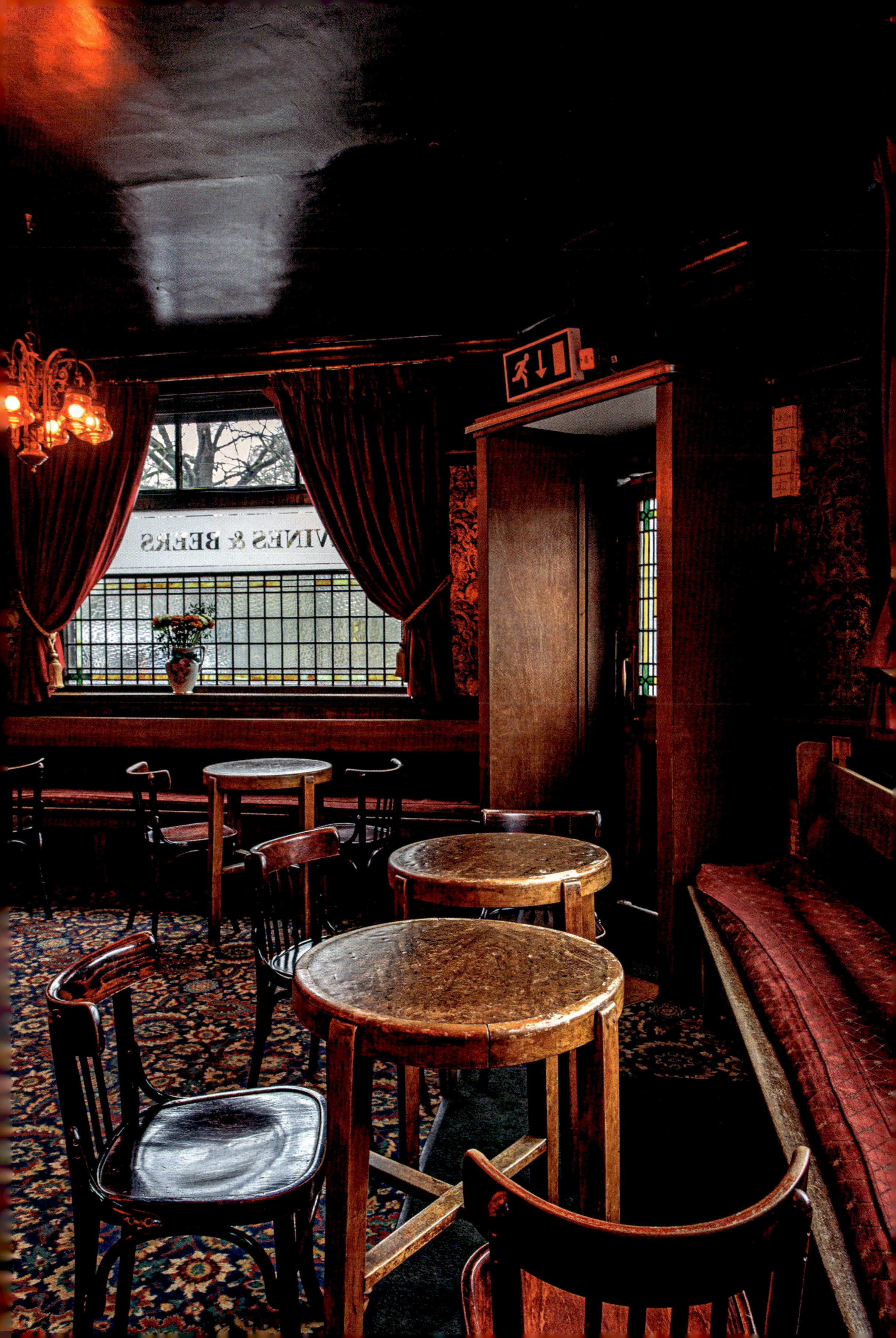

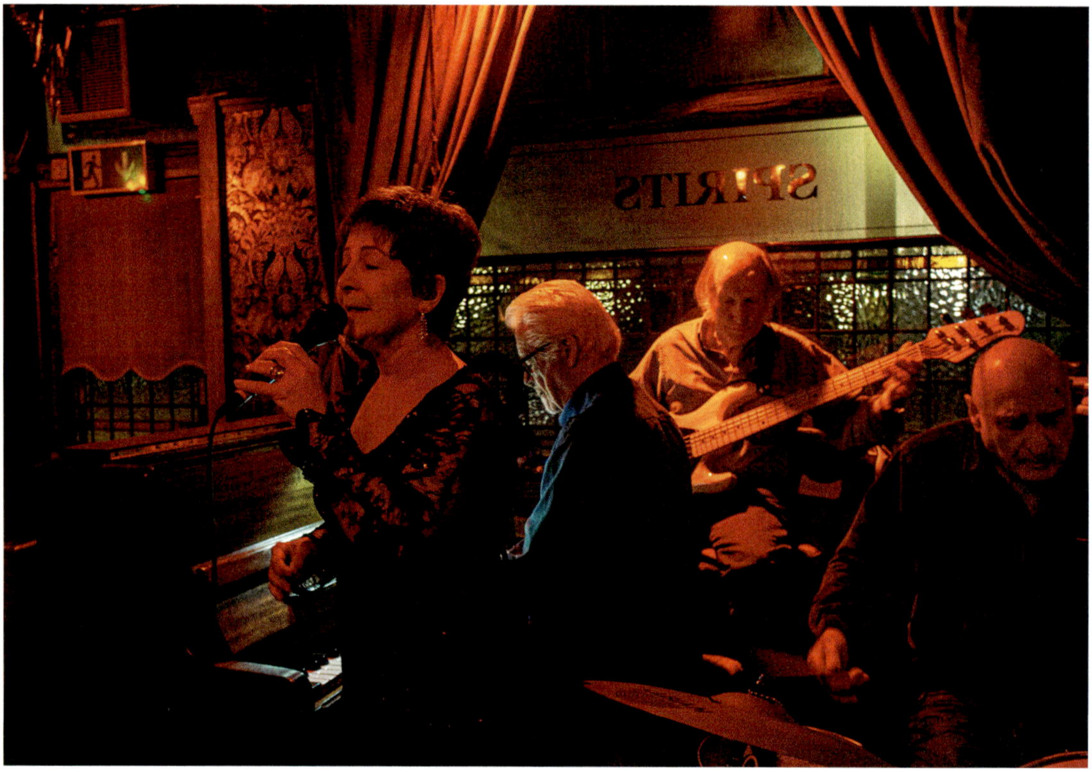

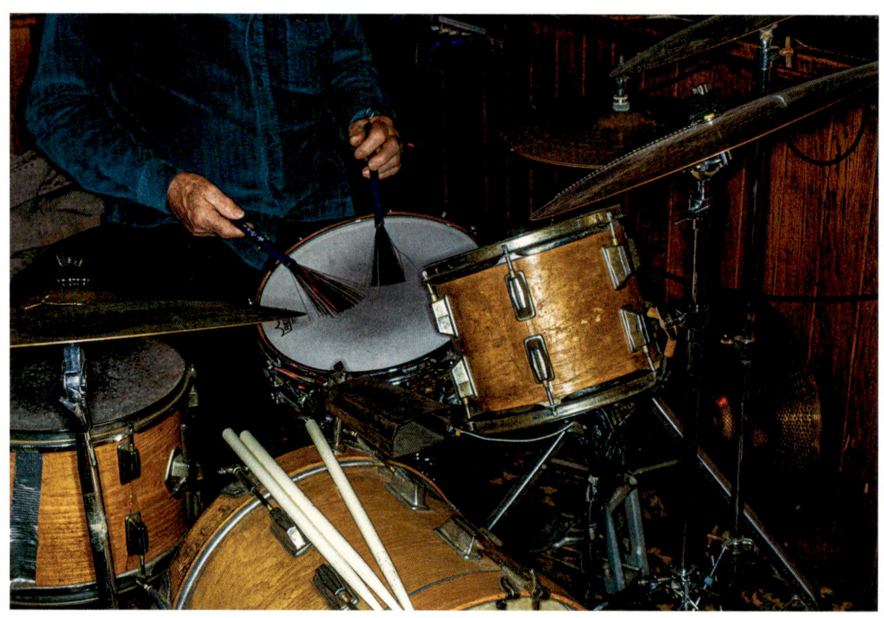

Home to legendary crooners and insouciant toe-tappers

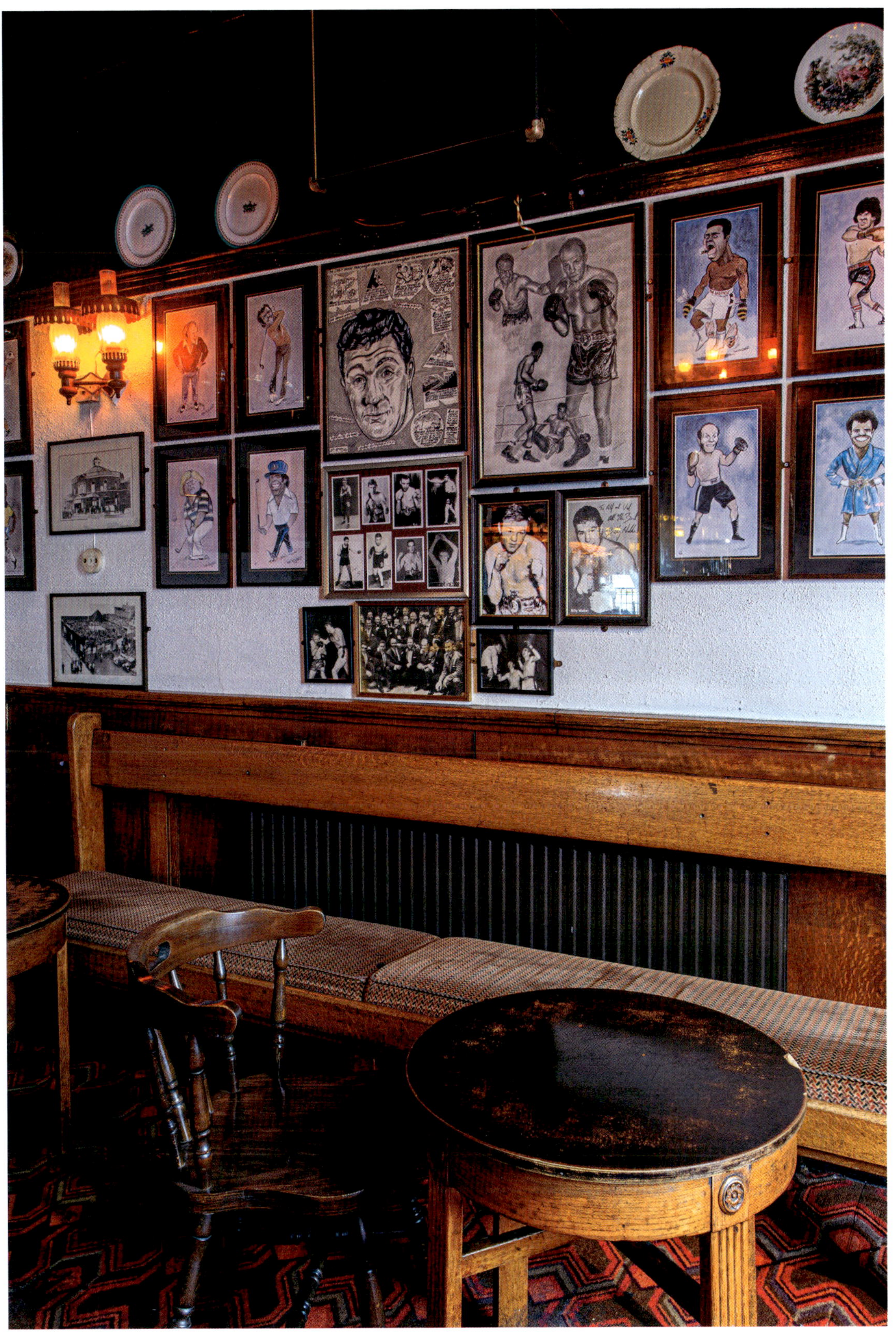

THE ELEANOR ARMS

There aren't many pool tables left in London pubs. And there are certainly not many pubs where you have to bring your own cue. But when landlord Frankie gets fed up with people snapping the house potting sticks, it doesn't matter how much you apologise. Bring your own cue or simply don't play.

Frankie and Leslie don't suffer fools gladly. In fact, they barely suffer them at all. The total number of people barred from this manor in the last fifteen years easily tops 100. It's a crowd with more hip replacements than hipsters, but all are welcome to this slightly eccentric house party in the Bermuda Triangle of Victoria Park, the Olympic Stadium and Bow.

The cumbersome opposing front doors offer perennial bafflement to newcomers. But once you're safely inside, it's all classically disarming. The dangling disco ball hints at livelier times, the curated art collection includes posters of LA art exhibitions and a Human League LP doubles as a wall clock. The lime green paint job might raise a few eyebrows, but it somehow successfully blends student union with bohemian house-party vibes. Even the khazis are pretty classy, with the door to the ladies' crafted from the same walnut burr that graces the dashboards of every Rolls-Royce in the land.

On taking up the tenancy, Frankie and Leslie were advised that no one would drink real ale in this urban desert. They pooh-poohed such naysayers, making it into the *Good Beer Guide* for over fourteen years in a row, and the whisky line-up doesn't disappoint either.

Frankie fills his role as party-loving uncle to a tee. From writing arcane pub quiz questions to digging deep into his forty-year-old music collection, he keeps the party going with his non-disco disco known simply as the "Minestrone of Sound". And when Frankie says "Relax", he means it. Sunday sees the pub morph into the Old Ford Jazz Club, and serious toe-tapping accompanies the tippling.

So, when Frankie and Leslie up sticks, they'll pack up their unique art and ephemera and take their idiosyncratic house-party vibes with them. It's unlikely anyone will fill those non-disco dancing shoes, replenish the vinyl back catalogue or write those devilish quizzes on a weekly basis. But when they are gone, I still hope that you'll get a decent pint of Spitfire, and maybe, just maybe, you won't even have to bring your own pool cue anymore.

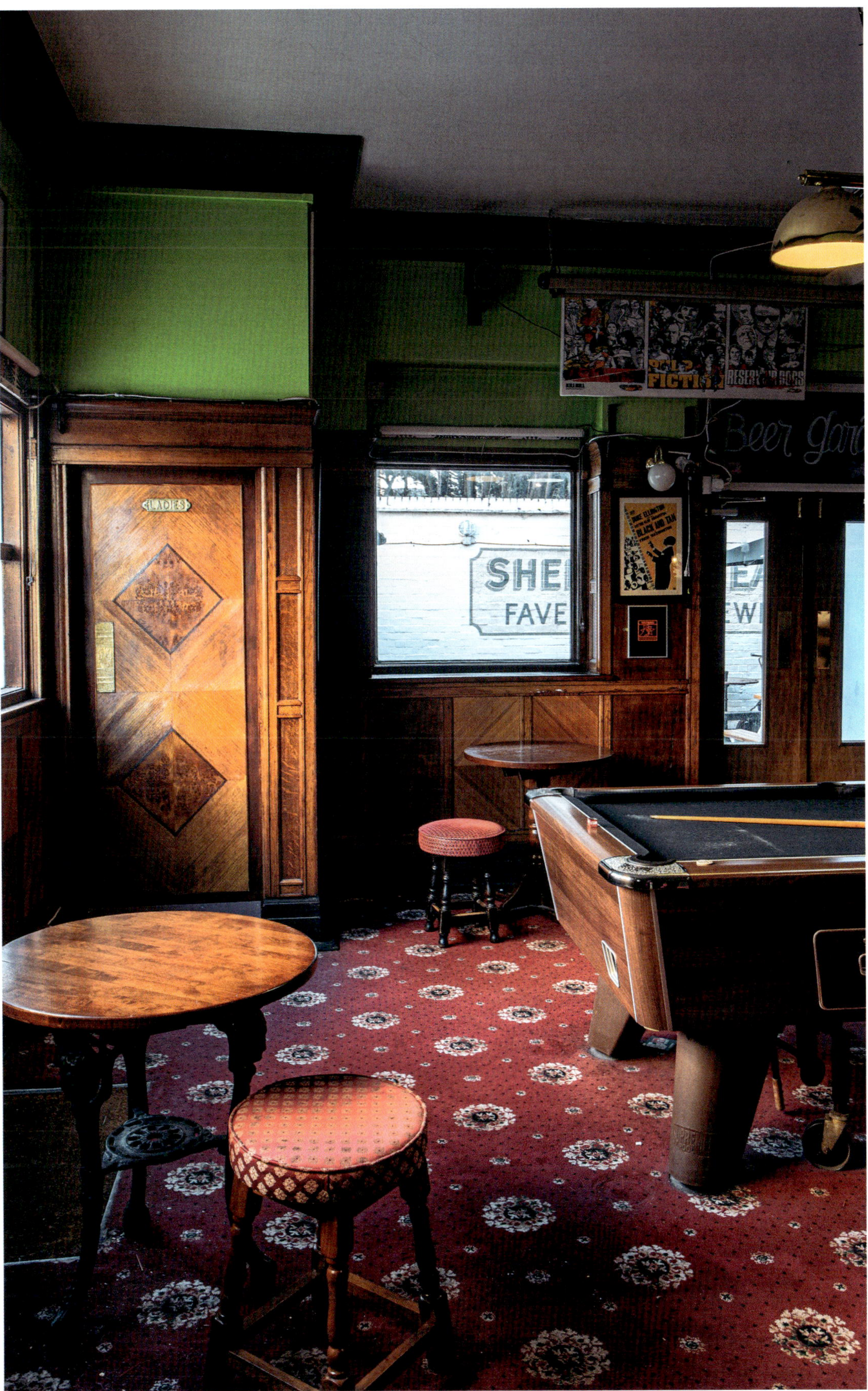

LADIES
SHER
FAVE
Beer gar

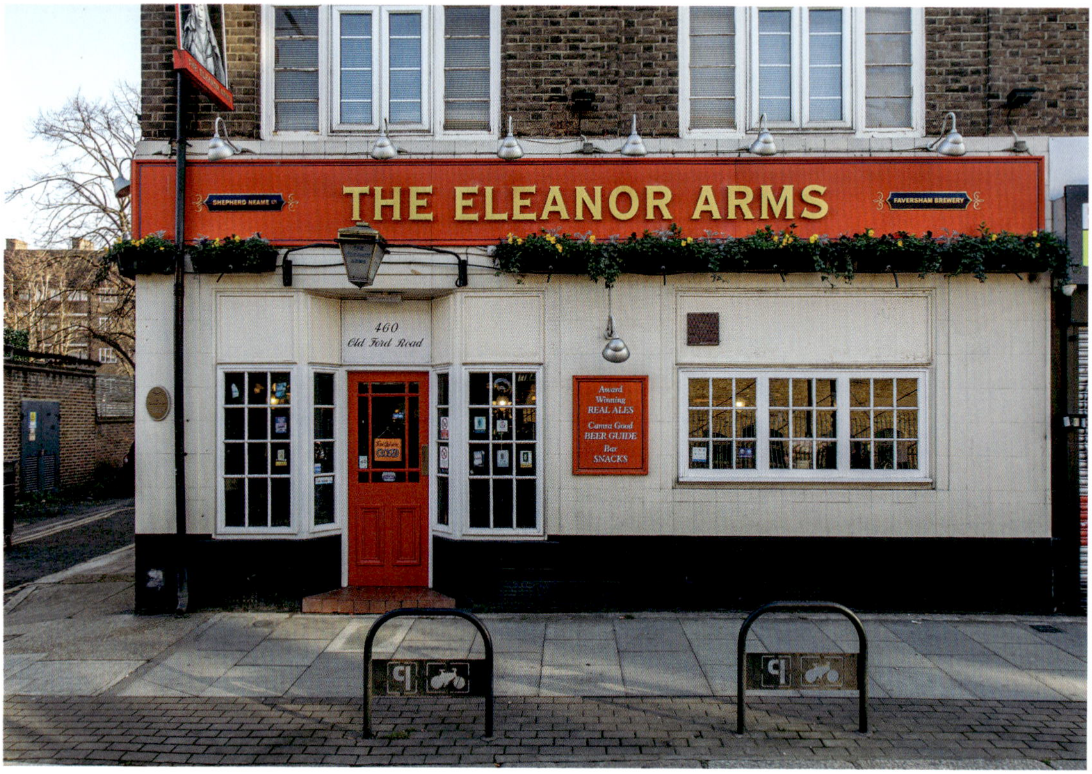

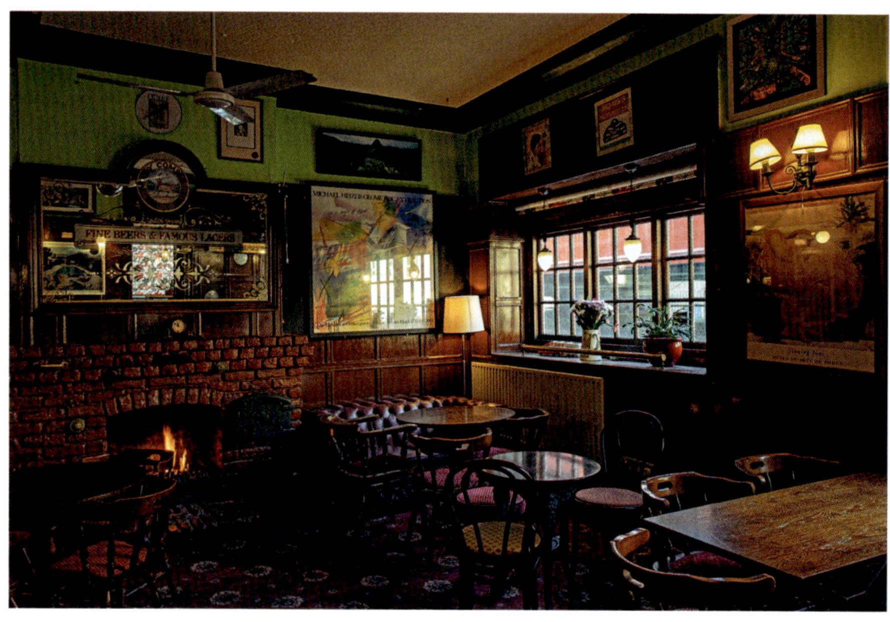

House party vibes and great beer are the key ingredients

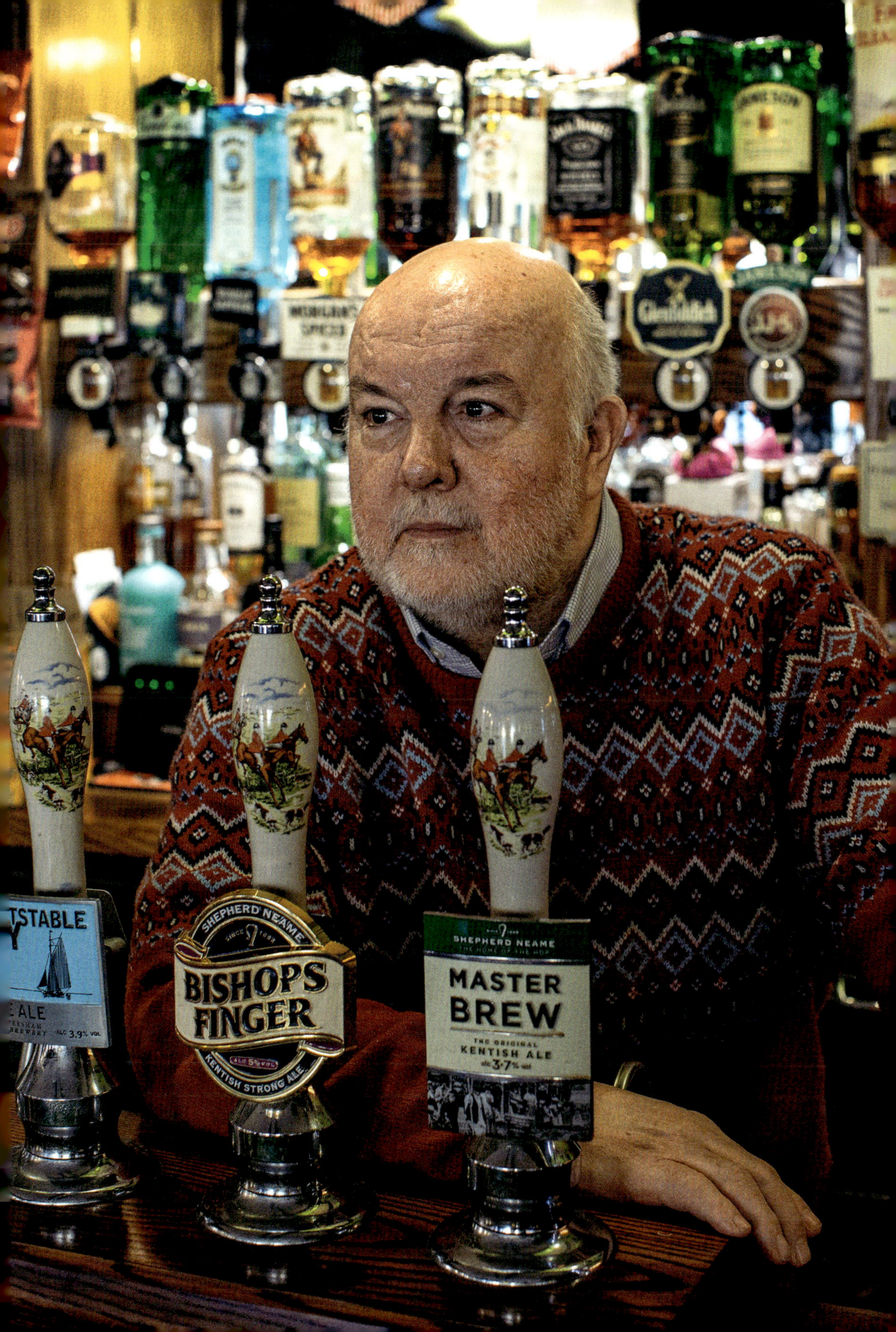

TSTABLE
ALE
3.9% VOL
SHEPHERD NEAME
BISHOPS FINGER
KENTISH STRONG ALE
ALE 5% VOL
SHEPHERD NEAME
THE HOME OF THE HOP
MASTER BREW
THE ORIGINAL
KENTISH ALE
ALC 3.7% VOL

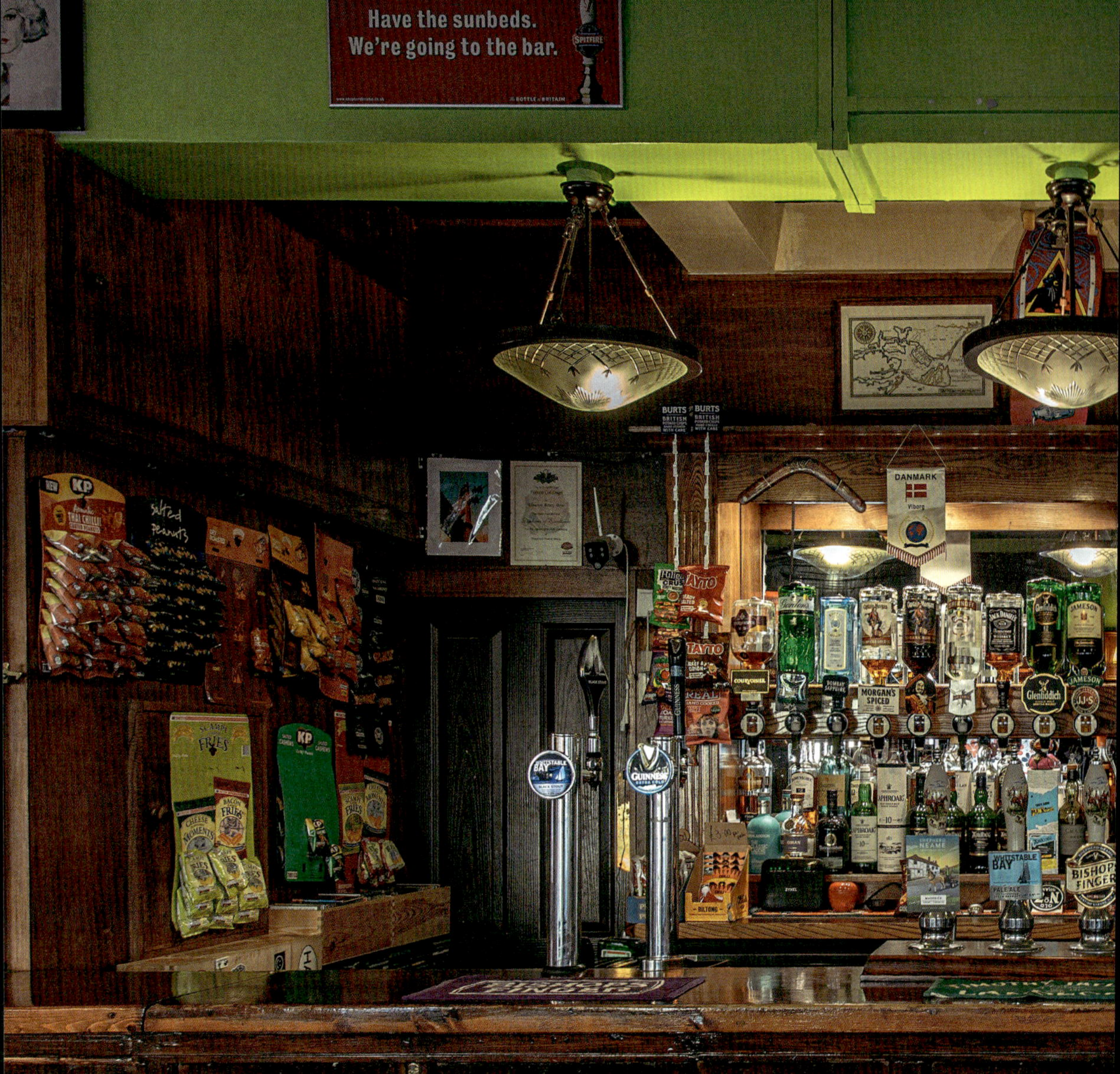

Have the sunbeds.
We're going to the bar.
SPITFIRE
THE BOTTLE of BRITAIN
DANMARK
Viborg
KP
THAI CHILLI
salted peanuts
SCAMPI FRIES
BACON FRIES
CHEESE MOMENTS
KP
FLAME GRILLED
TAYTO
REAL
HAND COOKED
GUINNESS
BURTS
BRITISH
BURTS
BRITISH
WHITSTABLE BAY
BLACK STOUT
GUINNESS
EXTRA COLD
COURVOISIER
BOMBAY SAPPHIRE
MORGAN'S SPICED
GLENFIDDICH
JAMESON
JAMESON
LAPHROAIG
10
OBAN
SHEPHERD NEAME
WHITSTABLE BAY
PALE ALE
BISHOP'S FINGER
ZYXEL
BILTONG

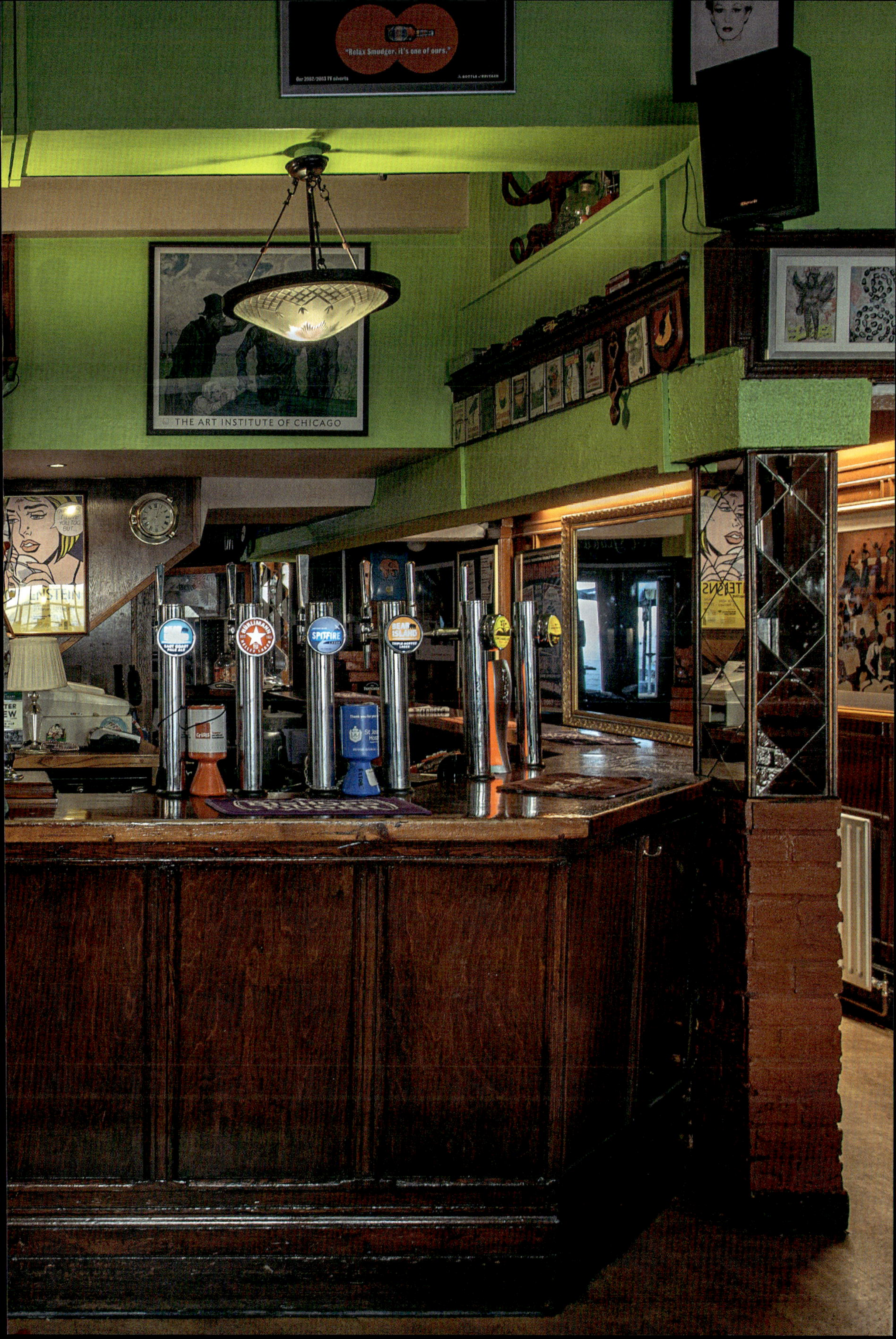

"Relax Smudger, it's one of ours."
THE ART INSTITUTE OF CHICAGO
SPITFIRE
BEAR ISLAND

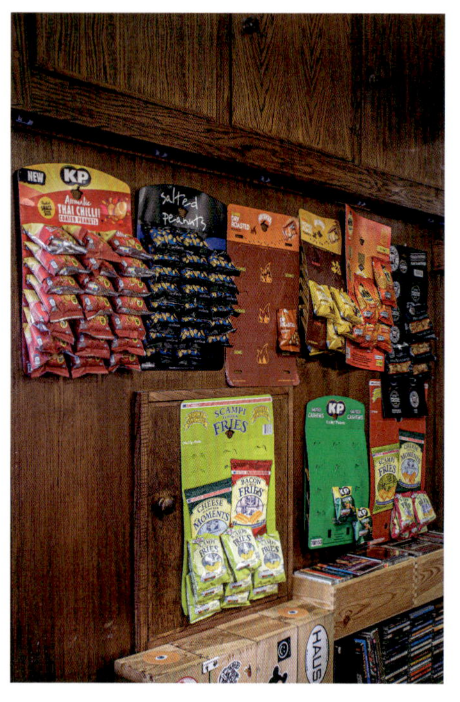

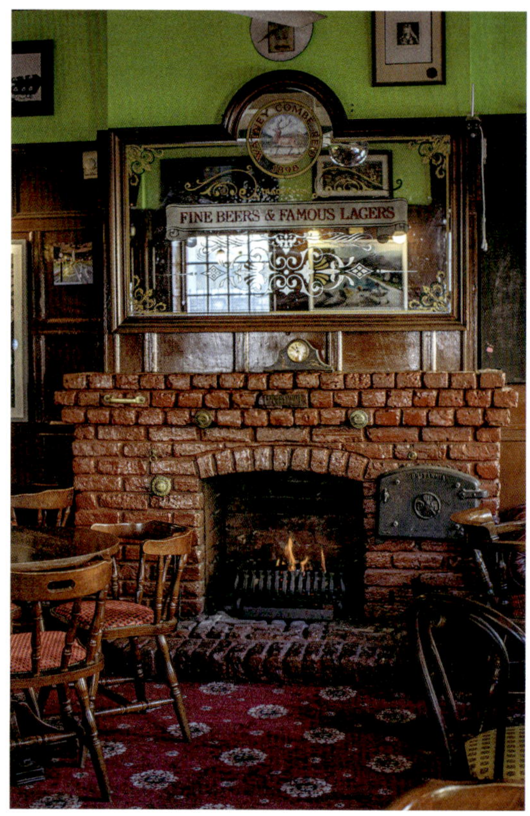

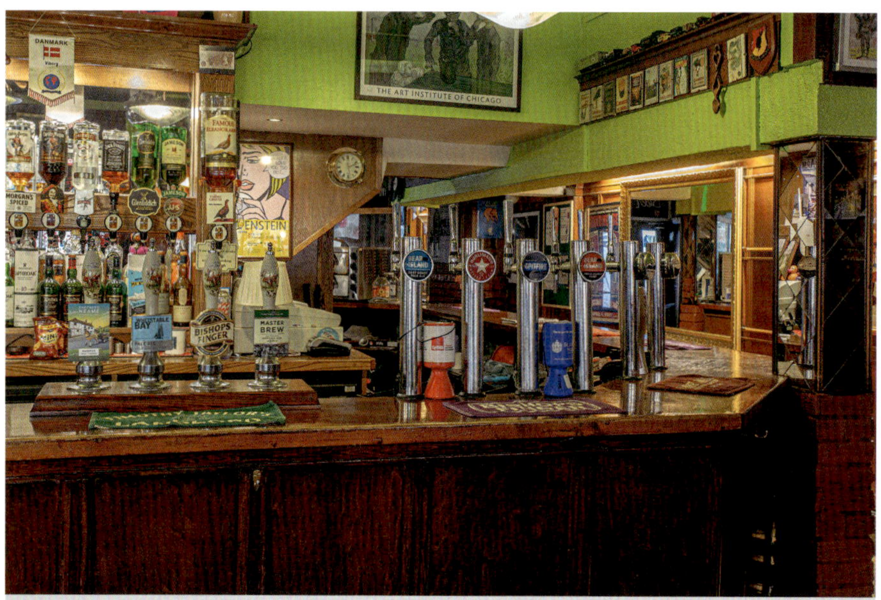

Low on pretension... high on fun

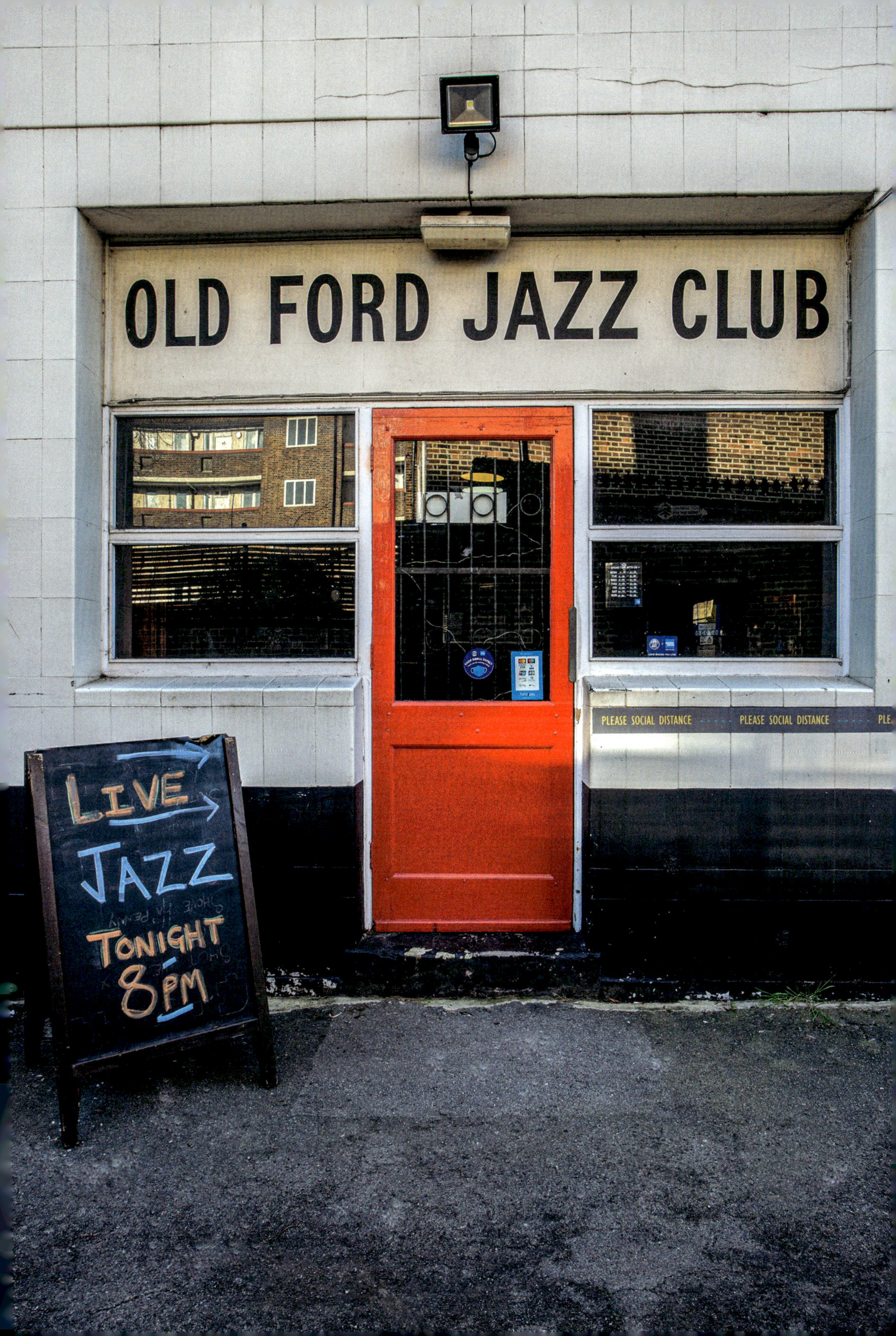
OLD FORD JAZZ CLUB
LIVE
JAZZ
TONIGHT
8 PM
PLEASE SOCIAL DISTANCE
PLEASE SOCIAL DISTANCE
PLE

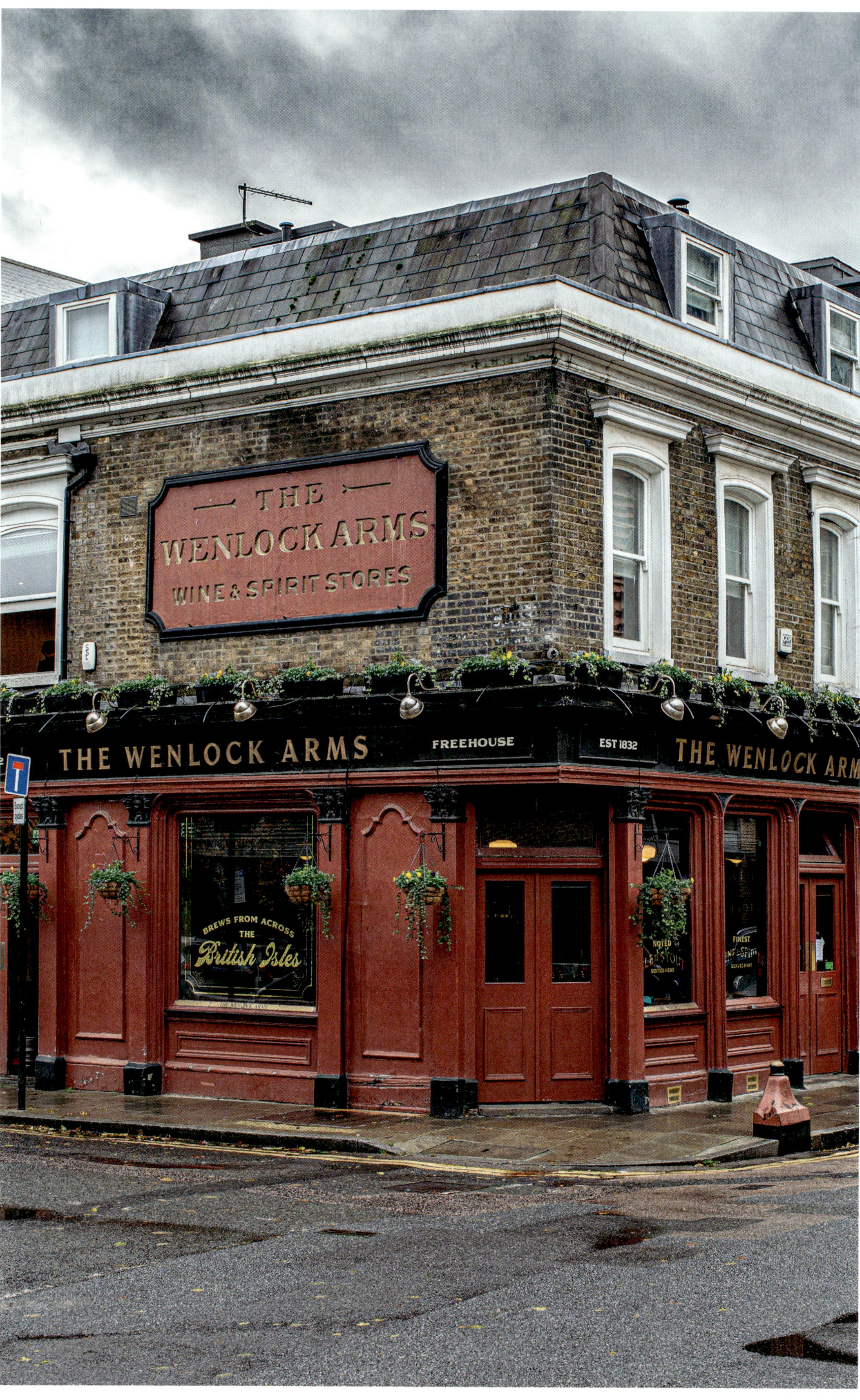
THE
WENLOCK ARMS
WINE & SPIRIT STORES
THE WENLOCK ARMS
FREEHOUSE
EST 1832
THE WENLOCK ARMS
BREWS FROM ACROSS
THE
British Isles

THE WENLOCK ARMS

Property developers are total cunts. You were thinking it, I've just written it. At best, we can make their excuses and file them under "Necessary Evil". Building a city like London is far from easy and fraught with all manner of side-line protests. Don't block the view of St Paul's or excavate too close to the Northern Line and don't forget Bazalgette's leaky poo pipe is only millimetres away. They know that everyone hates them, so are born into this world with thick skin, selective hearing and few moral values. Without these attributes they simply couldn't operate, and London would literally be stuck in the Dark Ages.

The planning powers that be let them pop in a proposal or two and local protest groups chain themselves to a few bits of street furniture until some government bod takes a backhander before allowing them to get the wrecking ball out. It produces a wonderful architectural hotchpotch. Old versus new. Private housing abutting Peabody Estates. Elizabethan, Georgian and faux Tudor all living cheek by jowl.

But try and knock a pub down, and a line shall be crossed. The local residents might never drink in that pub, not actually even like that pub, but will fight you tooth and nail until it's left well alone. There is some unwritten, dewy-eyed nostalgia for pubs that gets people's hackles right up when under threat.

Having poured its first pint in 1836, The Wenlock Arms has been under existential threat ever since. The Luftwaffe peppered the local area, the brewery closed next door, and by 2010 the property vultures were circling. Old Street had become "Silicon Roundabout", Banksy was now a household hero rather than the scourge of the British Transport Police, and the YBAs, including Damien Hirst, had moved west. The Wenlock had become prime property. But the locals were having none of this demolition nonsense, and a vociferous "Save The Wenlock" campaign was launched. The council kindly snuck The Wenlock into a conservation area, thwarting the forces of evil forever. Hurrah! The new owners painted and polished this beauty up. No reinvention of the wheel here, but looking backwards in time to determine their way forward. Choosing historic livery on the outside, uncovering vintage mosaics and adding... wait for it... ten cask ales, ten keg lines and real cider galore. Pub-loving Punters 1: Property Developers 0.

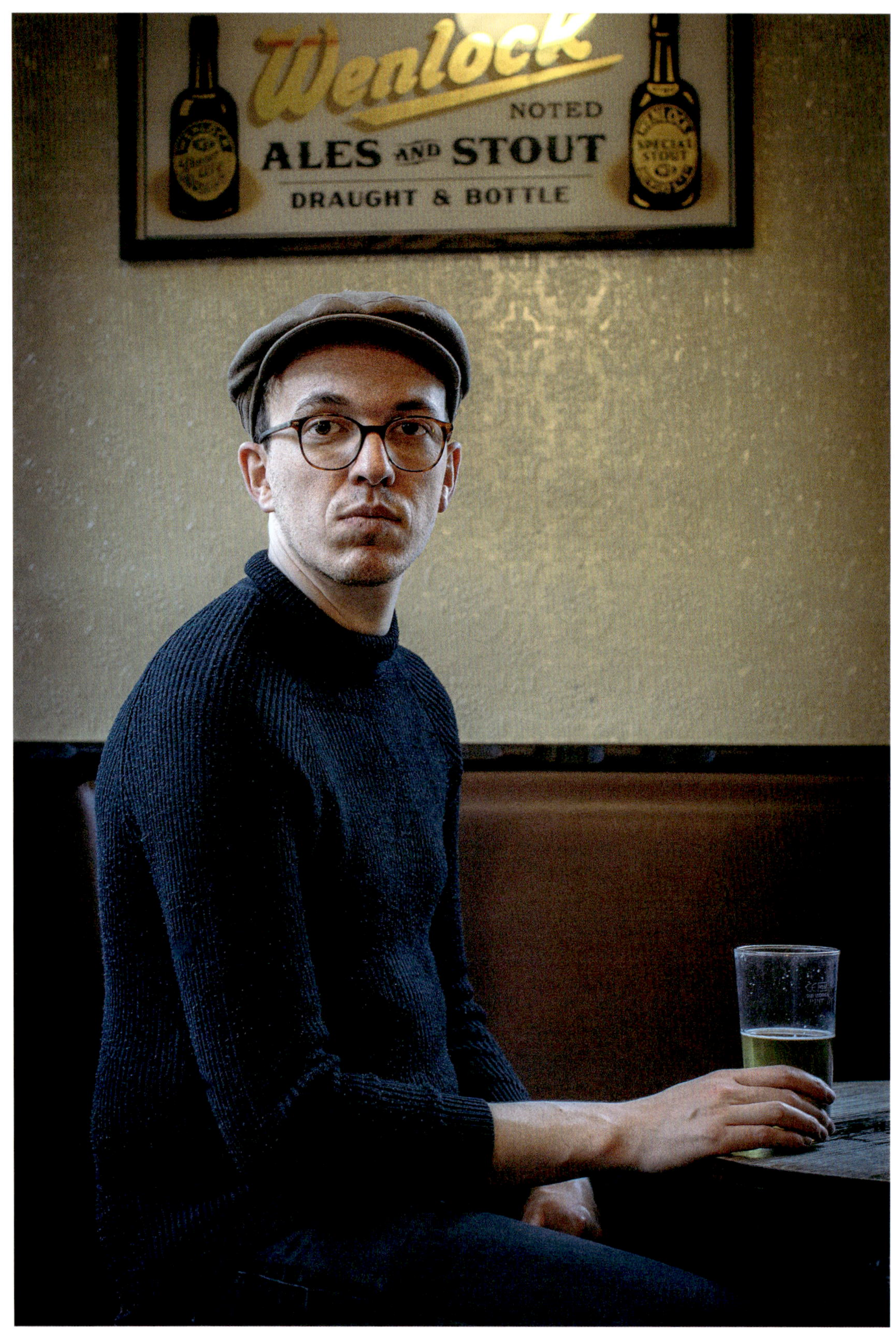

Dispensing good beer and good times

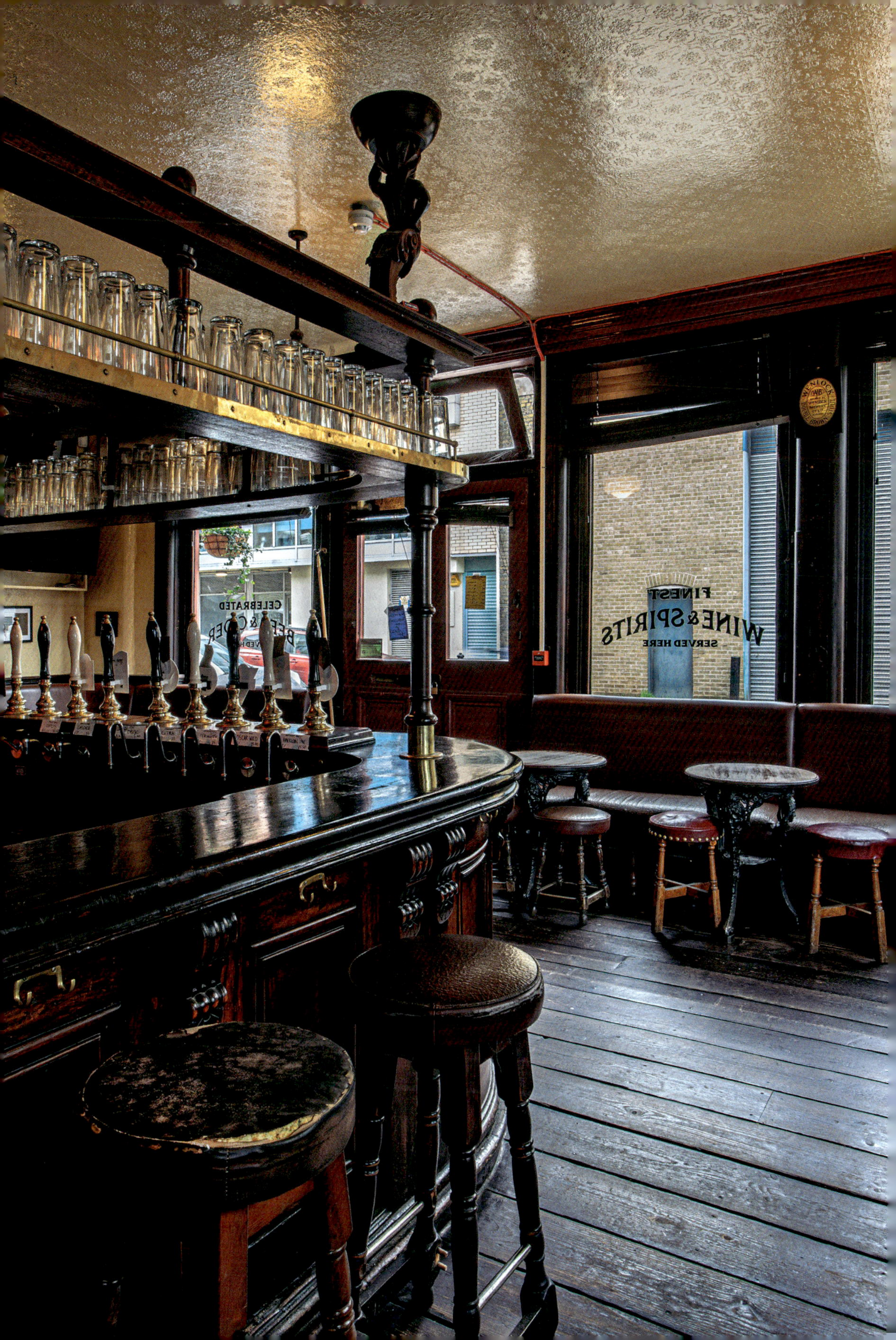
CELEBRATED
BEER & CIDER
FINEST
WINE & SPIRITS
SERVED HERE
WENLOCK

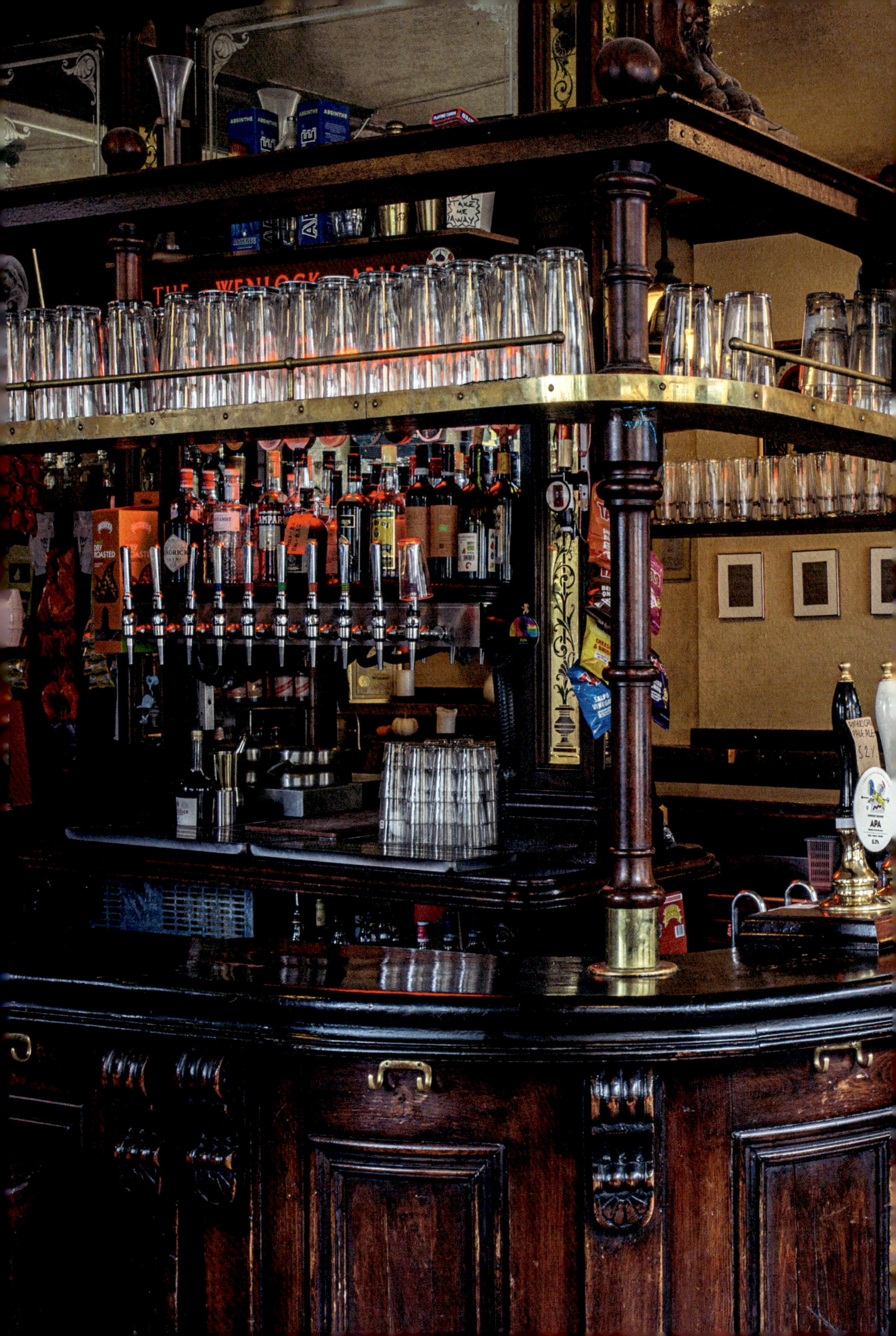

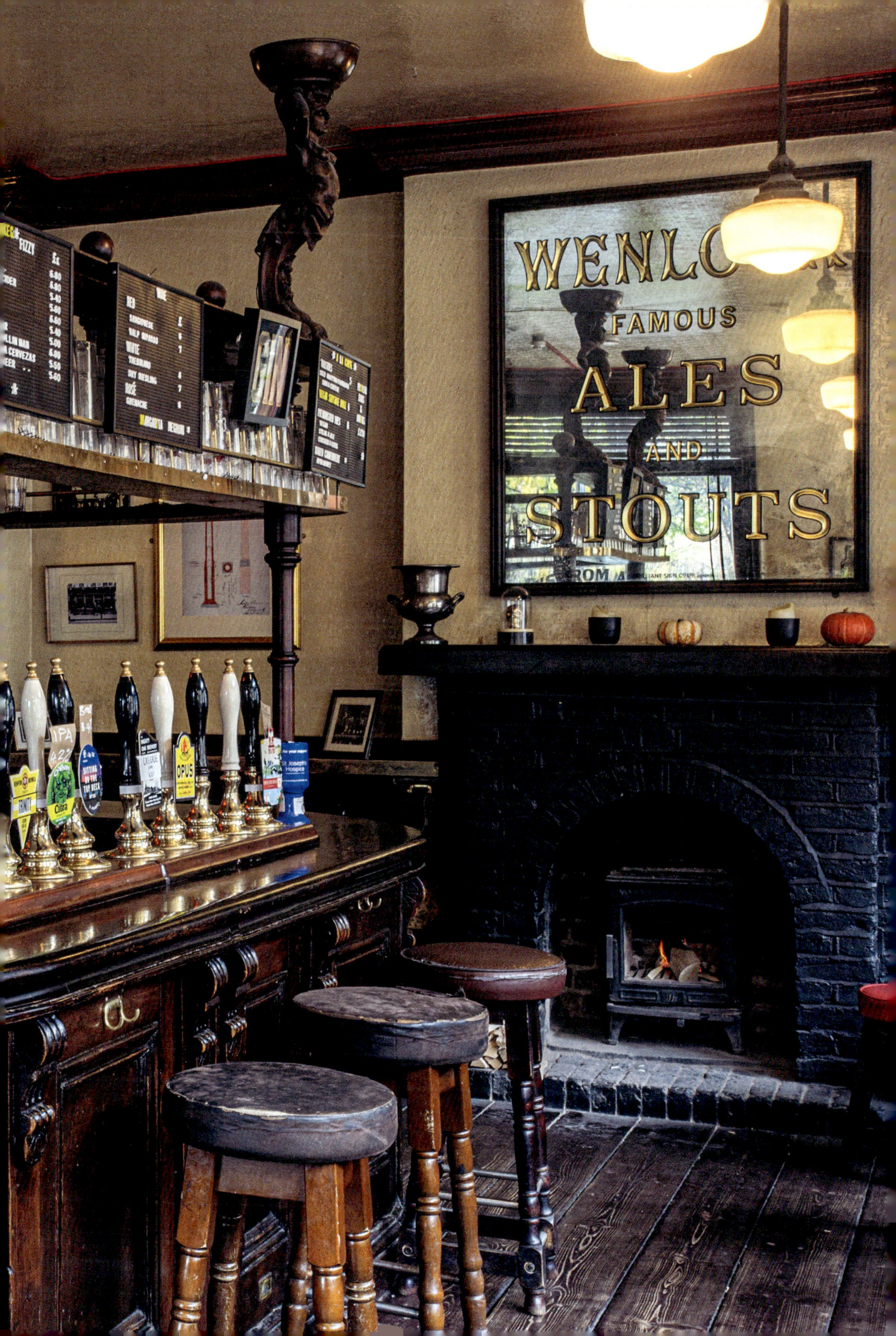

WENLOCK
FAMOUS
ALES
AND
STOUTS
OPUS

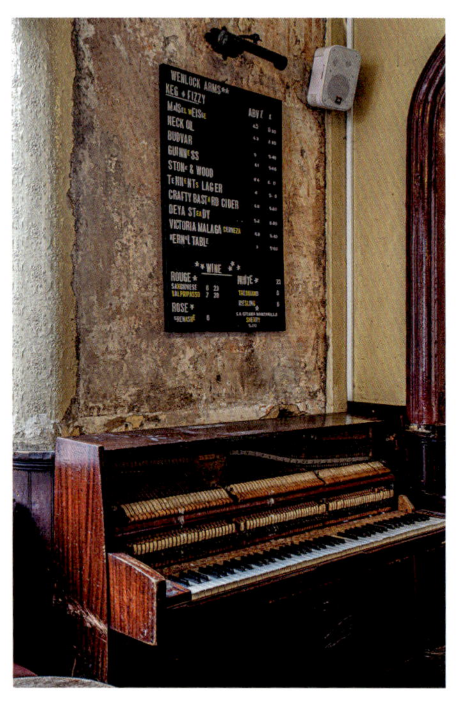

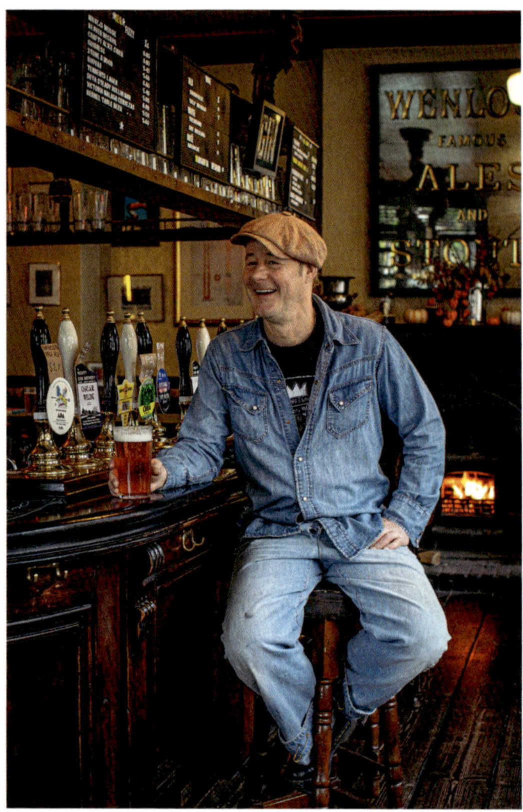

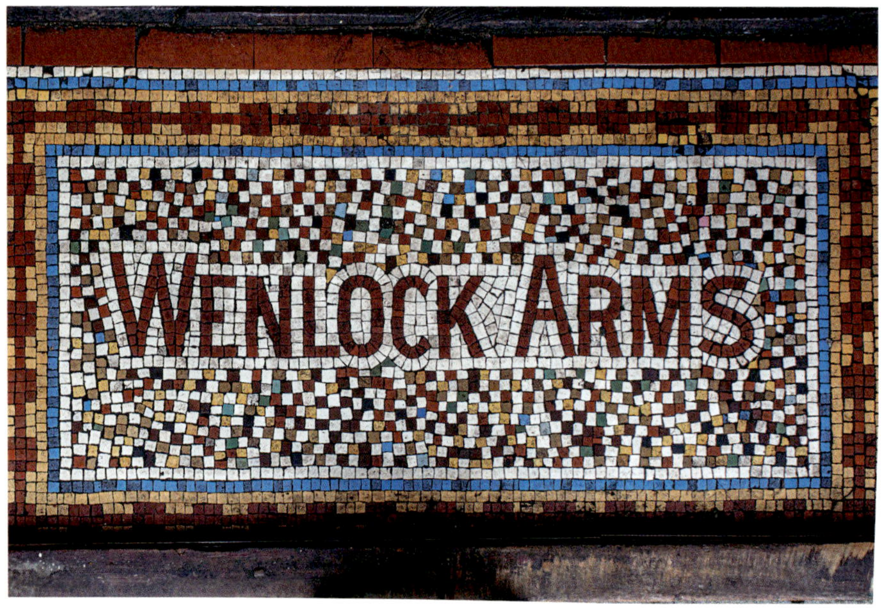

A back-to-basics refurb revealed some hidden architectural gems

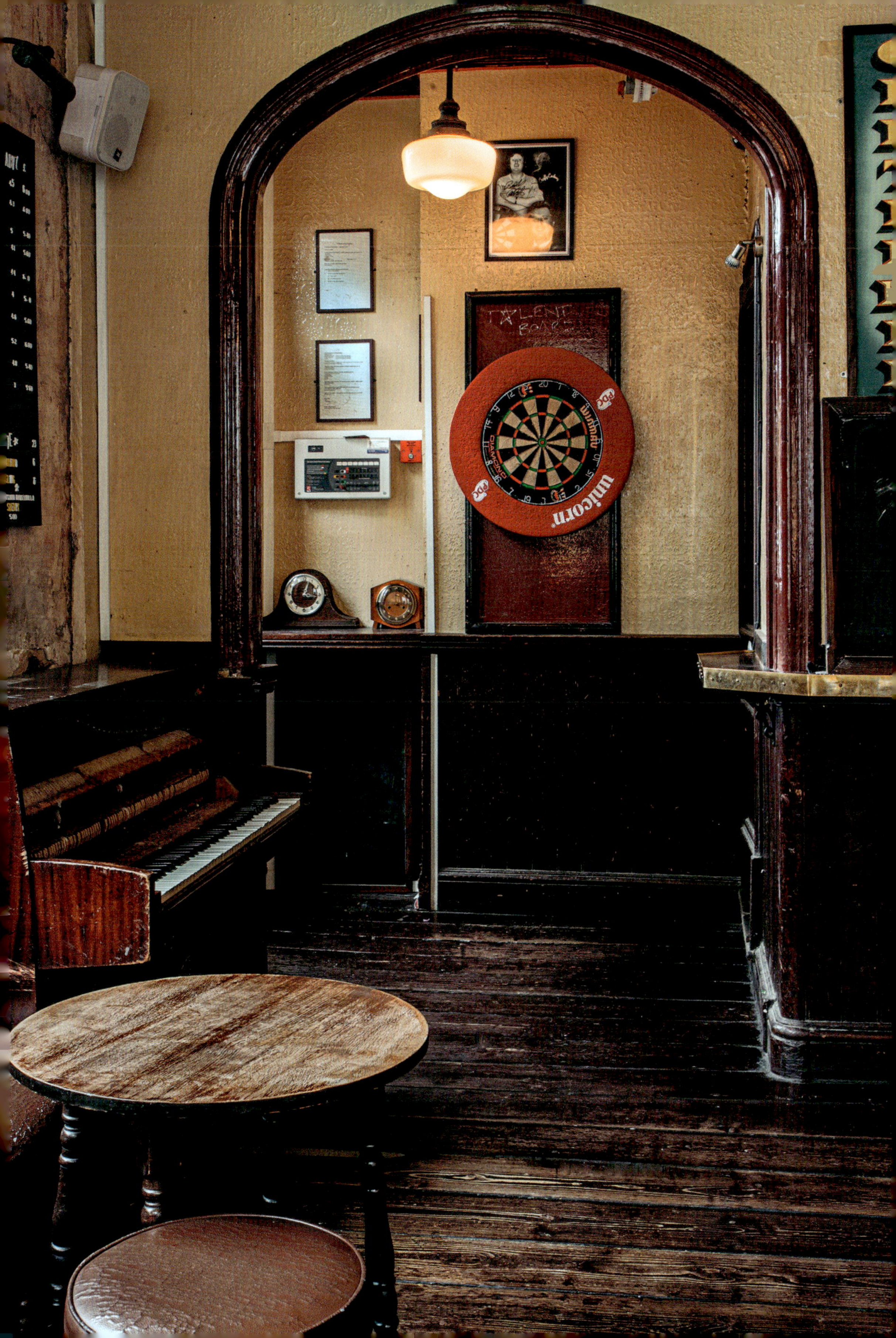

KING CHARLES I

This pub might look fit for a king, but it certainly isn't owned by one. The people still rule OK here, and this is their hard-won happy palace. You'll find more mild anarchy than monarchy in these King's Cross backstreets. Fifteen locals joined forces and bid for the leasehold in 2015, ring-fencing it from beady-eyed property chaps. The local council then agreed to award it an asset of community value status, in agreement that the pub "furthers the social wellbeing and interests of the local community, whilst also acknowledging the loyalty and dedication of the staff and customers who make this wonderful and unassuming local treasure what it is." Lovely stuff.

The jaunty paint job beckons you in off the fuggy thoroughfare and hints at its former self, known as the "Craic House". This is a pub that doesn't take itself too seriously. All the decapitated taxidermy hanging around the place doffs the historical cap to the fate of Charles I, losing his own head outside the Banqueting House on 30 January 1649. Power to the people.

Happiness here derives from what they give, not what they take

It's a small, one-room kingdom here, coated in brown from head to toe. Theatre masks and posters jostle between the dead animals. The pub is stuffed full of both characters and character. It runs a self-proclaimed "batshit crazy" pub quiz, and the Nude Alpine Club have been known to practise their passion here. Scrambling around the pub in the buff without touching the floor, they get up close and personal with all the well-hung ephemera. So, it is a pub where you can clearly see everyone's nuts. The jukebox and fire allow for more traditional relaxation, whilst claustrophobes should beware their trip to the gents.

Live music sessions support local artists. Restaurant menus found at the bar support local eateries. Happiness here definitely derives from what they give, not what they take.

Charles I believed in the divine right of kings, governing by conscience rather than consensus, and enforcing his sole right to make the rules. His namesake pub now appears to be the master of its own destiny. And they've honed their own rule-making down to one simple and spectacularly singular entry policy: "Strictly no wankers."

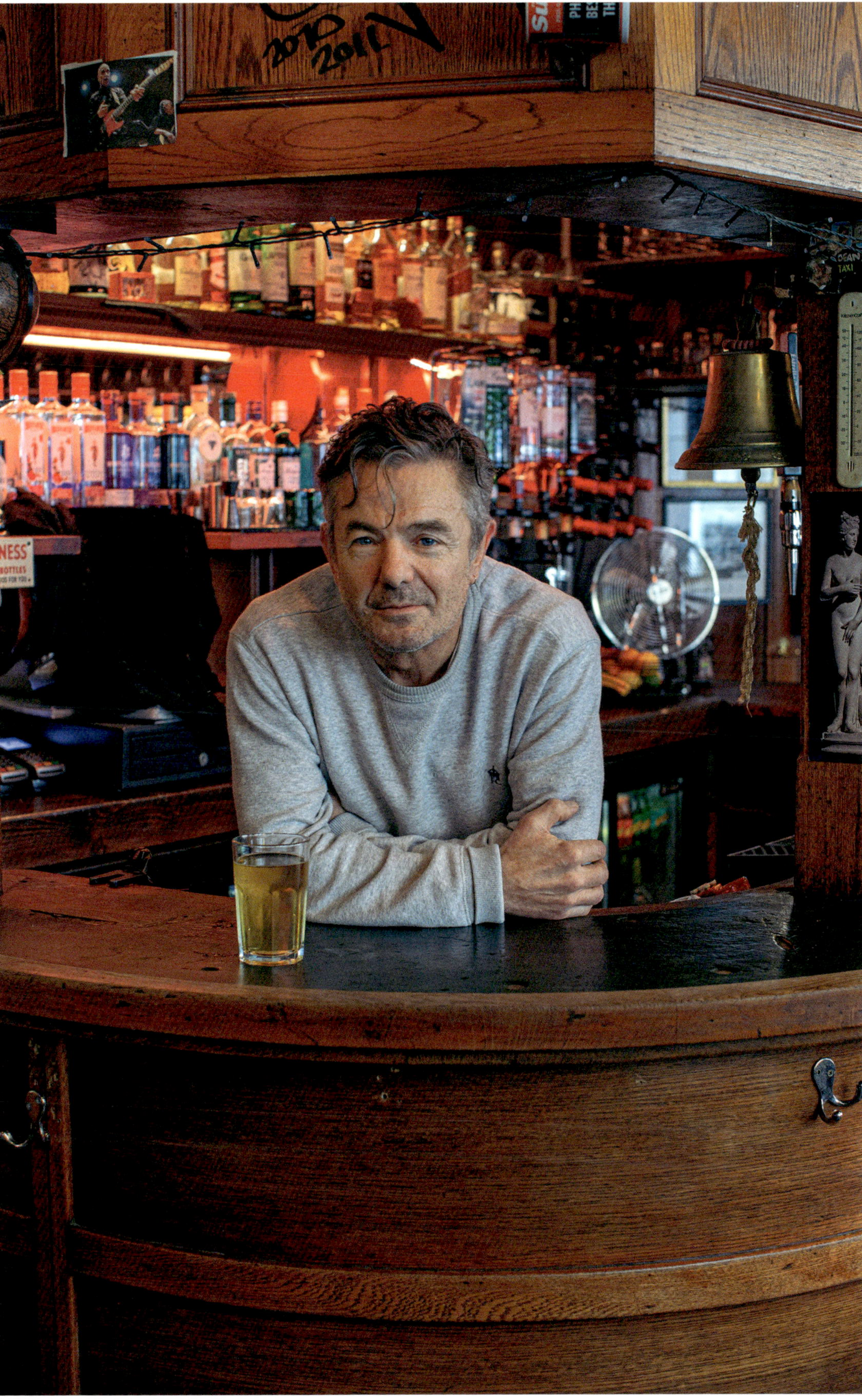

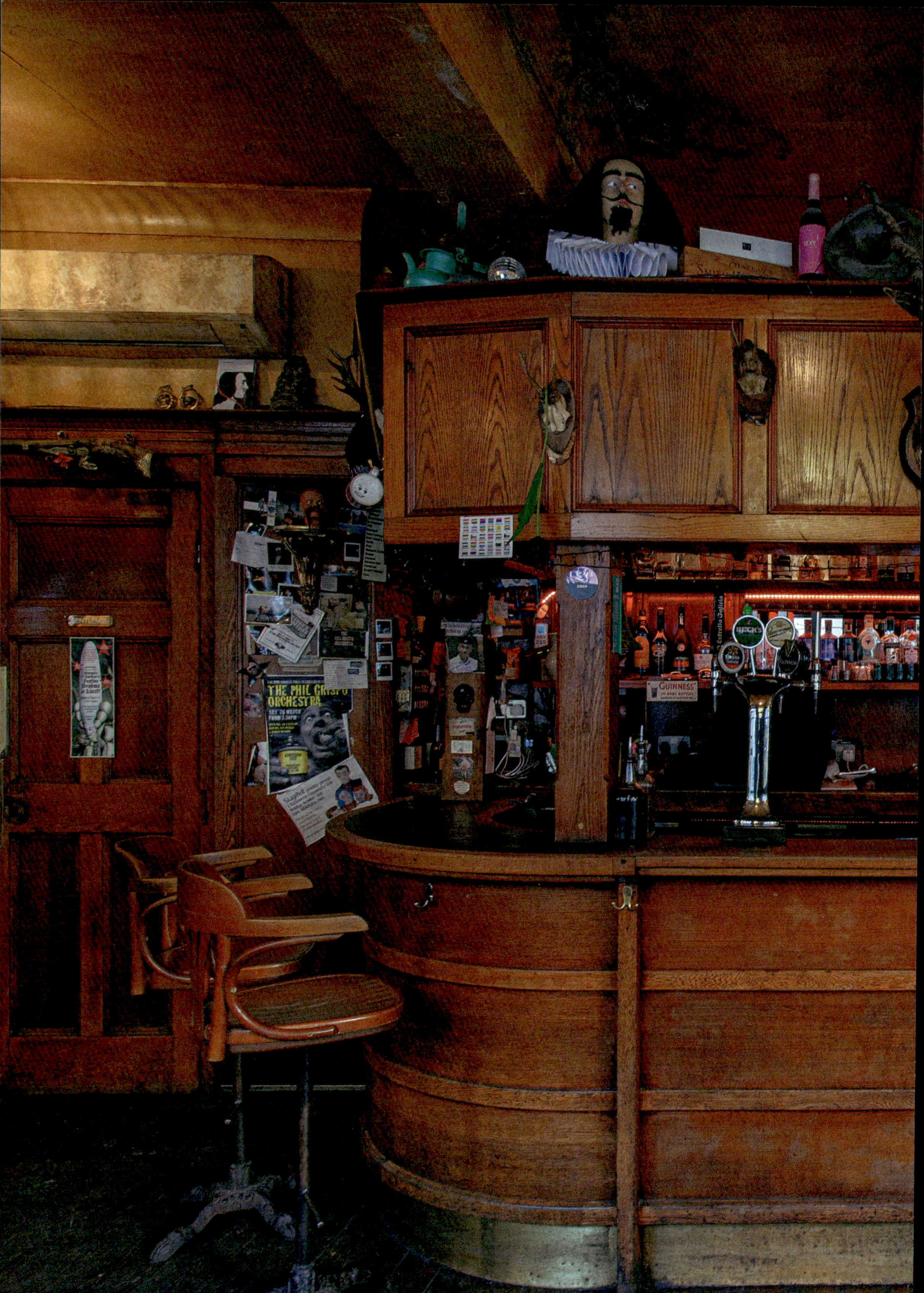

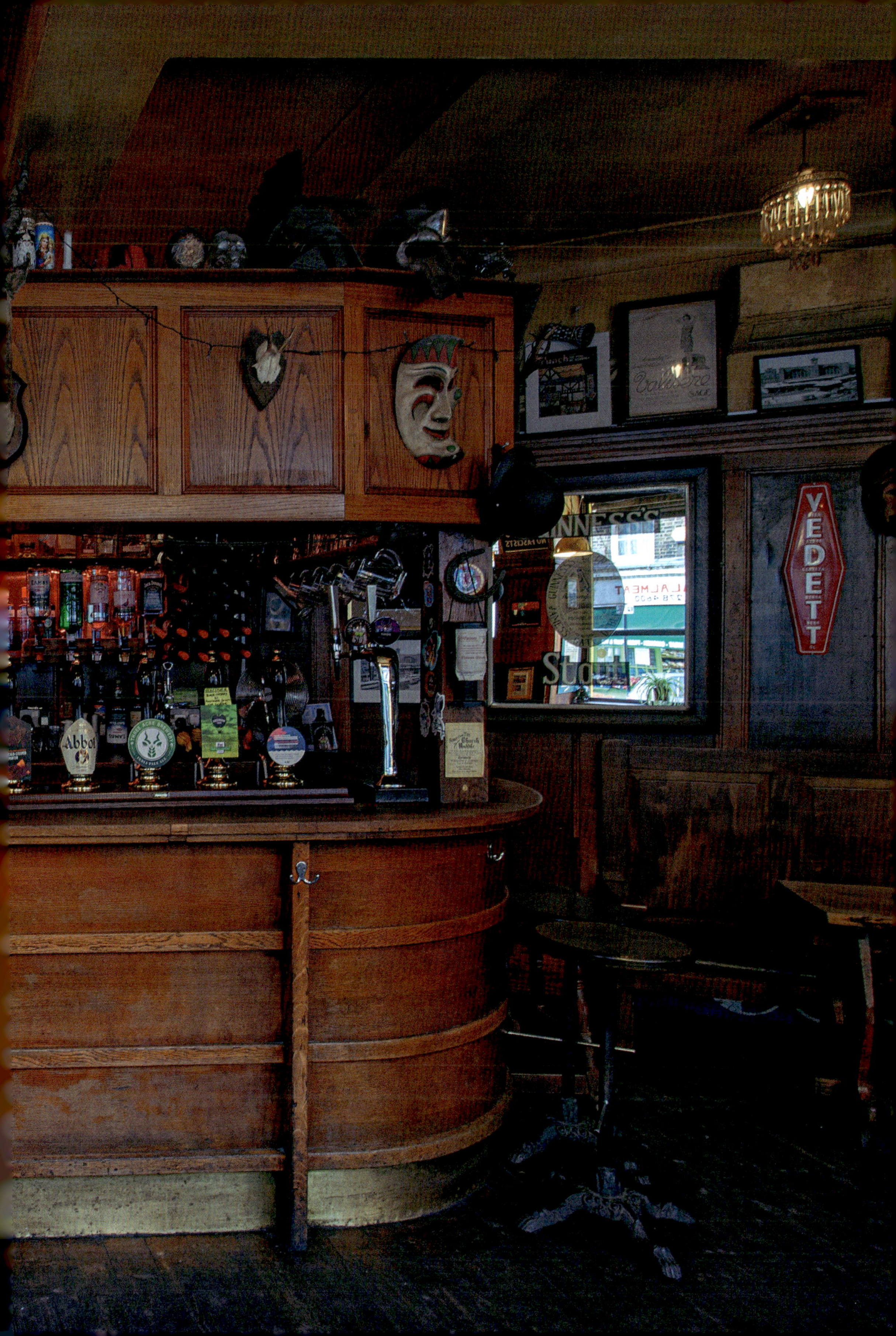

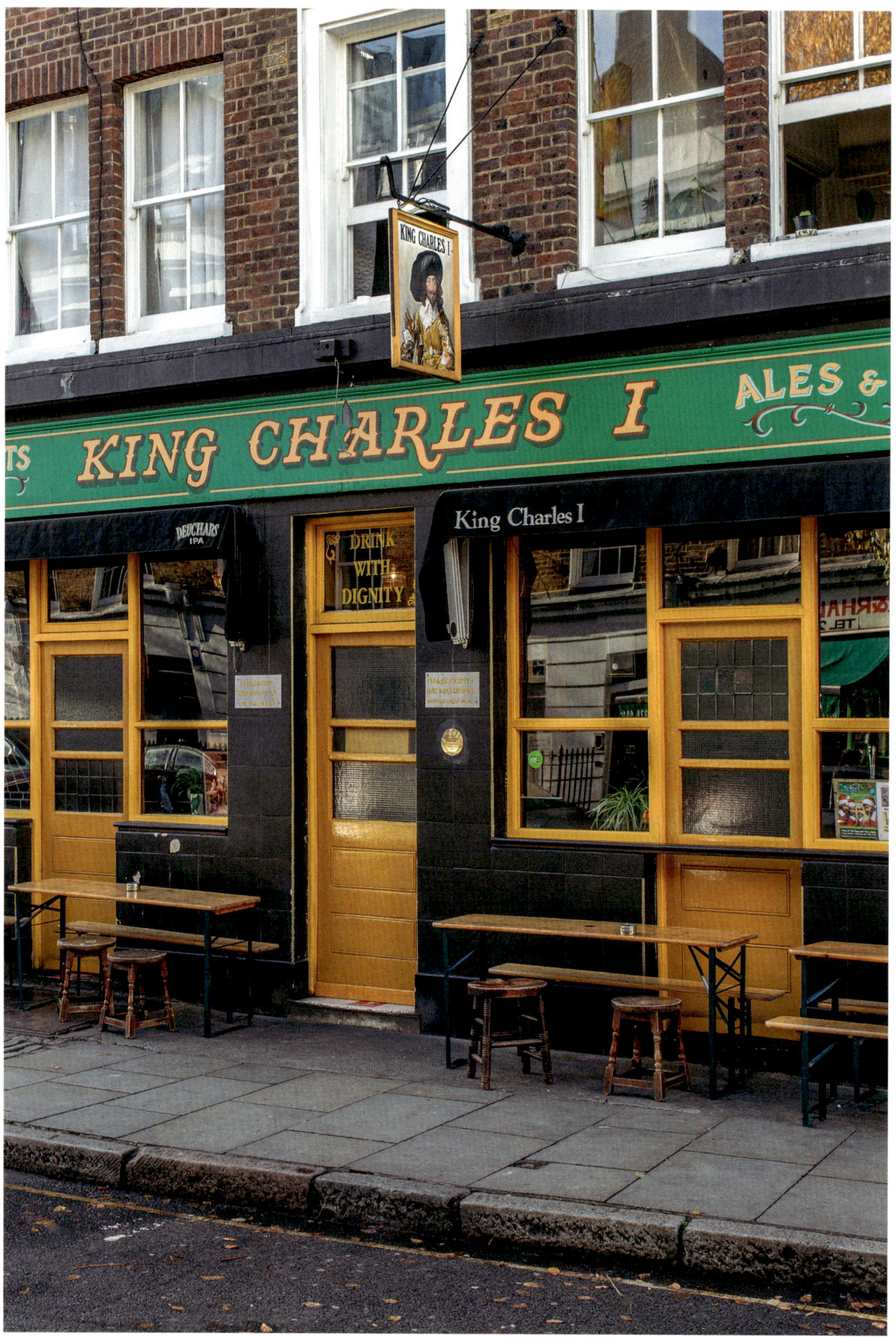

The jaunty paint job beckons you in

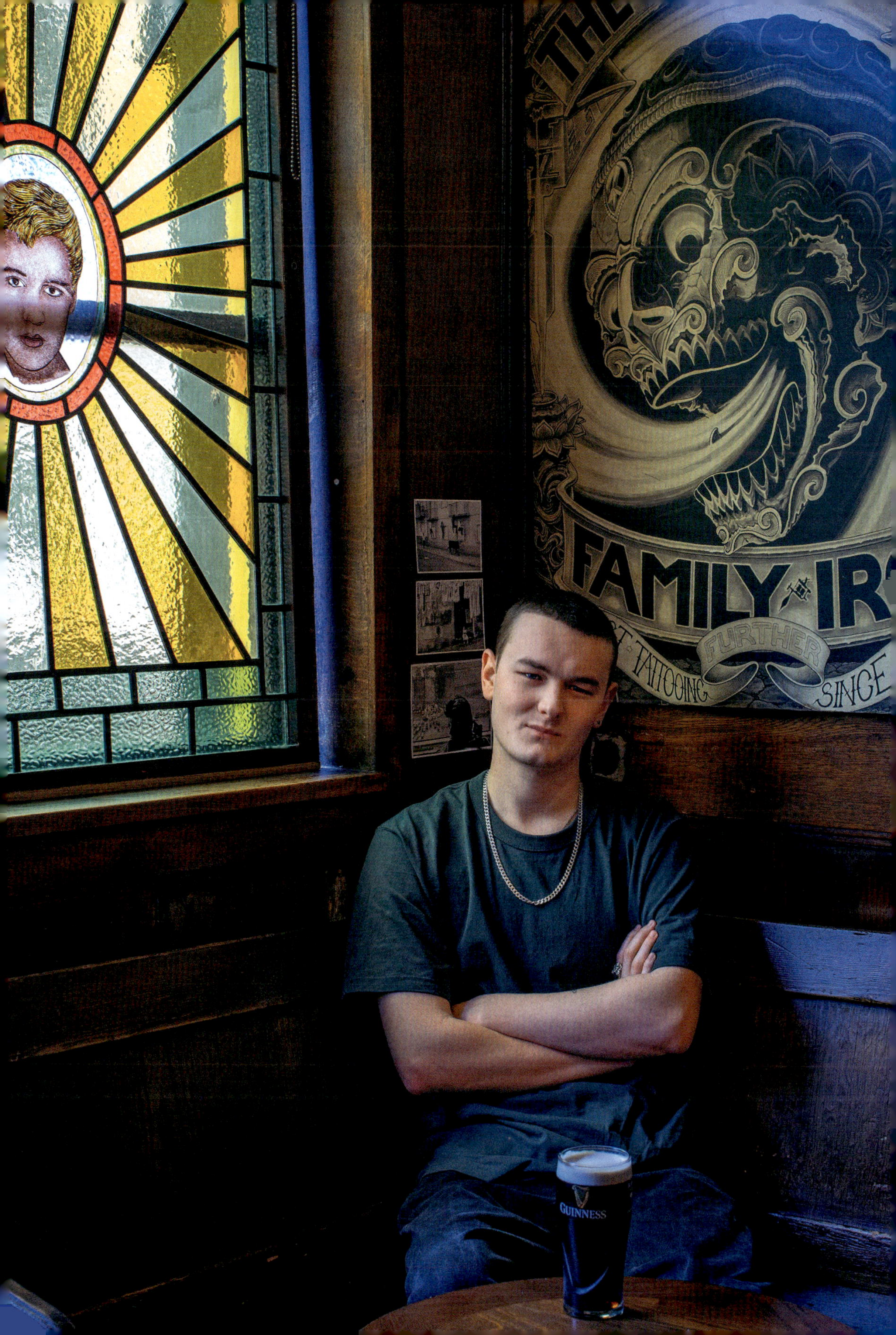
THE
FAMILY IR
FURTHER
TATTOOING
SINCE
GUINNESS

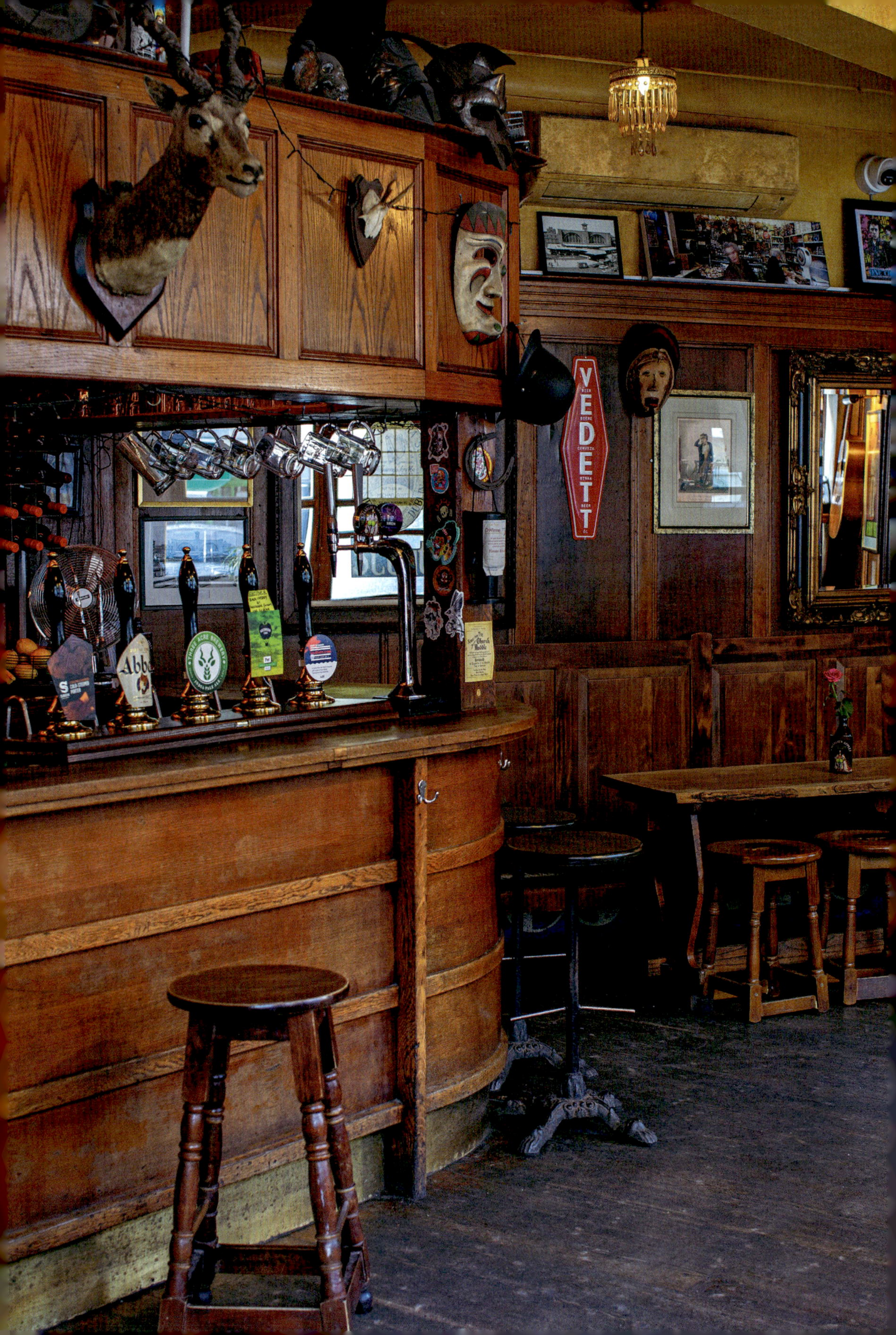

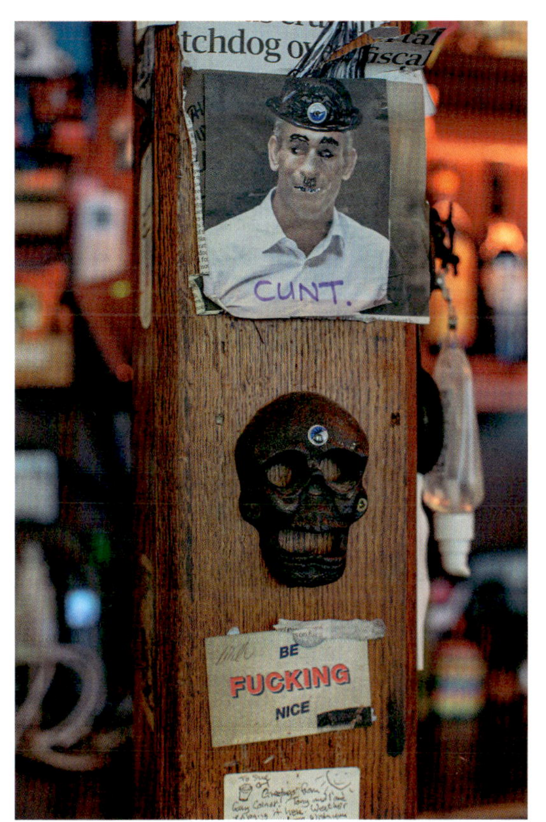

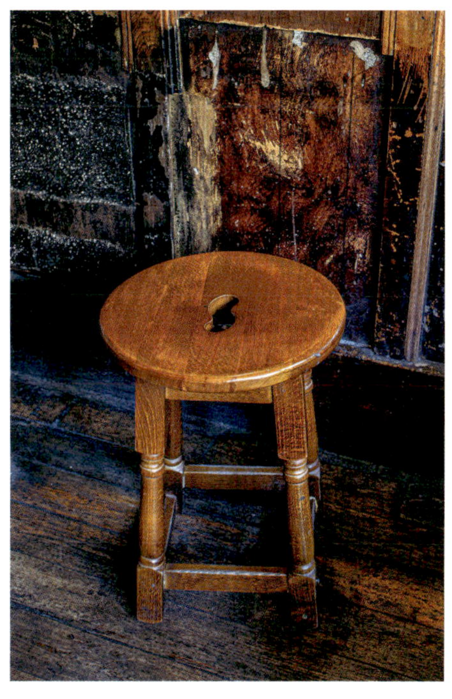

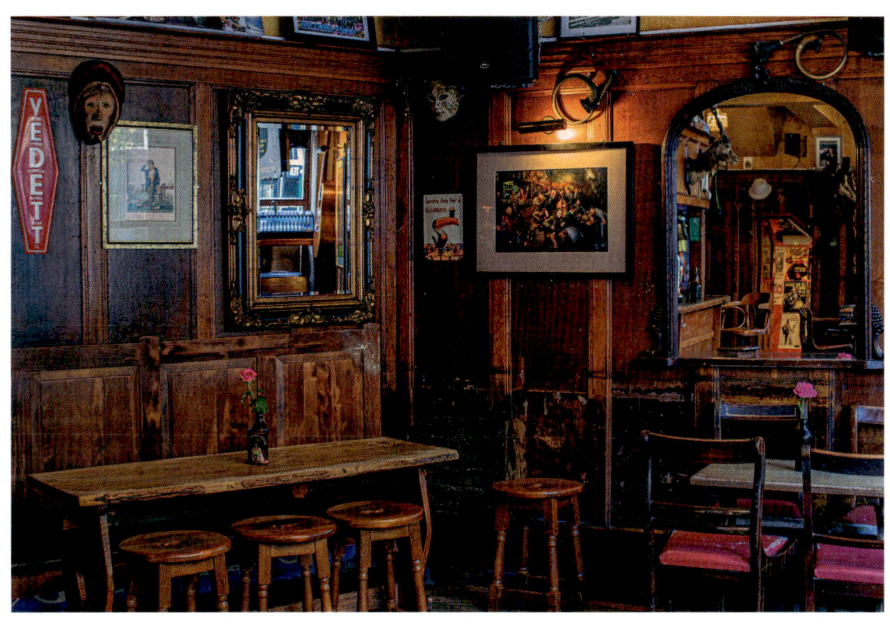

Amiable anarchy fills every corner

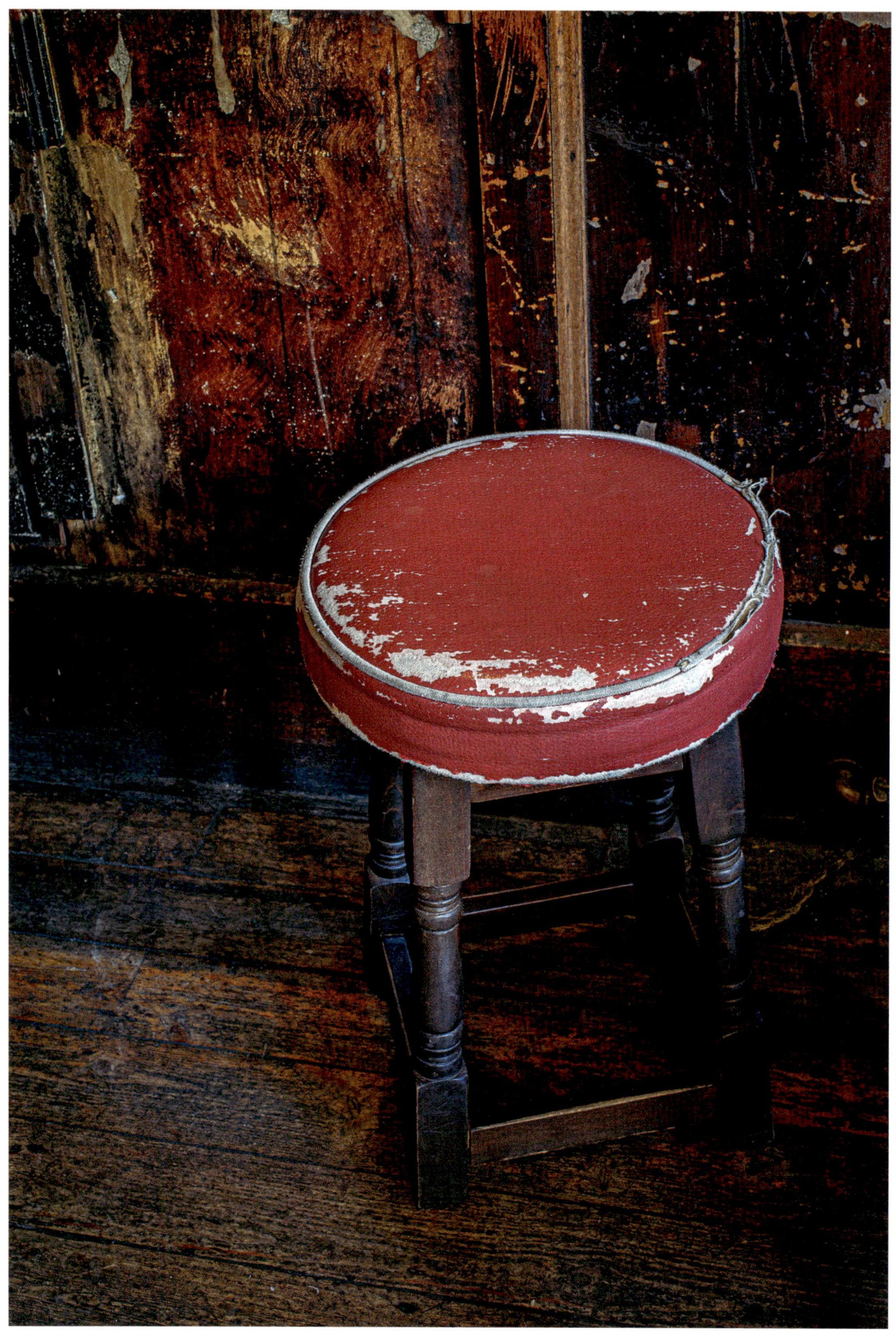

A true asset of community value

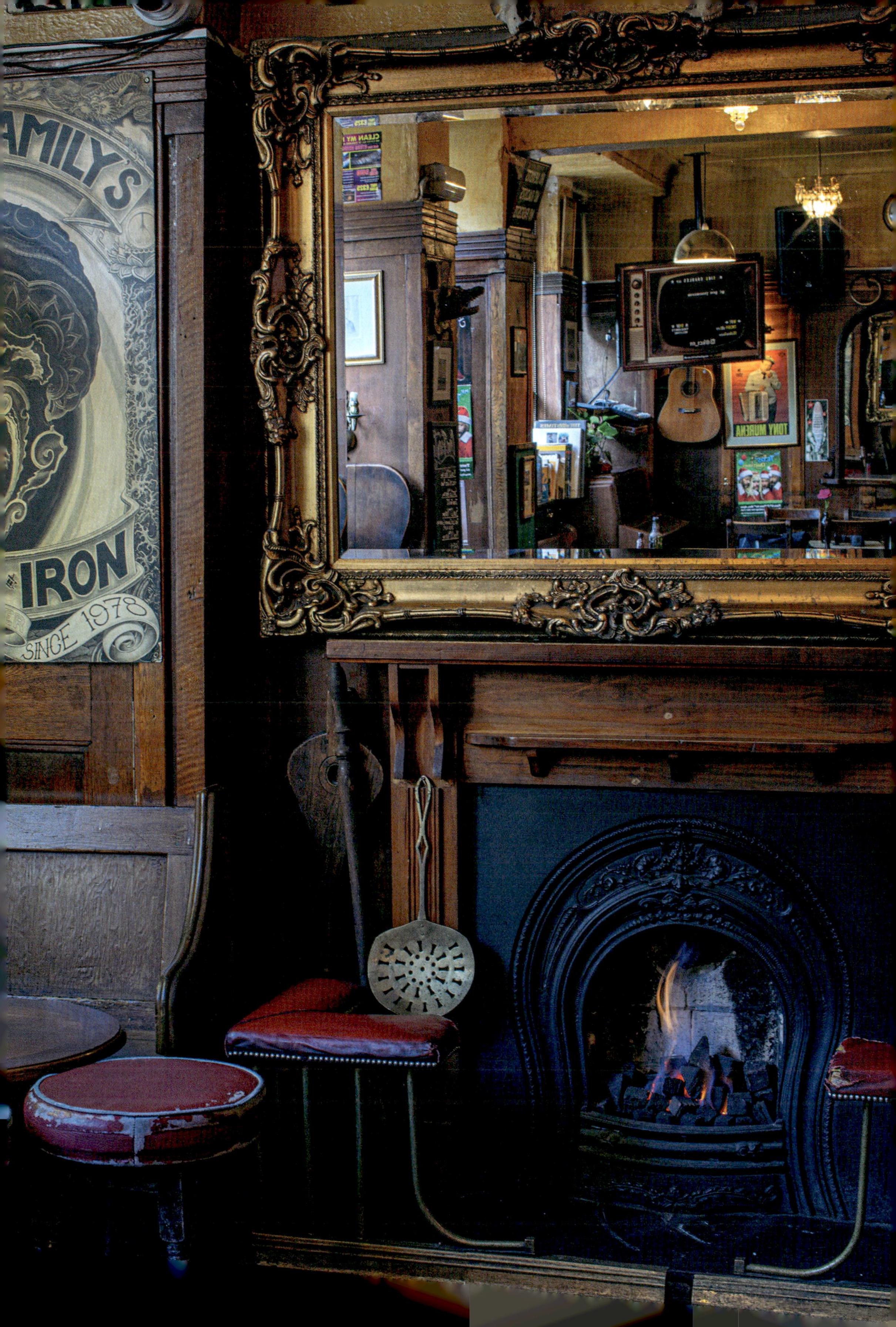

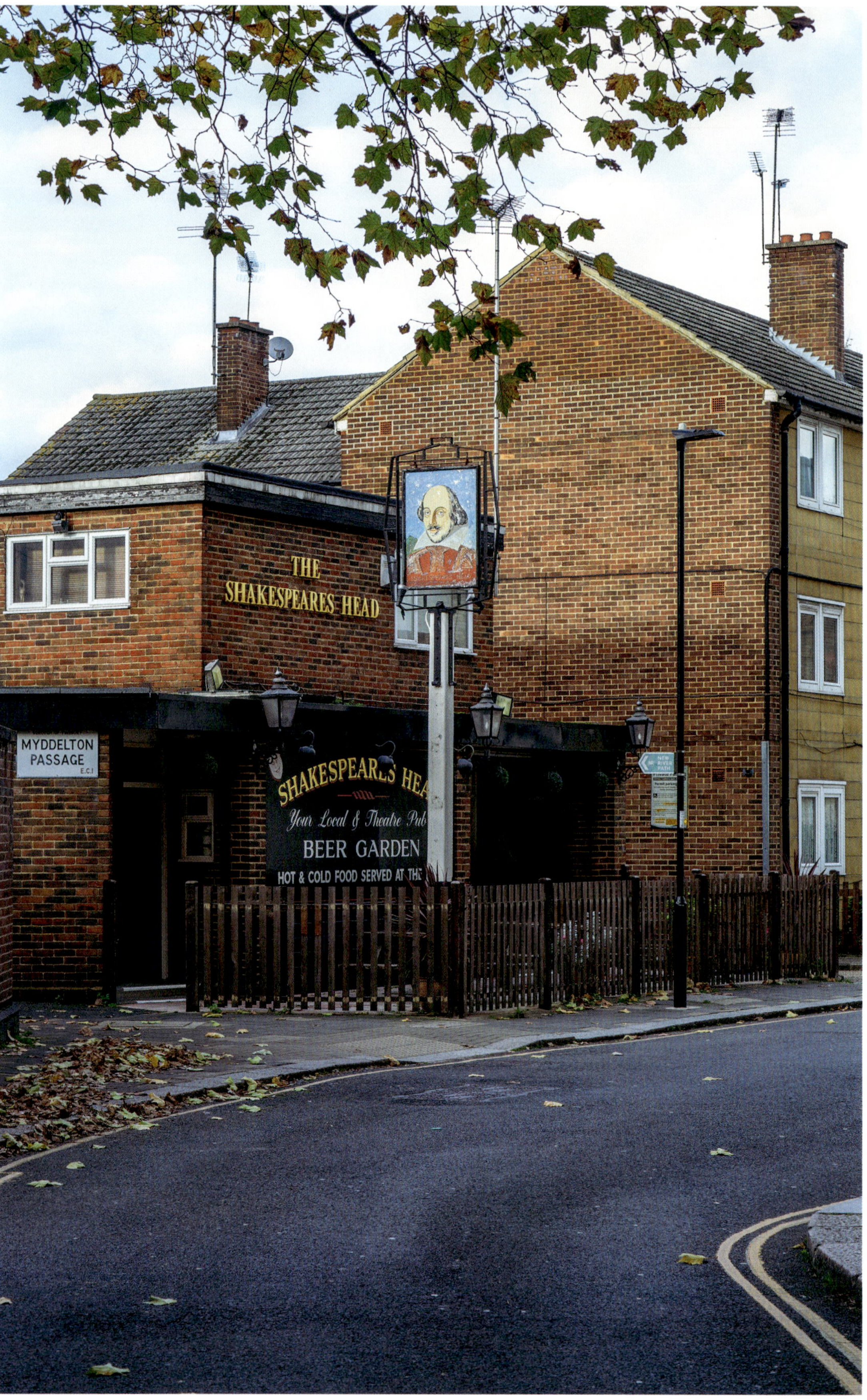
THE
SHAKESPEARES HEAD
MYDDELTON
PASSAGE
E.C.1
SHAKESPEARES HEAD
Your Local & Theatre Pub
BEER GARDEN
HOT & COLD FOOD SERVED AT THE
NEW RIVER PATH

THE SHAKESPEARE'S HEAD

It's 11.59 am and in they trickle. They're not here for the booze: they've come for the debrief on the grandkids, to bemoan the Gunners' most recent capitulation or to snatch a tip for the 2.30 at Chepstow.

To judge a book by its cover, you probably wouldn't fancy your chances in this slightly foreboding flat-roofer. There's no glass in the doors and net curtains obscure the rest. Historically, the area was indeed a bit rough around the edges, with Bobbies stationed in the passage alongside the pub. You can still see where they engraved their collar numbers on the wall whilst awaiting their prey.

With nearly three decades of profiling practice under their belts, teenage sweethearts George and Marie can sniff out a wrong'un in seconds. After ten years of pulling pints at The Harlequin, they staggered across the street to the stage door of Sadler's Wells Theatre. Removing the divide between the public and saloon bar is possibly the only intervention they've undertaken since then. Reminiscent of a working men's club, flat caps are still de rigueur, and if you want to know what this pub looked like when first built in the 1960s, just go there now.

While resembling an estate boozer, this is actually a mint-condition theatre pub. Old-timers, thirsty thesps and ballet stagehands drift in through the day. You might find celebrated choreographer Sir Matthew Bourne supping away in the corner and by night you could be clinking G&Ts with Kylie Minogue, Daniel Craig or the cast from *Stomp*. The walls resemble a who's who of stage and screen who have frequented this impromptu theatre bar over the decades, alongside a Great Train Robber or two.

It's a pub where the Pearly Kings and Queens still pay their respects on Remembrance Day and regulars turn out in their Sunday best. A pub where children are shown the door by 6 pm, but the pub cat is always welcome. Even the beer comes with no frills. You won't find a more rudimentary rundown on the pumps; a nostalgic pint of John Smith's hits all the right vintage notes in this period drama.

Like all great plays, the show must go on. As George and Marie begin to leave the limelight, their family understudies are waiting in the wings. Jason and Sharon know the ropes inside out, so they're not about to fluff their lines. The Shakespeare is ready for its next act.

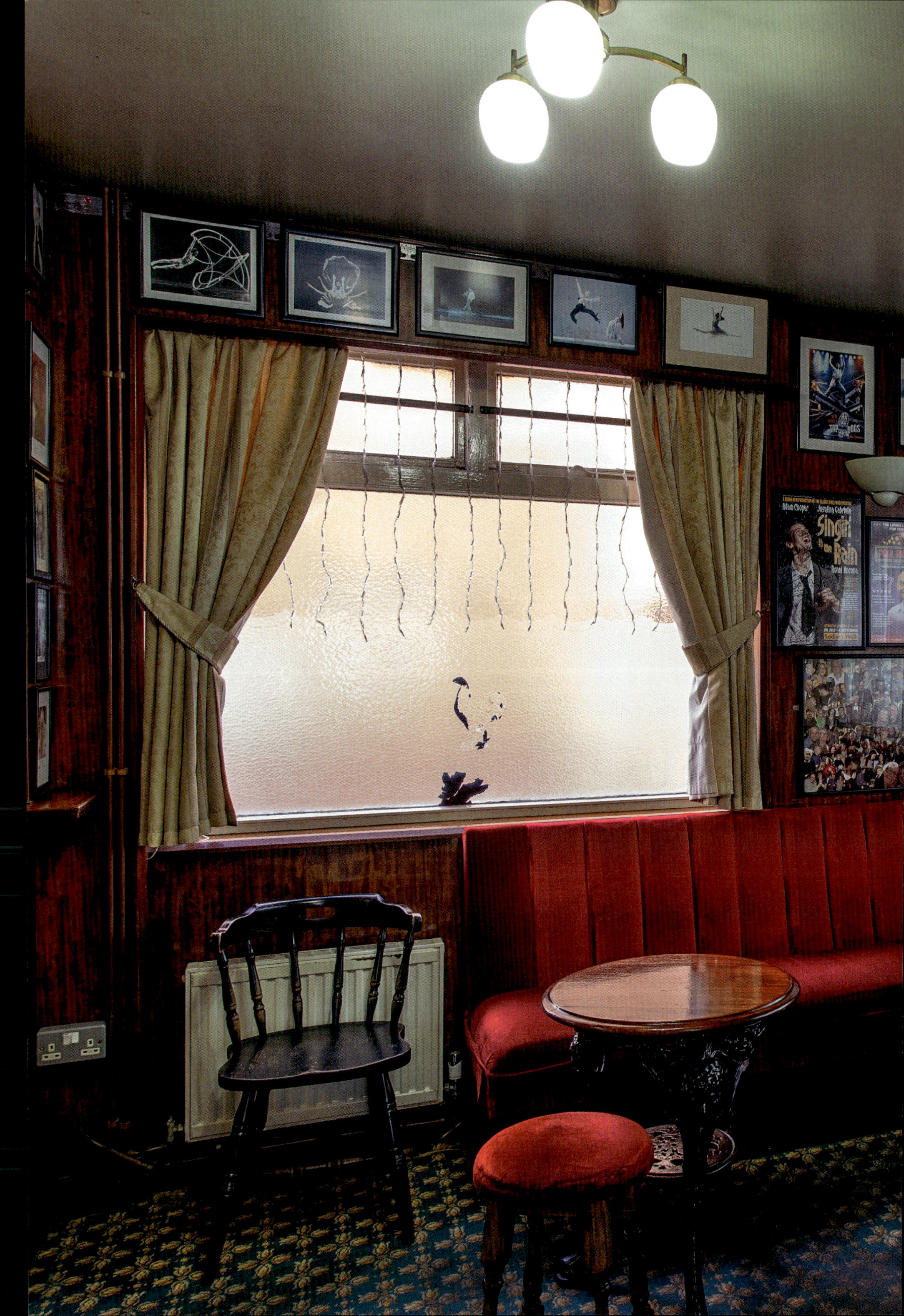

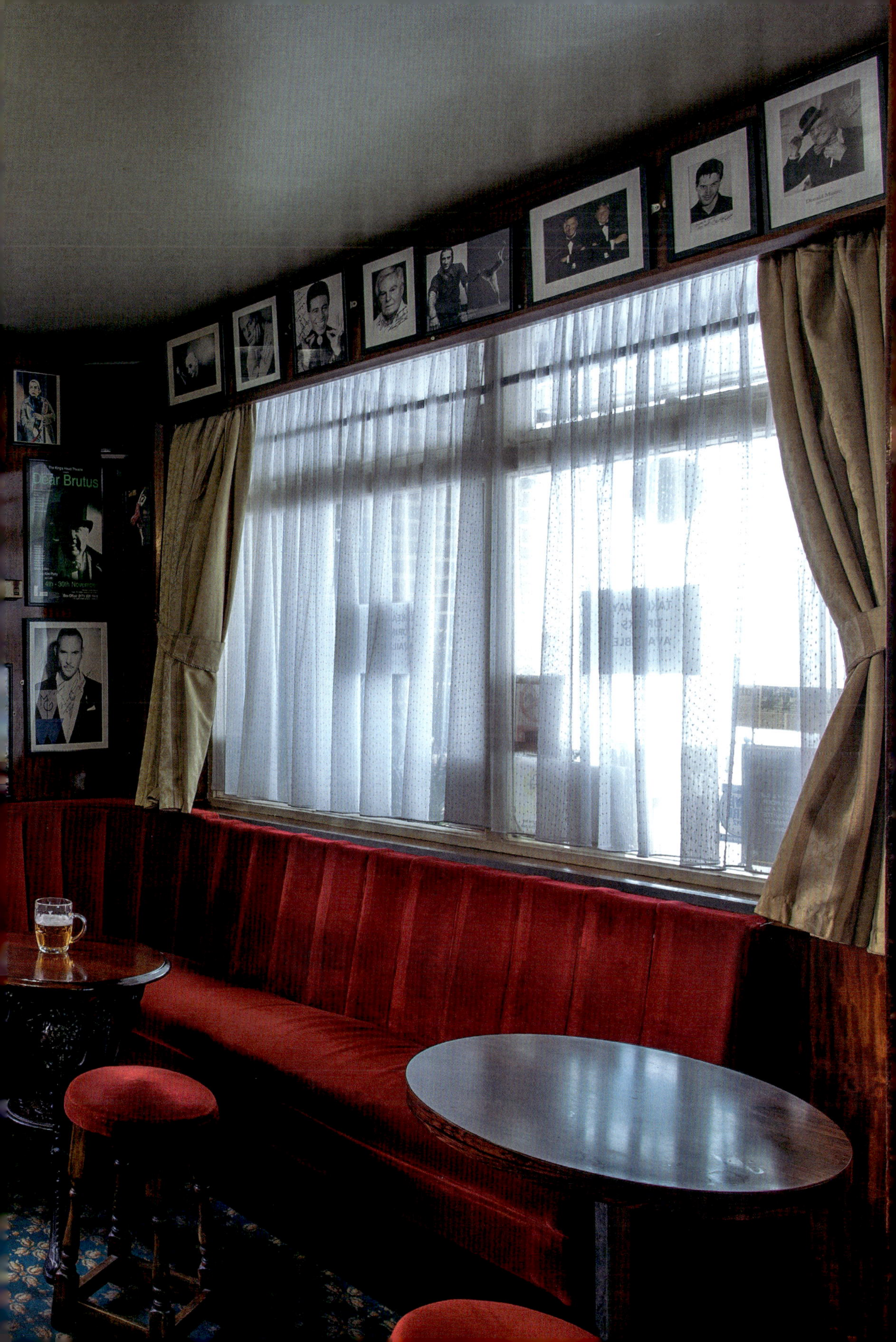

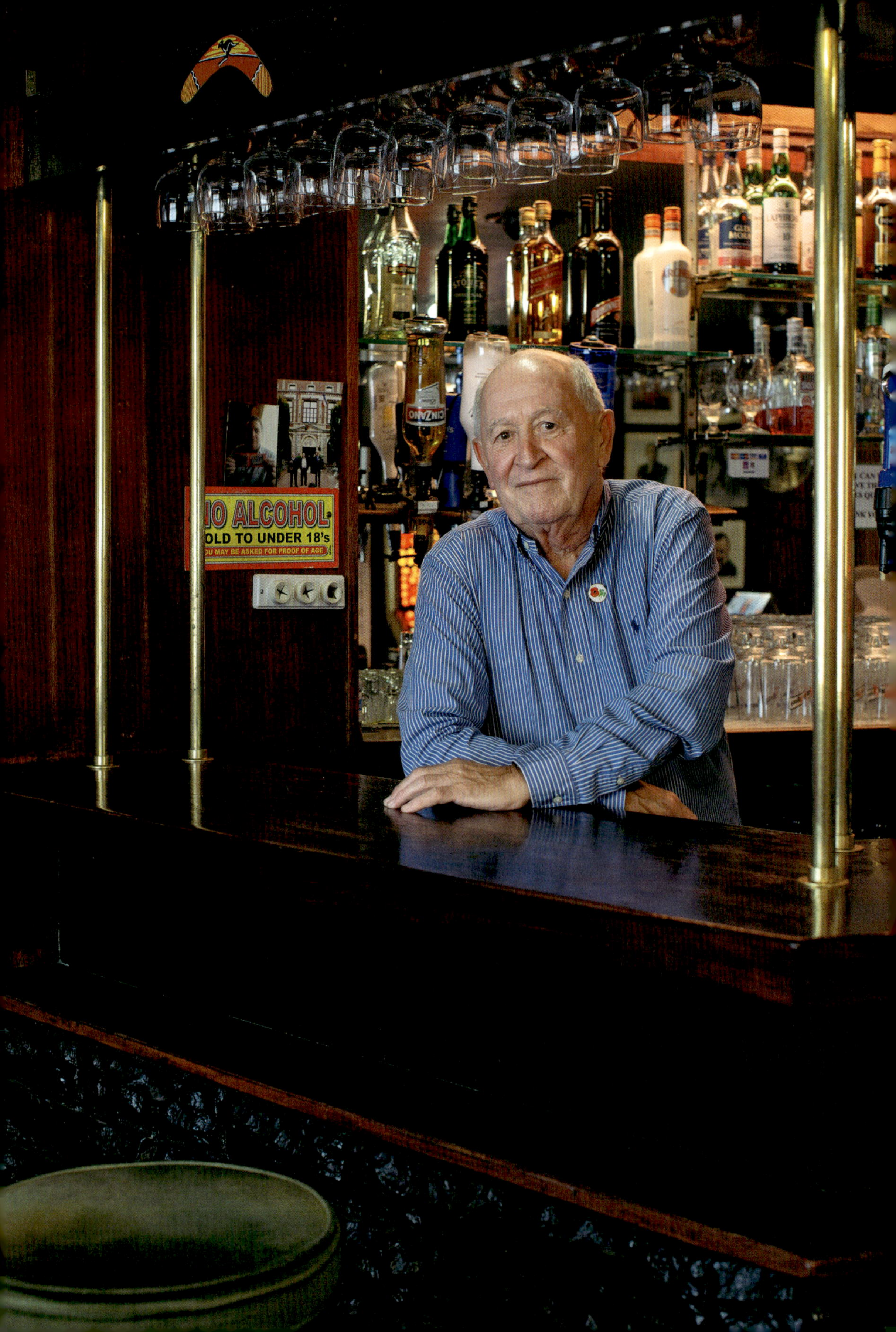
NO ALCOHOL
SOLD TO UNDER 18's
YOU MAY BE ASKED FOR PROOF OF AGE

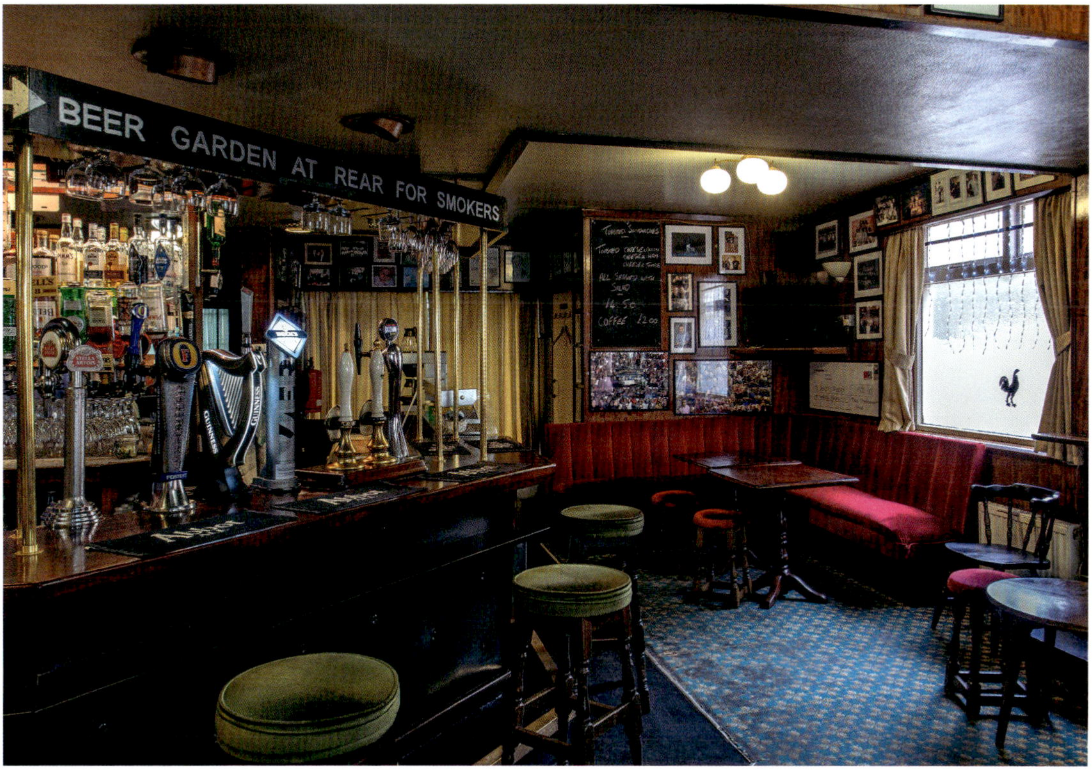

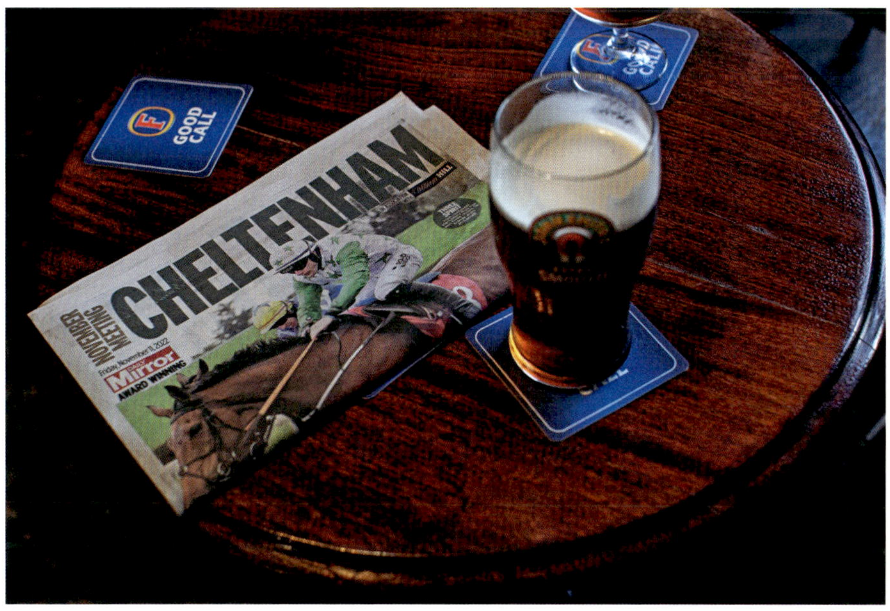

A convivial working men's club atmosphere blends with theatrical themes

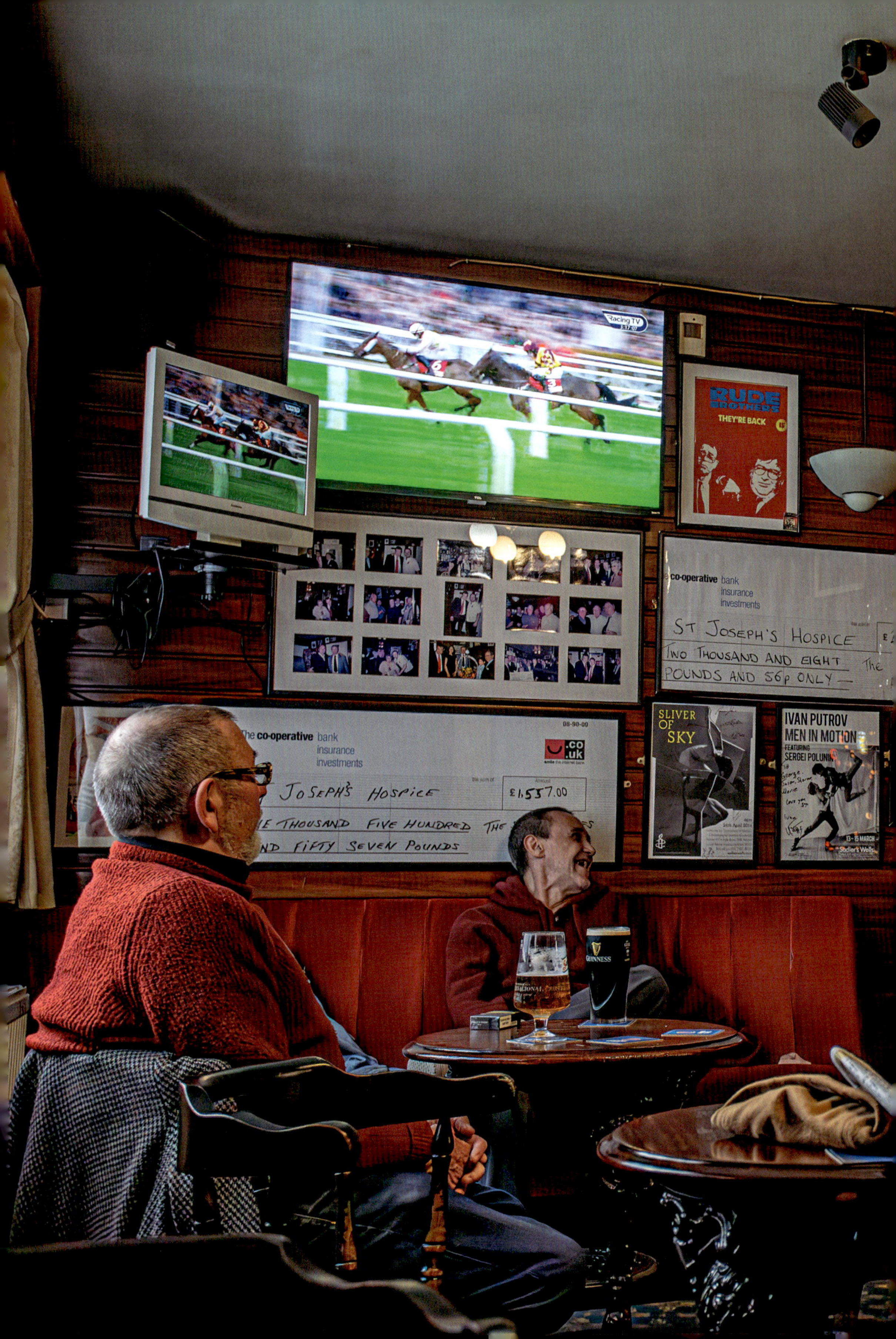

Racing TV
RUDE BROTHERS
THEY'RE BACK
the co-operative bank
insurance
investments
St JOSEPH'S HOSPICE
TWO THOUSAND AND EIGHT
POUNDS AND 56p ONLY
The co-operative bank
insurance
investments
08-90-00
.co.uk
smile the internet bank
JOSEPH'S HOSPICE
£1,557.00
THOUSAND FIVE HUNDRED
AND FIFTY SEVEN POUNDS
SLIVER OF SKY
IVAN PUTROV
MEN IN MOTION
FEATURING
SERGEI POLUNIN
GUINNESS

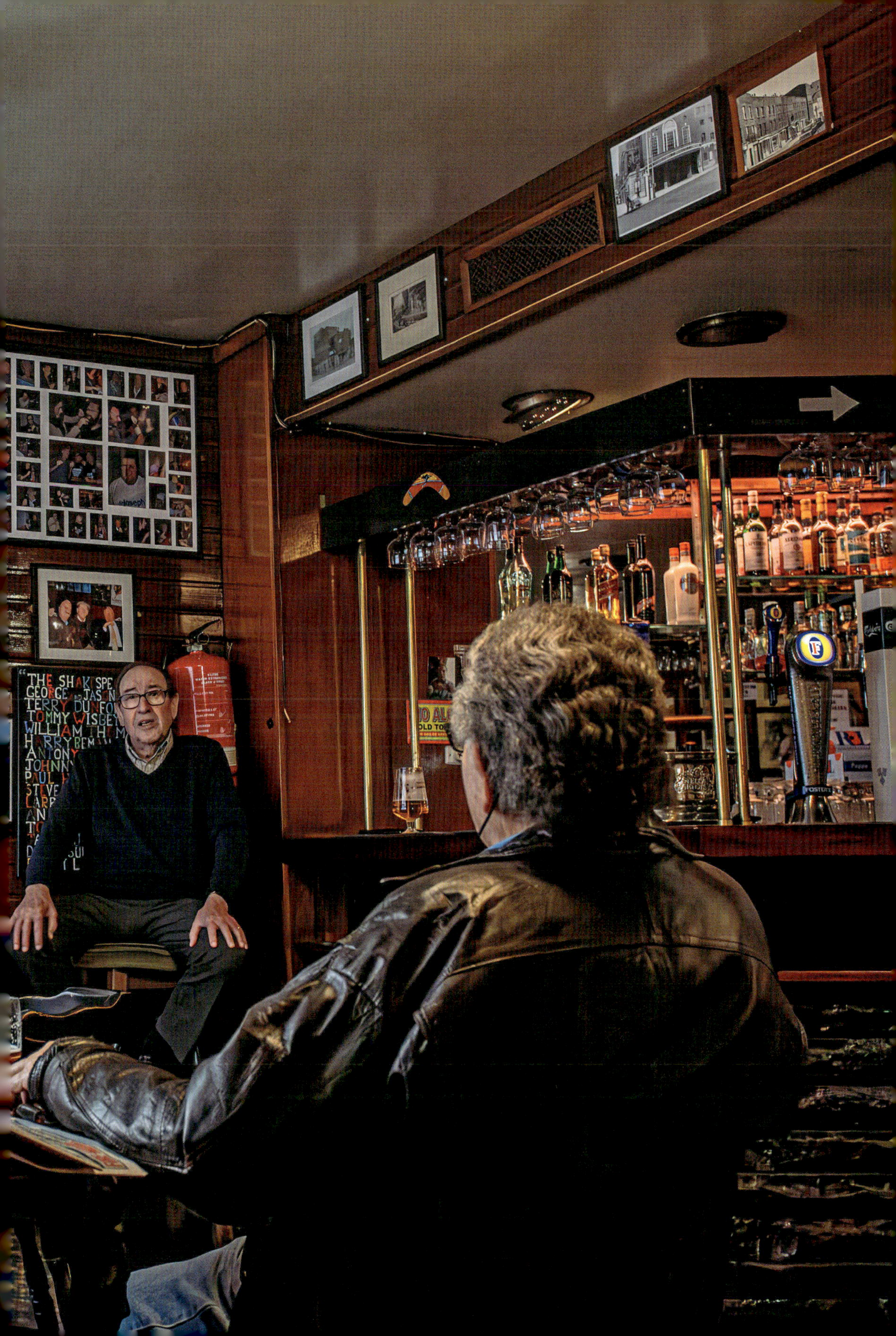

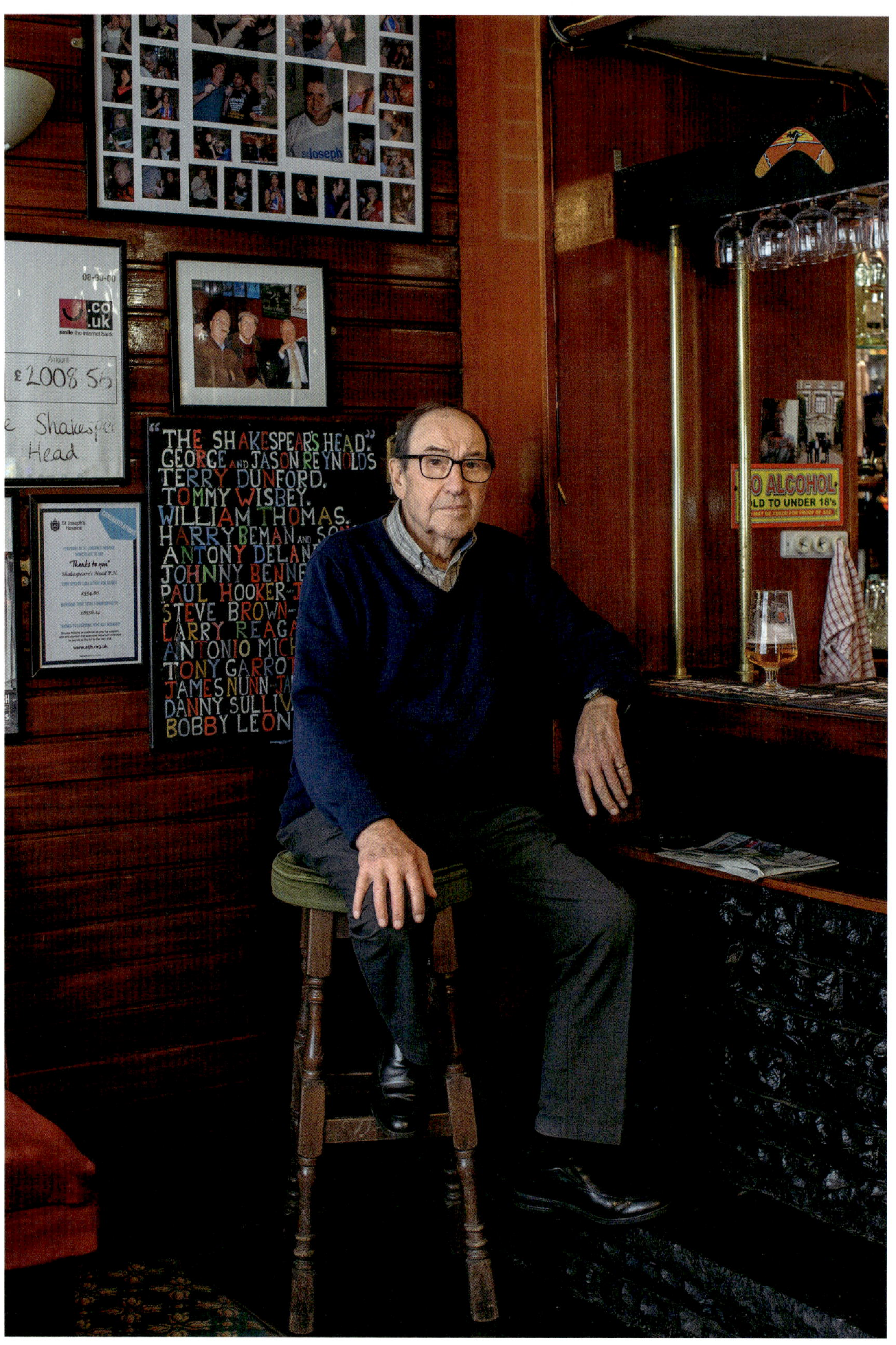

Old-timers, off-duty posties and stage-hands all drift through these doors

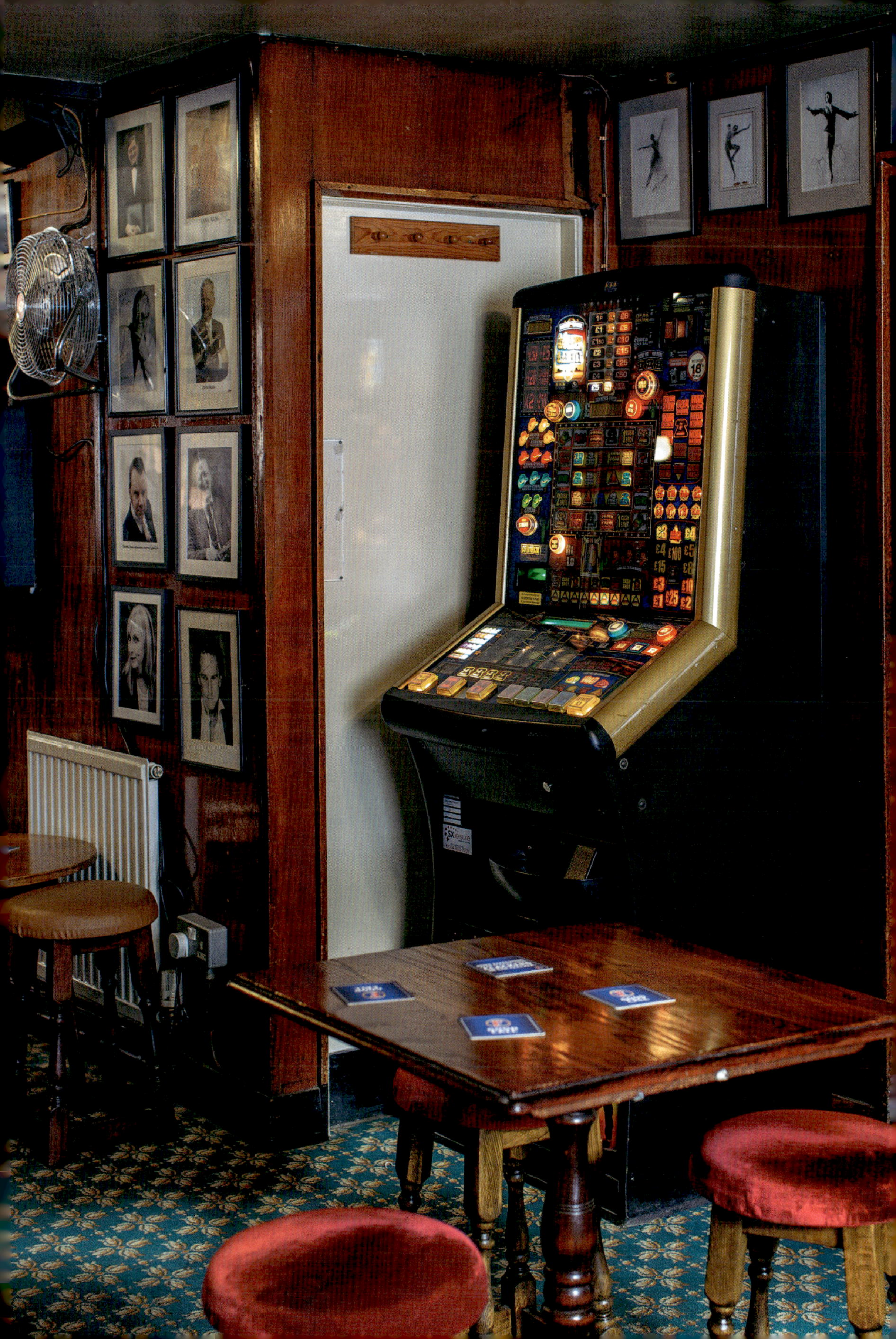

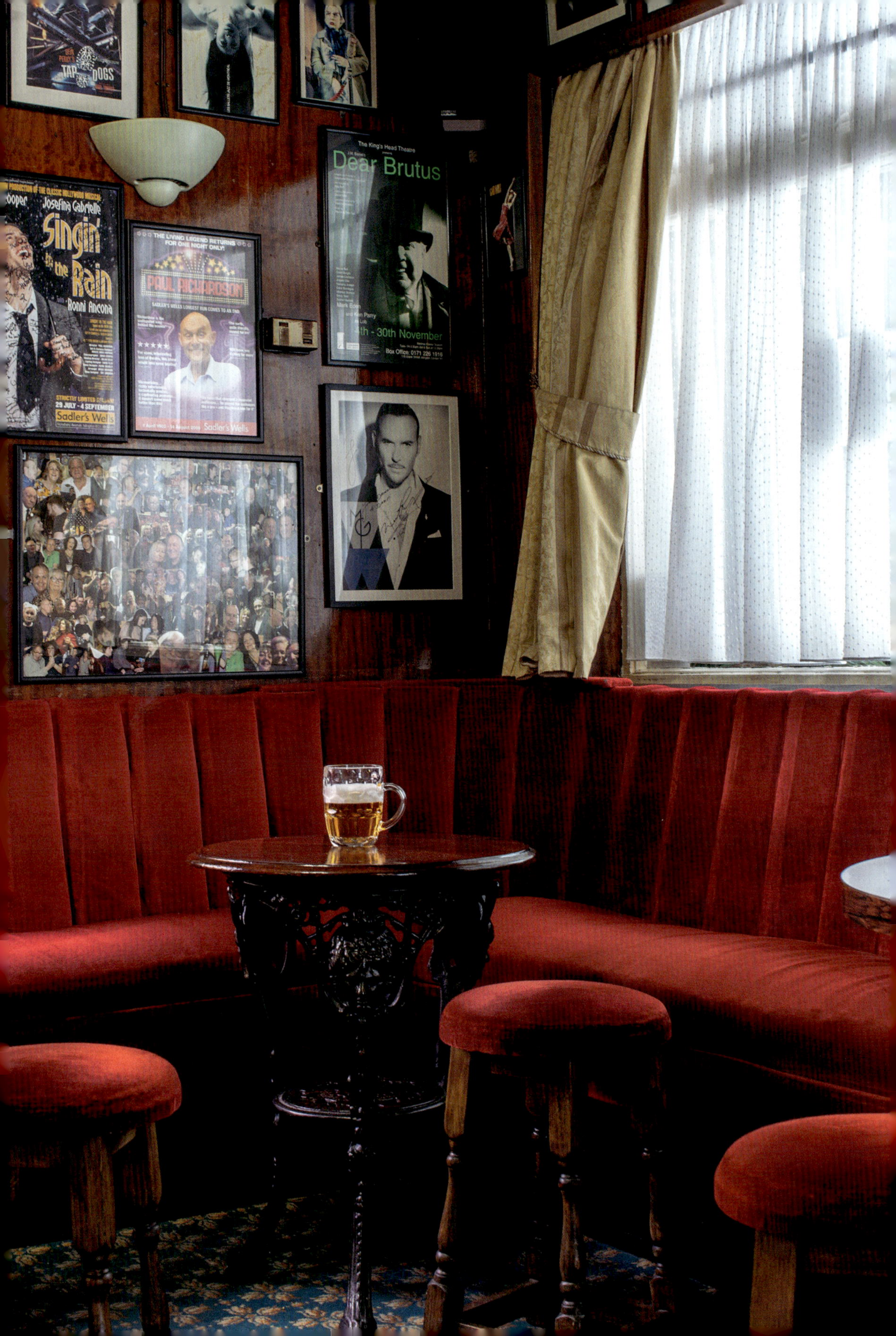
TAP DOGS
Josefina Gabrielle
Singin' in the Rain
with Bonni Ancona
29 JULY – 4 SEPTEMBER
Sadler's Wells
THE LIVING LEGEND RETURNS FOR ONE NIGHT ONLY!
PAUL RICHARDSON
SADLER'S WELLS LONGEST RUN COMES TO AN END.
Sadler's Wells
The King's Head Theatre
Dear Brutus
4th – 30th November
Box Office: 0171 226 1916

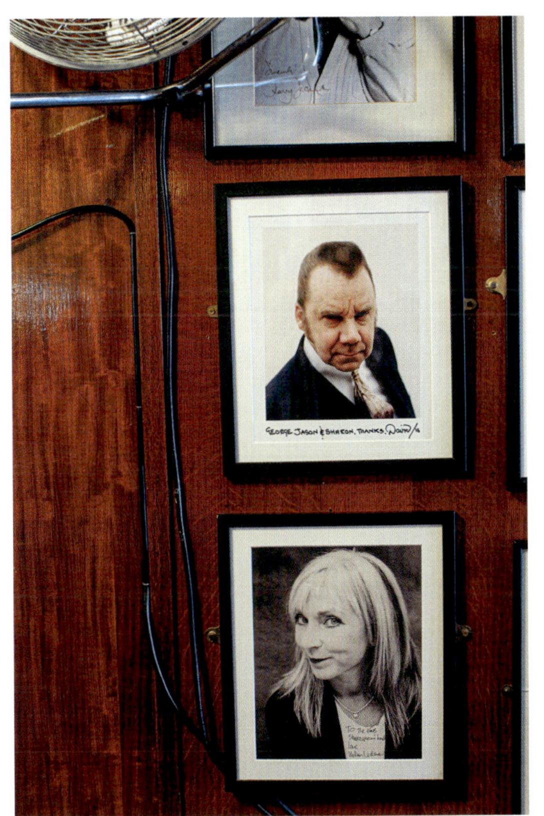

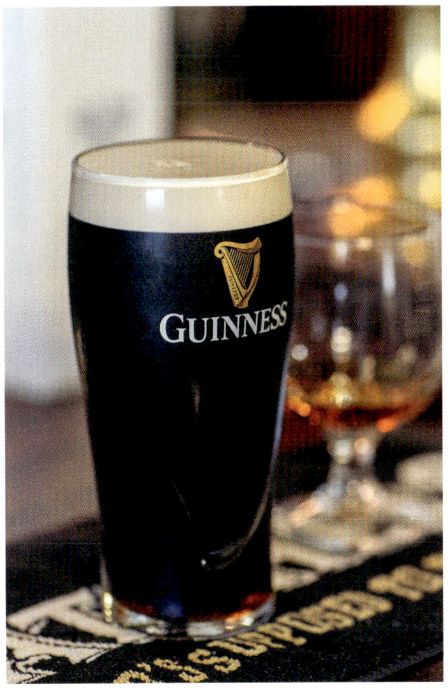

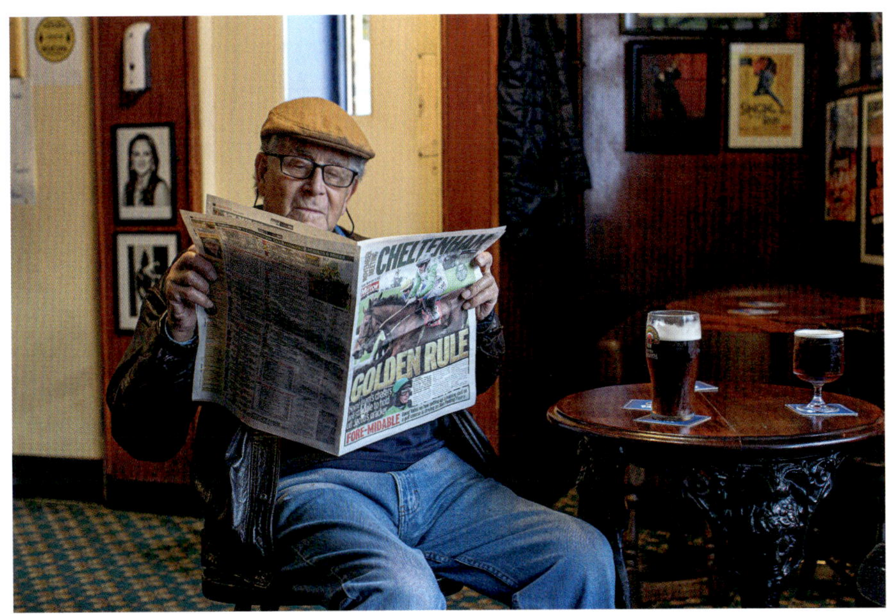

Nags and a natter are a good common denominator

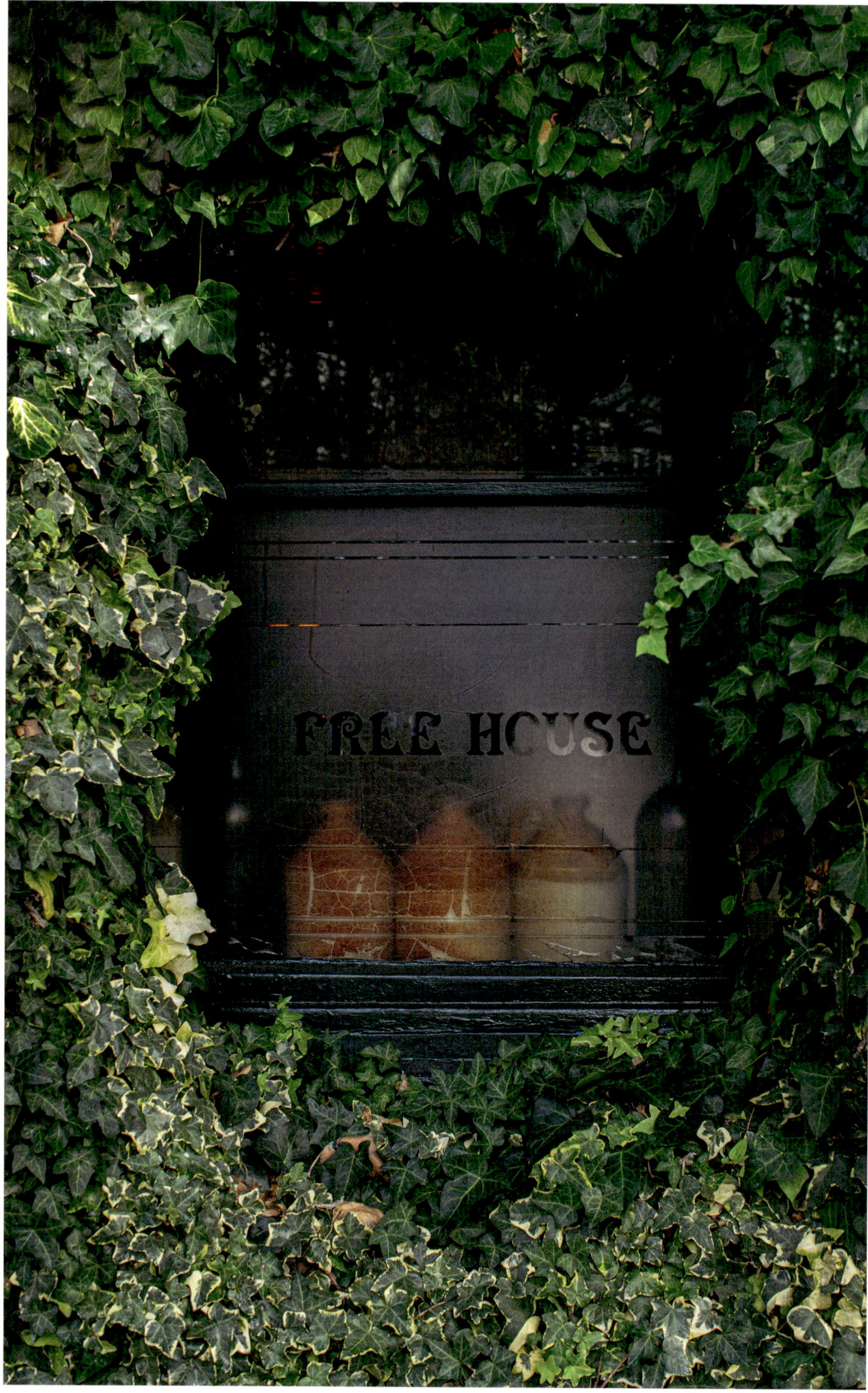
FREE HOUSE

THE HEMINGFORD ARMS

TIED HOUSE, THAI FOOD

158 HEMINGFORD RD, BARNSBURY N1 1DF

The majority of pubs in this book hold elusive freehold status, free from brewery tie and with no cookie-cutter pub company to answer to. Their swashbuckling, independent spirit is clear to see, from the beers that they serve to the hours that they wish to keep. These are London's artisans of autonomy, carving unique caverns of urban communion. But we had to let a few slip through our net. These are the ones that tend to wear any commercial association so thinly that you barely notice. Would you forego another pint at Ye Olde Mitre or at The Guinea Grill based purely on their lineage?

It's sometimes hard to be sure on which side of the law the patrons fall.

The pub's mothership might be a financial behemoth gobbling up all in its path, but the place itself still merits its position in our Ivy League of pubs. Quite literally. It's covered in the stuff. Rambling all over the façade, it's often hard to see the wooden bar for the trees in this horticultural hemline. Once inside this barn of a bar, surreal bric-a-brac and vintage film posters create quite the bohemian atmosphere. It's perfect for a pint when popping into the palace of penitence just up the road at Pentonville Prison, and indeed it's sometimes hard to be sure on which side of the law the patrons fall.

The faintest whiff of the salty Irish Sea blows through these parts, with County Holloway not far away. So, as sure as night follows day, Thai food shall be served. We don't know why: it's just the unwritten law that Irish pubs and Thai cooking are a match made in heaven. Gaeng Keow Wan paired with your Guinness is never a bad thing, and it keeps the local sundried-tomato-and-cappuccino crowd safely tucked up in the Islington gastropubs that encircle "The Hemmie".

This boozer continues to keep it real with trad music nights, a spot of bingo, quirky quizzes and locally sourced brews. The classic picnic tables allow punters to soak up some rays and marvel at the balletic kinetic motion of cars spinning around the double roundabout.

So, try not to hold The Hemmie's dubious ownership against it. After a few cold ones and some Thai crackers, you'll forgive this eccentric little bolthole almost anything.

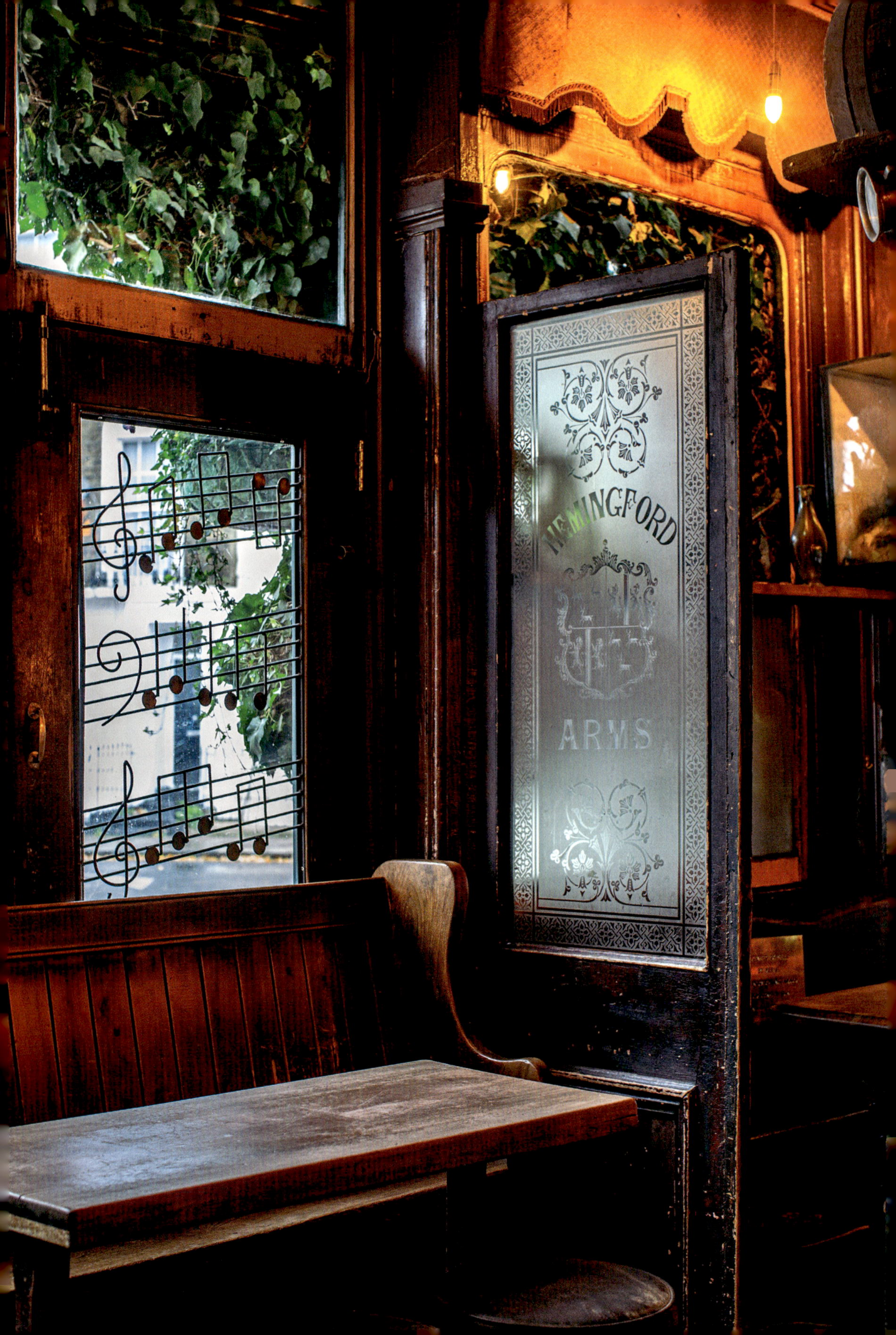

HEMINGFORD
ARMS

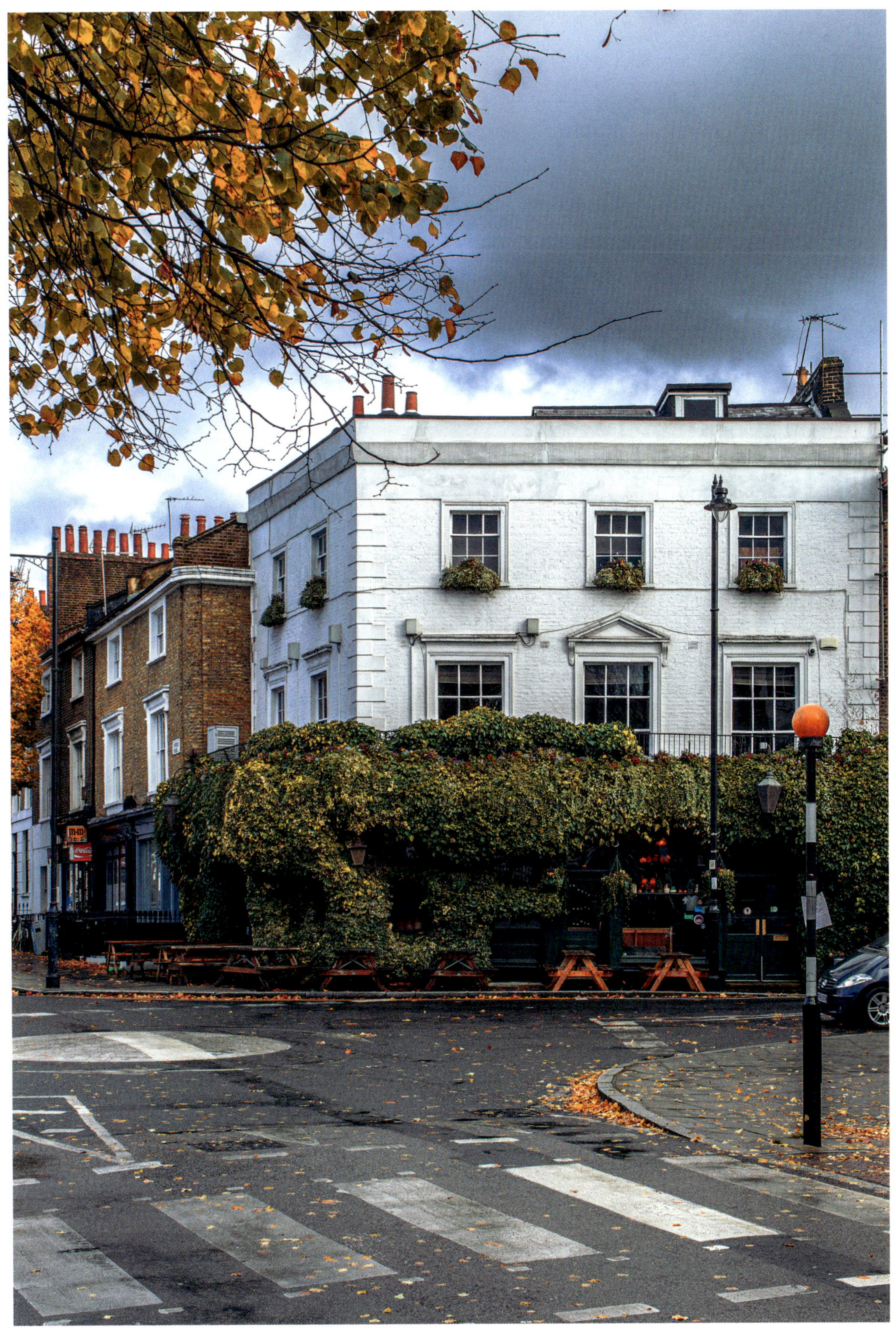

A verdant evergreen exterior gives way to a dark and moody bar scene

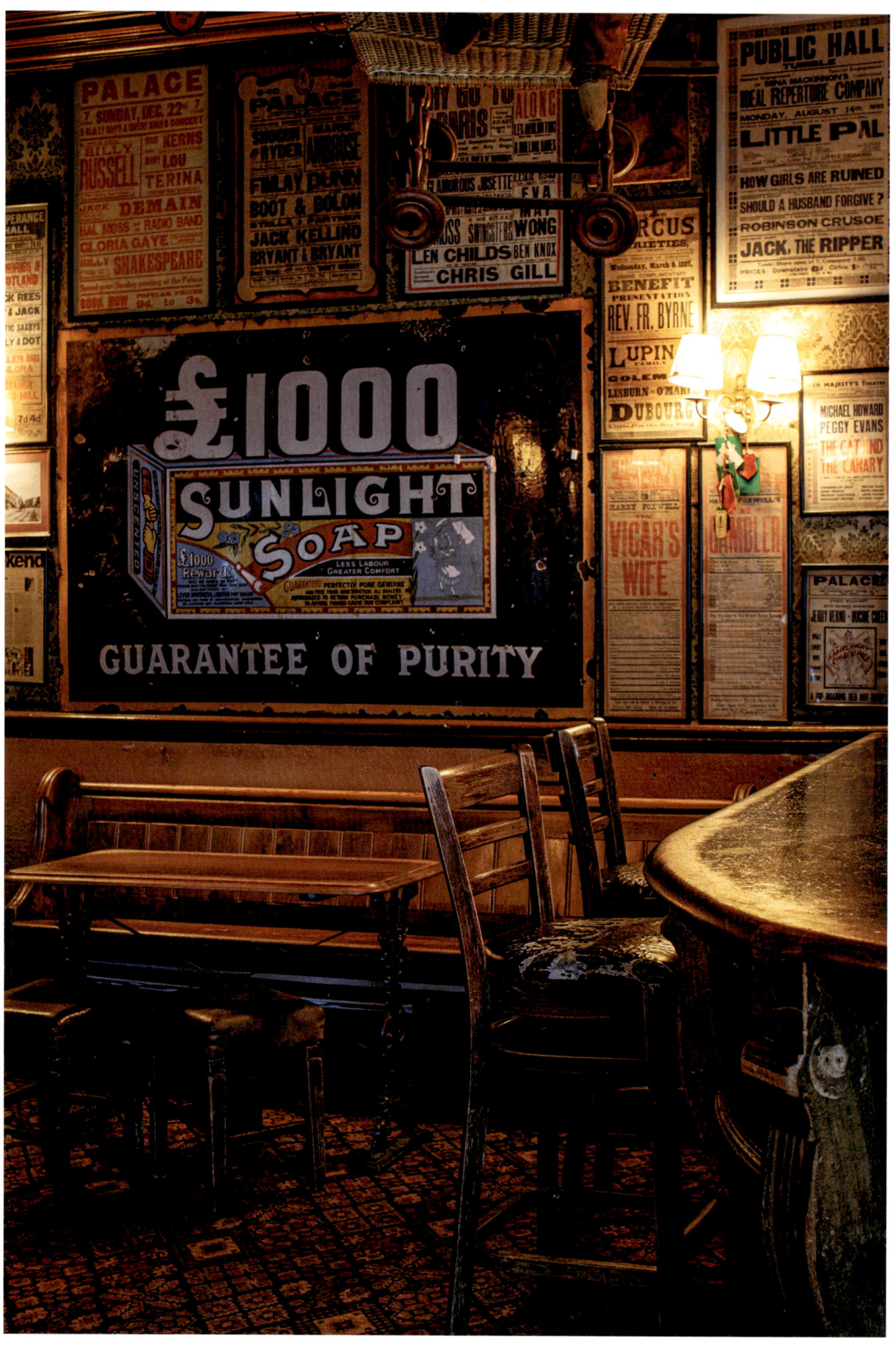

Eclectic bric-a-brac and vintage posters line the walls

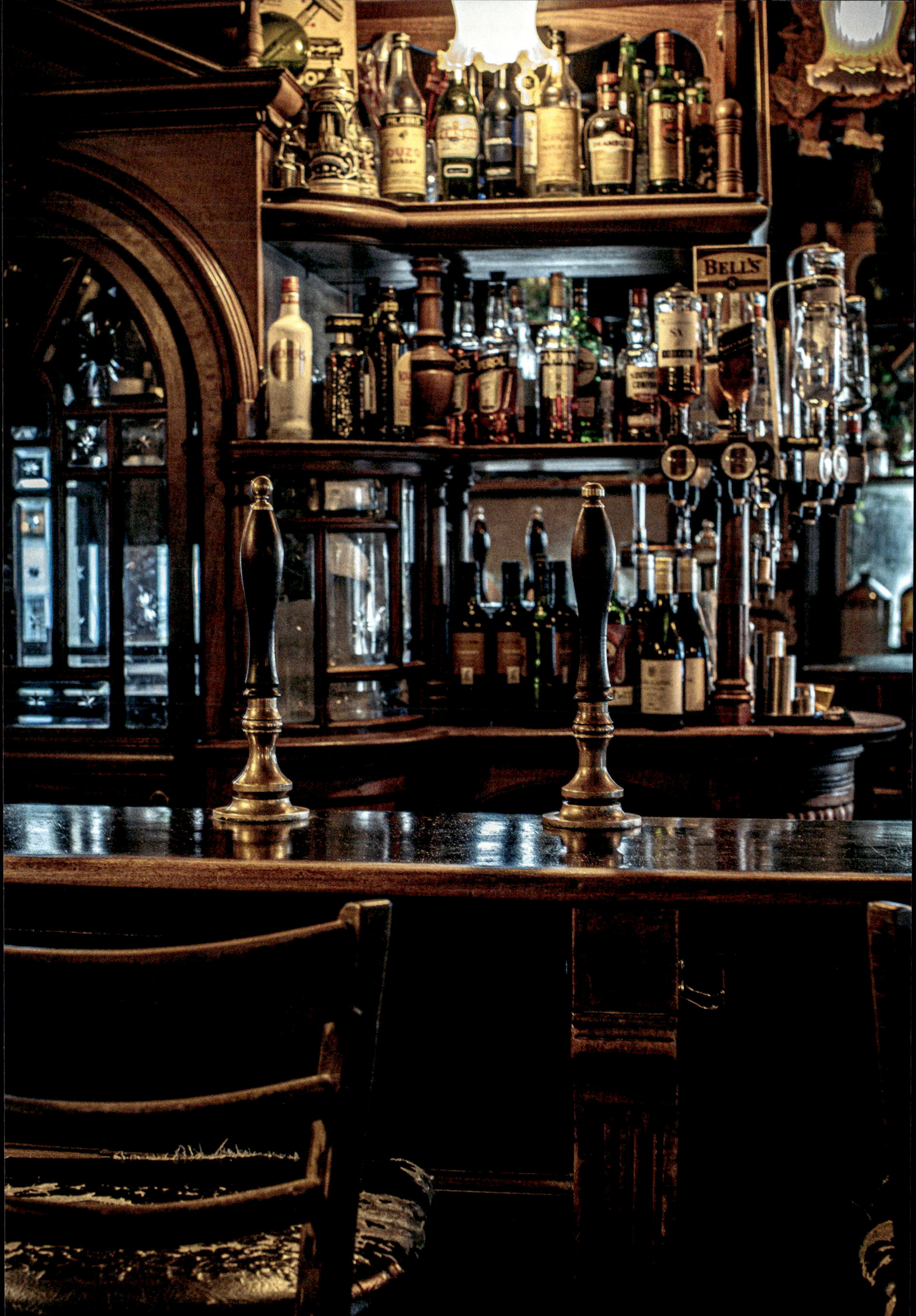

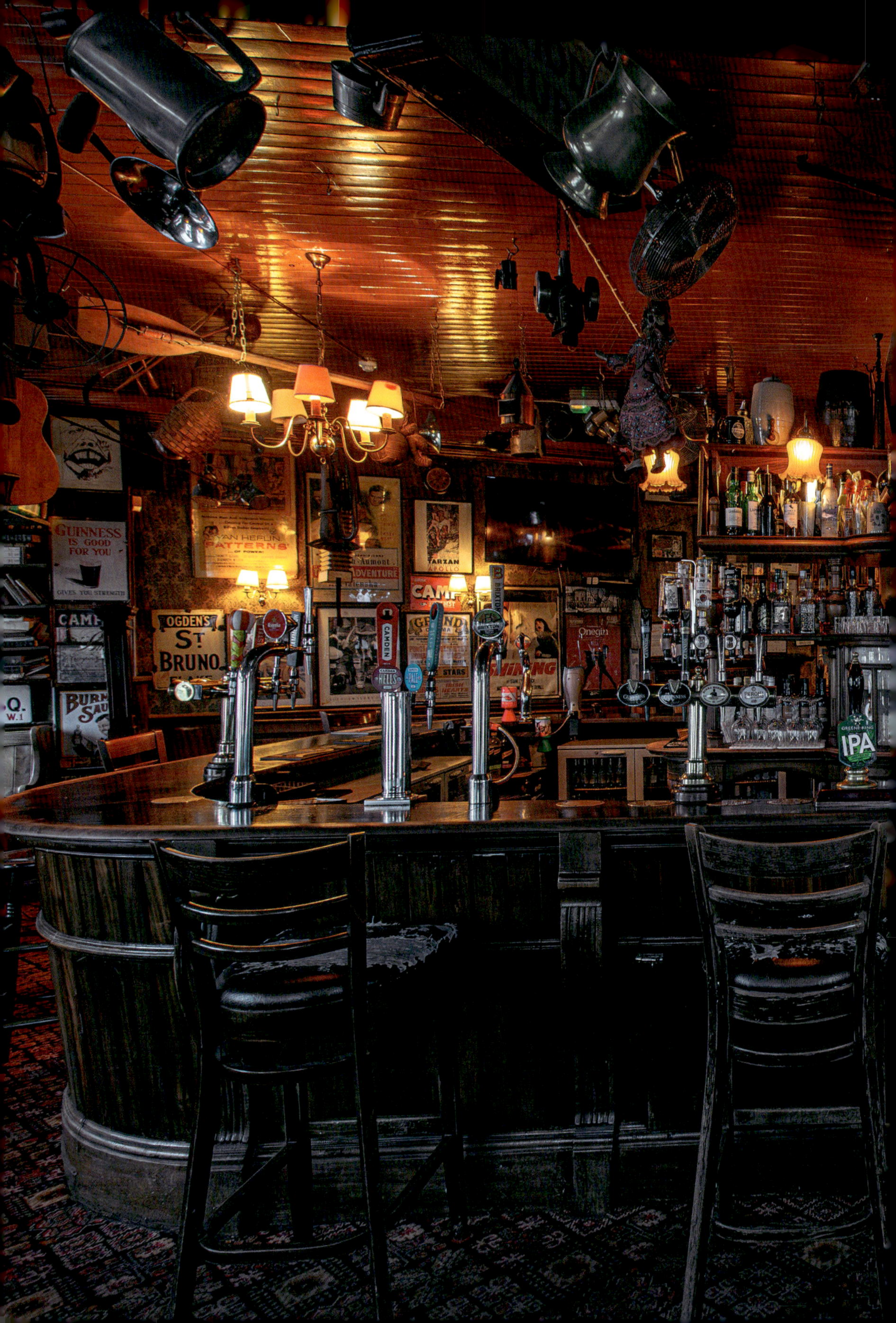

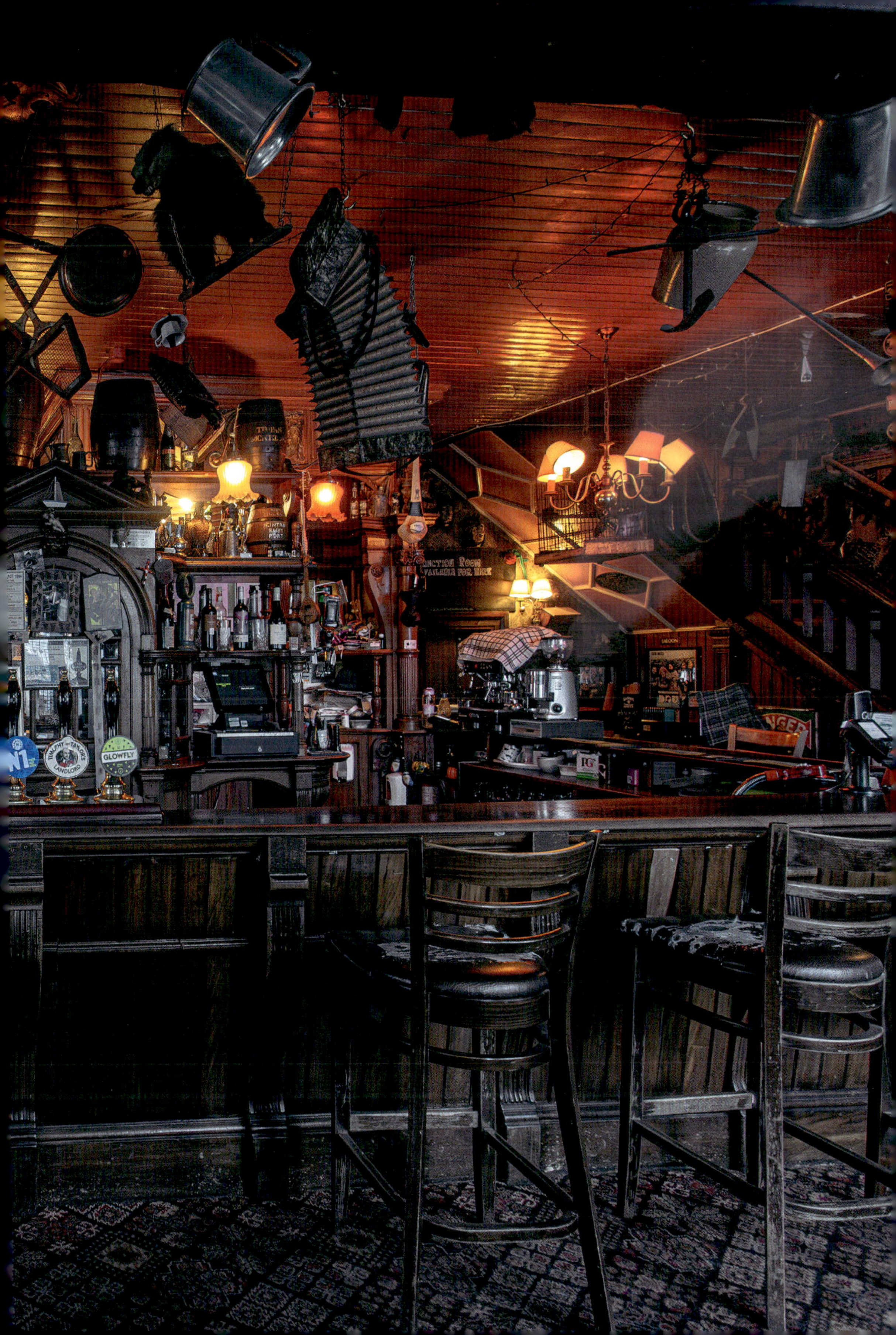

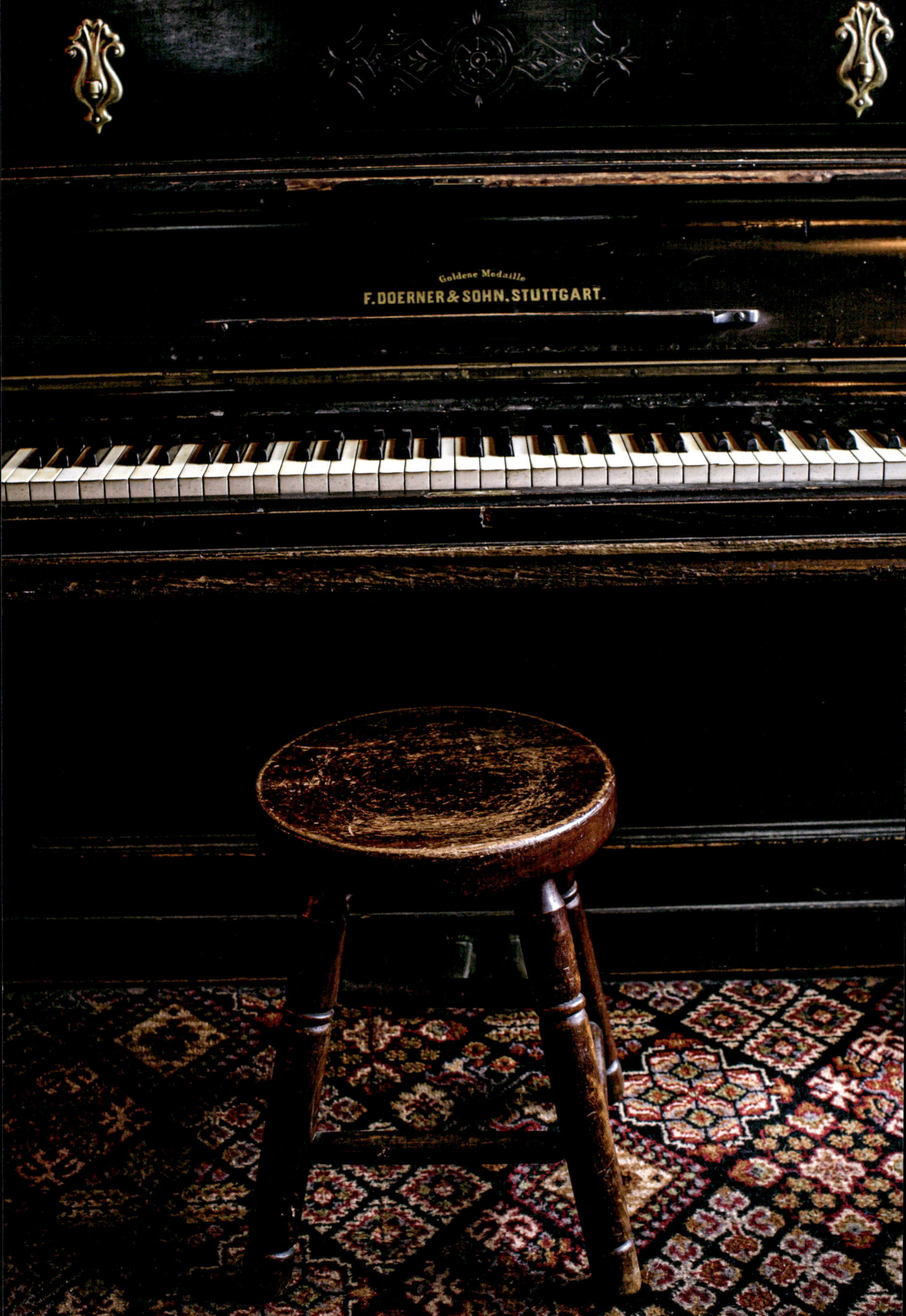

Goldene Medaille
F. DOERNER & SOHN. STUTTGART.

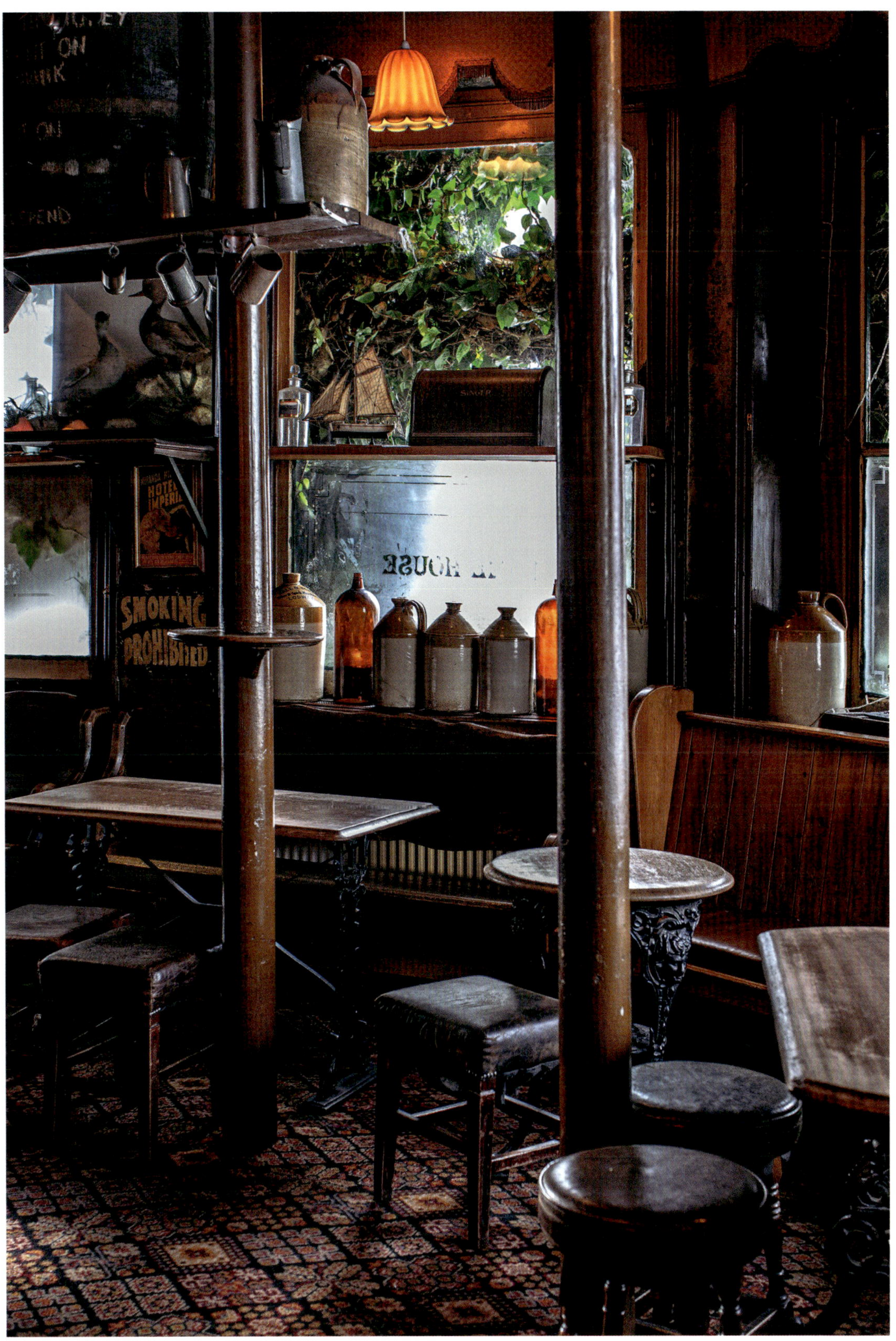

Never judge a pub by its cover

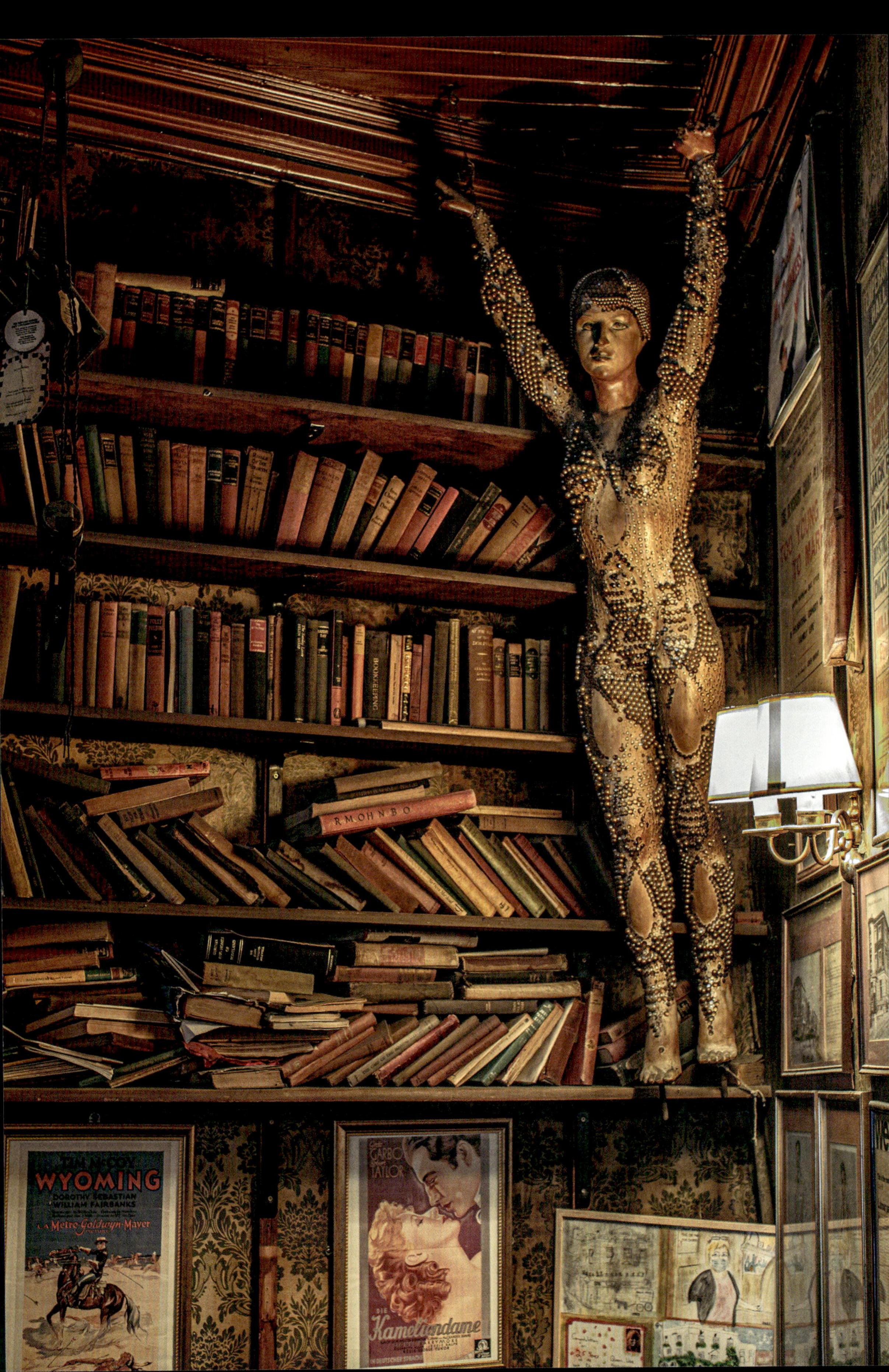
TIM McCOY
WYOMING
DOROTHY SEBASTIAN
WILLIAM FAIRBANKS
A Metro-Goldwyn-Mayer
GARBO
TAYLOR
Die Kameliendame

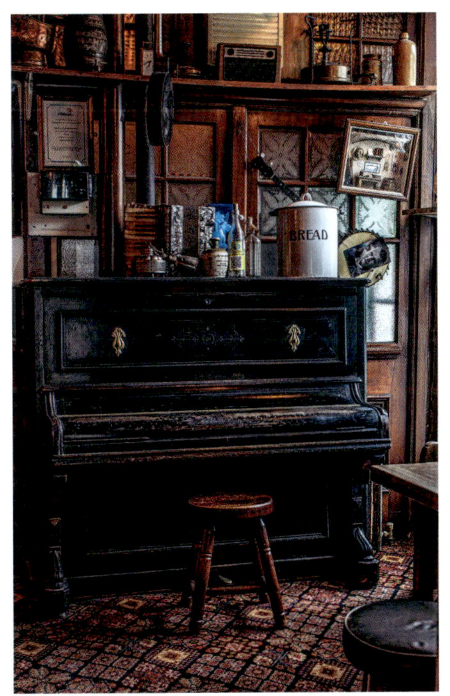

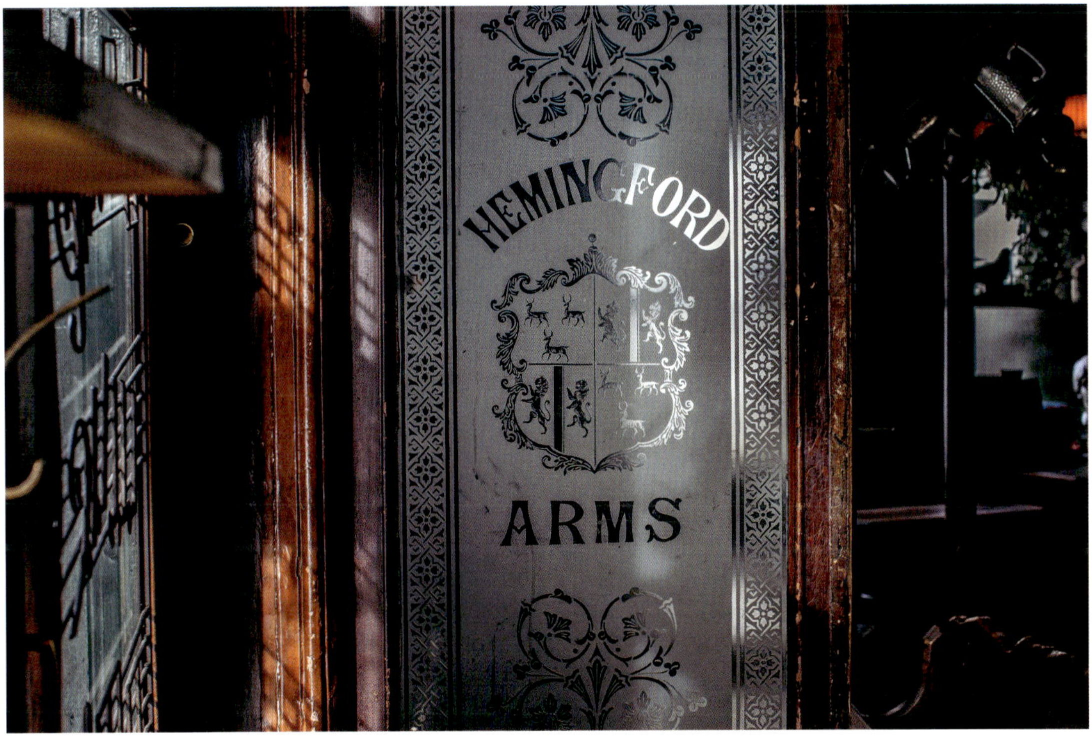

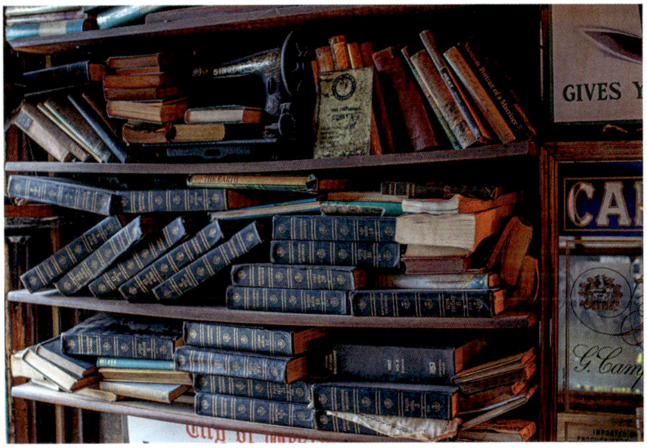

A free-spirited interior runs wild with imagination

THE QUEEN'S HEAD

66 ACTON ST, LONDON WC1X 8DU

King's Cross. What a hole. The more money they spend, the worse it gets. Long gone are the halcyon days of go-karting around railway sidings, spirits pouring down your gullet in the dentist's chair and pulling all-nighters at the warehouse rave mecca that was Bagley's followed by all-day worship at The Church. Inventor Sir Clive Sinclair would look down from his penthouse on high as the oldest profession in the world turned tricks 24/7. These days, it's just TikTokkers queuing for bacon naans for reasons as yet unknown and boutique shopping malls whilst Bagley's is now... wait for it. A Waitrose. Lord have mercy on London's malnourished souls!

No gimmicks, no ephemera or knick-knacks cluttering the space. Less can definitely be more, with simple landlording pleasures often being the hardest to find.

The billion-dollar development bucks dragged starchitects and titans of tech to the area north of platform 9¾, but head south of the station and it's still a no-man's land of indifferent architecture, with hotels dangling a mild promise of bed bugs and rooms available by the hour. It's certainly not an area you'd expect to find a crackerjack of a pub, but The Queen's Head presents a shining beacon of beer brilliance where you expect it least.

It's a pub that makes running a pub appear all so simple. Bold and brassy, with a correct apostrophe on the outside. Tick. The details matter, people, and you know that you're in safe hands before you even enter. An ever-friendly welcome, and a sense that they might just be genuinely glad to see you. Tick. Up top it's a cornucopia of delights, with some of the finest beers hand-picked from across the city and an eclectic whisky selection providing backup at the rear. Tick. When your tummy rumbles then treat yourself to some Brapas (British tapas) in the form of quality pork pies, meats and top cheeses from the best suppliers in the game. Tick. What more could one possibly desire from a London pub? Music, you say? No problem, sir. The ivories get tinkled regularly, and jazz nights make the living easy. Tick.

All sounds rather straightforward, doesn't it? No gimmicks, no ephemera or knick-knacks cluttering the space. Less can definitely be more, with simple landlording pleasures often being the hardest to find.

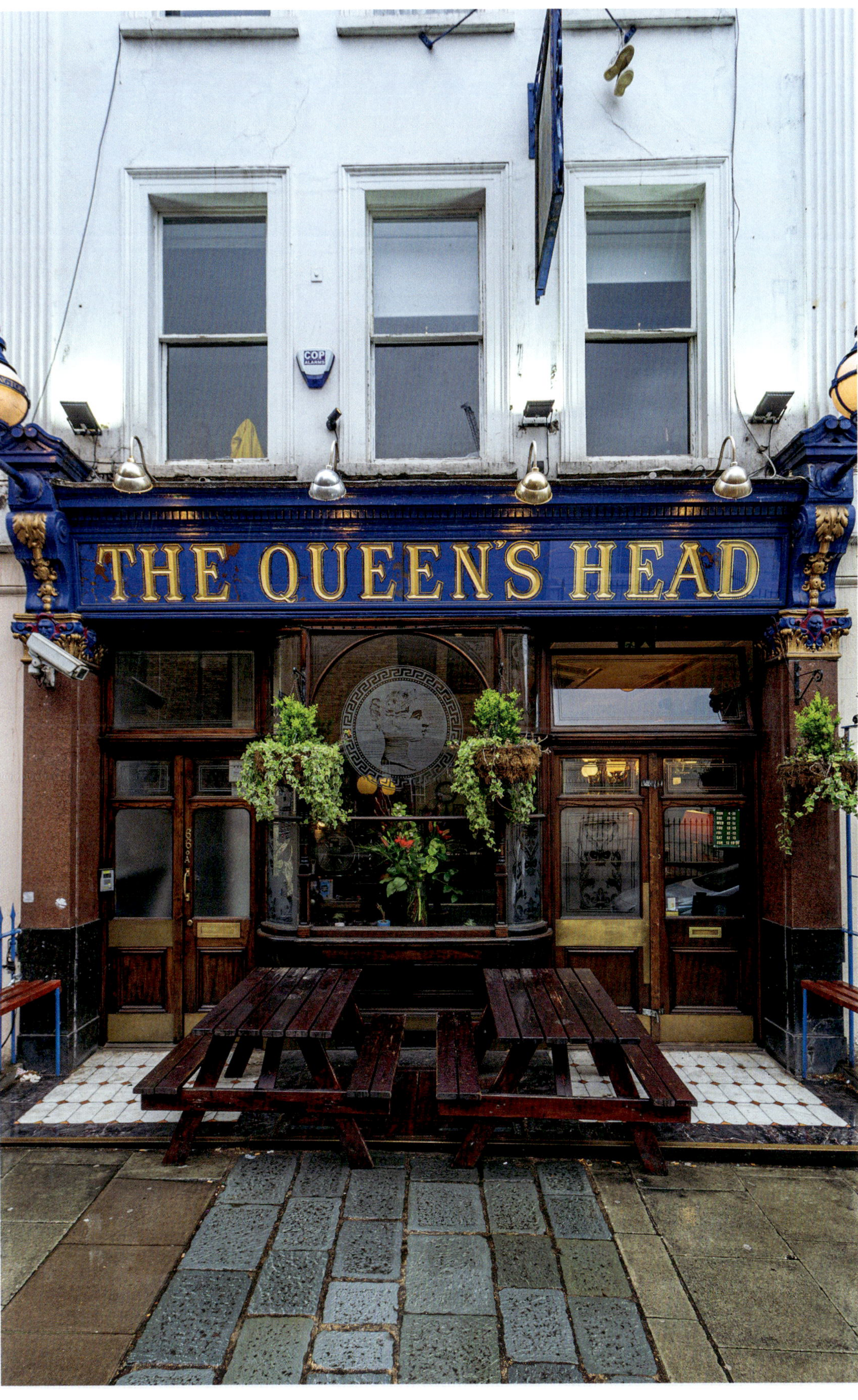
THE QUEEN'S HEAD

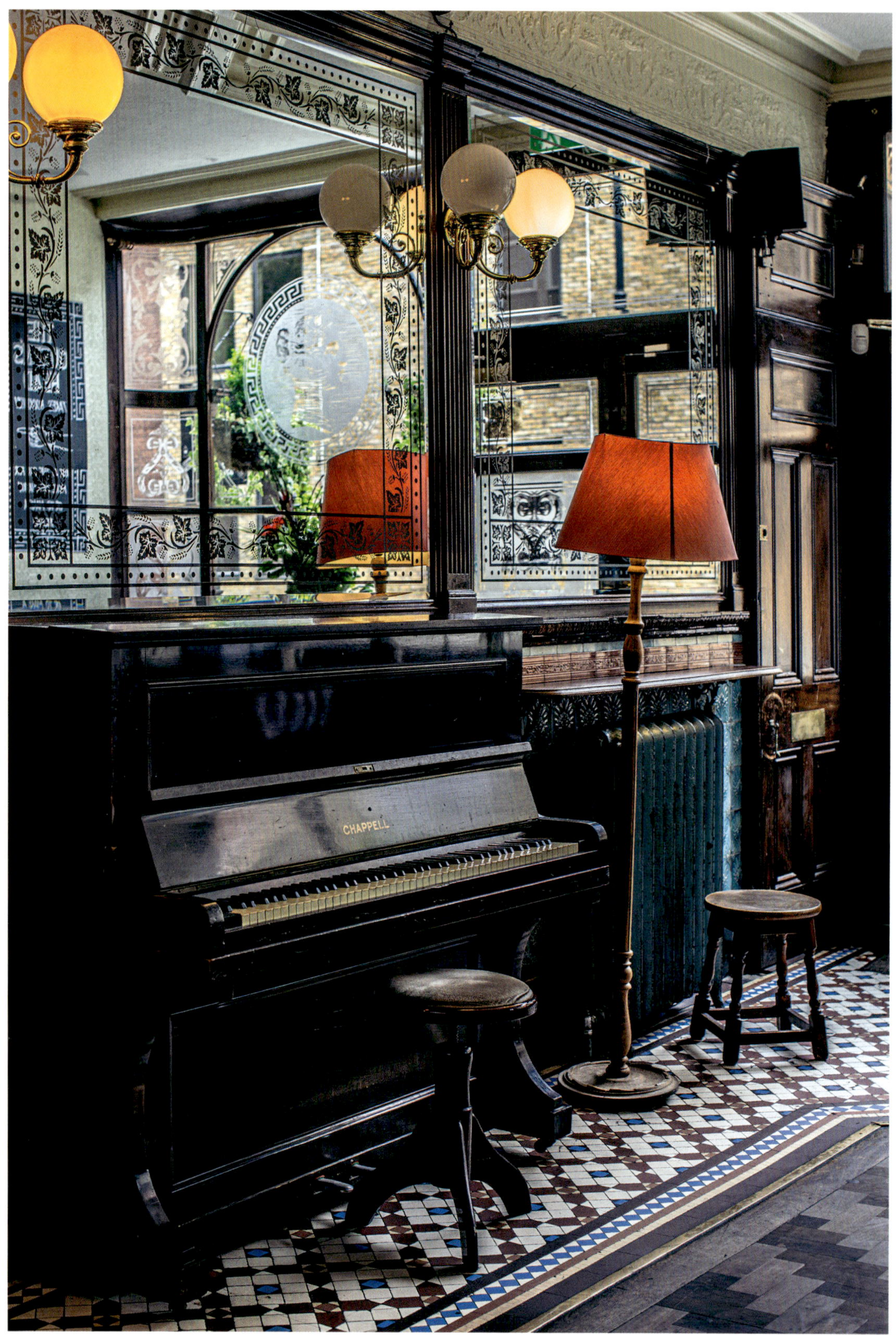

Time to tinkle the ivories!

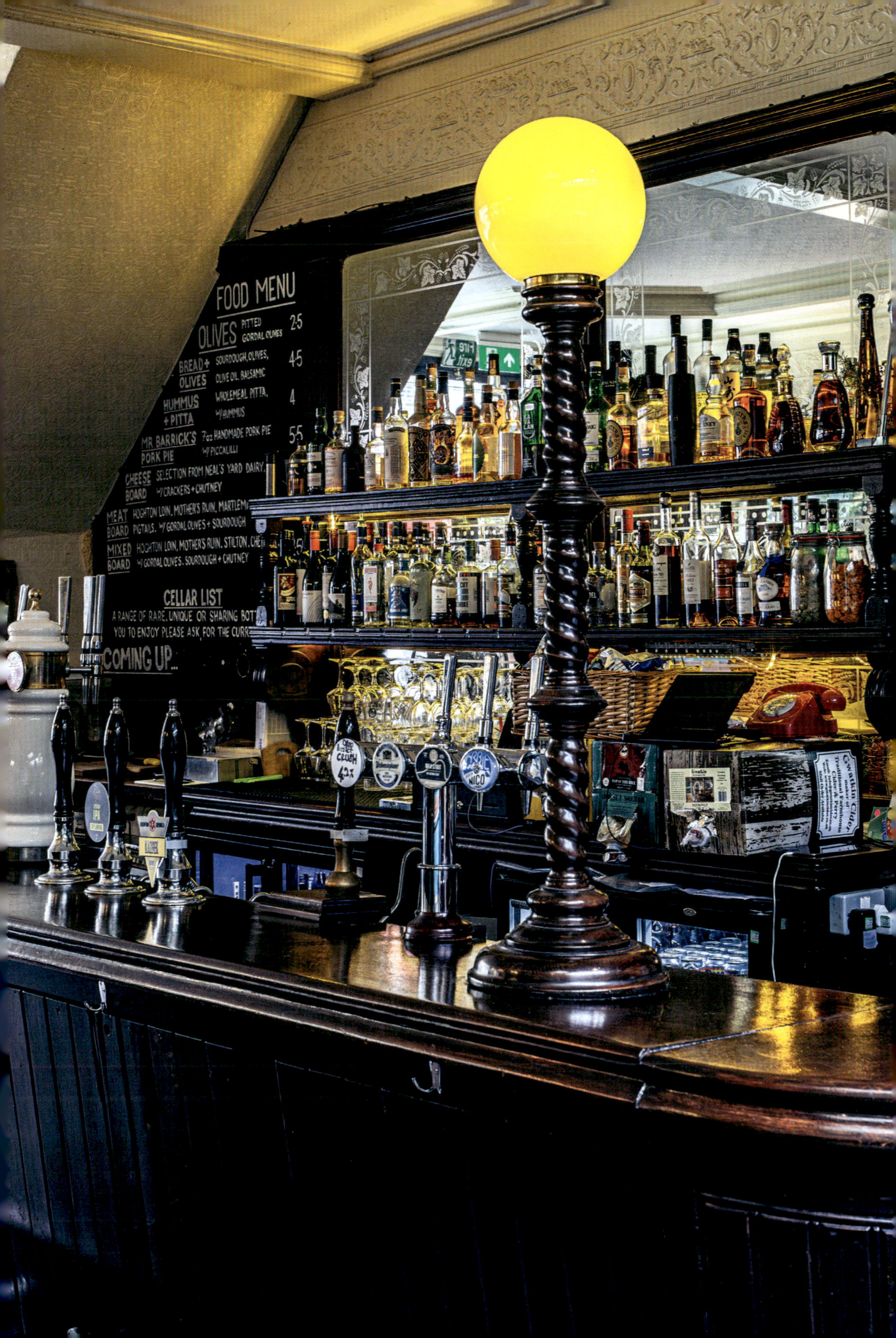

FOOD MENU
OLIVES   PITTED GORDAL OLIVES   2.5
BREAD + OLIVES   SOURDOUGH, OLIVES, OLIVE OIL, BALSAMIC   4.5
HUMMUS + PITTA   WHOLEMEAL PITTA, W/ HUMMUS   4
MR BARRICK'S PORK PIE   7oz HANDMADE PORK PIE W/ PICCALILLI   5.5
CHEESE BOARD   SELECTION FROM NEAL'S YARD DAIRY. W/ CRACKERS + CHUTNEY
MEAT BOARD   HOGHTON LOIN, MOTHER'S RUIN, MARTLEMA PIGTAILS, W/ GORDAL OLIVES + SOURDOUGH
MIXED BOARD   HOGHTON LOIN, MOTHER'S RUIN, STILTON, CHE W/ GORDAL OLIVES, SOURDOUGH + CHUTNEY
CELLAR LIST
A RANGE OF RARE, UNIQUE OR SHARING BOTT
YOU TO ENJOY PLEASE ASK FOR THE CURR
COMING UP...

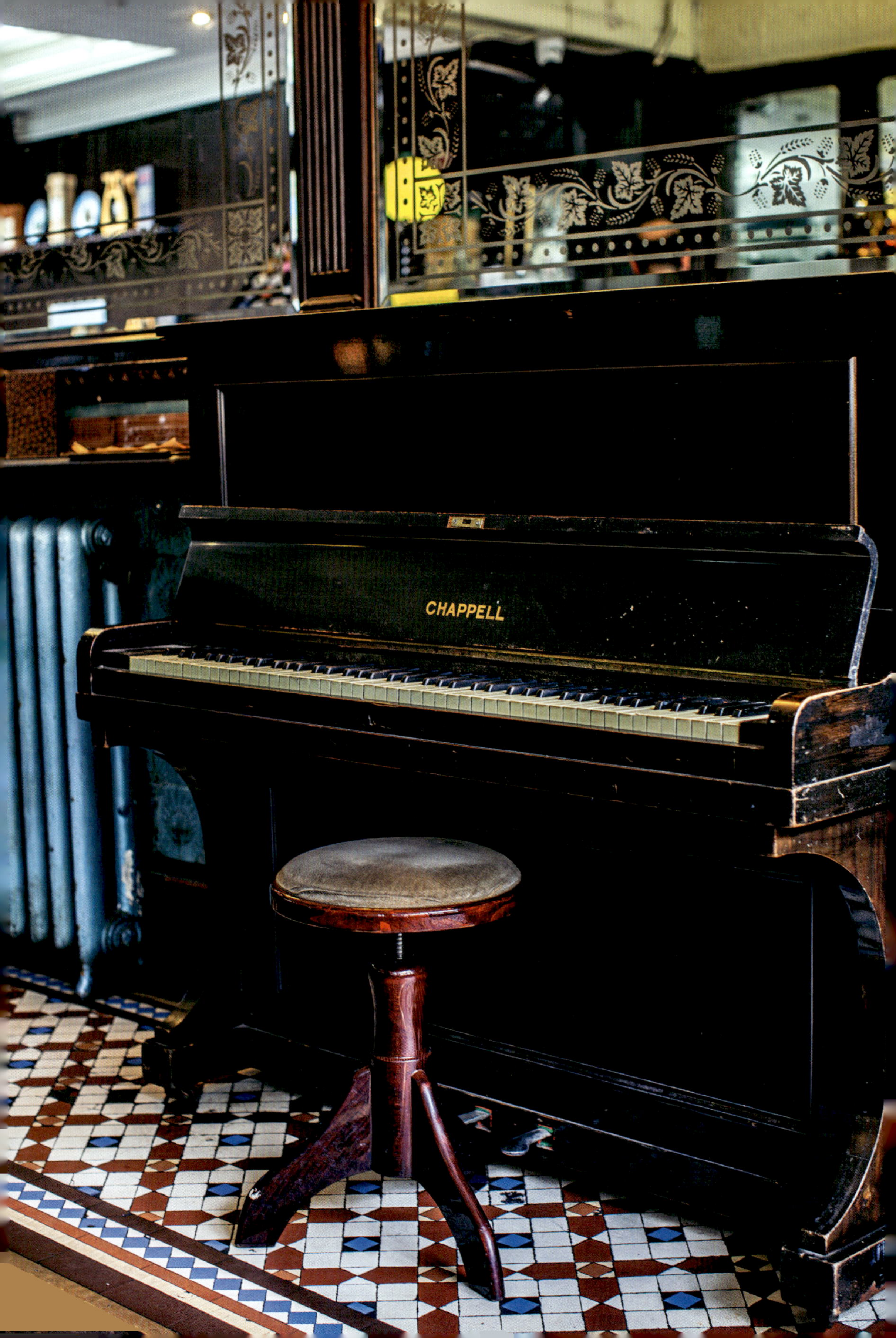
CHAPPELL

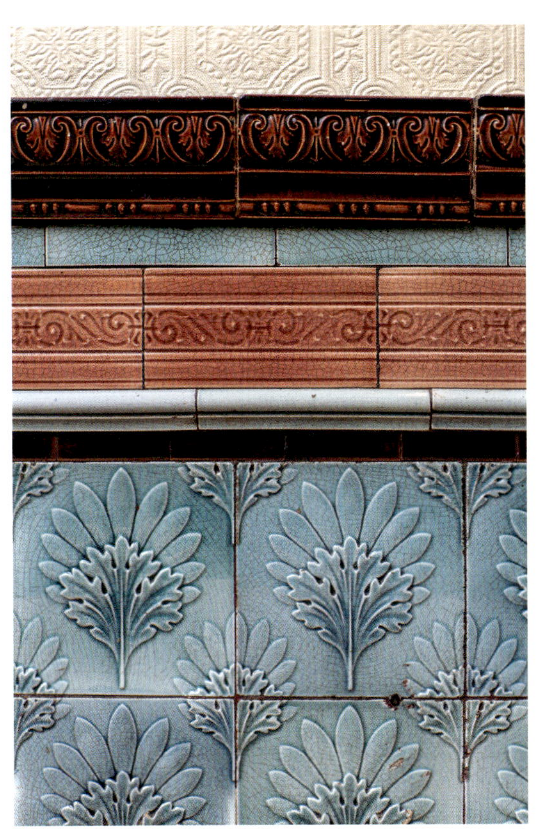

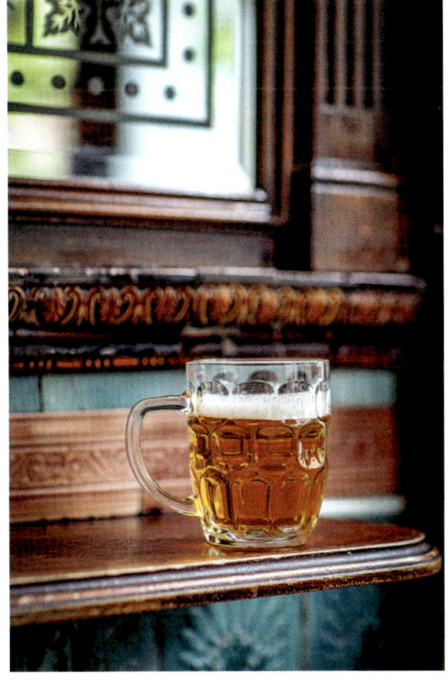

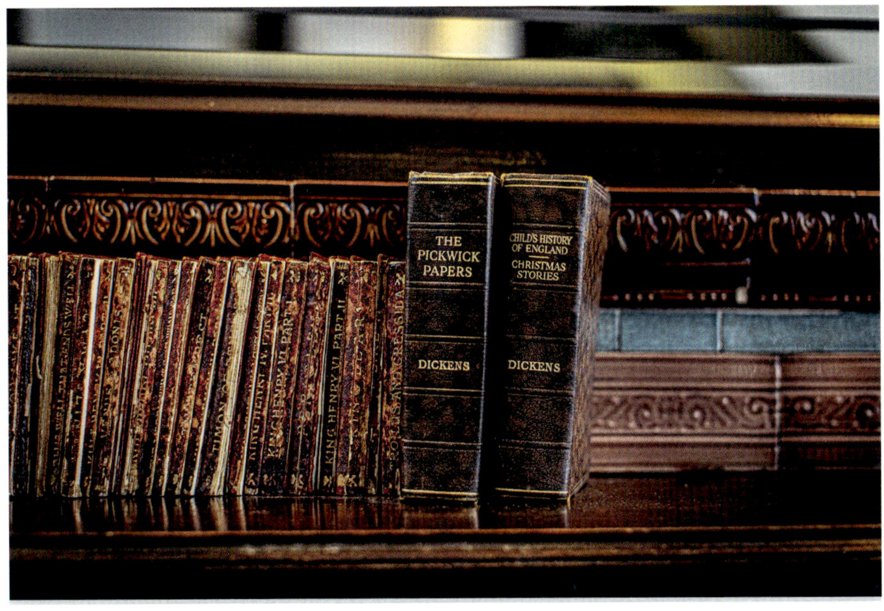

Simple pleasures. Simply good times

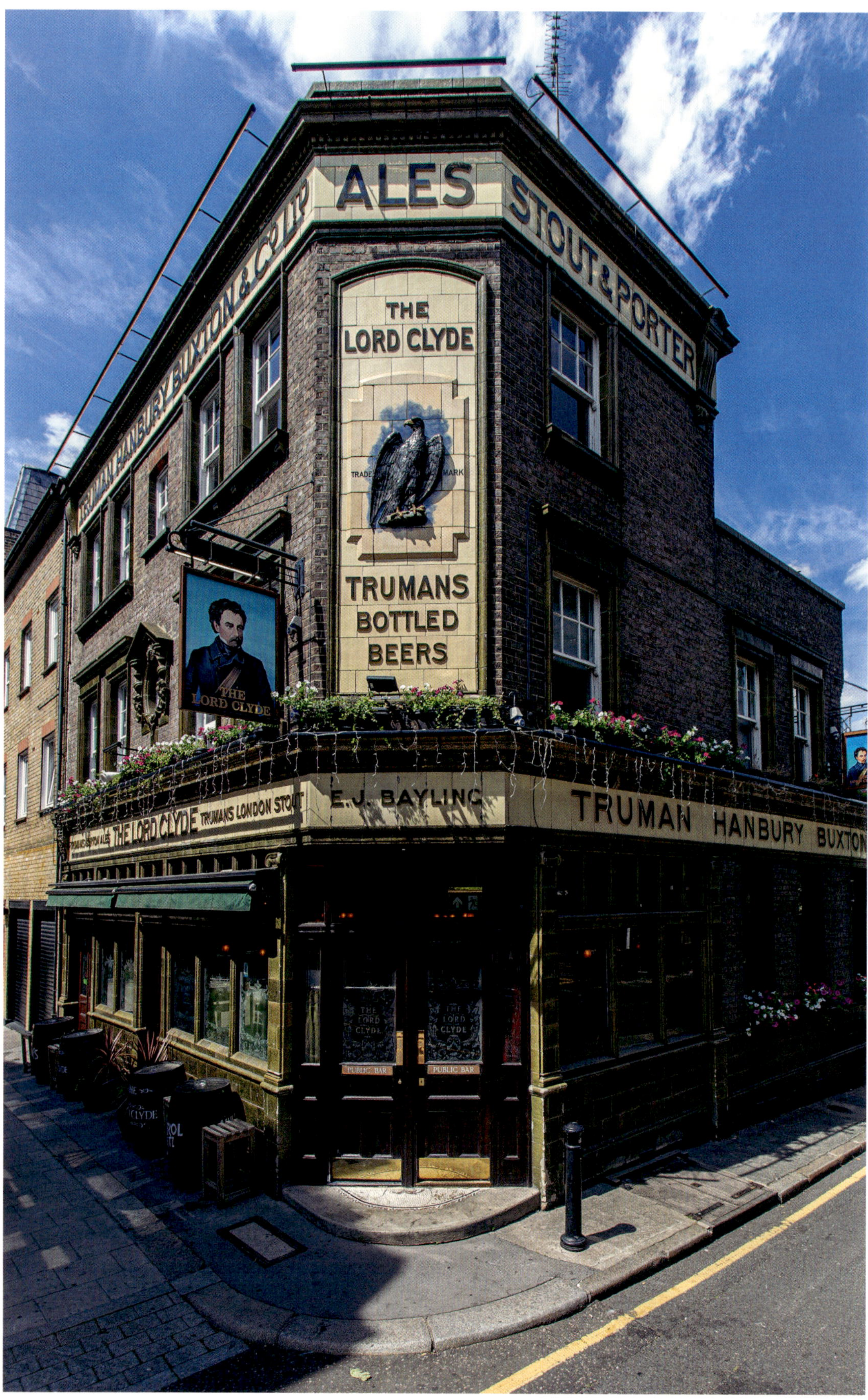
ALES
STOUT & PORTER
THE
LORD CLYDE
TRADE MARK
TRUMANS
BOTTLED
BEERS
THE
LORD CLYDE
E.J. BAYLING
TRUMAN HANBURY BUXTON
THE LORD CLYDE
TRUMANS LONDON STOUT
PUBLIC BAR
PUBLIC BAR

THE LORD CLYDE

UNSULLIED BASTION OF BOOZE

27 CLENNAM STREET, BOROUGH SE1 1ER

Oh Lord, what a pub! Tucked far enough away from the maddening crowds of Borough Market, and with its back turned on the world around it, this unpretentious wonder will only reveal itself if you're either very lost or very lucky. The pub's tiled exterior is jaw-droppingly splendiferous. It was built in 1913 by Truman, Hanbury, Buxton & Co., then one of the biggest breweries in the world – and they certainly wanted the world to know it.

The interior, however, is just straight-up solid boozer. Entering through velvet drapes, lucky locals sink into blood-red leather banquettes for some ardent elbow-bending or escape for a game of arrows in the rear whilst being served through a hatch. Antique etched glass mirrors share wall space with vintage Truman price lists, with the racing often flickering away in the corner. All acting as a reminder of the bookmaking and pawnbroking activity at the bar in years gone by. And the name? Colin Campbell, or Lord Clyde, famously defended Crimea with only his "thin red line" of men before going on to become Commander-in-Chief of India. Unluckily for him, he was never alive to visit this fine establishment named in his honour, but doubtless he would have appreciated how the baton of innkeeping excellence has been passed on and the stiff resistance to modernity and unnecessary change holds firm.

There is a subtle art to not tweaking, updating or modifying too fast or even, sometimes, at all. The secret to the pub's unspoilt and unfussy decor is six decades of landlording by the Fitzpatrick family. When they unlocked the doors in 1956, Elvis had just entered the charts with "Heartbreak Hotel", Eisenhower was still US president and Jim Laker was taking nineteen wickets in an Ashes test at Old Trafford.

However, in January 2020, just two months before the planet spiralled into pandemic lockdown, the Fitzpatricks bolted the doors one final time. A changing of the guard can precede a slow death by a thousand paper cuts and this would have been a very painful way to compromise an unadulterated Edwardian gem like this.

But huzzah and big sighs of relief all round! The new owners read the rule book and have left well alone. The khazis may have finally been dragged into the twenty-first century and you might find a few new brews on tap, but all in all, this unadulterated charmer remains blissfully unchanged.

A true example of "if it ain't broke, don't fix it".

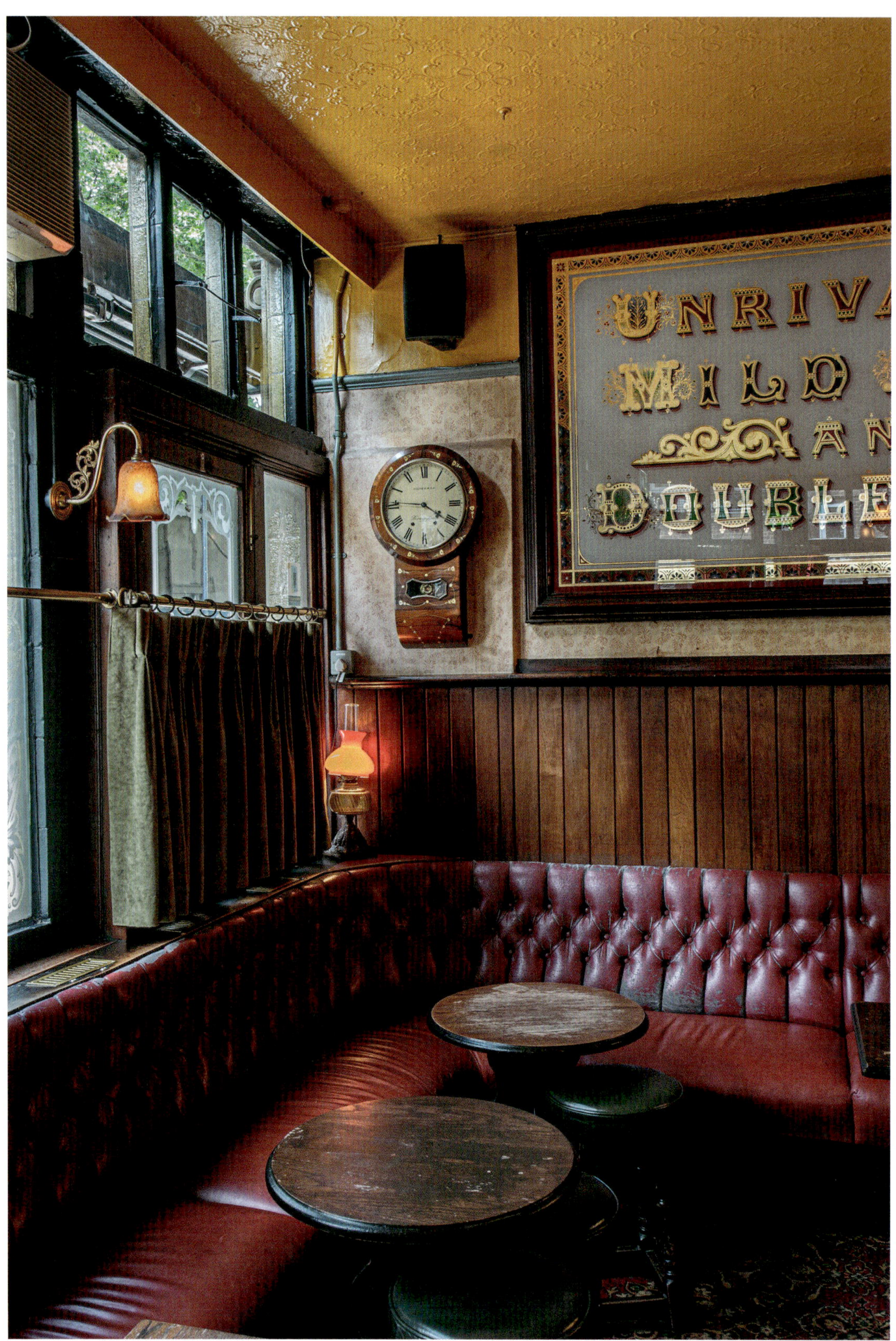

Settle in for a session at one of South London's finest

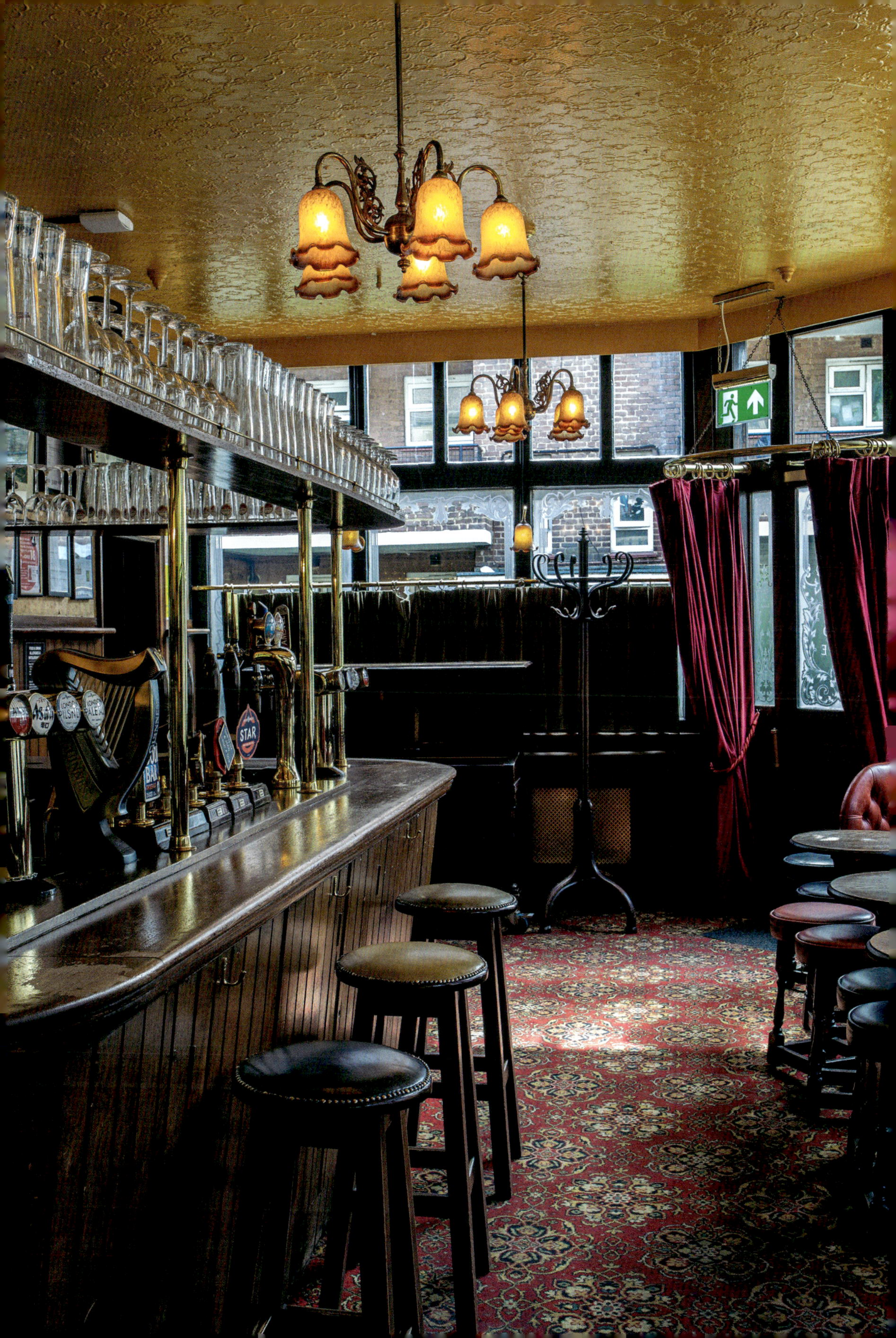

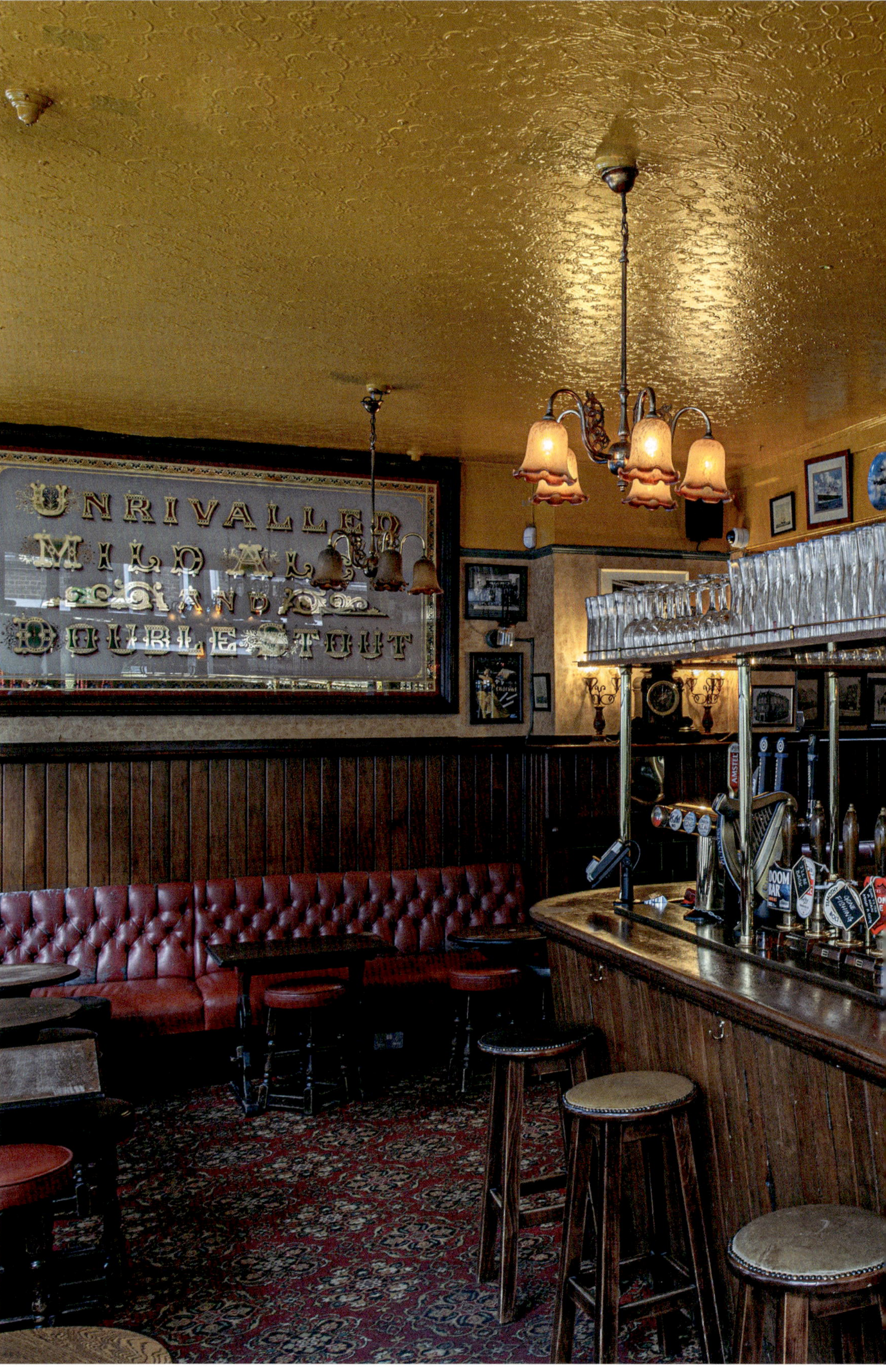
UNRIVALLED
MILD ALE
AND
DOUBLE STOUT

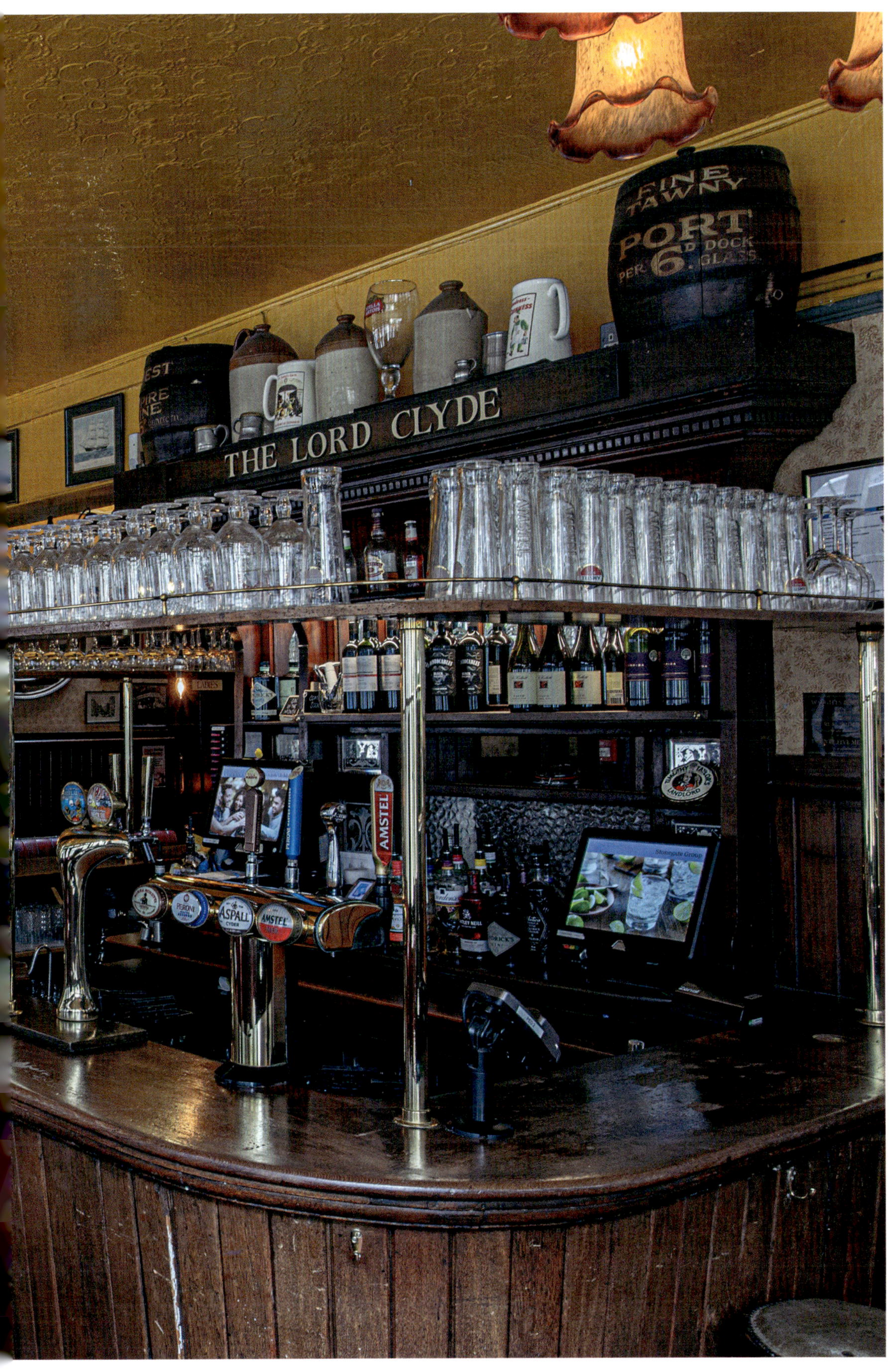

FINE
TAWNY
PORT
PER 6D DOCK GLASS
THE LORD CLYDE

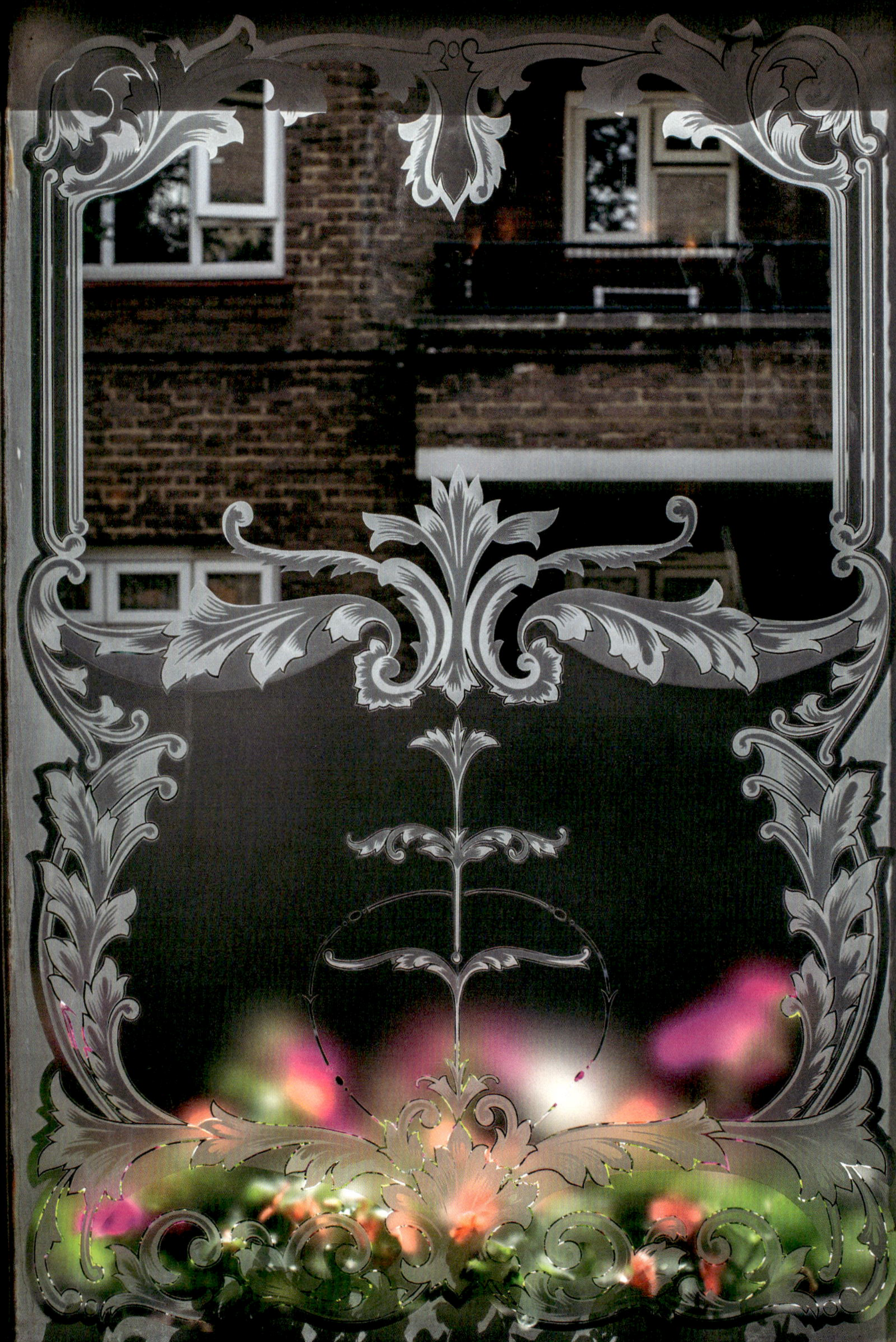

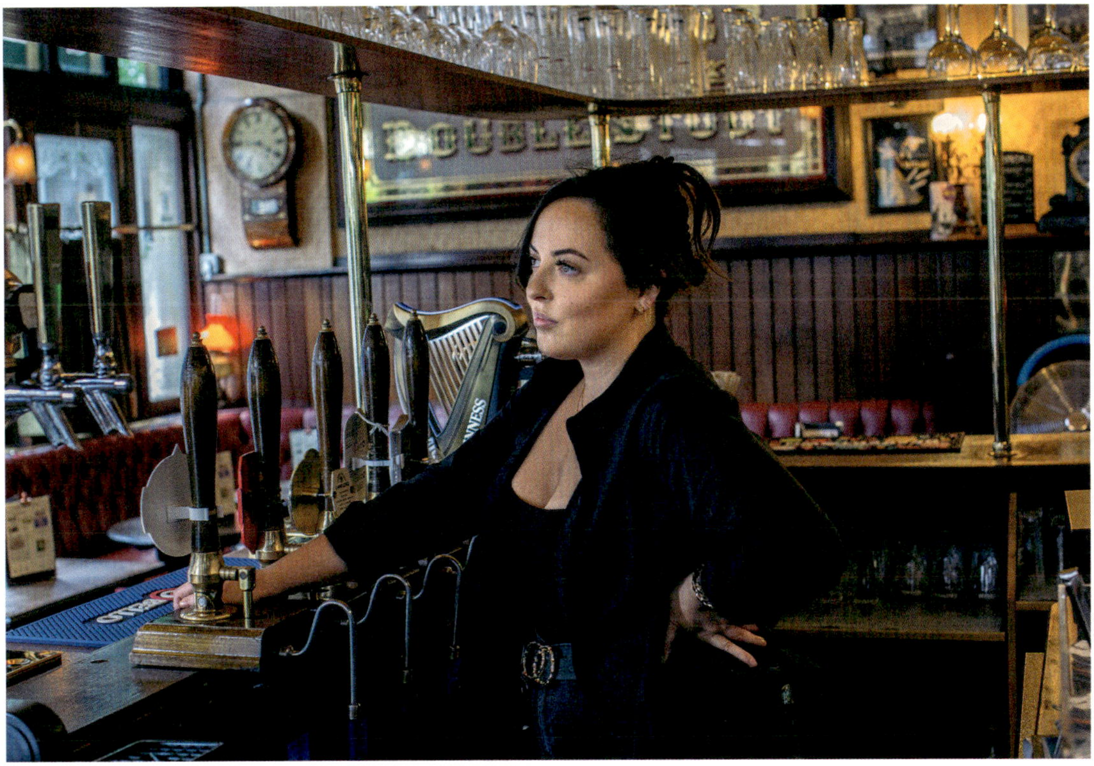

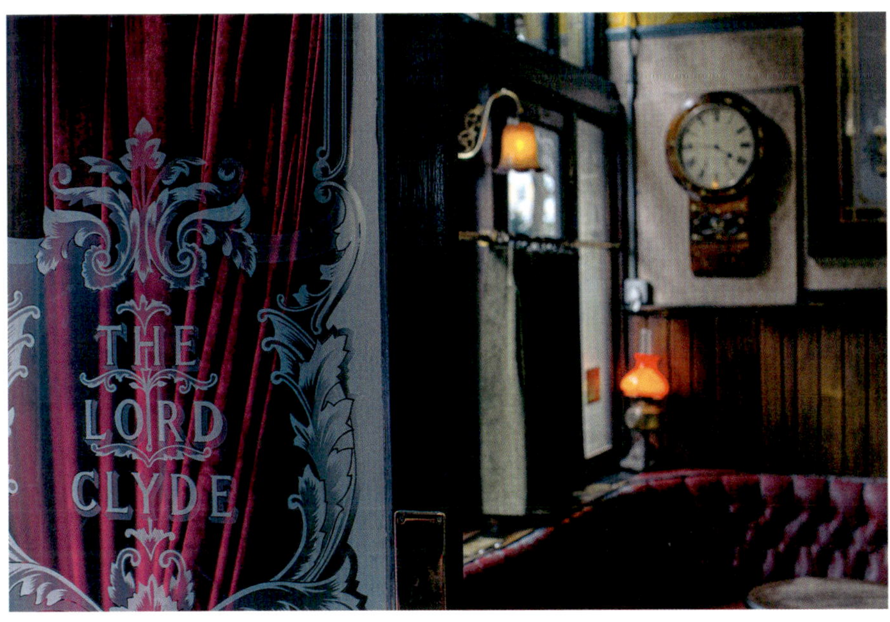

A class act all the way from the pavement to the pumps

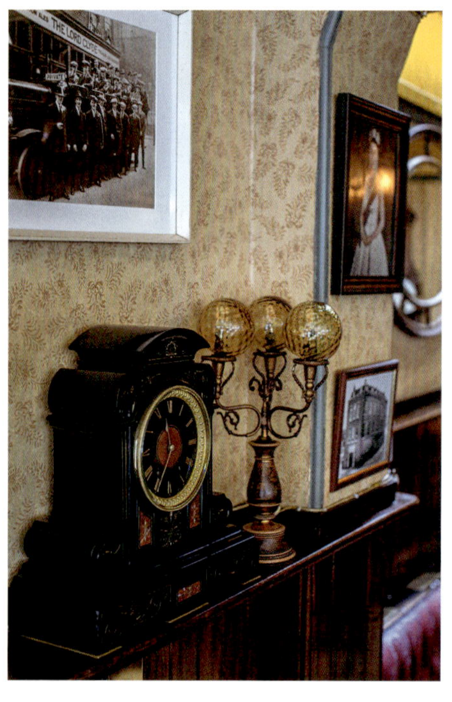

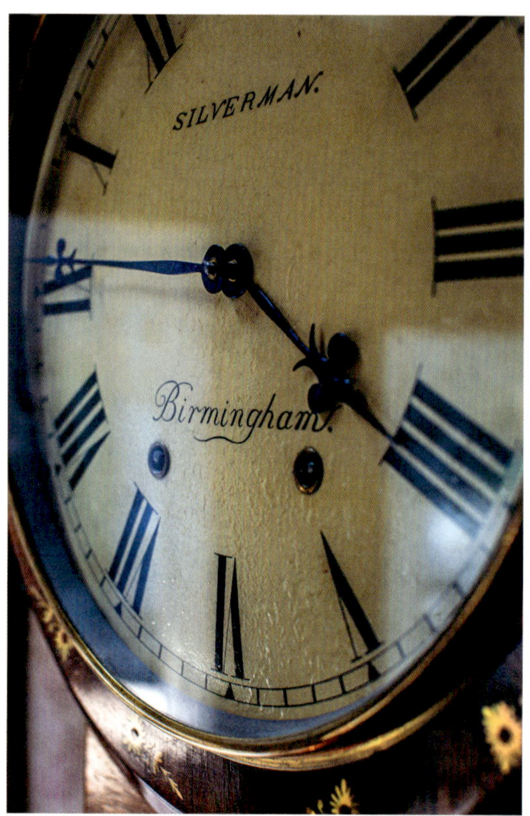

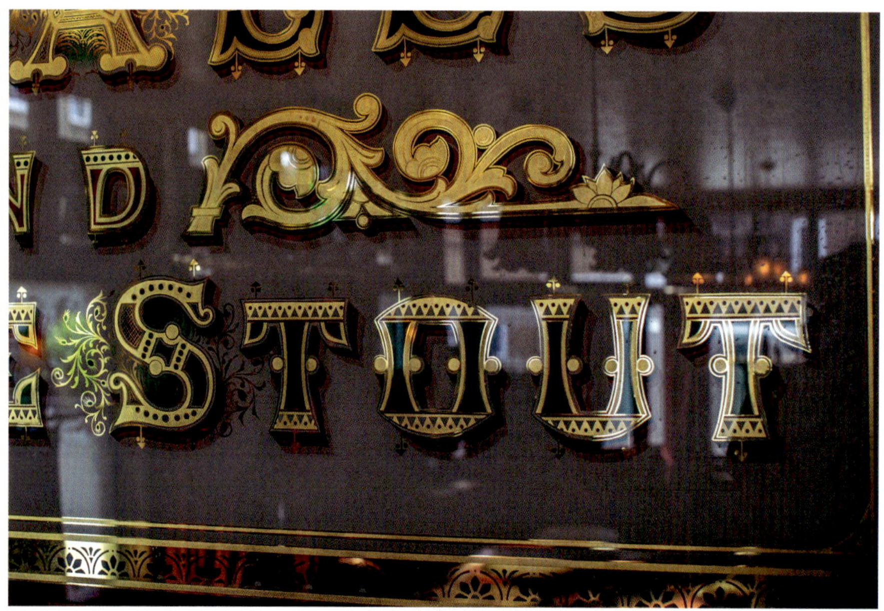

Clocks pawned for cash at the bar still await collection on the mantlepiece

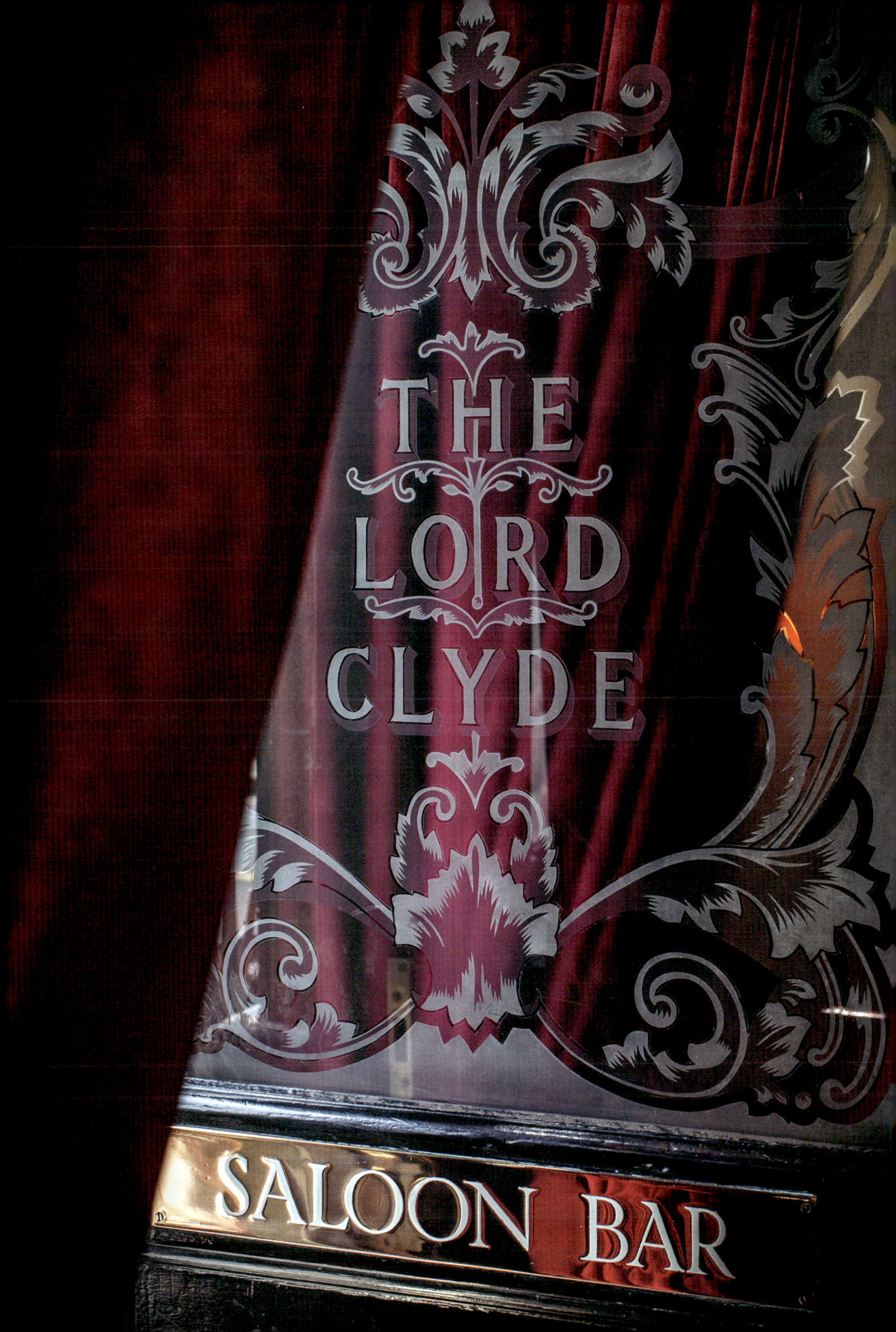

THE
LORD
CLYDE
SALOON BAR

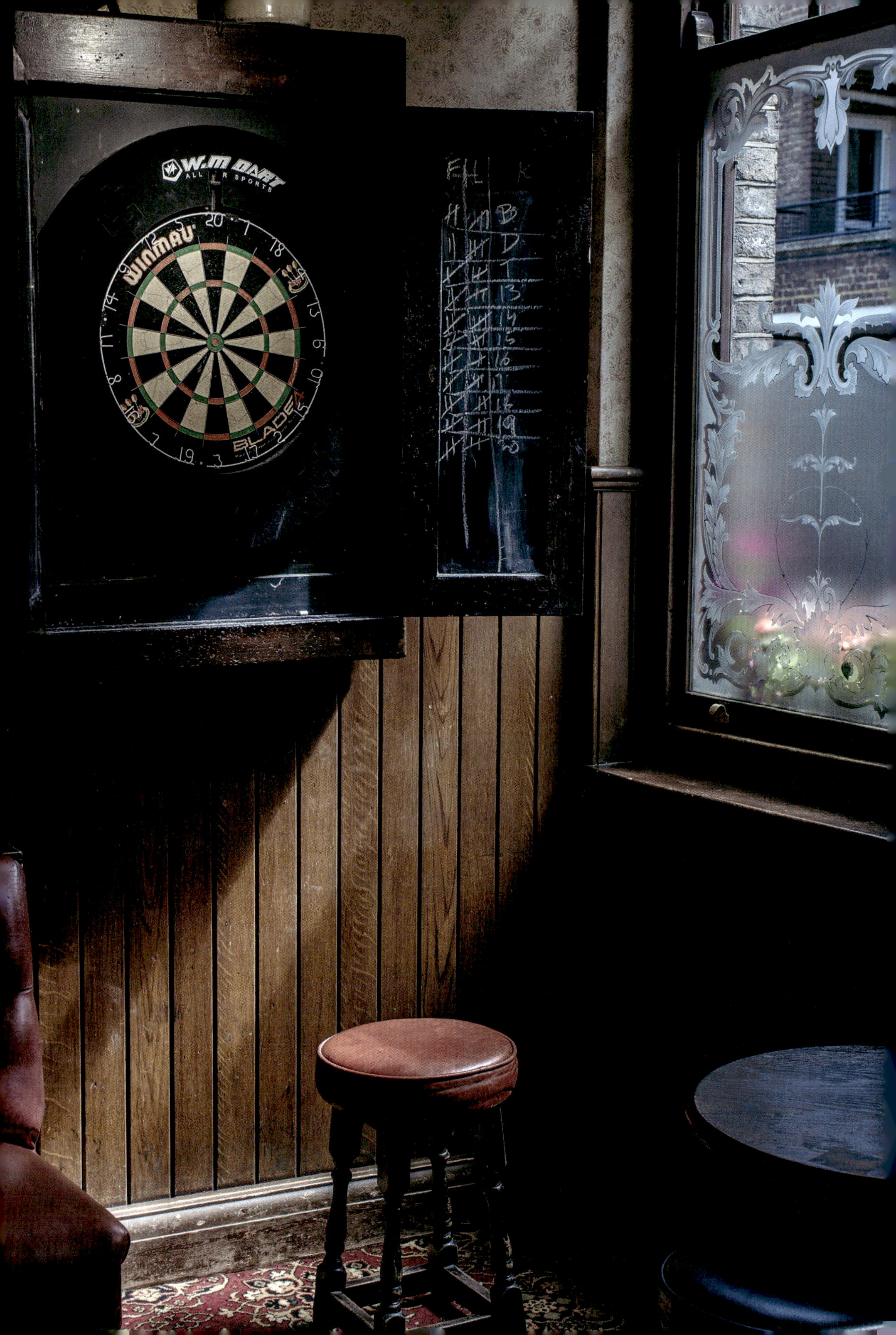

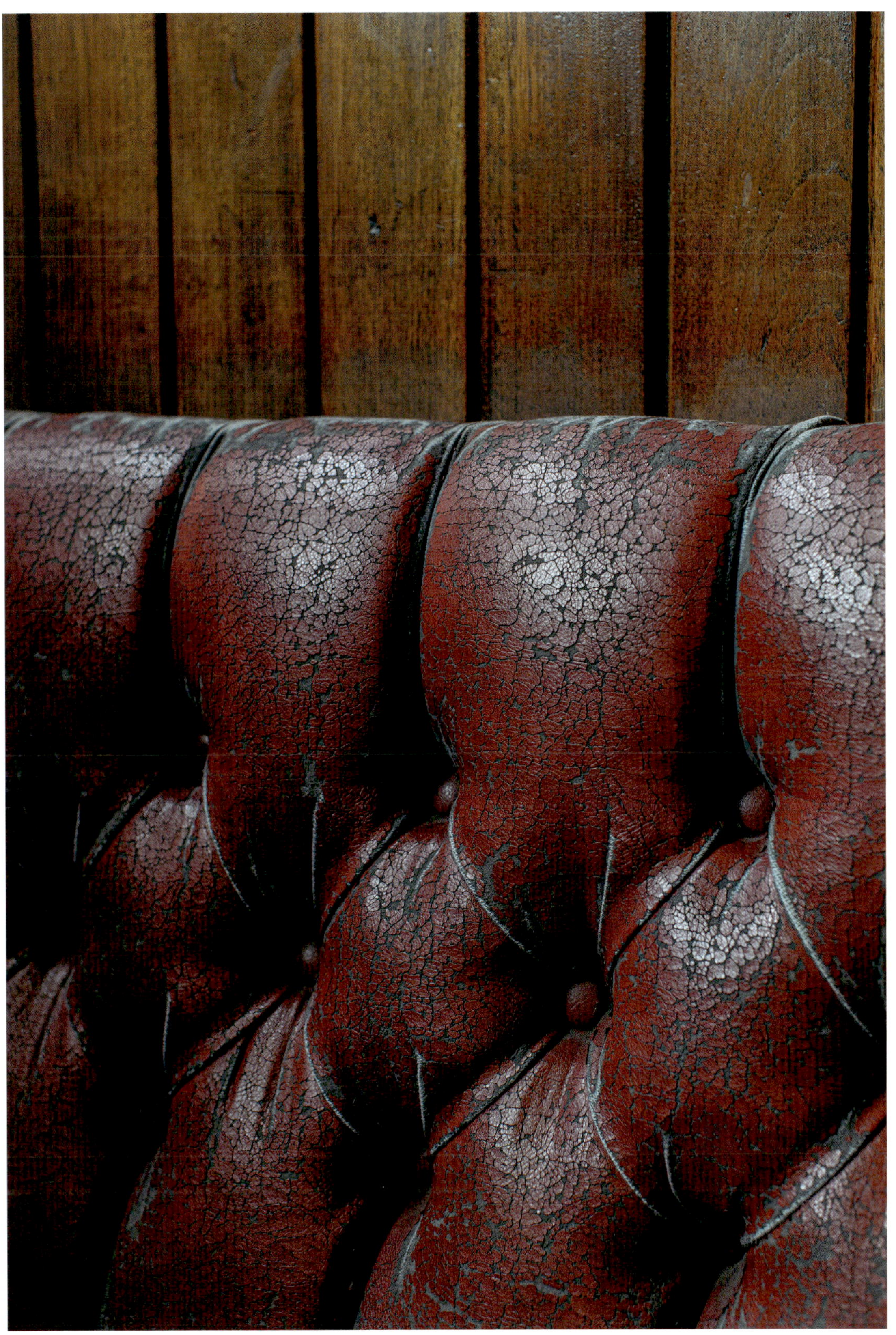

House rules: "If it ain't broke, don't fix it"

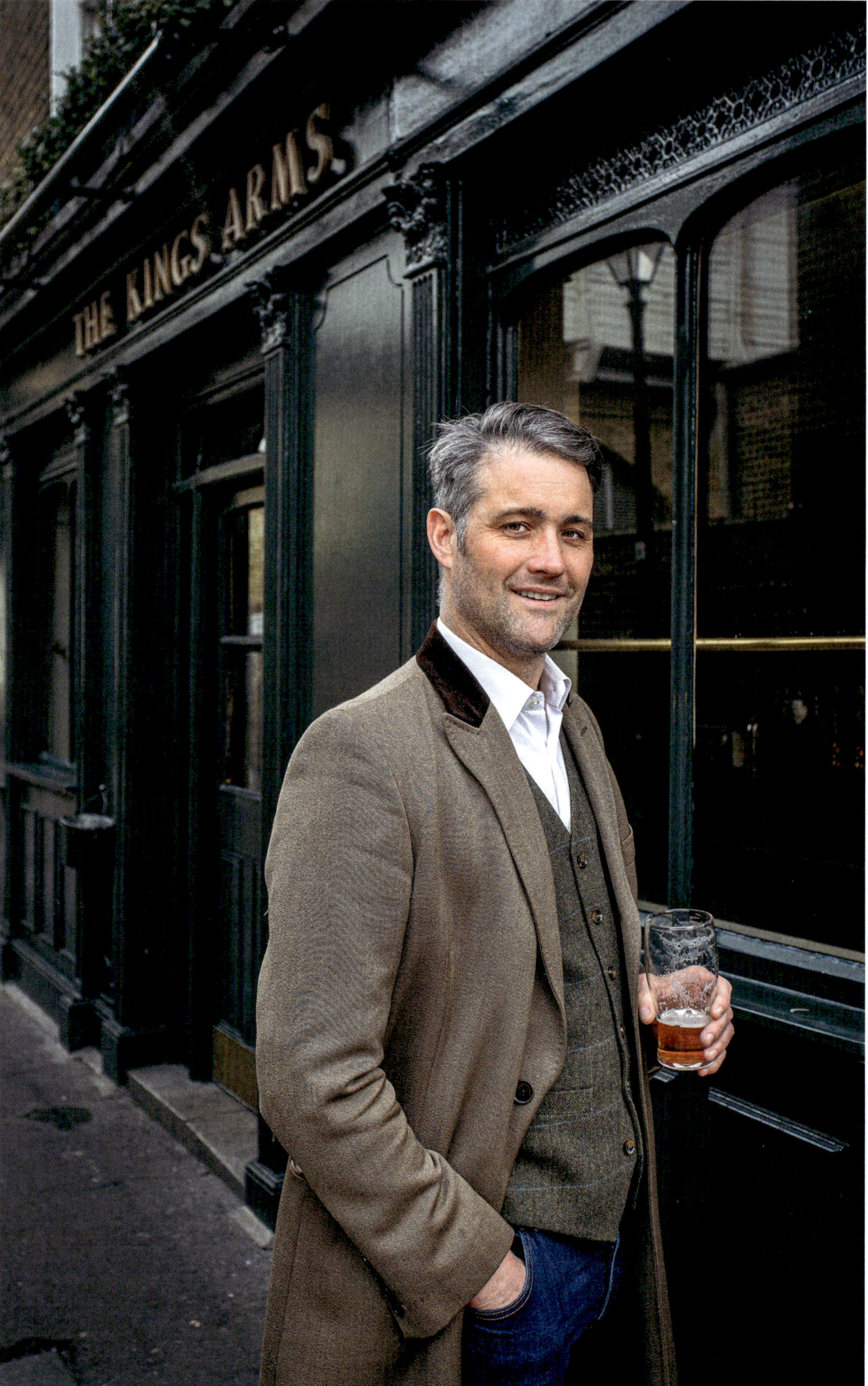
THE KINGS ARMS.

THE KINGS ARMS

Father-and-son relationships are a funny thing. Sons spend their first decades rebelling and fleeing, only to be drawn back by the realisation that family are pretty much all you've got.

My dad once lived behind the red door you see here. He moved to No. 60 Roupell Street after the breakdown of his marriage. This is where he came to rebuild his life. He became a "man about town" for the first time in over twenty-five years, bringing with him the promise of new horizons and urban adventure. But leaving the family home was no doubt cloaked in a mild fog of loneliness. Perhaps higher forces guided him to live opposite The Kings Arms (it no doubt saved on a larger therapy bill). The hubbub of humanity seeped through the thinly glazed windows until late at night, meaning he was never completely alone. When the evening crush became too much, he could grab a pint of freshly pulled Marston's ale and retreat across the road to the sanctuary of his very own beer garden.

On a street so cinematic you'll find it starring as the backdrop in many a movie or fashion shoot.

It is family that provides the mortar in The Kings Arms. With over five decades of industry experience, Jack McElhinney is still the pub patriarch and old-school guvnor. Sons Ryan and Johnny returned to the pub in the late nineties to add some experiential flavour. The boys even opened a bar in their father's name not far away in homage to the original "Jack's Bar", which began in Ireland over fifty years ago. Their new bars take the Mc & Sons moniker.

It's why this pub *feels* so right. It's full of love, and they make you feel human. Solid in classic corner-pub style, but with a big heart in the middle. Sitting fair and square on a street so cinematic you'll find it starring as the backdrop in many a movie or fashion shoot. People travel far for the reliable line-up on the servery, whilst rat-race commuters flood the sunny corner located almost directly under the platforms of Waterloo East station.

That's my dad in the flat cap. Supping solo and gazing back at his old front door. Over two decades later, Marston's might no longer be on tap and access to his private beer garden at No. 60 is no more. But if I fancy a decent afternoon pint with my old man, then this place shall be ours.

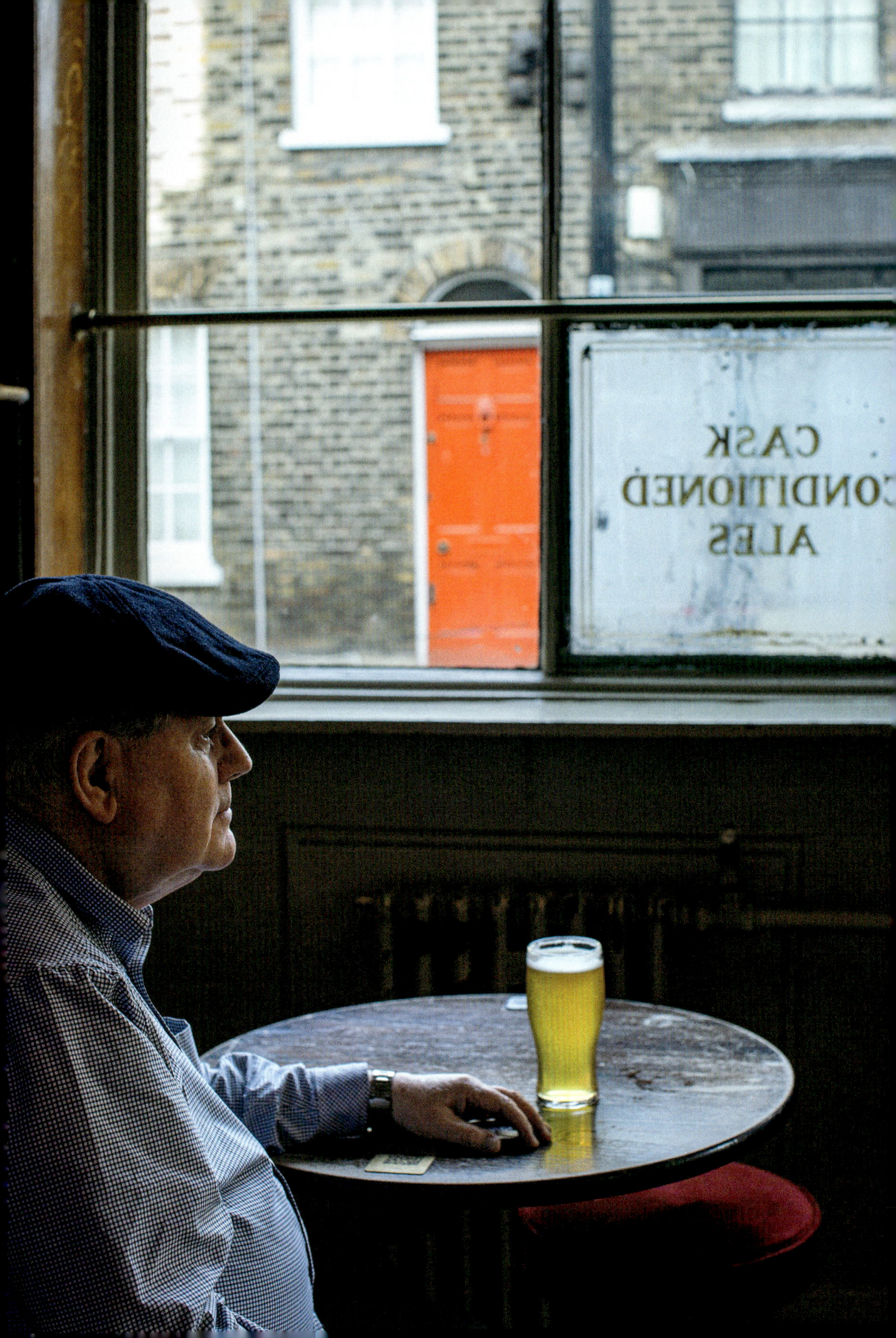

CASK
CONDITIONED
ALES

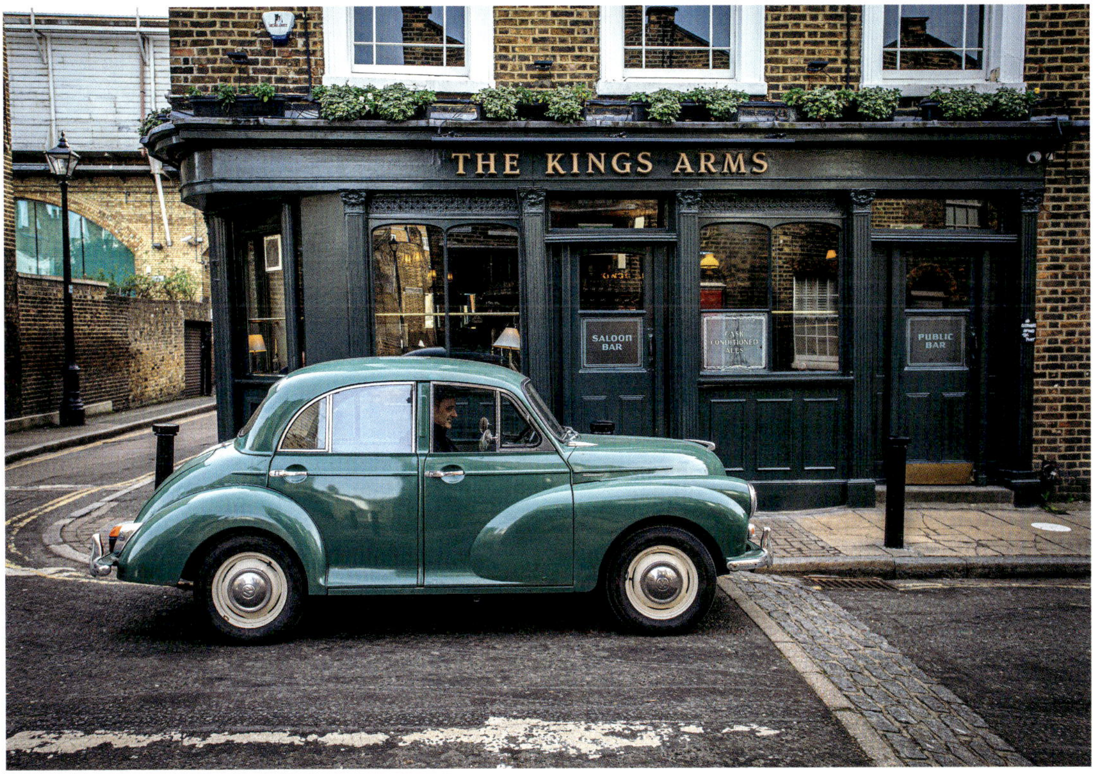

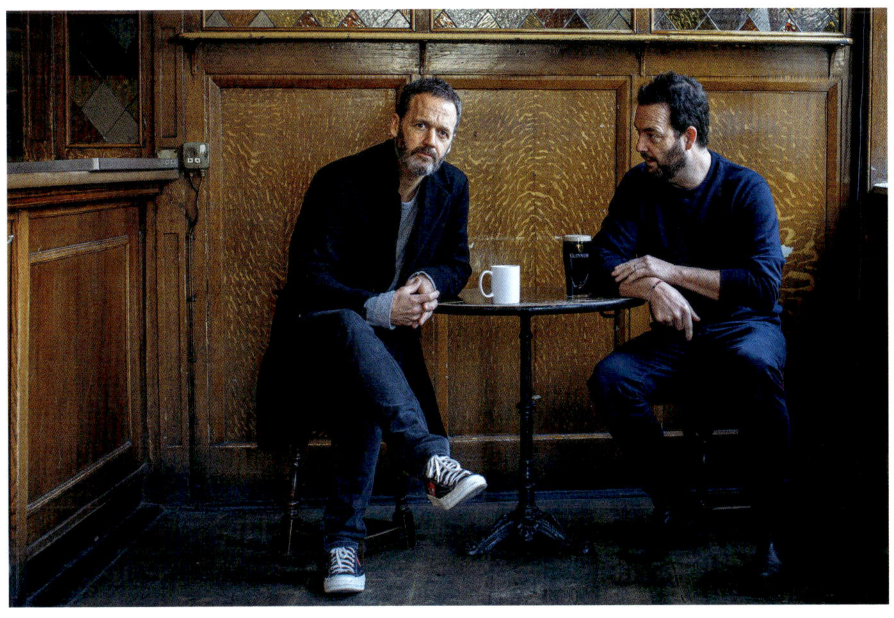

The McElhinney brothers keep family at the heart of the pub

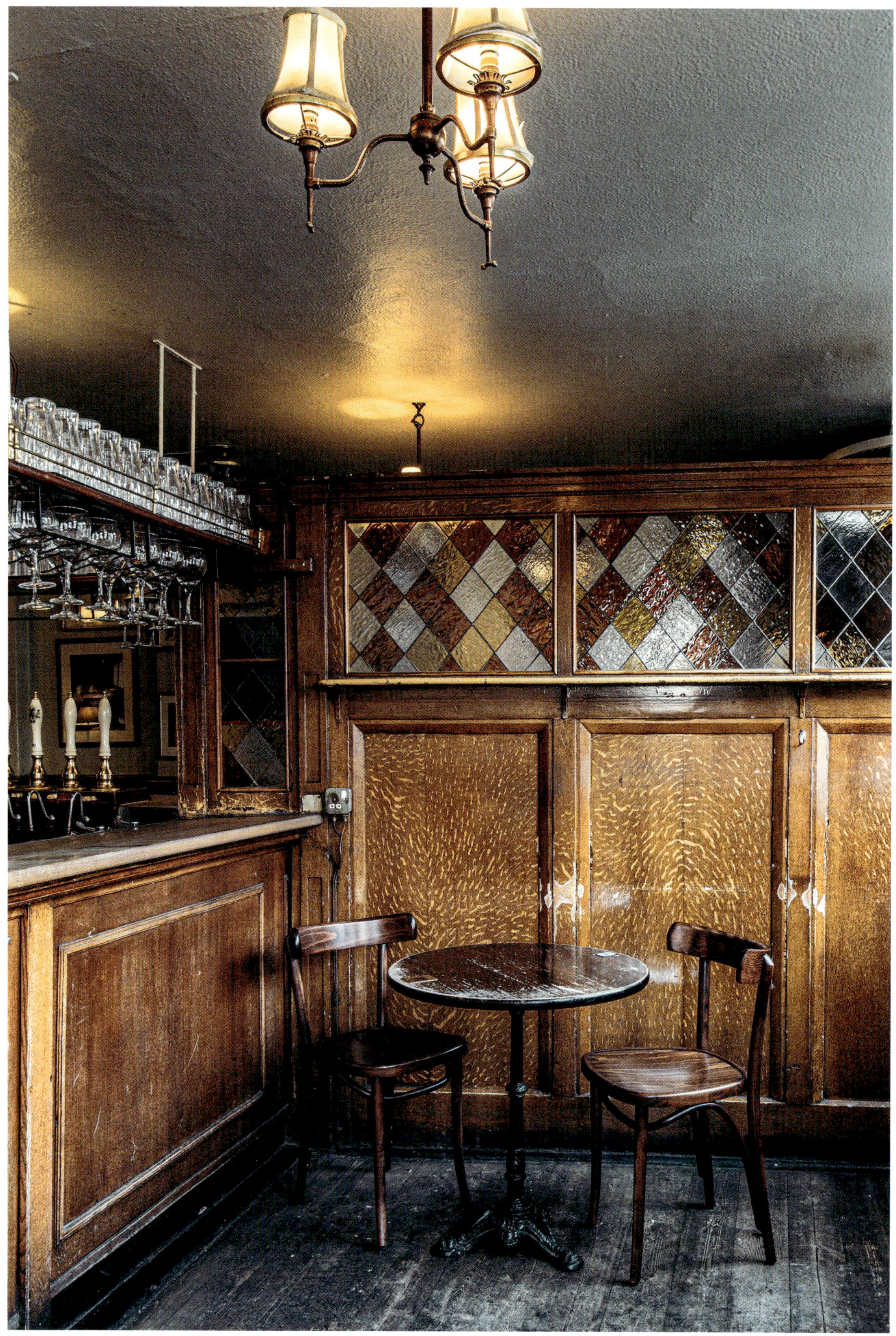

Sepia tones wash the rooms

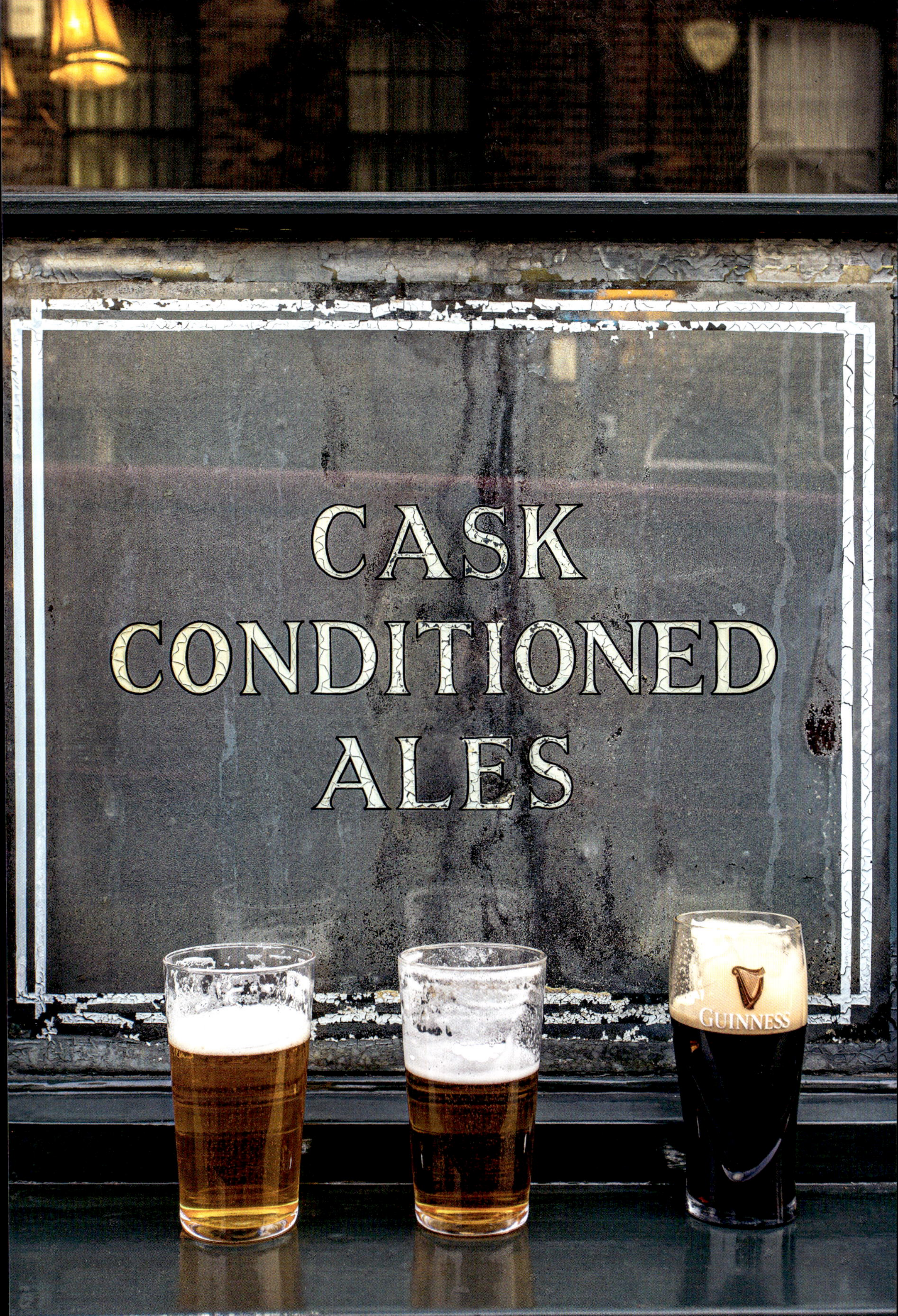
CASK
CONDITIONED
ALES
GUINNESS

THE PLUME OF FEATHERS

Every longitude on earth is measured in terms of its distance east or west from this pub, give or take a few yards. The Plume of Feathers in Greenwich appears to straddle time itself. The historic meridian line runs mere yards from the front door. When you traverse the threshold, your time travel is complete as you fall into a perfectly preserved backstreet boozer. This is a place to forget time, not be reminded of it. Once you're behind the door, the rain doesn't matter anymore, this month's credit card bill becomes a minor irrelevance and your focus fades to the glowing optics and hand pulls behind the bar.

This is a place to forget time, not be reminded of it.

There are many important dates in The Plume's back catalogue, from 1691, when first built, to 1884, when the Greenwich meridian was adopted by almost the entire world (except for the French, who unusually were the last to surrender in 1911). But the biggest date in the diary was not when the current owners (mother-and-son duo Susan and James) got the keys to the pub over forty years ago, but 1999, when they became free of tie. Total emancipation from the brewery shackles. Unheralded freedom was theirs. The stabilisers were off. Open when you want. Sell what you want. With "Ich dien" – I serve – being the motto for the Prince of Wales, this is a promise the pub has kept to its local community for the last four decades.

This family dream team came up smelling of roses. Their award-winning hanging baskets burst with pride and are emblematic in proving that God is indeed found in the details. The front bar is all solid brick fireplace, carpets and authentically boozy vibes, whilst the rear allows for decent pub grub to be dispensed and there's a sun-trap garden to enjoy with your four-legged friends after a yomp in Greenwich Park.

Salvador Dalí was right about his melting clocks. Time is both liquid and moveable. In 1984 the world decided that, as the earth's crust shifted, the historic meridian was no longer quite on the money. With the help of satellites and an atomic clock or two, the prime meridian moved 102.5 metres eastwards down the road. Goodbye Greenwich, hello Charlton! This left The Plume in a newly created no man's land between the two prime meridians. I'm no scientist, but I'd suggest this makes The Plume of Feathers almost timeless. And you certainly wouldn't argue with that.

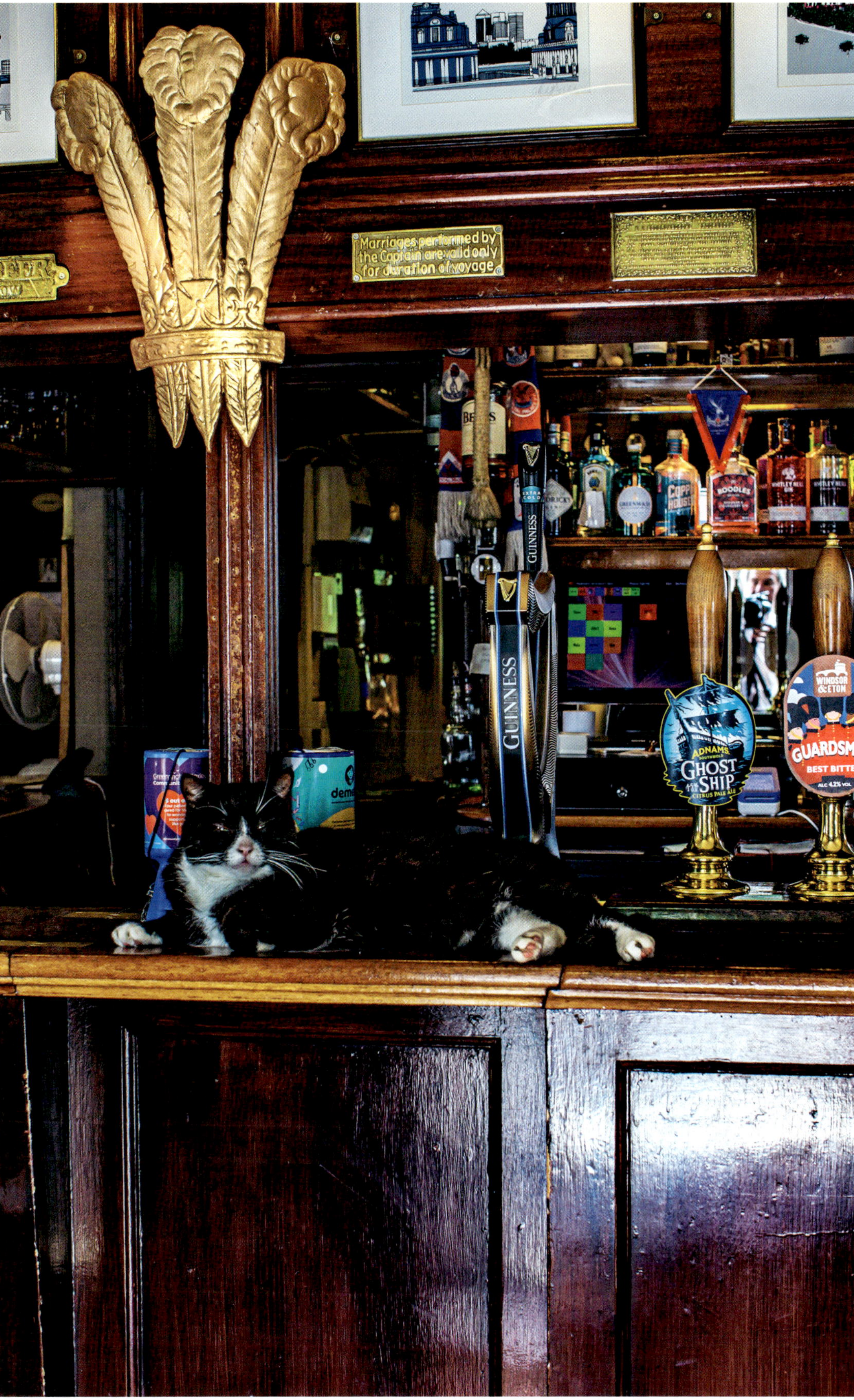

Marriages performed by
the Captain are valid only
for duration of voyage
GUINNESS
GHOST SHIP
ADNAMS
CITRUS PALE ALE
GUARDSMAN
WINDSOR & ETON
BEST BITTER
ALC 4.2% VOL

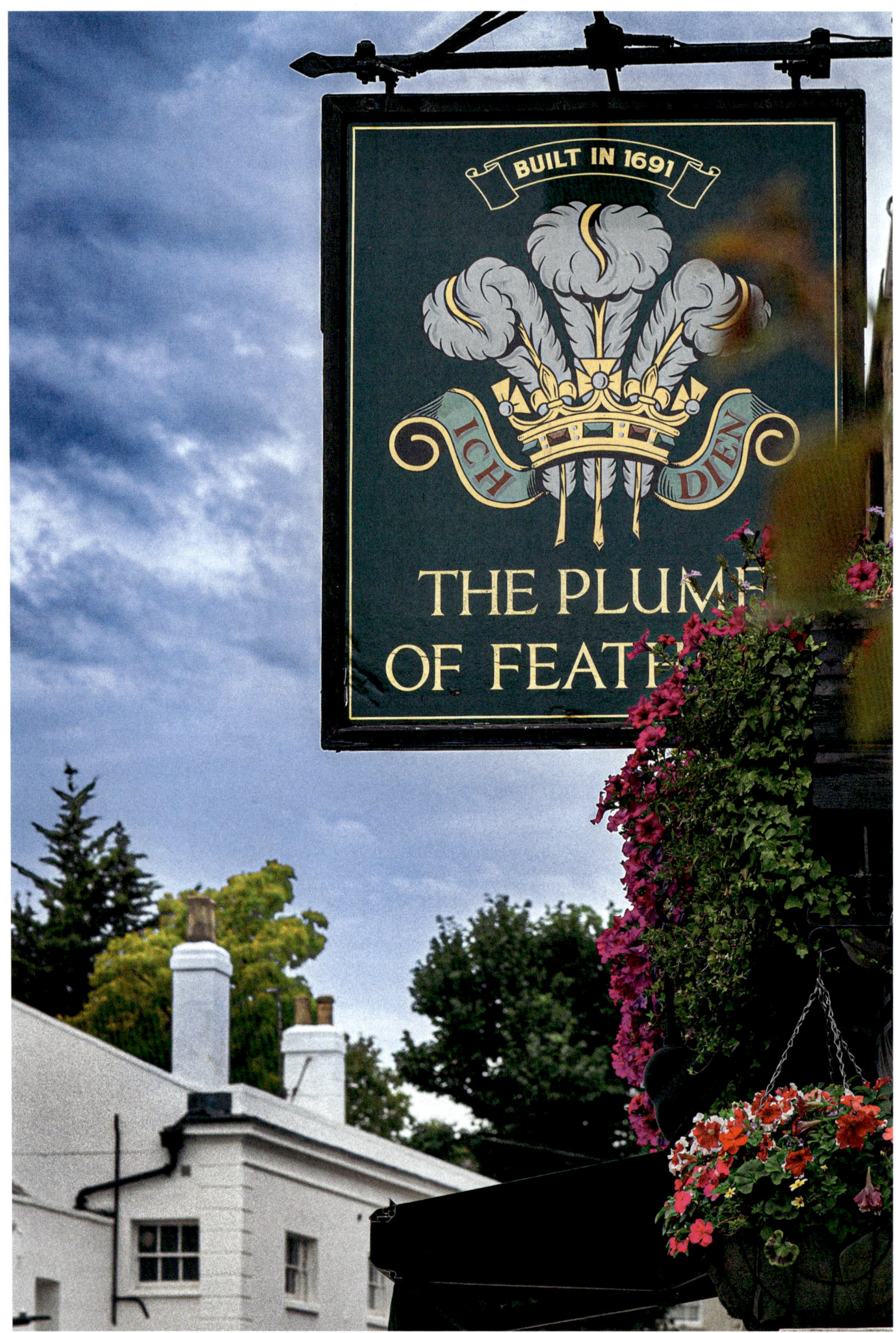

Homegrown blooms bursting with pride

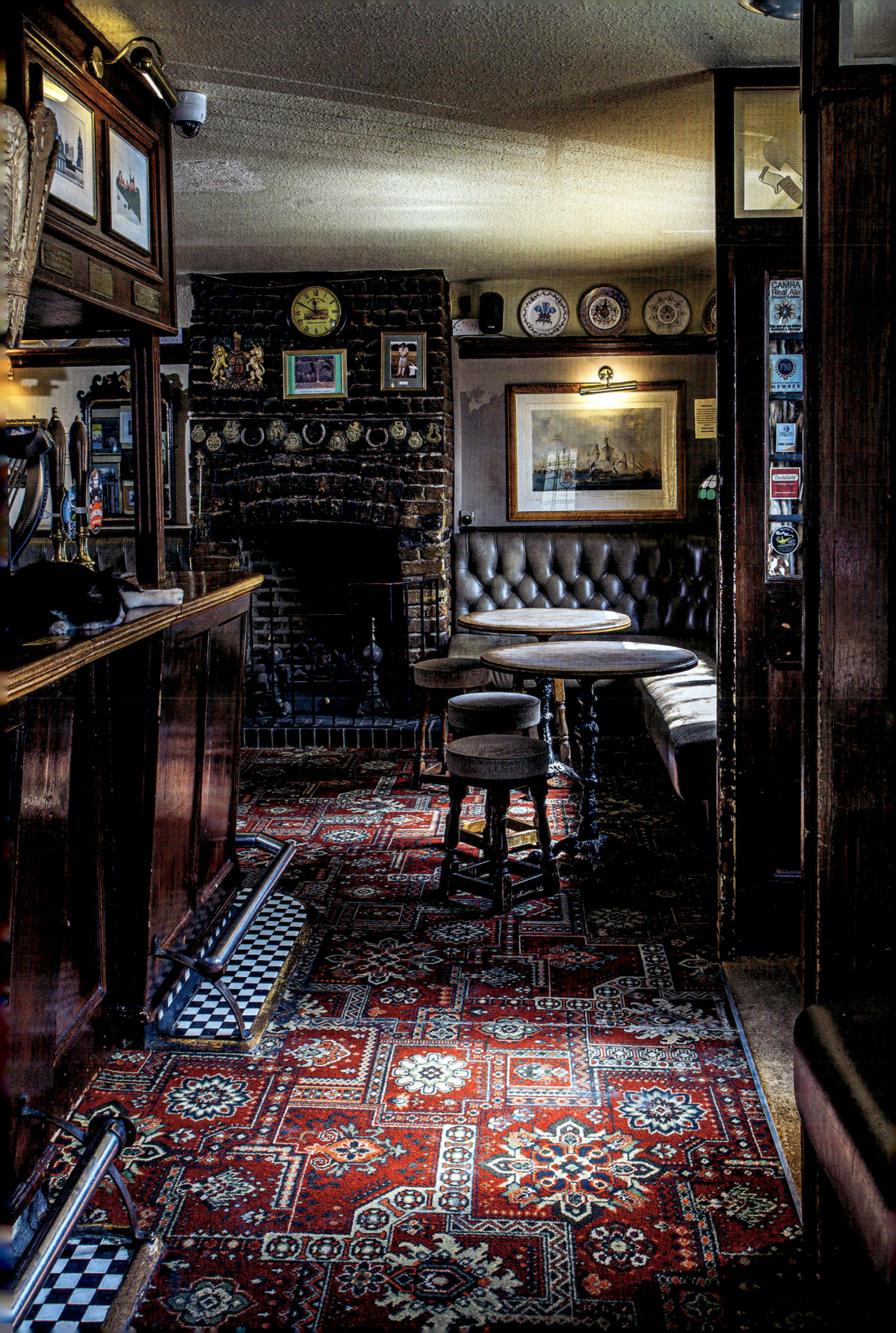

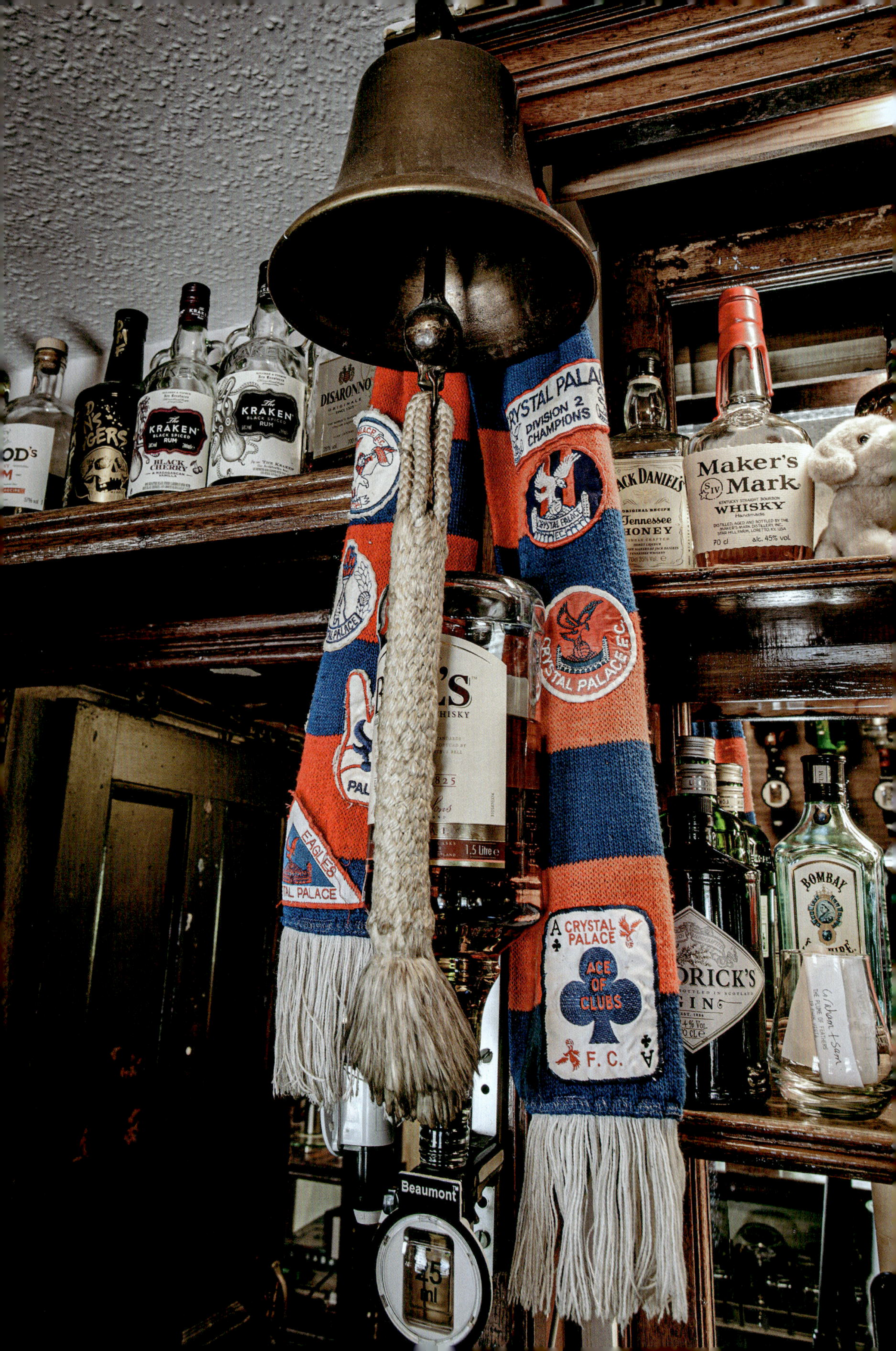

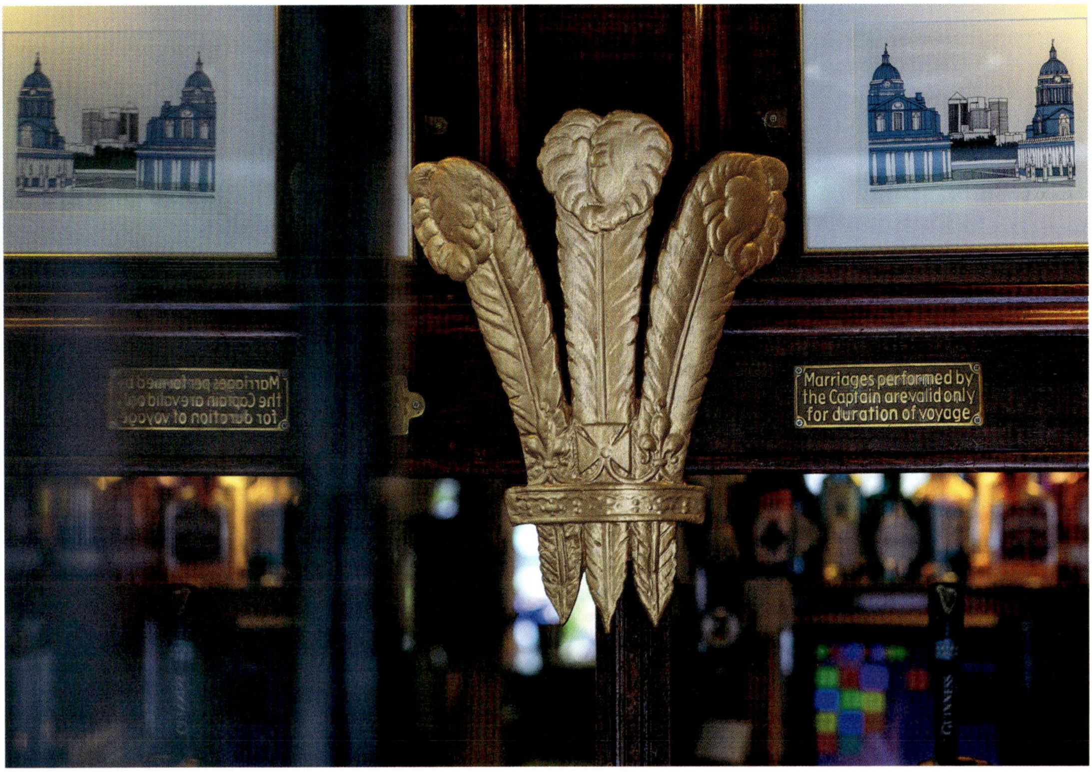

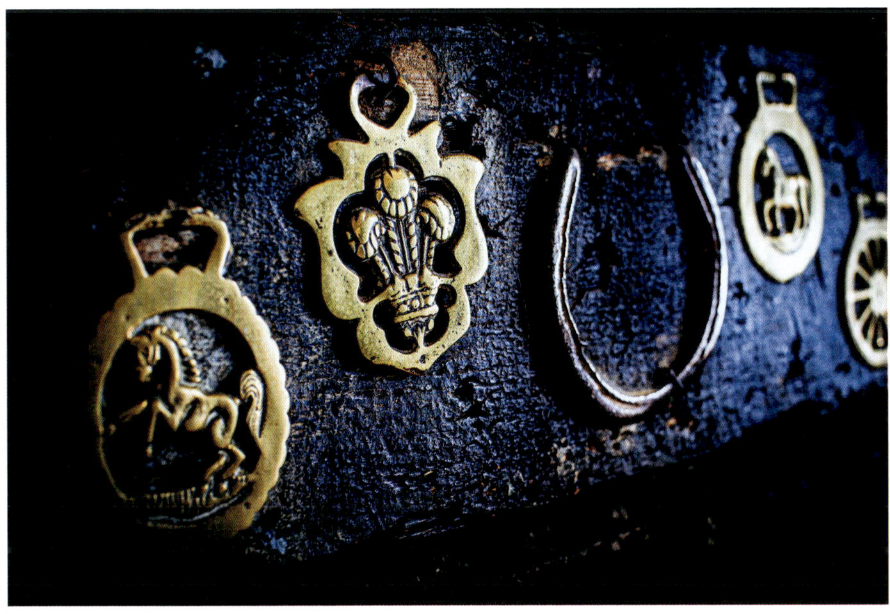

The house motto..."Ich dien: I serve"

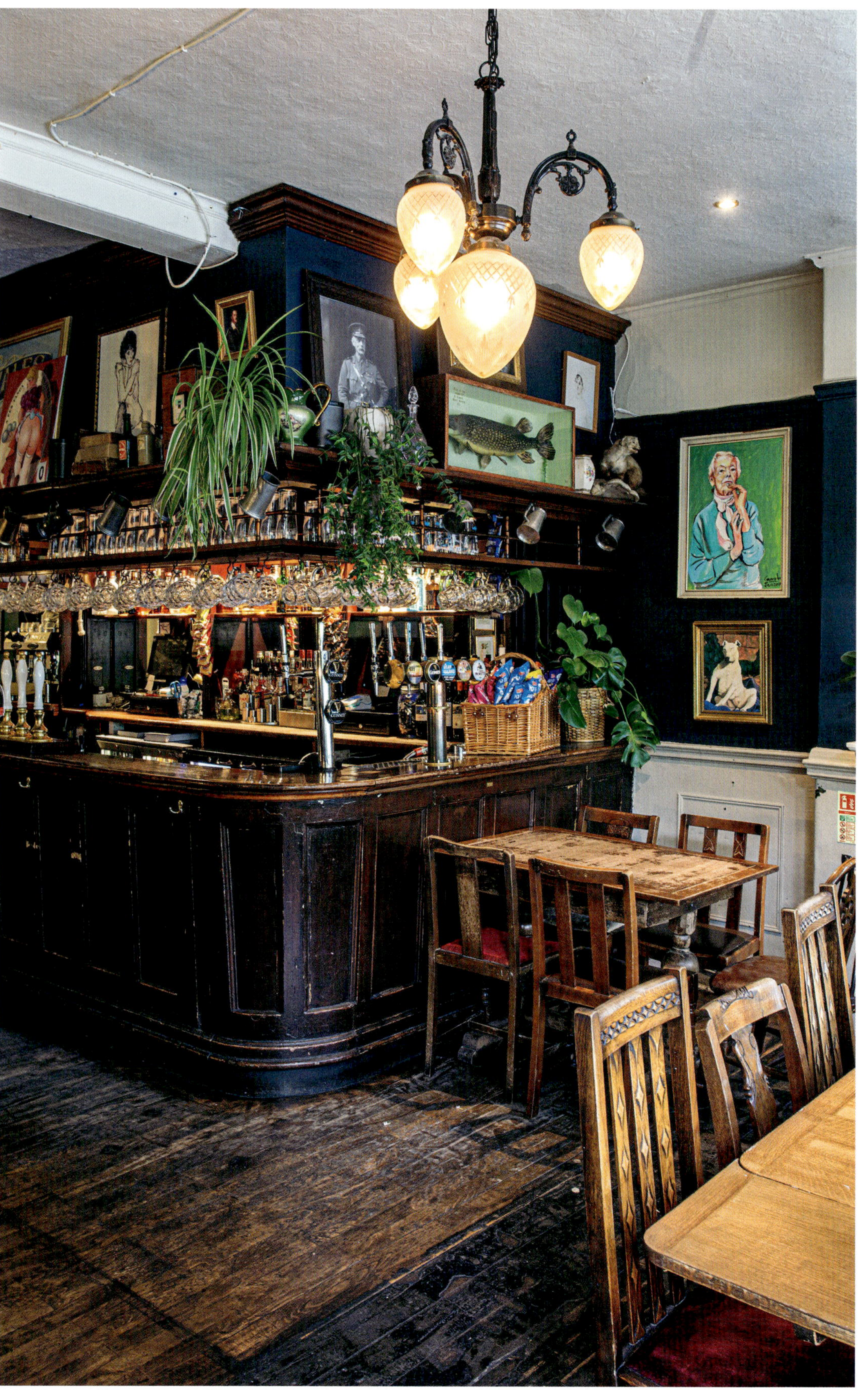

THE PRINCE OF WALES

PINTS AND PETANQUE IN A SHADY SOUTH LONDON SQUARE

This pub is one of the few bits of Kennington where the landlord is not actually the Prince of Wales. He still owns The Oval cricket ground and the Duchy Arms not far away. If you're driving up the Kennington Road, then you pass most of the Duchy on the left-hand side (ahem). Drift slightly further south, squeeze through the narrow streets seemingly leading you nowhere, and you'll emerge into one of the earliest and finest Georgian squares in London. Avenues of trees frame the gravelled square, creating a fine village green effect. And where there is a fine village green, you shall find a fine village pub.

> ### ... you can fling balls around the dust
> ### and just for a moment imagine
> ### you are in Provence

Nestled in one corner, with a wonderfully warm welcome and unembellished vibe, it makes one wonder two things. Firstly, how have I never visited this pub before, and secondly, how much is a house on this secret South London square? A young Charlie Chaplin would have known the accommodation as working class, but now it's generally full of poshos and politicians. Pea-loving former prime minister John Major lived here to be both within the eight-minute dash for the division bell at the Houses of Parliament and a light leg-stretch to watch the first ball from the Pavilion End. If you're stumped for good options in the area after some leather-on-willow action, then this is one for your little black book.

Inside, it's small yet handsome, as if decorated by an aristocrat who has left all the really natty Persian rugs and trophy art pieces at their place in the country. Is that a Freud on the wall? But they have certainly made this place feel like a country pub. One can imagine the current Prince of Wales arriving by mighty steed after a quick estate inspection and refreshing himself liberally before riding back to Kensington, laughing that the only difference in the two boroughs is a single vowel and a zero on the price of property.

Although pub conversation can drift to rah-rah talk of Tuscan villas, school fees or financial tittle-tattle, you can easily escape the pink trouser brigade and head *en plein air* to the square, famous for its beer and boules action. With drink in hand (pastis if you must live the dream), you can fling balls around the dust and just for a moment imagine you are in Provence. Now, how much were these houses again?

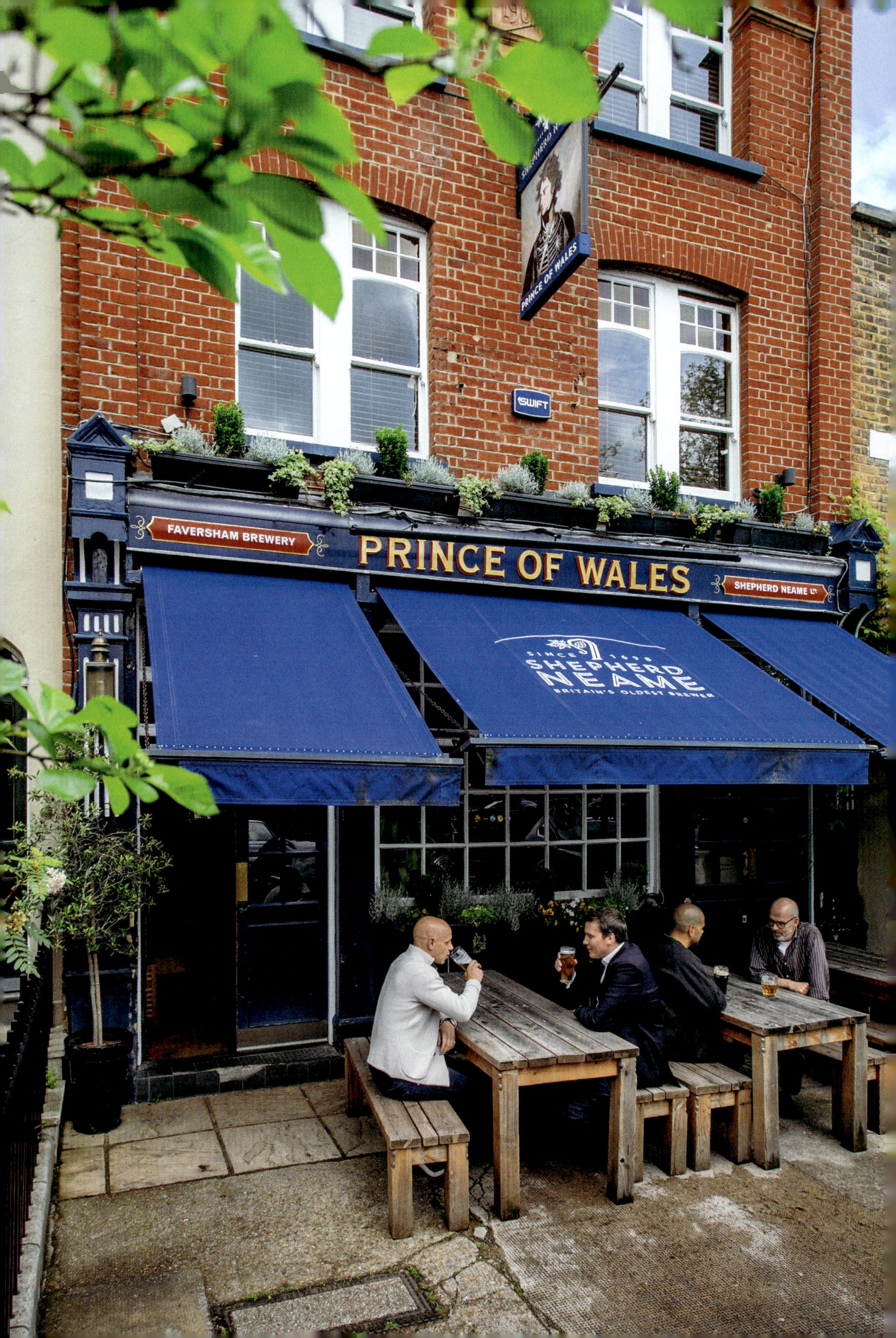

PRINCE OF WALES
FAVERSHAM BREWERY
SHEPHERD NEAME L.TD
SINCE 1698
SHEPHERD NEAME
BRITAIN'S OLDEST BREWER
PRINCE OF WALES
SWIFT

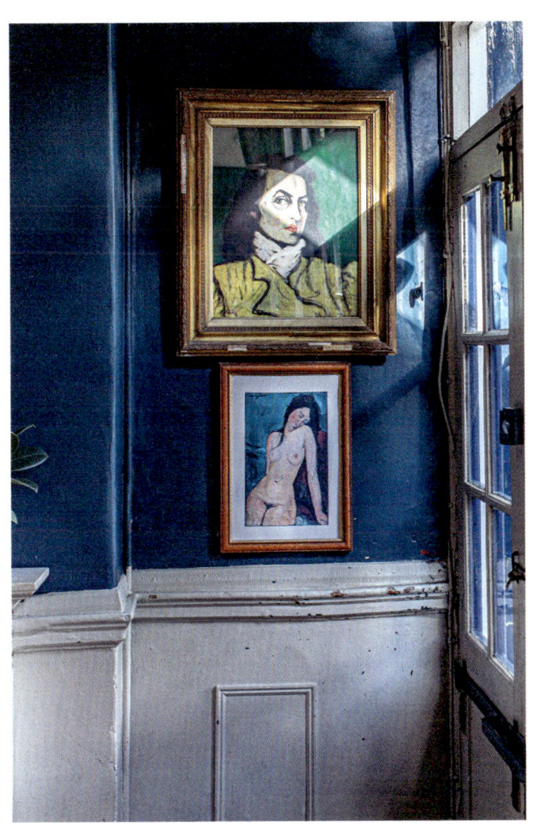

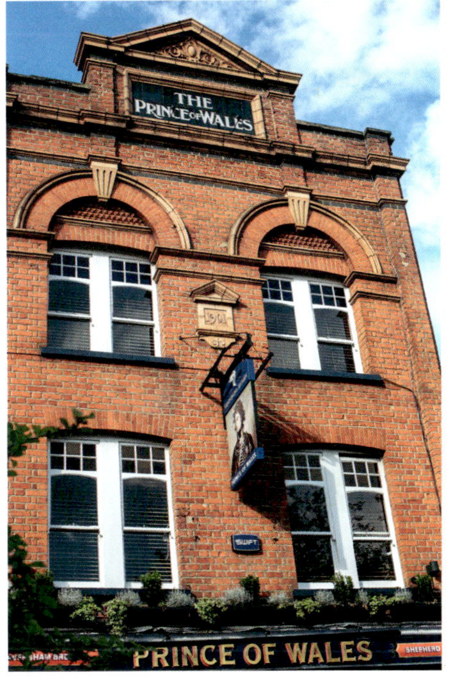

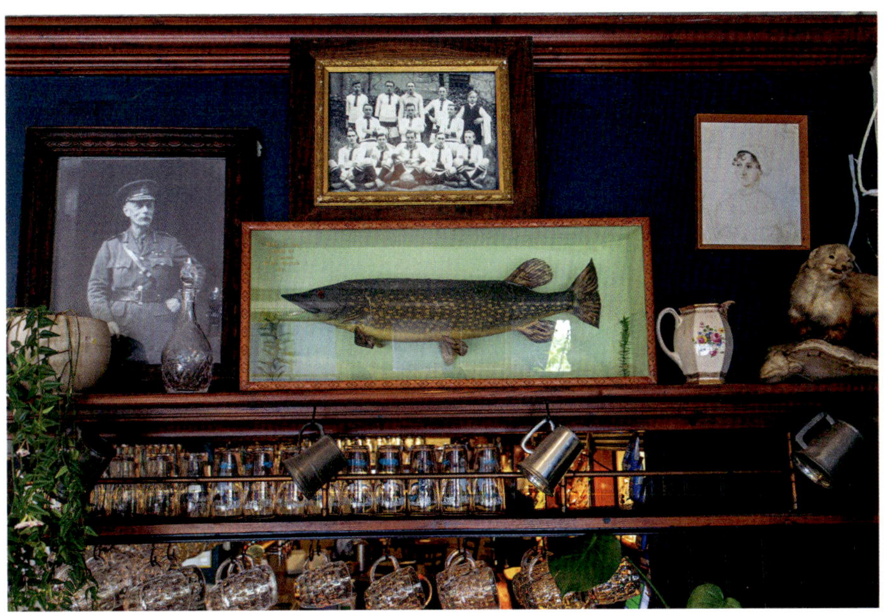

A bold eye for the art collection and antique rugs add a homely dimension

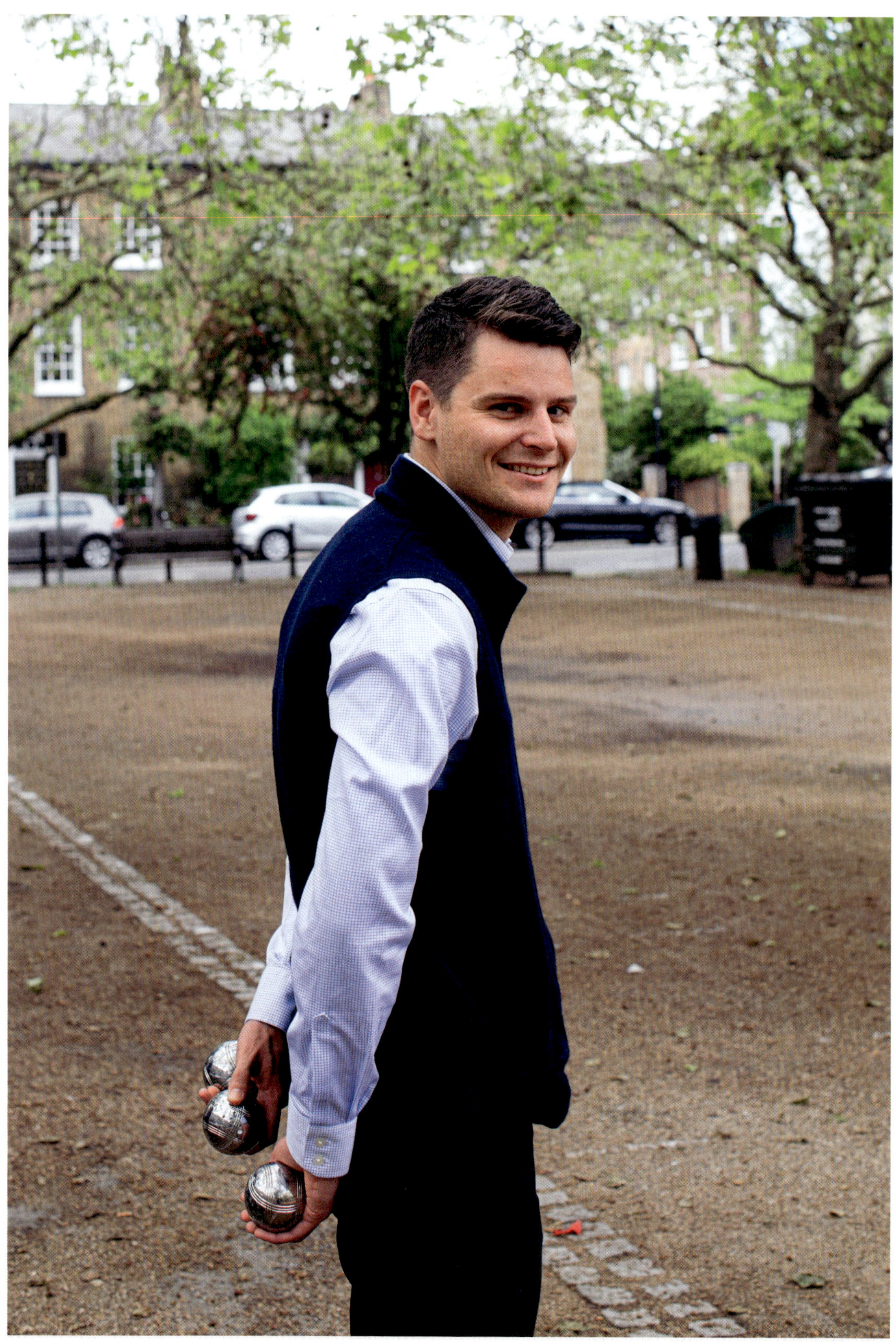

Pints and pétanque are de rigueur here

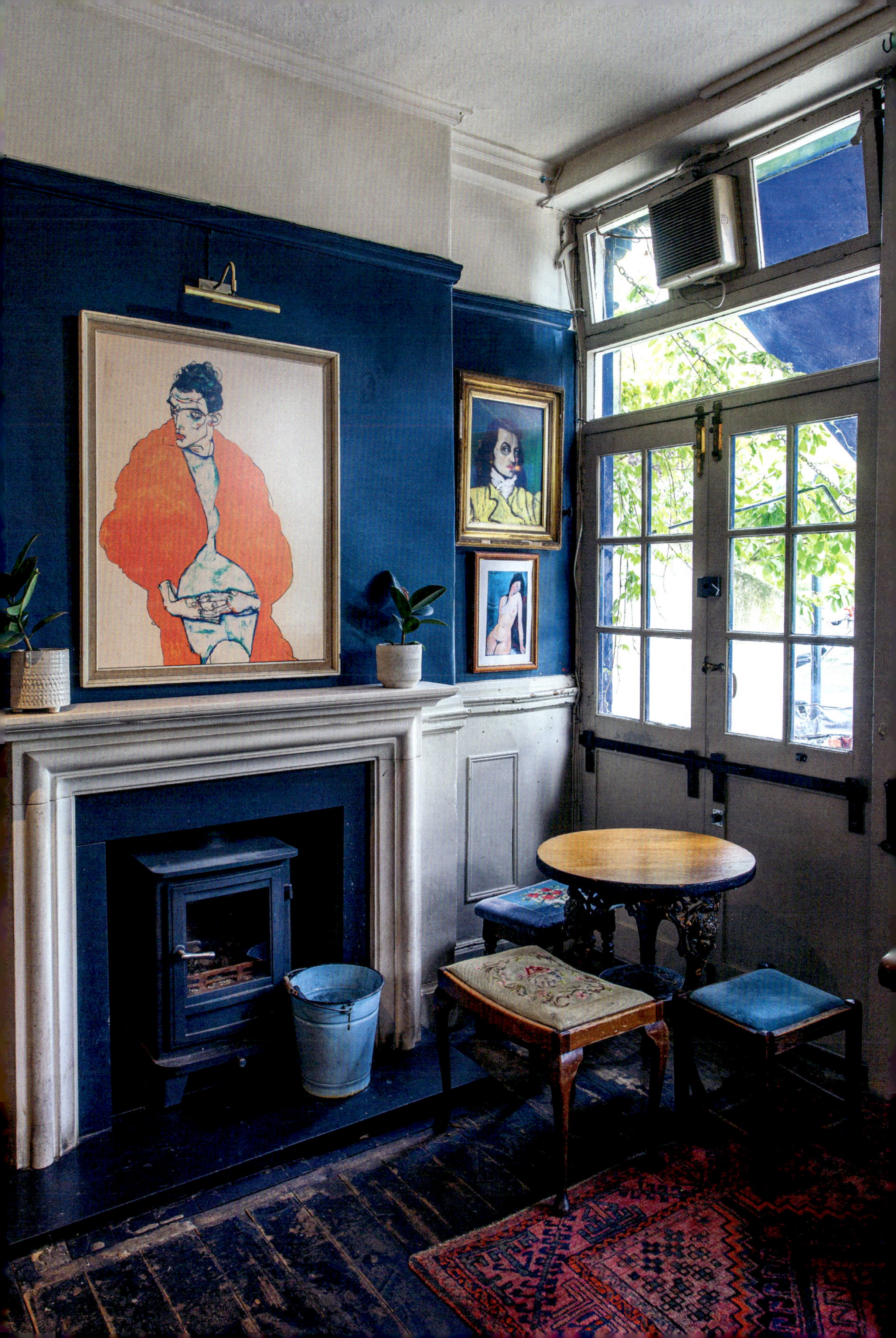

THE DOG & BELL

Deptford. Not a natural choice for first dates. But drift back a few centuries to when Samuel Pepys and John Evelyn ruled the roost here. By the early 1700s, Deptford Creek had the highest output of navy ship production anywhere in the country, making Deptford the unlikely epicentre of the Empire. It was here that Elizabeth I greeted Francis Drake with a knighthood for his successful circumnavigation of the globe on the *Golden Hinde* and Tsar Peter of Russia used priceless paintings for target practice. And don't forget Christopher Marlowe being stabbed through the eye after a well-lubricated lunch. Deptford really was quite the place.

Other pubs simply gave up the ghost and the world passed this place by for a century or two.

Shipbuilders, porters and dockers thronged the area and Napoleonic prisoners cobbled the streets. But the Empire inevitably faded, the dockyard closed in the nineteenth century and these streets became a no man's land of northern Kent. Wedged between old Father Thames and the A2 artery, other pubs simply gave up the ghost and the world passed this place by for a century or two.

Charlie and Eileen Gallagher took up the reins at The Dog & Bell in 1988 and have poured their love into one of the best pubs south (or, for that matter, north) of the river. With its pillar-box red paint job and Celtic braids, it looks like it has been dropped straight in from Dublin's Temple Bar (and it does indeed serve a good pint of the black custard). An ale-led consistency behind the pumps (plus Belgian beers) continues to be the secret, and your pint glass is guaranteed to runneth over with liquid delights here.

The home cooking is just like your mum's (but better). Bar billiards and vintage arcade games offer humble amusement and the pickle festival hints at the eccentric character underlying the whole ensemble. Whether it's Morris Men on May Day or the Green Man come Twelfth Night, they do enjoy a sausage sizzle and cider session here. The stained-glass windows enhance the near-religious experience of many who complete their pilgrimage to this high altar of ale. An old dog with absolutely no requirement for new tricks. The old ones appear to be working just fine, thank you.

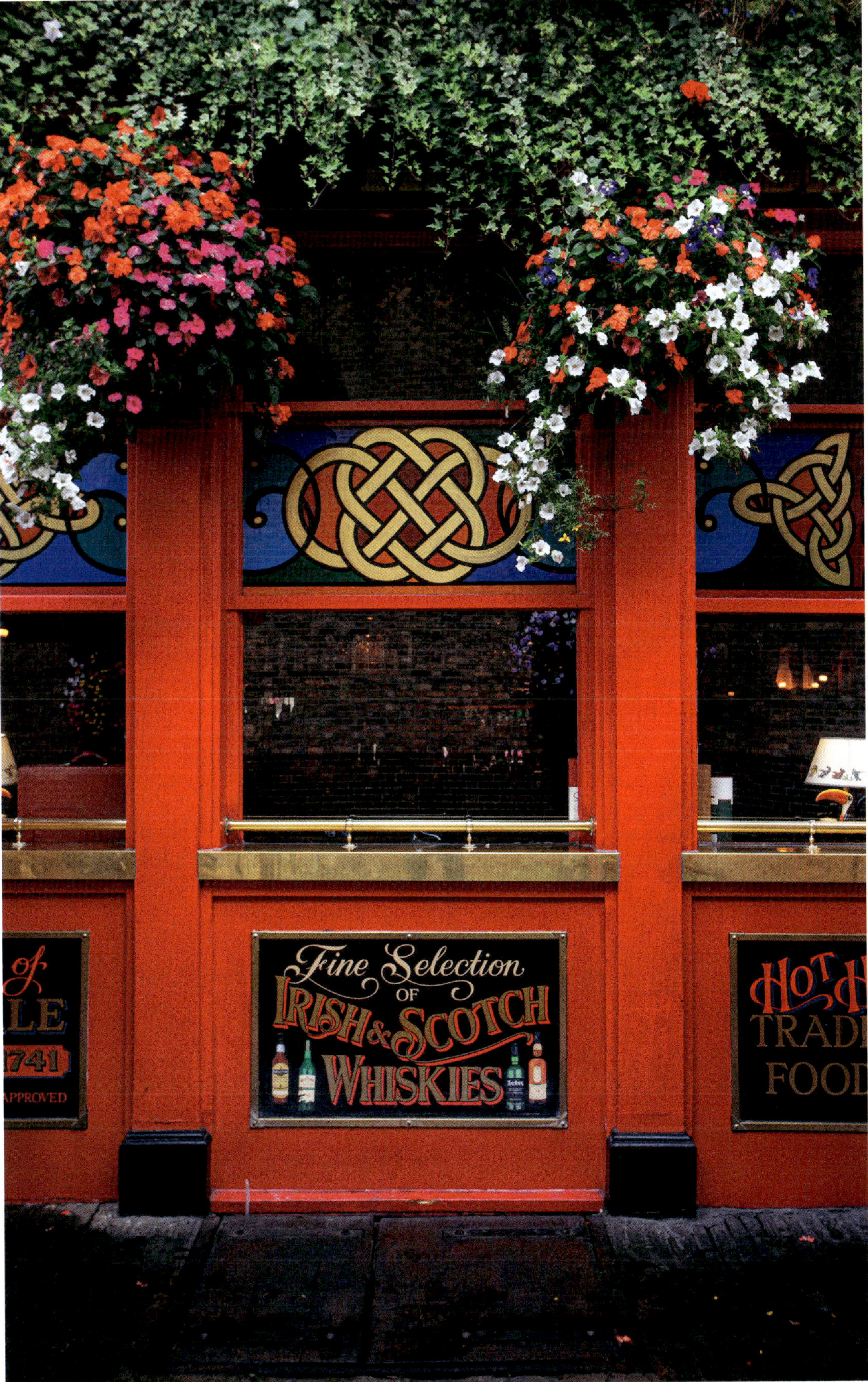
Fine Selection
OF
IRISH & SCOTCH
WHISKIES
of
LE
1741
APPROVED
HOT H
TRADI
FOOD

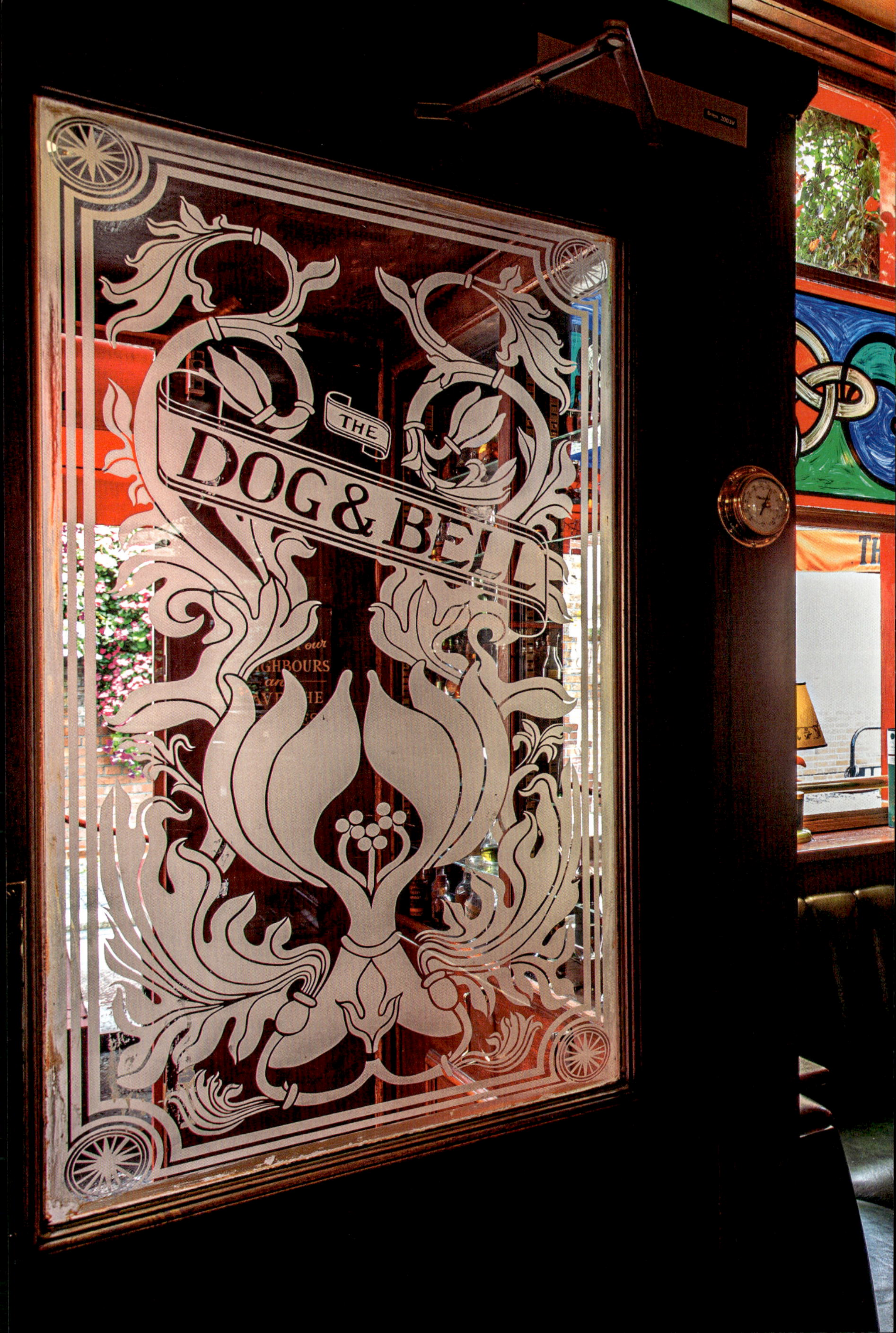
THE
DOG & BELL

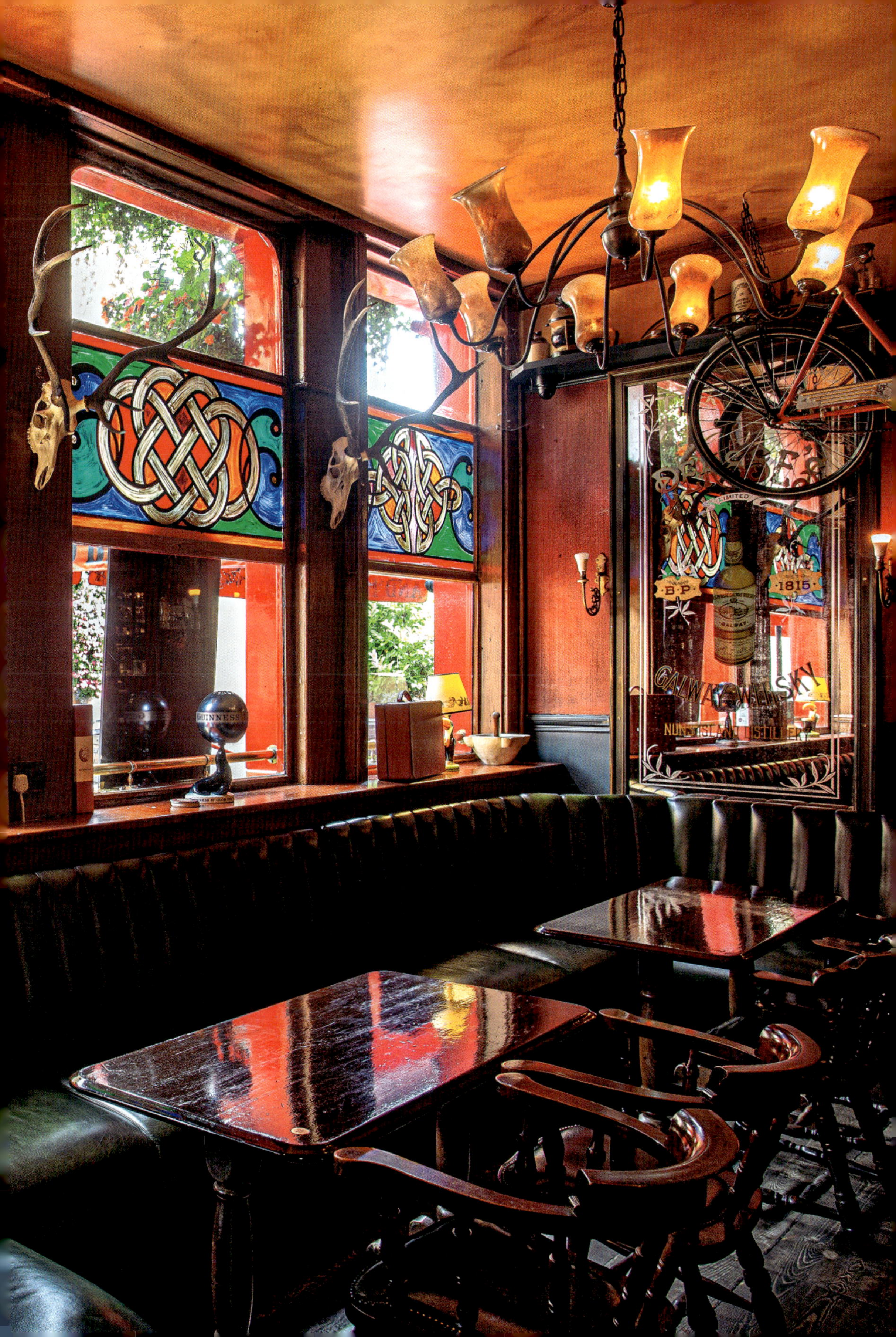

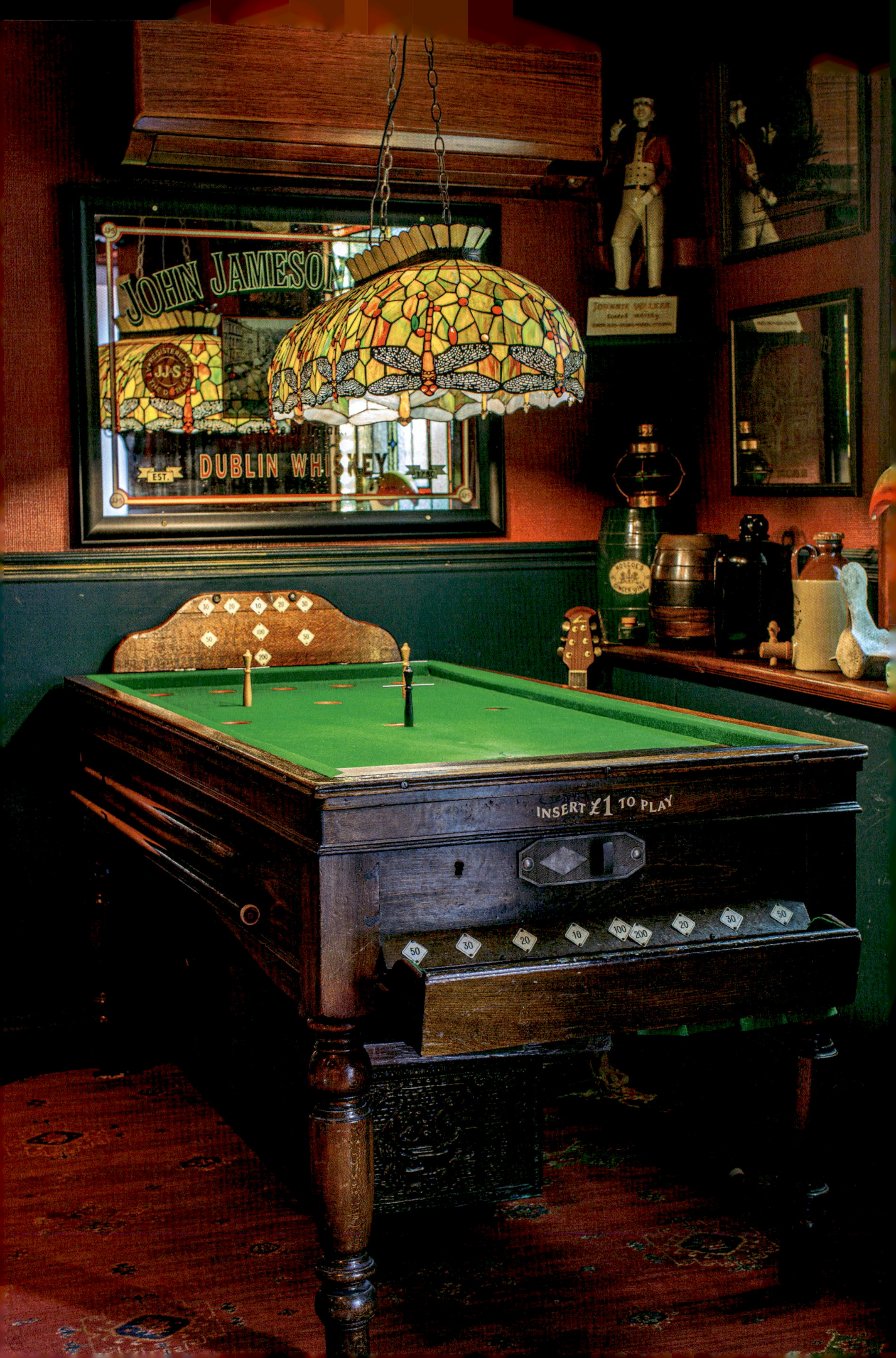

JOHN JAMESON
DUBLIN WHISKEY
INSERT £1 TO PLAY

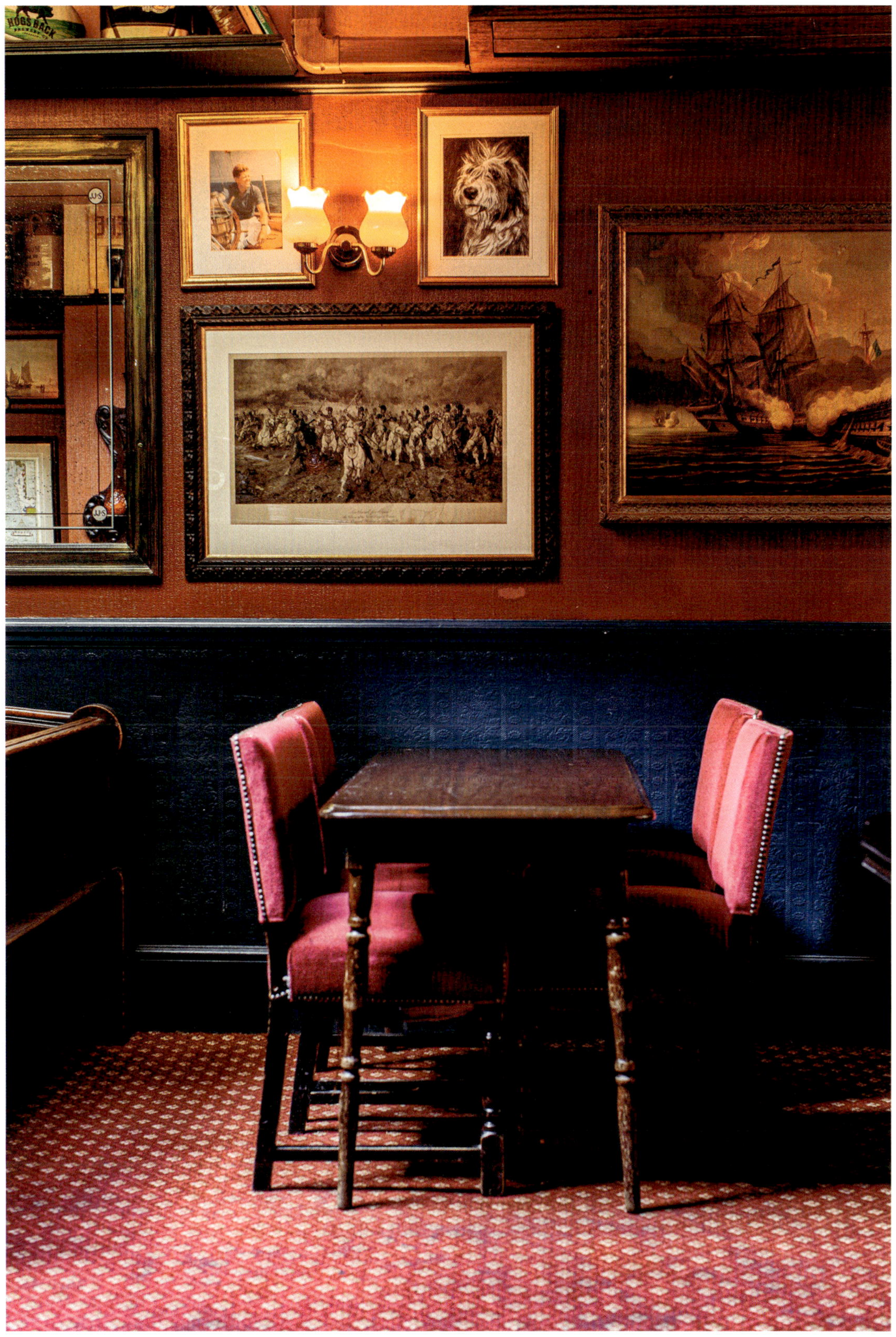

Vintage bar billiards offers a rare time-gone-by treat

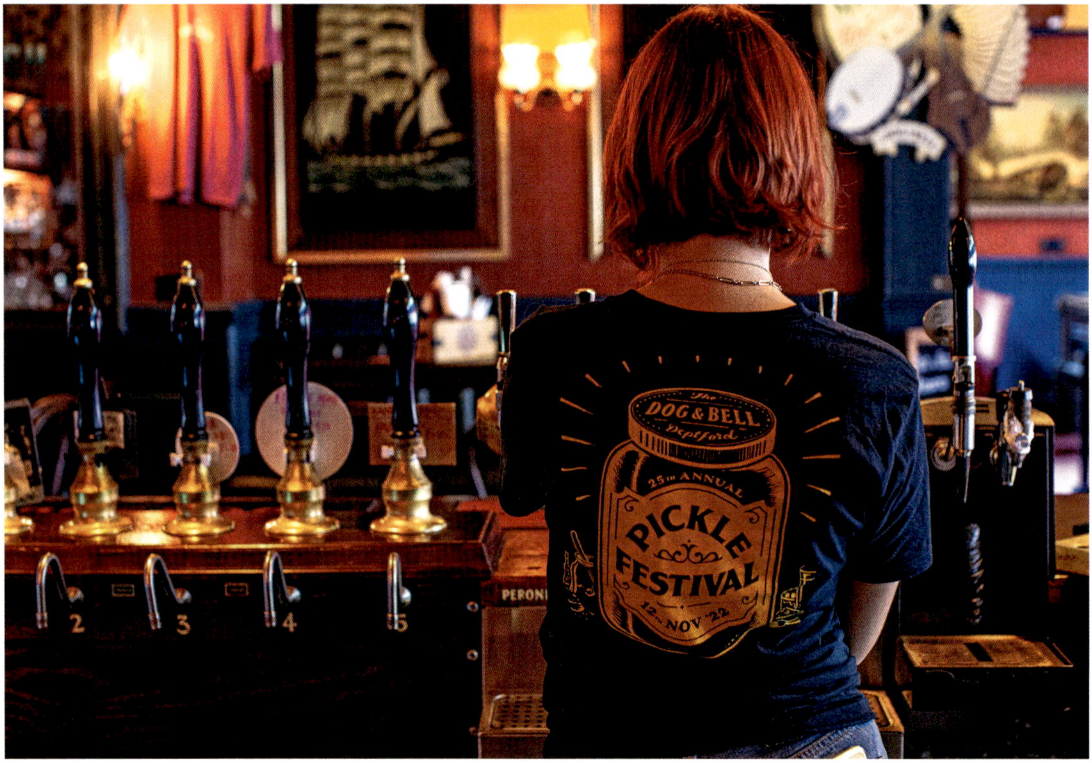

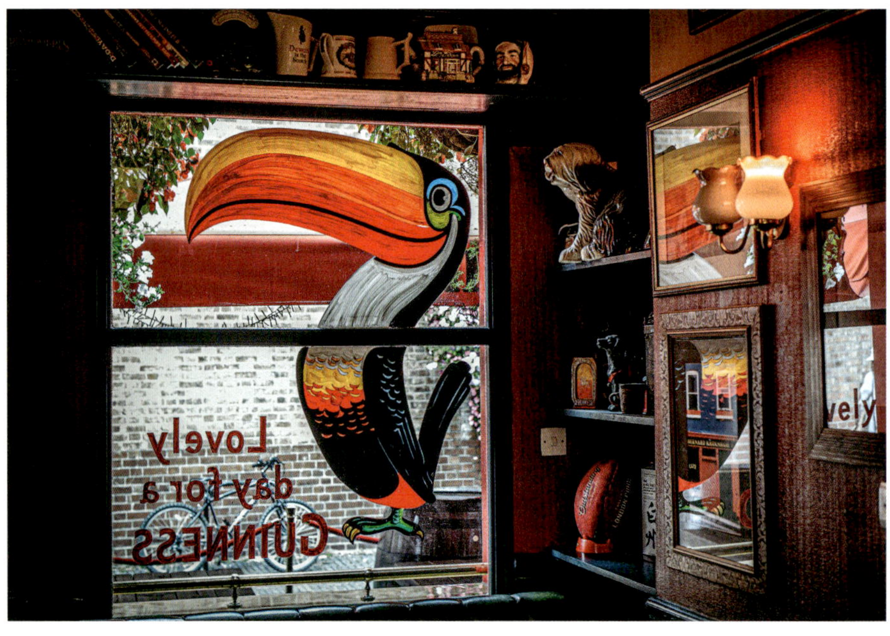

The annual pickle festival adds a suitably eccentric flavour

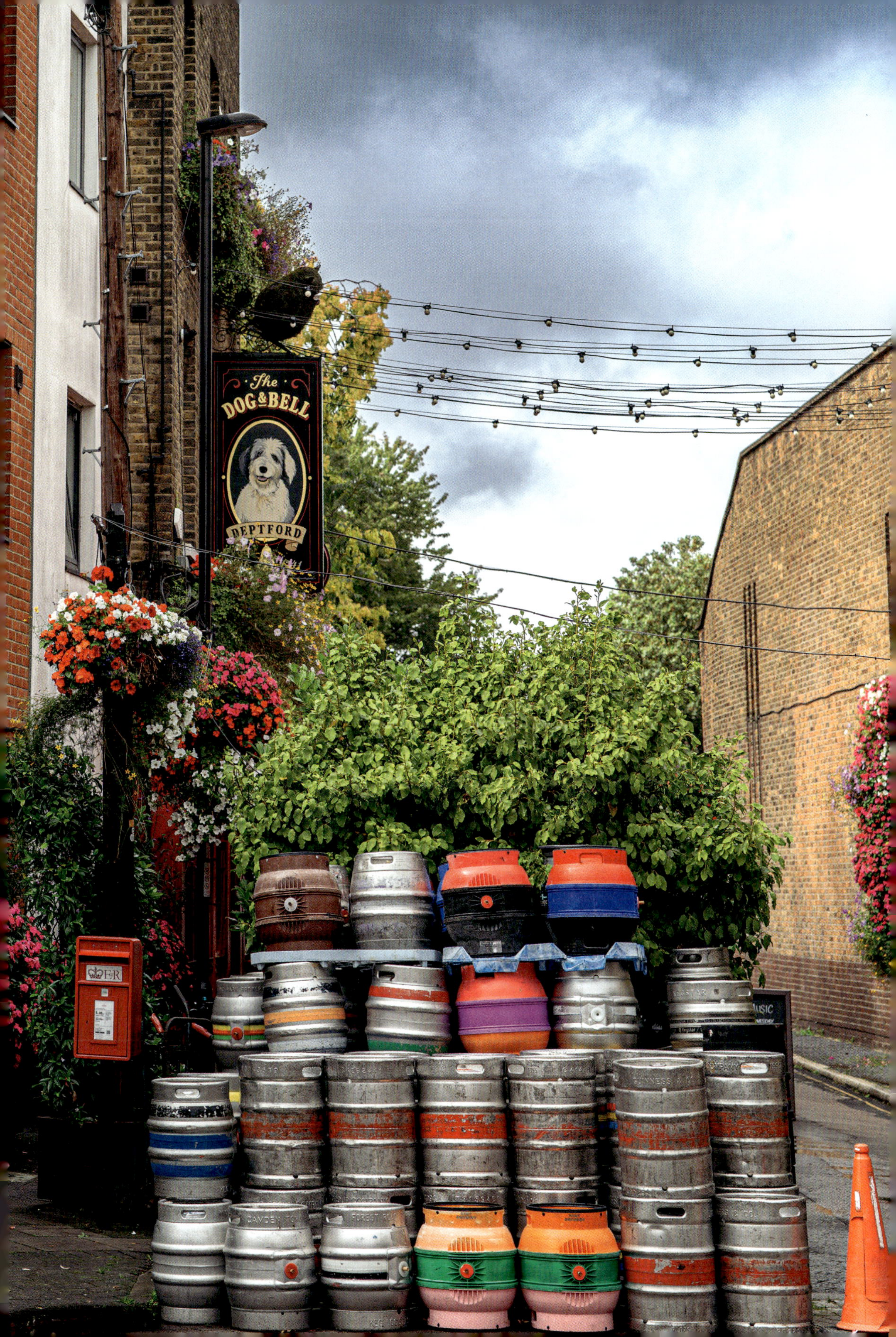
The
DOG & BELL
DEPTFORD

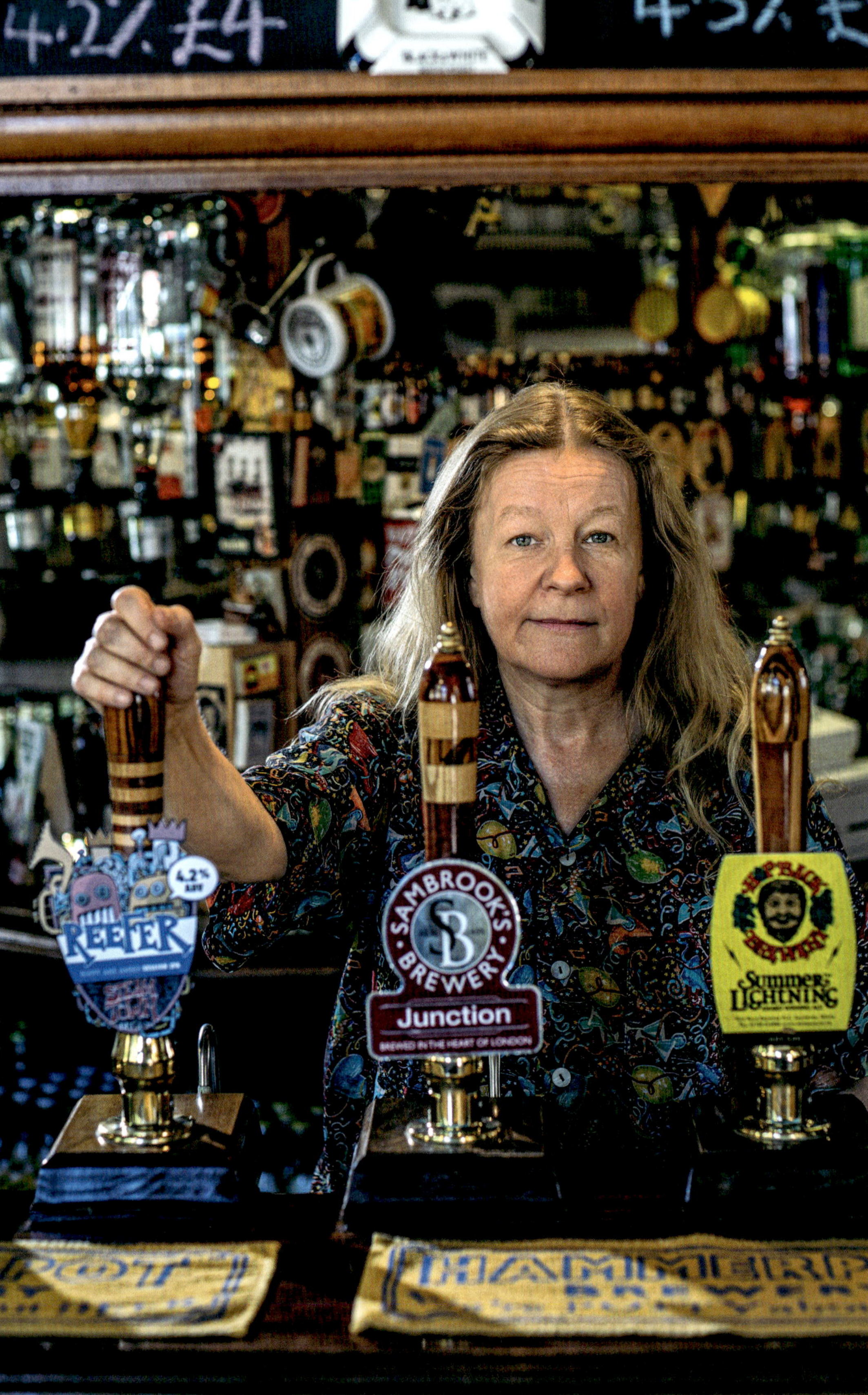

4.2, £4
4.5,
REEFER
4.2%
SAMBROOK'S BREWERY
Junction
BREWED IN THE HEART OF LONDON
SUMMER LIGHTNING

THE MASONS ARMS

The nearby Thameside taverns mop up the less discerning suburban pot walloper, leaving the backwater delights of The Masons Arms (no apostrophe required here: it's that kind of place) to the all-knowing local or in-the-know outsider. After travelling the world, Rae Williams got a job here with zero bar-keeping experience after reassuring the landlord that she had a lifetime of beer-drinking down her gullet. Thirty years later, she still lives above the shop.

Rae loves talking about beer and loves serving good people good beer. The pub's wall-to-wall breweriana is a true temple to tippling and makes it the perfect sister establishment to The Roebuck down the road.

> **"Please, please. Whatever you do. Don't. Write. About. This. Pub."** Michael, *Masons Arms barfly*

There is a kitchen here, but Rae has no desire to use it: it gets in the way of pouring pints of the good stuff. But during the colder months, she'll fire up the stoves to cook a mid-week roast so that customers who live on their own can convene, family-style, at the pub. If that doesn't make you want to jump on a train to Teddington right now, then I just don't know what will. On arrival, you'll be greeted by an amphitheatre of locals hunched over the bar or in flanking positions either side amongst the low-stool seating. A light profiling and gentle joshing are not uncommon as you enter and await service. Escape to the rear horticultural idyll if you must.

And then the magic slowly unfolds. "Would you like to start a tab?" is the leading question that makes you realise that you'll likely be staying longer than for just a quick half. Just have your name scribbled down (no card required) and your entrance to this wonderful world has begun.

There are four charity tins on the bar to gobble up loose coinage and a sponsored pram race on occasion. Rae managed to keep the doors to the pub open every single day during the pandemic: reinventing the place as the local corner shop, and even pivoting into local theatre, they were able to carry on supporting the community through the hardest of times. A pub often only discovered by word-of-mouth recommendation. A pub so good that you might linger in the estate agent windows on your return to the station. And of course, a pub that we simply mustn't tell anyone about. Sorry, Michael.

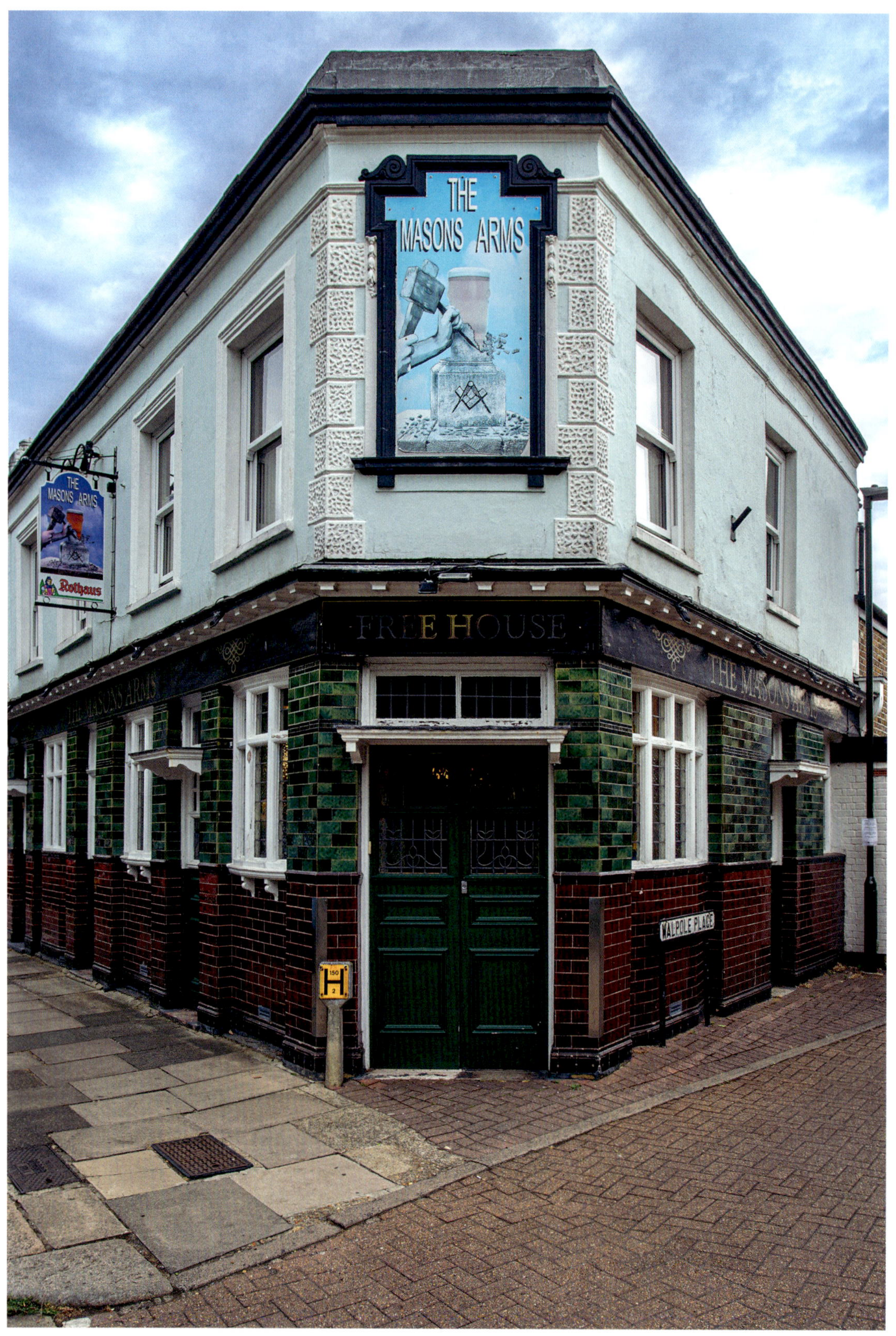

Unassuming brilliance tucked just off Teddington High Street

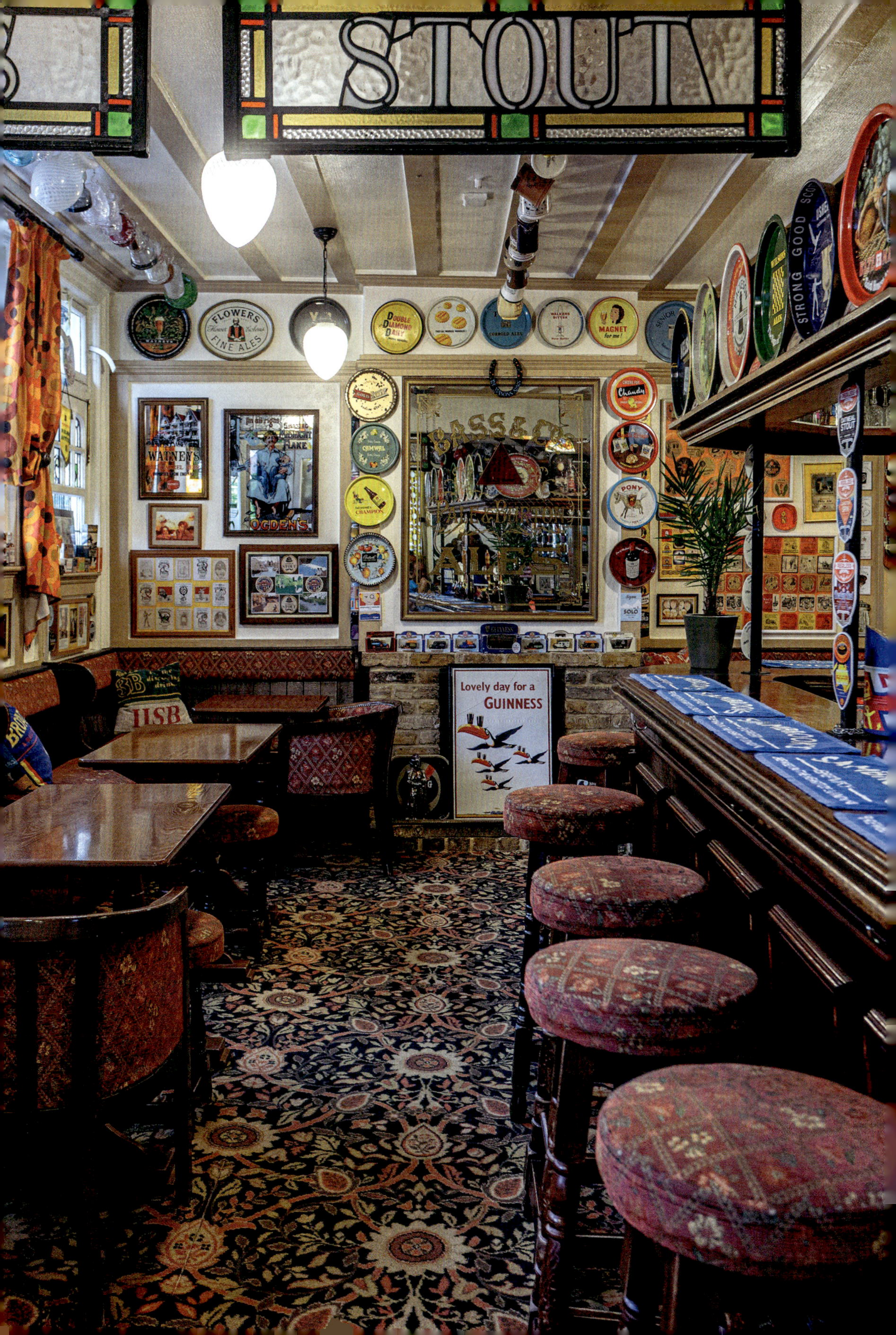

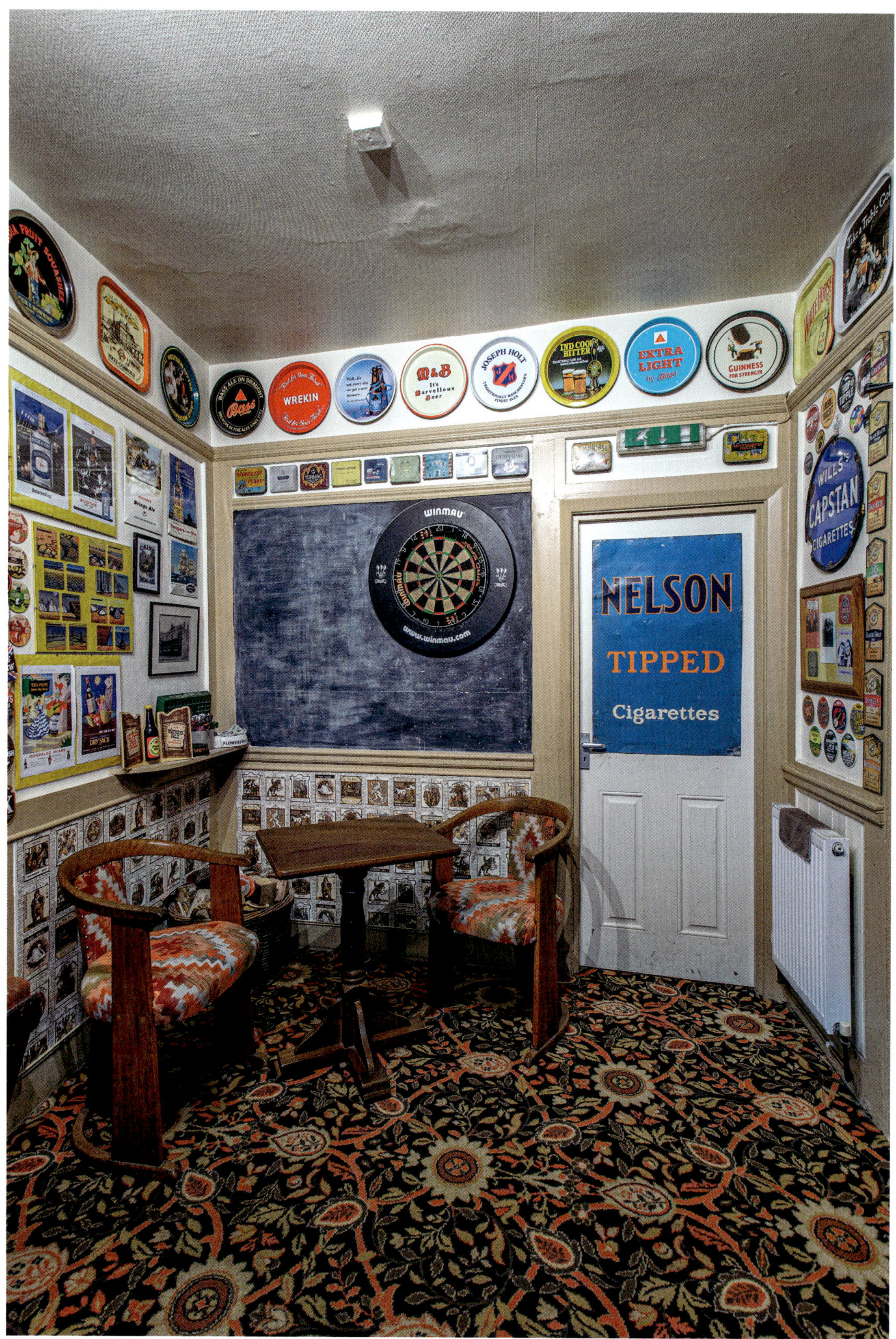

A life-long passion for the wet stuff runs through every vein

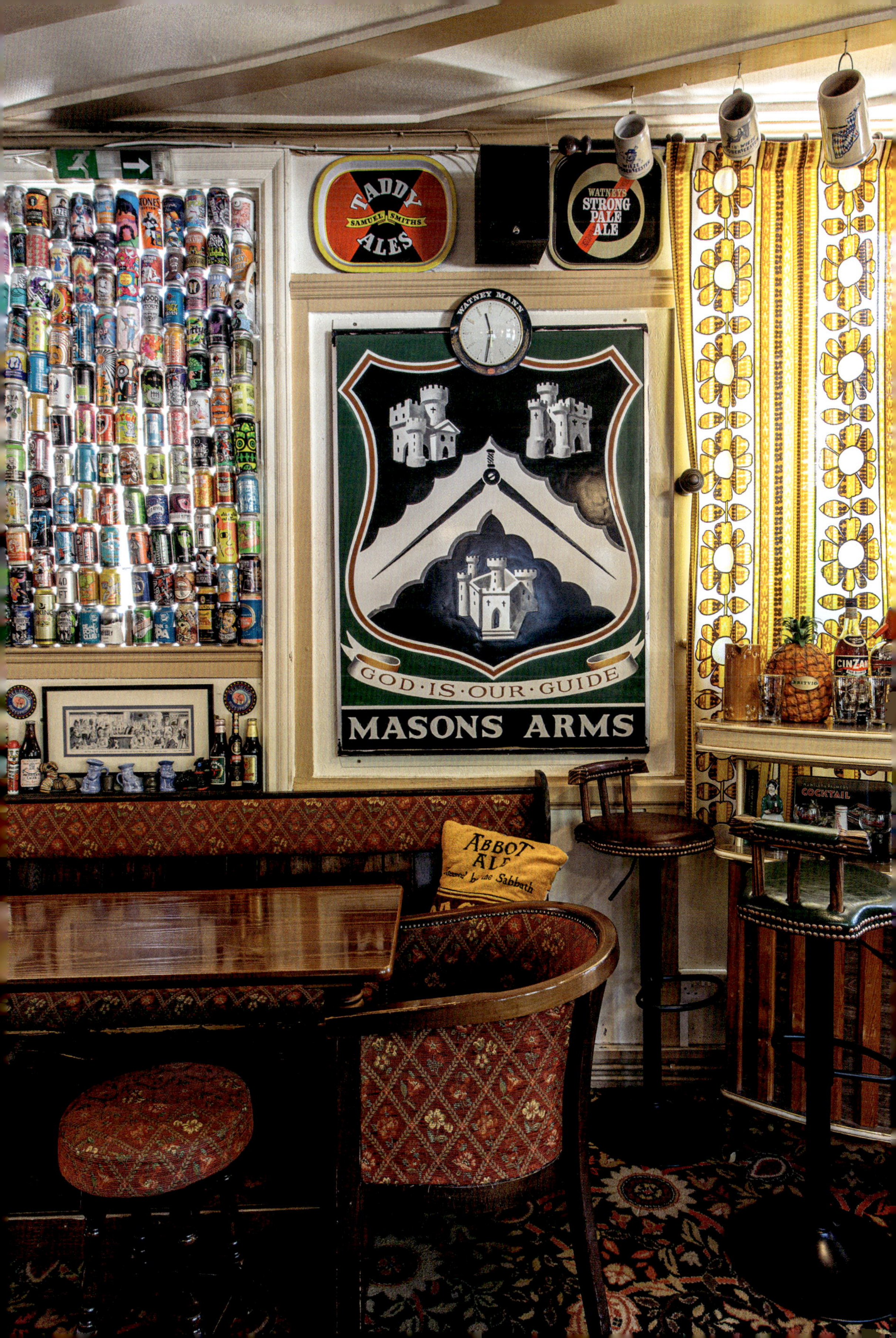

TADDY
SAMUEL SMITHS
ALES
WATNEYS
STRONG
PALE
ALE
WATNEY MANN
GOD · IS · OUR · GUIDE
MASONS ARMS
ABBOT
ALE
CINZANO
COCKTAIL

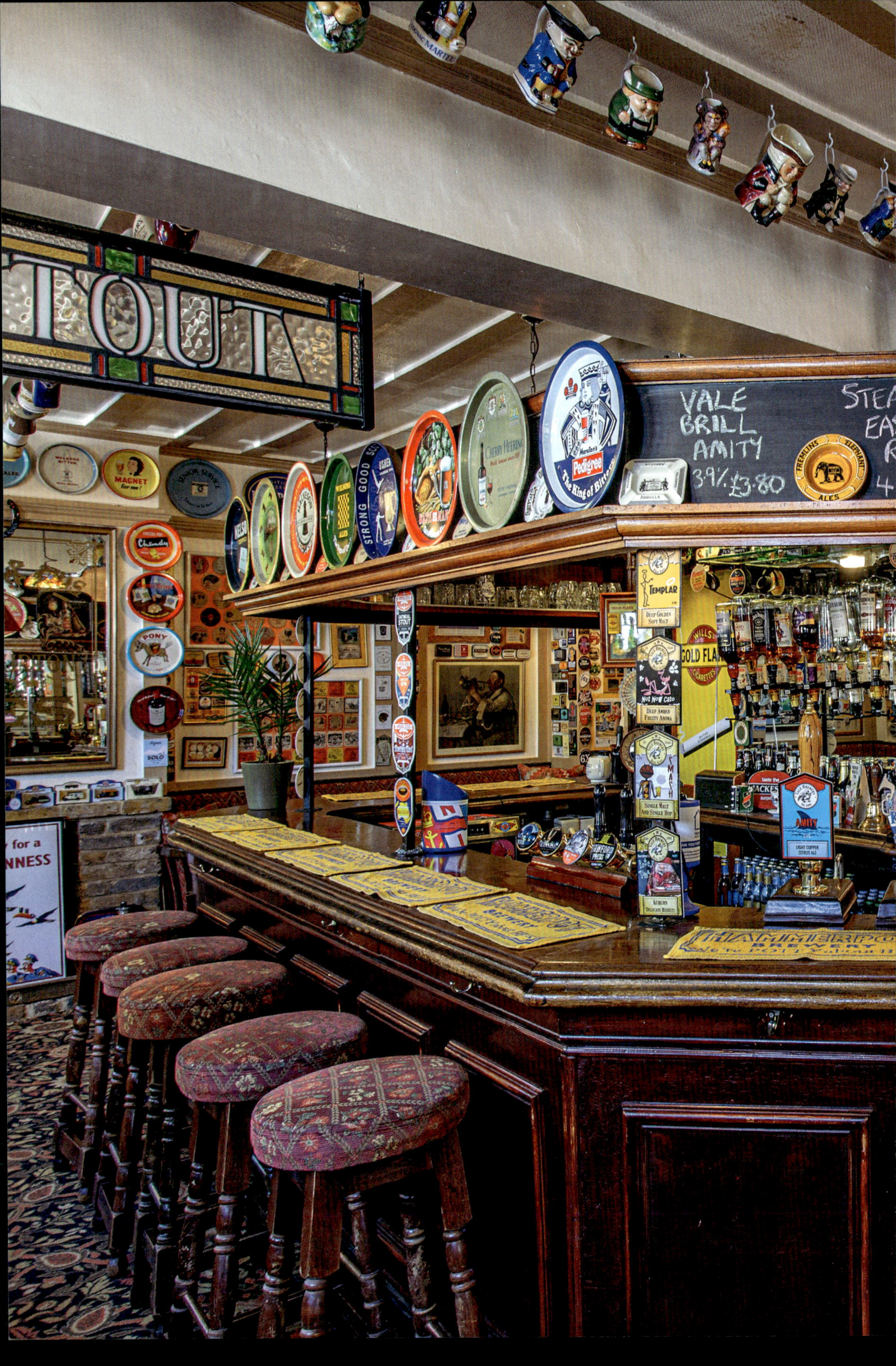

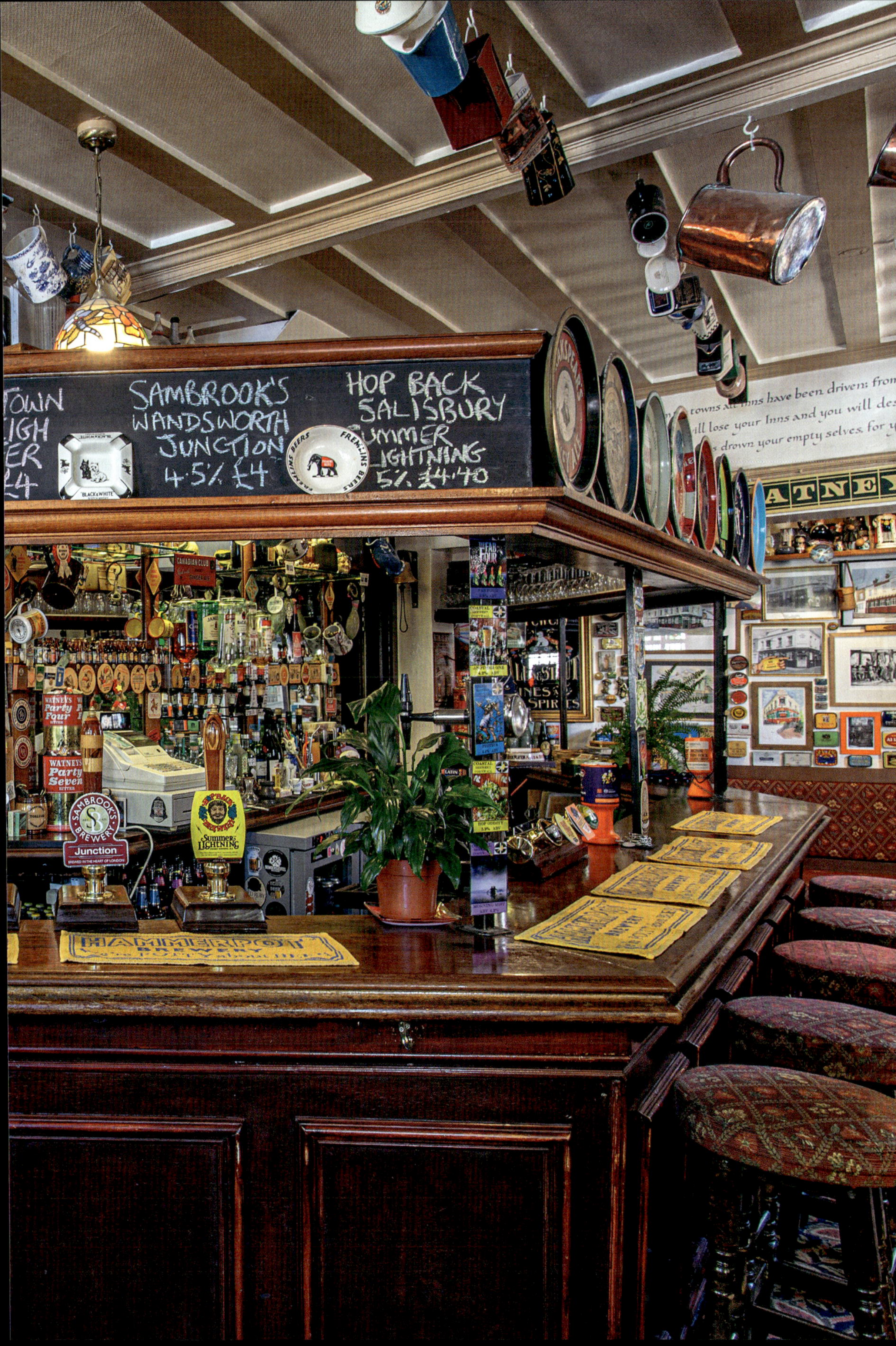

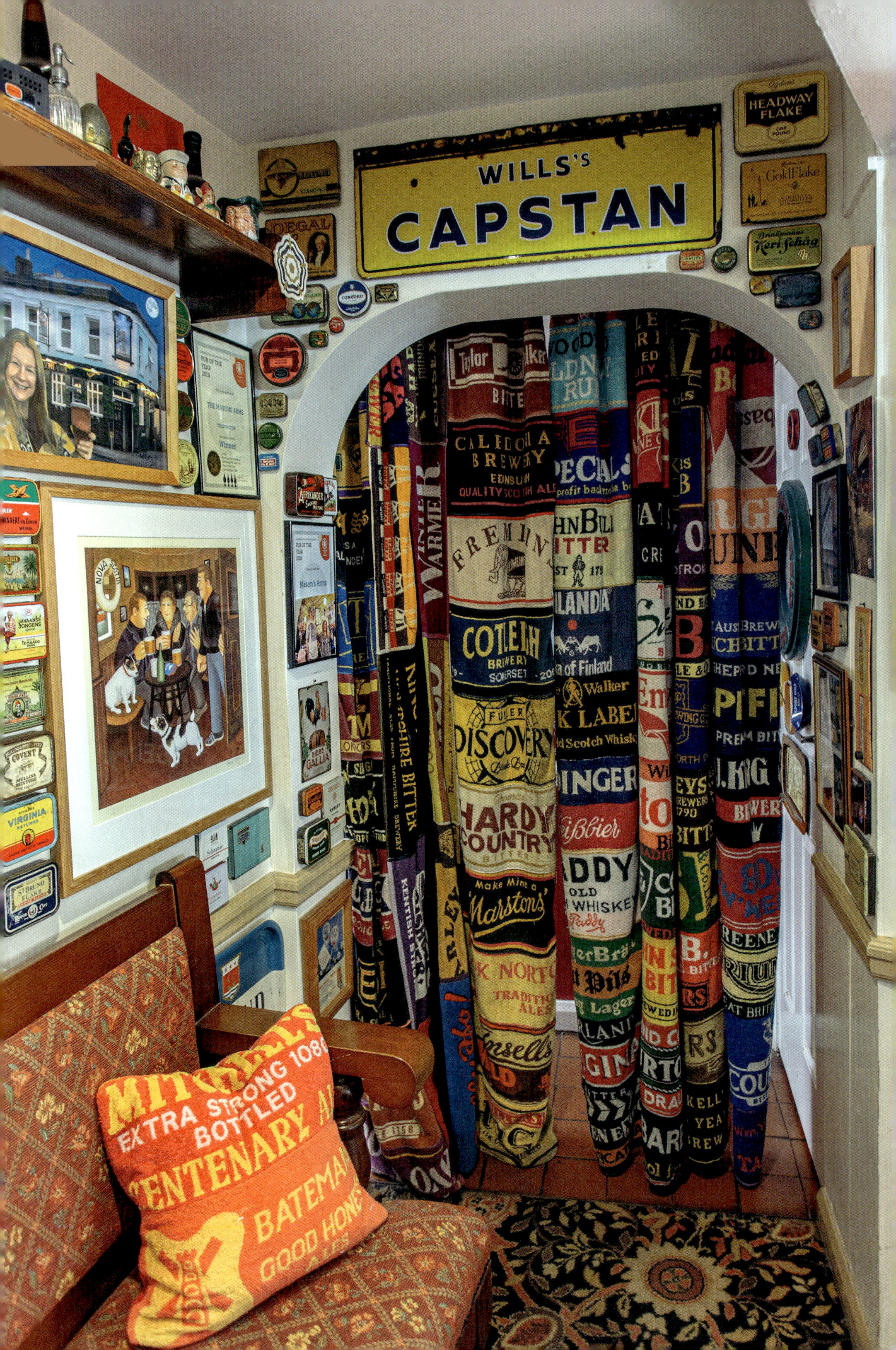

HEADWAY FLAKE
GoldFlake
WILLS'S
CAPSTAN
Taylor Walker
BITTER
CALEDONIAN
BREWERY
EDINBURGH
QUALITY SCOTCH ALES
FREMLIN
COTLEIGH
BREWERY
SOMERSET
DISCOVERY
HARDY
COUNTRY
BITTER
Marstons'
JohnBull
BITTER
EST 178
PIFI
MITCHELLS
EXTRA STRONG 1080
BOTTLED
CENTENARY A
BATEMAN
GOOD HONE

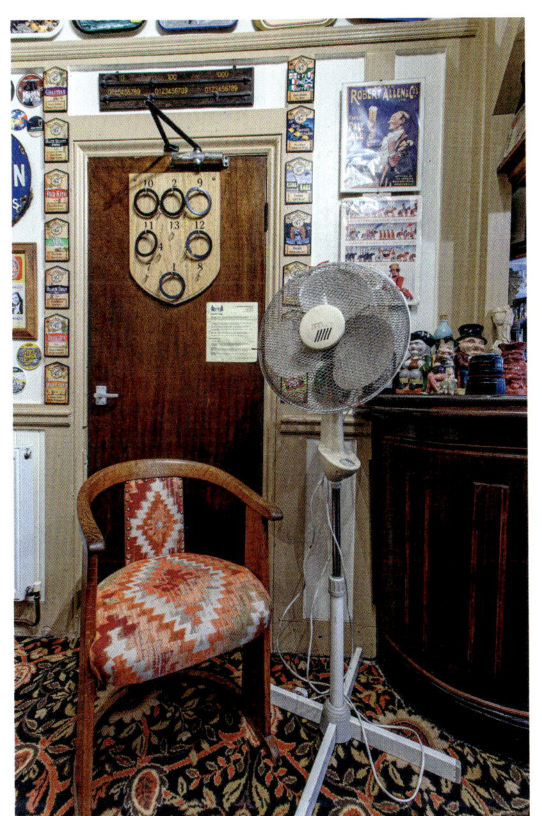

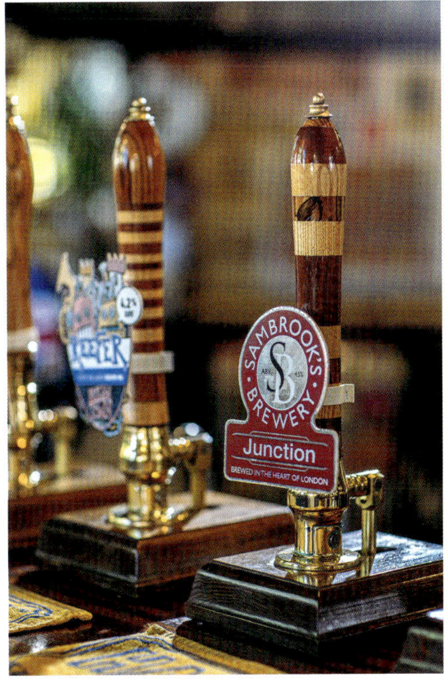

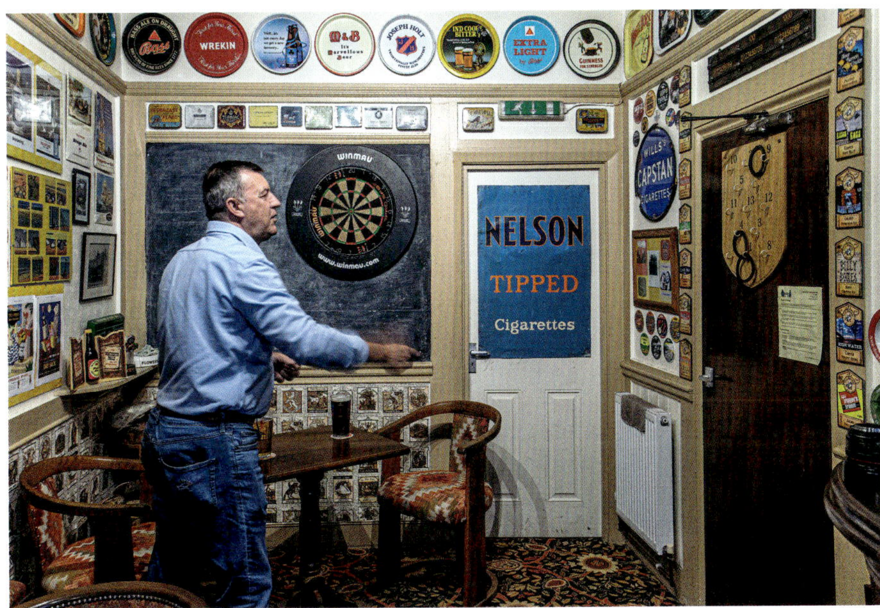

A humble game of hoops provides ample entertainment

BLYTHE HILL TAVERN

To blithely go: to proceed without concern and move forward in a light-hearted and happy way. Forest Hill, here we come! Thousands of motorists pootle past this treasure chest every day without giving it a glance. Driving around London, you'll pass hundreds of pubs that look just like this one: two-a-penny solid, brick corner affairs with large windows, all far from exceptional. Your eye might be caught here by the old Courage cockerel or the hand-painted Toucan hinting at something special within. But it's a stealth pub, hiding all its riches from the casual passer-by through a veil of apparent mediocrity. The pub equivalent of a Q-car, its unassuming exterior hides peak pub performance under the bonnet. Underestimate it from the outside at your peril.

You know you're in safe hands when the landlord and team wear their Sunday best to pull your pint.

Take one step inside here and it's a museum-quality timepiece. The perfect portal to the past. Where most Victorian pubs have been gutted and refurbed at least once or twice in the last 100 years, this beauty remains largely unfettered and unfiddled with. A magical three-room layout gives you an idea of just how special going to the pub used to be. It's an interior so unspoilt that it enjoys a rare heritage listing and certainly shows that they really don't make 'em like they used to. A series of perfect rooms and a garden allow the drinker to take their pick. Squeeze through the service area to the front for quiet chat or gather at the rear for gregarious sports-watching times. A well-curated selection of Irish paraphernalia and brewery mirrors adorn the early 1900s panelling, and it's a pub full of pure passion. A masterclass in understated ordinariness.

The classy tone continues behind the bar, where Con Riordan and his team don shirt and tie. Innkeeping is a serious art form, so you know you're in safe hands when the landlord and team wear their Sunday best to pull your pint. Respect. But don't expect a formal welcome just because of the formal dress. The gentle craic flows as freely as the Guinness brought directly to your table. It's the personal touch and pride in pouring some of the best pints in London that help "The Blythe" to win award after award. Putting the customer and community first has seen Con through over three decades behind the bar here. A most remarkable pub in a most unremarkable location.

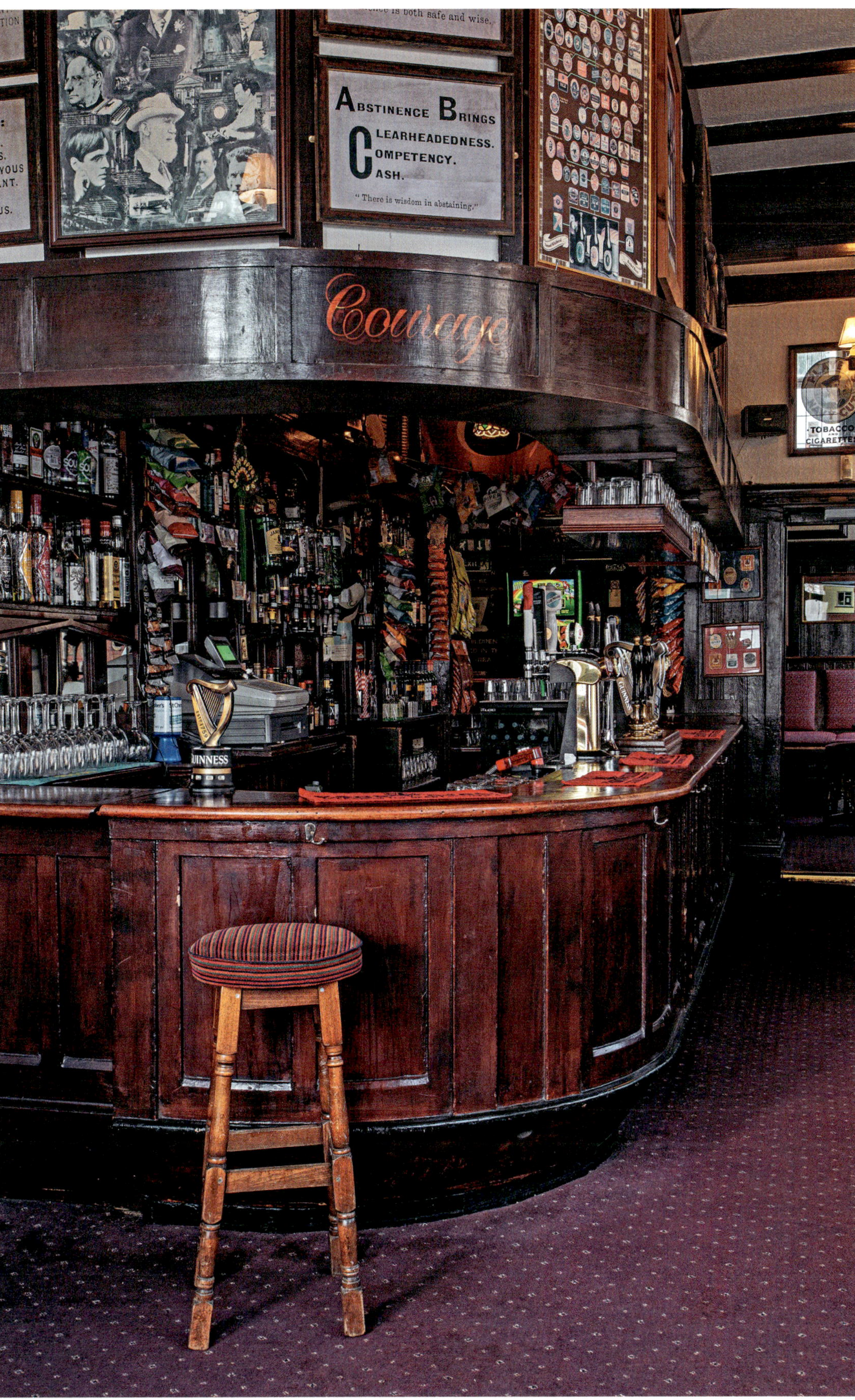

ABSTINENCE BRINGS
CLEARHEADEDNESS.
COMPETENCY.
CASH.
"There is wisdom in abstaining."
Courage
GUINNESS
TOBACCO
CIGARETTES

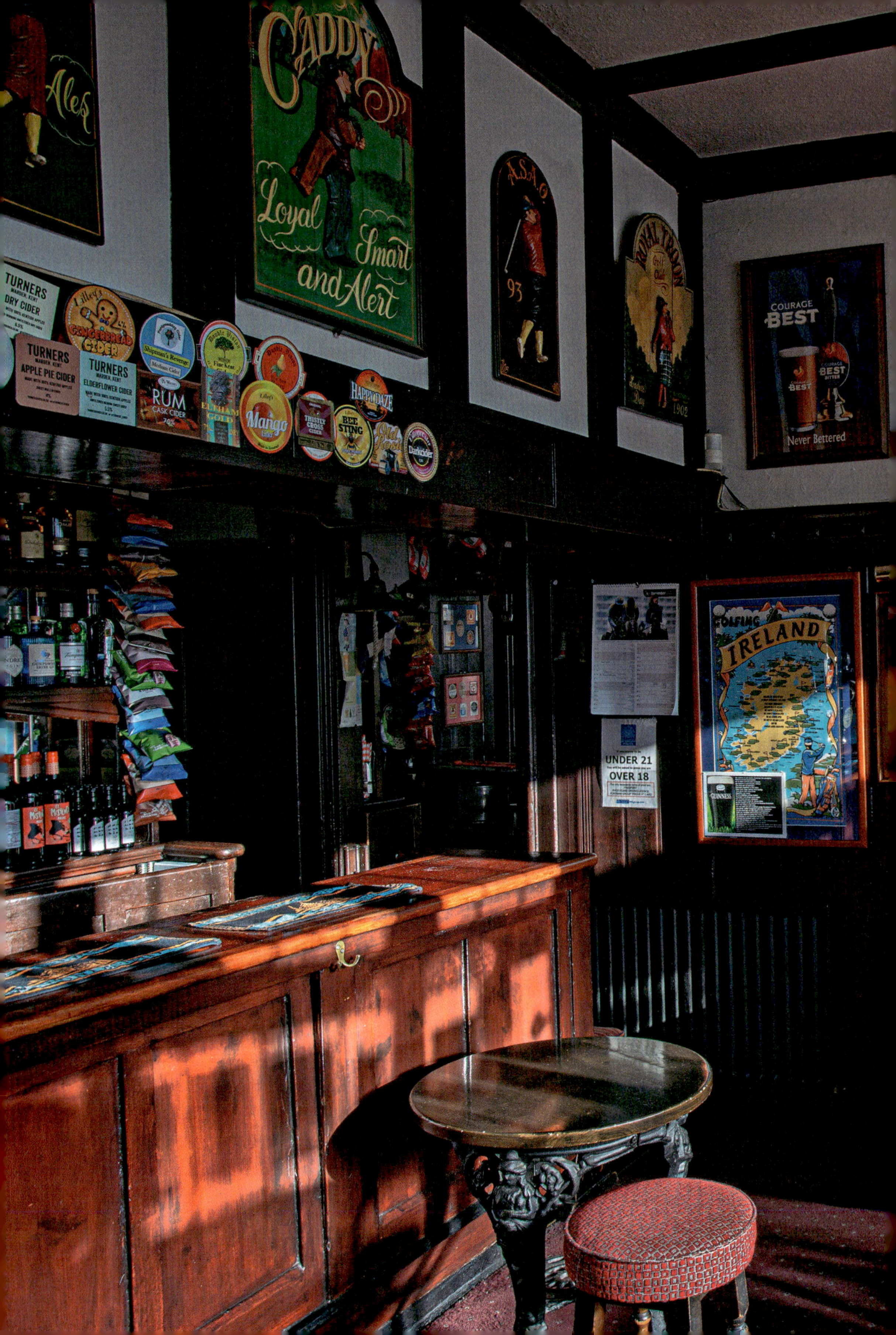

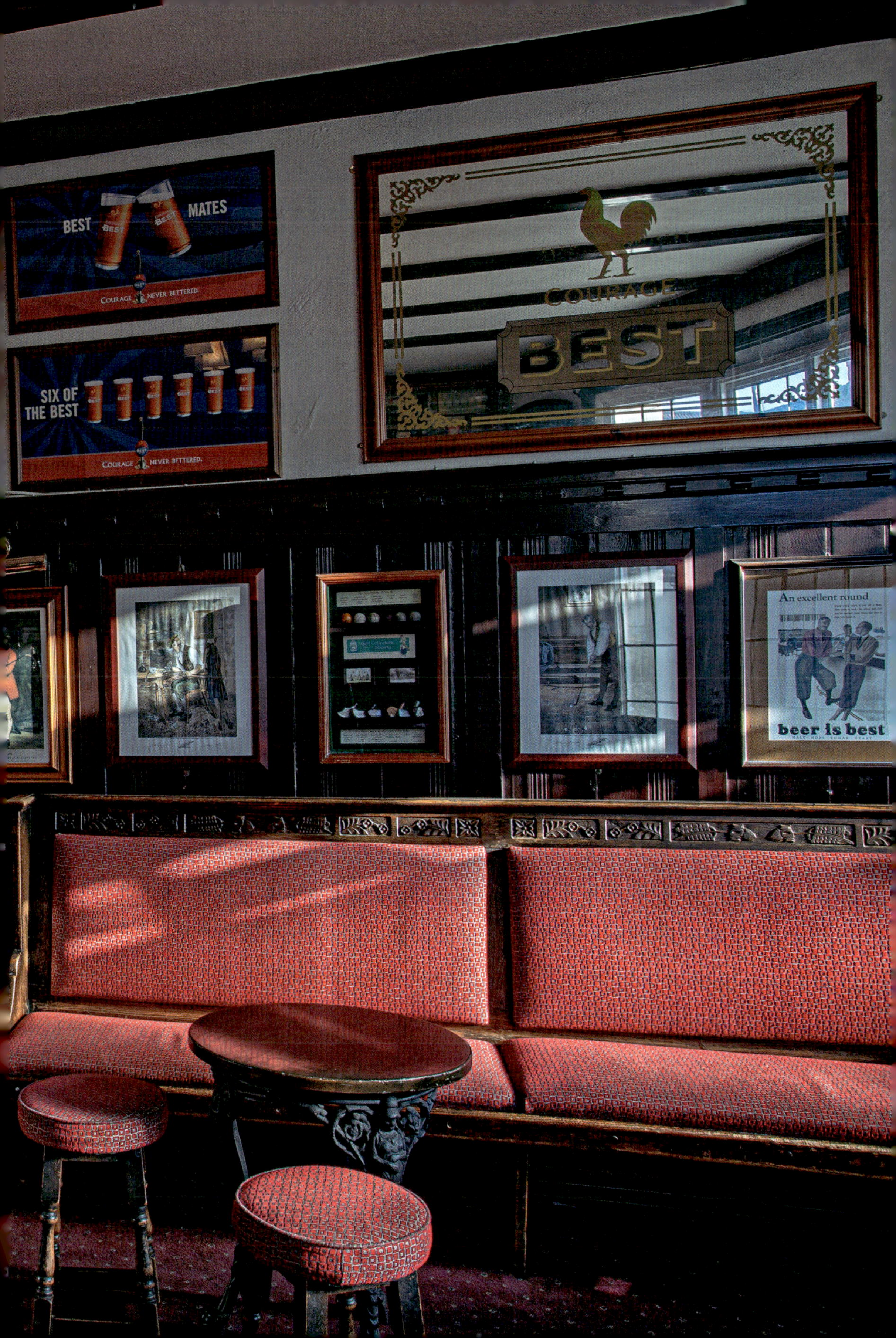
BEST MATES
COURAGE NEVER BETTERED.
SIX OF THE BEST
COURAGE NEVER BETTERED.
COURAGE
BEST
An excellent round
beer is best
MALT · HOPS · SUGAR · YEAST

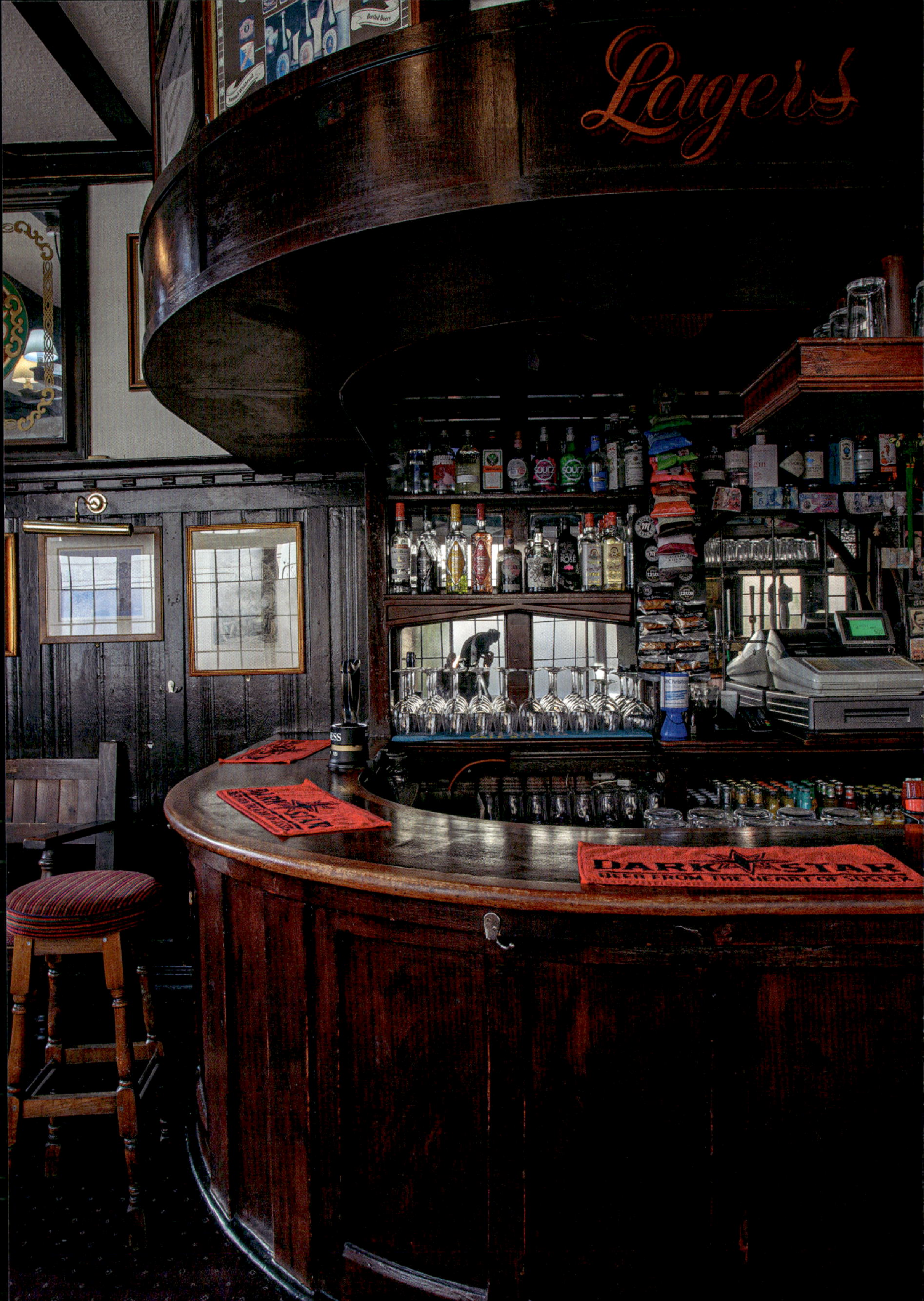

Lagers
DARK STAR
DARK STAR

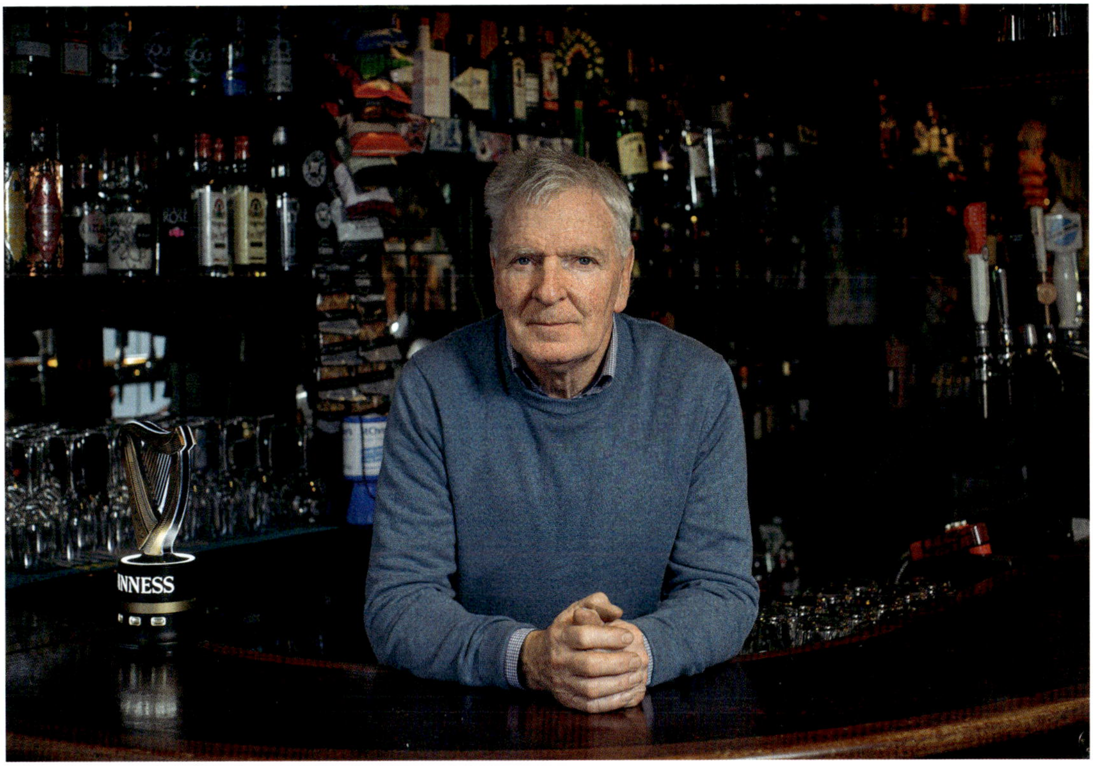

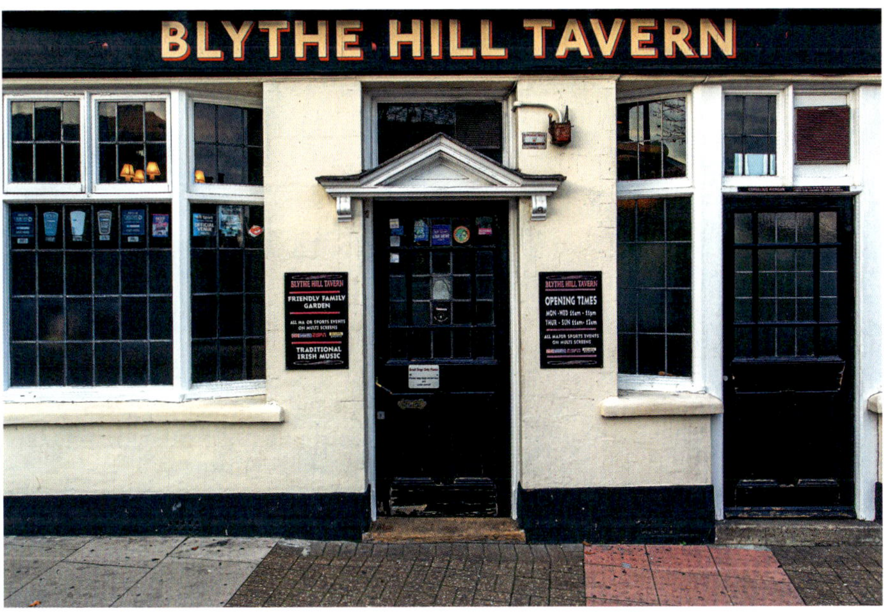

Expect warm welcomes and conversation that flows as easily as the real ales

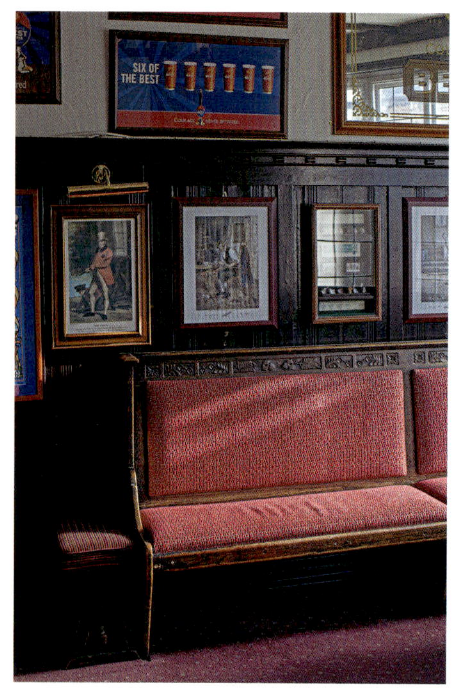

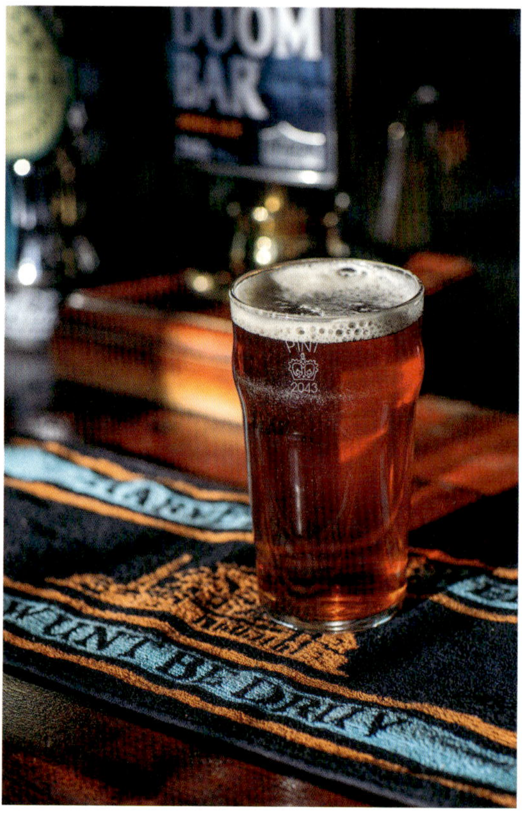

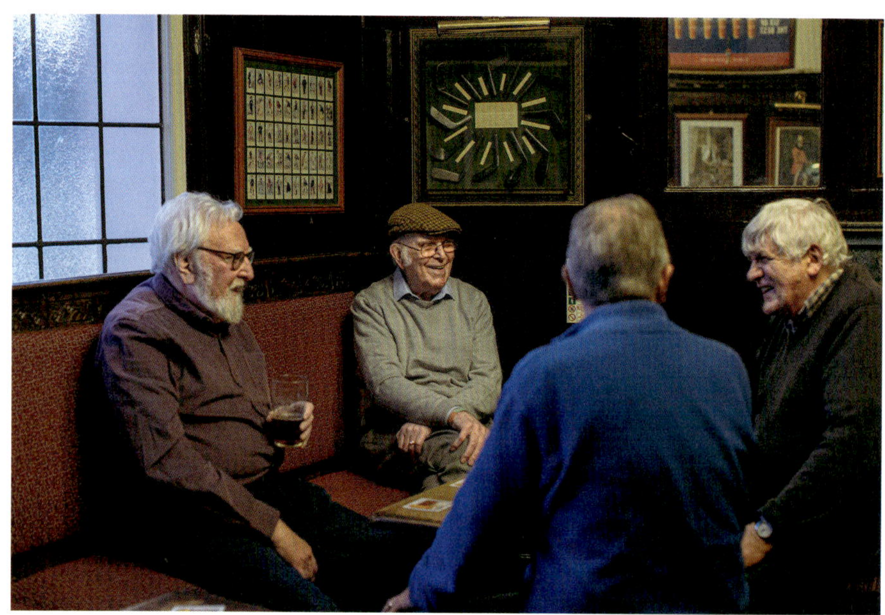

Savouring the gentle craic

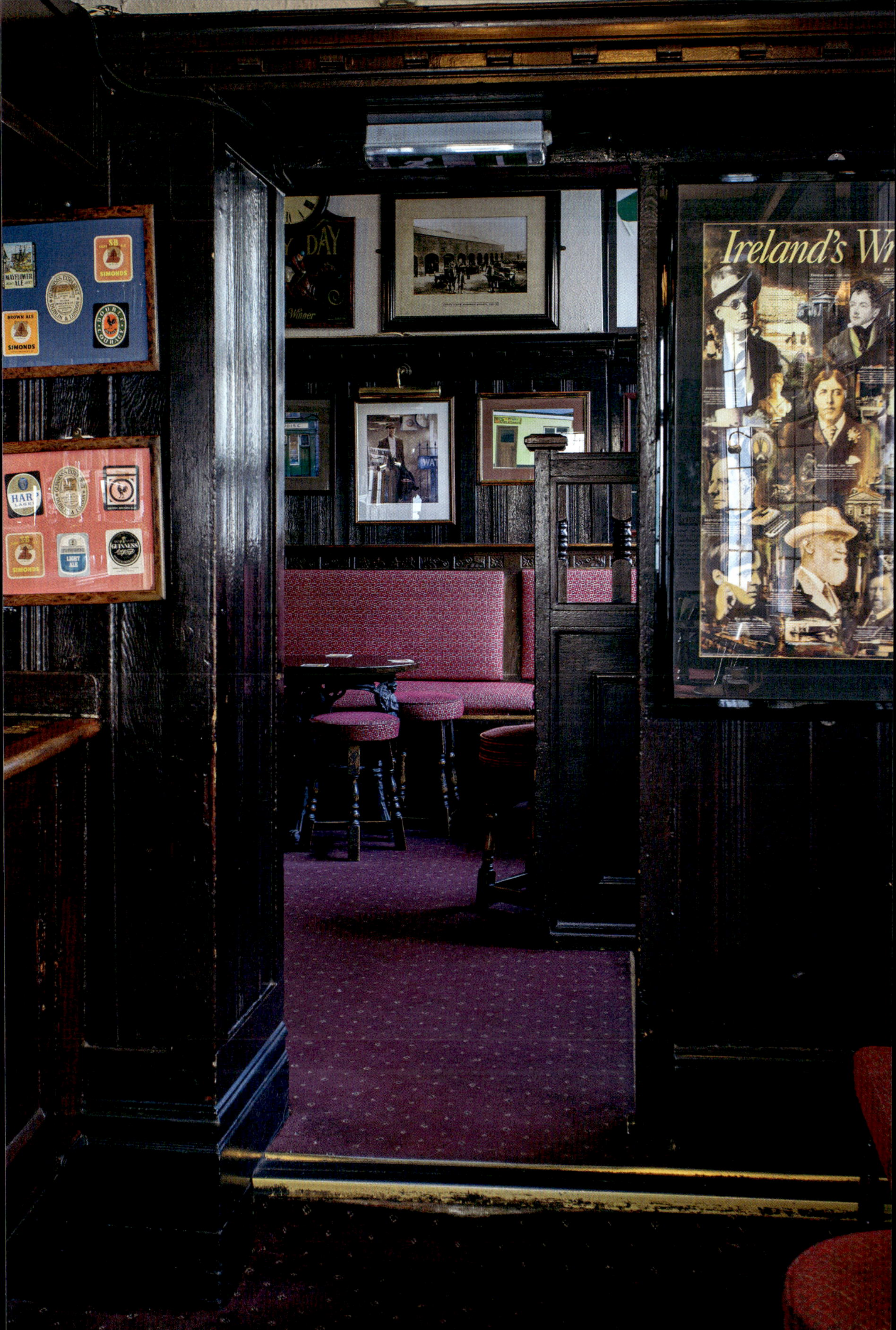

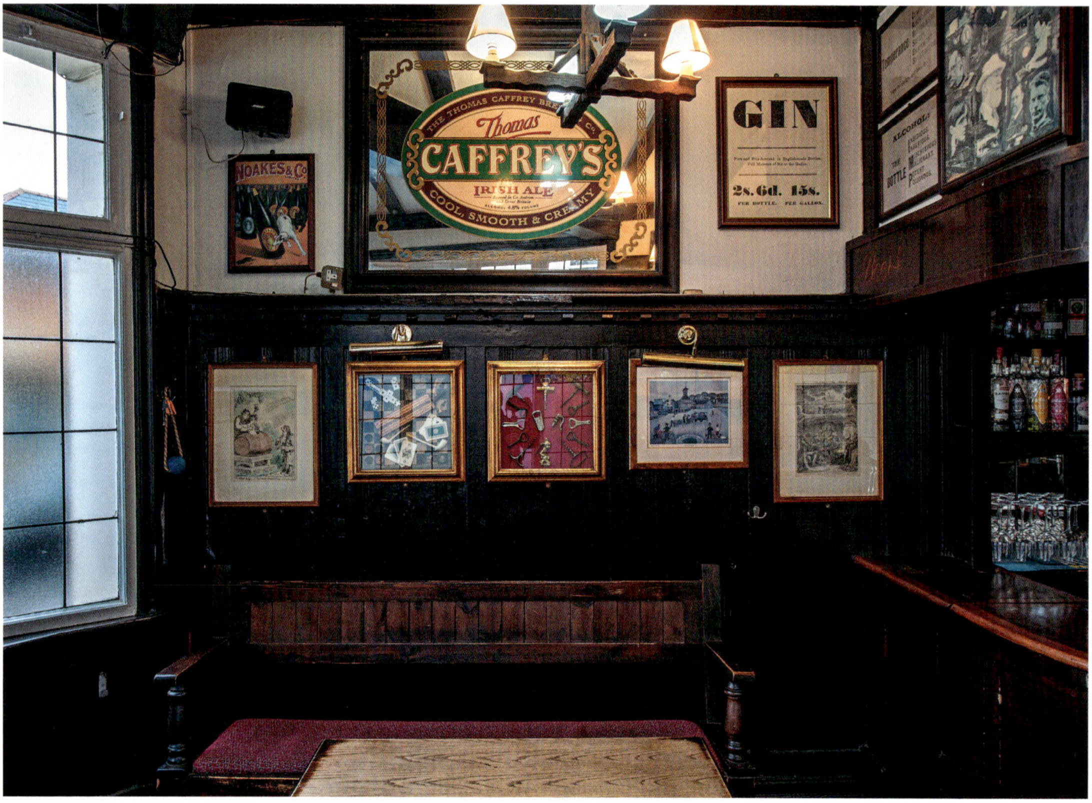

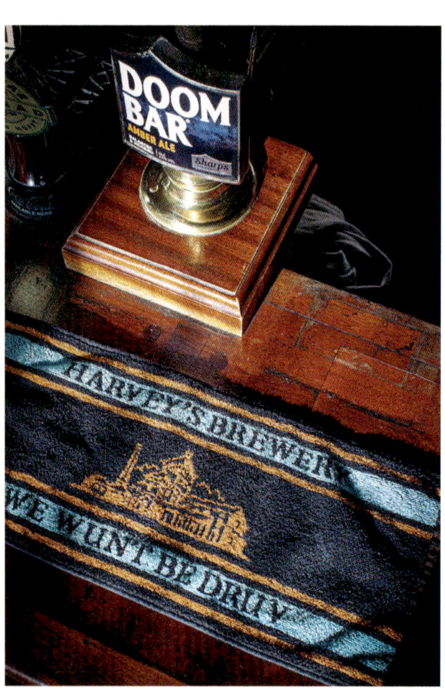

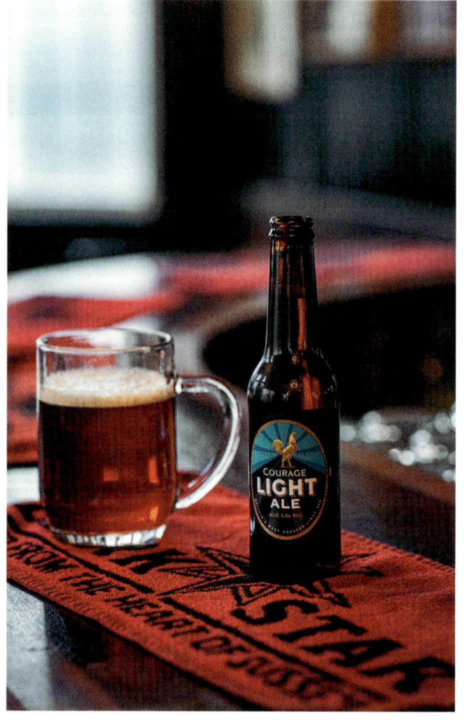

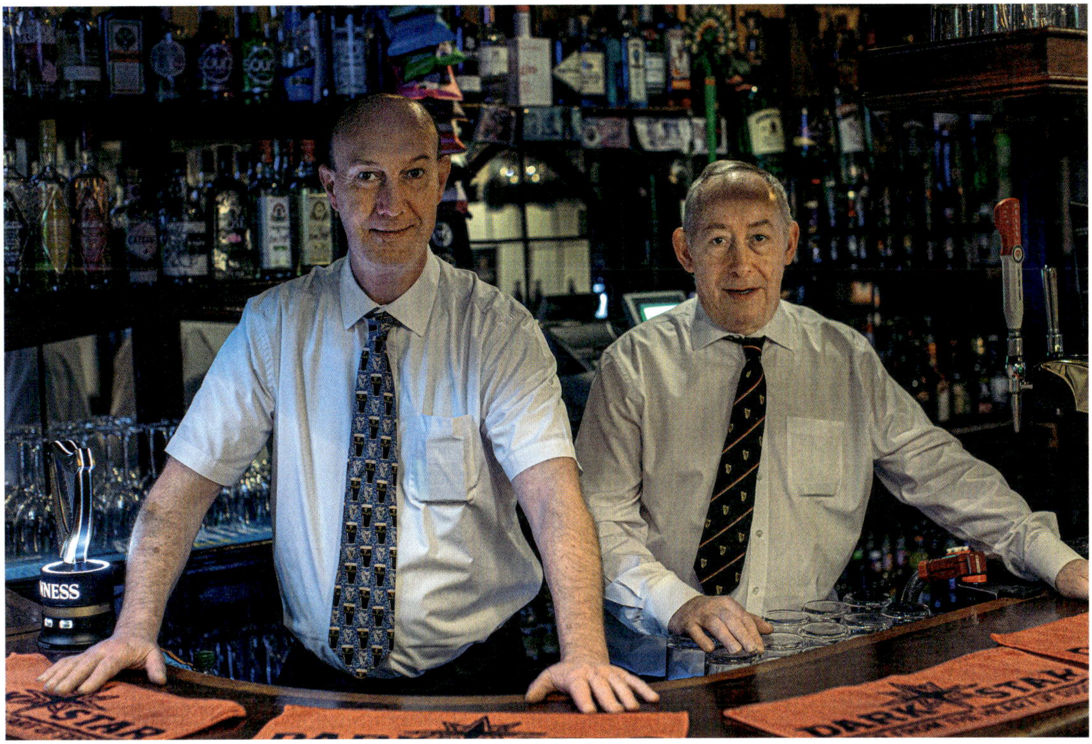

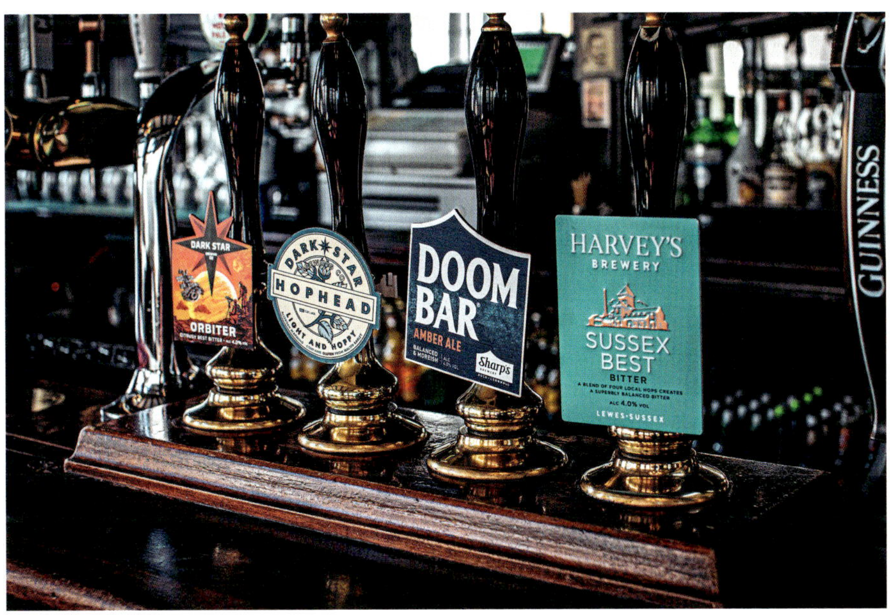

The serious art of traditional innkeeping is ever-present

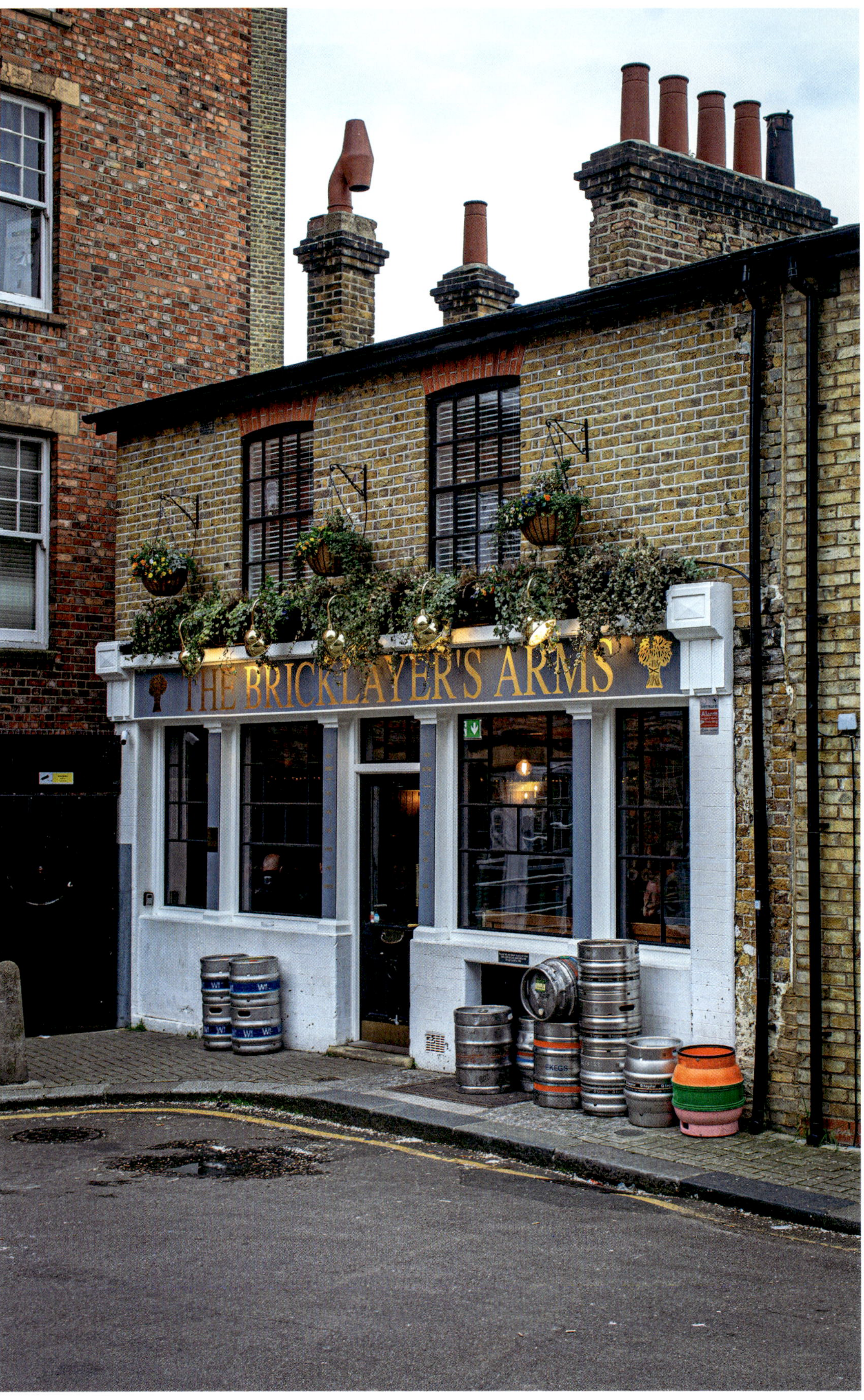
THE BRICKLAYER'S ARMS

THE BRICKLAYER'S ARMS

Who doesn't love a traditional pub game? No, I don't mean the forlorn collection of tattered and battered family classics such as Monopoly and Risk piled up in a corner by the bogs, and I certainly don't mean beer pong (You're not in Kansas now, Tonto). I'm talking about the ones handcrafted from solid wood, green baize and metal pins. Shove Ha'penny, bagatelle, skittles, hoops and bar billiards: unless you have read the rules, you'd assume they were either designed as an instrument of torture or sexual pleasure (I hear it's often a fine line between the two). These are games only to be found in proper pubs.

The Bricklayer's Arms is certainly a proper pub. Mark Steward, one of their regulars, has hewn a fine compendium of bar games for patrons to battle over. Crafted by his own fair hand, made with love and shared with pride. Literally investing in the built material of this pub's relaunch brick by brick, game by game. The pump clip ceiling is also expanding at a commendable rate, and much of the framed memorabilia was donated by long-time locals.

The locals who dipped into their pockets to keep it alive now pour their love into The Brick to make it feel just like home.

This is a lovely backstreet bastion of booze with a formidable reputation: a sole Georgian survivor bookended by modern housing estates. An actress saved the pub from closure and likely redevelopment and it was then reopened to wide acclaim on Boat Race Day in 2005. With beer festivals galore, CAMRA and even the *National Geographic* awarded it every plaudit going. But then the magic faded and the passion slowly seeped through the cellar door.

Under new stewardship, "The Brick" lives again! The joyous full range of Timmy Taylors is no longer guaranteed on the ramp, but they have spliced in their own back-of-the-net brews for pre-match pints for Fulham fans. When feeling a bit Hank Marvin, you simply order a takeaway to dine at your table. It's an open, inclusive and progressive ownership steering their course to forge a new identity. The locals who dipped into their pockets to keep it alive now pour their love into The Brick to make it feel just like home. So, grab a pint of Boltmaker, swing the skittles, join in with a folk singalong and raise a toast to the fact that it didn't become just another brick in the wall.

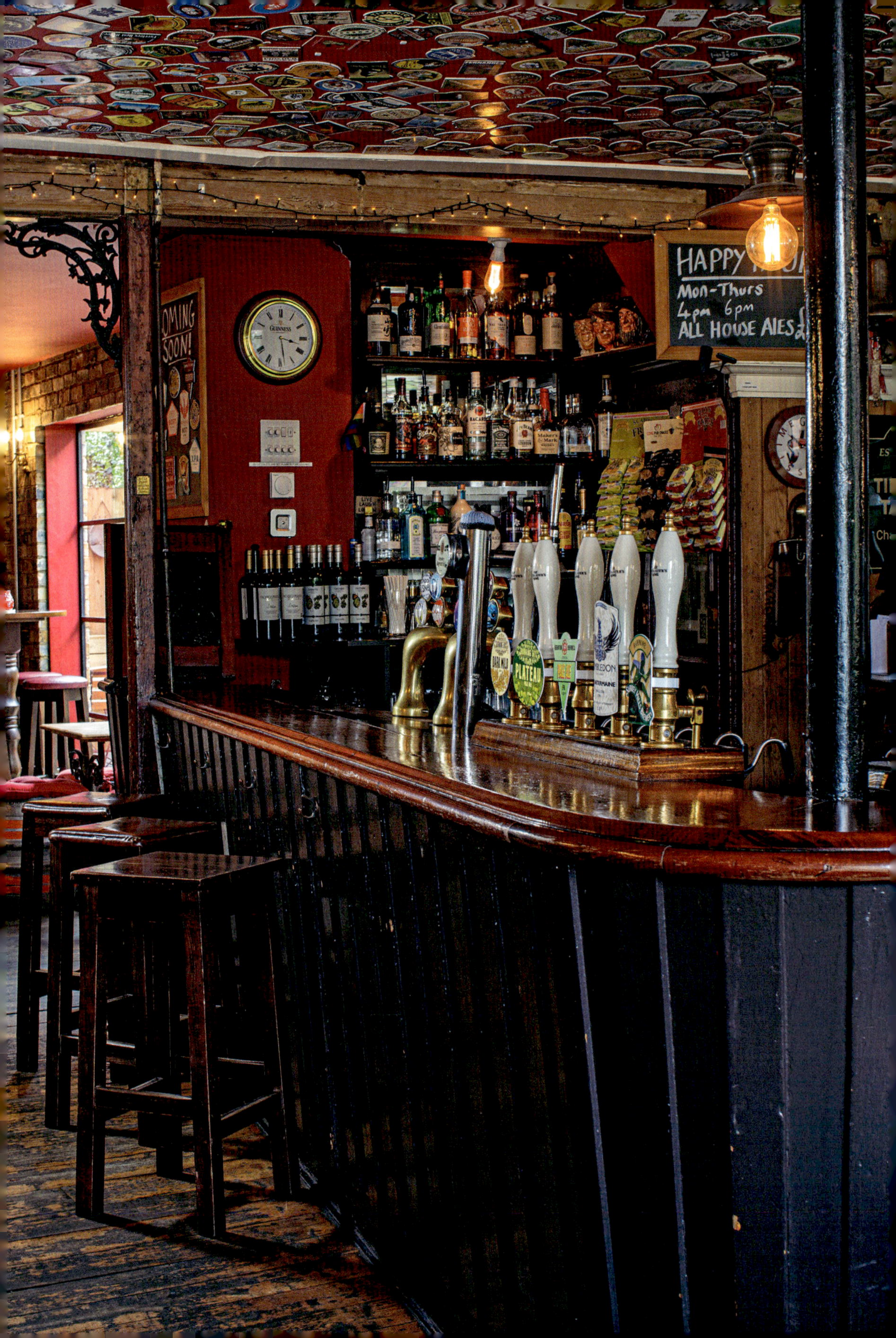

COMING SOON!
GUINNESS
HAPPY HOUR
Mon-Thurs
4pm - 6pm
ALL HOUSE ALES
PLATEAU

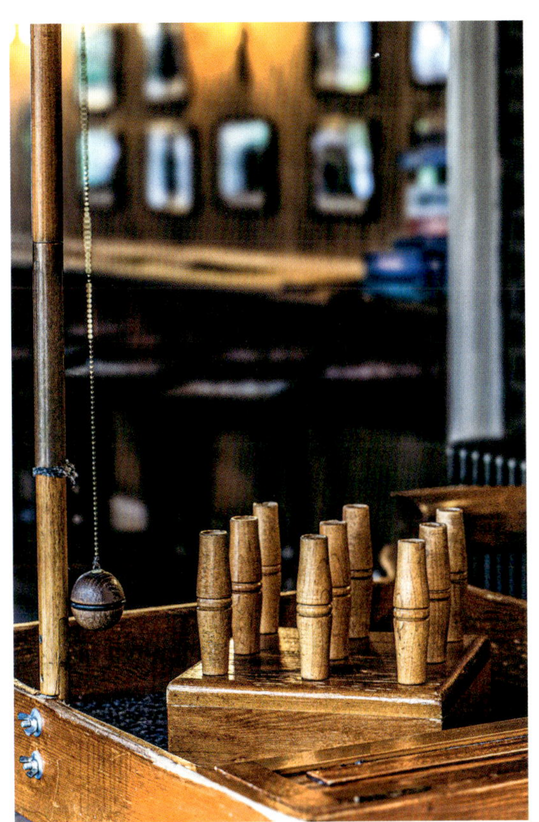

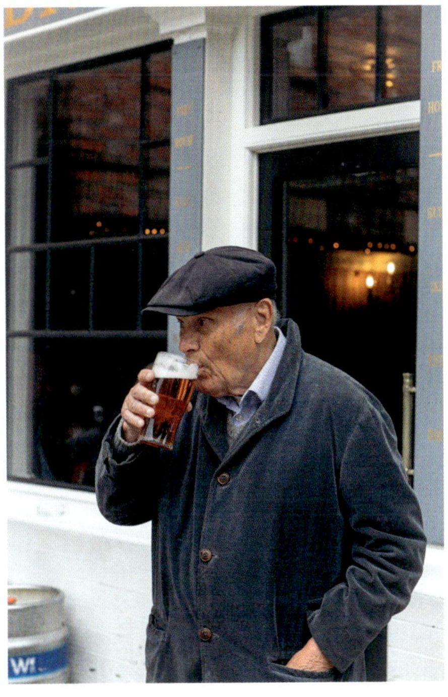

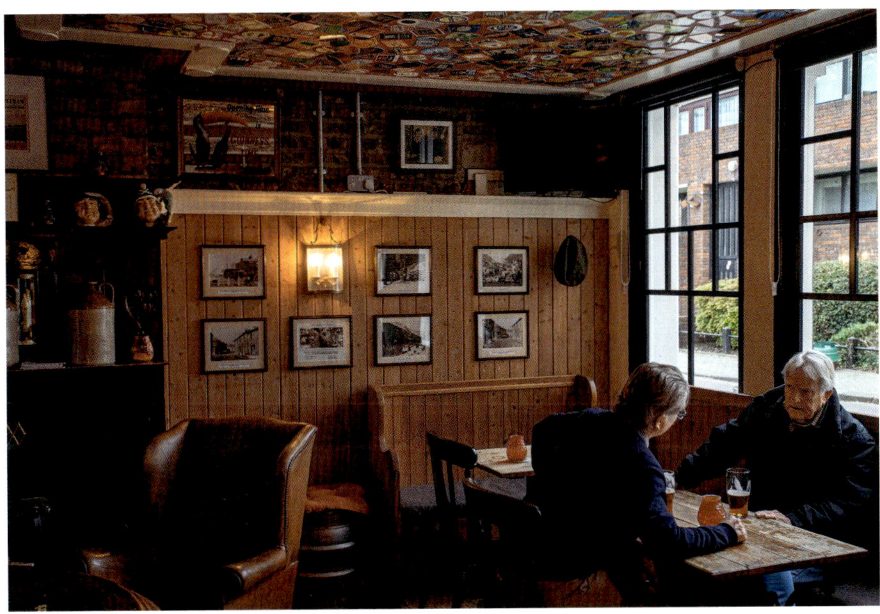

The handcrafted collection of bar games are all made with love

THE PARK TAVERN

NON–GASTRO PUB SIMPLY SERVING TRADITIONAL GOOD TIMES

19 NEW RD, KINGSTON UPON THAMES KT2 6AP

You'll probably never visit The Park Tavern. It took me twenty-five years of rub-a-dub-hunting across the Great Wen to stumble across this gem. It's rarely mentioned because it's so tucked away that only the most devoted of pub-goers will darken its doors. It is also a pub so brilliant that there is almost an unspoken rule not to tout its virtues for fear of spoiling it with hoi polloi. One to be filed under "I could tell you, but then I'd have to kill you."

Horst (the touted lensman for this book) has lived around the corner from The Park Tavern for over thirteen years and never knew about it, so there you go. The acclaimed Willoughby Arms and Wych Elm pubs snaffle up the plaudits and crowds, leaving The Park Tavern to potter on doing what it does best: being a locals' local and a most excellent cavern of camaraderie. It does its best to deter entry by the uninitiated, sitting innocuously midway up a quiet residential street, set back just enough to be cloaked in a wall of greenery (and floriferous wisteria come springtime). The jaunty flagpole offers a mere hint that this is no mere domestic residence.

Squeeze through the garden gazebo and a low-ceilinged, richly carpeted, pump clip-painted ambience awaits. Described by the McFarlane family landlords as "traditionalist to the end", it's a self-proclaimed "non-gastro pub" where the "coffee is instant, our tea is builders' and our ale is spot-on". Well-behaved children are shown the door by 6 pm, and good dogs "get a pat and a biscuit". The bar hosts some crowd-pleasing gut rot and a quirky guest ale or two and the beer pumps themselves are of true vintage calibre. Sport on the box dominates the right-hand side of the pub and, with the Cabbage Patch not far away, rugby is the main passion here. Over on the left, you can always grab a quiet pint, dry Fido by the fire after a Richmond Park yomp and numb your buttocks on an unforgiving church pew.

After watching England win a World Cup game, the bar staff dispensed free pizza to its patrons. Unannounced. Just genuine family hospitality to keep the good times rolling. It's that kind of place, and it's why the pub begins to justify its website address as www.perfectpub.co.uk. An incredible pub run by a fine family, on fine family values, patronised by a sport-loving and loyal crowd and just a short walk from one the finest urban parklands in the world. I guess it's just a shame that you're never going to visit.

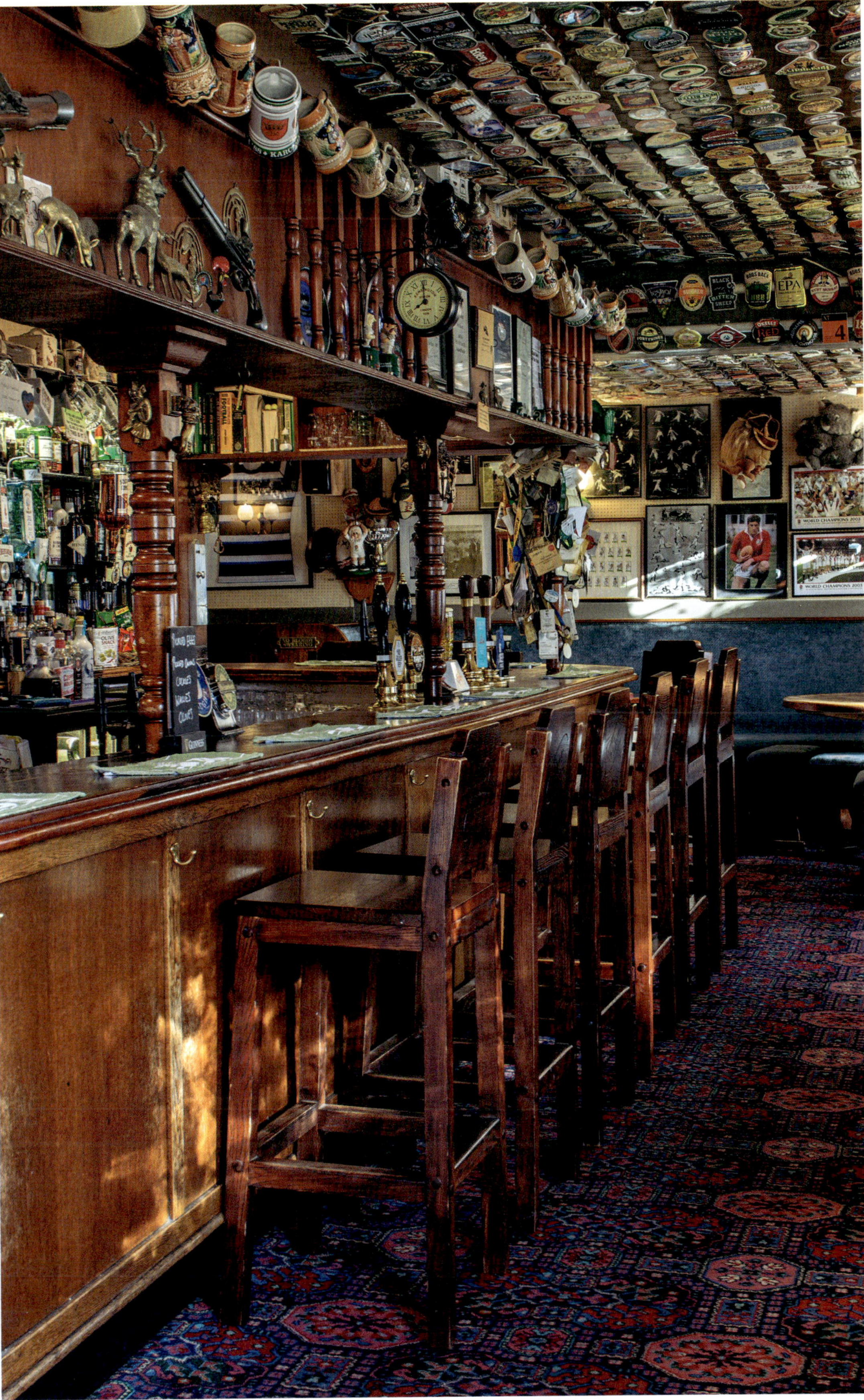

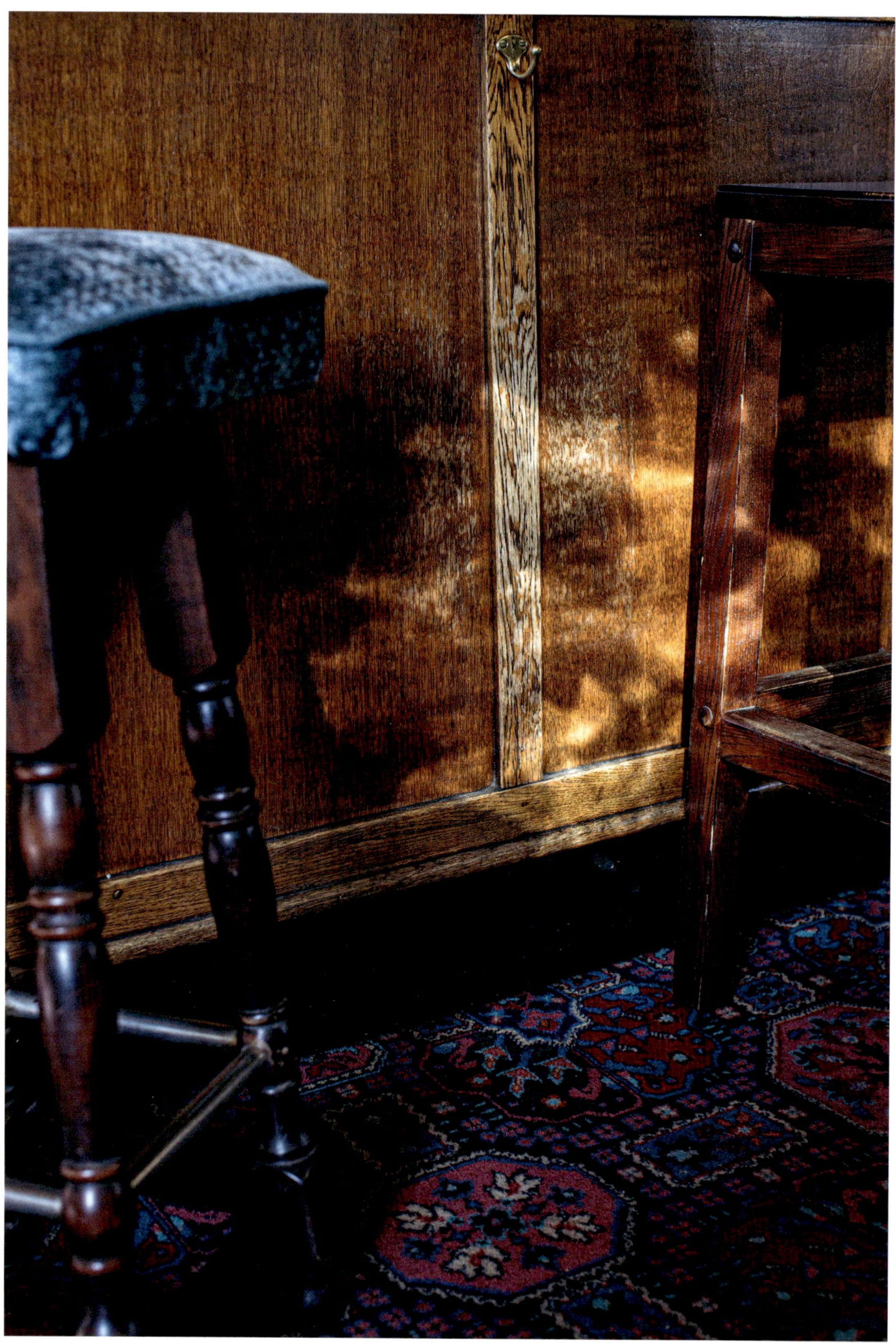

A quiet suburban side street hides a real crackerjack of a pub

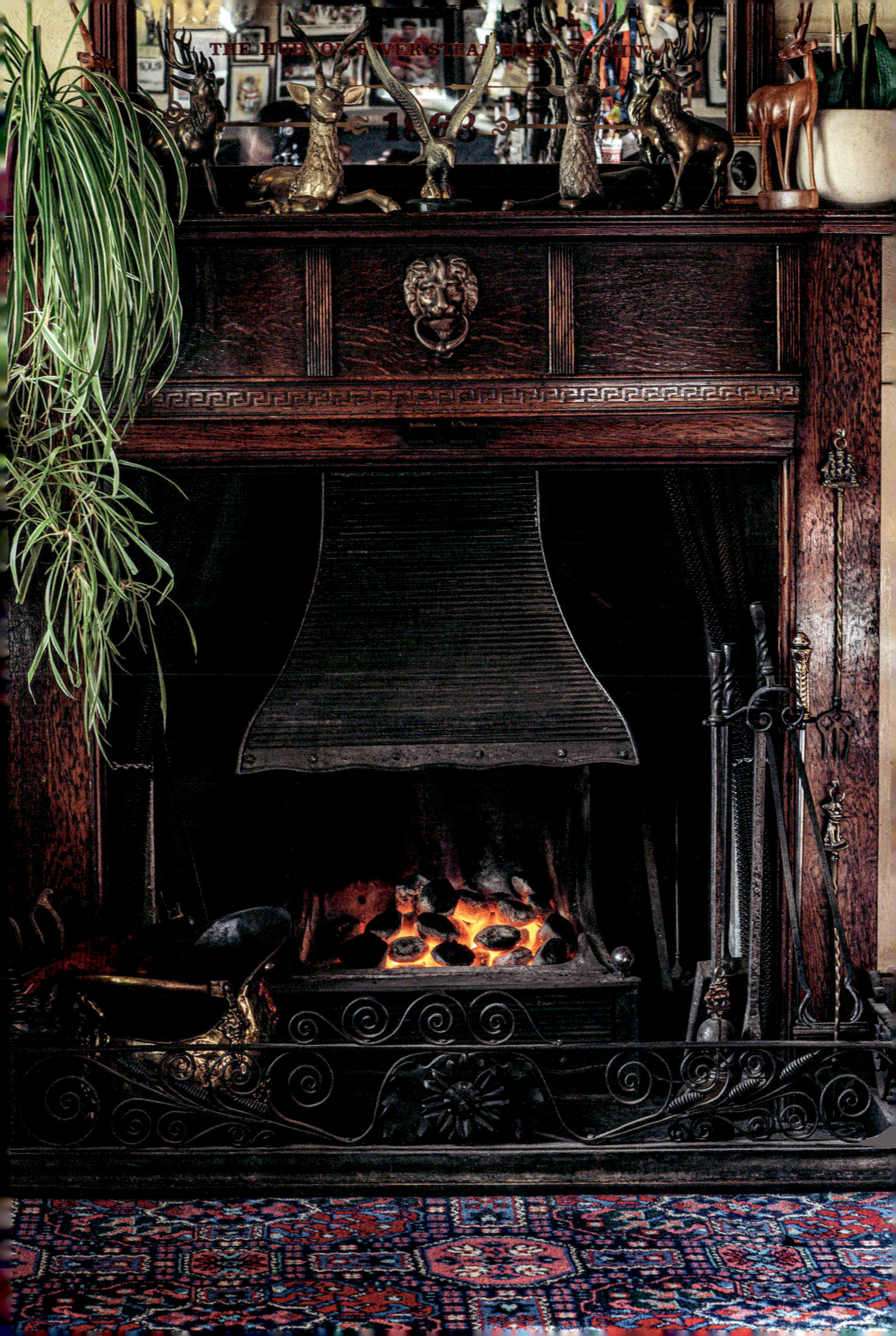

THE HUDSON RIVER STEAM BOAT YACHT
1863

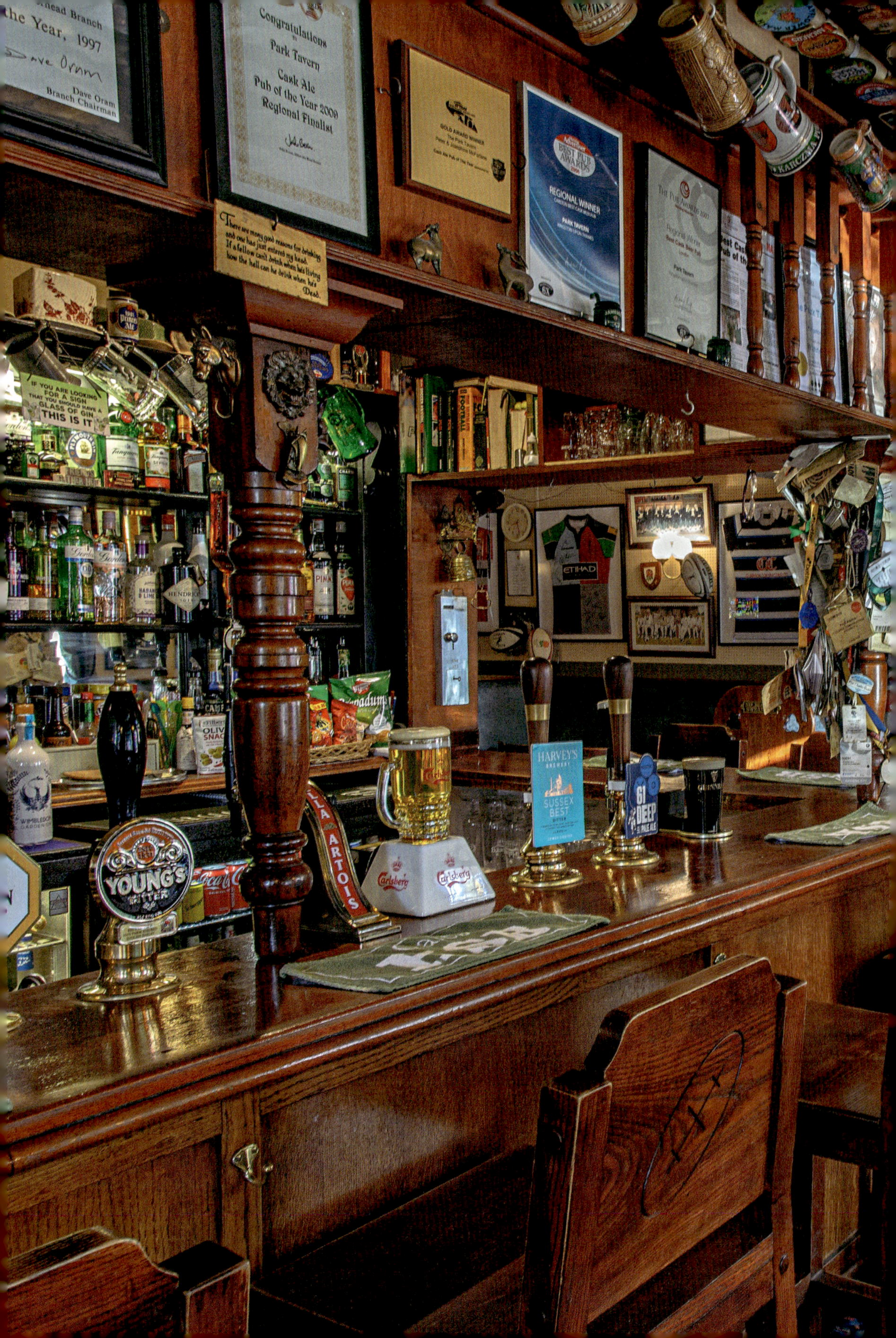

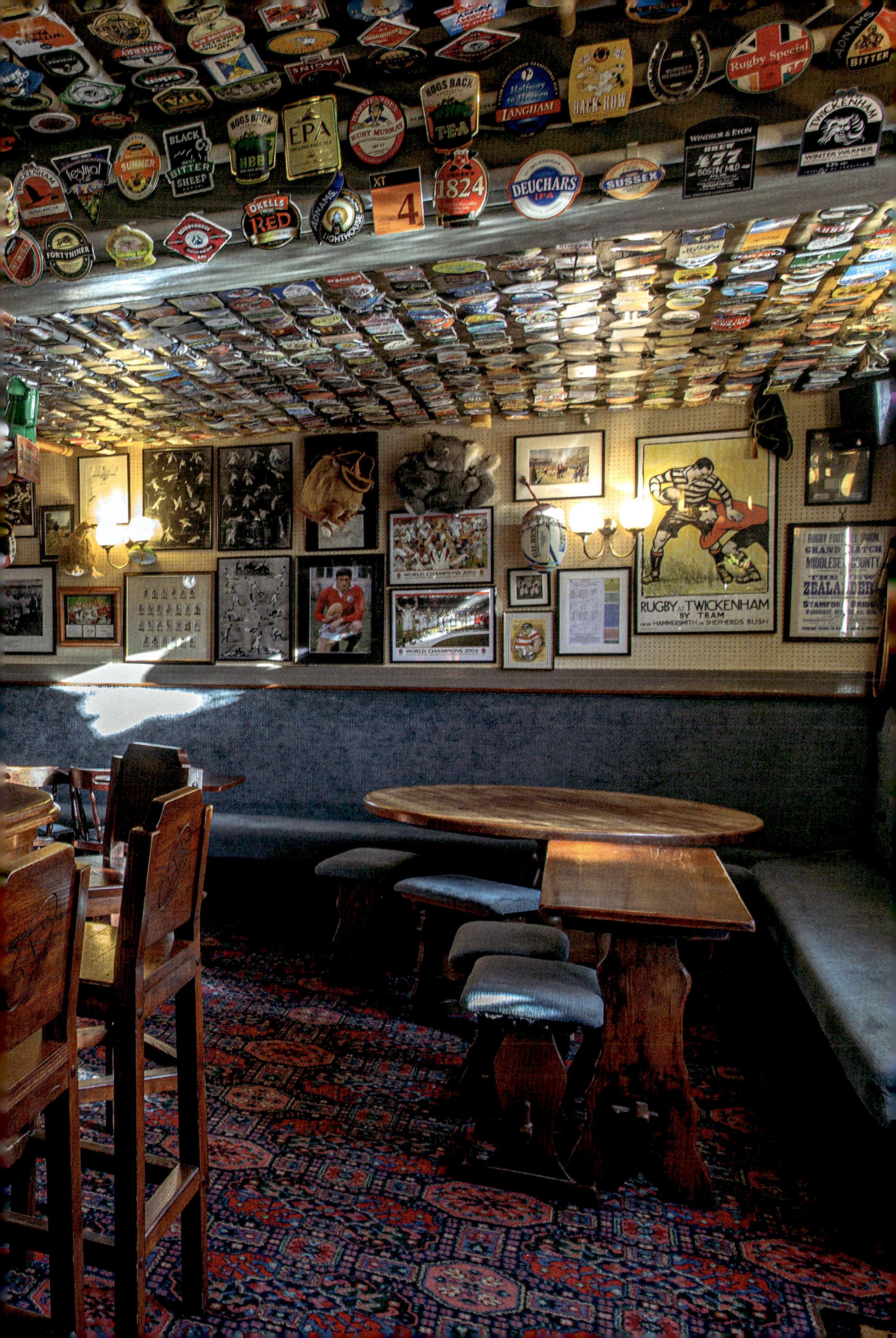

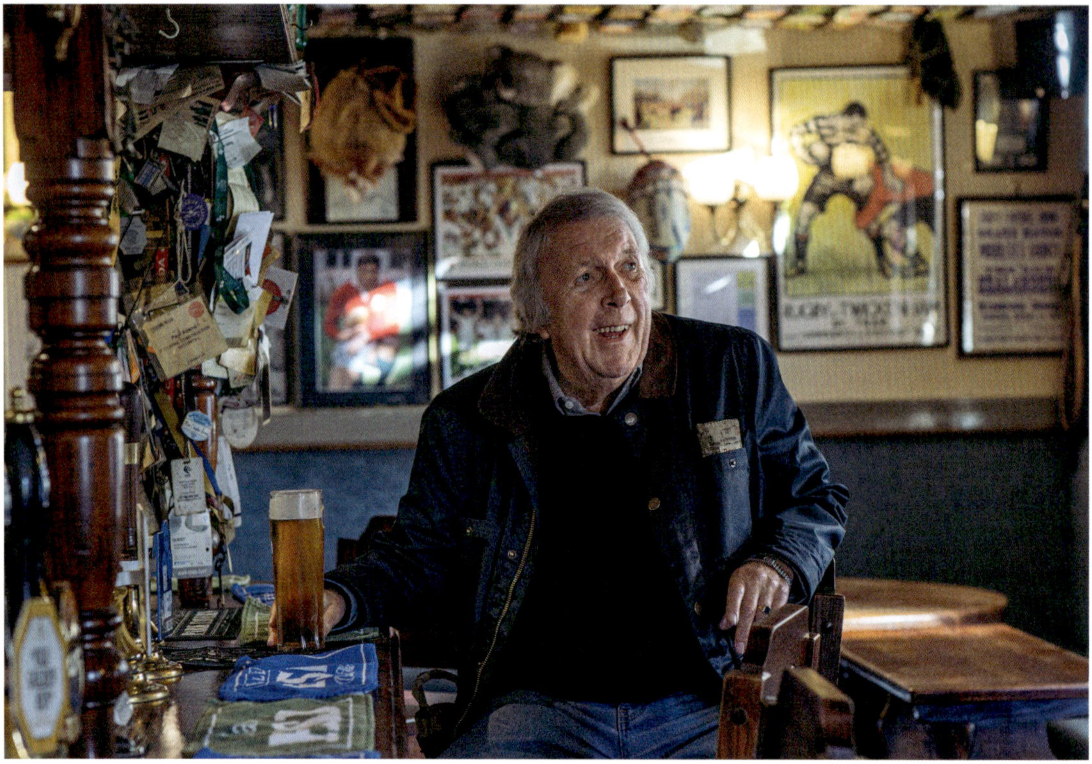

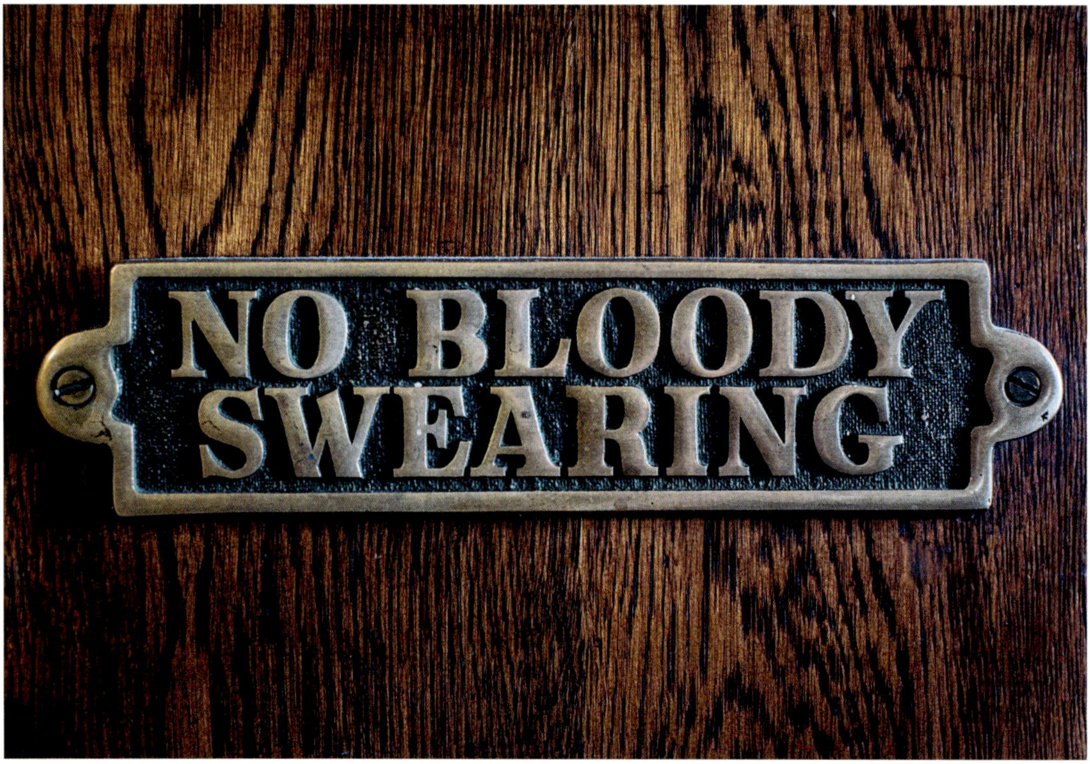

Pickled egg or wally? It's all reassuringly non-gastro.

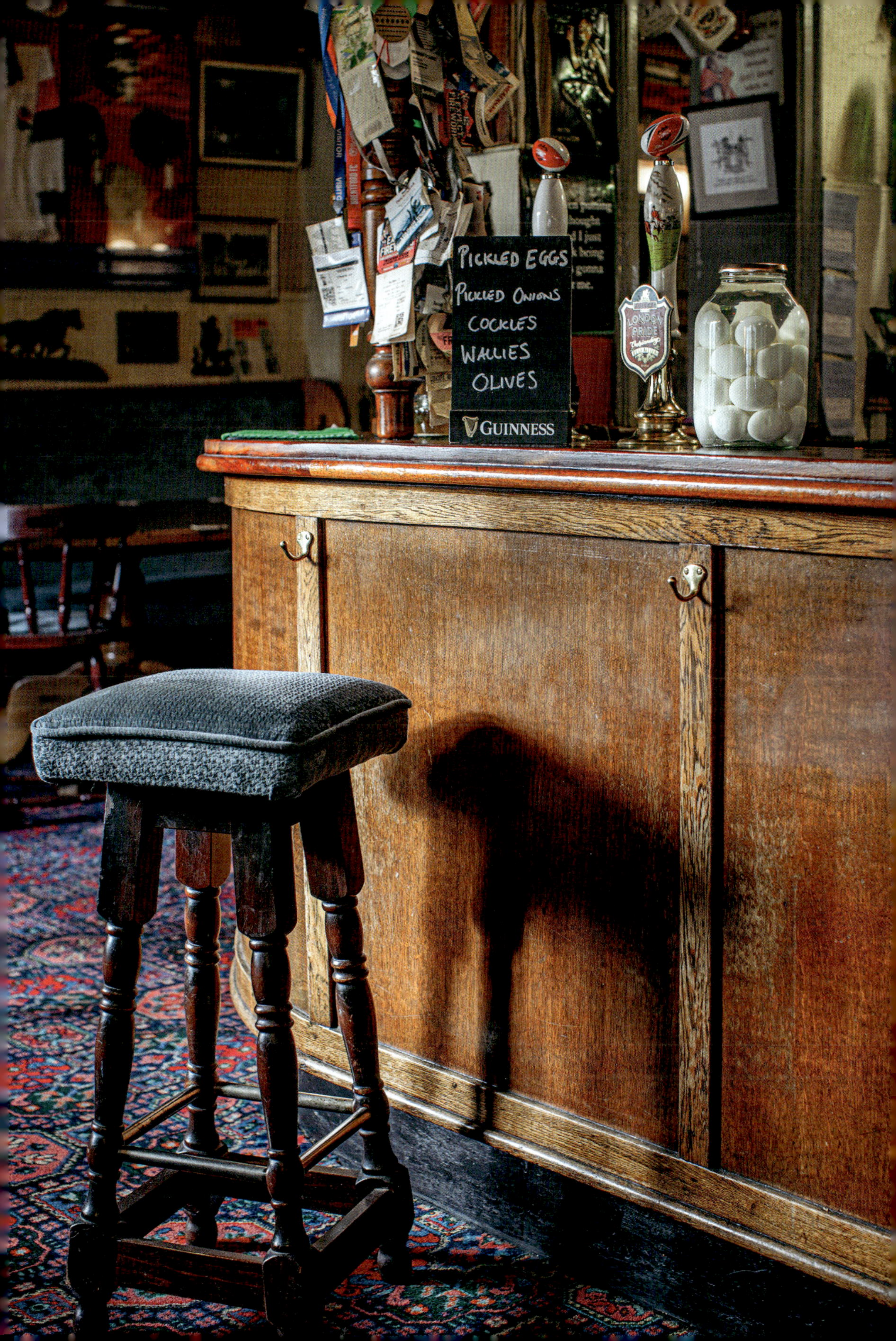

PICKLED EGGS
PICKLED ONIONS
COCKLES
WALLIES
OLIVES
GUINNESS
LONDON PRIDE

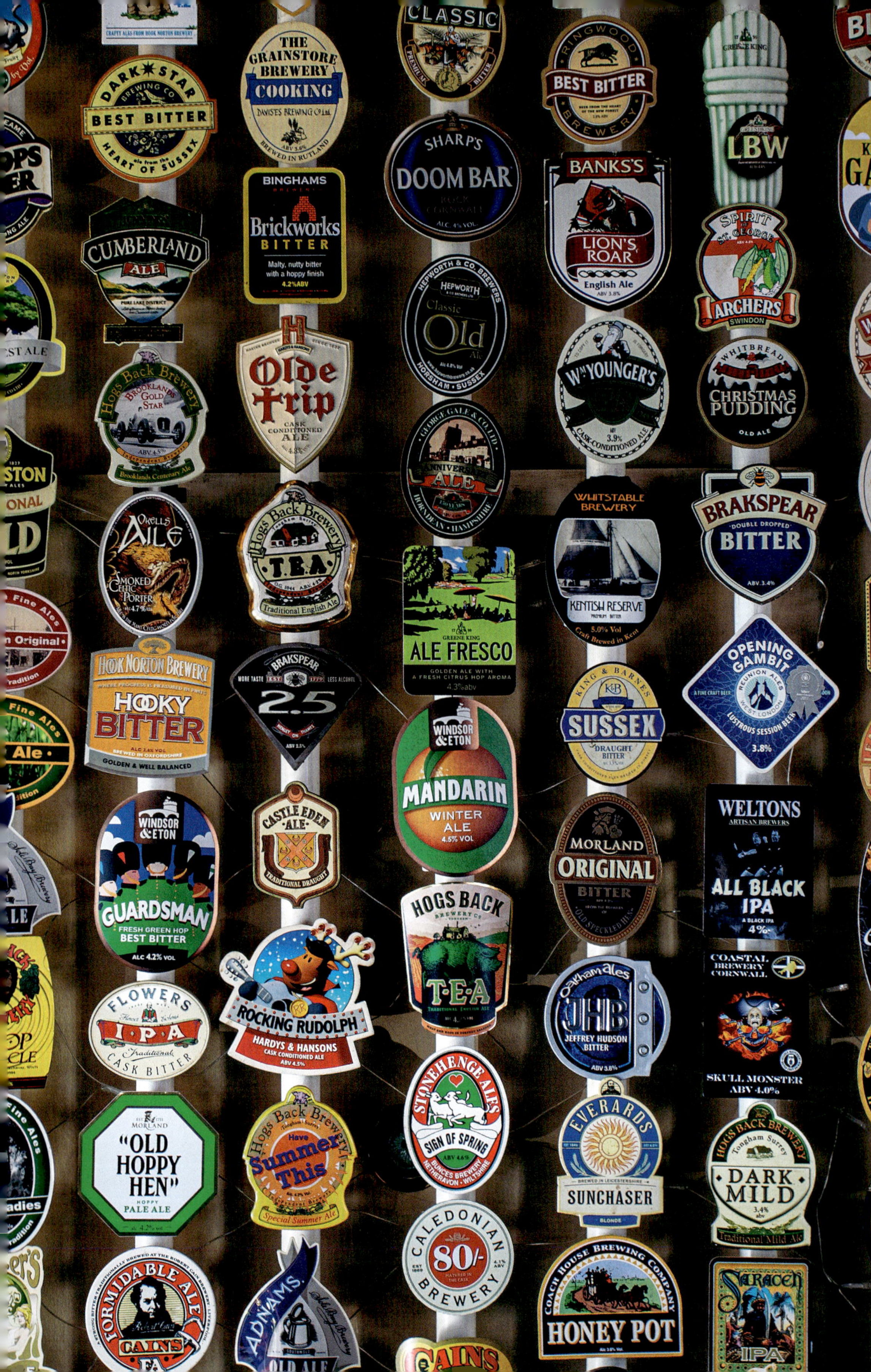

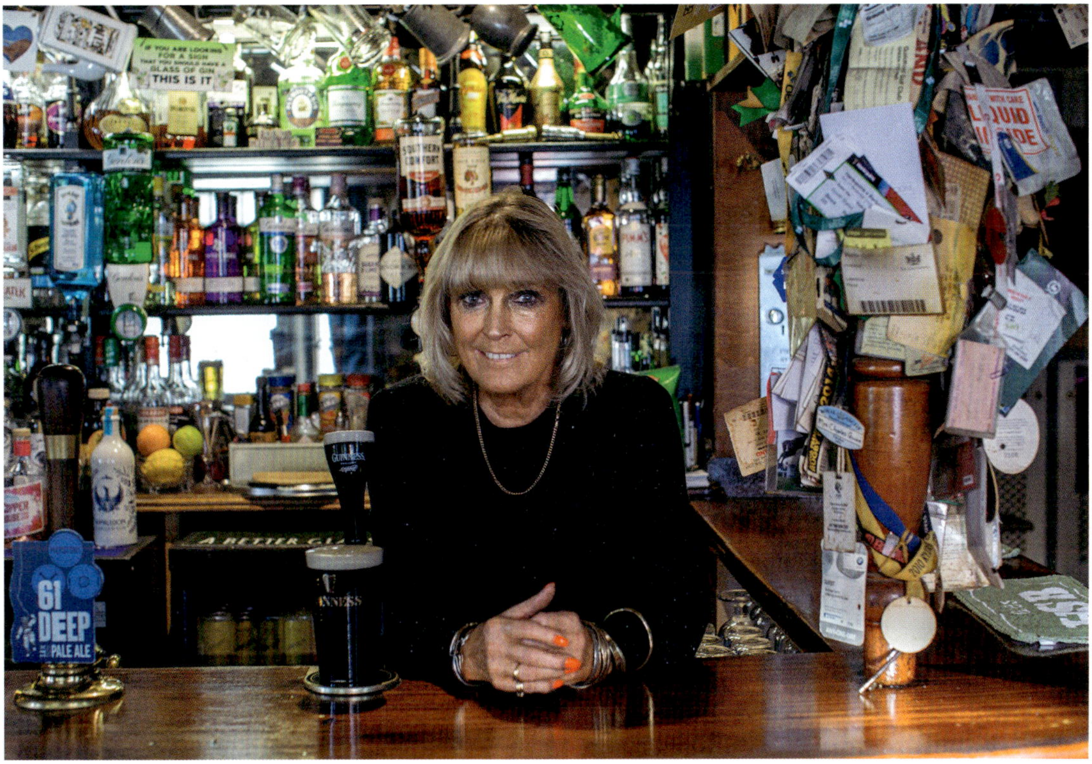

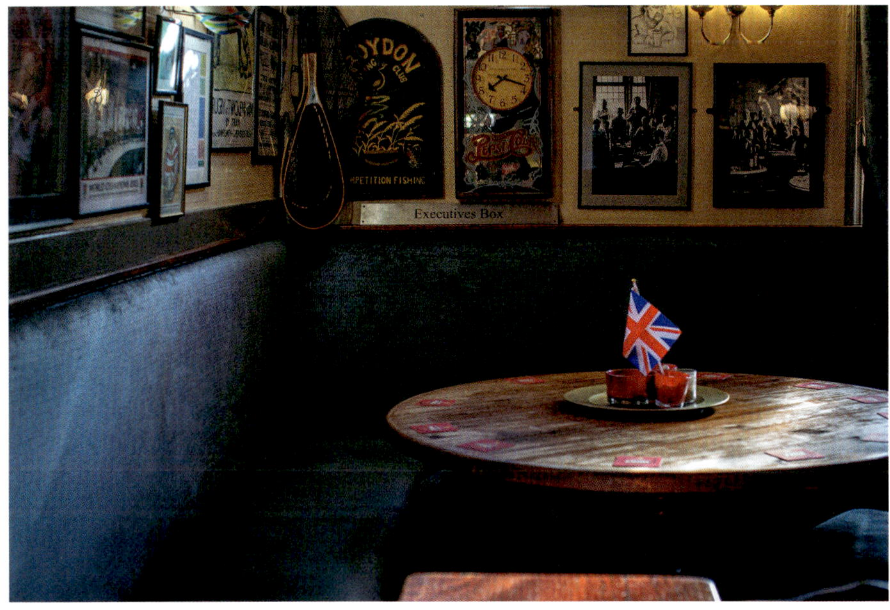

Traditionalist to the end

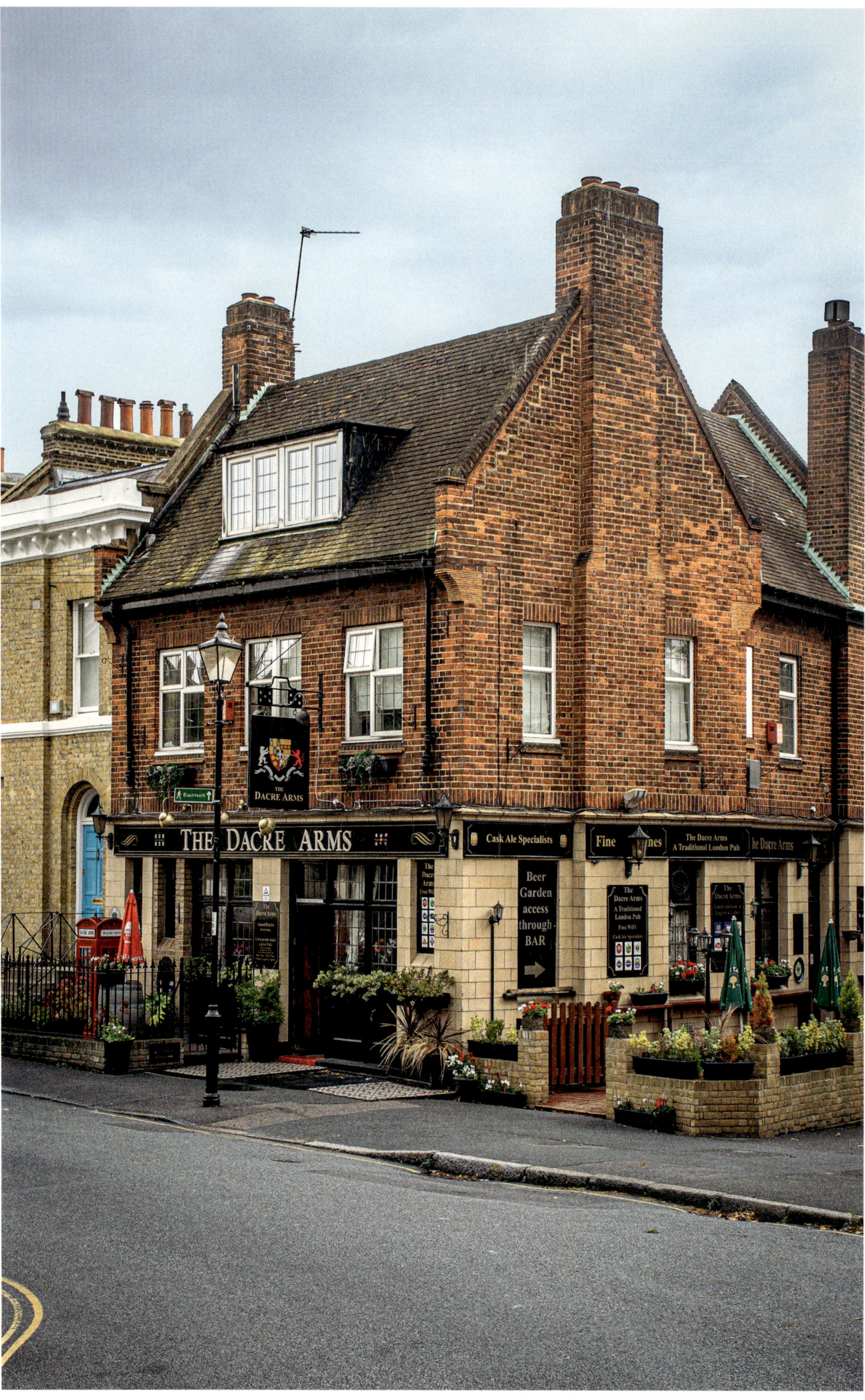
THE DACRE ARMS
Cask Ale Specialists
Fine Wines
The Dacre Arms
A Traditional London Pub
he Dacre Arms
Beer Garden access through BAR
The Dacre Arms
A Traditional London Pub
Free WiFi
Cask Ale Specialists

THE DACRE ARMS

A Traditional London Pub.

That's what it says over the pub fireplace, and The Dacre Arms keeps this promise rather well. Located between the arse-end of upmarket Blackheath, and "down-at-heel" Lee, this is a most unsuspecting outpost of destination drinking. This stoic outlier doesn't survive on passing trade. It's not a stop on the way or a mere detour. Unless you're lucky to live around the corner, then The Dacre Arms IS the destination.

Buried deep in these Blackheath backstreets, it's a "well, there's can't be a cracking boozer round here… ooh, wait a minute… that's a bingo!" location. Appearing as an architectural end-of-terrace afterthought, this 1930s suburban pub is both charming and disarming in equal measure. Enter into this inter-war time warp, acknowledge the old soaks sitting at the ramp and let the fine pub atmosphere wash over you. It's a very special kind of ordinary. Dark panelled walls, net-clad leaded windows and hop bines dangling from the ceiling create the alchemy. Toby jugs, horse brass, old radios and telephones set the domestic tone. Softly furnished corner comforts, carriage clocks atop the mantelpiece, and a vintage plate collection have you feeling right at home in no time. It does feel like your nan's front room, but this is no bad thing.

For over twenty-five years, the lord of the manor has been gaffer Terry and his family. They have saved this remarkable unsullied survivor from any misplaced refurbishment. History suggests the bar used to divide the public and saloon bars from front to back, but that's the only revolution to be found here. Just polish it, clean it, open the doors and serve well-kept pints to the chirpy community around you. Cash discounts still apply to keep the old-timers ticking over, and the capacious garden is a fine spot to sink a few cooking lagers. It's a country village local just missing its village.

Frequented by pint-nursers poring over the form in the papers, and the occasional one man and his dog drifting through for a sharpener, it's an exemplar of an old-man fiefdom and a reminder of what London's sprawling suburbs have lost over the years. Seemingly the only thing that I can find wrong with this pub is that it's not at the bottom of my street.

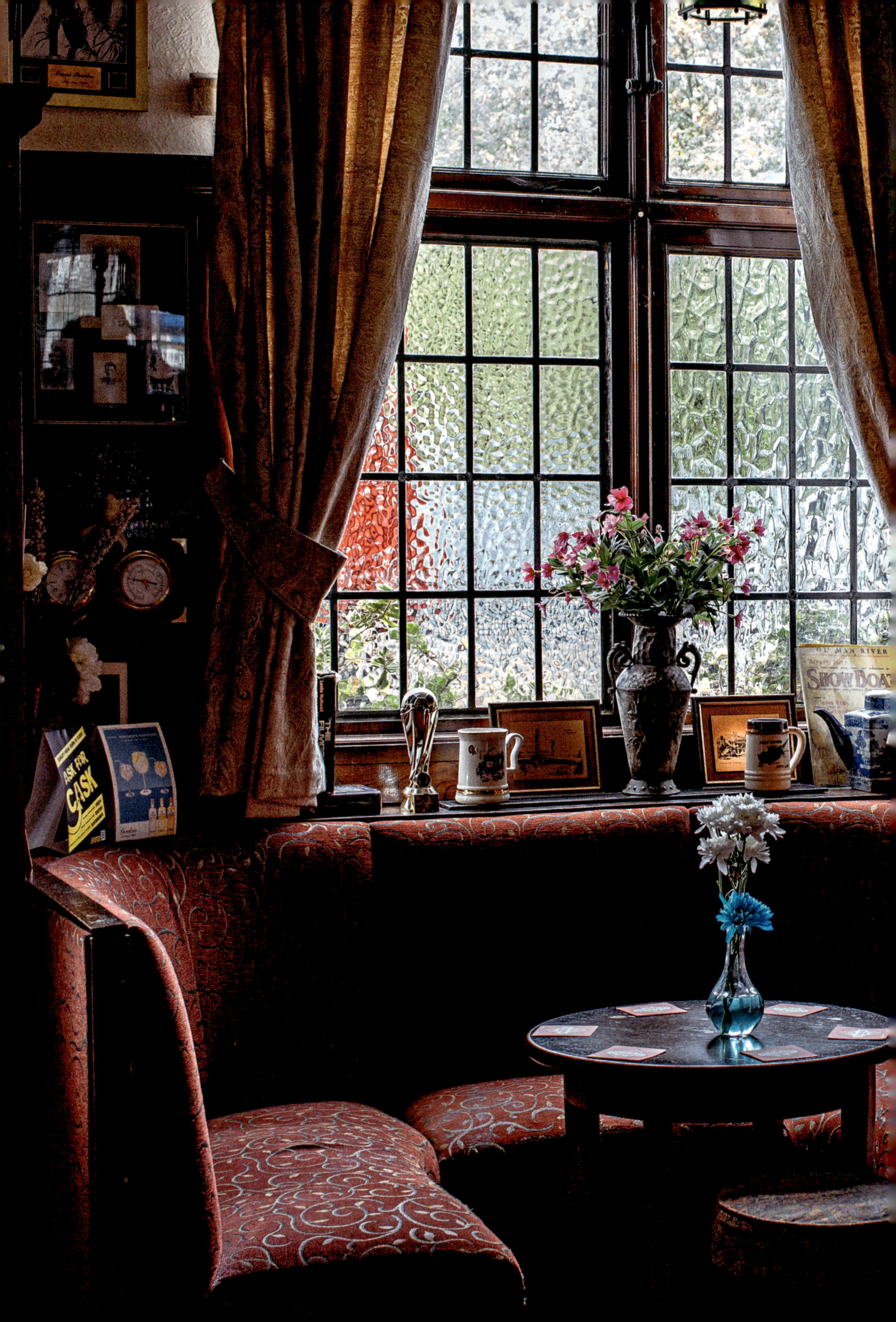

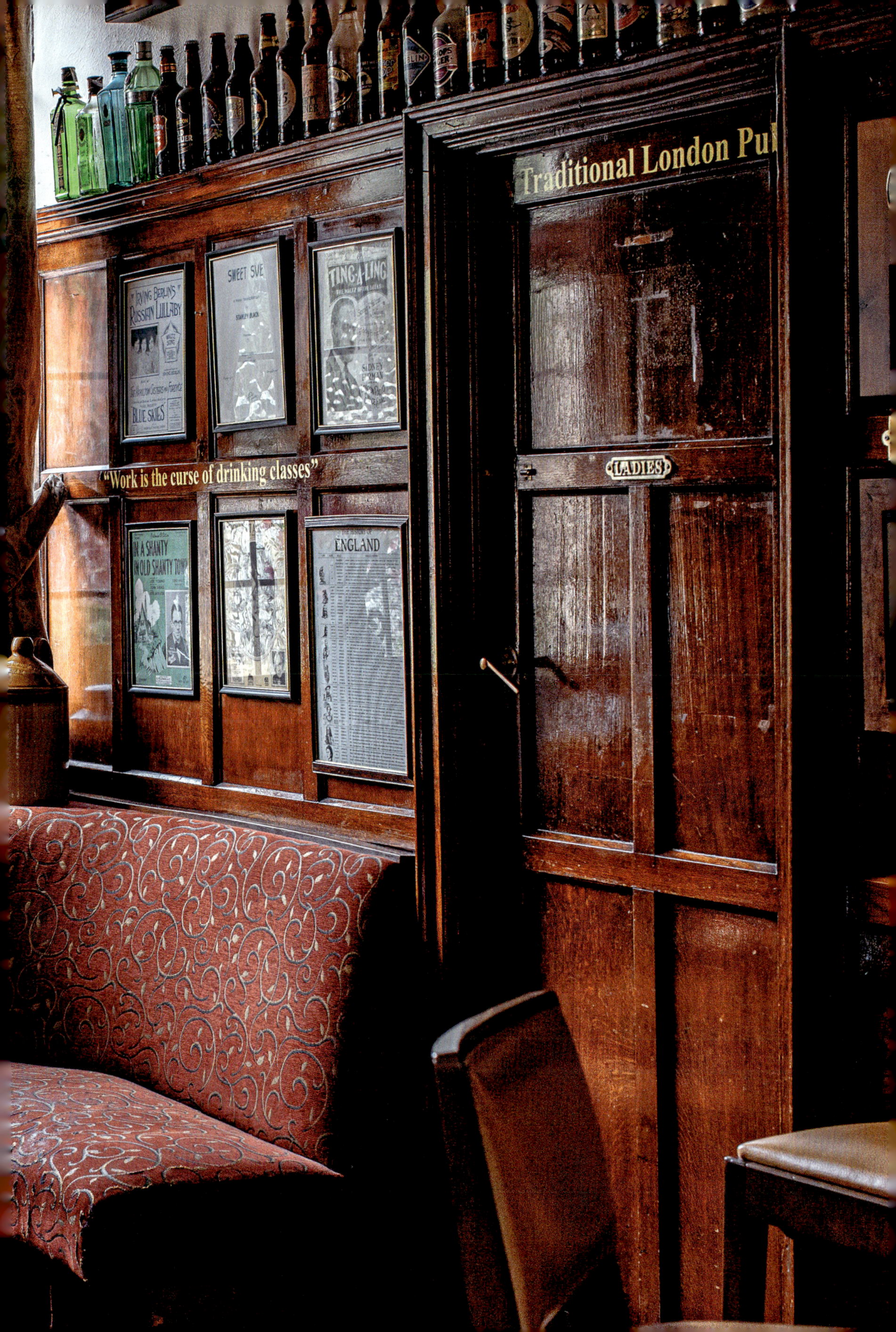

Traditional London Pub
LADIES
"Work is the curse of drinking classes"
IRVING BERLIN'S
RUSSIAN LULLABY
BLUE SKIES
SWEET SUE
STANLEY BLACK
TING-A-LING
SIDNEY BOWMAN
IN A SHANTY
IN OLD SHANTY TOWN
THE HISTORY OF
ENGLAND

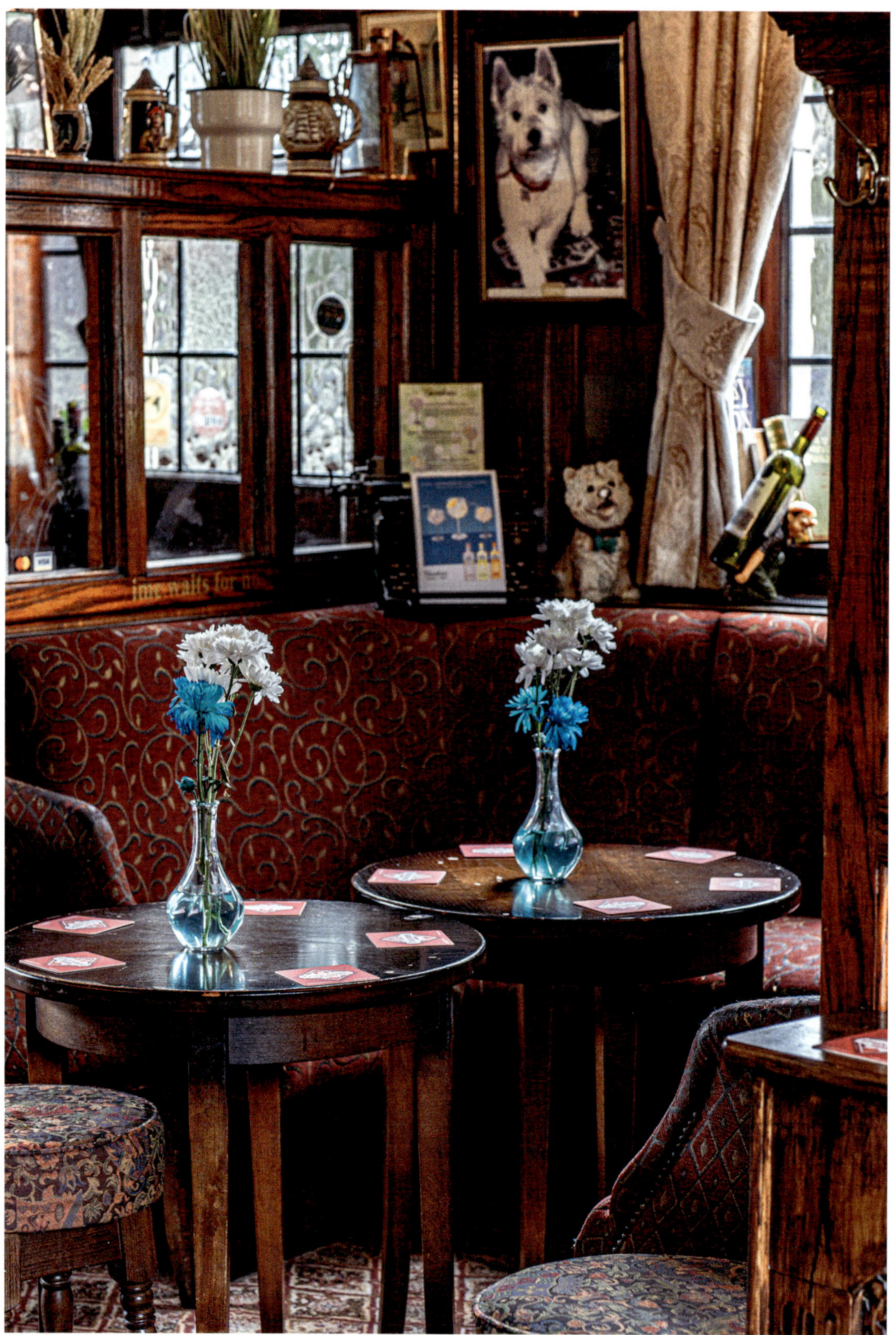

Trinkets and knick-knacks add a nostalgic waft of your Nan's house

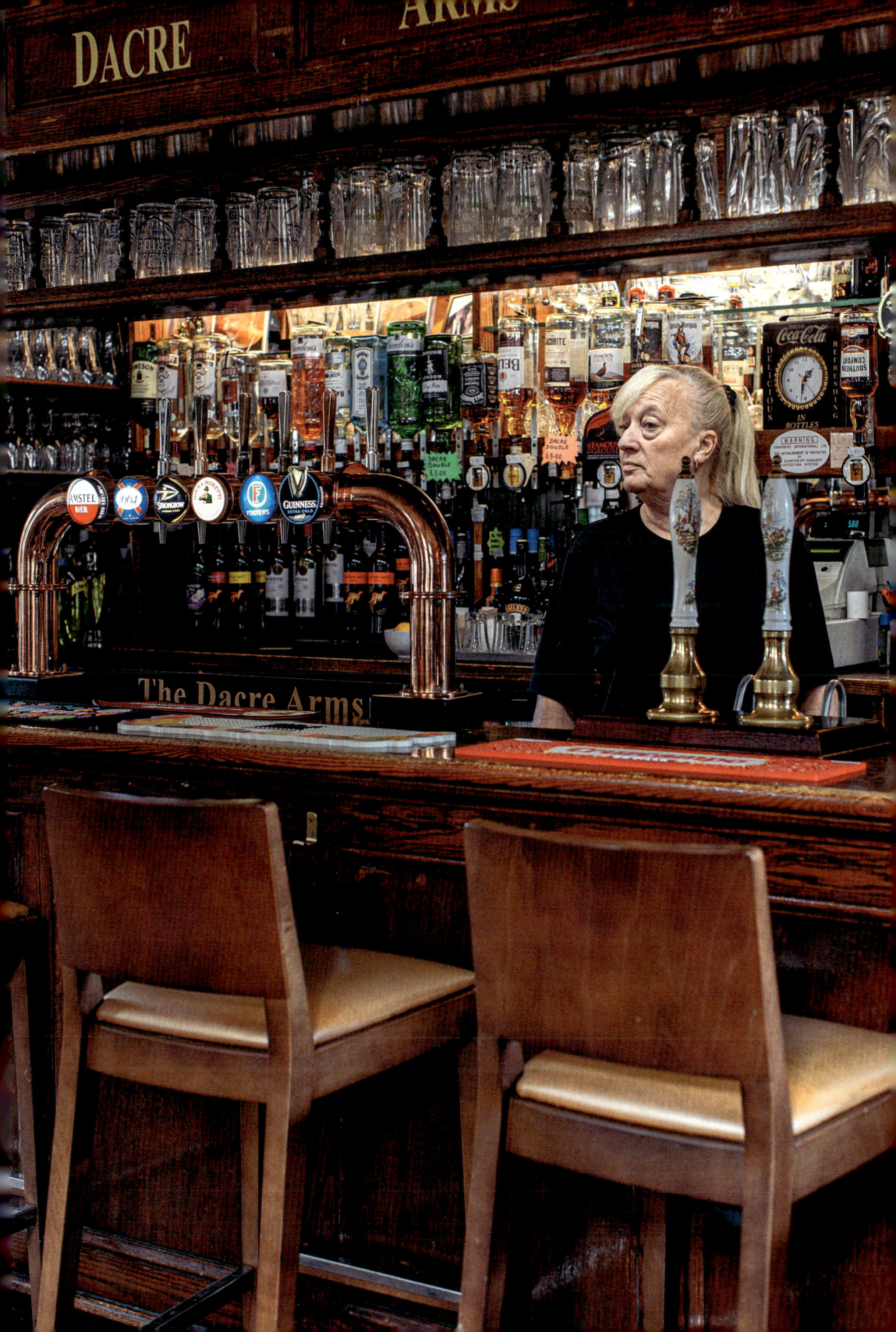

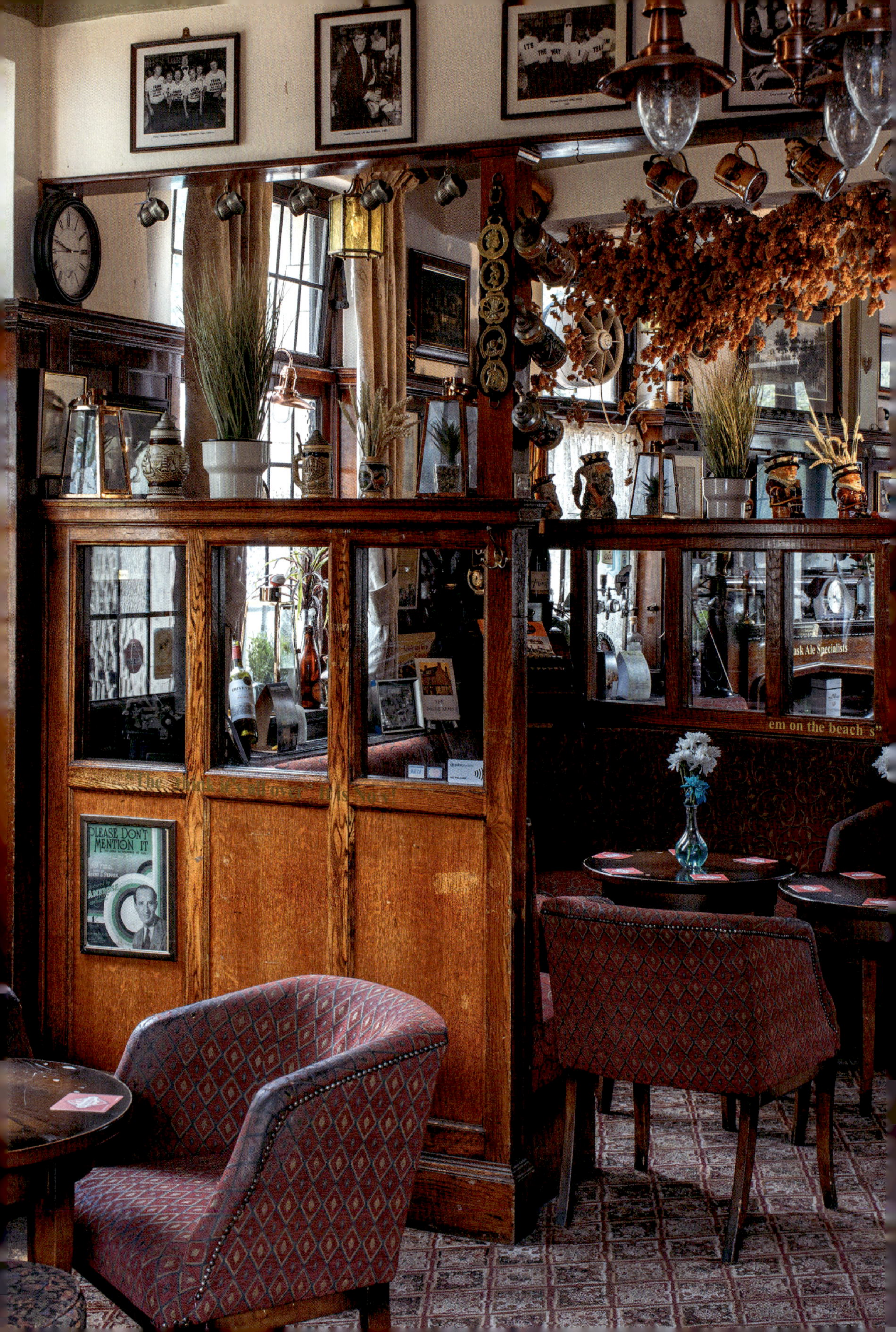

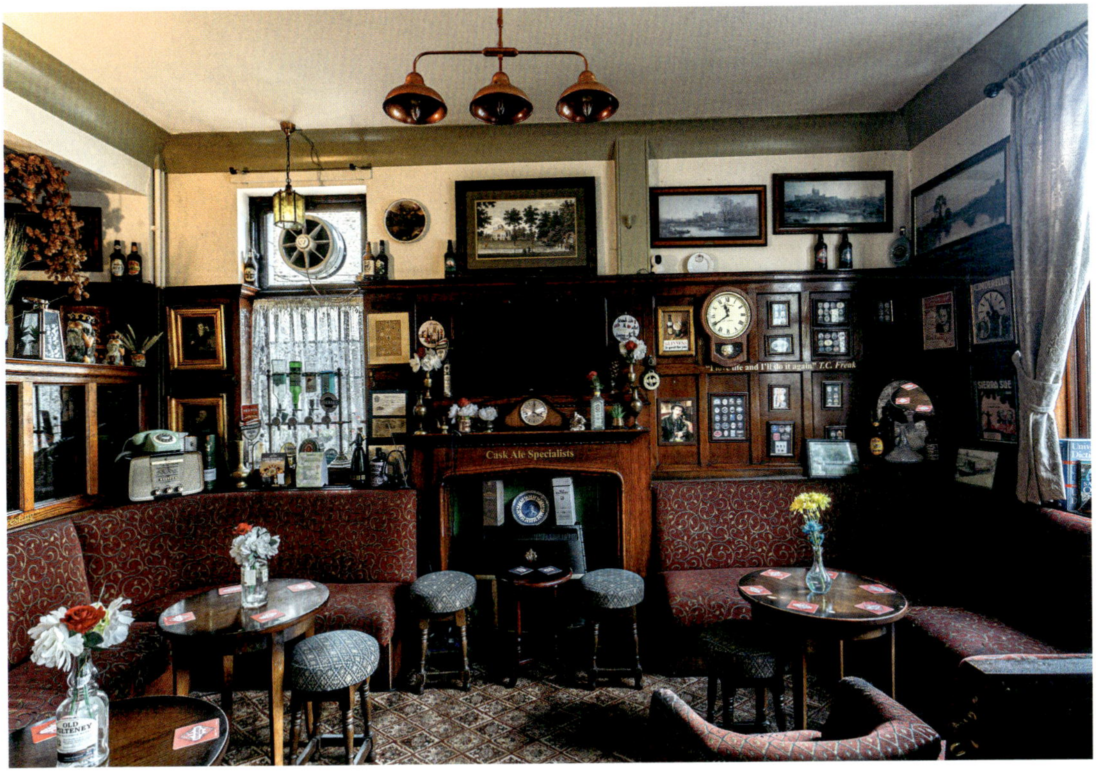

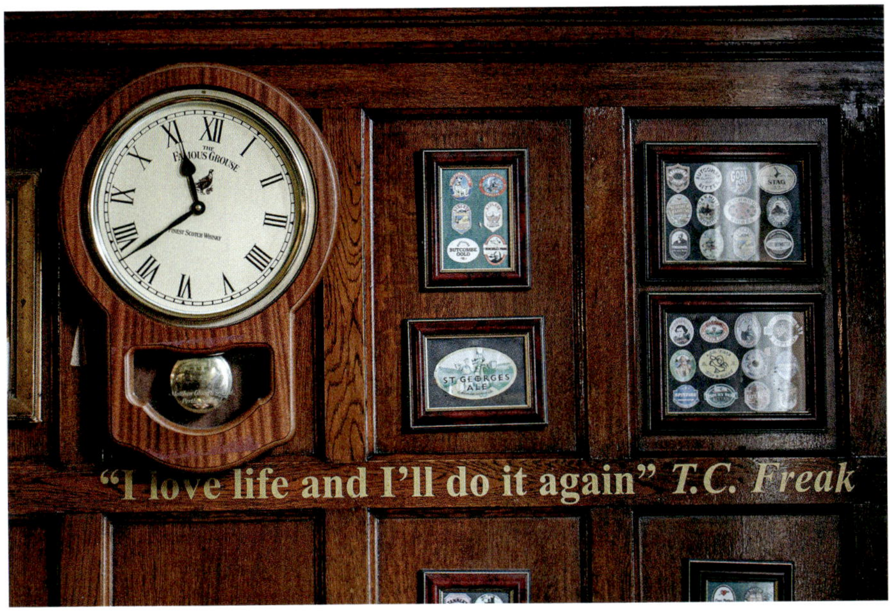

South London suburban splendour

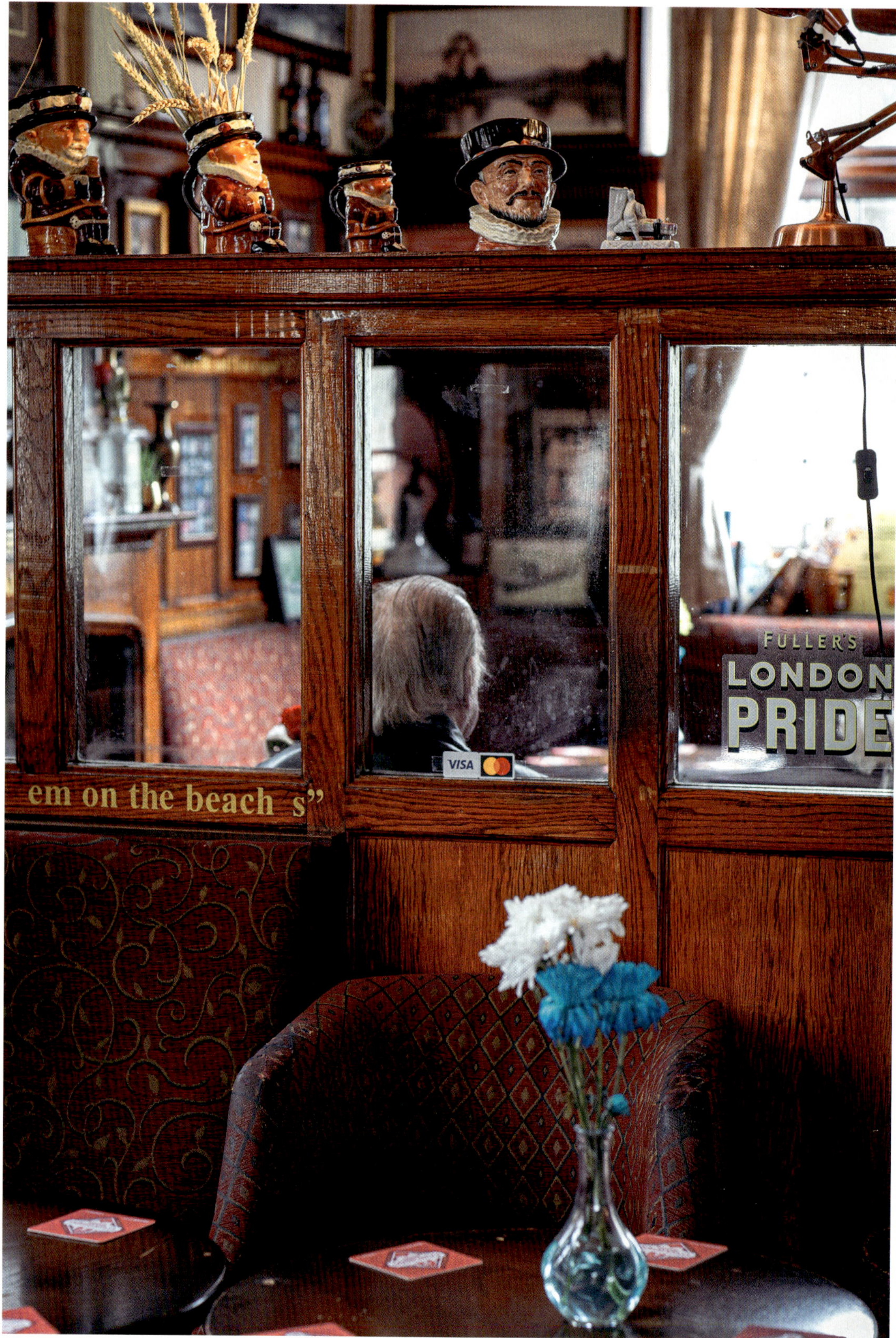

A truly traditional London pub

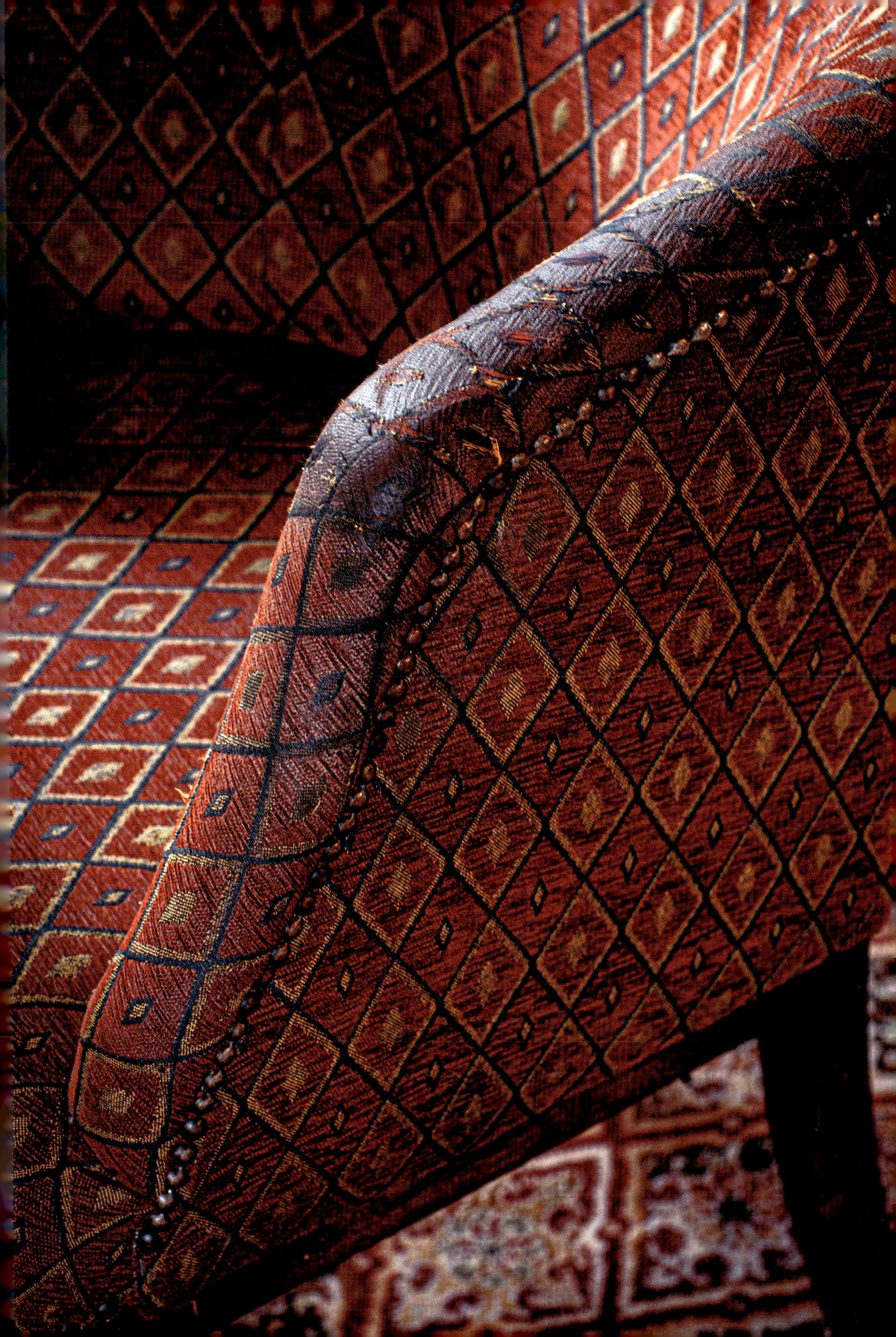

AUTHORS

HORST A. FRIEDRICHS

is an internationally renowned photographer, well known for documenting subcultures and architecture that bring out his fierce and excitable passion. He has published numerous books, including the bestselling *Cycle Style*, *I'm One: 21st Century Mods*, *Denim Style*, *Coffee Style* and *Best of British*. He currently lives in London, a short stroll from The Park Tavern. Lucky chap.

JOHN WARLAND

is the founder of Liquid History Tours, guided walking itineraries that explore London's rich hostelry heritage, and author of *Liquid History: An Illustrated Guide to London's Greatest Pubs*. He's also a noted garden designer, winning six RHS gold medals at Chelsea and Hampton Court Flower shows. Little wonder that a beer garden is his happy place.
h (Suggs, Phil, Tim, Sam, Lionel, the Handlebar Moustache Club and David for mobilising

"When you have lost your inns, drown your empty selves, for you will have lost the last of England."

Hilaire Belloc

ACKNOWLEDGEMENTS

THANKS

We raise our glasses to the legendary pint-pulling innkeepers of London, proffering traditional hospitality and warm welcomes to any that cross their threshold. The pride and professionalism they have shared with us on our pilgrimage across The Big Smoke has been emblematic of an old-school soul to the city that looked like it might be on its last legs. These are the true heroes of hospitality, and the reason for creating this book. Cheers to you all!

Judith *(Ye Olde Mitre)*, Cookie, Candice and Ricky *(The Cockpit)*, Roxy *(The Seven Stars)*, Karl *(The Hand & Shears)*, Maddie and Bill *(The Duke)*, Freya *(The Holy Tavern)*, Kathryn and Steve *(The Jamaica Wine House)*, Kevin *(The Nags Head)*, Sally *(Cask & Glass)*, Will and Clare *(The Barley Mow)*, Sam *(The Champion)*, Jan *(Bradley's Spanish Bar)*, Colin *(The Toucan)*, Gina and Jack *(The Golden Eagle)*, Eric *(The Cross Keys)*, Daniel *(The Nell Gwynne Tavern)*, Colin *(The Heron)*, Anne and Marc *(The Pride of Spitalfields)*, Janet and Darren *(Princess of Prussia)*, Paul and Bernice *(Turner's Old Star)*, Tomás and Aonghus *(The Auld Shillelagh)*, Alf and Kerry *(The Palm Tree)*, Frankie *(The Eleanor Arms)*, Marcus *(The Wenlock Arms)*, Simon *(King Charles I)*, George *(The Shakespeare's Head)*, Una *(The Hemingford Arms)*, Sinéad and Jim *(The Queen's Head)*, Jo and Emily *(The Lord Clyde)*, Ryan and Jodie *(The Kings Arms)*, Susan and James *(The Plume of Feathers)*, Luke *(The Prince of Wales)*, Séamus *(The Dog & Bell)*, Rae *(The Masons Arms)*, Con *(Blythe Hill Tavern)*, Chris *(The Bricklayer's Arms)*, Sue and James *(The Park Tavern)*, Terry *(The Dacre Arms)* and Leslie at *The French House* for her ongoing patronage of le bon vivant!

Thank you to all the participants who gave generously of their time, especially Suggs, Phil, Tim, Sam, Lionel, the Handlebar Moustache Club and David for mobilising his Morris Minor.

To Prestel: Andrew Hansen, Will Westall and Kate Luxton. Special thanks to Curt Holtz, Corinna Pickart and Christian Rieker for their immense support.

Our amazing creative director Lars Harmsen, the greatest book designer we could ever imagine. Thank you to photo assistant Jake Egelnick for your creativity and such lovely memories.

Cheers to David McGrath, Clare Button, Kevin Alderman and Andrew Ashmore for sharing hidden pub nuggets and helping to tweak the text along the way.

From Horst: Special thanks to my wife Adriana and my daughters Greta and Zoe, for their love, faith and inspiration.

From John: Eternal love to my ever-supportive wife Catherine and our incorrigible Alfie dog for proving that four-legged friends always deserve a place at the pub fireside.

© Prestel Verlag, Munich · London · New York, 2024
A member of Penguin Random House Verlagsgruppe GmbH
Neumarkter Straße 28 · 81673 Munich

Front Cover: The Cockpit, see page 19
Back Cover: Turner's Old Star, see page 165

Library of Congress Control Number is available; a CIP catalogue record for this book is available from the British Library.

Editorial direction: Curt Holtz
Copy-editing: Jonathan Fox
Design, layout and typesetting: Lars Harmsen, Melville Brand Design
Production: Corinna Pickart
Separations: Reproline Mediateam
Printing and binding: Alföldi Nyomda Zrt., Debrecen
Paper: Condat matt Périgord

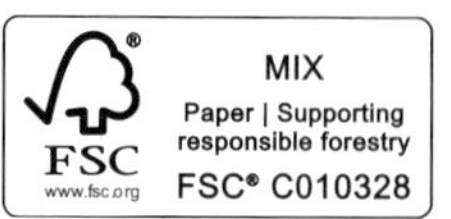

Penguin Random House Verlagsgruppe FSC® N001967
Printed in Hungary
ISBN 978-3-7913-8973-8

www.prestel.com

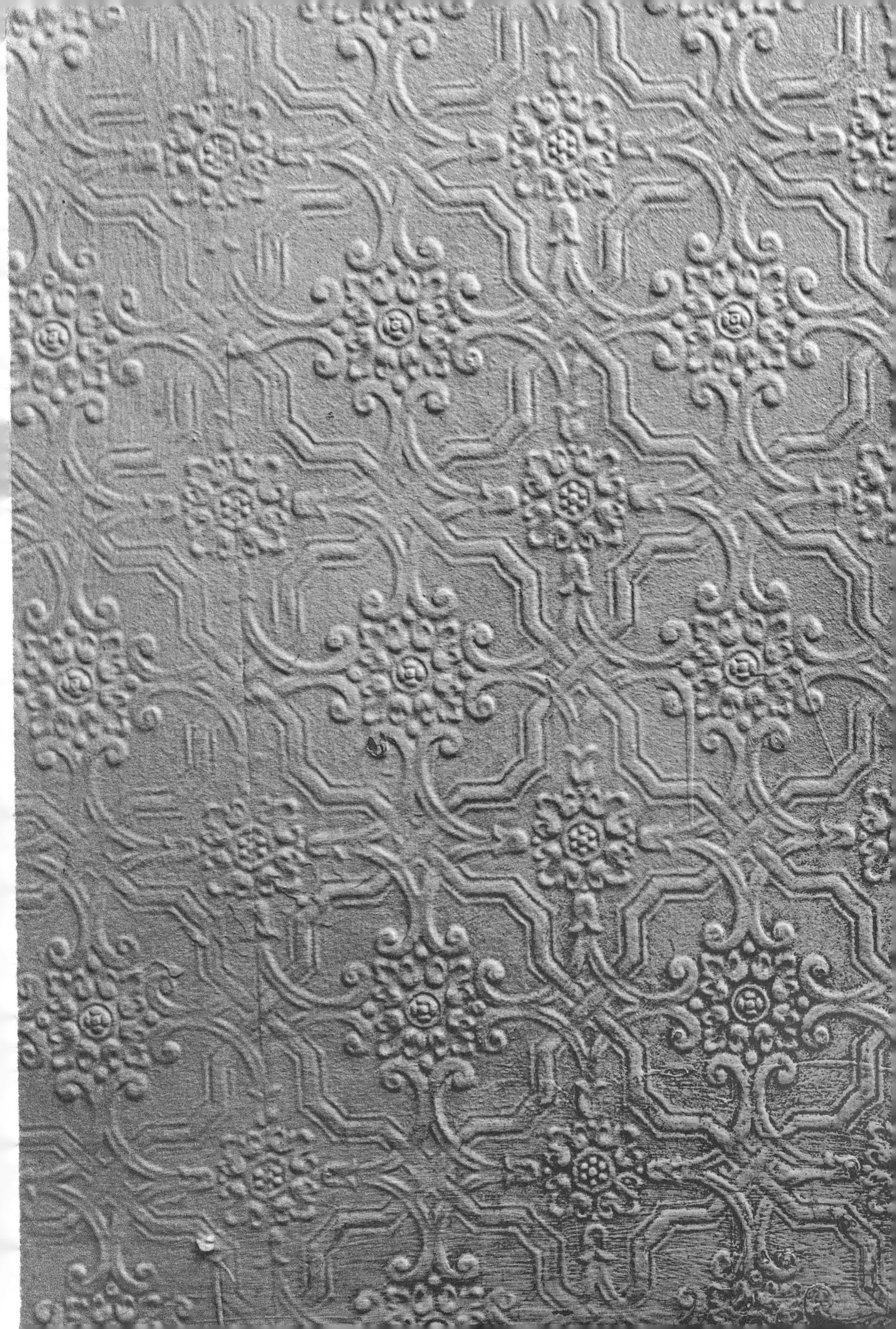

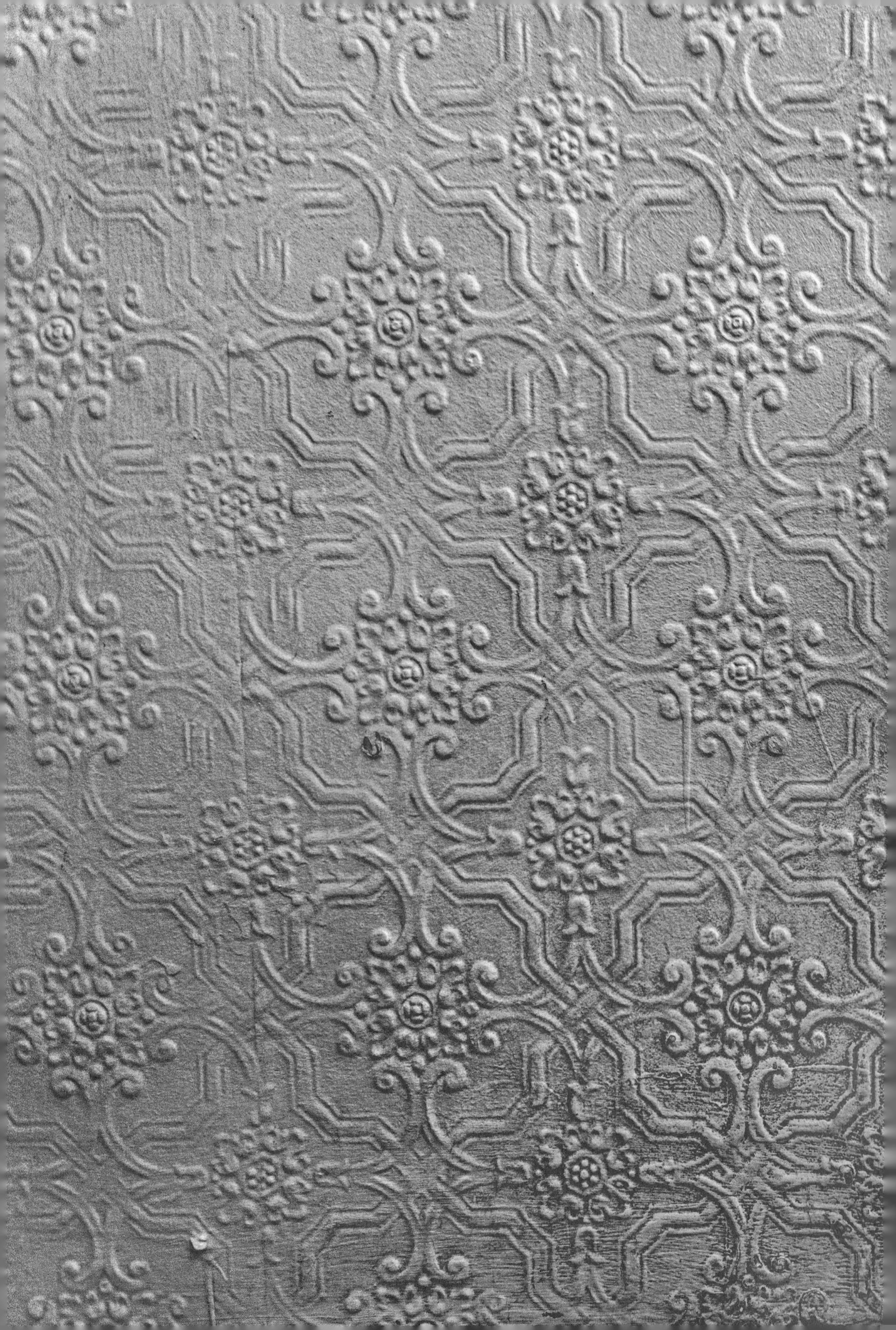